The publisher gratefully acknowledges the generous contribution
to this book provided by the Stephen Bechtel Fund.

The Fall and Rise of the Wetlands of California's Great Central Valley

The Fall and Rise of the Wetlands of California's Great Central Valley

Philip Garone

UNIVERSITY OF CALIFORNIA PRESS

Berkeley   Los Angeles   London

University of California Press, one of the most distinguished university
presses in the United States, enriches lives around the world by
advancing scholarship in the humanities, social sciences, and natural
sciences. Its activities are supported by the UC Press Foundation and by
philanthropic contributions from individuals and institutions. For more
information, visit www.ucpress.edu.

University of California Press
Berkeley and Los Angeles, California

University of California Press, Ltd.
London, England

Library of Congress Cataloging-in-Publication Data

Garone, Philip, 1961–
    The fall and rise of the wetlands of California's Great Central Valley /
Philip Garone.—1st ed.
        p.   cm.
    Includes bibliographical references and index.
    ISBN 978-0-520-26663-6 (cloth : alk. paper)
    1. Wetland conservation—California—Central Valley.
2. Wetlands—California—Central Valley.   3. Central Valley (Calif.)
I. Title.
    QH76.5.C2G37 2011
    333.91'8097945—dc22   2010040364

Manufactured in the United States of America

20   19   18   17   16   15   14   13   12   11
10 9 8 7 6 5 4 3 2 1

This book is printed on Cascades Enviro 100, a 100% post consumer
waste, recycled, de-inked fiber. FSC recycled certified and processed
chlorine free. It is acid free, Ecologo certified, and manufactured by
BioGas energy.

For my parents, Anna and Joseph Garone

CONTENTS

ILLUSTRATIONS

FIGURES

ACKNOWLEDGMENTS

During the decade that I have dedicated to this book since its origins as a doctoral dissertation at the University of California, Davis, I have benefited from the help, support, and encouragement of literally hundreds of people; along the way, many of them have become trusted friends. Starting from the beginning, I am extremely grateful to present and former faculty in the History Department at UC Davis. Lucy Barber, Dan Brower, Ruth Rosen, Alan Taylor, and Clarence Walker offered seminars that challenged me to think deeply and critically about history. My colleagues in the department brought a wealth of knowledge and a generosity of spirit to the program. I am thankful for the friendship of David Barber, Christina Bueno, Mark Carey, Robert Chester, Kathleen Duval, Steve Fountain, George Jarrett, Mike Meloy, and many others. The staff of the department did much to smooth my passage through graduate school, and I am especially grateful to Debbie Lyon.

For my dissertation, I could not have chosen a more supportive committee. Louis Warren graciously agreed to serve as chair shortly after joining the History Department at UC Davis. He consistently provided incisive and extensive commentary—as well as unconditional support—and is responsible for making this work immeasurably better. Michael Smith, formerly in the History Department and now in the American Studies Program, has been a friend and mentor since my first days as a graduate student. His inimitable teaching style has been an inspiration, and his insightful wit made graduate school even more of a pleasure than it might otherwise have been. Peter Lindert, in the Economics Department and, at that time, director of the Agricultural History Center, provided unflagging support and encouraged me to present my work-in-progress to the

xii ACKNOWLEDGMENTS

distinguished faculty and associates of the center, an experience from which I gained many indispensable suggestions. Peter Richerson, in the Department of Environmental Sciences and Policy as well as the Graduate Group in Ecology, contributed mightily to my understanding of both human ecology and environmental science; provided a close, critical read of my dissertation; and hosted numerous wonderful dinners for me and my colleagues. I thank each of my committee members for offering their time, expertise, and friendship.

Graduate school provides an opportunity to explore a range of interests. I am grateful to the History Department, and to Alan Taylor in particular, for supporting my unconventional request to choose ecology as my minor field. That choice, based on the premise that a strong background in ecology would be immensely helpful to an environmental historian, ultimately led me to pursue a concurrent MS in ecology, and to have an entirely new field of knowledge opened to me. The faculty of the Graduate Group in Ecology—especially Michael Barbour, Ted Foin, Rick Karban, Monique Borgerhoff Mulder, Ben Orlove, Kevin Rice, Don Strong, and Truman Young—were always supportive and encouraging, even if slightly bemused to have a historian in their midst. Geologist Jeffrey Mount and soil scientist Michael Singer expanded my knowledge in new and relevant directions. I am also grateful to Holly Doremus, formerly of the UC Davis School of Law, who taught me wildlife law and offered much useful advice. I found many close, supportive friends in the Graduate Group in Ecology and related disciplines, with whom I enjoyed a variety of wonderful adventures. My thanks to Josh and Alexis Ackerman, Monica Bueno, Sudeep Chandra, Charles Efferson, Erin Foresman, Maggie Franzen, Zeb Hogan, Mary Brooke McEachern, Marc Meyer, Kim Reever Morghan, Sarah Null, Jen Neale, Steve Newbold, Mark and Kai Rains, Bruce Roberts, Ben Sacks, Melanie Truan, and a host of others.

Beyond the walls of the academy, I received the benefit of the knowledge and firsthand experience of a number of scientists and resource managers who for many years have been involved with efforts to protect the Central Valley's wetlands. Many of them have read all or part of this book and have provided a great deal of helpful feedback, including a number of corrections that have saved me from embarrassing errors. Before this project was even a completed seminar paper, Jack Erickson, Des Hayes, and Brian Smith of the California Department of Water Resources introduced me to the complexity of California water issues. For a tremendous amount of help in the years that followed, I especially thank Howard Leach, retired from the California Department of Fish and Game, and Felix Smith, retired from the U.S. Fish and Wildlife Service. My travels in the Sacramento and San Joaquin valleys with these veterans of California water politics, who have directly experienced more than I could ever hope to learn, have been memorable. Joseph Skorupa, with the U.S. Fish and Wildlife Service, took an early and sustained interest in my work; he has offered detailed commentary and supplied me with many important sources. Harry Ohlendorf, formerly with the U.S. Fish and Wildlife Service, offered much patient explanation and generously provided access to his personal files as well as numerous slides. Frank Hall, retired from the California Department of Fish and Game, provided historical data and other unpublished information about the Central Valley's duck clubs. Lloyd Carter, an attorney and former journalist who has written about California water issues for decades, provided many helpful insights. Gary Zahm, former manager of the San Luis National Wildlife Refuge Complex, generously provided numerous documents from his personal files, provided detailed commentary on the Kesterson chapter, and shared his reminiscences. Environmental writer and photographer Tim Palmer has also kindly allowed me to use his photographic work in this book. Kevin Petrik of Ducks Unlimited produced the map of protected wetland areas in the Central Valley that appears in the epilogue. Ranger Mike Whelan of Caswell Memorial State Park has, on more than one occasion, shared his considerable knowledge of riparian forests with me and my students.

The managers and staff of the national wildlife refuges in the Central Valley have allowed me access to their archives, helpful information, and a comfortable environment in which to work during my research trips up and down the Central Valley. My thanks to Joe Silveira and Greg Mensik of the Sacramento National Wildlife Refuge Complex, Kim Forrest and Dennis Woolington of the San Luis National Wildlife Refuge Complex, and Dave Hardt of the Kern National Wildlife Refuge Complex. Prior to his untimely death, Don Marciochi, general manager of the Grassland Water District, was a gracious and helpful host during my visits to the district's archives in Los Banos, as was Veronica Woodruff. I would also like to thank collectively the dozens of librarians and archive staff throughout California who have consistently been helpful and have gone out of their way to track down documents and accommodate my many requests.

Numerous institutions provided financial support for the research that has resulted in this book. At UC Davis, the History Department, the Agricultural History Center, and the Public Service Research Program awarded me fellowships and grants. The Society of Wetland Scientists provided a research grant, and the American Society for Environmental History supplied a travel grant. The Huntington Library offered me a monthlong research fellowship that was both professionally and personally rewarding. The U.S. Environmental Protection Agency's Science to Achieve Results (STAR) Graduate Fellowship provided three years of funding that allowed me to complete my dissertation free from interruptions, and introduced me to a wonderful community of environmental scholars.

I have benefited as well from many colleagues in environmental history and ecology, who have commented on my presentations of various portions of this work at meetings of the American Society for Environmental History, the Society of Wetland Scientists, and the First World Congress of Environmental History.

Among them I would like to thank Peter Alagona, who has discussed the book with me at length on many occasions and commented on earlier versions of chapters. I am grateful also to Bill Cronon for providing a number of challenging and helpful suggestions that helped me transform my voluminous dissertation into a book manuscript. Few books about wetlands have been written by environmental historians, but among that small circle of authors, I would like to acknowledge Ann Vileisis, Robert Wilson, and Nancy Langston for the insights I have gained from their work.

I have been especially fortunate in having Jenny Wapner as my editor at the University of California Press for all but the final few months of this project. From the outset, she was entirely supportive and helpful, offered numerous suggestions about better ways to organize the book, and graciously worked with me as I struggled to meet deadlines while working in a university system that mandates a very heavy teaching load. At UC Press, I also wish to thank Lynn Meinhardt, who guided the book through the production process. I am grateful to UC Press's editorial board, and Peter Moyle in particular, for providing constructive commentary, as well as to David Igler, Donald Pisani, and the anonymous reviewers who read this work and offered detailed commentary and suggestions at various stages in the review process. Any errors that remain are solely my own.

Some material in chapter 7 appeared previously in *Natural Protest: Essays on the History of American Environmentalism*, edited by Michael Egan and Jeff Crane (New York and London: Routledge, 2009). An early version of some material in chapters 8 and 9 appeared previously in *Environs* 22, no. 2 (Spring 1999), the environmental law and policy journal of the UC Davis School of Law. These materials are used with permission.

There is something about moving to California—with its stunning landscapes, fascinating geology, and vast wilderness areas—that turns one's interest toward the environment. After arriving in the San Francisco Bay area from the East with degrees in history and medieval studies, I found myself teaching at The Athenian School, a high school with a strong reputation for outdoor and environmental education. Influenced by that physically and intellectually stimulating environment, I soon began working summers as a ranger naturalist in Sequoia National Park, high in the Sierra Nevada but within view of the Central Valley lying far below. In a happy coincidence, Rick Higashi and Teresa Fan, researchers at UC Davis whom I had recently met, appeared unexpectedly in the park one day and first told me about toxicity issues that were affecting waterfowl in the valley, a topic they correctly suggested might be of interest to me. In the Central Valley I sensed a different kind of nature, one that has been remarkably transformed by human actions but still presents glimpses of what it once was and offers tantalizing possibilities for exploration and investigation. With these observations in mind, as I entered the history doctoral program at UC Davis, the kernel of what has now become this book began taking shape.

It seemed fortuitous that, upon completing my time at Davis, I should find a position at a university in the Central Valley. I would like to thank each and every one of my colleagues and friends in the History Department at California State University, Stanislaus—Bret Carroll, Sam Regalado, Katherine Royer, Marjorie Sanchez-Walker, Nancy Taniguchi, Shuo Wang, Richard Weikart, and Jonathan David, who has recently moved on—for their support since I joined the department as a new assistant professor in 2006. California's unprecedented budget crisis began shortly thereafter, and even as this crisis has precipitated draconian budget cuts that threaten the very core of public higher education in the state, including the jobs of faculty, my spirits have been consistently buoyed by these individuals, who bring to the department a combination of intellectual rigor and conviviality that is most welcome. Additionally, I must thank our administrative assistant, Cathy Lanzon, who has been helpful in too many ways for me possibly to describe.

From my earliest memories, my family has always been a wonderful source of support. My parents, Anna and Joseph Garone, read my entire dissertation and offered suggestions for making it more accessible to a broad audience. My brother Stephen, a professional editor, combed through my first version of this manuscript with a level of detail that I found truly astounding. I especially thank him for innumerable corrections to minuscule errors that did not escape his critical eye.

Finally, I am grateful to my partner, Teresa Bergman, an accomplished scholar in her own right, whom I met on the fateful day I submitted the completed prospectus for my dissertation to my committee. As a fellow academic, she has understood and stoically endured the long periods of physical and emotional absence from a relationship that writing a book requires. She has read—and reread—every chapter, and has offered countless suggestions that have made this an infinitely better project. She has also made my life infinitely better, and for her love and support, I thank her.

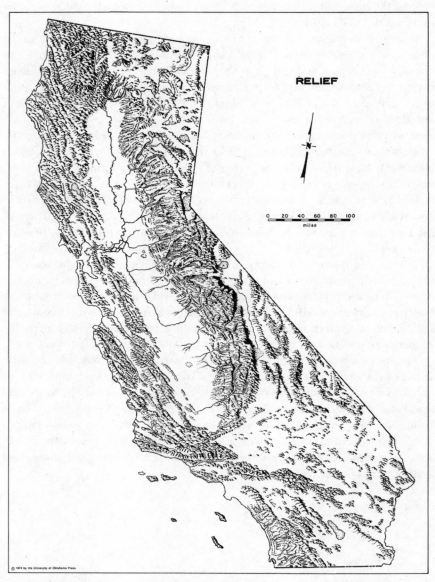

RELIEF

0 20 40 60 80 100
          miles

MAP 1. Relief map of California. The Central Valley occupies the center of the state and extends for more than four hundred miles from north to south. The Sacramento River drains the northern portion of the valley, and the San Joaquin River drains the southern portion. The two rivers meet near the center of the state in the Sacramento–San Joaquin Delta. Source: Warren A. Beck and Ynez D. Haase, *Historical Atlas of California* (Norman: University of Oklahoma Press, 1974). Used with permission.

Introduction

Every autumn and early winter, millions of aquatic birds—ducks, geese, swans, and shorebirds—descend upon the Great Central Valley of California. Dozens of species of long-distance travelers return to their ancestral wintering grounds to feed and rest in the freshwater marshes, shallow lakes, and river systems of California's heartland. Breeding, for the most part, in the northern wetlands of Alaska and western Canada, these birds have sought seasonal refuge for at least the past ten thousand centuries in the relative warmth of the Central Valley wetlands—California's most important contribution to the Pacific Flyway, the westernmost of four North American migratory bird corridors, which stretch from the Arctic to Mexico and beyond.

Today's migrating waterbirds have been arriving in a valley far different from the one known by their forebears. From the time of California statehood in 1850, the wetlands of the Central Valley experienced nearly a century of accelerating losses as they were drained—or "reclaimed"—usually for conversion to agricultural uses. This trend began to change during the middle third of the twentieth century, when efforts to protect and restore wetlands in the Central Valley slowly gained momentum, a momentum that has been carried to the present day. This book explains why that change took place, and why it is important to an understanding of crucial aspects of U.S. conservation history. As the title suggests, at its heart this book is not a declension story, a "classic narrative of regret" (to borrow a phrase from one historian of the Central Valley) about a fall from a pristine past to an environmentally degraded present.[1] Rather, although the sheer volume of wetland losses has been enormous, this book suggests reasons for a cautious

1

optimism about the future of wetlands in California's Central Valley and across the nation as a whole.

The fate of California's Central Valley wetlands over the past two centuries has paralleled broader trends across the United States. In the 1780s, the earliest decade for which estimates are available, there were approximately 392 million acres of wetlands in what are now the fifty states; 221 million of these acres were in the forty-eight contiguous states.[2] By the end of the twentieth century, only 105.5 million acres of wetlands remained in the contiguous states, representing a loss of more than 52 percent.[3] The disappearance of America's wetlands represents, quite simply, a loss of one of our greatest natural treasures. In addition to protecting biodiversity by providing habitat for migratory waterfowl and other wetland-dependent animals and plants, wetlands provide immense economic and ecological benefits. Economic benefits stem largely from fishing, hunting, and recreation; ecological benefits are myriad: wetland ecosystems function as rechargers and dischargers of aquifers; they absorb and store floodwaters; and they recycle nutrients and transform wastes, thereby ameliorating pollution problems.[4]

As profound as the nationwide losses of wetlands surely are, they pale in comparison to those suffered by California, which by the 1980s had lost 91 percent of its original estimated 5 million wetland acres.[5] Overwhelmingly, the losses were in the permanent and seasonal wetlands of the Central Valley, which had declined from at least 4 million acres to approximately 379,000 acres (see map 2).[6] The bright spot in this otherwise bleak picture is that the rate of loss in California's Central Valley and nationally slowed dramatically during the late twentieth century, and in the Central Valley, wetlands have begun to rebound.[7] The details of the California story differ in significant and meaningful ways from events elsewhere in the nation. But the consequences of wetland loss—whether a result of direct destruction of habitat for nonhuman creatures, lost or degraded ecosystem functionality, or the vanishing of a significant portion of our aesthetic heritage— are similar.

In California, the pursuit of a mythic vision of the state as an agricultural empire came close to destroying all of its wetlands, but once the ecological consequences of this loss for waterfowl and other wetland-dependent species became apparent, concerted efforts to save the state's remaining wetlands gained traction. The history of wetlands in California is thus intimately tied to the history of the growth and development of agriculture, and of the massive irrigation and reclamation projects that support the state's agricultural industry. This book is therefore as much about the agricultural history of California as it is about the history of the wetlands themselves. Linking the two histories reveals many of the unintended consequences of the unrestrained manipulation of nature and brings to light nuanced and at times surprising motivations behind the protection of wetlands.

What we as a society do with our water—from whom and where we take it, and to whom and where we deliver it—reveals much about our values and our relationship with nature. Recent efforts to protect and restore wetlands in the Central Valley and nationally tell us a great deal about how priorities for water use have shifted during the twentieth century and into the twenty-first. We have witnessed a modest, gradual shift from the prioritization of agriculture to that of environmental protection and restoration. Changes in public and scientific perceptions about the inherent value of wetlands have altered the focus and direction of public policy initiatives, with the result that economic incentives to drain wetlands have been gradually overshadowed by ecological justifications to preserve them.

The Central Valley possesses a richly textured history, the significance of which is compounded by the valley's enormous size. Larger than many states, the Central Valley extends approximately 430 miles from north to south, averages 50 miles wide, and accounts for more than 13 million of California's 101,563,520 acres.[8] This valley is ancient by human time scales, but not by geological ones. When the ancestral Sierra Nevada was first uplifted, perhaps two hundred million years ago, its peaks formed the western edge of what is now California. The future Central Valley, to the west of the Sierra Nevada, was still part of the Pacific Ocean floor. Beginning tens of millions of years ago, complex tectonic forces, resulting from the ongoing collision of the Pacific and North American plates, uplifted California's jumbled northern Coast Ranges. The place that is now the Central Valley was transformed from open expanse of ocean to inland sea by these new mountains to the west. This inland sea appears to have receded from the Central Valley about the same time that the much younger southern Coast Ranges rose above sea level, only a few million years ago. While the Coast Ranges were slowly rising from the sea, the Sierra Nevada, which had gradually eroded down to a gently rising plain, was rejuvenated and began to rise to its present height of more than fourteen thousand feet.[9] The Central Valley's placement between the Coast Ranges and the Sierra Nevada accounts for no small part of its modern history. Sediments thousands of feet deep have accumulated as alluvial deposits washed out of both the Sierra Nevada and the Coast Ranges, creating the rich, fertile soil that has yielded the valley's famed agricultural bounty.[10]

The Central Valley actually comprises two distinct valleys, the Sacramento Valley in the north and the larger San Joaquin Valley in the south; the latter is, in turn, composed of two separate basins, the San Joaquin Basin in the north and the Tulare Basin in the south. In full or in large part, eighteen of the state's fifty-eight counties are included in the Central Valley: Shasta, Tehama, Butte, Glenn, Colusa, Sutter, Yuba, Placer, Yolo, and Sacramento counties in the Sacramento Valley; and San Joaquin, Stanislaus, Merced, Madera, Fresno, Kings, Tulare, and Kern counties in the San Joaquin Valley (see map 3).[11] Almost completely flat, the Central Valley rises gradually in each direction from near sea level at its center,

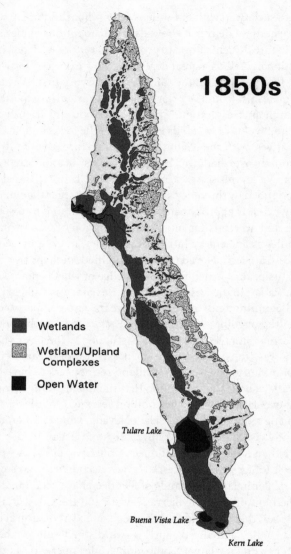

1850s

Wetlands

Wetland/Upland
Complexes

Open Water

Tulare Lake

Buena Vista Lake

Kern Lake

MAP 2. The extent of wetlands in the Central Valley in the 1850s (left) and the 1990s. In addition to the pronounced wetland decline throughout the valley, note the elimination of open water in the valley's southernmost reaches. Courtesy of the U.S. Fish and Wildlife Service, Division of Habitat Conservation, Branch of Habitat Assessment.

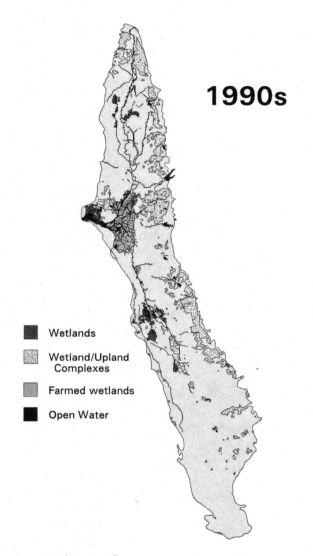

1990s

■ Wetlands

▦ Wetland/Upland
   Complexes

▨ Farmed wetlands

■ Open Water

MAP 2. (continued)

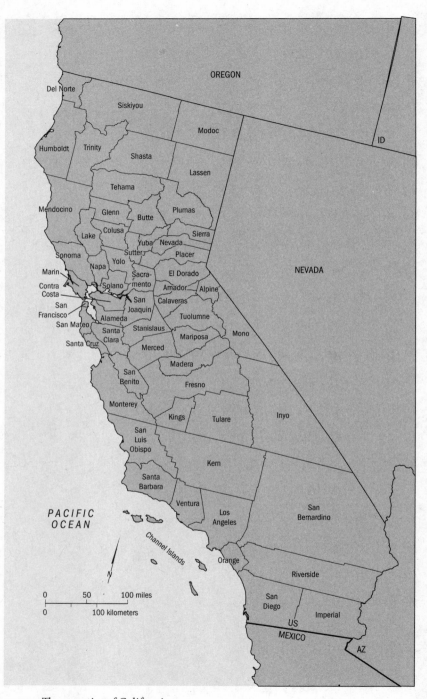

OREGON

Del Norte

Siskiyou

Modoc

ID

Humboldt Trinity Shasta

Lassen

Tehama

Mendocino Glenn Butte Plumas

Lake Colusa Sierra

Yuba Nevada

Sutter Placer

Sonoma Yolo

Napa

Marin Sacra-
mento El Dorado

NEVADA

Contra
Costa Solano Amador Alpine

San
Francisco San
Joaquin Calaveras

San Mateo Alameda Tuolumne

Santa
Clara Stanislaus Mariposa

Santa Cruz Merced Mono

San
Benito Madera

Monterey Fresno

Kings Tulare Inyo

San
Luis
Obispo

Kern

Santa
Barbara

PACIFIC
OCEAN Ventura Los
Angeles San
Bernardino

Channel Islands Orange

Riverside

N

San
Diego Imperial

US
MEXICO AZ

0   50   100 miles
0   100 kilometers

MAP 3. The counties of California.

reaching elevations approaching four hundred feet at its northern and southern extremes. The volcanic Sutter Buttes, rising from the middle of the northern valley floor and reaching an elevation of approximately two thousand feet, offer the only significant topographical relief along the entire length of the valley.

The Central Valley is drained by the Sacramento and San Joaquin rivers, the first and second longest rivers, respectively, that flow entirely within the state of California.[12] At the confluence of the rivers, near the center of the valley, lies one of the world's great inland deltas, the Sacramento–San Joaquin Delta. From the Delta the combined flow of the Sacramento and San Joaquin rivers drains westward through a break in the Coast Ranges into San Francisco Bay and the Pacific Ocean beyond. During most of the 1.6 million years of the Pleistocene epoch, expansive shallow lakes occupied the Central Valley, particularly in its southern portion. A number of these lakes survived through the ten thousand years of the current Holocene epoch, disappearing only as nineteenth- and twentieth-century Californians drained them, largely for agricultural purposes.[13]

While the Central Valley has been endowed with rich soils, it has been denied abundant moisture. Annual rainfall in the valley declines dramatically from north to south, with Redding, at the northern end, averaging a generous 33.5 inches; Sacramento, near the center, averaging just below 20 inches; and Bakersfield, at the southern end, averaging a mere 6.5 inches. In pursuit of irrigation water for agriculture—and later of drinking water for southern cities—Californians have struggled to bring water from the relatively moist Sacramento Valley to the semi-arid San Joaquin Valley. In the process, they have dammed and diverted rivers, drained ancient lakes, destroyed millions of acres of wetlands, and, overall, reshaped the landscape to an almost unimaginable degree.

For hundreds of millennia before the first European settlers arrived, the Central Valley was a rich, diverse landscape that supported large populations of both resident and migratory species of fish and wildlife. Its freshwater lakes and marshes, riparian forests, and grasslands dotted with vernal pools provided habitat for tule elk and pronghorn antelope, grizzly bears that migrated annually from the foothills of the Sierra Nevada, and waterfowl in such concentrations that they darkened the sky as they flew overhead. During the nineteenth century, tens of millions of Pacific Flyway waterfowl wintered annually in the wetlands of the Central Valley. The waterfowl were drawn to the valley's open water and vast tule marshes, named after the common tule, or hardstem bulrush, the defining plant of California's Central Valley freshwater marshes.[14] By the early twentieth century, as wetland acreage in the Central Valley plummeted, the number of waterfowl wintering in the valley declined precipitously.

Many of the Central Valley's wetlands were first drained by diverting and channelizing the rivers that fed them. Enormous dams then further tamed the valley's rivers and prevented them from overflowing their banks and recharging the wetlands. California leads the nation both in the number of large dams and reservoirs and in their total water storage capacity. More than fourteen hundred state and federal dams and their reservoirs capture 42 million acre-feet of water, almost 60 percent of the average annual runoff for the entire state.[15] The main purposes of the dams are flood control for the Sacramento Valley and the provision of irrigation and drinking water for the San Joaquin Valley and Southern California. Despite dams and irrigation diversions, the wetlands of the Central Valley continue to be vitally important for the wintering waterfowl of the Pacific Flyway. Central Valley wetlands provide wintering habitat for approximately 60 percent of the migratory waterfowl of that flyway, and a remarkable 19 percent of all the waterfowl in the continental United States. Central Valley wetlands also shelter numerous federal and state endangered and threatened species.[16]

Throughout most of the nineteenth century, the ecological benefits of wetlands were largely unknown. Beginning with the Swamp and Overflowed Lands Act of 1849, which was extended to include California in 1850, the policy of the United States government was to promote the drainage of wetlands by the states for conversion to agriculture.[17] This policy reflected the long-standing belief that wetlands were wastelands that not only failed to provide economic benefits, but also posed a significant health risk from malaria. Such a view of wetlands differed sharply from that of the Native American inhabitants of the Central Valley, who found them a valuable source of both sustenance and raw materials—and later used them as a place of refuge from Spanish and Mexican authorities seeking to confine them to California's missions. As Californians rapidly converted Central Valley wetland habitat to agriculture during the late nineteenth and early twentieth centuries, waterfowl appeared to them more a nuisance than a resource, as geese fed in their wheat fields and, later, ducks devoured their rice crops. In this environment, waterfowl were widely hunted for the market—an activity that served as much to inhibit crop depredations as to supply the restaurants and hotels of San Francisco and the state capital, Sacramento. As market hunting led to the noticeable decline of waterfowl and other game bird populations, state and federal laws were passed to protect migratory birds, culminating in the Migratory Bird Treaty with Canada in 1916.

The first national bird-banding program, begun in 1920 under the auspices of the U.S. Bureau of Biological Survey, accelerated the mapping of the four great migratory flyways—the Pacific, Central, Mississippi, and Atlantic—that traverse the continent.[18] The discovery of the importance of wetland habitat for maintaining migratory waterfowl populations laid the foundation for the shift in scientific and public perceptions of wetlands that took place during the twentieth century. Scientists began to realize that the decline of waterfowl populations was no longer primarily caused by market hunting, as may have been the case in the late nineteenth century, but rather resulted from the loss of wetland habitat because of drainage and reclamation. Beginning in the 1930s, private citizens, notably those who formed Ducks Unlimited, launched efforts to protect the breeding grounds of North America's waterfowl.[19] At the same time, state and federal officials initiated an era of wildlife refuge creation in the Central Valley to protect the wintering grounds of the Pacific Flyway waterfowl.

During the second half of the twentieth century, as the ecological importance of wetlands became increasingly clear, a number of formal scientific and legal definitions were formulated to further their study and to enable their preservation. In the early 1950s the U.S. Fish and Wildlife Service conducted the first systematic inventory of the nation's wetlands. The agency's 1956 report, *Wetlands of the United States,* introduced the new term *wetland* to replace older, more value-laden terms, such as *swamp, marsh, bog, fen, mire,* and *moor.*[20] The Fish and Wildlife Service emphasized that wetlands are important as waterfowl habitat and identified twenty types of wetlands, which remained the basis of wetland classification in the United States for more than two decades. In 1979 the service introduced the most comprehensive definition of wetlands to date, defining them as lands that are transitional between terrestrial and aquatic ecosystems. The new definition introduced the terms *hydrophytes* (plants adapted to wet conditions) and *hydric soils* (anaerobic soils formed under conditions of saturation), attributes that indicate the presence of a wetland.[21]

To facilitate greater precision in the study of wetlands, the Fish and Wildlife Service developed a hierarchical classification scheme, analogous to the taxonomic classifications for plants and animals that assign them to genera and species. Under this classification system, there are two main categories of wetlands (as opposed to deepwater habitats, such as lakes, reservoirs, rivers, and streams) present in the Central Valley. In the mid-1980s the service found that tidal, or estuarine, wetlands accounted for approximately 60,000 acres, or 16 percent, of the valley's extant 379,000 acres of wetlands. These tidal wetlands are located primarily in and adjacent to the Sacramento–San Joaquin Delta. Nontidal, or palustrine, wetlands accounted for much more, approximately 319,000 acres, or 84 percent, of the valley's surviving wetlands.[22]

Each of the Central Valley's four major physiographic regions—the Sacramento Valley, the Sacramento–San Joaquin Delta, the San Joaquin Basin, and the Tulare Basin—has been dramatically altered by human action.[23] The common threads that link their physical transformation have been the draining of their permanent and seasonal wetlands, and the simplification and homogenization of their biota. Yet the history of each region, while interwoven with and influencing the history of the others, has followed a unique trajectory. These four histories can tell us much about the ways in which nineteenth- and twentieth-century Americans valued the natural world, and how these value systems began to change—and continue to change—in the face of ecological limits.

Most of the first half of this book, "The Fall" (chapters 2–5), examines the history of the Central Valley's four regions from well before statehood through the early twentieth century, a period when the valley's wetlands were declining precipitously. Yet even during this early period there were signs of change on the horizon, indications that the plight of wetland-dependent waterfowl was entering the public consciousness. The beginning of restrictions on the hunting and sale of wild game in California augured the far-reaching changes in attitudes about the protection of waterfowl and wetlands that lay ahead. The second half of the book, "The Rise" (chapters 6–10), begins with a discussion of the pathbreaking Migratory Bird Treaty with Canada, the discovery of the Pacific Flyway, and the origins of the Central Valley's first waterfowl refuges. Subsequent chapters analyze the reasons behind the revival of each of the region's wetlands in the middle and later twentieth century and beyond. But here again, that recovery was not absolute, as the Central Valley's wetlands continued to face serious challenges and setbacks. While wetlands were restored, to a greater or lesser degree, in each of the valley's four regions, this time period also witnessed the destruction of a significant portion of the San Joaquin River (which would not begin to be reversed until late in the first decade of the twenty-first century) and the widespread poisoning of wildlife on one of the Central Valley's national wildlife refuges. The "fall and rise" of the Central Valley's wetlands in the book's title thus signifies a broad shift in direction from the destruction of wetlands to their recovery, rather than a linear trajectory. Along similar lines, the title of the book is not intended to suggest that the rise has been commensurate with the fall. With millions of people now calling the Central Valley their home, the extent of the valley's wetlands cannot realistically be restored to what it once was, but it is nevertheless significant that since the second half of the twentieth century, California's Central Valley wetlands have been ascendant, reversing a lengthy period of decline.

In the Central Valley overall, the greatest single wetland area that has been lost is Tulare Lake with its surrounding tule marshes in the Tulare Basin, the southern portion of the San Joaquin Valley. From a historic maximum area of 760 square miles and a maximum depth approaching forty feet, Tulare Lake today is entirely gone, and its bed and the basin's former tule marshes have been converted almost completely to agriculture.[24] The Tulare Basin was drained piecemeal, beginning in the 1850s with small-scale irrigation projects along the rivers—especially the Kings, Kaweah, and Tule—that fed Tulare Lake. The 1870s witnessed an influx of new land-hungry settlers, following the construction of a Southern Pacific railroad line through the basin. As farmers diverted the rivers and streams that fed Tulare Lake and the tule marshes that it supported, the lake inexorably shrank until, by the early twentieth century, it had ceased to exist in all but extreme flood years. More so than any other region in the Central Valley, the

Tulare Basin has been irrevocably altered, and restoration efforts there face the most daunting challenges.

In contrast to the Tulare Basin, where drainage was more a consequence of settlement than a prerequisite, the Sacramento Valley could not develop until the threat of frequent, devastating floods along the Sacramento River and its tributaries was removed. This threat increased as nineteenth-century hydraulic mining enterprises deposited massive quantities of debris in the valley's rivers, raising their beds and increasing the likelihood that high flows would overtop their banks.[25] Although hydraulic mining in California was effectively terminated in federal court in 1884, decades elapsed before the Sacramento Valley received effective flood protection.[26] Despite more than a half-century of reclamation and flood control efforts by large landowners and urban boosters from throughout the valley, protection ultimately could not come about as a result of local or even regional efforts, but only as a direct result of the state's Flood Control Act of 1911 and the landmark federal Flood Control Act of 1917, which for the first time made flood control a federal responsibility.[27] These two acts made possible the construction of the Sacramento Flood Control Project, a system of levees, weirs, and bypasses that protects the Sacramento Valley to this day. Only after the Sacramento River was finally tamed could the reclamation of the Sacramento Valley's tremendous wetland basins and their conversion to agriculture proceed successfully.[28]

The history of the Sacramento Valley offers an opportunity to investigate some of the unintended consequences of manipulating the natural world and the ironies associated with wetland protection. During the early decades of the twentieth century, much of the Sacramento Valley was converted to profitable rice production. However, because the valley's natural wetlands had been reclaimed, hungry migratory ducks were drawn to the private rice fields. The large-scale crop depredations that followed led to a crescendo of calls by the same farmers who had benefited from the valley's reclamation to create wetland refuges in the valley. Some of the earliest motivations behind the creation of these refuges in the Sacramento Valley stemmed, therefore, more from economic interests than from an ecological awareness of the importance of wetlands as wintering habitat for the migratory waterfowl of the Pacific Flyway.

The Sacramento–San Joaquin Delta, in the heart of the Central Valley, has been profoundly altered by the development of an extensive levee system to protect its many low-lying islands, the dredging of its channels for navigation, the hydrologic effects of upstream dams, and a decline in water quality caused by the diversion of fresh water for agricultural and municipal use. Historically, Delta islands had regularly been inundated by flood flows from the Sacramento and San Joaquin rivers, but the Delta was almost completely reclaimed for agriculture during the seven decades from 1860 to 1930, and formerly extensive habitat for waterfowl and other wetland animals and plants was destroyed.[29] As the islands were surrounded by levees, drained, and converted to agricultural use, their organic peat soils began to erode. Consequently, the interior portions of many of the Delta islands have subsided to twenty or more feet below sea level, increasing the risk of levee failures and threatening the state's complex engineering system of water transfers from the Sacramento Valley through the Delta to the San Joaquin Valley and Southern California. The same water transfers have contributed to the endangerment of native species and the state's once-significant salmon runs.

In contrast to the gradual draining of the Tulare Basin, containment of the raging floodwaters of the Sacramento River, and reclamation of the Sacramento–San Joaquin Delta, hydraulic engineering in California has at times had immediate consequences for wetlands. The Central Valley Project, California's largest water storage and diversion undertaking, was authorized for construction as a federal reclamation project in 1935.[30] It posed a direct threat to the wetlands of the northern San Joaquin Valley, in a region of the San Joaquin Basin known as the Grasslands, home to one-third of the remaining wetland acreage in all of the Central Valley.

Throughout the late nineteenth and early twentieth centuries, much of the overflow grasslands along the San Joaquin River lay within the cattle empire of Henry Miller and Charles Lux, two of California's largest landowners of that era. For decades, Miller and Lux reaped the benefits of the flood flows of the San Joaquin River, which produced valuable crops of annual grasses for their cattle and provided habitat for migratory waterfowl. During the early twentieth century, after the death of both of its founders, the firm of Miller and Lux sold much of these overflow grasslands to private duck hunting clubs, establishing a regional economy in which cattle ranching and waterfowl hunting successfully coexisted. But the construction of Friant Dam—a major component of the Central Valley Project—on the San Joaquin River in the 1940s dewatered the river below the dam and deprived the Grasslands of its historic water supply, thereby threatening to obliterate its wetlands. Among the many ironies explored in this book is the fact that at the same time that government agencies were creating state and federal wetland refuges throughout the Central Valley to protect Pacific Flyway waterfowl, the Central Valley Project was threatening to destroy private wetlands. As a result of the persistent political efforts of local duck hunting clubs and their allies dedicated to preserving these private lands, Congress passed a historic reauthorization of the Central Valley Project in 1954 that for the first time recognized the protection of fish and wildlife as a purpose of the project.[31]

A generation later, the Grasslands of the San Joaquin Basin were again threatened by the consequences of the Central Valley Project. This time the threat came in the form of elevated levels of selenium, a naturally occurring element that was leached by irrigation water from agricultural soils on the western side of the San Joaquin Valley, and then channeled by a drainage system into the ponds of the newly created Kesterson National Wildlife Refuge. Accumulating there in high concentrations, the selenium caused widespread avian death and deformity in the early 1980s.[32] In the aftermath of this particularly tragic episode at Kesterson, the consequences of irrigated agriculture were reevaluated and a new era of unprecedented protection and restoration of California's Central Valley wetlands was born.

. . .

The scientific community has demonstrated a strong interest in wetlands for decades, and historians have begun to wade into this promising field of scholarship as well, with the completion of several fine studies.[33] This interdisciplinary study of wetlands is thus intended, in part, to serve the needs of historians seeking a more detailed understanding of wetlands, but also to provide wetland ecologists, environmental scientists, and policy makers a longer-term historical perspective within which to situate their work. At the same time, I hope that this book will foster increased public interest in wetlands and their protection.

To the growing body of historical scholarship on wetlands, this book adds a dimension of natural history and ecology that attempts to return waterfowl to their deserved central place in the narrative. Had it not been for the discovery of the importance of wetlands for maintaining waterfowl populations, the impetus for halting the destruction of wetlands in California's Central Valley and across the nation would have been long delayed, and untold numbers of additional wetland acres would have been lost. To emphasize the indissoluble nexus between wetlands and the waterfowl they support, chapter 1 of this book is dedicated to a discussion of the natural wetland environments of the Central Valley, as well as to the breeding and wintering habitat requirements of the waterfowl species most important to the Pacific Flyway in general and to California's Central Valley in particular. (Scientific names of these and other species discussed in the book are provided in an appendix.) Because the waterfowl that winter in the wetlands of the Central Valley breed, for the most part, thousands of miles away in Alaska and Canada, a study of the life cycle of these birds requires analysis on a variety of scales.[34] These scales range from tiny microhabitats within a single wetland to the length of the transcontinental flyway. Only by coming to know the birds themselves, on all the relevant scales, can we truly come to an appreciation of their intrinsic value, above and beyond anthropocentric considerations such as economic value, and therefore better understand the motivations and passions of those who fought, and continue to fight, to save them.

In addition to introducing a distinctly ecological component to the story of the Central Valley wetlands, this book relates the changing fortunes of these wetlands to agricultural and western history. At the core of this inquiry are the questions of why public and private attitudes about wetlands have changed so dramatically, and when those changes occurred. Ecologists have made tremendous advances toward understanding the physical and biological processes that take place in wetlands, and therefore in demonstrating their importance to both human and nonhuman organisms. The rise of contemporary environmentalism since the 1960s and 1970s has further effected a dramatic reevaluation of our relationship with the natural world. With that reevaluation has come a critical new look at the stories that we tell ourselves about the past. One of the historical myths that has come under attack is the myth of the predestined transformation of the U.S. West from an untamed wilderness to an agricultural Eden. It has become increasingly clear that this myth of inevitability obscures the fact that the conversion of western lands—including wetlands—to agriculture was the result of social and political processes driven by individual and institutional decisions.[35] But how has this transformation been largely halted and in some places reversed? What kinds of dissent and protest have arisen against the continuing destruction of wetlands in favor of agricultural development? How and why has the expertise of engineers from the U.S. Bureau of Reclamation and the U.S. Army Corps of Engineers, builders of dams and reclamation projects, been questioned and partially superseded by the expertise of ecologists and other natural resource managers? Finally, what do the state and federal creation of wildlife refuges and the private creation of managed wetlands for waterfowl conservation tell us about public and private commitment to environmental protection?

In answering these questions, this book offers a further critique of the "agricultural mystique" of the West—the belief that agriculture, and the control of nature it implies, represents the optimal use for western lands.[36] The conversion of wetlands for agriculture, whether as a direct result of reclamation projects or as a consequence of flood control measures, was clearly intended to domesticate the landscape and create a productive garden in the Central Valley. However, there were profound—and largely unforeseen—ecological consequences. Drastic reduction of their wintering habitat led to critical food shortages for migratory waterfowl, which in turn resulted in crop depredations that were severe enough to threaten the valley's agricultural economy. The increasing concentration of waterfowl on rapidly diminishing habitat resulted in severe outbreaks of fatal diseases such as avian botulism and cholera. In the case of the Kesterson National Wildlife Refuge, reliance on agricultural wastewater resulted in the death and deformity of both waterfowl and shorebirds from selenium poisoning.

In part as a result of these unfortunate ecological consequences, the base of support for wetlands and waterfowl has broadened in recent years to include academic and government scientists, especially the biologists and ecologists of the U.S. Fish and Wildlife Service; nonprofit organizations, such as Ducks Unlimited and the Nature Conservancy; and the general public, which has embraced wetland-friendly legislation.[37] Through domestic legislation, executive orders, and international treaties, wetland conservation has become a focus of national policy. The United States National Wetlands Inventory Program, begun in 1974 by the U.S. Fish and Wildlife Service, has generated detailed maps and has led to a series of *Status and Trends* reports on U.S. wetlands.[38] On a global scale, international conventions such as the Convention on Wetlands of International Importance, held in Ramsar, Iran, in 1971, have recognized the importance of intergovernmental cooperation on wetland conservation.[39] This broadened base of support has led to a number of pathbreaking new directions in public policy, many of which directly affect California's Central Valley. Those policy initiatives, discussed in detail in chapter 10, have resulted in the protection and restoration of hundreds of thousands of acres of Central Valley wetlands.

Despite such substantial gains, the wetlands of California's Great Central Valley face an uncertain future, subject to continuing pressures from population growth, urban expansion, and economic development, as well as the threat of global climate change. However, there are grounds for optimism as the policy pendulum has swung, perhaps irrevocably, from promoting the destruction of wetlands at all costs to devoting scarce resources, even at the expense of irrigated agriculture, to their protection. Underlying these efforts on behalf of Central Valley wetlands is an evolving understanding of their ecological importance not only for providing habitat for the wintering waterfowl of the Pacific Flyway, but also for sustaining the rich diversity of the valley's wetland-dependent species.

PART ONE

Wetlands and Waterfowl

The Nature of the Great Central Valley and the Pacific Flyway

Before the arrival of European Americans, wetlands were present across the length and breadth of the Central Valley. Waterfowl and other waterbirds swam on the surface or stood in the shallows of permanent and seasonal freshwater marshes, which were renewed annually by the spring flooding of the valley's rivers. Thundering honks and quacks of enormous flocks of geese and ducks, descending from the sky or taking flight en masse from the water, revealed from afar the locations of these marshes, clustered in the low-lying and poorly drained basins (or troughs) of the valley. Ephemeral vernal pools and larger playa pools, filled with aquatic invertebrates and surrounded by brilliantly colored flowers, lay scattered amid millions of acres of native valley grasslands. Expansive riparian forests with their massive valley oaks, as well as evergreen oaks, cottonwoods, and sycamores, lined the major rivers and creeks, creating thick ribbons of green and vertical relief from the flat valley floor. Within these seasonally flooded forests, herons, egrets, and cormorants roosted in colonies, and brightly colored wood ducks nested and raised their young in tree cavities.

Each of these three natural communities—freshwater marsh, valley grassland, and riparian woodland—either was defined by wetlands or contained a wetland element, and at least some of the plants and animals in each community were adapted to live in wetlands. Over the past two centuries, each community has been dramatically altered and numerous species of flora and fauna have been displaced, waterfowl not least among them. The history of each community therefore reveals a distinct component of the overall ecological transformation of the Central Valley and the disappearance of its wetlands.[1]

VALLEY GRASSLAND

Valley grassland was the most extensive of the Central Valley's three natural communities. Once believed to have been dominated by perennial bunchgrasses—including needlegrasses, three-awn grasses, bluegrasses, and ryegrasses—which grow upright in dense tufts of stems that rise several feet above the ground from their root crowns, native grassland vegetation was far more likely a complex mosaic of plant communities that included perennial bunchgrasses, annual grasses, annual and perennial forbs, and, in the extreme southern end of the valley, desert scrub vegetation.[2] Historically, during the spring, wildflowers dominated parts of the valley grassland community and produced startling displays that carpeted parts of the valley floor in dazzling color. The great nineteenth-century conservationist John Muir famously characterized these flowering lands as "bee pastures" and described their magnificence:

> The Great Central Plain of California, during the months of March, April, and May, was one smooth, continuous bed of honey-bloom, so marvelously rich that, in walking from one end of it to the other, a distance of more than 400 miles, your foot would press about a hundred flowers at every step. Mints, gilias, nemophilas, castilleias, and innumerable compositae were so crowded together that, had ninety-nine percent of them been taken away, the plain would still have seemed to any but Californians extravagantly flowery. The radiant, honeyful corollas, touching and overlapping, and rising above one another, glowed in the living light like a sunset sky—one sheet of purple and gold, with the bright Sacramento pouring through the midst of it from the north, the San Joaquin from the south, and their many tributaries sweeping in at right angles from the mountains, dividing the plain into sections fringed with trees.[3]

Although Muir may have taken some literary license in claiming that the entire Central Valley was covered in wildflowers, this passage is worth savoring, because we are unlikely ever to see such a scene. Only about 1 percent of the native valley grassland remains.[4] As historical geographer William Preston has written, "The most dramatic alterations anywhere in continental America occurred within California's grasslands."[5]

Unlike the riparian woodlands and freshwater marshes, Central Valley grasslands were already significantly altered during the years before California statehood in 1850. Alien grasses of Mediterranean origin appear to have become established prior to the beginning of the Spanish mission period in 1769, perhaps from seeds disseminated during earlier exploratory voyages. One of the most telling pieces of evidence for this early establishment has been the discovery of specimens of introduced grasses in the adobe bricks of the earliest Spanish missions. During the Spanish period, cattle grazed widely in coastal California; after the Mexican government began granting large ranchos under the terms of the

Colonization Act of 1824, cattle spread into the Central Valley as well. Overgrazing and extended periods of drought, such as that from 1828 to 1830, weakened the competitive abilities of native grasses compared to nonnatives. Native perennial grasses in particular were inferior competitors to nonnative annual grasses because annual grasses produce deep and extensive root systems more rapidly than perennials and thus can acquire a larger share of soil nutrients and soil moisture. Under these conditions, the grasses wild oats and ripgut brome became established near the missions along the southern and central coasts and spread inland, expanding first into the San Joaquin Valley and, by the time of the Gold Rush, into the Sacramento Valley as well.[6]

Accounts by early travelers corroborate this chronology. During his travels in California from July 1833 to July 1834, fur trader Zenas Leonard reported seeing "a large prairie covered with wild oats," which he called the "Oat Plain," in the lower San Joaquin Valley, near the confluence of the Merced and San Joaquin rivers.[7] Farther north, near the Mokelumne River, Edwin Bryant recorded on September 14, 1846, "We passed through large tracts of wild oats during the day; the stalks are generally from three to five feet in length."[8] Thus, archaeological evidence and travelers' accounts suggest that long before the first marshes were drained or riparian woodlands cleared, the matrix of valley grasslands in which they lay had already been transformed.

The Gold Rush led to a dramatic increase in grazing pressure, especially in the Central Valley. Native grasses and forbs were adapted to seasonal grazing by herds of pronghorn and tule elk, as well as deer, rabbits, and rodents, but not to the continuous and heavy grazing of millions of domesticated sheep and cattle. By 1860, at the height of the cattle boom, there were one million domestic cattle grazing in California.[9] Drought conditions during the 1860s led to the widespread replacement of cattle by sheep, which could survive on less forage, and by 1880 the number of sheep in California had peaked at 5.7 million. By this time, the combination of drought and overgrazing had destroyed much of the native valley grassland.[10] As a result, today the most common grassland species are all introduced European annuals: filaree, soft chess, wild oat, ripgut brome, annual ryegrass, foxtail, fescue, and California burclover.[11]

In the poorly drained alkali soils of the southern and western portions of the San Joaquin Valley, a region characterized by sinks that lack drainage to the ocean, the grassland is composed of alkali-tolerant species such as saltgrass, iodine bush, and various kinds of saltbushes, which provide a desertlike visage. This sparse desert scrub vegetation often borders completely barren soils that contain the highest percentages of alkali salts.[12] William H. Brewer, a member of Josiah Dwight Whitney's California State Geological Survey of 1860–1864, provided a striking description of these lands. Brewer's journal details more than fourteen thousand miles of travel up and down California. Writing during the

FIGURE 1. Alkali grassland at the San Luis National Wildlife Refuge, northern San Joaquin Valley. In this harsh environment, alkali salts cover the ground surface of the barren patches. Photo by the author.

drought of 1864, he described the valley plain between the Kings River and the town of Visalia in the southern San Joaquin Valley: "In a few miles we passed the belt of oaks that skirts the [Kings] river for a couple of miles on each side; then across the barren, treeless plain, still perfectly level—in places entirely bare, in others with some alkali grass. The surface of the soil was so alkaline that it was crisp under the horses' feet, as if covered with a thin sheet of frozen ground."[13] These arid, alkali lands (see figure 1) offer a striking contrast to Muir's "bee pastures" elsewhere in the Central Valley.

Scattered throughout much of the valley grassland are complexes of vernal pools, seasonal ephemeral wetlands that form in shallow depressions underlain by an impermeable surface such as claypan, hardpan, or rock.[14] They are fed primarily by winter precipitation, but also by surface swales and subsurface water flow.[15] As the pools dry up in the spring and hot summer months, a number of annual plant species flower, often in conspicuous concentric rings of vibrant colors. Among the most common plants are meadowfoam, goldfields, popcornflowers, and downingia. The soil and hydrologic conditions in vernal pools render it difficult for exotic plant species to invade, with the result that they are one of the few low-elevation habitats still dominated by native species.[16]

Despite increasing fragmentation and overall estimated losses of 60 to 85 percent, vernal pool habitat remains in every county of the Central Valley, forming a ring along the valley's perimeter and a swath in the basin lands along the valley's floor.[17] Central Valley vernal pools and their adjacent uplands provide habitat for plants, aquatic invertebrates, amphibians, reptiles, birds, and mammals, including approximately eighty species of plants and animals that are listed as endangered, threatened, or of special concern.[18] The larger vernal pools, known as playa pools, provide important foraging and courtship areas for numerous species of migrating ducks, as well as locally breeding mallards, gadwalls, and cinnamon teal. The abundant invertebrate fauna in the pools provide an important source of protein and calcium necessary for the ducks' migration and reproduction. The pools also support many additional species of wetland birds, including tundra swans, great egrets, great blue herons, black-necked stilts, and American avocets. The protein-rich grasses of the adjacent uplands provide an optimal food source for Ross's, white-fronted, Canada, and cackling geese, as well as American wigeon, a grazing duck species.[19] Thus, despite their relatively small size and ephemeral nature, vernal pool landscapes provide vital links in the Central Valley portion of the Pacific Flyway.[20]

RIPARIAN WOODLAND

Historically, the two major river systems of the Central Valley, the Sacramento and the San Joaquin, flooded their banks in winter and spring, inundating the once-vast riparian forests that lined the riverbanks and forming extensive seasonal wetlands. These riparian wetlands accounted for approximately 1.6 million of the 4 million original acres of Central Valley wetlands.[21] These riparian ecosystems formed—and their remnants continue to form—a conspicuous feature in the landscape (see figure 2), in contrast to the adjacent arid or semiarid grassland.

The largest and most diverse riparian forests occurred on those rivers having well-developed natural levees, but riparian systems were found along virtually all of the numerous watercourses in the Central Valley. In the Sacramento Valley, the Feather, Yuba, Bear, and American rivers, as well as the substantial Butte Creek, drain westward into the Sacramento River from the Sierra Nevada. Natural levees of the Sacramento River and naturally occurring flood basins historically blocked some streams from reaching the main river system. Instead, these streams, including Putah and Cache creeks, which flow eastward out of the Coast Ranges, spread out over the valley floor, typically pooling in expansive sinks of tule marsh, and connecting to the Sacramento River only by subsurface flow.[22] The San Joaquin Valley—drier on the whole than the Sacramento Valley—possesses few significant drainages from the Coast Ranges but a greater number of major rivers draining from the Sierra Nevada, including, in addition to the San Joaquin River itself, the Cosumnes, Mokelumne, Stanislaus, Tuolumne, Merced, Kings, Kaweah, Tule, and Kern rivers.

FIGURE 2. Riparian woodland along the lower Stanislaus River. Throughout the Central Valley, watercourses can generally be located from a distance by the meandering line of riparian vegetation present along their banks. Photo courtesy of Tim Palmer.

Riparian forests along these rivers and creeks extended from the banks to the edge of the moist soil zone, and, in many cases, as far as the hundred-year flood line. These complexly structured forests achieved their greatest widths, four to five miles on each side, on the banks of the lower Sacramento River, where natural levees are widest. Forming the canopy was the signature tree of the Central Valley, the massive, sprawling, deciduous valley oak, along with the broad evergreen interior live oak, the Fremont cottonwood, and the western sycamore. Intermediate layers were composed of box elder, Oregon ash, alder, and various species of willow. The diverse undergrowth included such species as wild rose, blackberry, and poison oak. Vines, including wild grape, often grew through the various layers.[23]

The valley oak, in particular, captured the attention of early visitors to the valley. Along his journey up the Sacramento River in 1837, Captain Sir Edward Belcher of the British Royal Navy reported, "Within, and at the very edge of the banks, oaks of immense size were plentiful. These appeared to form a band on each side, about three hundred yards in depth. . . . Several of these oaks were examined, and some of the smaller felled. The two most remarkable measured respectively twenty-seven and nineteen feet in circumference, at three feet above ground. The latter rose perpendicularly at a (computed) height of sixty feet before expanding its branches, and was truly a noble sight."[24] Riparian vegetation in the Central Valley was quickly destroyed in the wake of the Gold Rush, when many prospectors turned toward agriculture as a source of a more stable livelihood. Growing agricultural communities utilized the riparian forests, which were often the only significant woody vegetation on the valley floor, for fencing, lumber, and fuel. The soil on the rivers' natural levees, which supported these forests, was highly fertile, easily managed, and not subject to the seasonal flooding of lower ground just beyond. Orchards, in particular, were suited to these well-drained soils, and much riparian vegetation was therefore removed to make way for fruit trees.[25]

The ecological importance of these riparian forests was not fully realized until the second half of the twentieth century, by which time only an estimated 2 percent to 6 percent of historical riparian areas remained.[26] Riparian trees reinforce riverbanks and provide greater stability to river channels, and they act as windbreaks and reduce evaporation. The forests provide critical habitat for aquatic, terrestrial, and arboreal wildlife, including mammals, reptiles, amphibians, and birds. Waterbirds—especially great blue herons, great egrets, snowy egrets, black-crowned night herons, and double-crested cormorants—roost there in sizable colonies. Among waterfowl, wood ducks and common mergansers raise their young in tree cavities. The disappearance of the riparian forests is particularly associated with a historical decline in the abundance of the beautiful, artfully colored wood duck, once a common year-round resident in the Central Valley, and now the object of conservation efforts.[27]

FRESHWATER MARSH

Of the three types of Central Valley freshwater wetlands—the vernal pools within the grassland, the riparian wetlands, and the marshes that filled the valley's basins—the marshes were by far the most important for waterfowl. Most of the seasonal and permanent freshwater marshes present in the Central Valley are classified, in the U.S. Fish and Wildlife Service's hierarchical approach, as persistent emergent wetlands.[28] This precise designation is useful for visualizing the valley's wetlands; it implies the presence of species of vegetation that are rooted in the marsh soils, emerge above the water level, and generally persist, or remain standing, until the beginning of the next growing season. Much of the tremendous productivity of wetlands is contributed by these rooted herbaceous emergent plants, which include cattail and tule in deeper water, and, in shallower water, rushes, spikerushes, knotweeds and smartweeds, docks, and aquatic grasses such as wild millet. Along pond edges and in moist soils, saltgrass is prevalent, along with arrowhead, water plantain, and bur-reed. A typical flooded marsh is often a mosaic not only of emergents and moist-soil plants, but also of floating

FIGURE 3. Tule-lined freshwater marsh, with red-winged blackbirds, at the San Luis National Wildlife Refuge. Photo by the author.

plants and of submergents, plants lying below the surface. Floating plants include those that float freely on the surface of the water, taking their nutrients directly from the water column, as well as those that are rooted in the substrate and extend their leaves to the surface on long stalks (petioles). The tiny duckweed is an example of the former; the invasive water lily provides a well-known example of the latter. Submergents are usually rooted in the substrate and are able effectively to capture light underwater. The seed-bearing pondweeds, such as sago pondweed, are among the most important groups of submergent plants, which also include hornwort, ditch-grass, and common water-nymph. Emergents, moist-soil plants, floating plants, and submergents, along with algae, are the primary producers in a marsh. They form the base of the food chain, and provide food as well as nesting habitat and cover for waterfowl (see figure 3).[29]

The Central Valley's seasonal and permanent freshwater marshes were historically located in the numerous river overflow basins of the Sacramento and San Joaquin valleys as well as in the tidal channels of the Sacramento–San Joaquin Delta. The Sacramento Valley contains five major flood basins, three—Butte, Sutter, and American—to the east of the Sacramento River, and two—Colusa and Yolo—to the west. The basins were initially formed and then repeatedly flooded by the Sacramento River itself.[30] After descending into the valley from its head-

waters in the Klamath Mountains to the north, during flood stages the Sacramento River deposited sediments beyond its banks. Because the velocity of
floodwaters decreases as soon as they escape a river channel, the Sacramento
River deposited its coarse, heavier sediments first, thereby creating natural levees. As the floodwaters extended farther out onto the floodplain and lost their
remaining velocity, they dropped the rest of their sediment load. These finer
sediments became the basis for the valley's adobe (clay) soils. This land reaches
low points (troughs) on either side of the river before beginning to rise again
onto alluvial deposits from the Sierra Nevada to the east and the Coast Ranges to
the west.[31] These natural basins acted as reservoirs for winter floodwaters and
could remain inundated well into the spring, providing vast breeding as well as
wintering areas for waterfowl. While the other basins have been largely reclaimed, the Butte Basin, farthest to the north, continues to support the highest
concentration of waterfowl anywhere in the Sacramento Valley.[32]

Lying between the Sacramento and San Joaquin valleys, the Sacramento–San
Joaquin Delta is the hydrological linchpin of California. A complex labyrinth of
sloughs and marshes, the Delta is a product of its topography. As the Sacramento
and San Joaquin rivers descend toward sea level near their confluence in the
Delta, their gradients decrease dramatically, reducing their velocity and ability
to incise their channels. Consequently, the rivers distribute their flow into numerous sloughs that meander across the landscape.[33] The roughly triangular
Delta that is created by this sluggish hydrological regime also includes the lower
reaches of the San Joaquin's northernmost tributaries, the Cosumnes, Mokelumne, and Calaveras rivers. This vast, sparsely populated region in the center of
California (see map 4) stretches approximately twenty-four miles from east to
west and forty-eight miles from north to south, and is bounded by the cities of
Sacramento to the north, Stockton to the east, Tracy to the south, and Antioch
to the west. The Delta encompasses more than eleven hundred square miles—
or 700,000 acres—of which approximately 340,000 acres were ancestral tidal
marsh. Although Delta waters are tidal, they are generally not saline except during late summer and early fall, when flows from the Sacramento and San Joaquin
rivers and their tributaries are at their nadir, allowing salt water from the Pacific
Ocean to intrude inland. Because of its vast expanses of freshwater marsh, before
reclamation the Delta supported one of the most significant concentrations of
waterfowl in California.[34]

Just beyond the western apex of the Delta lies the brackish Suisun Marsh.
Technically beyond the boundaries of the Central Valley, Suisun Marsh is part of
the coastal estuary that includes San Francisco Bay, the largest estuarine system
on the Pacific Coast of the Americas.[35] Despite its peripheral location relative to
the Central Valley, Suisun Marsh is of great importance to the wintering waterfowl

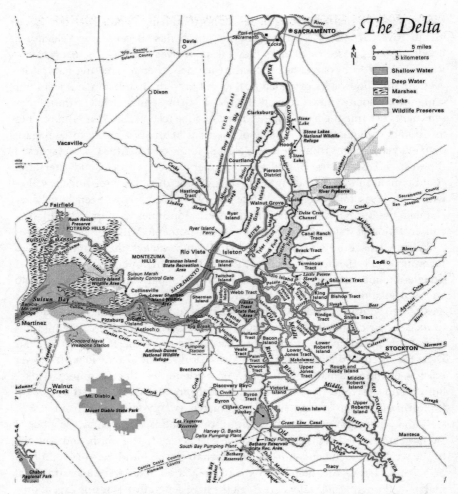

MAP 4. The waterways, islands, and tracts of the Sacramento–San Joaquin Delta and, to the west, Suisun Marsh. Source: John Hart and David Sanger, *San Francisco Bay: Portrait of an Estuary* (Berkeley and Los Angeles: University of California Press, 2003). Used with permission.

of the valley, and therefore is often included in Central Valley habitat studies.[36] Encompassing approximately 116,000 acres of tidal wetlands, managed wetlands, bays, sloughs, and associated uplands, every fall Suisun Marsh provides for early-arriving waterfowl from the north until winter precipitation makes new habitat and food sources available in the Central Valley.[37]

Draining into the Delta from the south, the San Joaquin River has its origins high in the southern Sierra Nevada, at Thousand Island Lake in the towering thirteen-thousand-foot Ritter Range. When the river reaches the San Joaquin Valley floor it first flows to the west, defining the southern limit of the San Joaquin Basin. After passing north of the city of Fresno, the river turns sharply northward and flows through the middle of the basin on its journey to the Delta. Overflow wetlands in the San Joaquin Basin were historically associated with the San Joaquin River, as well as its major Sierran tributaries, the Merced, Tuolumne, and Stanislaus rivers. Floodwaters created extensive wetland habitat consisting of permanent lakes, sloughs, and ponds as well as both permanent and seasonal marshes. The most significant marshes still remaining are in an area of overflow lands—known as the Grasslands—that lie astride the San Joaquin River, largely in Merced County.[38] The Grasslands continues to be of tremendous importance to waterfowl, and, as later chapters will demonstrate, its history is inextricably woven into the story of the changing fortunes of the Central Valley's wetlands and waterfowl.

Located south of the San Joaquin River, the Tulare Basin occupies the broadest portion of the San Joaquin Valley. At the basin's southernmost extreme rise the Transverse Ranges, which separate the San Joaquin Valley from the Los Angeles Basin and Southern California. Watered by the Kings, Kaweah, Tule, and Kern rivers, all of which flow out of the Sierra Nevada, the Tulare Basin has no direct outlet to the Pacific Ocean. As a result, before large-scale diversions for agriculture, these rivers filled several enormous lakes at the lowest points in the basin, including Tulare, Buena Vista, and Kern lakes. Together with their surrounding marshes, these lakes provided the largest single block of wetland habitat in the Central Valley, and in all of California.[39] Yet virtually all the wetland habitat in the Tulare Basin has been lost, resulting in a dramatic decline in the basin's waterfowl populations.

WATERFOWL OF THE CENTRAL VALLEY WETLANDS

The waterfowl that depended on the Central Valley's extensive wetlands—and that still rely on the remaining wetlands—are far more ancient than the Central Valley itself. These birds first appeared on Earth during the early Cenozoic era, approximately fifty million years ago, many millions of years before the Central Valley emerged from the depths of the sea.[40] Waterfowl are found on all continents and many isolated islands worldwide. They compose the family Anatidae, which includes ducks, geese, and swans, and they number approximately 150 species in at least 45 genera; one-third of these species occur in North America, and most can be found along the Pacific Flyway, including California's Central Valley.[41]

All waterfowl species are dependent on wetlands, and every waterfowl species has precise dietary requirements that are satisfied by wetlands. Swans and geese are almost entirely vegetarian in their diets. Swans forage primarily on submergent vegetation but may also graze in meadows. Geese are specialized as grazers in meadows and adjacent uplands but may also feed in wetter areas on tuberous plants. In most species of geese the cutting edges of the upper and lower mandibles are coarsely serrated, providing an effective method of clipping off vegetation close to the ground.[42] Important species of swans and geese that winter in the Central Valley are the tundra swan, greater white-fronted goose, snow goose, Ross's goose, and various subspecies of Canada and cackling goose.[43]

Ducks are classified as dabbling (or surface-feeding) ducks and diving ducks, the latter including pochards (bay ducks), stiff-tailed ducks, and sea ducks and mergansers.[44] Dabbling ducks, the most widespread of all waterbirds, are considered the most adaptable of all waterfowl. They are flexible in food choices and are pioneers in new habitats. During nonbreeding seasons they eat seeds and other plant reproductive parts that provide carbohydrates for energy and fat storage. During prebreeding and molting periods, the diet of the adults of most species shifts toward protein-rich aquatic insects and other invertebrates, which are also essential for growth in juveniles.[45] Dabbling ducks are easily distinguished by their endearing habit of "tilting up" in shallow water, bill down and tail up, to feed on submerged vegetation and benthic (bottom-dwelling) invertebrates. Dabbling ducks also feed by filtering surface water through the comblike lamellae along the sides of their bills. Their feet are located relatively far forward on their bodies, giving them a moderately good walking ability, and they are able to take off and land abruptly from small areas of water or land.[46] Dabbling ducks are by far the most numerous of Central Valley ducks. Mallard—the most widely distributed duck of the Pacific Flyway—northern pintail, American wigeon, northern shoveler, gadwall, and green-winged and cinnamon teal are important species that winter in the valley.[47]

Diving ducks, though nearly as widespread as dabblers, constitute a much smaller proportion—less than 10 percent—of the total duck population of the Pacific Flyway.[48] Diving ducks require more permanent waters than dabblers. As their name suggests, they feed by diving completely below the surface, searching for submergent plant material and invertebrates. They further differ from dabbling ducks in several important respects. Their legs are situated farther back on their body, making them less adept at walking on land. Their generally heavier bodies, relative to wing surface area, require them to run some distance over water prior to reaching minimum flight speed. Their feet and webbing are larger, increasing diving effectiveness, and their bills are generally broad, heavy, and adapted for underwater foraging.[49]

Of the diving ducks that winter in the Central Valley, the canvasback, prized by hunters, is numerous, but other pochards, including the lesser scaup, ring-necked duck, and redhead, are also present. Only one species of stiff-tailed duck, the ruddy duck, inhabits the Central Valley. These diving ducks, characterized by upturned, elongated tail feathers, may either reside permanently in the valley or only winter there. They feed mainly on benthic invertebrates for much of the year, but also on submergent foliage and seeds during the winter. Several species of sea ducks, arctic-adapted diving ducks, overwinter in the Central Valley, most notably the common goldeneye and the bufflehead. Unlike dabbling ducks and most other diving ducks, these sea ducks depend predominantly on animal sources of food, including crustaceans, mollusks, and other aquatic invertebrates. The common merganser, possessing a long, thin, serrated bill, adds fish to this diet as well. Common goldeneyes, buffleheads, and common mergansers all breed in riparian woodlands to the north, where they nest in tree cavities. During the winter, they inhabit the Central Valley's rivers and freshwater and estuarine marshes.[50]

THE PACIFIC FLYWAY: A WEB OF LIFE

The wetlands of the Central Valley compose part of a larger system of wetlands that stretches from the Arctic regions of Alaska and western Canada, across the western United States and western Mexico, and beyond to Central America and South America. The migratory routes along this chain of wetlands constitute the Pacific Flyway.[51] Every spring and fall, migratory waterfowl may travel entire continents as they migrate along the flyway between their northern breeding grounds and their southern wintering grounds, including the Great Central Valley of California. It is the migratory waterfowl, above all, that tie together these wetland ecosystems. Thus the destruction—and restoration—of individual wetlands in the Central Valley has ecological repercussions on a range of scales from a particular wetland to, quite literally, the western half of North America.[52] In order to manage the waterfowl of the Pacific Flyway successfully, resource managers have had to come to terms with the ecological processes that unfold on these diverse scales.[53]

During the late fall and winter, in any large wetland area in the Central Valley, we are likely to find several species of geese, numerous species of ducks, and perhaps tundra swans as well.[54] For this brief period, these birds form a community, each species present in a particular area because that area meets its biological requirements for resting and feeding, such as shallow water for dabbling ducks and deeper water for diving ducks. Each species occupies a different ecological niche, or functional role, in this community.[55] Resident species are further differentiated by their nesting requirements. Mallards, for example, build their nests on or near the edges of water where the ground is only slightly marshy and where they are concealed by tall emergent plants such as cattails. Northern pintail, on the other hand, almost always nest on dry ground, at times as much as a half-mile from water. The manner in which species of ducks occupy different nesting and feeding spaces, or different niche spaces, may be a result of ecological interactions among species, such as competition for resources, or abiotic considerations, such as water depth and percent of open water to plant cover. These community-level and ecosystem-level considerations, respectively, are essential for successful wetland management.

The theory of island biogeography has shown that the spatial area and degree of isolation of islands affect avian species richness by altering the equilibrium between the rate of extinction of species already established and the rate of colonization by new species. Larger and less isolated islands tend to have greater species diversity; smaller and more isolated islands tend to have less.[56] This theory has been successfully applied to nonliteral "island" habitats as well, such as freshwater marshes, which exist as the functional equivalent of islands in a sea of agricultural lands.[57] Consequently, the placement of wetlands in the landscape has implications for both species richness and the regulation of marsh bird populations. A cluster of marshes, or a wetland complex, provides greater habitat heterogeneity for waterfowl than a single, isolated marsh. Heterogeneity, which includes individual marshes at different flooding and drying stages, allows a marsh complex to meet the ecological requirements of a larger number of species than a single large, isolated wetland; at the same time, the presence of more than one marsh reduces the risk of the spread of disease. Seasonally, the heterogeneity offered by a marsh complex is also important in the regulation of breeding duck populations. The number of breeding pairs that a particular wetland can accommodate has been found to be primarily a function of the surface area, rather than the productivity, of the wetland. By contrast, late-summer populations of fledged and adult ducks seek out the most productive ponds, regardless of size.[58] It is clear, then, that wetland managers must take into account landscape-level considerations, and not simply those of individual wetlands.

Regardless of how well we may manage an individual wetland, or even a complex of wetlands, these efforts will be to little avail if there are serious problems on successively larger spatial scales. If important wintering habitat, such as that provided by California's Central Valley, disappears—whether the cause is conversion to agricultural land, water development projects, or urban encroachment—migrating waterfowl will suffer high mortality rates from lack of life-sustaining resources and diseases such as avian botulism and cholera, outbreaks of which are intensified by overcrowding on fewer and smaller remaining habitat areas. Alternatively, even if vast expanses of wintering habitat are protected, populations of migratory waterfowl will continue to plummet if the birds' breeding habitat is compromised. Because the overwhelming majority of North American water-fowl breed in Canada and Alaska, ecologists and land-use planners must consider and manage wetlands on vast spatial scales.

Waterfowl of the Pacific Flyway constitute the biotic link between distinct river systems and wetland complexes across western North America. Drawing nutrients and water from these systems, waterfowl are themselves literally a product of wetlands. In ecological terms, they are obligate wetland species, dependent on wetlands for the entirety of their life cycle. Within the enormous expanses of wetlands that exist in this region, millions of migratory waterfowl carry out their life cycles, breeding during the spring and summer, often in the Far North, and wintering in southern and more temperate climes.

Yet it has perhaps been too easy to take for granted the existence of these millions of Pacific Flyway waterfowl, and the apparent inevitability of their annual return to the Central Valley. Extended periods of drought on the breeding grounds, excessive hunting and the ravages of disease on the wintering grounds, and the widespread destruction of habitat on both breeding and wintering grounds have operated synergistically to produce dramatic reductions in waterfowl populations, which were once so extensive as to darken the sky during their migrations. The precipitous decline of Pacific Flyway waterfowl during the brief century and a half since California statehood highlights the inescapable fact that the system of wetlands and waterfowl that compose the flyway is a historically contingent system, dependent in part on climate but, more important, on the choices made by humanity.

Waterfowl are adaptable to changing habitat conditions, but adaptation has its limits. In the wintering grounds of the Central Valley, migratory geese quickly learned to feed on the wheat crops of the late nineteenth century, and migrating ducks learned just as quickly during the early twentieth century that rice fields provided an excellent food source. But wintering waterfowl need more than grains to survive. They require a variety of foods, including aquatic invertebrates, which are found in great numbers in natural wetlands but not in grain fields; they require resting areas where they are protected from predators, including humans; and they require enough wetland habitat to be protected from the spread of disease.

Waterfowl are not alone in their dependence on wetlands. Throughout the Central Valley, bald eagles, peregrine falcons, and other birds of prey rely on wetland areas for food. The Butte Basin in the Sacramento Valley is one of the last strongholds of the riparian yellow-billed cuckoo, and the few remaining permanent wetlands of the San Joaquin Valley are crucial to the survival of the giant garter snake. Additionally, many waterbird and upland bird species are associated with the remaining wetland and adjacent upland habitat of the Central Valley.

A partial listing of these species includes white pelicans, great and snowy egrets, several grebe species, greater and lesser sandhill cranes, great blue herons, green herons, black-crowned night herons, double-crested cormorants, white-faced ibis, American bitterns, American avocets, black-necked stilts, common snipe, long-billed curlews, and tricolored blackbirds.[59]

Conservation policies enacted on local, regional, national, and continental scales have rescued waterfowl from their nadir during the 1930s and have stabilized populations of most waterfowl species, albeit at levels far below those that once prevailed in North America.[60] The uneven success of these efforts points to levels of ecological complexity that we may not yet fully understand and to ecological processes that we may not be fully able to reverse. The overwhelming impetus to protect wetlands in the late twentieth and early twenty-first centuries has come from recognition of the need to protect continental waterfowl populations. In this sense, while waterfowl are clearly dependent on wetlands, wetlands themselves became dependent on waterfowl for their continued existence in the face of pressures from reclamation and development.

Waterfowl and other waterbirds can directly affect wetland ecosystems in a number of important ways. They can maintain or increase biological diversity in wetlands by transporting invertebrates and invertebrate eggs, as well as plant seeds, in or on their plumage. In addition, ducks transport seeds in their digestive tracts, a small percentage of which remain viable after passage. Herbivorous birds such as snow geese and white-fronted geese can significantly reduce emergent vegetation and, by digging out tubers, can deepen basins, thereby retarding plant succession and the filling in of marshes. Carnivorous birds such as mergansers, cormorants, pelicans, and herons can remove a substantial amount of biomass in the form of aquatic invertebrates, fish, and amphibians, as well as small mammals and other birds. Less direct, but more widespread, is the influence of waterbirds on wetlands owing to nutrients excreted into the water column and substrate. Flocks of waterfowl attracted to wetland sites deposit nutrients in amounts significant enough to increase the growth of algae, thus influencing food webs and larger ecosystem processes. In each of these ways, waterfowl and other waterbirds influence wetland development and community structure.[61] The fundamental relationship between waterfowl and wetlands, manifested in the transfer of resources between them, necessitates that this system be studied on a wide range of scales, from individual wetlands nestled in the Central Valley to the Pacific Flyway as a whole.

Though totaling only a fraction of their historic magnitude, waterfowl numbers along the Pacific Flyway remain daunting. Midwinter inventories compiled annually by the U.S. Fish and Wildlife Service since 1955 record an average of more than 6.6 million waterfowl wintering in the U.S. portion of the flyway.[62] Midwinter inventory data from a representative five-year period, 1973–1977,

The Pacific Flyway

Important nesting, staging, and wintering areas of flyway waterfowl.

❶ Klamath Basin
❷ Summer Lake Area
❸ Malheur Marshes
❹ Skagit Flats
❺ Stikine Flats
❻ Copper River Delta
❼ Susitna River Delta
❽ Kuskokwim River Delta
❾ Yukon Delta
❿ Seward Peninsula
⓫ Yukon Flats
⓬ Old Crow Flats
⓭ Mackenzie River Delta
⓮ Anderson River Delta
⓯ Banks Island
⓰ Great Bear Lake
⓱ Mills Lake
⓲ Great Slave Lake
⓳ Parklands
⓴ Western Prairies
㉑ Great Salt Lake
㉒ Imperial Valley

MAP 5. The Pacific Flyway in Canada and the United States, featuring many of the most important nesting, staging, and wintering areas for waterfowl. The majority of these locations are discussed in the text. This map highlights the state-owned Gray Lodge Wildlife Area in the Sacramento Valley, one of the first refuges established in the Central Valley. Source: John B. Cowan, *A Jewel in the Pacific Flyway: The Story of Gray Lodge Wildlife Area* (Sacramento: California Waterfowl Association, 2002). Used with permission.

record that 60 percent of the total Pacific Flyway population, including nearly 4.7 million ducks and 570,000 geese, were found in the Central Valley.[63] These numbers are conservative because the midwinter counts do not necessarily reflect peak populations of ducks and geese, nor do they reflect the total waterfowl population that utilizes the Central Valley during the winter. Birds en route to and from wintering grounds farther south in California's Imperial Valley, western Mexico, and beyond utilize Central Valley waterfowl habitat as migration staging areas. A more comprehensive range that reflects this transitional use is ten million to twelve million ducks and geese, accompanied by hundreds of thousands of shorebirds and other waterbirds, that either winter in or migrate through the Central Valley of California.[64]

This story of the Central Valley wetlands would not be complete without consideration of the geographic range of the millions of Pacific Flyway waterfowl that annually descend on the valley. The extensive range of Pacific Flyway migratory waterfowl includes geographically separate regions for breeding, wintering, and other needs, such as staging prior to migration and seeking protected habitat during molting periods, when the birds are flightless and vulnerable.[65] As one historian of the Pacific Flyway has suggested, "a bioregional history of the Pacific Flyway would encompass much of the western half of North America."[66] The remainder of this chapter provides, in a limited fashion, that bioregional history by reviewing those areas of western North America (see map 5) that provide critical breeding and staging habitat for the waterfowl of the Pacific Flyway, the majority of which winter in the Central Valley.

IMPORTANT BREEDING AND STAGING AREAS OF THE FLYWAY

The overwhelming majority of Pacific Flyway waterfowl breed in the vast wetlands of western Canada and Alaska, which together contain approximately 550,000 square miles of wetlands, 25 percent of the estimated world's total.[67] Of that amount, approximately 266,000 square miles, or a little less than half, are concentrated in Alaska. The relatively limited development that has taken place in Alaska has cost that state, unlike the rest of the United States, only a fraction of 1 percent of its wetland heritage.[68] The most important waterfowl production areas in western Canada and Alaska are watersheds and deltas, and forests and tundra. Farther to the south and east, the prairie pothole region of south-central Canada and the north-central United States is the major duck production area for North America. Although the pothole region supplies only a small portion of its duck production to the Pacific Flyway, it is important to the flyway nonetheless. The western region of the contiguous United States, including California's Great Central Valley, contributes to Pacific Flyway populations as well, though on a smaller scale.

Watersheds and Deltas

The Yukon-Kuskokwim Delta bears the names of Alaska's first and second largest rivers, which create its expanse of 26,000 square miles, preserved in the Yukon Delta National Wildlife Refuge. Flowing westward toward the Bering Sea, the Yukon and Kuskokwim rivers approach within twenty-five miles of each other and then diverge sharply for the last hundred miles of their journey, the Yukon veering to the northwest and the Kuskokwim to the southwest. The delta that lies between them—a vast, sprawling, treeless wetland plain—is North America's most productive waterfowl nursery.[69] The delta's rivers, streams, sloughs, lakes, and ponds support roughly 750,000 geese and swans, two million ducks, and more than five million shorebirds. Included among these are major proportions of the North American populations of tundra swans and greater white-fronted and cackling geese.[70]

Many northern wetlands, the Yukon-Kuskokwim Delta included, serve as both breeding areas and staging areas for migration. Cackling geese migrate southward from their staging areas in the delta across the Alaska Peninsula and the Gulf of Alaska, and then follow the coast of British Columbia across the Canadian border as far as the mouth of the Columbia River, which forms the border between the states of Washington and Oregon. Proceeding inland along the Columbia, they then turn southward again to their wintering grounds in the Sacramento Valley and northern San Joaquin Valley.[71] The Central Valley is the destination for many white-fronted geese as well. These geese have been recorded flying nonstop from their staging areas in the Yukon-Kuskokwim Delta to Summer Lake in Oregon or Tule and Klamath lakes on the California-Oregon border, a distance of 2,300 miles. Flying at an average speed of forty-five miles per hour, this continuous flight lasts for more than fifty hours, making it one of the longest nonstop flights of any goose species. After resting and refueling for a week or two, the geese then make one last overnight flight to their wintering grounds in the Sacramento Valley.[72]

In contrast to the open, treeless tundra of the coast, the Yukon Flats area of interior northeastern Alaska is clothed in willow, aspen, and spruce. There are an estimated forty thousand lakes and potholes in this broad, crescent-shaped valley, which lies within the Yukon Flats National Wildlife Refuge. The lakes are extremely productive, perhaps because of deep-burning fires in the area that release minerals and other nutrients otherwise bound up in undecayed peat bogs. One million to two million ducks nest annually at Yukon Flats. The predominant species include canvasback, mallard, northern pintail, lesser scaup, American wigeon, and northern shoveler; roughly ten thousand to fifteen thousand geese of various species are present as well. Yukon Flats and the Yukon-Kuskokwim Delta combined are responsible for about half of Alaska's annual waterfowl crop.

Both regions are also important breeding areas for the lesser sandhill crane.[73] The cranes are popular winter visitors in California's Central Valley, where these stately three-foot-tall birds may be found in refuges and flooded rice fields.

Across the Canadian border from Yukon Flats, in the western Yukon Territory, lies Old Crow Flats, a basin of nearly two thousand square miles. The basin is a fossil delta of the Old Crow River, a tributary of the Porcupine River, itself a tributary of the Yukon. The basin is laced with shallow lakes and ponds that are bordered by both open and forest tundra. Historically, it has supported, on average, nearly half as many breeding ducks as Yukon Flats, and is a particularly important area for diving ducks. In addition to its role as an important breeding ground, Old Crow Flats serves as a major staging area for migrating ducks, geese, and swans.[74]

The Peace-Athabasca Delta in northeastern Alberta, occupying twelve hundred square miles, is the largest freshwater inland boreal delta in the world, and is the southernmost of the Canadian deltas of major importance for breeding Pacific Flyway waterfowl.[75] Comprising the Athabasca River Delta, the Peace River Delta, and the much smaller Birch River Delta, this wetland paradise is one of the most important waterfowl nesting and staging areas in North America. The major lakes of the delta are shallow and foster a thick growth of submergent and emergent vegetation during the growing season. The shallow water, high fertility, and relatively long growing season for such northern latitudes make the delta an abundant food source, one of particular importance during drought years in the breeding grounds of the prairie pothole region to the south. In the spring and fall, more than one million birds use the Peace-Athabaska Delta, including the world's entire nesting population of the endangered whooping crane. The delta is a vital link in the migration of the lesser snow goose, greater white-fronted goose, Canada goose, tundra swan, and at least fourteen duck species. The Peace-Athabaska Delta occupies the southeastern corner of the tremendous Wood Buffalo National Park, the largest national park in Canada. In the park, the most expansive undisturbed grass and sedge meadows in North America support an estimated population of ten thousand wood and plains buffalo.[76]

The enormous Mackenzie River system connects the Peace-Athabasca Delta to the Arctic Ocean. More than 2,600 miles long including its headstreams, the Mackenzie River is the longest river in North America, draining a basin of nearly 700,000 square miles. North of the Peace-Athabasca Delta, the Peace and Athabasca rivers merge as the Slave River, which flows northward to Great Slave Lake in the Northwest Territories, where it forms an important delta for waterfowl in its own right. The outflow from Great Slave Lake is the Mackenzie River proper, which, unfrozen for only five months of the year, flows northward for almost eleven hundred miles through boreal forests and then forest tundra before finally emptying into the Beaufort Sea in the Arctic. As the river approaches the Beaufort Sea, its main stem divides into multiple channels, which fan out across its hundred-mile-long delta. Along the Mackenzie Delta, spruce trees give way to willows, then to sedge meadows, and finally to bare mudflats. Nearly five thousand square miles in area, the delta is rich in duck food—submerged aquatic vegetation, and aquatic insects and other invertebrates. Aerial surveys suggest that the delta has supported populations of well over a quarter of a million ducks. Of the many species that breed in the Mackenzie Delta, the northern pintail, American wigeon, mallard, common goldeneye, green-winged teal, northern shoveler, and canvasback migrate to the Central Valley. The delta serves as a major staging area as well. Snow geese that nest on Banks Island, four hundred miles to the northeast, and on the Arctic coast gather at the delta before beginning their journey to the Central Valley of California and beyond, as far as the highlands of central Mexico.[77]

The waterfowl of the Pacific Flyway that breed in these watersheds and deltas of the interior of Alaska and Canada migrate southward through Canada's prairie provinces of Alberta, Saskatchewan, and Manitoba, at which latitude the flyways are not yet distinct. The routes branch near the international border. Some birds turn southeastward into the Central and Mississippi flyways. Those that use the Pacific Flyway turn southwestward across northwestern Montana and the Idaho panhandle, follow along the Snake River and Columbia River valleys, and then turn southward again across central Oregon to their final destination in the Central Valley of California.[78]

Forests and Tundra

The northern woodlands of Canada and Alaska are part of a vast expanse of approximately 3.5 million square miles of North American boreal forest that stretches from Alaska to Canada's Atlantic Coast. This forest, also known as taiga, lies between tundra to the north and deciduous forests and grasslands to the south and is characterized by spruce, fir, and other coniferous trees, as well as aspen and birch. Much of the ground surface of the boreal forest is covered with lichen and, during the summer months, is often marshy. Waterfowl densities in these woodlands are lower than those of the northern watersheds and deltas, averaging between one and five breeding birds, mostly ducks, per square mile, but the region's vast expanse, filled with lakes and streams, still results in a substantial contribution to the continent's total waterfowl population.[79]

North of the woodlands, the treeless tundra is especially important for goose production. Permafrost lying only inches below the ground surface precludes drainage, and the short summer thaw of the uppermost topsoil therefore produces wet and marshy conditions and fine breeding habitat. Along the coastline and on the coastal plain of Canada and Alaska, as well as on the Canadian Arctic Archipelago, all species of geese nest in tundra, and it is there that most North

American geese are produced.[80] The tundra of the western and central Canadian Arctic is especially important for the white goose species of the Pacific Flyway, which nest in this region in enormous colonies.

The tundra of the lower basin and delta of the Egg River on Banks Island, the westernmost island in the Arctic Archipelago, is probably the greatest single snow goose production area in North America. More than two hundred thousand nesting pairs of these white geese have been found on the island. They arrive at their nesting grounds in May and must carry out their entire breeding cycle in the short span of the high Arctic summer. Eggs incubate for twenty-eight days. Goslings fledge in fifty-six days. Then the snow geese are on the move again. Their migration route is from Banks Island to Freezeout Lake in Montana via the lakes of southern Saskatchewan and Alberta. From Montana they veer westward to Oregon's Summer Lake and Tule and Klamath lakes on the California-Oregon border. When the lakes freeze in mid-November to early December, they fly to their final winter destination, the Central Valley of California.[81]

The main breeding area of the Ross's goose, the other North American white goose, lies farther east in the central Canadian Arctic, on the tundra near Queen Maud Gulf. Half a million Ross's geese have been recorded nesting in this region, where a single colony has numbered as many as 291,000 birds. Approximately one-third of these Ross's geese migrate along the Pacific Flyway to their wintering grounds in the Central Valley, with the remainder going to the Central and Mississippi flyways.[82]

Prairie Potholes

The prairie pothole region stretches across the semiarid, treeless prairies of the southern third of the provinces of Alberta, Saskatchewan, and Manitoba, and continues south of the United States border into northeastern Montana, North Dakota, South Dakota, western Minnesota, and Iowa, demonstrating the stubborn resistance of ecosystems to respecting national boundaries. The landscape here is dotted with more than four million small wetlands, known simply as potholes. They were formed approximately eleven thousand years ago as the glaciers of the Wisconsin Ice Age, the last glacial period of the Pleistocene, receded and molded the landscape into a "poorly drained terrain pock-marked with millions of relatively small depressions, the potholes."[83] Of a total of 300,000 square miles, approximately 65 percent, or 194,000 square miles, of the prairie pothole region lies in Canada; the remaining 35 percent, or 106,000 square miles, lies in the United States.[84]

Known as North America's "duck factory," the prairie pothole region is the most important area for duck production on the entire continent. Its numerous shallow lakes and marshes, rich soils, and warm summers also render it one of the most important wetland regions in the world. Historically, from 50 percent to as much as 75 percent of all the ducks originating in North America have come from the pothole region, yet it accounts for only 10 percent of the total waterfowl breeding area on the continent.[85] The prairie pothole region contributes fewer ducks to the Pacific Flyway than to the Central and Mississippi flyways to the east, but its contribution to the Pacific Flyway is nevertheless substantial. Alberta, the westernmost province of the region, is a particularly important breeding area for Pacific Flyway ducks, and, overall, the ponds and lakes of the western prairies provide resting habitat for many Pacific Flyway waterfowl on their migrations to and from the northern interior.[86]

In the short term, the greatest regulator of prairie duck numbers is drought. But in the longer term the greatest threat to the production of waterfowl in this region of North America is the destruction of the potholes themselves. Much like the freshwater marshes of the Central Valley, the potholes have been under intense pressure from agricultural development. By the early years of the twentieth century, railroads had cut across the breeding grounds of the prairie pothole region in both the United States and Canada, opening up the region to settlement and agriculture.[87] The direct loss of the wetland basins through artificial drainage and the accompanying deterioration of marsh-edge vegetation—the essential upland component of waterfowl habitat—has been a major factor in the diminishing annual production of waterfowl. In the 1850s, wetlands covered between 16 percent and 18 percent of the prairie regions of Minnesota, the Dakotas, and Iowa. By the 1990s, at least half of this wetland area had been lost; only 8 percent of these prairie regions remained as wetlands.[88] Canadian losses are even greater. By the late twentieth century, as much as 71 percent of the original wetland area of the prairie provinces may have been lost.[89] Widespread recognition of the importance of this dwindling "duck factory" has led to impressive conservation efforts on both sides of the border. The Canadian Wildlife Service, the U.S. Fish and Wildlife Service, and private organizations such as Ducks Unlimited and the Nature Conservancy have been working together since the late 1980s to protect the remaining prairie potholes.[90]

Western United States

A small percentage of the waterfowl of the Pacific Flyway breeds in the western United States, a region that is generally more important for its wintering grounds than for its breeding grounds. Despite widespread wetland reclamation, some important waterfowl production areas remain, many of which are managed by the federal or state governments. In the Klamath Basin, Lower Klamath and Tule lakes on the California-Oregon border were once expansive marshes and overflow lands of the Klamath River and Lost River drainages. Although the federal government reclaimed much of this area for agriculture during the early years of the twentieth century, high-quality duck production habitat still exists in the

Klamath Basin on Lower Klamath, Tule Lake, and other national wildlife refuges, which also serve as important migratory stopovers for approximately three-quarters of the waterfowl of the Pacific Flyway. Other important western production areas include the Malheur National Wildlife Refuge and Summer Lake in southeastern Oregon, Stillwater National Wildlife Refuge in western Nevada, and the Great Salt Lake marshes of the Bear River National Wildlife Refuge in northern Utah.[91] The Bear River marshes, the easternmost of these areas, provide waterfowl not only to the Pacific Flyway, but also to the Central and Atlantic flyways. Those ducks that join the Pacific Flyway routes enter California via two parallel routes, either through the northeastern part of the state or over the Sierra Nevada near Lake Tahoe. They converge in the Central Valley near the Sacramento–San Joaquin Delta.[92]

The Central Valley itself was once an important production, as well as wintering, area for ducks. Similar to other inland freshwater wetlands, the valley's basin wetlands lack current and have little wave energy except that produced by wind, and therefore have little impact on nests, young, or food resources, making them especially appealing to breeding waterfowl.[93] Historically, important nesters included northern pintail, mallards, gadwalls, cinnamon teal, northern shovelers, redheads, and ruddy ducks.[94] This production function diminished in the Central Valley as wetland acreage plummeted; but by the early twenty-first century wetland restoration efforts had begun to reverse this prolonged decline. Breeding waterfowl populations, though never more than a fraction of the number of the valley's wintering waterfowl, began to rise.[95]

A LOOK AHEAD

Efforts to protect the breeding grounds of waterfowl—ranging from the creation of national wildlife refuges in Alaska to the establishment of conservation programs in the prairie potholes—have numerous parallels to efforts to protect the more southerly wintering grounds of waterfowl in the Central Valley of California. Most of the remainder of this book will narrow the focus from western North America back to the Central Valley, investigating the human and non-human history of the valley's wetlands over the past two centuries.

When the wetlands of California's Great Central Valley were first drained, the protection of the migratory waterfowl that inhabited them was simply not a consideration. During the course of the twentieth century, however, the ducks and geese of the Pacific Flyway became the paramount reason for the protection and restoration of these wetlands. Before Californians could reverse the course of their actions, it was first necessary for them to perceive that land use changes at the local level have unambiguous repercussions for waterfowl on regional and continental scales. And in order for those repercussions to *matter*, Californians needed to rethink the place of humans in nature, to shift—at least a little—from an anthropocentric to a biocentric view of the world.[96]

Foreshadowing this biocentric view a generation ago, in the introduction to his highly esteemed book on North American waterfowl, Paul A. Johnsgard wrote,

> Whatever values we place on them, we must recognize the special relationship we share with our waterfowl resource. They were not created for us, but only exist with us, traversing the same continent, drinking the same water, breathing the same air. . . .
>
> We cannot expect to learn directly from or communicate with waterfowl; they speak separate languages, hear different voices, know other sensory worlds. They transcend our own perceptions, make mockery of our national boundaries, ignore our flyway concepts. They have their own innate maps, calendars, and compasses, each older and more remarkable than our own. We can only delight in their flying skills, marvel at their regular and precise movements across the continent, take example in their persistence in the face of repeated disaster. They are a microcosm of nature, of violent death and abundant rebirth, of untrammeled beauty and instinctive grace. We should be content to ask no more of them than that they simply exist, and we can hope for no more than that our children might know them and enjoy them as we do.[97]

PART TWO

The Fall

2

From Native American Lands
of Plenty to "Waste" Lands

The nineteenth century witnessed a remarkable transformation of California's Great Central Valley. As the century opened, Native American peoples inhabited the valley at density levels that were among the highest in North America north of central Mexico, supported by the plant and animal resources of its rich wetlands, grasslands, and riparian forests. Spanish settlements, in the form of missions, presidios (forts), pueblos, and ranchos, had been multiplying along the Pacific Coast from San Diego to San Francisco since 1769. Except for a few exploratory expeditions—notably those of Pedro Fages and Friar Francisco Garcés into the San Joaquin Valley in 1772 and 1776, respectively; Juan Bautista de Anza along the western margins of the Sacramento–San Joaquin Delta in 1776; and Gabriel Moraga into the Sacramento Valley in 1808—there had yet been little penetration into the Central Valley.[1] In 1812 the Russians established a coastal colony at Fort Ross, less than one hundred miles north of San Francisco, as a base for hunting sea otters for the fur trade and for shipping food to the Russian-American Fur Company's outpost in Sitka, Alaska. Ultimately unable to sustain itself, this colony exercised little lasting effect on the interior.[2] In 1841 the Russians sold out to John Sutter, the Swiss émigré whose mill near Sacramento would be at the epicenter of the California Gold Rush when his partner, James Marshall, discovered the precious flakes there seven years later.

The most significant event to affect native peoples in the Central Valley during the early nineteenth century was the malaria epidemic of 1833, which may have carried off as much as three-fourths of their population.[3] The disease, most likely brought into the Central Valley by British fur trappers coming south from Oregon, presaged the near-demise of California's indigenous population in the face of foreigners and the disease organisms they carried. By the early 1840s permanent settlers had begun to arrive from the States, and before the decade was out the United States had wrested California from Mexico, which had won its independence from Spain in 1821. The Treaty of Guadalupe Hidalgo, which ended the war between Mexico and the United States, was signed on February 2, 1848, just nine days after Marshall's discovery.

As Americans began to settle in the Central Valley during the second half of the century, they looked at the valley's wetlands, along with the plant and animal resources they harbored, much less as sources of subsistence—as Native Americans had viewed them—than as malaria-ridden obstacles to settlement, the spread of agriculture, and the procurement of wealth. The story of their attempts to drain the wetlands, some more successful than others, are inextricably tied to seminal issues in California's history, especially irrigation and reclamation. Reclaiming the land meant draining the wetlands and redesigning natural waterways to prevent flooding, and, as a consequence of these processes, simplifying and homogenizing the landscape. But *reclamation* meant more than that, for the term also encompassed irrigation, by which land—whether drained wetland or arid grassland—could be brought into agricultural production and therefore "reclaimed" from its supposedly flawed natural condition.[4] With the passage of the federal Swamp and Overflowed Lands Act in 1850, designed to encourage the draining of wetlands for conversion to agriculture, Californians began that long and arduous process of ecological transformation.

NATIVE AMERICANS IN THE CENTRAL VALLEY

Before the physical landscape of the Central Valley began to be reconfigured by irrigation and reclamation projects, the human landscape was dramatically altered, as Native Americans died or were displaced by the direct or indirect effects of colonization. Population estimates of Native Americans for the beginning of the Spanish, or mission, period in 1769 place approximately 76,100 indigenous people in the Sacramento Valley and 83,800 in the San Joaquin Valley, a combined total that exceeds one-half of the 310,000 Native Americans thought to have been living in all of California at that time.[5] The Native American population of the Central Valley was far from homogeneous, and comprised four major linguistic groups. Tribal territories (see map 6) further demarcated the speakers of distinct languages or dialects within these groups.[6]

For at least ten thousand years, from the end of the last Pleistocene ice age until the mid-nineteenth century, these Native American peoples relied on the wetlands of California's Central Valley. They exploited them as a source of food, in the form of fish, waterfowl, and edible plant roots and seeds, and of raw materials, such as tule reeds, from which they wove rafts for hunting on rivers and

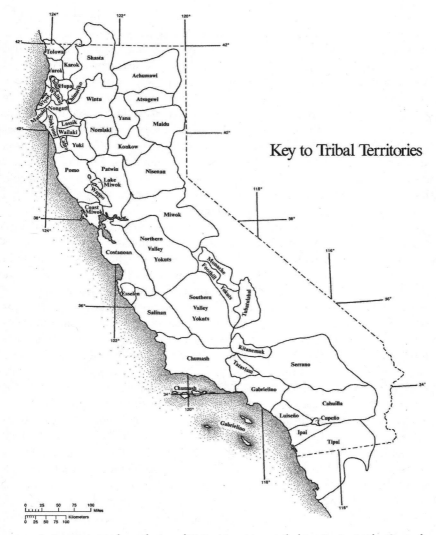

Key to Tribal Territories

MAP 6. Approximate boundaries of Native American tribal territories in the Central Valley and surrounding parts of California. Source: Robert F. Heizer, ed., *Handbook of North American Indians,* vol. 8: *California* (Washington, D.C.: Smithsonian Institution, 1978). Courtesy of the Smithsonian Institution.

lakes. Much as they used fire in the grasslands to enhance the growth of new grasses and forbs, Native Americans also burned and altered wetlands to increase productivity.[7] The Wukchumni Yokuts of the San Joaquin Valley burned freshwater marshes to remove old growth, to provide space for emergent plants that served as animal forage, and to stimulate the production of new long, straight tules. Regular burning cleared out reed-choked marshlands, allowing space for waterfowl movement and nesting activities, and increased the amount of light that reached the soil at the marsh edges, thereby heightening plant species diversity. Controlled burning also reduced the invasion of woody vegetation and therefore maintained and enhanced wetland habitats for wildlife.[8] A century would pass after the nearly complete disappearance of Native Americans from the Central Valley before modern preservation and restoration attempts revived this ancient method of wetland enhancement.[9]

Native Americans were proficient hunters of waterfowl in these wetlands. Waterfowl were taken most often by nooses or nets; some were hunted with bows and arrows. In the Sacramento Valley, the Konkow caught ducks and geese in nooses that they hung from a cord above the surface of the water, or used a live decoy to attract them under a row of nets, and then enmeshed them by the pull of a string grasped by a hunter. The centrality of waterfowl to Konkow culture was reflected in the Duck Dance, part of an annual dance and celebration cycle dedicated to the different animal spirits believed by the Konkow to inhabit their world. The Patwin also netted ducks and geese and employed duck decoys, and the Nisenan used the feathers of ducks that they hunted to wrap into two-ply cordage and weave into blankets. Native Americans appear to have also exploited waterfowl that made use of vernal pool wetlands nestled in the grasslands. Net weights, known as charmstones, have been found at vernal pool locations in both Placer and Solano counties in the Sacramento Valley. In the Delta region, with its maze of tule swamps and sloughs and abundant waterfowl resources, the Plains Miwok captured ducks and geese with nets in two distinct ways, either pulling a net over them while they were feeding or raising a net in the path of a flock of low-flying birds, presumably as they were landing or taking flight. In the San Joaquin Valley, migratory waterfowl gathered by the thousands among the tules. Next to fishing, waterfowling was probably the most important source of animal protein for Native Americans in this region. The Southern Valley Yokuts, in particular, hunted ducks and geese in ingenious ways. They trapped waterfowl in snares set up in the tules, and captured them with long-handled nets as the birds flew overhead. On dark nights, they set alight piles of brush to attract flocks of geese. As the geese swooped down unsuspectingly, they were easily killed.[10]

One of the most intriguing accounts of waterfowl hunting by the Southern Valley Yokuts comes from the reminiscences of Thomas Jefferson Mayfield, who as a boy lived among the Choinumne Yokuts of the lower Kings River from 1850 to 1862 while his widowed father, William Mayfield, was often absent, seeking economic opportunities in the region. Mayfield's account, recorded by San Joaquin Valley historian and ethnographer Frank F. Latta in 1928, the year of Mayfield's death, is the only account by an outsider who lived among California Indians while they were still following their traditional ways.[11] Known to valley residents as "Uncle Jeff" in his later years, Mayfield offered an unparalleled description of the intimate details of day-to-day life among the Southern Valley Yokuts and of the natural beauty and abundant wildlife in the primeval San Joaquin. He describes white geese with black wing tips (snow geese) "flying so thickly that I am positive one band of them would cover four square miles of land."[12] Mayfield explains how, for fishing and hunting on Tulare Lake, the Indians constructed wide, flat tule rafts capable of passing over very shallow water. He describes the uses of these rafts that he witnessed on a trip to Tulare Lake:

> Sometimes three or four Indians would go out on the lake on one of the fishing rafts and hunt ducks and geese and stay out there for as long as a week. During this time they poled the raft around through the tules and ate and slept on it.
>
> They would throw loose tules over the raft and themselves, forming a blind. Then, through the hole in the center they would slowly pole the raft wherever they wanted to go. In this way they would approach within a few feet of ducks and geese and shoot them from the blind with bows and arrows.
>
> Sometimes they would catch the ducks that flew overhead in a net. This net was a good deal like the net fishermen use to take trout out of the water after they have hooked them. It was about two feet across at the mouth. They also snared ducks and geese among the tules.[13]

Nowhere else in the Central Valley would Mayfield have found a still-thriving indigenous culture in the 1850s. By 1852 Tulare County, which included the territory of the Choinumne, was the only region in interior California where large communities remained the basis of Indian social life. The sparseness of white settlement left large areas open to Indian exploitation and allowed the Choinumne and other neighboring tribes to remain mostly autonomous for a few years longer than their northern neighbors.[14] Nevertheless, their way of life was coming to an end. In 1857 the federal government settled most of the remaining Southern Valley Yokuts on a reservation three miles east of Porterville, on the eastern edge of the valley. In response to pressure from settlers, in 1876 the government relocated this reservation farther eastward into the Sierra Nevada foothills, placing nearly twelve hundred dispossessed people on 42,500 acres along the Tule River.[15]

The destruction of the Native Americans of California, nearly complete by the 1860s, had its origins in the Spanish and Mexican periods of the future state's history. The Spanish period began in 1769 with the expedition of Gaspar de Portolá and Franciscan priest Junípero Serra to establish the new colony of Alta

California. Intended to fortify the northern frontier of New Spain and to restrict potential southward expansion of the Russian fur-trading enterprise in Alaska, the colony was to be governed by Portolá, while the zealous Serra was to establish a string of new missions. By 1823, under Serra's successors, the Franciscans had established twenty-one missions along the California coast from San Diego to Sonoma, north of San Francisco. By the early nineteenth century, twenty thousand Native American converts, or neophytes, lived within the mission system, where they found their daily lives strictly regulated by the missionaries. Ravaged by European diseases, forced into new labor routines, and subject to strict social and sexual controls, neophytes fled the missions by the thousands, often seeking the protection of tribes in the interior. As fugitivism became an increasingly serious problem, the Spanish, along with Indian auxiliaries from allied coastal tribes, began to pursue the fleeing converts into the Central Valley.[16]

The tule marshes and riparian wetlands of the valley provided not only food and materials for Native Americans, but also a place of refuge. Time after time, the neophytes managed to escape their would-be captors by disappearing into the impenetrable tules and riparian corridors of the Delta and the San Joaquin Valley. In 1813, José Argüello led the first punitive expedition into the interior against runaway neophytes, in this case from Mission San José.[17] Following them across the Delta, the Spaniards "gained no decision because of the difficulties of the terrain, where it was necessary in places to walk in water up to the knees. The Indians were much favored by very close thickets in which they could hide. Although they were dislodged from that place, the river was very near and they all jumped in to swim, some crossing to the opposite island, others hiding in the dense tule swamps where they could not be followed. For this reason it was not possible to capture anyone."[18] Two years later, Juan Ortega and José Dolores Pico each led a party of a joint expedition into the Tulare Basin from Mission San Miguel and Mission San Juan Bautista, respectively. The combined expedition returned only nine prisoners, as the Spaniards were foiled by the tule marshes around Tulare Lake, into which the Indians repeatedly fled to escape capture.[19]

Central Valley tribes became increasingly embroiled in brutal colonial campaigns to recapture runaway neophytes; some groups, including the Yokuts and Miwoks, adopted the horse, and became more mobile and militaristic as they resisted colonial expeditions.[20] The secularization of the missions, rumored since 1826 and initiated in earnest in 1834, led to increased social instability and rebellion. Spanish and then Mexican authorities exacerbated the problem by sending armies into the interior not only to recapture runaway neophytes, but also to capture gentiles (nonconverts) and impress them into the mission community. Estanislao, a Northern Valley Yokut, was one such captive. Removed to Mission San José by the 1820s, he rose to the position of alcalde, the highest Indian office in the mission hierarchy. In late 1828 and 1829, Estanislao led a rebellion of neophytes from the mission, hundreds of whom refused to return after visiting relatives along the Stanislaus River in the northern San Joaquin Valley. No less than four military expeditions were required to dislodge Estanislao and his followers from protected positions within the riparian wetlands of the Stanislaus and nearby Tuolumne rivers.[21]

It will never be known how powerful a force the Native Americans of the Central Valley might have become because in 1833 they were struck down by a fearful malaria epidemic.[22] The outbreak began in 1830 at the Hudson Bay Company's headquarters at Fort Vancouver in the Oregon Territory, and then spread along the Columbia River. The disease may have been introduced by infected sailors arriving at Fort Vancouver from semitropical locations in the Pacific, or by traders and trappers arriving from the east. Late in 1832, malaria entered the Central Valley, following in the wake of British fur trappers entering California from Oregon. The epidemic expanded from the head of the valley, first down the Sacramento River to the Sacramento–San Joaquin Delta and then up the San Joaquin River. Numerous accounts from the period point to the epidemic's extent and severity, citing the classic malarial symptoms of fever and ague.

John Work's detailed account of the fur brigade of 1832–1833 from Fort Vancouver to California provides a chronology of the onset and spread of the disease. On December 2, 1832, Work noted, "There appears to be some sickness resembling an ague prevailing among [the natives]" in the vicinity of the Feather River in the northern Sacramento Valley. This is the first mention in the account of disease in California. After journeying as far south as the San Joaquin portion of the Delta, Work's party returned northward in 1833. As they passed through the Sacramento Valley in the vicinity of the Feather River once again, fever struck members of his party in late July. On August 1 Work recorded, "A great many of the Indians are sick[,] some of them with the fever." From August 6 to August 19, the trapping party appears to have witnessed the most severe effects of the epidemic. On August 6: "The villages which were so populous and swarming with inhabitants when we passed that way in Jany or Febry [sic] last seem now almost deserted and have a desolate appearance. The few wretched Indians who remain . . . are lying apparently scarcely able to move." Only after the party climbed northward out of the valley floor did Work report on August 19 that the Indians "don't appear to be sick like those below."[23]

Among the most moving accounts of the epidemic is that attributed to Colonel J.J. Warner, a member of Ewing Young's American trapping expedition of 1832–1833:

> In the fall of 1832 there were a number of Indian villages on King's [sic] River, between its mouth and the mountains; also on the San Joaquin River from the base of the mountains down to, and some distance below, the great slough. . . . [M]any of

these villages contained from fifty to one hundred dwellings. . . . The banks of the Sacramento River, in its whole course through the valley, were studded with Indian villages. . . .

On our return, late in the summer of 1833 we found the valleys depopulated. From the head of the Sacramento to the great bend and slough of the San Joaquin, we did not see more than six or eight Indians; while large numbers of their skulls and dead bodies were to be seen under almost every shade-tree near water, where the uninhabited and deserted villages had been converted into graveyards; and, on the San Joaquin River, in the immediate neighborhood of the larger class of villages, which, in the preceding year, were the abodes of a large number of those Indians, we found not only graves, but the vestiges of a funeral pyre.[24]

At least twenty thousand Native Americans died on the river systems of the Central Valley, from Red Bluff in the north to Tulare Lake in the south, in 1833 alone, and the Native American population in the affected parts of the valley may have been reduced by as much as 75 percent between 1833 and 1846, in the wake of successive outbreaks.[25] Such profound depopulation, and the material and psychological consequences that it wrought, reduced survivors' resistance to the wave of white settlers about to pour into the valley in search of gold—and then of grain.[26]

CHANGING DEMOGRAPHICS

Under the 1824 General Law of Colonization, the Mexican government had established rules for grants of national lands to stimulate settlement in California.[27] The number of grants approved during the next decade was small, perhaps fifty in all, but after the secularization of the missions in 1834 the number increased dramatically, reaching more than eight hundred by the end of the Mexican period in 1846. During the 1840s, Mexican authorities granted a number of ranchos to recent emigrants from the United States who settled in the Central Valley along the Sacramento and San Joaquin rivers.[28] These grants represented an attempt to encourage the establishment of cattle ranches in the interior as a buffer for the established coastal settlements and as an impediment to potential American occupation.

The unease of the Mexican government concerning American designs was not unfounded. Mexico had lost Texas to American rebels in 1836, and many in the United States were beginning to eye Mexican territory in the Southwest. In 1826 Jedediah Smith had led a party of trappers to California, only to be ordered out by the Mexican governor, José María Echeandía, the next year. Nevertheless, other mountain men soon followed, including Joseph Walker, who in 1833 became the first to lead a party across the Sierra Nevada from east to west. By 1840 California had a permanent foreign resident population of several hundred, most of whom were drawn by the hide-and-tallow or beaver trades. In 1841 the first organized company of settlers, the Bidwell-Bartleson party, arrived from Missouri, and the political calculus changed in California. Although the term *manifest destiny* was not coined until 1845, the expansionist sentiment it embodied was ascendant.[29]

The United States stripped Mexico of its northern possessions in the Mexican War of 1846–1848. Under the Treaty of Guadalupe Hidalgo, the United States agreed to honor existing rights in land.[30] The boundaries of the Mexican land grants, however, were at times vague and overlapping, and titles to the grants did not always comply fully with the letter of the law. To sort out the quagmire, Congress passed the Land Act of 1851, which established a land commission to adjudicate.[31] Despite the legal guarantees to land rights in articles VIII and IX of the Treaty of Guadalupe Hidalgo, the Land Act placed the burden of proof on every Californian who claimed land. Ultimately, before it concluded its work in 1856, the commission approved 553 of 813 grants claimed. Adjudication on others continued for decades, averaging seventeen years in length, during which time many of the original grants passed into the hands of wealthy Anglo speculators as the original claimants were forced to sell land to pay for legal fees, taxes, and debts.[32] These shifting fortunes laid the groundwork for a pattern of concentrated land ownership in California, one that would be reinforced by federal land disposal policies during the state's formative decades. Concentrated private ownership of vast tracts of land, which often included wetlands and the watercourses that fed them, would have future consequences of the utmost significance for wetlands in the Central Valley.

THE DISEASE ENVIRONMENT
IN THE CENTRAL VALLEY

Centered on the valley's wetlands, the malaria epidemic of 1833 belied California's early reputation as a salubrious locale, with its sunny skies and mild temperatures. The Central Valley, with its expansive seasonal and permanent wetlands, presented a much less healthful picture.[33] Malaria remained a threat, and an obstacle to settlement, long after it decimated the Native American population of the Central Valley in the 1830s. Malaria tends to debilitate rather than kill victims whose ancestors had faced the disease, including those of European stock. Therefore, for those who streamed into California at mid-century, victims far less commonly experienced death than such varied symptoms as extreme anemia, enlargement of the spleen, muscular weakness, and mental depression.[34]

During the nineteenth century, malaria was one of the most common and most widespread diseases in North America. Prior to the development of the germ theory of disease, late in the century, malaria was believed to be caused by miasma, noxious gas released by the decomposition of organic matter. Described as fever and ague, or "intermittent" fever, malaria was associated with poorly drained, swampy areas, which, of course, are rich in decomposing plant matter.[35] Despite such associations, the disease remained poorly understood. Witness the confession of the United States Sanitary Commission in 1863: "Of the intimate nature of . . . 'marsh miasmata,' or 'malaria,' we are in complete ignorance."[36]

The medical profession may have been at a loss to explain malaria, but its members clearly recognized those areas that presented the greatest threat. Comparing wetland areas of the Central Valley with the lower Mississippi Valley, a region of notorious malaria endemicity, a California physician wrote in 1850, "I was greatly surprised and disappointed with the Sacramento. The shores were flat and marshy, being overgrown with thulé [sic]. . . . For many miles from its entrance into Suisun Bay, the country is cut up with "sloughs," and extensive thulé marshes are the consequence; fit nurseries of disease which prevails here to an alarming extent during the latter part of summer, and in the fall months, when the water is low. I can conceive of no part of the Mississippi valley more prolific of disease, than the valley of the Sacramento must be."[37]

A full generation later, the insalubriousness of the lowest portions of the Central Valley had not much changed. Malaria cases continued to complicate the construction of railroads through the swampy lowlands of both the Sacramento and the San Joaquin valleys. Records of the Central Pacific Railroad Hospital for the year 1883 indicate that of the 2,525 railroad employees admitted that year, fully 1,200 of them required treatment for "fevers, malarial."[38] California railroads continued to promote the healthful properties of the state, especially in advertisements for the sale of their lands; but even there they could not escape including one mild caveat: "During the rainy season it is usually too cool to facilitate fermentation, and the result is, *except along some of the river valleys,* an absolutely pure atmosphere."[39]

We now know that malaria is caused not by the fermentation of miasmatic gases in swampy regions but by the presence of parasitic protozoa of the genus *Plasmodium* in red blood cells.[40] Its etiology was not discovered until a series of seminal developments in the late nineteenth century. In 1880 Charles Louis Alphonse Laveran discovered malarial parasites in the blood cells of his patients. In 1897 Sir Ronald Ross published his proof that malaria is transmitted by mosquitoes. The next year, Giovanni Battista Grassi demonstrated that the malaria parasite goes through the sexual reproductive phase of its life cycle only in the *Anopheles* mosquito.[41] The discovery of the life cycle of *Plasmodium* proved that malaria is transmitted from humans to mosquitoes and back to humans. Thus, a person suffering from malaria can introduce the disease into any previously healthy locale in which there are *Anopheles* mosquitoes.[42] Since mosquito larvae develop in stagnant water, these findings made it clear why poorly drained wetlands, especially those with a large surface area, tended to be associated with high malaria endemicity. They also help explain why malaria began to decline in the Central Valley after 1880, paralleling the large-scale loss of wetlands because of diversion and drainage.[43]

Diversion of the watercourses that fed swampy areas in the valley, in order to support irrigated agriculture, led to the early disappearance of hundreds of thousands of acres of potentially malarious wetlands. But for several decades in the late nineteenth century, there was substantial debate over whether irrigation itself might not contribute to an increase in malaria. Considering the question in 1873, Thomas M. Logan, secretary of the State Board of Health, wrote, "The census map discloses the fact that the whole State is more or less subject to malarial diseases, in a slight degree. The broad level plains of the Sacramento and San Joaquin Valleys are specially proclivious to ague and other fevers, and it is very questionable whether the extensive systems of irrigation, now under discussion, will not add to their insalubrity."[44] George Perkins Marsh, a highly esteemed American diplomat, accomplished philologist, and pathbreaking early conservationist, addressed the potential dangers and benefits of irrigation in his wide-ranging paper prepared for Congress, *Irrigation: Its Evils, the Remedies, and the Compensations.* After first cautioning that "all irrigation, except where the configuration of the surface and the character of the soil are such as to promote the rapid draining of the water, or where special precautions are taken against its influence, is prejudicial to health," Marsh concluded that it is possible to take "*prophylactic* measures" to prevent the proliferation of disease. These measures included the prohibition of rice and other crops grown in standing water, the draining of swamps, and the proper discharge of water from irrigated lands to prevent stagnation.[45]

Such cautious statements about irrigation in California may suggest white settlers' awareness of their physical vulnerability in a new environment, one in which heat and disease were more suggestive of tropical climes than of European or American landscapes. Such fears about an alien landscape, perhaps unsuitable for white bodies, certainly seem to have underlain the reservations of some early Californians concerning irrigation.[46] Despite malarial warnings, however, irrigation efforts proliferated, and by 1879 there were nearly 300,000 acres of irrigated land in California, the majority of which were in the San Joaquin Valley.[47] By the 1880s attitudes had shifted to such an extent that irrigation's salubrious effects were touted. The sandy, well-drained soils of parts of Kern County, at the extreme southern end of the valley, appeared to contemporaries to be one area where irrigation, combined with reclamation of wetlands, was beneficial to public health. A late-nineteenth-century account describes changes in the area then known as Kern Island, near present-day Bakersfield: "The change for the better in the climate of the country, since the general introduction of irrigation, has been as marked as the improvement in the soil. Old sloughs containing stagnant water have been purified by the introduction of fresh running water through them. Jungles of miasma-breeding willows have been cleared, swamps drained and dried out, and much decaying vegetation destroyed. Malarious fevers were formerly very prevalent, but have been much abated by these measures."[48]

THE SWAMP AND OVERFLOWED LANDS ACT

The attempt to eradicate malaria was but one incentive to reclaim wetlands. It was part of a much more broadly based drive to open swamplands to settlement and to convert them to productive agricultural use. The wetlands of the Central Valley were drained, or reclaimed, by a complex nexus of public and private efforts. The Swamp and Overflowed Lands Act of 1850 provided the initial thrust for reclamation in California. The act was an extension of the first Swamp Land Act of March 1849, by which Congress had granted to the state of Louisiana "the whole of those swamp and overflowed lands which may be or are found unfit for cultivation."[49] The purpose of the act was to aid the state in constructing levees and drainage systems necessary to reclaim its hitherto relatively inaccessible and underutilized swamplands, created and sustained by the floodwaters of the Mississippi River. It quickly became apparent that Congress could not justifiably make such a land grant to Louisiana alone while other states, such as Mississippi and Arkansas, faced a similar situation, and still others farther north in the Mississippi Valley contained substantial tracts of undrained land of limited use, except perhaps as pasture. Florida and California, too, contained vast areas so wet as to be "unfit for cultivation."[50]

In this context Congress passed the general Swamp and Overflowed Lands Act—commonly known as the Arkansas Act, for the one state it specifically names—on September 28, 1850. The act extended the federal land grant offered to Louisiana the previous year to twelve other states, including California.[51] It directed the secretary of the interior to "make out an accurate list and plats of the lands" that qualified as swampland in each state. Upon receipt of a patent from the secretary, the swamplands would be granted to the states to dispose of as they saw fit, provided that any proceeds generated be applied to reclaiming them.[52]

The General Land Office, which assumed responsibility for the land surveys under the secretary of the interior, failed to develop a consistent plan. The commissioner of the Land Office, Justin Butterfield, complicated the situation by allowing states to choose either to use the plats and field notes of the federal government surveys or to make their own surveys, provided they proved that their selections were in accordance with the act.[53] Fairly predictably, those states that conducted their own surveys (all states except Michigan, Minnesota, and Wisconsin) became embroiled in protracted controversies with federal officials in the General Land Office over their claims. The greatest point of contention revolved around what truly constituted swamp and overflowed lands, with the states claiming greater acreage than federal authorities would concede. In California, one issue stemmed from the seasonality of flooding. In parts of the state, especially along the great river systems, lands that flooded during the winter and spring tended to be dry by the summer and fall. J. F. Houghton, California's surveyor general from 1862 to 1867, noted pointedly in 1862 that federal authorities usually surveyed during the driest part of the year, thereby underrepresenting the acreage of swamp and overflowed land. Additionally, the U.S. surveys made no attempt to determine the condition of the land in 1850, when the grant to the state was made. In the intervening years, many tracts had been "reclaimed and rendered fit for cultivation, by means of levees, drains, stopping the mouths of sloughs, etc., which they [federal surveyors] have returned as high land." As a result, there was a discrepancy of nearly 85,000 acres between lands segregated by the state as swampland and those returned by federal surveyors as dry land. All of this land was located in five counties along the lower Sacramento and lower San Joaquin rivers, where the seasonality of flooding is marked, and where reclamation projects were already under way.[54]

Owing in part to such widely varying assessments of exactly what constituted swamp and overflowed land, by 1860 the federal government still had not recognized California's title to a single acre of swampland. One litigious result of this policy was that the federal government surveyed, and offered for sale, public land that had previously been sold by the state as swampland.[55] This conflict between the state and federal governments over the delineation of swamplands was not resolved until the passage of a congressional act in July 1866. The act confirmed that all public domain lands previously claimed as swamp and overflowed land by California, and then sold, were in fact deeded by the federal government to the state, thus securing the titles of those who had purchased them.[56]

Ultimately, the federal government deeded 2,193,965 acres of swamplands to California.[57] The state attempted, with only limited success, to devise an orderly method of disposing of this grant, which, while occupying just over 2 percent of its land area, accounted for half of its total freshwater wetlands. In 1855 the California legislature had passed the state's first act providing for the sale of swamp and overflowed lands.[58] The act authorized county surveyors to survey tracts of land upon the application of anyone wishing to acquire them, and also provided for the filing and recording of the surveys with the state surveyor general. The price was one dollar per acre, and individual acquisitions were limited to 320 acres of land. In 1858, the year in which California finally established its State Land Office, the 1855 law was repealed and replaced by a new act providing that all revenues received from the swampland purchases should be placed in a state swampland fund.[59] The 1858 act, in turn, was amended the next year, raising the maximum land purchase to 640 acres.[60] As of this date, the state had not yet made provision for actually reclaiming the lands purchased.

Accordingly, in 1861 California entered what proved to be a short-lived—but pivotal—experiment in coordinated reclamation. That year the legislature passed "An Act to provide for the Reclamation and Segregation of Swamp and Overflowed, and Salt Marsh and Tide, Lands, donated to the State of California by Act of Congress," thereby creating the five-member State Board of Swamp Land Commissioners.[61] The Swamp Land Commission owed its existence in part to a period of Republican ascendancy in California politics. Republican Leland Stanford was elected governor of California in 1861, and the state legislature was also tilting toward the Republicans, although they would not formally take control until 1863, only seven years after their first state convention. Many Republican leaders saw in the flooded "wasteland" of California's Central Valley the potential for an ordered and lucrative agricultural empire, but only if the state were to play an active, centralized role in making that bountiful future a reality. California's Republicans contended that reclamation efforts left in the hands of county governments and private individuals were doomed to failure, and that no amount of reclamation could ever be permanently achieved without a valleywide flood control system.[62]

One of the board's first actions was to establish a system whereby purchasers of swamp and overflowed lands could petition to organize a "reclamation district." The district was a new entity in the California polity, and it set a precedent of localized control under centralized supervision that would be emulated time and time again in the state, not least importantly in the form of irrigation districts. The district, which came to be regarded by the courts as a municipal corporation, had specified governing powers, soon to include taxation, over the lands within its borders.[63] By the end of 1861 organization petitions had been filed by twenty-eight reclamation districts. Together they encompassed 381,035 acres of land in eleven counties in the Sacramento and San Joaquin valleys and in the San Francisco Bay region. Upon petition of the purchasers of one-third of a tract of swamp and overflowed land, the commissioners were authorized to appoint an engineer to plan the reclamation of the tract. However, the act offered no means by which lands could be reclaimed if the cost of such reclamation exceeded the purchase price of one dollar per acre. Keenly aware of this problem, and recognizing that large tracts of reclaimed land would increase many times over in value, the commission, in its first report to the legislature in December 1861, recommended the passage of a law for taxing the lands in each reclamation district.[64] The legislature responded in 1862 by granting authority to the county boards of supervisors to levy an assessment to complete reclamation. Funds raised under this assessment were set aside by the state in a special swampland fund for each district.[65]

Despite its newly granted power of taxation, the Swamp Land Commission faced an overwhelming task for which it was hopelessly outmatched. The knowledge, expertise, and technology necessary to institute an effective flood control program for the Central Valley were almost completely lacking. Engineers did not possess information on stream flows or flood flow patterns, and mechanical dredges and levee-building equipment were still in a nascent state. The flood of 1862, the greatest in the historical record of California, compounded the problem. Unprecedented rains, beginning in early November 1861, had by January 1862 flooded vast portions of the Sacramento and San Joaquin valleys. Newspaper coverage of the event was extensive, and detailed accounts of the floods were preserved in a series of county histories produced in the state in the 1880s.[66]

One of the more literary accounts is that of William H. Brewer. Writing from San Francisco on January 19, 1862, Brewer evokes a powerful image: "The great central valley of the state is under water—the Sacramento and San Joaquin valleys—a region 250 to 300 miles long and an average of at least twenty miles wide, a district of five thousand or six thousand square miles, or probably three to three and a half millions of acres! Although much of it is not cultivated, yet a part of it is the garden of the state. Thousands of farms are entirely under water—cattle starving and drowning."[67]

On February 9 he added,

> The "lake" was at that point sixty miles wide, from the mountains on one side to the hills on the other. This was in the Sacramento Valley. *Steamers* ran back over the ranches fourteen miles from the river, carrying stock, etc., to the hills.
>
> Nearly every house and farm over this immense region is gone. There was such a body of water—250 to 300 miles long and 20 to 60 miles wide, the water ice cold and muddy—that the winds made high waves which beat the farm houses in [sic] pieces.[68]

In a valley subject to flooding on so extensive a scale, many questioned the wisdom of the Board of Swamp Land Commissioners' engineers, who called for closing off the sloughs, the natural overflow channels that siphoned water away from the rivers and into the adjacent flood basins. By blocking these natural escape routes for floodwaters, this plan forced the rivers to carry a greater volume in their main channels. The inevitable result was that when floodwaters burst out of the channels, they did so with a greater force and greater destructiveness to the surrounding lands.[69] The problem of flooding, particularly in the Sacramento Valley, was exacerbated by hydraulic mining, the use of water under high pressure to blast away entire hillsides in search of gold. First developed in 1853 near the mines of Nevada City and generally credited to Edward E. Matteson, hydraulic mining deposited millions of cubic yards of debris in the rivers of the Sierra Nevada, raising their beds far above their natural levels and intensifying the frequency and magnitude of flooding.[70]

Opposition to the Board of Commissioners stemmed from fundamental disagreements not only with the board's flood control policy, but also with its power of taxation. Settlers with farms on relatively high land that seldom overflowed were reluctant to pay taxes for levees that would primarily benefit their lower-lying neighbors. Some landowners held narrow frontages along rivers and were unwilling to lose part of that land for the construction of levees. Still others simply could not afford the taxes for levee construction. Some opposed reclamation on principle. Stock raisers who relied on seasonal floods to nurture grasses for their cattle, sheep, horses, and hogs were opposed to reclamation because it would damage their range. Similarly, grain farmers who relied on the natural floods as an inexpensive substitute for artificial irrigation argued against improving the swamplands.[71]

Upon the commissioners' own recommendation for increased efficiency, the board was reconstituted in 1863 with three, rather than five, commissioners and an office engineer.[72] Nevertheless, progress remained halting for the next two years. In 1865 the board expressed frustration that the General Land Office still had not approved any of the state's swampland segregations (and would not do so until 1866). Nonetheless, by 1865 a total of fifty-four swampland districts had been recognized. Of these, fourteen had advanced to the point that monies received into the Swamp Land Fund had been separately appropriated for reclamation. Surveys were in progress in thirteen others.[73] The largest district, and the one in which the board could report the most progress, was No. 18, the Yolo Basin, encompassing 164,318 acres west of the Sacramento River in Yolo and Solano counties. By 1864 the district had constructed a twenty-five-mile drainage canal to facilitate flood runoff and thereby allow use of the basin's pastures. In the Delta, ten miles of levee were built on Ryer Island in 1865; and between 1861 and 1872 Grand Island was reclaimed with a six-foot levee. Operations began to reclaim Andrus, Brannan, Tyler, and Staten islands as well, but these enclosures were not completed until the 1870s.[74]

Despite having made measurable progress in the lower Sacramento Valley and the Delta, the board was criticized for not having achieved more. It was unable to effectively reclaim District No. 1, the American Basin, which lay between the Sacramento and American rivers, adjacent to the capital city of Sacramento. This state of affairs proved disappointing to the legislature. By early 1866, facing unexpectedly high costs of reclamation, many of the swampland districts had sunk deeply into debt, further strengthening the arguments of the commission's opponents. Finally, the forces opposing the Swamp Land Commission and favoring more local autonomy prevailed in April 1866, when the legislature abolished the Board of Swamp Land Commissioners and discharged the district engineers.[75] All the swamp and overflowed lands belonging to the state, and all the funds raised from the sale of such lands, were granted to the various counties, to be held in trust for the purpose of constructing the levees and drains necessary to reclaim those lands. In effect, the authority of the Swamp Land Commission

devolved to individual county boards of supervisors, which inherited the obliga-
tions that the commission had held since 1861. Thus any semblance of a unified,
systematic statewide approach to the reclamation of swamp and overflowed
lands was lost.[76]

The decentralized reclamation system established in 1866, with authority resting in the county boards of supervisors, survived for only two years, when it was
replaced by a new apparatus by which reclamation was further localized. A legislative act of March 28, 1868—commonly known as the Green Act, after its cre-
ator, Will S. Green of Colusa County—revised not only the swampland laws, but
also all the state's public land laws, and integrated them into a single bill.[77] Will
Green was one of the more influential figures in California's first half-century of
statehood, particularly in terms of the reclamation and development of the Sacramento Valley. Born in 1832 in rural Kentucky and raised with little formal education, Green left his home state for California in August 1849, drawn by the
Gold Rush. He arrived at San Francisco, via Panama, in October and took up
residence in the small town of Colusa the following July. Over the next few years,
Green held the occupations of shopkeeper, hotelier, baker, vegetable gardener,
and farmer. During this time he took up the study of mathematics, and in 1857
was elected to the position of county surveyor, an office he held for ten years.[78]
During his tenure, he learned in detail the lay of the land, including the locations
of the Sacramento Valley's natural flood basins and the most suitable avenues for
drainage canals. He developed a relentless vision of a future Sacramento Valley
made wealthy by reclamation and irrigated agriculture.[79]

In 1863 Green purchased the *Colusa Sun* newspaper, which he used for the
next four decades as his bully pulpit to argue for reclaiming the Sacramento Valley.
While the Republicans had favored centralized planning for reclamation, Democratic ideology at this time tended toward local control of such efforts.[80] Green
brought this agenda to the state assembly in 1867 when, as part of a Democratic
resurgence in California that resulted in a sweep of the legislature and the governorship, he was elected to represent Colusa and Tehama counties. Green's bill,
which he negotiated through the legislature during the spring of 1868, placed the
power to plan and execute the construction of levees in the hands of the boards
of trustees of each reclamation district. The county boards of supervisors were
deprived of their authority to examine and rule on the plans of the individual
reclamation districts, even if such plans interfered with the valley's natural
drainage patterns. Furthermore, taxes collected from the districts were now to
be placed in the county treasuries rather than in the state treasury.[81]

The Green Act of 1868 signaled the triumph of the trend toward localism and
laissez-faire over centralized planning that had begun with the dissolution of the
Board of Swamp Land Commissioners in 1866. The act contained no limitation
on the number of acres of swamp and overflowed lands that any individual could

purchase. Under the previous 320 and 640-acre limitations, sales were restricted largely to the higher lands, upon which it was possible to settle. In order for the deep tule lands to be reclaimed, larger capitalist efforts would be required.[82] The Green Act intended to encourage these efforts, but it inaugurated a period of widespread land speculation. Since the only requirement for receiving a refund on the purchase price was the submission of a sworn statement that the land had been reclaimed, abuses were rife.[83] Within a few years, millions of acres of California's swamplands passed into private hands. In 1872 the disposal of swamp and overflowed lands was carried into the California *Political Code,* which indicated a reversion to the 640-acre limitation that had existed until 1868.[84] But by that point the acreage restriction was meaningless. By the end of 1871, the state had sold all except a few small tracts.[85] The beneficiaries of the 1868 act included the best known of California's land barons, men who already owned huge parcels of real estate: William S. Chapman, Isaac Friedlander, Henry Miller and Charles Lux, and James Ben Ali Haggin and Lloyd Tevis. As of 1872, Miller and Lux had purchased 80,350 acres, and Haggin and Tevis had procured 34,000 acres.[86]

As a result of the decentralization of reclamation planning, coordinated flood control remained an elusive dream in the Central Valley for the next half-century. Nevertheless, the Swamp and Overflowed Lands Act, and the short-lived policies initiated by the Board of Swamp Land Commissioners to implement that act, were of lasting significance for California's wetlands in three ways. First, the act led to the initial sequence of reclamation projects in the Central Valley. Second, by exposing the difficulties and tremendous expenses of reclamation, the act ushered in a period of contentious debate, which lasted well into the twentieth century, about whether reclamation could be best achieved by private local enterprises, quasi-public regional entities (reclamation and irrigation districts), the state, or the federal government. It quickly became apparent that it was impossible to separate the reclamation of swamp and overflow wetlands from the larger concepts of flood control and irrigation. The trend over time was toward larger public projects, culminating in the Sacramento Flood Control Project, the Central Valley Project, and the State Water Project of the twentieth century. Third, the act contributed to increased concentration of land ownership in California and to titanic conflicts over the monopolization of water rights that would be resolved only in the state's highest courts. The acquisition by the federal government of privately held water rights would prove to be a prerequisite for construction of California's greatest twentieth-century irrigation and reclamation project, the Central Valley Project, which, in turn, threatened some of the state's most important remaining wetlands.

3

The San Joaquin Valley

A Tale of Two Basins

In the decades immediately following the dissolution of the Swamp Land Commission and the failure of the state's first attempt at coordinated reclamation, private reclamation efforts began significantly to reduce the extent of the Great Central Valley's wetlands. In the San Joaquin Valley, the conversion of wetlands for agriculture, by small farmers and land barons alike, proceeded in both the San Joaquin and the Tulare basins, but nowhere were the ecological effects of this conversion of the landscape as profound, and as visually apparent, as in the Tulare Basin, the southernmost part of the Central Valley.[1]

THE TULARE BASIN

When California entered the Union as the thirty-first state in 1850, the Tulare Basin contained its largest single expanse of freshwater wetlands. Covered by freshwater lakes for most of the Pleistocene, the Tulare Basin included Tulare, Buena Vista, and Kern lakes, along with their bordering tule marshes, sloughs, and connecting channels. Although the size of these lakes and watercourses varied tremendously based on precipitation patterns, estimates suggest that there were more than 2,100 miles of shoreline marsh habitat in the middle of the nineteenth century. The Tulare Basin was the single most important wintering area for Pacific Flyway waterfowl in California.[2]

Tulare Lake—at that time, the largest body, in surface area, of fresh water in the United States west of the Great Lakes—lay in the Tulare Basin's trough, which has been evocatively described as "a trough within a basin within a valley."[3] The Tulare Lake Basin, which includes Tulare Lake and its environs, is a sub-basin of the larger Tulare Basin. Before diversions for agriculture, Tulare Lake was directly fed by, from north to south, the Kings, Kaweah, and Tule rivers, as well as the smaller Deer Creek and White River, all of which originate in the Sierra Nevada. Another major Sierran river, the Kern, flows southward through a deep canyon before turning westward through foothills and then onto the Tulare Basin floor. The Kern River fed Kern and Buena Vista lakes, situated at the extreme southern end of the basin, and connected to each other by a slough. Buena Vista Lake drained northward into the sixty-mile-long Buena Vista Slough, then through Goose Lake, which lay among the slough's channels, and ultimately into Tulare Lake. Prior to damming and diversions, the four largest watercourses—the Kings, Kaweah, Tule, and Kern—contributed a mean annual flow of 3.25 million acre-feet to the Tulare Basin. As these rivers spilled out of the mountains onto the valley floor, they deposited vast amounts of alluvium, creating fertile deltas that were covered by riparian forest.[4]

Historically, the trough of the Tulare Lake Basin was bisected by a series of sand dunes, fifteen to twenty-five feet in height, several hundred yards wide, and several miles long, running across the southern margin of the lake bed. In times of high water, these ridges—Atwell's Island, Skull Island, and Pelican Island—divided Tulare Lake from marshlands to the south. When the water was exceptionally high, the marshlands became a lake as well, and the dunes then divided Tulare Lake into two lakes, which early Spanish explorers referred to as the Tachi to the north and the Ton Tachi to the south. The lakes were named after a Yokut tribelet, the Tachi, whose members resided near the lake's northern and northwestern shores.[5] The highest lake level ever recorded was reached during the flood of the winter and spring of 1862, when heavy rains turned the rivers into raging torrents. Three hundred billion cubic feet, or 6.9 million acre-feet, of water poured into the Tulare Lake Basin, and Tulare Lake reached a depth of thirty-seven feet near its northwestern shore.[6] The engorged lake then covered approximately 760 square miles. Overflow waters from the smaller, but still substantial, Buena Vista and Kern lakes to the south contributed to this deluge via Buena Vista Slough.

At the northern end of the Tulare Lake Basin, the alluvial fan of the Kings River coalesces with that of Los Gatos Creek, which flows eastward out of the Coast Ranges. These fans form a ridge that stands approximately thirty feet higher than the lake bed. In most years, this ridge contained Tulare Lake in its basin, depriving it of any natural outlet to the sea. But in exceptionally wet years, such as 1862, the lake spilled over the ridge, filled tiny Summit Lake, and drained northward via Fresno Slough, a northern distributary of the Kings River, to the San Joaquin River.[7] A continuous watercourse was thus formed from Tulare Lake all the way through the San Joaquin Valley to the Sacramento–San Joaquin Delta, San Francisco Bay, and the Pacific Ocean.

Early explorers and topographers have left vivid descriptions of the Tulare Lake region. Jedediah Smith camped along Kern and Tulare lakes during his southwest expedition of 1826–1827.[8] John C. Fremont, George H. Derby, and R. S. Williamson led expeditions to the Tulare Basin for the U.S. Army Corps of Topographical Engineers in 1844, 1850, and 1853, respectively. Fremont produced one of the earliest maps of the basin and aroused American interest in the region. Derby's map was far more precise (see map 7), and his report to Congress, rich in detail and broad in scope, contained especially revealing passages about both Tulare and Buena Vista lakes. Passing eastward out of the Coast Ranges toward the southern shore of Tulare Lake on May 3, 1850, Derby wrote,

> We found here a ridge of sand about one hundred yards in width, and about twelve feet above the level of the lake, which divides the water of the northern or Taché from the bed (now nearly dry) of the southern or Ton Taché lake. This last is little more than a very extensive swamp, covering the plain for fifteen miles in a southerly direction, and is about ten in width. It is filled with sloughs and small tulé [sic] lakes, and is of course impassible, except with the assistance of boats or rafts. The gradual receding of the water is distinctly marked by the ridges of decayed tulé upon its shore, and I was informed, and see no reason to disbelieve, that ten years ago it was nearly as extensive a sheet of water as the northern lake, having been gradually drained by the connecting sloughs, and its beds filled by the encroachments of the tulé.[9]

Derby's description of the Ton Taché supports the historical evidence for dramatic fluctuations in the size and depth of the lake. Traveling southward, Derby found himself a week later on the northern shore of Buena Vista Lake:

> Buena Vista lake is a sheet of water about ten miles in length and from four to six miles in width; it lies about eight miles from the head of the valley formed by the junction of the ridges of the coast range and Sierra Nevada. Like the other bodies of water in the valley it is nearly surrounded with tulé [sic], and upon its north and east banks is found a heavy growth of willows. A slough some sixty miles in length [Buena Vista Slough] connects it with the swamps and bodies of standing water in the bed of the Ton Taché, and through them with the great northern lake [Taché].[10]

Having circled back northward, on May 20 Derby reached the Sanjon de San Jose (Fresno Slough), hoping to follow it from Tulare Lake to the San Joaquin River. He was disappointed: "We . . . were unable to get further on account of the mire, the ground between the lake and the San Joaquin being entirely cut up by small sloughs which had overflown in every direction, making the country a perfect swamp, which I found it a matter of great difficulty to cross."[11]

Perhaps most amazing to a modern reader of Derby's account is that Tulare Lake is now gone, Buena Vista Lake exists only as a much-reduced reservoir for fishing and boating, and the sloughs and marshes that once surrounded and connected

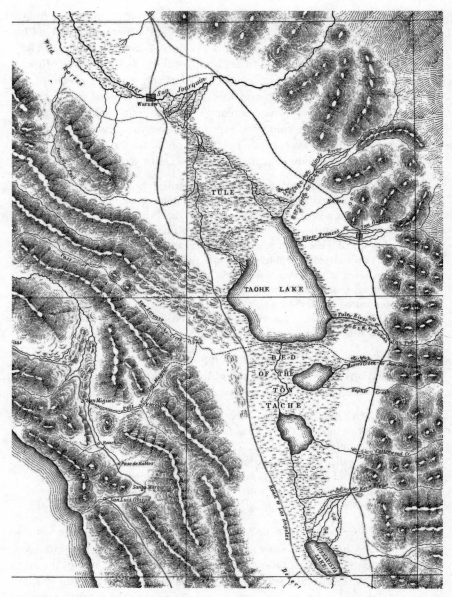

MAP 7. The central portion of Lieutenant George Horatio Derby's 1850 map "Reconnaissance of the Tulares Valley." Note the nearly continuous stretch of marshland across the Tulare Basin and northward into the San Joaquin Basin. Source: Senate Executive Document no. 110, 32d Congress, 1st session, 1852.

them have been either dried up or converted to irrigation channels. Kern, Goose, and Summit lakes have vanished as well. Of perhaps 625,000 acres of original wetlands in the basin, no more than a few thousand remain.[12] There has been no greater percentage loss of wetlands anywhere in the Central Valley. The disappearance of these wetlands represents a tremendous loss to the waterfowl that inhabit the Tulare Basin. Mary Austin, the accomplished nature writer, has left us a timeless account of the life that the tules (often called *tulares,* following Spanish usage) once supported:

> Wild fowl, quacking hordes of them, nest in the tulares. Any day's venture will raise from open shallows the great blue heron on his hollow wings. Chill evenings the mallard drakes cry continually from the glassy pools, the bittern's hollow boom rolls along the water paths. Strange and far-flown fowl drop down against the saffron, autumn sky. All day wings beat above it hazy with speed; long flights of cranes glimmer in the twilight. By night one wakes to hear the clanging geese go over. One wishes for, but gets no nearer speech from those the reedy ferns have swallowed up. What they do there, how fare, what find, is the secret of the tulares.[13]

Three factors interacting synergistically led to the destruction of the tule wetlands of the Tulare Basin. During the flood of 1862, the Kings and Kern rivers changed their courses. The Kings River reapportioned its flow among its distributary sloughs so that the main stream of the river now flowed northwest into Fresno Slough toward the San Joaquin River, rather than southwest toward Tulare Lake. The Kern River, for its part, cut a new channel to the north, largely bypassing Kern Lake and flowing instead into the slough connecting Kern Lake to the east with the slightly lower Buena Vista Lake to the west. Kern Lake then slowly began to dry up. By 1872 the lake had become so putrid and salty that the aquatic biota died. Soon afterward the lake disappeared completely. Following the wet years of 1867 and 1868, the Kern again changed its course, now largely bypassing Buena Vista Lake as well and flowing directly into Buena Vista Slough toward Tulare Lake. These events dramatically reshaped the waterscape of the Tulare Basin and resulted in the natural conversion of what were once well-defined wetland areas.[14] Precipitation, widely variable in California, declined to below-average levels during the last decades of the nineteenth century, further desiccating the basin.[15] Complementing natural changes in watercourses and variations in precipitation, irrigation diversions in the Tulare Basin drastically reduced inflow into Tulare Lake, and ultimately starved the lake into oblivion.

THE DESTRUCTION OF TULARE LAKE

The alluvial lands of the wooded deltas of the Kings and Kaweah rivers, the largest watercourses that directly fed Tulare Lake, had impressed Spanish explorers during the early decades of the nineteenth century, but the Tulare Lake Basin's remoteness from the coastal settlements and the intransigence of the Yokuts prohibited economic development in the region until after California statehood. The earliest diversions were made in the mid-1850s along the Kaweah River near Visalia, as well as along the upper Tule River, the Kings River, and Deer Creek. Many natural distributaries and sloughs were straightened or deepened and integrated into irrigation systems. Grain, especially wheat and barley, grew easily on the delta bottomlands, and within two decades wheat became the dominant crop in the basin. Wheat did not require irrigation except in drought years, but irrigation fostered increased yields, allowing small farmers to remain competitive with large-scale dryland grain farmers. Irrigation also opened possibilities for crop diversification.[16]

The tule lands surrounding Tulare Lake were developed more slowly than the alluvial delta lands to the east. Early settlers in the basin had avoided the tule lands because of the risk of malaria, but during the 1860s growing statewide confidence in reclamation led to a reappraisal of the marshland surrounding Tulare Lake. Once it became clear that wheat could grow on the adobe soils of reclaimed marshland as well as on the better-drained river alluvium, settlers quickly turned the tule lands bordering the lake over to that grain.[17] Few individuals at the time viewed these tule lands through the naturalist lens of Mary Austin. For most, the tules were an obstacle to cultivation and settlement.

By the early 1870s, most of the Tulare Lake Basin had passed into private hands, and irrigation had become a significant feature of the region. Diversions of the Kings, Kaweah, Tule, and White rivers, as well as Deer Creek, began to reduce water levels in Tulare Lake by the late 1870s. After this time, Tulare Lake no longer reached its overflow stage to discharge into the San Joaquin Basin.[18] As early as 1881, settlers began filing claims along the margins of the retreating lake itself. As the lake receded and agriculture advanced westward toward the basin trough, farmers constructed irrigation ditches to deliver water over ever-increasing distances. The marshlands of the basin were replaced by well-ordered fields irrigated by the rivers that had once nourished them. By the late nineteenth century the natural landscapes of the Tulare Lake Basin had been reordered "into cultural landscapes of geometrical forms."[19]

Developments in the Tulare Lake Basin paralleled those in the state as a whole. California was then at the height of its wheat boom, the defining economic feature of the state from the 1870s through the early 1890s. In 1890 alone, California produced more than forty million bushels of wheat and competed with Minnesota for the distinction of the top wheat-producing state in the nation.[20] This accomplishment would not have been possible were it not for the growth of railroads across the state.[21] In the Central Valley, an expanding network of rail lines enabled the easy transport of wheat growers' crops to the ports of Stockton and

San Francisco, from which they could be shipped to international markets.[22] By 1872 the Central Pacific Railroad (of transcontinental fame) had constructed its San Joaquin Valley line as far south as Tulare County. Between 1872 and 1874, operating as the Southern Pacific, the railroad extended its line southward through the Tulare Basin, reaching Bakersfield in Kern County.[23] Two years later, the Southern Pacific built a branch westward from its main line to the fertile country north of Tulare Lake known as the Mussel Slough district.[24] The quantities of produce transported from the Tulare Basin were astounding. By the early 1880s it required approximately 2,400 rail cars, each carrying twenty thousand pounds of wheat, to deliver the crop of Tulare County alone.[25]

Despite their transportation and marketing advantages, however, wheat growers in the Tulare Basin, like those in the rest of California, faced increasing competition in the 1880s and 1890s from other regions of the United States, especially the Great Plains, and from abroad, as vast tracts were turned over to wheat in India, Australia, Argentina, Canada, and the Ukraine. Profits in the basin reached their nadir in 1894, and it was only after this collapse that basin farmers fully diversified into fruits, vegetables, and dairy products, accelerating a transition from extensive to intensive agriculture. Despite this trend toward diversification, huge grain ranches persisted after the collapse of the wheat boom, especially in the newly reclaimed lake bed, establishing a pattern that would prevail throughout the twentieth century, when the bed would be converted to cotton production on the largest scale.[26]

By the beginning of the twentieth century, the effects of decades of irrigation diversions in the basin had taken their toll on Tulare Lake. In 1898 the lake went completely dry for the first time in recorded history, and remained so for about a year.[27] During the first two decades of the twentieth century, as wet years alternated with dry years, the lake level rose and fell, in some years flooding tens of thousands of acres of crops and in other years receding completely. Continued agricultural encroachment upon the lake area necessitated the construction of massive protective levees. Tulare Lake itself was reduced to thirty-six square miles, the size of a single township, and the land surrounding the lake was now irrigated by canals stretching from the rivers that had once sustained it.[28]

Irrigated acreage in the Tulare Basin as a whole increased dramatically, from just below 180,000 acres in 1900 to more than 680,000 acres in 1930.[29] This increase was driven by groundwater as well as surface flows. When the first wells were drilled in the basin during the late 1870s, they penetrated the clay layer that underlies much of the western half of the San Joaquin Valley and tapped into a series of aquifers confined beneath it.[30] Because the water in the aquifers was at greater than atmospheric pressure, the water rose freely to the surface without pumping. These artesian wells were part of a broad belt that stretched from Kern County, at the valley's southern end, northward through Tulare, Fresno, Merced, and Stanislaus counties; the largest wells were found in Kern and Tulare counties, in the Tulare Basin.[31] By 1885 artesian flow began to diminish, and continued overdrafts through the end of century so reduced water pressure that many former artesian wells now required pumping. Irrigation withdrawals continued to exceed the aquifers' recharge capacity by significant amounts, and groundwater levels plummeted during the first decades of the twentieth century, falling to depths that were not economically feasible to exploit. By the 1930s, with the Tulare Basin's once-vast wetlands gone and its aquifers depleted, farmers could no longer expand irrigated acreage without an additional source of water.[32] More than three decades would pass before that water finally arrived in the western side of the basin, via the San Luis Unit of the Central Valley Project and the California Aqueduct of the State Water Project.

THE KERN RIVER, BUENA VISTA SLOUGH, AND *LUX V. HAGGIN*

Irrigation and reclamation issues attained paramount importance in the southern portion of the Tulare Basin, along the Kern River and Buena Vista Slough. Here, the basin's wetlands came to occupy center stage in a titanic legal struggle that ultimately defined California's complicated system of water rights and destined those wetlands for oblivion. Once known as Kern Island, the often-flooded Kern River delta in the southeastern portion of the Tulare Basin was largely reclaimed by the enterprise of James Ben Ali Haggin, Lloyd Tevis, and William B. Carr. Together they amassed tremendous landholdings and extensive water rights in Kern County. Their Kern County Land and Water Company, founded in 1875 and reorganized as the Kern County Land Company in 1890, dominated and shaped that region's economic development for generations. Haggin had arrived in San Francisco from Kentucky in 1850, and shortly thereafter established a partnership in law with his brother-in-law, Lloyd Tevis. The firm's success brought wealth to the partners, which they translated into investments in mining, banking, manufacturing, and the urban development of San Francisco.[33] During the early 1870s Haggin purchased Kern and Buena Vista lakes and much of the lowland swamp around them, "with a view of draining and reclaiming them."[34]

Haggin expanded his empire under the terms of the Desert Land Act of March 3, 1877, a congressional measure intended to stimulate farming on the arid lands of the West.[35] Despite the tremendous amount of water that its rivers delivered to the Tulare Basin, that region was indeed a desert. In the city of Bakersfield, rainfall measured 5.00 inches in the year 1875–1876 and only 2.85 inches in the following dry year, 1876–1877.[36] Having already acquired tens of thousands of acres of railroad lands in Kern County during the 1870s with the help of his agent in the San Joaquin Valley, William B. Carr—a Republican Party boss and lobbyist for the Southern Pacific Railroad—Haggin used the Desert Land Act to accumulate more than a hundred thousand acres of land north of Bakersfield and adjoining the new Southern Pacific Railroad line. The Desert Land Act permitted settlers to purchase a section (640 acres) of land for $1.25 an acre, provided that the claimant irrigated all the land within three years of purchase.[37] Haggin's claim that the lands of the Tulare Basin were desert lands was legitimate, but the ways in which he and his associates took advantage of the act were not. The Desert Land Act was subject to widespread abuse, as Haggin and Carr and many other wealthy individuals utilized "dummy" claims, taken out in someone else's name, to acquire vast holdings.[38]

Haggin's acquisitions of desert lands in 1877 included a solid block of land on the Kern River. After purchasing local water rights, Haggin began to construct a network of canals intended to irrigate the Kern Delta and the surrounding plains and to "utilize effectually all the surplus water of [the Kern] river."[39] The largest and most important of these canals was the Calloway Canal, which tapped the Kern River above Bakersfield, where the river emerges from the foothills of the Sierra Nevada onto the valley plains and its low, sandy banks allow for the relatively easy diversion of water. Started by a rival firm in 1875, the canal was acquired by the Kern County Land and Water Company in 1877. Expanded to more than thirty miles in length in 1879, the canal was 80 feet wide at the bottom, 120 feet wide at the top, and 7 feet deep. Its capacity—never reached—was nearly 1,000 cubic feet of water per second (cfs), essentially the maximum flow of the river, enough to irrigate 70,000 acres of the parched plains north of Bakersfield.[40]

A diversion dam constructed for the Calloway Canal on the Kern River in 1877 appropriated most of the water supply for the Buena Vista Slough downstream, along with the swamp and overflowed lands adjacent to it. These lands had been acquired since 1868 by Haggin's rivals in the Tulare Basin, the powerful landowners Henry Miller and Charles Lux, in partnership with a local rancher, James C. Crocker. Charles Lux and Henry Miller (born Heinrich Alfred Kreiser), both German émigrés, arrived independently in San Francisco via New York in 1850. Beginning as butchers, within a few years they entered the cattle trade, and in 1858 they established a partnership that would last until Lux's death in 1887; Miller died nearly thirty years later, in 1916. Together they accumulated 1.25 million acres of land in the San Joaquin Valley as well as in Nevada and Oregon. Already the most important landowners in the San Joaquin Basin to the north, by 1879 Miller and Lux had taken possession of 78,908 acres along Buena Vista Slough.[41] By that year, diversions through the Calloway Canal had so affected the basin's hydrology that "the sloughs and natural streams of the Kern River below the Calloway weir changed from clear, rushing streams to limpid, stagnated marshes good for almost nothing."[42] Yet the Calloway Canal was only one of at least twenty-seven major diversion canals purchased or constructed by the Kern

County Land and Water Company that spread like tentacles north and south of the Kern River's alluvial delta.[43]

Miller and Lux, Crocker, and six other riparian owners filed suit in May 1879 against James B. Haggin, the Kern County Land and Water Company, and 117 other appropriators in order to halt the diversions. This suit, *Lux v. Haggin,* was one of eighty-four lawsuits filed by the Riparian Suits Association, organized by Miller and Lux the previous year to defend the rights of riparian owners along Buena Vista Slough.[44] Henry Miller and Charles Lux were not interested in maintaining their right to the full flow of the Kern River through Buena Vista Slough; rather, they wanted to be guaranteed just enough water to irrigate their pastures and croplands: too much water flowing through the slough would flood their lands and hinder their reclamation efforts. In 1876 Miller and Lux had organized the Kern Valley Water Company for the purpose of reclaiming the several hundred square miles of swampland surrounding the slough. To accomplish this ambitious goal, they diverted the Kern River from Buena Vista Slough to the new Kern Valley Water Company Canal, running twenty-one miles along the western side of the slough's marshlands. The canal had a capacity of 5,026 cubic feet per second, more than five times that of Haggin's Calloway Canal. By the time *Lux v. Haggin* made it to the courtroom, Miller and Lux had reclaimed nearly 50,000 acres of wetlands along Buena Vista Slough by diverting its waters to the dry lands to its west.[45] Thus the actions of both riparians and appropriators tended to diminish the wetlands of Buena Vista Slough. Whether the diversions were made higher up on the Kern, through Haggin's canals, or at the slough itself, through Miller and Lux's canal, the wetlands of Buena Vista Slough were destined for obliteration.

The trial of *Lux v. Haggin* began in April 1881, and it pitted the San Joaquin Valley's largest landowners against each other in a battle that spanned five years and three court rulings. *Lux v. Haggin* would determine not simply the immediate fate of the wetlands of Buena Vista Slough but, more broadly, the future of California's system of riparian and appropriative water rights. Possession—and contestation—of water rights, in turn, would shape the future development of the Central Valley and the fate of significant portions of the valley's wetlands.

From the first years of statehood, California established a legal and judicial framework that recognized both riparian and appropriative rights. Conflicts between the two systems of rights were inevitable. The doctrine of riparian rights, or riparianism, guaranteed owners of land bordering a stream the full natural flow of that watercourse. It allowed withdrawals for domestic needs and the watering of livestock, but did not allow for irrigation. Riparian doctrine traces its origins to English common law and was carried to the eastern United States, where rainfall is abundant, rivers flow year-round, and irrigation is rarely necessary. The doctrine also took hold in several western states, including California, where a constitutional provision passed by the first legislature in April 1850 recognized English common law and provided the legal basis for its acceptance on private lands.[46]

The competing doctrine of prior appropriation—based on the principle of "first in time, first in right"—allowed for diversions to be made from streams without regard to ownership and without fear that other individuals could later deprive claimants of their water. Unlike riparian rights, which were inseparable from the land they adjoined, appropriative rights could be bought and sold, in part or in their entirety. In California, prior appropriation was first developed on the public lands of the state's mining districts in the early 1850s, where diversions of water were necessary to work a claim, and where riparian doctrine could not apply because the miners did not hold title to the claims they worked.[47] Prior appropriation was ratified by the state legislature for the gold-bearing "mother lode" country in 1851, and by the U.S. Congress for public lands generally in 1866.[48] In 1872 the California legislature instituted a system for regulating water rights through the state's *Civil Code*. The *Civil Code* reflected common usage, which by this time had established that the water gained by appropriative right could be used on any land, regardless of the distance from the watercourse, provided that the water was put to "some useful or beneficial purpose."[49]

Though originally developed to serve the needs of miners, the doctrine of prior appropriation was embraced by irrigators, large and small, in the Central Valley. Haggin and Carr relied on their appropriative rights to the Kern River to irrigate their Kern County lands, and these rights clashed directly with Miller and Lux's riparian rights to their lands along Buena Vista Slough. The crux of the issue in *Lux v. Haggin* was whether Buena Vista Slough constituted a watercourse, and therefore had riparian rights attached to it that could not be diminished by upstream appropriations, or whether the slough was indistinguishable from the Buena Vista swamplands, in which case Haggin's appropriations on the Kern River would be justified.[50]

The first ruling in *Lux v. Haggin* came in November 1881. Judge Benjamin Brundage of the Kern County Superior Court decided in favor of Haggin and his fellow appropriators, arguing that riparian doctrine was subject to certain limitations based on the special conditions of the arid West. Miller and Lux appealed, and the California Supreme Court heard the case in 1883 and 1884. In a brief decision issued in October 1884, Judge J. R. Sharpstein reversed Brundage's decision, ruling that swamplands carried riparian rights.[51] However, Sharpstein's ruling was too narrow to address fully a number of contentious issues concerning the nature of riparian and appropriative rights, and, in the context of an urgent need to clarify and reform California water law, the court agreed to rehear the case. Judge E. W. McKinstry issued the final decision on April 26, 1886.[52] McKinstry affirmed Miller and Lux's riparian rights along Buena Vista Slough, arguing that unrestrained appropriation would lead to monopoly. But McKinstry also held that irrigation was a "public use" of water, and allowed for several methods by which appropriators could gain access to water held by riparian rights, including purchase and condemnation. Because irrigation was a "public use," irrigation companies and irrigation districts could legally condemn riparian rights on condition of proper compensation.[53] *Lux v. Haggin* thus established the dual doctrine of riparian and appropriative rights. Known subsequently as the California Doctrine, this legal precept spread to eight other states: Washington and Oregon in the Far West, and North Dakota, South Dakota, Nebraska, Kansas, Oklahoma, and Texas on the Great Plains.[54]

Ironically, the decision in *Lux v. Haggin* did little to benefit the wetlands along Buena Vista Slough. With the case finally decided, the two sides reached an agreement to apportion the waters of the Kern River, but neither party intended that solution to protect the wetlands fed by the river.[55] Instead, Miller and Lux would receive adequate water for their pastures and croplands while continuing to reclaim the swamplands surrounding Buena Vista Slough. Haggin and the other appropriators would continue to divert much of the upstream flow of the Kern River and thereby prevent flooding in the basin. The combination of Miller and Lux's reclamation project and Haggin's appropriations contributed to the demise of Buena Vista Slough and Tulare Lake. Its waters diverted for the irrigation of alfalfa and natural pasture, the slough no longer replenished Tulare Lake. Instead, it grew the grasses that fed the cattle of the men who ruled the Tulare Basin during the last quarter of the nineteenth century.

ECOLOGICAL CONSEQUENCES OF WETLAND LOSS IN THE TULARE BASIN

The reclamation of Tulare Lake and the destruction of wetlands throughout the Tulare Basin destroyed a rich and complex ecosystem upon which myriad organisms depended.[56] Tule elk once inhabited the marshes and sloughs surrounding Tulare, Buena Vista, and Kern lakes, as well as overflow grasslands bordering the San Joaquin and Sacramento rivers. The elk came to the wetlands during the summer to browse on marshland grasses, but by the late nineteenth century, hunting, encroachment on their habitat, and the decline of Tulare Lake drove them to a final refuge along the shores of Buena Vista Lake near Miller and Lux's Buttonwillow Ranch. In the late 1870s Henry Miller offered protection to the last surviving animals and is reported to have annually planted a field reserved solely for elk forage.[57] In 1904 Miller and Lux offered to turn the elk over to the federal government, through the Department of Agriculture's Division of Biological Survey, for protection. As a result of these and subsequent efforts, tule elk were saved from probable extinction, and nearly two dozen thriving herds (see figure 4) were

FIGURE 4. Tule elk at the San Luis National Wildlife Refuge. These elk are part of a herd of approximately forty to fifty animals that are protected on the refuge. Photo by the author.

established in the Central Valley and throughout California during the course of the twentieth century.[58]

While the elk that browsed along the edges of the lakes were saved from extinction, organisms that resided in Tulare Lake itself fared far less well. The lake had supported a thriving terrapin population, which were sold for $2.25 to $4.50 a dozen to San Francisco's restaurants. Large boats sailed the lake's waters, the most famous of which was the thirty-two-foot schooner *Water Witch* (see figure 5). This boat was used on the lake for catching and transporting terrapin, and for fishing and hunting expeditions, from 1878 until it was destroyed by a violent storm in the early 1880s.[59]

The lake also supported a tremendous fish population, the extent of which was not discovered until 1884, when the lake level was already declining. For the previous several dry years, the Kings and Tule rivers had been fully tapped for irrigation, and no water from them had reached the lake. When the spring freshet reached the lake in 1884, the fish, which had been surviving in the increasingly alkalized water, came to meet the fresh water on the eastern side of the lake in solid masses. By the fall of that year, the first market seines appeared on Tulare Lake. These enormous fishing nets were a thousand yards in length and approximately fourteen feet in width at their center. The seines were taken out from one

NORTH END OF TULARE LAKE, & MOUTH OF KINGS RIVER. LAST VOYAGE OF THE "WATER WITCH". STUMPS OF SUBMERGED FOREST.

FIGURE 5. This illustration of the schooner *Water Witch* provides a sense of the tremendous size of Tulare Lake during the nineteenth century. Source: Wallace W. Elliott & Co., *History of Tulare County, California* (San Francisco: Wallace W. Elliott, 1883).

to one and a half miles into the shallow lake and drawn in by horse-powered windlasses. Two hauls were generally made per day, each seine bringing in a catch of as much as a ton of marketable fish daily. Most of the fish caught were native Sacramento perch, which can grow up to two feet in length. Fish weighing three and a half pounds were common, and five-pounders frequent. They were shipped to markets in San Francisco at an average profit of three cents per pound. Such unsustainable harvesting could not last indefinitely, and by 1889 the perch population had been drastically reduced by the market seines.[60] In the end, however, it mattered little that overfishing was eliminating the perch; the lake itself was doomed. William J. Browning, a market hunter, fished Tulare Lake with seines from 1884 to 1894, after which time "it was so reduced in size and had become so filled with catfish that it was no longer profitable."[61] By the 1890s remaining lake fish had begun to die off as years of evaporation without replenishment concentrated the alkali in the lake to levels that would no longer support life. Commercial fishing in Tulare Lake was dead.[62]

Waterfowl hunting on Tulare and Buena Vista lakes had been phenomenal during the decades preceding the lakes' disappearance. Waterfowl were described as "plentiful, sometimes innumerable," and for many years professional hunters shipped large numbers of ducks, geese, and swans to the markets of San Francisco and Stockton.[63] The gathering of bird eggs for market was so lucrative that it threatened the viability of local populations. By 1899 the Kern County Board of Supervisors felt it necessary to pass an ordinance prohibiting the gathering of the eggs of the "brown ibis," considered to be a fine game bird, on the lowlands surrounding the shores of Buena Vista Lake.[64] The diminution of both Tulare and Buena Vista lakes most severely affected avifauna that required large bodies of water for habitat. Local populations of game birds and nongame birds alike declined, including the eared grebe, western grebe, white pelican, double-crested cormorant, great blue heron, black-crowned night heron, tundra swan, and two species of diving ducks, the canvasback and the redhead.[65] Concentrated on ever-shrinking habitat, the birds also became more susceptible to outbreaks of avian diseases, especially botulism and, from the mid-twentieth century, cholera.[66]

THE SAN JOAQUIN BASIN: MILLER AND LUX, WATER RIGHTS, AND WATERFOWL

Historically, the San Joaquin Basin, which includes the course of the San Joaquin River from its emergence onto the valley floor north to its discharge into the Sacramento–San Joaquin Delta, lacked the large fluctuating but permanent lakes that characterized the Tulare Basin.[67] Instead, its wetlands consisted of riparian corridors and seasonally flooded grasslands. Riparian zones stretched along the San Joaquin River and its major tributaries in the basin, the Merced, Tuolumne, and Stanislaus rivers. These corridors were more substantial than those of the Tulare Basin, and are conservatively estimated at 185,000 acres, compared to perhaps 50,000 acres in the Tulare Basin.[68] The majority of the approximately one million acres of wetlands in the San Joaquin Basin, however, were seasonally flooded grasslands that extended along the western side of the San Joaquin River.[69] In those extremely wet years when water from Tulare Lake overflowed into the San Joaquin Basin, the San Joaquin River poured over its banks, inundating the land for miles from northwestern Fresno County to the Delta. The high flows of 1862 flooded the lands on the San Joaquin River's western side to a depth of four feet in an area estimated at from five to twenty miles wide.[70] But the San Joaquin River did not require an extrabasin water source to flood its banks. In all but the driest years, winter rains and high spring flows from snowmelt in the Sierra Nevada were sufficient to cause the river to spill over its low banks into the marshy, slough-laced land to its west.

The center of this wetland habitat, which was of tremendous importance to wintering waterfowl, lay in Merced County, where concentration of land ownership and struggles over water rights have repeatedly risen to center stage in the history of California's water development. In large part, this region owes its importance in California history to the fact that the natural overflow that provided habitat for millions of migratory birds also nourished the growth of grasses, making the region particularly well suited for raising cattle and for the enterprises of Henry Miller and Charles Lux. Miller and Lux were the primary landowners along Buena Vista Slough in the Tulare Basin, but in the long run their land and water rights in the San Joaquin Basin were to prove more important for the San Joaquin Valley's remaining wetlands. Their holdings in the San Joaquin Basin were concentrated in the arid and sparsely populated Westside, as it was known, the land west of the San Joaquin River. The dominance of Miller and Lux both reflected and perpetuated the separate development of the Westside, a fact not lost on nineteenth-century contemporaries.[71] By adopting a policy of neither subdividing their properties for sale nor opening them to agricultural settlement, Miller and Lux ensured control over the water rights of the region, and, as a fortuitous consequence for migratory waterfowl, prevented the permanent drainage of the Westside's extensive overflow lands.

In the heart of the Westside lay Rancho Sanjon de Santa Rita, one of fewer than twenty Mexican land grants in the San Joaquin Valley, and the one that was to become the core of Miller and Lux's cattle empire in the San Joaquin Basin (see map 8). Encompassing 48,823.84 acres, or approximately eleven square leagues, Rancho Sanjon de Santa Rita fronted the west bank of the San Joaquin River for approximately twenty-eight miles in Merced County.[72] Stretching along a roughly north-south axis parallel to the river, the grant was dissected by a series of sloughs. On slightly higher ground between the sloughs lay the most fertile and productive grasslands in the valley. The ownership history of Rancho Sanjon de Santa Rita is long and convoluted, and, representative of many of the Mexican land grants, it had passed out of the hands of the original grantee before it was ever confirmed by the United States government. Rancho Sanjon de Santa Rita had been granted to Don Francisco Soberanes in September 1841.[73] Under the terms of the Land Act of 1851, Soberanes appeared before the Land Claims Commission in 1853 to seek confirmation of his grant. When that confirmation finally came nine years later, in November 1862, Soberanes had long since divested himself of the property, selling it in various parcels. Henry Miller and Charles Lux gradually purchased these tracts and, by 1865, had acquired all of Rancho Sanjon de Santa Rita.[74]

Miller and Lux quickly extended their holdings in the San Joaquin Basin, both to the north and to the south of Rancho Sanjon de Santa Rita. Expanding northward, in 1868 they purchased the majority of Rancho Orestimba, another Mexican land grant, which lay almost equally astride the Merced-Stanislaus county line. Like Rancho Sanjon de Santa Rita, Rancho Orestimba bordered the San Joaquin River to the east. In addition to taking advantage of opportunities to purchase Mexican land grants, Miller and Lux successfully exploited federal land laws to acquire acreage in the basin. Between 1866 and 1880, the partners accumulated at least 126,800 acres of the public domain in Merced County alone. Of these, more than 13,207 acres were "swampland" along the San Joaquin River. Keen to take advantage of the seasonal overflow of the grasslands along the river

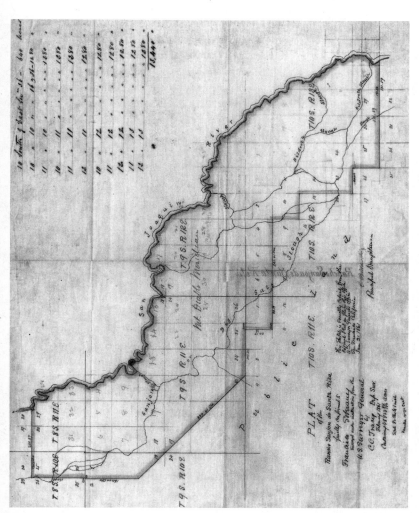

MAP 8. Plat of the Rancho Sanjon de Santa Rita, produced in 1861 by the office of the U.S. Surveyor General. Seasonally flooded grassland adjacent to the San Joaquin River and a maze of sloughs provided excellent grazing for cattle—and habitat for waterfowl. Source: Spanish and Mexican land grant maps, 1855–75. *Records of the United States Surveyor General for California.* Courtesy of the California State Archives, Sacramento, California.

to support their expanding cattle herds, in 1869 Miller and Lux hired William G. Collier, the Merced County surveyor, to map the lands along the San Joaquin River in Stanislaus, Merced, and northern Fresno counties and identify the swamplands.[75] The partners were able to purchase thousands of acres of these overflow lands, including 11,520 acres paralleling the San Joaquin River running south from Rancho Sanjon de Santa Rita.[76] By 1881 Miller and Lux's holdings extended for sixty-eight contiguous miles along the western side of the river, and were from five to forty miles wide.[77] Edward F. Treadwell, chief counsel for Miller and Lux from 1907 to 1922, and Miller's near-hagiographical biographer, described how Miller and Lux efficiently and productively used these overflow lands: "The arrangement of the land to receive the benefit of this water was intricate and ingenious. Land lying so low under natural conditions that it was practically in perpetual inundation was protected by levees so as to receive the flood for shorter periods, and then drained so that the sun could reach the soil and produce grasses. The great acreage of tules and cattails were thus dried out and burned over, and then flooded for a shorter period and crops of rich grasses produced."[78]

Miller and Lux not only reconfigured the natural landscape of the San Joaquin Basin by levying low-lying lands adjacent to the San Joaquin River and its sloughs, but over the course of several decades they also constructed a prodigious network of canals to water the lands of the arid Westside. The partners gained control of their most important canal, the Main Canal, from the failed San Joaquin and Kings River Canal and Irrigation Company.[79] Founded by San Francisco capitalist John Bensley in 1866, the company had envisioned reclaiming the San Joaquin Valley by constructing a 160-mile irrigation canal from Tulare Lake in the south to the city of Antioch, at the western edge of the Delta, in the north. With promises from Miller and Lux to grant the right-of-way and to purchase a portion of the canal's water to irrigate pastureland, the company began work on the canal in August 1871 at Firebaugh's Ferry on the San Joaquin River in northern Fresno County, and proceeded northward across Miller and Lux's properties. When the finances of the San Joaquin and Kings River Canal and Irrigation Company collapsed in the late 1870s, Miller and Lux acquired controlling interest in the company as well as the forty-mile segment of the canal that it had completed to date. The canal, which measured 32 feet wide at the bottom, 42 feet wide at the top, and 6 feet deep, was capable of delivering 726 cubic feet of water per second, enough to irrigate 145,000 acres of land.[80] By 1880 Miller and Lux had extended the canal an additional twenty-seven miles north to Orestimba Creek, which flows out of the Coast Ranges in southwestern Stanislaus County. By the turn of the century, hundreds of miles of Miller and Lux canals and ditches brought San Joaquin River water to northwestern Fresno County and western Merced and Stanislaus counties. While maintaining the overflow lands adjacent to the river, Miller and Lux rationally apportioned the once-uncontrollable floodwaters of the San Joaquin across the landscape. Agriculture flourished on the irrigated lands of the Westside, but the contrast between irrigated and nonirrigated land remained always stark:

> The line of sterility is sharply drawn between the soil reached by the water taken from the upper San Joaquin, and the unwatered region adjoining. At irrigated places the grain is often breast high and the alfalfa fields are covered with a strong growth of succulent herbage. Root crops of every description are growing to perfection, and an abundance of fruit and shade trees, grape vines, and berry bushes, all in the best possible condition, indicate the general fertility of the soil under the influence of abundant water. Only a few yards away from the moistened land famine commences.[81]

In the last decades of the nineteenth century and the first decades of the twentieth, the overflow grasslands of the Westside provided an avian paradise for birds migrating along the Pacific Flyway. William J. Browning recalled, "Late in the evening, and just at the first streak of daylight, all of the ducks and geese and sand-hill cranes for many miles around would come to feed, along with the beef cattle on the trampled grain hay."[82] Henry Miller was reported to have been particularly hostile toward the geese, which consumed prodigious quantities of the grasses upon which his cattle fed. Geese caused other problems as well. According to L. A. Sischo, "What made it still worse was the fact that the geese dirties [sic] so much other grass besides what they ate. The cattle would not feed where the geese had dirtied the grass."[83] Over the course of several decades, Miller personally granted permission to selected individuals to hunt waterfowl on his properties in an effort to reduce depredations. Browning reported that he earned $965 during his first three weeks of hunting on Miller and Lux property in 1882. Sischo, who first came to the Westside settlement of Los Banos in 1903, was given written permission by Miller to hunt geese to protect the grass, after Miller came upon him standing with about fifty dead geese at his feet. Using the oversize guns typical of that period, Sischo reportedly had taken them down with a single shot.

Although Miller and Lux kept their properties open to hunters, and fishermen as well, they went to great lengths to keep out those who hunted without permission, particularly those who hunted for market. As Edward Treadwell reported: "The 'market hunter' would break locks and leave gates open, shoot without regard to the presence of cattle, stalk behind old stags, use high powered and forbidden firearms, and his occupation as market hunter was frequently a blind for his real occupation as cattle rustler."[84] To keep the market hunters away, "Miller and Lux had men riding with guns" across the length and breadth of their property.[85]

Instead of forbidding hunting completely, Miller and Lux leased the best hunting lands to duck clubs, whose members could be relied on to obey the law and to protect the property from market hunters.

For as long as Miller and Lux held on to their San Joaquin Basin properties, or at least the water rights associated with them, the overflow grasslands of the Westside remained a land of irrigated pastures, of cattle that grazed on them, and of ducks and geese and those who hunted them, legally or not. But as the twentieth century dawned, the firm faced a number of escalating challenges, both ecological and economic. Rising groundwater tables and increasing soil salinity levels, the result of decades of flood irrigation, reduced yields of alfalfa and pasturage grasses and forced the firm to curtail its operations.[86] In 1913 Congress lifted the tariff on imported beef, opening the market to competition from Australian beef, which arrived in refrigerated containers. The sudden increase in supply led to a dramatic fall in the price of cattle, and Miller and Lux lost the ability to control the supply or price of beef in the region.[87]

When Miller died in 1916, the firm's finances were already in decline, and by the mid-1920s Miller and Lux had begun the widespread sale of its land into smaller parcels.[88] Much of it passed into the hands of private duck clubs, especially in the Westside region of overflow grasslands. The firm deliberately marketed these lands to appeal to hunters, and made clear the connection between organized duck hunting and cattle raising that came to define the Westside during much of the twentieth century. This marketing strategy is clearly seen in one of the firm's sale pamphlets from that era. The section titled "Duck Clubs" is particularly revealing:

> Ever since the first shotguns were brought across the plains the Western San Joaquin has been known as the duck hunter's paradise. The many square miles of swamp land dotted with lakes and ponds not only afford a great stop-over for northern birds on their annual migration, but they also serve as breeding grounds for many thousands which remain the year round.
>
> The greater part of this natural water fowl territory is on Miller & Lux property. It is desirable for pasture, and during the livestock operating years of the company, supported thousands of cattle. It was the custom of the company to lease portions of the grass and swamp lands to gun clubs. . . .
>
> The land, being excellent pasture, can be leased for cattle purposes. In fact several of the duck clubs expect to combine pleasure and business by renting much of their acreage for pasturing stock.[89]

Although the firm could not have predicted it at that time, those duck clubs that purchased Miller and Lux's Westside holdings would lead the fight during the 1940s and 1950s to protect the region's wetlands from the ecological consequences of the Central Valley Project, an irrigation and reclamation project made possible—ironically—by the eventual sale of Miller and Lux's water rights to the federal government in 1939. This struggle would become one of the great twentieth-century California water wars, in which the duck clubs of the overflow grasslands and their allies would eventually secure a guaranteed water supply to this region, the largest remaining area of privately held wetlands in the Central Valley.

By the time that Miller and Lux was disposing of its holdings in the San Joaquin Basin during the 1920s, wetlands elsewhere in the Central Valley were in short supply. Not only had the freshwater lakes and marshes of the Tulare Basin been largely obliterated, but the vast tule basins of the Sacramento Valley and the overflow islands of the Delta had also been reclaimed in the face of the relentless expansion of agriculture. We thus turn next to the late-nineteenth- and early-twentieth-century destruction of wetlands in the Sacramento Valley and the Delta, and to the discovery of the Pacific Flyway, which provided a rationale for those who would come to oppose the further wholesale destruction of wetlands, regardless of ecological cost.

4

Reclamation and Conservation
in the Sacramento Valley

VISIONS

When the Bidwell-Bartleson party, the first wagon train of American settlers bound for California, arrived in the Sacramento Valley in 1841, the valley contained approximately 1.5 million acres of wetlands, composed predominantly of riparian forests and the semipermanently flooded tule marshes that occupied the valley's five great overflow basins (see map 9).[1] Of the five basins that compose the Sacramento Valley—Butte, Sutter, American, Colusa, and Yolo— only the Yolo Basin witnessed any measurable progress toward reclamation under the auspices of the Swamp Land Commission during the first half of the 1860s. Because of the unpredictable flood flows of the Sacramento River, reclamation would prove more difficult, and would take decades longer, than elsewhere in the Central Valley. Nevertheless, despite the daunting nature of the task, throughout the late nineteenth century influential voices continued to call for coordinated planning of flood control and reclamation works in the Sacramento Valley.

Among the most notable of such visionaries was John Bidwell of Chico. Bidwell represents the confluence of several important trends in the history of late-nineteenth-century California. He was a leader in the fight against the environmental destruction caused by hydraulic mining that buried thousands of acres of productive farmland, and he possessed a vibrant vision for the future of the state's agricultural economy, calling for an elaborate statewide system of irrigation canals, reservoirs, dams, and levees in order to facilitate diversified agricultural development. Bidwell fell squarely in the tradition of late-nineteenth-century

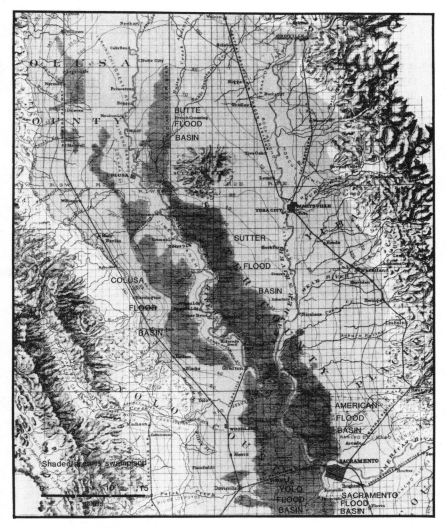

MAP 9. The flood basins of the Sacramento Valley, 1887. The shaded areas are unreclaimed swampland, almost the entirety of which lay within the valley's natural basins. Source: John Thompson and Edward A. Dutra, *The Tule Breakers: The Story of the California Dredge* (Stockton, Calif.: Stockton Corral of Westerners International and University of the Pacific, 1983). Used with permission.

environmental reformers who sought to create among California's wheat fields and rangelands a "garden landscape," based on diversified horticulture, which would be both profitable and beautiful and would support the democratic ideal of the small-scale farmer.[2]

Having been in the employ of John Sutter since shortly after his arrival in California in 1841, Bidwell amassed a fortune during the Gold Rush. The location of his gold strike in 1848 along the Middle Fork of the Feather River, the main tributary of the Sacramento, soon became known as Bidwell's Bar. Using the profits from his mining operations and from a store he opened at Bidwell's Bar to supply miners in the region, by 1851 Bidwell had acquired the five-square-league Rancho del Arroyo Chico in the Sacramento Valley's Butte County.[3] He quickly became one of the new state's leading citizens, joining the California State Agricultural Society in 1858, founding the city of Chico in 1860, and serving as a Republican member of Congress from 1865 to 1867. Bidwell used his position of prominence within the California State Agricultural Society to argue for the hydraulic reengineering of the Central Valley. In his 1867 annual address to the Agricultural Society, Bidwell called for the reclamation of the tule marshes that occupied so dominant a place in the valley's topography: "That the drainage of the vast tule marshes is important, nay, a necessity, none will deny. That these vast regions, which occupy the central and most accessible part of our great interior valleys, would be the very best lands as regards fertility, and their capacity to yield almost everything required to supply human wants, is an undeniable fact."[4]

Despite the urgency of Bidwell's appeal, the tule basins would not be definitively reclaimed until the early twentieth century. During the intervening years, California was drawn inexorably into the realm of coordinated statewide and federal planning of its water development—and the draining of its wetlands. By the late twentieth century only 80,000 acres of Sacramento Valley wetlands remained, most of them on protected national wildlife refuges and state wildlife areas.[5]

FLOOD CONTROL FOR THE SACRAMENTO VALLEY

In order to reclaim the great tule basins of the Sacramento Valley, it was first necessary to constrain the Sacramento River, which repeatedly overflowed its banks and inundated the valley, most notably in the years 1850–1852 and 1861–1862. The decades-long struggle to contain the Sacramento River and prevent the inundations of the valley's tule basins would eventually culminate in the Sacramento Flood Control Project of the early twentieth century.[6] A central point of contention in this battle was whether to restrain the river in its main channel between high, closely spaced levees, or to construct a bypass system that would use weirs to divert the river's high flows into some of the basins, thereby allowing for controlled flooding at specific locations, in effect ending the river's unpredictability. The U.S. Army Corps of Engineers steadfastly maintained a main channel, or "levees only," plan for decades.[7] This strategy had been developed by Captain Andrew A. Humphreys of the corps based on his commissioned study of flooding in the lower Mississippi River Basin, and espoused in his 1861 report to Congress. The levees-only doctrine rested on the premise that by increasing the velocity of flow, the levees would force streams to scour and deepen their beds, allowing them to carry off all floodwaters.[8] The geomorphology of the Sacramento River eventually proved otherwise, but the levees-only strategy would remain corps dogma through the early years of the twentieth century.

Will Green of Colusa, who during the ten years that he served as Colusa County surveyor had come to know the Sacramento River and its drainage basins better than perhaps anyone else, disagreed with the position of the corps, arguing that the Sacramento River's flow was simply too great to be restrained within its channel. A singular problem with any attempt at flood control planning was that neither the corps nor anyone else at this time knew exactly how much water was capable of flowing down the river during flood conditions.[9] As a member of a commission appointed in 1868 "to examine into the practicability of making a new outlet for the flood water of the Sacramento Valley," Green had developed an elaborate plan that included locks and canals (now called weirs and bypasses) constructed through the troughs of the basins.[10] Green's plan was rejected by the legislature, but it foreshadowed the one the corps would eventually adopt in the Sacramento Flood Control Project.[11]

While the state failed to take action, the accumulation of hydraulic mining debris, especially the fine silts known as slickens, steadily raised the beds of the rivers that flowed from the Sierra Nevada through the mining districts into the Sacramento Valley, and increased the likelihood and severity of flooding. The quantity of debris washing into the rivers was so substantial that by 1874, at a point twelve miles above the city of Marysville, the Yuba River was reported as flowing sixty feet above its original bed.[12] When rivers flowing along elevated beds escaped from their channels, tens of thousands of acres of fertile land in the valley were buried by mining debris deposited by floodwaters. As the sediments worked their way downstream along its tributaries, the Sacramento River also began to silt up, increasing flooding along the valley floor and impeding navigation. The floods pitted farmers against miners for decades, and it was not until the economic balance of power in the state shifted in favor of those who would farm the land rather than mine it for riches that an assault on the mines became feasible.

In this context, the flood of February 1878—one of the worst on record— exacerbated the controversy between agricultural and mining interests. Sacramento Valley farmers founded the Anti-Debris Association, through which they strengthened their demands for the restriction of hydraulic mining. This struggle reached its denouement in the historic 1884 decision by Judge Lorenzo Sawyer of the federal Ninth Circuit Court of Appeals in San Francisco, in the case of *Woodruff, Edwards v. North Bloomfield Gravel Mining Co. et al.*[13] In his comprehensive 225-page decision, Judge Sawyer declared that the dumping of mine tailings into the rivers constituted a public and private nuisance and must be halted. For all practical purposes, Sawyer's ruling marked the end of hydraulic mining in California.[14]

The year 1878 was important for the history of flood control in the Sacramento Valley not only because of the establishment of the Anti-Debris Association, but also because of the creation by the legislature of the office of state engineer, "to investigate the problems of irrigation of the plains, the condition and capacity of the great drainage lines of the state, and the improvement and navigation of rivers."[15] Governor Will Irwin appointed thirty-three-year-old William Hammond Hall to the post, which he held until 1889. Hall had received his training with the U.S. Army Corps of Engineers, and he became a forceful advocate for centralized state control over water policy and management, arguing for more rigorous definition and regulation of water rights, and for a statewide act to promote irrigation.[16]

Fulfilling his obligation to report back to the legislature at the beginning of 1880, Hall produced a monumental document that provided detailed information about virtually every aspect of the Central Valley's hydrology, including the extent to which mining operations had exacerbated the tendency of the valley to flood. Yet Hall also pointedly demonstrated how the Sacramento River had been designed by nature to flood even without the additional strain of mine tailings, noting that the river's channel constricted markedly between its upper and lower reaches: "For 106 miles and more above the head of Butte Slough, there is a channel of *greater grade and greater dimensions than there is below,* all the way to the mouth of the Feather River, a distance of 64½ miles."[17] The combination of a lower gradient, which reduces velocity of flow, and a constricted channel between Butte Slough and the mouth of the Feather River meant that without modification, during periods of high discharge the Sacramento River would inevitably overflow into the two basins that lay astride this stretch of the river in the heart of the valley, the Colusa Basin to the west and the Sutter Basin to the east.[18] Describing this phenomenon, Hall wrote, "The main river channels, and more particularly the Sacramento, as the main drain of the valley, being insufficient in capacity for the immediate passage to the bay of ordinary floods, these waters have, for ages past, poured over its banks and been temporarily lodged in the low basins by which it is flanked for miles of its course, to be drained off after the passage of the flood-water proper."[19]

Hall recognized that although engineers might try to contain the Sacramento River within a system of levees, "it should be fully understood that floods will occasionally come which must be allowed to spread." He argued that floods might come that would be greater than the greatest floods in the historical record, including that of 1862, and that such floods could potentially submerge levees, no matter how well constructed. The swamplands and basin lands would always be at risk of flooding, although it would be possible to reclaim them and greatly reduce the frequency of inundation "by a proper system of works and a wise government of them."[20]

With the passage of "An Act to Promote Drainage" in 1880, the legislature took a step toward implementing Hall's recommendation that the state take charge of drainage in the Sacramento Valley by overseeing a coordinated system of levees and debris dams.[21] But the Drainage Act was declared unconstitutional by the California Supreme Court in 1881 on the grounds that the Drainage Commission created under the act represented the delegation of legislative powers to executive officers.[22] Californians were not yet ready to accept the expansive vision of William Hammond Hall and like-minded men, which allowed for the centralized control of natural resource management by governmental entities other than the legislature.[23]

More than a decade was to pass before two events laid the groundwork for coordinated flood control in the Sacramento Valley. The 1893 federal Caminetti Act, designed by mining interests in what ultimately proved an unsuccessful attempt to revive hydraulic mining, created the California Debris Commission, a three-member federal body composed of officers of the Army Corps of Engineers. In a provision little noticed at the time, the act granted the Debris Commission authority "for affording relief . . . in flood time."[24] A federal agency now existed with authority to shape California's flood control planning. In the same year that the Caminetti Act created the Debris Commission, the California legislature created the office of the Commissioner of Public Works.[25] The new commissioner, A. H. Rose—a veteran of swampland reclamation attempts—understood the need for a comprehensive flood control plan for the valley. To prepare such a plan, he employed two prominent engineers, Marsden Manson and C. E. Grunsky, both of whom had served under William Hammond Hall. Their report strongly disagreed with the levees-only philosophy of the Army Corps of Engineers. It recommended that river channels be enlarged and utilized to their maximum capacity as "drainways." When that maximum capacity was exceeded, water was to be released into embanked "by-pass channels" running through the basins, in effect creating a second river channel through the Sacramento Valley, which would allow floodwaters to be carried quickly out of the valley to Suisun Bay at the western edge of the Delta.[26] Although no action was taken on this expensive plan, in part because of the nationwide economic crisis of the mid-1890s, the Manson-Grunsky Report was the first officially sanctioned plan for the system of levees and bypasses that was eventually to become the Sacramento Flood Control Project.[27]

Despite the well-documented figures and clear logic of the Manson-Grunsky Report, the Army Corps of Engineers remained unconvinced. As late as 1904 Major T. G. Dabney of the corps, the head of a commission appointed by the governor, rejected the prescriptions of the report. The commission found itself "unable to accept this plan as a permanent solution of the Sacramento river [sic] problem" and came down in favor of a levees-only main channel plan.[28] The Dabney Commission argued that the maximum flow that the Sacramento River was capable of producing was 250,000 cubic feet per second (cfs), well below the 300,000 cfs suggested by Manson and Grunsky. Such a flow, the commission held, could be restrained within main channel levees. Both of these flood flow predictions were blown asunder by the flood of 1907, during which time the U.S. Geological Survey found that 600,000 cfs had exploded out of the river's mouth into Suisun Bay, having first inundated vast regions of the Sacramento Valley along the way. The flood of 1907, and another of similar magnitude in 1909, made a mockery of the Dabney Commission's plan and ended any realistic hope of a single-channel plan.[29]

In the wake of the 1907 flood, the California Debris Commission initiated a detailed study of the Sacramento River and its tributaries. In 1910 the commission produced its compelling report, which quickly became known as the Jackson Report after its gifted young engineer, Thomas H. Jackson. Coming to an inevitable conclusion, the report argued that "the interests of navigation, debris control, and flood control in the case of this river are so inseparably connected that it is thought that they should be considered under one general project."[30] The report called for a Sacramento Flood Control Project that harkened back to the 1894 bypass plan of Manson and Grunsky, the main difference lying in the larger size of the floods now known to be possible.

Under the vigorous leadership of California's Progressive governor, Hiram Johnson, who served from 1911 to 1917, the state finally achieved coordinated flood control. The state Flood Control Act of 1911 officially adopted the Jackson Report "as a plan for controlling the flood waters of the Sacramento river [sic] and its tributaries for the improvement and preservation of navigation and the reclamation of the lands that are susceptible to overflow." The act created a State Reclamation Board with regulatory authority over the valley's reclamation districts, particularly with regard to evaluating and approving "plans of reclamation that contemplate the construction of levees, embankments, or canals along or near the banks of the Sacramento river [sic] or its tributaries or . . . the overflow basins."[31] Two years later, in 1913, the state amended the Flood Control Act to unite the entire region of the Central Valley subject to flooding within a single Sacramento and San Joaquin Drainage District, encompassing the Sacramento Valley, the Delta, and the lower San Joaquin Valley as far south as Fresno Slough, an area approximately 230 miles long, 8 to 27 miles wide, and comprising

1,515,300 acres in fourteen counties.[32] After more than half a century of failed and frustrated attempts to achieve a coordinated reclamation plan, California was finally ready to try to tame the Sacramento River. The state began to build the Sacramento Flood Control Project without federal support, a key ingredient that remained elusive until 1917.

Until this time, the federal government had resisted providing funds for flood control, limiting its responsibility to the maintenance of navigable streams. But widespread flooding in the Mississippi and Ohio valleys in 1912 and 1913 intensified public support for a federal flood control program. Finally, nearly six years after the Jackson Report was first presented to Congress, the House Flood Control Committee placed plans for Mississippi River flood control and an amended Jackson Report together in a single bill, which Congress passed in March 1917. The measure was the first national flood control act, and it marked a significant expansion in the responsibilities of the Army Corps of Engineers.[33] While offering flood protection for the Sacramento Valley, the combination of the new state and federal flood control acts also guaranteed the destruction of the valley's vast tule basins, the ancestral winter home for millions of migratory waterfowl.

The essential features of the Sacramento Flood Control Project include a continuous levee along both sides of the Sacramento River from Ord Bend, approximately thirty miles above Colusa—the point at which the river typically begins to spill over its banks into the adjacent tule basins—to the river's mouth at the westernmost apex of the Delta (see map 10). Along this stretch of more than two hundred river miles, the Sacramento River's waters and those of its tributaries are regulated by a system of weirs that control flow through the Sutter and Yolo bypasses, which channel excess water down the valley. In brief, the system works as follows: Moulton and Colusa weirs, upstream from Colusa, protect Colusa and the Colusa Basin by allowing Sacramento River water to flow eastward into the Butte Sink, the lowest part of the Butte Basin. This water flows southward past the western side of the Sutter Buttes and eventually drains into the mouth of the Sutter Bypass, which runs through the Sutter Basin, the low-lying land between the Sacramento and Feather rivers. At the confluence of the Sacramento and Feather rivers, the bypass system crosses from the east to the west of the Sacramento River. The flow from the Sutter Bypass joins the waters of the Sacramento River from the east and, through Fremont Weir, is channeled west of the river into the Yolo Bypass, which transects the Yolo Basin. Below Sacramento, the Yolo Bypass carries its water to Cache Slough, from which it rejoins the main body of the Sacramento River just above the small Delta city of Rio Vista. The river then flows through the Delta to its mouth at Collinsville, and beyond into Suisun Bay.[34] This remarkable system ties together the five basins of the Sacramento Valley, and it controls flooding in a manner that mimics many of the valley's natural overflow patterns. The primary differences are that the Colusa and

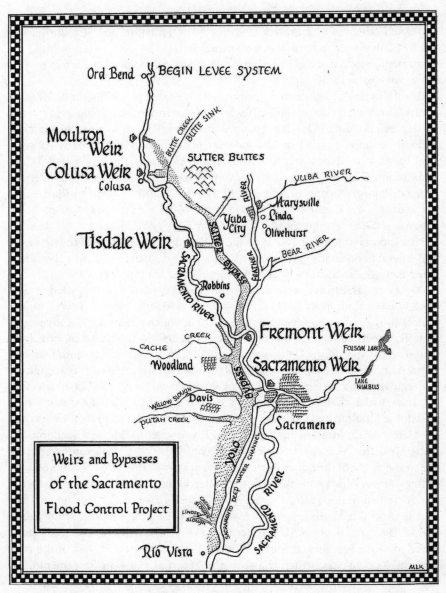

MAP 10. The main features of the Sacramento Flood Control Project, extending from the central Sacramento Valley southward to the Delta. Source: Robert Kelley, *Battling the Inland Sea: American Political Culture, Public Policy, and the Sacramento Valley, 1850–1986* (Berkeley and Los Angeles: University of California Press, 1989). Used with permission.

American basins are now isolated from the overflow of the Sacramento River, and floodwaters, which formerly spread out over entire basins and then drained slowly over the course of many months, now travel quickly through the Sutter and Yolo basins in channels constrained by high embankments.[35]

The state of California had begun extensive work on the Sacramento Flood Control Project even while it lobbied the federal government to come on board. As a result, the project's riverine levees and bypasses were largely completed within the first decade after the passage of the state Flood Control Act of 1911. The Yolo Bypass, between the mouth of the Feather River and Cache Slough, was largely built by 1917, although its west levee was not completed until 1923. The bypass lies between massive levees as much as 12,000 feet apart, and was designed to be capable of handling at least 500,000 cubic feet per second, five times the capacity of the parallel section of the Sacramento River itself. The Sutter Bypass, in contrast, turned into a more litigious project. Only after the matter of the final routing of the bypass through the Sutter Basin was settled in the California Supreme Court in 1917 was the Reclamation Board able to carry its work on the bypass's levees—which stood 20 feet high, 20 feet wide at the crown, and 120 feet wide at the base—to completion.[36]

The amount of earth that needed to be moved to build the great levees of the Sacramento Flood Control Project, and those of the reclamation districts privately reclaiming the basins, far exceeded anything that could be carried out economically with shovels, wheelbarrows, or horse-drawn scrapers. Only floating mechanical dredges—first developed for harbor work in San Francisco Bay during the 1850s, and later adopted by reclaimers of swamp and overflowed land—could handle the tremendous volumes of spoil required for constructing levees broad and high enough to withstand the great floods of the Sacramento Valley. Of at least a half-dozen varieties of dredges in use during the late nineteenth and early twentieth centuries, the most effective was the clamshell dredge. As its name suggests, this dredge was fitted with a single bucket composed of a pair of hinged shells that closed around the material to be excavated and emplaced (see figure 6). The clamshell bucket was suspended from a movable boom, a long rectangular beam that could reach a remarkable 240 feet in length. One of the most important advantages of the reach provided by the long boom was that a dredge could dig at a considerable distance from a levee and therefore not compromise the structure by excavating too close to it. In addition to working on levees along the Sacramento River and its sloughs, the floating dredges could also construct levees on higher ground if water were pumped into cuts, and those cuts were then dammed to float the dredges. In this manner the dredges were able to construct the bypass levees as well as the back levees of the Sacramento Valley's various reclamation districts.[37]

FIGURE 6. The dredge *Ryer Island*. Built in 1888, this relatively early clamshell dredge had a 130-foot boom and a bucket with a capacity of two cubic yards. Source: John Thompson and Edward A. Dutra, *The Tule Breakers: The Story of the California Dredge* (Stockton, Calif.: Stockton Corral of Westerners International and University of the Pacific, 1983). Used with permission.

RECLAIMING THE TULE BASINS

With the Sacramento Flood Control Project well under way, entrepreneurs fever-ishly renewed their attempts to reclaim the basins for agricultural use, the earli-est of which dated back to the 1860s. The task was no less than herculean. Occupy-ing perhaps one million acres of valley floodplain overall, these enormous basins contained in excess of 500,000 acres of tule marsh, with 62,000 in the Butte Ba-sin, 116,000 in the Sutter Basin, 93,000 in the Colusa Basin, 164,000 in the Yolo Basin, and 53,000 in the American Basin.[38] The basins were capable of holding tremendous amounts of water. The Sutter Basin could hold up to 39 billion cubic feet of water over an area of approximately 140 square miles; the Yolo Basin could hold up to 50 billion cubic feet spread over an area of approximately 300 square miles.[39] Yet despite their formidable size, the Colusa, Yolo, Sutter, and American basins were almost completely reclaimed by 1920.

On the western side of the Sacramento River, efforts to reclaim the Colusa Basin began in 1869 when Charles Reed, with a group of San Francisco investors that included A. H. Rose, later commissioner of public works, organized the Sac-ramento Valley Reclamation Company. In 1870 the company formed Reclamation District No. 108, one of the oldest reclamation districts still in existence, with

74,086 acres that "occup[y] the lowest, most central, and largest of the collabora- tively drained segments of the basin."[40] By constructing a levee forty-five miles long paralleling the Sacramento River's western bank from Sycamore Slough, six miles downstream from Colusa, to Knights Landing in Yolo County, Reclama- tion District No. 108 set off an uncoordinated levee-building spiral in which each district tried to protect itself at the expense of its neighbors across the river. The reclamation of the Colusa Basin was particularly challenging, as floodwaters were prone to enter the basin from three sides, the north, west, and east. Compounding the problem was the Knights Landing Ridge, an east-west-running alluvial de- posit at the southern end of the basin, created by depositions from Cache Creek, which flows out of the Coast Ranges. This ridge, about three miles across, rose ten feet higher than the floor of the Colusa Basin and prevented drainage into the Yolo Basin below. The most significant reclamation work in the Colusa Basin took place between 1910 and 1919. The Knights Landing Ridge Drainage District, created in 1913, finally cut through the problematic Knights Landing Ridge for a distance of about seven miles. The cut, four hundred feet wide at the bottom and with a maximum depth of nearly twenty feet, is capable of discharging 20,000 cubic feet per second from the Colusa Basin into the Yolo Bypass. Overall, in the process of protecting the Colusa Basin from flooding, the basin's reclamation and drainage districts excavated and emplaced at least 36 million cubic yards of fill during the decade of the 1910s, the work carried out at times by a dozen or more dredges working simultaneously.[41]

The first attempt to reclaim the Yolo Basin, immediately to the south of the Colusa Basin, was the construction in 1864 of a twenty-five-mile drainage canal by Swamp Land District No. 18. The reclamation of the last major segment of the basin did not begin until a half-century later, when the Netherlands Farm Com- pany in 1913 organized the formation of Reclamation District No. 999, consisting of 26,150 acres of land between the Sacramento River to the east and the Yolo Bypass to the west. Thirty miles of levees needed to be built, requiring more than 10 million cubic yards of fill. Facing insurmountable financial difficulties, the Netherlands Farm Company soon transferred ownership of its lands to the Holland Land Company, which carried out the work between 1916 and 1918. With the completion of this project, almost all of the 58,800 acres of the Yolo Basin that lay between the Sacramento River and the trough of the basin had been reclaimed.[42]

Across the Sacramento River from the Colusa Basin, the Sutter Basin was so consistently inundated that tules ten to fourteen feet high covered the land. The semipermanent flooding of much of the basin provided a vast breeding and win- tering area for waterfowl. Farmers who owned property around the edge of the basin were nicknamed "rimlanders," a reflection of the natural topography.[43] Large-scale reclamation attempts began with the Sutter Basin project of the early

1870s. The project, orchestrated by swampland owner William H. Parks, was intended to halt all Sacramento River overflows into the Sutter Basin. To protect the basin successfully, it would be necessary to construct a levee-dam that would cut off Sacramento River overflows through Butte Slough, which drained into the Sutter Basin from the Butte Basin to the north. Additionally, a forty-mile levee running along the eastern side of the Sacramento River from Butte Slough downriver to a point opposite Knights Landing would need to be raised, thus paralleling, literally and figuratively, the efforts of Reclamation District No. 108 in the Colusa Basin on the opposite side of the river. The Sutter Basin project was derailed by a lower-court decision in 1876, later confirmed twice by the California Supreme Court, which ruled that Parks' dam was damaging his neighbors in the valley by increasing their susceptibility to flooding.[44] Effective reclamation for the Sutter Basin became possible only a generation later with the construction of the Sutter Bypass, which channeled the floodwaters as they passed through the basin. Much of the reclamation of the basin was accomplished between 1913 and 1920 by the new Reclamation District No. 1500. The district's levees, overlapping with those of the Sacramento Flood Control Project, protected 67,850 acres of the basin. Combined, the efforts of the reclamation districts in the basin protected more than 100,000 acres of land, utilizing 52 million cubic yards of fill.[45]

In the American Basin, located to the south of the Sutter Basin, the first reclamation attempts began in 1865 but met with little success. Throughout the late nineteenth century, the Feather River to the north and west, and the American River to the south and east, flowed across beds elevated by mining debris and continued to flood the basin regularly as a result. Significant reclamation in the American Basin was not achieved until the years 1909 to 1915, following the acquisition of the majority of the swampland in the basin by a gold-dredging company, Natomas Consolidated of California, which intended to transform the tule swamps into irrigated farmland and then sell it. Along with neighboring landowners, the company organized Reclamation Districts No. 1000 and No. 1001, which by 1915 had reclaimed 82,650 acres in the basin.[46]

THE BUTTE BASIN EXCEPTION

The Butte Basin, northernmost and remotest of the five basins, was not reclaimed during the second decade of the twentieth century, nor has it been significantly reclaimed since. The reasons for its alternative fate lie both in its natural topography and in the decisions made by its rice farmers and waterfowl hunters. These groups actively resisted the reclamation of the Butte Basin, envisioning a different nature for their part of the valley. Rice growing in California would also have implications for the wetlands of the state far beyond the Butte Basin, and the origins and expansion of California's rice industry will be discussed later in this chapter.

The Butte Basin receives its waters from two primary sources, one natural and one an alteration of a natural process. Butte Creek, which originates above the city of Chico, flows into the basin from the north. Via the Moulton and Colusa weirs of the Sacramento Flood Control Project, but originally by natural over-bank flow, the Sacramento River deposits some of its excess waters into the Butte Basin from the west. The southernmost and lowest-lying portion of the basin, the Butte Sink, is a flat depression approximately a dozen miles long between the Sacramento River to the west and the Sutter Buttes to the east. The surface of the sink sits more than fifteen feet below that of the river. Therefore, the water entering the sink from the north and west does not drain directly back into the Sacramento River, but instead drains slowly southward through a narrow channel toward the Sutter Bypass. During major floods, the Butte Sink is transformed into an inland sea covering as much as 150 square miles and containing as much as 20 billion cubic feet of water. At the southern end of the Butte Sink, just above the Sutter Bypass, this water is joined by controlled outflows of the Sacramento River into Butte Slough. In its natural state, Butte Slough, which departs eastward from the Sacramento about five river miles downstream from Colusa, was more than one hundred feet wide and thirty feet deep, making it the largest slough flowing out of the Sacramento's east bank.[47]

As a consequence of topography, water is nearly omnipresent in much of the Butte Sink, creating a natural lowland swamp, an ecosystem now unique in California.[48] The sink and surrounding basin lands provide the most important habitat for migratory and resident waterfowl anywhere in the Sacramento Valley. Historically, the Butte Sink and adjacent lands have hosted the densest concentrations of waterfowl in the Central Valley as a whole. As many as 1.3 million birds have been counted at one time on 640 acres, or one square mile, on the lands immediately south of the sink. The seasonal presence of so many birds—and therefore of unsurpassed hunting—has been a major factor in protecting the Butte Basin from reclamation. An equally important factor has been the marginal quality of much of the basin's fine-textured clay soils, which exhibit very poor drainage and have proved suitable only for rice production. The presence of millions of ducks and geese on waterlogged land capable of supporting little agriculture has been responsible for setting the Butte Basin on a trajectory vastly different from that of the Sacramento Valley's other great tule basins.[49]

One of the most revealing sources concerning the development—or lack thereof—of the Butte Basin during the early years of the Sacramento Flood Control Project is the minutes of the California State Reclamation Board. The board's minutes reveal glacial progress on a proposed bypass in the Butte Basin, protests by Butte Basin landowners against inclusion in the Sacramento and San Joaquin Drainage District, and efforts by Butte Sink landowners to retain rice drainage water on their lands in order to increase waterfowl habitat for hunting. A "Butte

Slough By-Pass" had been part of the original Sacramento Flood Control Project. The bypass was intended to channelize the slough between its egress from the Sacramento River and its entrance into the mouth of the Sutter Bypass to the south. The lines of the bypass first needed to be approved by the California Debris Commission, and the Reclamation Board needed to obtain easements over the bypass lands and then contract for clearing that land.[50] The board discussed the matter of the bypass during no fewer than six meetings between November 1913 and June 1914, reporting little progress. In October 1915, the board noted that "the persons most interested in this matter [of the bypass] and whose assistance had been offered in the matter of securing rights of way, did not appear to be at all active in the matter, and no progress had been made."[51]

Why did the board have so much difficulty getting started on the Butte Bypass project, at the same time that significant advancements were being made on the much larger and more complex Yolo and Sutter bypasses? The first clear hint appears in the minutes of June 27, 1918, when a petition, dated a month earlier, was read before the board members. The petition was "signed by land owners representing approximately 78,000 acres in and north of the Butte Basin, protesting against the construction of levees or a by-pass system through the Butte Basin."[52]

Four new drainage districts had been formed in the upper Butte Basin between 1912 and 1920, largely for the purpose of controlling the drainage of rice waters, a reflection of the Sacramento Valley rice boom that began in the century's second decade. The valley's new rice growers purposely retained water in the basin in order to maintain their fields in a flooded condition during the spring and summer growing seasons. Rice is a high water-demand crop; on average, Sacramento Valley rice required seven feet of water per acre during a single growing season, far more than wheat or alfalfa, and twice as much as most row and orchard crops.[53] The rice fields of the upper Butte Basin caused a dramatic increase in the amount of drainage water flowing into the Butte Sink and affected grazing operations there to such an extent that landowners filed suit against the upslope rice farmers to prevent the flooding of their lands. This action led to a series of agreements in 1922 between the upper Butte Basin rice farmers and the Butte Sink landowners that gave the upslope farmers flowage rights for their agricultural drainwater over the Butte Sink lands in exchange for providing enough water to the Butte Sink landowners to maintain their properties in a flooded condition year-round.[54] These agreements reflected changing priorities among the Butte Sink landowners, and the opening of a new chapter in this part of the northern Sacramento Valley. As a result of the new water regime, Butte Sink properties were converted from grazing land to emergent marsh and riparian habitat, benefiting both waterfowl and waterfowl hunters. Waterfowling in the Butte Sink was certainly not new; indeed, it had been tremendously popular since the time of settlement. But the 1922 agreements signaled the beginning of the active management of the land for waterfowl, and waterfowl hunting became a primary use of the Butte Sink.

Because they prescribed the permanent flooding of much of the Butte Sink, the 1922 agreements reduced the need for a Butte Bypass to drain the basin. By 1923 the construction of the bypass appeared less than certain, as the Reclamation Board's minutes included the suggestive phrase, "*if Butte By-pass levees are ever built.*"[55] In late 1924, stakeholders in the Butte Basin made it clear to the board that they "did not desire reclamation."[56] Rather, they attempted to secede from the Sacramento and San Joaquin Drainage District, petitioning the board that "it was the consensus of all residents and landowners that there had been no benefits received by any of the landowners within this district, from assessments levied or to be levied by this Board, or from work done or work contemplated to be done by this Board."[57] The boundaries of the Sacramento and San Joaquin Drainage District had been set by the state legislature, however, and the board was unable to comply with this request.[58]

Despite this setback, the iconoclastic position regarding drainage adopted by Butte Basin residents required the Reclamation Board to adopt a more expansive view of appropriate land uses that included waterfowling. In October 1925 the Sutter County Water Users Organization applied to the board to construct a low levee along the southern boundary line of the properties owned by one of its members, the West Butte Country Club, "to regulate . . . the rice drainage water flowing through Butte Basin, for game preserve purposes."[59] Significantly, the majority of the constituents of the Sutter County Water Users Organization had names that clearly designated waterfowl hunting organizations.[60] The board unanimously approved the application in November 1925.[61]

With rice growers desiring to retain water in the basin to flood their fields during the spring and summer, and duck hunters desiring to pool rice drainage water to flood their duck clubs during the fall and winter, little incentive remained to drain the Butte Basin and convert it to irrigated agriculture. The bypass plan was never implemented and gradually faded from memory, as the basin's fate diverged from that of the Sacramento Valley's other tule basins. At first the waterfowl clubs in the Butte Sink were flooded year-round, as per the 1922 agreements. However, continuous inundation caused excessive growth of aquatic vegetation, hindering flows within the system and covering the open water that waterfowl required. Beginning in 1937, the drainage districts and duck clubs addressed these problems by constructing various water control structures that allowed the clubs to dry out during the summer and manage their vegetation. The annual management of emergent vegetation has since provided an appropriate mix of food, cover, and open water habitat for waterfowl.[62] Because of these land-use choices, made early in the twentieth century, the Butte Basin, alone of the five great tule basins, remained a viable habitat for migratory waterfowl and for wild-life in general, as well as a mecca for hunters who, with the passage of time, have been increasingly drawn from the ranks of the elite to this unsurpassed, and largely unreclaimed, waterfowl haven.

WATERFOWL HUNTING IN THE
SACRAMENTO VALLEY

The Butte Basin stands in stark contrast to the rest of the Sacramento Valley, but that contrast would have been less glaring during the late nineteenth century. Before the Sacramento Flood Control Project and the massive basin reclamation projects, vast numbers of geese and ducks occupied all of the valley's wetland basins. Native Americans had hunted waterfowl in the valley from time imme-morial; in 1828, after Jedediah Smith and his men shot into what they thought was a congregation of live standing geese, they learned that the Sacramento Val-ley's aboriginal inhabitants were skilled in the use of freshly killed geese as de-coys.[63] Yet it was not until the 1870s and 1880s that waterfowl in the valley, espe-cially geese, would be seriously affected by human activities. The planting of hundreds of thousands of acres of winter wheat on previously unused lands, char-acterized by alkali soil and sparse vegetation, created a major new food source for the valley's wintering geese. The sight and sound of their tremendous numbers left a lifelong impression on many of the valley's early settlers. One observer com-mented, "The unoccupied land of the plains, considered as worthless and usually referred to as 'goose land,' is where they flocked to roost, unmolested, by the bil-lions. . . . When a large flock arose they resembled a dark cloud. . . . In the air they scattered, the cloud disappeared, and you could see strings of geese in 'V' forma-tions as far as the eye could see. From daylight until midnight you could hear their continual squawk. Flock after flock arose in the morning and started for the wheat fields."[64]

The wheat farmers were understandably less impressed. Farmers had begun complaining as early as 1874 that geese were destroying their wheat, and by 1876 the practice of goose herding had been developed. Goose herders fired into flocks of geese to deter them from landing on sprouting grain. In some cases "cabin herders" operated out of one-room shacks that had been dragged by mules to the center of a quarter section, a 160-acre parcel. From the cabins, where they resided for up to six months, the herders were responsible for keeping geese off the sur-rounding land. At night, when it was difficult to observe marauding geese, herd-ers set out flashing acetylene lamps to produce both flashes of light and bursts of sound in efforts to discourage the hungry birds. Protecting one's wheat fields could become quite an expensive proposition. Dr. Hugh J. Glenn, California's largest wheat producer, hired twenty to forty goose herders each year and spent

$13,000 annually to supply them with ammunition to protect his 60,000-acre estate along the western bank of the Sacramento River.[65]

By the end of the 1870s, three decades of intensive hunting had largely depleted the populations of the Sacramento Valley's large game animals—elk, pronghorn antelope, deer, and grizzly bear. During the 1880s, market hunters turned their attention to waterfowl, and the wheat-consuming geese of the Sacramento Valley proved an enticing and lucrative target. No game laws protected wild geese, which were considered pests, and market hunters capitalized on the 75 cents to $1.25 price per dozen offered in the restaurant and hotel markets of San Francisco. Using sawed-off, double-barreled shotguns and often joining two guns together, hunters were able to kill close to two hundred geese at one time. In a technique known as "bull hunting," market hunters often approached unsuspecting geese by employing live animal blinds (hiding behind horses, cows, and oxen), tacking back and forth until within shooting range, and then firing over the animals' backs. Many hunters also shot from dug-out pit blinds, around which they tethered crippled or wing-clipped geese that served as live decoys. As hundreds of thousands of geese were harvested every season, their numbers began to plummet.[66]

Only as the nineteenth century drew to a close did California take steps to protect its wild bird populations, the efforts lagging behind those directed at fish and large game. The legislature had established a Board of Fish Commissioners in 1870, and in 1878 had expanded its powers to include game as well. But like its predecessor, the new Board of Fish and Game Commissioners lacked a staff to enforce its regulations, and therefore remained ineffective. In 1895 the legislature finally authorized the employment of fish and game wardens in each county, but it was not until 1913 that the state was divided into fish and game districts to facilitate enforcement of the law. Meanwhile, in response to diminishing waterfowl numbers across the state, in 1901 the legislature first introduced closed seasons and bag limits for ducks. Originally set at fifty per day, the limit was reduced to thirty-five in 1907 and then to twenty-five in 1909, the level at which it remained for the next twenty years. In 1909 the use of animal blinds was first prohibited for both ducks and geese. After a brief reprieve that reinstated bull hunting for geese in 1911, this method was again entirely prohibited in 1915. Other prohibitions focused on the marketing of wild game, rather than the methods by which it was killed. In 1911 dealers in wild game were required to obtain licenses and to keep records of game received, together with the names and addresses of their suppliers. Not easily deterred, dealers in San Francisco then formed game transfer companies to circumvent the restrictions. These companies operated through the fall of 1913, when a superior court judge ruled that they had been organized to evade the law. The same year, the state legislature passed the Flint-Cary Act, which for the first time prohibited the sale of game, although ducks were excepted during the month of November and geese at all times.[67] This new law faced immediate and hostile opposition, especially from wealthy hotel owners in San Francisco and Sacramento, who purchased game from market hunters and reaped large profits from its sale. In 1914 they successfully sponsored a referendum on the act, and it was repealed. This would be one of the last victories for those who profited from the sale of wild game.[68]

The opposition to the Flint-Cary Act accentuated the contentious relationship between sportsmen and market hunters, based on different notions of the appropriate use of natural resources.[69] The regulations that limited hunting for the market and restricted, and then prohibited, the sale of game can be seen as measures that pitted conservation-minded sportsmen and their allies against those hunters who relied on wildlife for money or subsistence, or both.[70] Reaching back to the 1870s, this struggle had deep roots that antedated the turn-of-the-century Progressive conservation movement. Perhaps the most sweeping call for ending the commercialization of game appeared in an 1894 editorial in the sportsmen's magazine *Forest and Stream*. The piece—apparently written by the magazine's editor, influential conservationist George Bird Grinnell, and his managing editor, Charles B. Reynolds—asked rhetorically, "Why should we not adopt as a plank in the sportsman's platform a declaration to this end—*That the sale of game should be forbidden at all seasons?*"[71] The nineteenth-century efforts of upper-class sportsmen to protect wildlife populations by circumscribing acceptable methods of hunting came to fruition as the twentieth century dawned, once those efforts coalesced with the support of a growing and increasingly sophisticated scientific community and the enhanced authority of state fish and game commissions. As a result, by 1900 or shortly thereafter most states, California included, had drafted a set of statutes that sought to protect many species of wildlife. Market hunters were among those who resisted these new regulations most often and, at times, most violently. Unlike their elite sportsmen counterparts, market hunters had little opportunity to defend their interests through political channels, and conflicts between market hunters and state, and later federal, authorities, in the Central Valley continued for decades.[72]

The restrictions on waterfowl hunting in California introduced in 1901 were promulgated in direct response to marked declines in waterfowl populations by the turn of the century. The decrease in the numbers of game birds in California had begun to be noticed as early as 1880, and during subsequent years reports to that effect came from all parts of the Central Valley. In the days before waterfowl censuses, populations could only be estimated, but those estimates were more than simply anecdotal, and were drawn from multiple sources. In their exhaustive work *The Game Birds of California*, published in 1918, Joseph Grinnell, the director of the University of California Museum of Vertebrate Zoology, and his colleagues at the museum, Harold Child Bryant and Tracy Irwin Storer, compiled evidence from "the judgments of dependable observers; the records of the kills of waterfowl on gun-club grounds; the records of market sales and shipments of game; and the toll taken by various agencies, natural as well as artificial" in order to evaluate the extent and causes of the decreasing number of waterfowl and other game birds in the state.[73] They found:

> The ducks and geese which were once distributed throughout the state are now crowded into the few ponds and marshes which are not yet reclaimed. It now takes a scientifically managed gun-club pond with every attraction that can be offered to wild fowl to bring the birds in large numbers. The same numbers of birds that can now be seen on baited ponds were present formerly on every small natural pond in the state. An example of this concentration is to be found in the vicinity of Gridley, Butte County [in the Butte Sink], where geese still congregate annually in immense numbers; but most of the localities in the San Joaquin and Sacramento Valleys which formerly favored the wintering of these birds, are completely devoid of them now.[74]

While acknowledging that the reclamation of land weighed heavily on waterfowl populations in the long term, the authors concluded that during the years of widespread and largely unregulated hunting in the late nineteenth and early twentieth centuries, the "sale of game on the open market has been fundamentally the most important factor in reducing California's supply of game birds." During the hunting year from July 1911 through June 1912, shortly before the final termination of bull hunting and the dissolution of the game transfer companies, 250,000 ducks were sold in the game markets of San Francisco alone, a large majority of the statewide total of 350,000. Largely as a result of these activities, it was "beyond question that waterfowl and upland game birds have both on the average decreased by fully one-half within the past forty years."[75]

One of the more intriguing parts of *The Game Birds of California* is the volume's positive assessment of the effect of gun clubs, the preserves of the sport hunter, on California's duck supply.[76] Duck clubs had existed in California since 1879, initially spurred by the construction of a Southern Pacific Railroad line from Benicia, east of San Francisco Bay, across Suisun Marsh to the small community of Suisun City. The new line made the marsh accessible to hunters in nearby San Francisco and Oakland.[77] Suisun Marsh, which was then privately owned, had been leased to two market hunters, Jim Payne and Seth Beckwith, who upon the completion of the railroad began subleasing their holdings on the western side of the marsh to the Ibis and Cordelia shooting clubs, the first organized duck clubs.[78] Waterfowl hunting clubs quickly proliferated in Suisun Marsh, where ducks congregated in enormous numbers from September to December before spreading throughout the Central Valley once the early winter rains brought water to the valley's seasonal wetlands. From December through March, many hunters turned their attention to the flocks of geese that descended on the valley as well, "where farmers were most glad to welcome shooters to drive the geese from their fields."[79] In the 1890s, sportsmen in the Sacramento Valley followed the precedent of their brethren in Suisun Marsh, organizing their own clubs and leasing or buying overflow land for use as private hunting preserves for their members. The largest of these was the Gridley Gun Club, which owned 6,000 acres along lower Butte Creek in the Butte Basin. Shortly after the turn of the century, duck clubs expanded into the San Joaquin Valley as well, where Miller and Lux began leasing their lands to duck hunters. The earliest of these clubs was the Gustine Gun Club, which by 1911 boasted 147 members.[80] Thus, by the time *The Game Birds of California* was published in 1918, gun clubs were widespread throughout the Central Valley and already had nearly a forty-year tradition behind them.

In evaluating the effects of these gun clubs, Grinnell and his colleagues weighed "detrimental" against "favorable" conditions. They addressed the undeniable fact that because of the improved conditions on these hunting grounds, especially when compared to surrounding reclaimed marshland, ducks congregate in high concentrations on small parcels of land, where they suffer a heavy toll from hunters. However, gun clubs maintained favorable grounds for feeding and loafing and provided additional food for ducks, both in the form of bait and by encouraging the growth of native plant foods, especially sago pondweed, "the best of the natural food plants for many kinds of ducks, both surface feeders [dabbling ducks] and diving ducks." In addition to providing valuable waterfowl habitat and food sources, gun clubs offered a refuge for ducks during the closed season and on nonshooting days. With all factors taken into account, the authors of *The Game Birds of California* concluded that "it would appear that the institution of the well regulated gun club . . . is to be looked upon as a propitious rather than as an adverse factor in the conservation of our duck supply. Whether or not, as further changes result from increased human population, this valuation of the preserve will persist, remains to be seen."[81]

RICE COMES TO THE SACRAMENTO VALLEY

While California passed increasingly restrictive measures against the hunting and marketing of waterfowl, and *The Game Birds of California* directed further attention to the plight of the state's waterfowl, migratory waterfowl in the Sacramento Valley also benefited from a new form of habitat—rice fields—that suddenly became available in the years after 1912. Interest in rice growing in California dated from as early as the 1850s, when rice was publicized as a crop adaptable to the climate and conditions of the state. In part, this interest was driven by California's large Chinese population, which by 1856 numbered between forty thousand and fifty thousand. Most had immigrated to work the gold fields of the Sierra Nevada, and soon they would find employment on the railroads. Based on a consumption rate of at least one pound of rice per person per day, contemporary estimates suggested that it was necessary to import from fifteen million to eighteen million pounds of rice per year simply to meet the needs of the Chinese populace. At an average cost of seven cents per pound, the cost of importing rice exceeded one million dollars per year, money that theoretically could have been going to California farmers. As early as 1858, the California State Agricultural Society offered a prize for the best quarter-acre of rice. Additional prizes were offered in 1859 and 1860, but the prizes failed to stimulate production. The California state legislature offered premiums as well in 1862, ranging from $250 for the first thousand pounds of rice grown in the state to $1,000 for the first ten thousand pounds. This legislative act was repealed in 1870, apparently without any money ever having been paid.[82] By 1875 more than fifty-four million pounds of rice were imported into California, primarily from China but also from Hawaii, and the need to develop a domestic supply intensified.[83]

The earliest attempts to grow rice in California were not successful. Rice-growing experiments in Los Angeles and Sonoma counties in 1881 ended in failure, as did trials in the mid-1890s conducted on Union Island in the Delta by Professor E. J. Wickson and J. Duert Davy of the University of California Agricultural Experiment Station. These early setbacks most likely stemmed from a failure to submerge the rice fields completely and from the inappropriate choice of long grain, late-maturing varieties from Honduras. While California rice-growing experiments were failing, the collapse of the wheat boom was exacting a heavy toll on the farmers of the Central Valley. The Sacramento Valley's Butte County, lying largely between the Sacramento and Feather rivers, was particularly vulnerable. Intensifying the hardships caused by falling prices, wheat production declined precipitously as the soils failed after several decades of continuous cropping, which had drained them of nitrogen and organic matter.[84]

A new round of rice experiments began in 1906, when the Bureau of Soils Survey of the U.S. Department of Agriculture sent W. W. Mackie to Fresno County in the San Joaquin Valley to conduct reclamation work on the soils there by growing rice and other crops. Several Japanese varieties matured and set seed, and appeared to be better suited for California conditions than the Honduran varieties. Mackie conducted additional trials in 1907 at several locations along the fringes of the Sacramento–San Joaquin Delta, but despite the region's fertile soils, these trials failed because late-afternoon and evening temperatures in the Delta were too cool for rice to mature. While Mackie was conducting his experiments in the Delta, interest in rice was mounting in economically depressed Butte County. Offered an experimental plot by a local rancher, Mackie came to that county in January 1908, where he planted 40 acres of rice on adobe soils southwest of the small city of Biggs. The long grain Honduras variety failed again, but the Japanese medium grain Kyushu rice matured. The experiment was a partial success.[85]

Rice-growing experiments continued in Butte County during each of the three subsequent years. The expertise of several Japanese immigrants, most notably Tokuya Yasuoka and Kenju Ikuta, contributed to the success of these experiments and helped launch the commercial rice industry in California. Rice was first grown profitably in 1912.[86] During that year, approximately 1,300 acres of commercial rice were seeded, with 1,000 acres in Butte County and the remaining 300 acres in Colusa County. The following year, more than 6,000 acres were planted commercially, with 5,000 in Butte County alone, and most of the remainder in Colusa and Sutter counties. Production increased nearly exponentially in the years that followed. A good measure of this success was due to the foresight of Charles Edward Chambliss, the head of the Department of Agriculture's Bureau of Plant Industry. Chambliss believed a successful rice industry could be established in California, and at his urging, local Butte County rice farmers organized the Sacramento Valley Grain Association in 1912 to provide the necessary land and plans for the Department of Agriculture to establish a Rice Experiment Station near Biggs. Since its origin, the Rice Experiment Station has been the focal point of rice research in California.[87]

The basins of the Sacramento Valley, and to a lesser extent the San Joaquin Valley, proved well suited to rice cultivation.[88] Significant portions of the Central Valley's basin areas are dominated by relatively impermeable heavy clay soils that allow rice fields to remain flooded during the growing season. The soils are also frequently saline. These textural and chemical qualities of basin soils pose much less of a problem for rice than for other crops. Rice is able to tolerate greater salinity than most other crops because it grows in standing water, which dilutes the salts and removes some of them by percolation. Rice could therefore be grown not only on the exhausted wheat lands of the valley, but also on some of the harshest basin soils, which had previously precluded cultivation almost entirely.[89]

In high demand because of the needs generated by World War I, rice brought economic prosperity to the Sacramento Valley. It also brought hungry ducks. After the collapse of the wheat boom and the expansion of rice production, ducks replaced geese as the primary depredators, and a new round of farmers versus waterfowl began. In 1917 losses from ducks totaled three hundred thousand bags of rice worth more than a million dollars. Rice growers used shotguns against this new agricultural pest and were at first arrested for violating game laws, but by 1918 federal and state authorities granted farmers licenses to kill ducks, geese, and mudhens (American coots) damaging their crops anytime between September 15 and February 1. As early as 1919, airplanes were used to frighten ducks off rice fields, a practice credited to Sam Purcell and Edmund Moffett of the Colusa area. Rice growers contracted with aviators at fifty cents per acre to patrol the fields from September 1 to December 10 of each year, while the rice plants reached maturity. The flyers fitted their biplanes with extra-heavy propellers so they could fly through flocks of ducks without having their blades shattered, and they herded ducks from the rice fields as far as the Coast Ranges to the west of the valley.[90] Effective as this method may have been at first, ducks and geese quickly became accustomed to the noise and were no longer frightened. Duck herding by airplane was abandoned in 1921, but aviation proved useful to rice production again in 1929 when two flyers in the Merced area of the San Joaquin Valley discovered that rice could be sown by airplane at a rate ten times faster than by ground machinery, raising capacity from 50 to 500 acres per day. Rice could now be sown in fields already flooded, thereby eliminating the problem of birds devouring much of the machine-planted seed before water could be released onto the fields.[91] However, depredation in the rice fields at harvesttime remained heavy, and by the 1930s the California Department of Fish and Game and the U.S. Fish and Wildlife Service would need to create refuges throughout the Central Valley to provide alternative feeding sites for the millions of waterfowl that annually descended on the valley for an autumnal feast. In this ironic turn of events, agriculture, which had been responsible for much of the destruction of California's Central Valley wetlands, now necessitated the restoration of a portion of those wetlands.

The explosion of the rice industry in the Central Valley—and the crop depredations that followed—foreshadow the impetus for creation of state and federal refuges near mid-century. A more immediate issue was that rice growing in the Sacramento Valley required much greater utilization of Sacramento River water than at any time in the past. As rice farmers increasingly tapped their limited supply of fresh water, less and less of the Sacramento River's flow reached the Sacramento–San Joaquin Delta, causing unprecedented problems of water supply and water quality in that ecologically fragile estuary. The reaction of Delta residents to their rice-growing neighbors to the north helped set in motion a chain of events that, within two decades, led to the Central Valley Project and the epic reconfiguration of the valley's hydrology that defines its possibilities and limitations to this day.

5

The Sacramento-San Joaquin Delta and the Central Valley Project's Origins

GEOGRAPHY AND HISTORY

More than in any other region of the Central Valley—save perhaps the Tulare Basin—the wetlands of the Delta were rapidly and thoroughly engineered out of existence during the decades following California statehood. While the geography, climate, and soils of the Delta shaped the details of its reclamation in distinctive ways, the goal of that reclamation was, once again, conversion of its wetlands to agricultural use. As was the case in 1850, the contemporary Delta remains largely defined by its numerous watercourses, rivers and sloughs that flow around its jigsaw-puzzle-like configuration of islands and low-lying tracts. But the nature of the land in the Delta has been completely transformed. Extensive tule marshes and overflow wetlands long ago gave way to row crops and orchards. As the wetlands disappeared, so too did the vast numbers of waterfowl that had relied on the Delta for their permanent or seasonal home.

Occupying 738,000 acres, the Sacramento–San Joaquin Delta lies in the heart of California's Great Central Valley.[1] Yet because of its lack of large cities, sparse population, and few roads, the Delta seems a place apart from the more developed Sacramento Valley to the north and San Joaquin Valley to the south. The bustling metropolis of the San Francisco Bay Area cities, situated not far to the west, is a different world. Nevertheless, these regions are intricately linked by hydrology, and the Delta connects them all. While the northern, eastern, and southern margins of the Delta merge into the Central Valley, the Delta's western tip is defined as the juncture of the Sacramento and San Joaquin rivers with Suisun Bay, the first of three connected bays—including San Pablo Bay and San

Francisco Bay—that lie between the Delta and the Pacific Ocean. Rising sea levels between six thousand and seven thousand years ago impeded the flow of the lower reaches of the Sacramento and San Joaquin rivers, creating a labyrinthine network of hundreds of miles of sloughs surrounding nearly one hundred low-lying islands—the historical Delta. Salt water intruded inland as far as Suisun Bay, and tidal marshes extended from San Francisco Bay to the Delta itself (see map 11). Most lands in the Delta were close to mean sea level, with the highest points only fifteen feet above that level. Swamp vegetation, partially decomposing over the thousands of years since the Delta had formed, created a layer of fertile peat soil, the depth of which ranges from a few inches on the eastern periphery to as much as sixty feet on Sherman Island in the west-central Delta.[2] These peat soils made the Delta an early target for reclamation.

Prior to reclamation, natural levees separated the main Delta channels from both tidal and river overflow areas. The Delta's dominant native plant cover was the tule, which was omnipresent in tidal and river backswamps; but it did not cover the entire estuarine marsh. In the centrally located tracts along the San Joaquin River, while tules covered the wettest lands, annual grasses on higher ground supported livestock grazing as early as the 1860s. Along the banks of the Delta portions of the Sacramento and San Joaquin rivers grew a luxurious forest of oak, sycamore, alder, and cottonwood.[3] In the tules and along the riverbanks could be found "thousands of raccoons, otter, badger, beaver, and other fur bearing animals." Waterfowl were abundant in this "tule or peat land [which] became, during the winter season, the feeding place of thousands of ducks and geese that flew from the north at the first approach of the Arctic winters."[4] Through the 1880s, hunters annually burned the tules to drive out flocks of ducks and geese. Observers vividly described this spectacle of burning tules: "One of the beautiful sights annually occurring in the fall of the year was the burning of miles and miles of tules. They were set on fire by the hunters to clear the land and drive out the game, making it easier to locate a flock of ducks or geese. It was indeed a beautiful sight, especially at night—'the ocean of fire'— . . . the flames rushing along at racehorse speed, licking up with their red-forked tongues the dry tules."[5]

As in all other regions of the Central Valley, the Delta was altered hydrologically and ecologically during the second half of the nineteenth century. Mining debris choked its channels, while would-be agriculturalists burned off the tules and reclaimed the land. The effects of hydraulic mining were similar to those in the Sacramento Valley, but delayed by the few years that it took for the tailings to travel downstream to the Delta. Sierran rivers transported the tailings down from the mines to the Sacramento River and, to a lesser degree, the San Joaquin River, which in turn carried them to the Delta and beyond, on their unalterable course to the Pacific. It is estimated that in the years between 1860 and 1914, more than eight hundred million cubic yards of mining debris passed through the Delta.

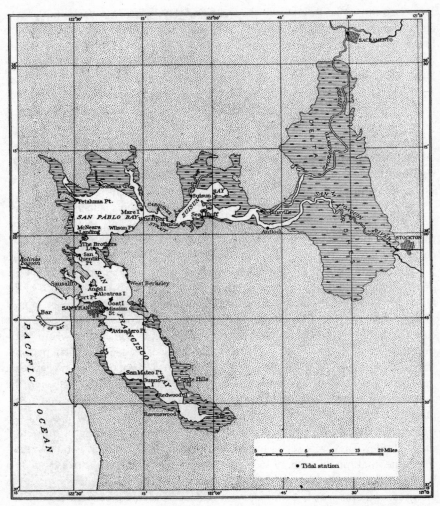

MAP 11. Historical tidal marsh areas of the Sacramento–San Joaquin Delta, Suisun Bay, San Pablo Bay, and San Francisco Bay. Source: John Thompson and Edward A. Dutra, *The Tule Breakers: The Story of the California Dredge* (Stockton, Calif.: Stockton Corral of Westerners International and University of the Pacific, 1983). Used with permission.

Mine tailings raised and constricted the beds of all channels, thereby increasing the extent and frequency of flooding. As the rivers rose, tidal influence from the Pacific Ocean was correspondingly reduced. Tidal fluctuations declined from an average of two feet in Sacramento, at the Delta's northern tip, until they disappeared entirely between 1883 and 1898. Alluviation became so great that the tide, where still present at all, no longer assisted deeper-draft vessels over certain shoals. Following the cessation of hydraulic mining, however, Delta channels were gradually cleared by a combination of natural scouring and the dredging work associated with the Sacramento Flood Control Project.[6]

The physical effects on the Delta of mining were severe, but in the long run, less important than the effects of reclamation. Under the Swamp Land Commission, significant reclamation progress was made on Ryer and Grand islands in the northern Delta, and projects were begun immediately south of them on Brannan, Andrus, Tyler, and Staten islands. Reclamation of the peat islands of the west-central Delta, however, did not begin in earnest until after the Green Act of 1868 removed the limitation on the acreage of swamp and overflowed land that a single individual could hold, at which time "the process of enclosing, burning, and planting the tule lands progressed rapidly."[7] The first coordinated attempts to build a levee in the peatlands of the Delta were on Sherman Island in 1868 and 1869. Over the next half-century, private efforts were responsible for reclaiming more than 300,000 acres of the Delta (see map 12).[8] Ultimately, of the 340,000 acres of the Delta that were wetlands in 1850, all except 18,000 acres were reclaimed, the overwhelming majority having been leveed, drained, and converted to agricultural use by the early twentieth century.[9]

Who built these levees that transformed the Delta? As early as 1852, Californians had proposed the use of Chinese laborers for the reclamation of the "tule lands." At that time, however, the Chinese were working claims in the gold mines, until they were systematically driven out by beatings, lynchings, and the burning of Chinatowns by white miners.[10] In the 1860s, thousands of Chinese found employment on the transcontinental railroad, but by the end of that decade they were available to work on reclamation projects. Recruited from Chinatown boarding houses in Sacramento, Stockton, and San Francisco and working with only the minimalist technology of shovels and wheelbarrows, Chinese workers "dammed sloughs, cut drainage ditches, built floodgates, and piled up levees." These levees encircled entire islands and were usually from 3 to 5 feet high, from 10 to 15 feet wide at the base, and 5 feet wide at the crest. Some workers remained to farm—as laborers and as tenants—the land they had reclaimed. Their numbers were swelled by a new generation of Chinese, Japanese, and, later, Hindu immigrants. Nowhere in the Central Valley was the influence of the Chinese felt more than in the Delta, where they settled in the communities of Walnut Grove, Isleton, Courtland, and Rio Vista and later founded the town of Locke.[11]

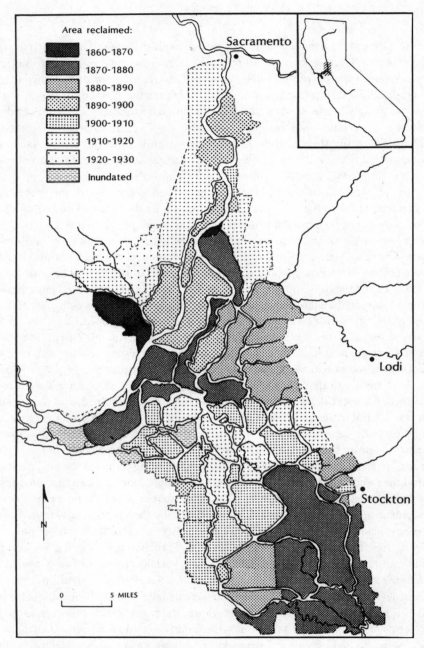

Area reclaimed:

1860-1870
1870-1880
1880-1890
1890-1900
1900-1910
1910-1920
1920-1930
Inundated

Sacramento

Lodi

Stockton

N

0   5 MILES

MAP 12. Reclamation of the Delta, 1860–1930. The lowest-lying peat islands in the south-central Delta were among the most difficult to reclaim, and hence—as the map indicates—reclamation efforts there proceeded slowly. Source: John Thompson, "The Settlement Geography of the Sacramento–San Joaquin Delta, California," PhD diss., Stanford University, 1957. Courtesy of John Thompson.

After levees were completed, the process of clearing the land began. Burning was the accepted method of removing stands of tules, not only because it produced good seedbeds, but also because it was believed to prevent miasma. The tules were burned in the fall, after the tops of the plants had died and the sod was the driest. Sometimes they were first mowed or rolled to ensure more thorough destruction of the vegetation.[12] The process of rolling is described in an early history of Contra Costa County: "The rollers are heavily weighted, double, ten feet in diameter, and are *pushed* into the *tules* by four horses, a man steering their course by means of a rudder wheel. The land is then plowed up in deep, wide furrows, and the roots of the weeds burned out."[13] Joel Parker Whitney, a leading entrepreneur in Delta reclamation, described how the tules were burned: "The tule, deprived of water, dies, and one man with a box of matches clears twenty acres per day, not only burning off the tule but the tussocks or roots, the ground being allowed to dry to the condition that permits from six to twelve inches of the upper surface of soft, dead tule roots to burn off, when the absorbed moisture from below prevent [sic] further consumption."[14] Once the seedbed had been prepared by these methods, reclaimers often planted first potatoes and then beans, harvesting two crops during the first year.

As the pace of Delta reclamation accelerated, technological advances— including the horse-drawn Fresno scraper and, later, mechanically powered earth-moving equipment—gradually displaced the Chinese laborers. Dredges and ditchers were introduced around 1870, and came into general use after 1876. Clamshell dredges were used in the Delta at least as early as 1879. Mighty dredges, with names that included *Samson, Goliath, Atlas,* and *Hercules,* leveed the islands and low-lying tracts of the Delta over the course of the next generation. The peak years for dredging were from 1900 until about the end of World War I, by which time the majority of the land had been reclaimed.[15]

By 1920 even the difficult peat lands of the central Delta had been brought under the plow. Throughout this arduous process, peat, which is buoyant, perennially proved a difficult material for levee construction. Peat subsides or compresses in unpredictable ways; it shrinks and cracks with oxidation, the process by which organic matter lying above the water table is decomposed. It also becomes increasingly susceptible to wind and wave erosion and to seepage as it oxidizes, and it burns easily.[16] Complicating the situation further, peat levees, even those that withstood these inherent disadvantages, could be undermined by the peat soils that they enclosed. The combination of oxidation, wind erosion, and compaction resulted in a fall of ground elevation in the enclosed areas, which in turn led to accelerated seepage through levees and their foundations. On Sherman Island, the elevation in the interior was rapidly reduced by as much as five or six feet. A combination of flood and subsidence has caused levees on that Delta island, along with many others, to fail repeatedly. Tillage of the peat lands continues to lead to the reduction of surface elevations by an average of up to three inches per year. Substantial areas of the Delta have dropped to between ten and twenty feet below mean sea level.[17]

By the early twentieth century the Delta had been transformed from a tidal swampland with natural levees into an intensively cultivated agricultural landscape. Tules and other wetland plants were restricted to waterway margins, overflowed tracts, unreclaimed islets, and sloughs and drainage ditches within leveed districts. The dense concentrations of wildlife that had thrived in and around the tules vanished with them. The Delta's wetlands, which once provided habitat for millions of waterfowl, were converted into fields of asparagus, potatoes, beans, barley, celery, onions, corn, and orchard crops, principally pears.[18]

For a time it appeared that Suisun Marsh would share the fate of the neighboring Delta, its wetlands hemmed in by levees, drained, and then plowed. The first duck clubs in California had originated in the wetlands of Suisun Marsh in 1879, but beginning in the 1880s much of the marsh was diked and reclaimed for agriculture, the reclamation efforts proceeding generally from east to west. Dairy farms and cattle ranches were established first, followed by wheat, asparagus, and potatoes. Unlike the situation in the Delta, agriculture faltered in Suisun Marsh, largely because of salt water from the Pacific Ocean, which moved up the sloughs in dry years. As a result, within a few decades islands in the marsh were intentionally reflooded within their encircling dikes to establish new wetlands for ducks and hunters.[19]

Lying farther inland than Suisun Marsh, the predominantly freshwater Delta was not as consistently affected by saltwater intrusion. The extent to which salinity penetrates into the Delta from the Pacific Ocean to the west depends on the volume of flow discharged through the Delta by Central Valley rivers to hold that salinity at bay. Historically, the inflow of Central Valley drainage into the Delta exceeded an annual mean of thirty million acre-feet, approximately 74 percent of which originated in the Sacramento Valley watershed, with the highest flows recorded during winter and spring.[20] Any significant reductions in this water supply would inevitably affect Delta water quality.

Salinity in the Delta became an increasing problem as irrigation diversions from the San Joaquin and Sacramento river systems increased. The first diversions in the San Joaquin Basin were along the Merced River in 1852, and by 1870 enough water had been withdrawn from the San Joaquin River and its tributaries to cause a noticeable reduction in the flow into the Delta. In the Sacramento Valley, the overall acreage irrigated by the Sacramento River more than tripled between 1902 and 1919, from 206,000 to 640,000 acres. The explosion of the rice industry after 1912 dramatically increased diversions. Rice cultivation demanded complete inundation, and—with an average annual requirement in the Sacramento Valley of seven feet of water per acre—rice culture was primarily responsible for a doubling of Sacramento River diversions, from 1,154,000 acre-feet in 1915 to 2,300,000 acre-feet in 1919. Although perhaps 35 percent to 40 percent of that water reentered the Sacramento River by return flow, the effect of the diversions was enough to reduce drastically the inflow of the Sacramento River to the Delta, and Delta and Suisun Bay area water users alike held the rice producers in the Sacramento Valley largely responsible for the increasing penetration of ocean salinity.[21]

When a record 164,000 acres of rice cultivation coincided with a serious drought in 1920, the salinity problem in the Delta reached crisis proportions. In July of that year, the western Delta city of Antioch, situated near the mouth of the San Joaquin River, together with ninety-seven Delta landowners, brought suit against upstream irrigators in the Sacramento Valley. The plaintiffs requested that the irrigators be enjoined from diverting so much water from the Sacramento River and its tributaries that tidal salinity would advance far enough into the Delta to threaten Antioch's municipal water supply, which was drawn from the San Joaquin River. The city argued that a Sacramento River flow of 3,500 cubic feet per second past the city of Sacramento (where the river enters the Delta) was necessary to achieve this protection. In August, this flow fell below 500 cubic feet per second. In January 1921 the Alameda Superior Court granted a temporary injunction against upstream diversions, but the California Supreme Court overturned this decision in March of the following year.[22] In ruling against the city of Antioch, the court held, "Our conclusion is that an appropriator of fresh water from one of these streams at a point near its outlet to the sea does not, by such appropriation, acquire the right to insist that subsequent appropriators above shall leave enough water flowing in the stream to hold the salt water of the incoming tides below his point of diversion. Further than this we need not go."[23]

Although the Antioch case was unsuccessful, it "was a landmark in the history of the fight against salinity," and led to discussions by the state Division of Engineering and Irrigation about the feasibility of constructing a physical barrier somewhere below the Delta to separate salt water from fresh water and permanently limit the upstream incursion of salinity.[24] The idea of a barrier, as a flood control measure rather than as a potential barrier to salinity, had been investigated by C. E. Grunsky, later the author of the Manson-Grunsky Report, as early as 1880. The idea proved impractical and was abandoned, but at the time of the Antioch suit, the irrigators of the Sacramento Valley revived the barrier idea as an alternative to legal action. Delta landowners accepted the feasibility of constructing a barrier but were deeply concerned that such a barrier would raise water levels behind it during periods of high river flow, increasing the stress on already fragile levees.[25] However, another physical solution was possible. Dams could be built on the headwaters and tributaries of the Sacramento and San Joaquin rivers to store floodwaters for release during the dry season, providing water for irrigation and salinity control. By the 1930s, the latter solution would take shape as the federal Central Valley Project.

IRRIGATION PRECEDENTS

The move toward state—and ultimately federal—control of water planning marked the culmination of a series of developments, in California and the nation at large, that reached well back into the nineteenth century. In 1873 Robert Maitland Brereton, the accomplished chief engineer of the struggling San Joaquin and Kings River Canal and Irrigation Company, had lobbied Congress on behalf of the company for a federal land grant of 256,000 acres, the sale of which could be used to finance further construction of the company's Main Canal. Facing a Congress skeptical of both the project's feasibility and the propriety of contributing to the monopolistic control of land and water by Henry Miller and Charles Lux, the main beneficiaries of the canal, Brereton failed in his quest.[26] Instead, Nevada senator William Morris Stewart introduced a bill, signed by President Grant in March 1873, calling for the creation of a commission "to make a full report to the President on the best system of irrigation for . . . [the Sacramento and San Joaquin] valleys."[27] General B. S. Alexander of the Army Corps of Engineers headed the commission, which completed its survey work in the summer of 1873 and published its report the following year. The commission did not endorse the San Joaquin and Kings River Canal and Irrigation Company's request, and stopped short of proposing a valleywide plan for reclamation. Instead, it argued the need for further detailed studies of the Central Valley's hydrology and for a system of centralized planning to construct the valley's irrigation systems efficiently and properly. The commission's conclusions heralded a new way of thinking about irrigation and reclamation in the arid West: "It is the duty of government, both State and national, to encourage irrigation, and the first step in that direction ought to be to make a complete instrumental reconnaissance of the country to be irrigated, embracing the sources from whence the irrigating-canals ought to commence, gauging the flow of the rivers and streams, and defining the boundaries of the natural districts of irrigation into which the country is divided."[28]

The Alexander Commission report of 1874 clearly suggested that government intervention in irrigation enterprises was desirable, and it was "significant as representing the first congressional appropriation to use irrigation as an agent of economic growth."[29] The report had little immediate direct effect, however, and irrigation remained a local matter in California for decades longer. The 1884 and 1886 decisions in *Lux v. Haggin,* which had favored riparian rights, left behind much bitterness toward riparian proprietors and the monopolistic control of water that they symbolized. In the wake of those decisions, nonriparian owners resorted to the irrigation district, an ostensibly equitable instrument for distributing the existing water supply. The concept of the irrigation district, partially modeled on the swampland districts of the 1860s, developed during the 1870s and received support from the California Grange, whose members promoted irrigation as a cooperative endeavor to increase productivity and land values. The first attempts to establish irrigation districts in California were unsuccessful.[30] Yet despite setbacks, the irrigation district idea remained alive and was endorsed by William Hammond Hall in his 1880 report to the governor, in which he called for the state legislature to pass "an act to promote irrigation," the first principle of which was to "provide for the organization of irrigation districts." Hall argued that irrigation increased the tendency for large landowners to break up their holdings into small tracts that could provide a home and a livelihood for large numbers of farmers.[31]

In 1886 C. C. Wright, a lawyer from Modesto in the San Joaquin Valley's Stanislaus County, was elected to the state assembly, where he presented a bill that would allow local communities to build and operate their own irrigation works. Although the bill was opposed by large landowners, including Haggin and Carr and Miller and Lux, who possessed extensive water rights, it passed the assembly unanimously, and in March 1887 was signed by the governor. The Wright Act provided that "whenever fifty or a majority" of landowners whose lands were irrigable from a common source desired to develop irrigation for those lands, they could petition their county board of supervisors to create an irrigation district.[32] Each district was to be governed by a board of five directors, whose responsibilities included purchasing or condemning water rights and rights-of-way, supervising construction of dams and canals, and distributing the water supply based on the apportionment of individual taxes. Between 1887 and 1895, forty-nine irrigation districts were formed in California under the Wright Act. Of these, thirty were in Southern California and nineteen were distributed throughout the Central Valley, with seven in the Sacramento Valley and twelve in the San Joaquin Valley.[33]

Initially, the Wright Act was considered a success and many Californians became convinced that centralized state reclamation was unnecessary. However, numerous districts soon found themselves in financial difficulty and facing various legal challenges, and the majority of them failed. Only eight of the original forty-nine districts formed under the act were still operating in 1916.[34] The Wright Act was amended four times between 1889 and 1895, but its shortcomings were not adequately addressed until 1897, when the legislature superseded it with the Bridgeford Act, which imposed more stringent regulations on the creation of irrigation districts.[35] Ultimately, the Wright Act fell far short of the hopes that Californians had placed in it. Irrigated acreage increased from one million acres in 1889, by which time California already led the nation in irrigated agriculture, to 1.5 million acres in 1900. Much of this modest gain occurred on large estates, and, overall, the Wright Act did little to reduce the average size of farms, which fell only from 426 acres to 397 acres between 1880 and 1900.[36] Yet although the Wright Act "failed to transform California's vast wheat ranchos into small, intensively cultivated family farms," together with the Alexander Commission Report it stimulated nationwide discussion of federal irrigation in the arid West, a discussion that would soon have profound consequences for California's Great Central Valley.[37]

THE LEGITIMATION OF FEDERAL RECLAMATION

Congress had authorized the U.S. Geological Survey to conduct the first water resources investigation of the nation's arid lands in 1888, an investigation that Major John Wesley Powell, chief of the survey, had proposed nearly a decade earlier in his classic *Report on the Lands of the Arid Region of the United States*.[38] The irrigation survey of 1888–1890—under Powell's leadership and including the talented engineer Frederick Haynes Newell—coined the terms "run-off" and "acre-feet," and envisaged the West as a series of "hydrographic basins," or watersheds, which would form the basis of locally controlled irrigation districts. Despite its importance, the irrigation survey was killed after two years by eastern politicians, who opposed irrigation spending in general, and by their western counterparts, who opposed Powell's insistence on scientific planning and communitarian ownership of natural resources, rather than laissez-faire economic development, in the West.[39]

Drought, beginning on the Great Plains in 1890, finally served as the catalyst for federally sponsored irrigation legislation. The dry years of the 1890s ignited a national irrigation crusade that was initially led by William Smythe, a Nebraska journalist. Smythe promoted irrigation development both by regulated private enterprise and by public ownership of canals, reservoirs, and related facilities. At a state irrigation convention in Lincoln, Nebraska, in February 1891, he was named chairman of a commission to arrange for the first National Irrigation Congress, which met in Salt Lake City in the Utah Territory later that year. For Smythe, who founded the influential journal *Irrigation Age*, irrigation came to represent the omnipotent instrument for transforming society in America's arid West. Irrigation provided hope for the liberty of the individual, enabling people to settle on small family farms and to ward off the stifling challenges from syndicates and corporations, and from the urban malaise that was undermining the social order in the East. As Smythe wrote in *The Conquest of Arid America*, "I had taken the cross of a new crusade. To my mind, irrigation seemed the biggest thing in the world. It was not merely a matter of ditches and acres, but a philosophy, a religion, and a programme of practical statesmanship rolled into one."[40] At first,

Smythe believed that the individual states should play the major role in sponsoring irrigation projects, but he gradually accepted the idea that only the federal government possessed the resources and the expertise to carry out such grandiose projects.[41]

In California, where the Wright Act had temporarily dampened the desire for centralized irrigation planning, the irrigation crusade regained momentum during the drought of 1898–1900, fortified by discontent over falling prices for wheat and declining land values. By that time George H. Maxwell, a young lawyer, had assumed its leadership. In 1897 Maxwell organized the National Irrigation Association, based in Chicago, and he lobbied leaders of both the Democratic and the Republican parties for support. By 1900 the platforms of both parties included planks in favor of the reclamation of arid lands in the West.[42] Nevada congressman and future senator Francis G. Newlands proposed legislation the next year that provided for the federal government to finance irrigation through the sale of western public lands. On June 17, 1902, Theodore Roosevelt, having assumed the presidency the previous year upon the assassination of William McKinley, signed the landmark Newlands Reclamation Act into law.[43] He defended his stance to the American public by arguing that just as public works for rivers and harbors had benefited the East, now irrigation dams would represent an equivalent appropriation for the West.[44]

The Reclamation Act originally applied to sixteen western states and territories, and provided that "all monies received from the sale and disposal of public lands" be set aside in a special "reclamation fund," to be used for the surveying of arid and semiarid lands, and for the storage, diversion, and development of waters for the reclamation of those lands.[45] Significantly, the Reclamation Act specifically provided that "no right to the use of water for land in private ownership shall be sold for a tract exceeding one hundred and sixty acres to any one landowner, and no such sale shall be made to any landowner unless he be an actual bona fide resident on such land, or occupant thereof residing in the neighborhood of said land."[46] The 160-acre limitation established continuity with the Homestead Act of 1862, which had prescribed 160 acres—a quarter-section of land—as the appropriate size of farms to be established on public lands.[47] The acreage limitation and the residency requirement reflect the spirit and intention of the Reclamation Act. Keeping true to the goals of the national irrigation crusade, the act was designed to encourage smallholdings and prevent the monopolistic control of land and water in the West. Nevertheless, acreage and residency requirements were routinely disregarded during the early years of the reclamation program, which was plagued by speculation. Particularly contentious was the issue of the sale of excess lands, those lands above 160 acres in the possession of a single individual.[48] The lawmakers seemed to assume that landowners would sell their excess lands to eligible farmers so that they would all receive water from the project. But the law contained no provisions for the sale of excess lands in project areas, or for the prices at which such lands could be sold.[49]

To carry out the policies of the Reclamation Act, in 1902 the secretary of the interior created the Reclamation Service as part of the U.S. Geological Survey. In 1907 the Reclamation Service was separated from the Geological Survey, and Frederick Haynes Newell, who had been the survey's chief engineer, assumed the new title of director of reclamation. As the Reclamation Service began to construct reservoirs to store water for irrigation, it adopted the Geological Survey's position that the nation's water resources could be harnessed for multiple uses, and began to explore the possibility of combining reservoir storage with the production of hydroelectric power. The federal government's role in water development had gradually expanded from the maintenance of navigation to include flood control, irrigation, and now power generation. This shift toward multiple-purpose basin development would later be fully manifested in the Central Valley Project.

In its early years, the Reclamation Service had little effect on the Central Valley, initiating only one small irrigation project on the western side of the Sacramento Valley. The Orland Project, approved by Newell in 1906 and completed a decade later, created East Park Reservoir on Stony Creek, a Coast Range tributary of the Sacramento River, in northern Colusa County, approximately forty miles southwest of the city of Orland. Originally including only 14,000 acres of land and later expanded to 20,000 acres—less than 1 percent of the 3,874,000 acres of irrigable land in the Sacramento Valley—the Orland Project remained a small, isolated endeavor and failed to inaugurate the full development of the Sacramento Valley.[50] The limited effectiveness of the Reclamation Service's attempts to reclaim land in California caused the state to turn, once again, toward developing its own water supply.[51]

FROM STATE WATER PLAN TO FEDERAL PROJECT

By the 1920s, the prevailing mood within the state government was favorable for consideration of statewide water planning. In 1911, during the governorship of Hiram Johnson, the state legislature had created the Conservation Commission for the purpose of investigating and recommending necessary laws pertaining to irrigation, water power, and other natural resource issues.[52] In accordance with one of the recommendations of the Conservation Commission, in 1913 the legislature established the State Water Commission, California's first water rights governing agency, to regulate the appropriation and use of water.[53] Subsequently, the State Water Problems Conference of 1916 examined in detail concerns over irrigation, reclamation, water storage, flood control, drainage, and municipal water supplies, with the goal of moving toward a unified statewide plan.[54] The need for such a plan was accentuated by a serious drought from 1918 to 1920, which caused extensive abandonment of newly irrigated lands in the San Joaquin Valley, where excessive pumping of groundwater had depleted the water supply. Meanwhile, massive withdrawals of Sacramento River water by rice growers in the Sacramento Valley were contributing to saltwater intrusion into the Delta. California was rapidly approaching a water crisis, and it was in this context that the legislature in 1921 called for a statewide water investigation, to be completed no later than the legislative session of 1923, "of the possibilities of the storage, control, and diversion of water for public use and public protection."[55]

While the state water bureaucracy was growing, political realignments among both Republicans and Democrats were reducing the obstacles to centralized water planning.[56] During the 1920s and 1930s, Republicans were moving away from their Progressive predecessors' support of activist government directed toward social reform, but they remained committed to government activism for the promotion of business and economic development. At the same time, Democrats—while remaining distrustful of powerful business interests—were moving away from their traditional laissez-faire position toward a preference for a strong, activist government and centralized planning. Thus, despite their ideological differences, both parties were able to come together to support a state water project.[57]

In 1923 the Division of Engineering and Irrigation of the California Department of Public Works issued the results of the statewide water investigation in its Bulletin no. 4, titled *Water Resources of California*.[58] This report to the legislature offered a state plan that provided for the irrigation of a total of 18 million acres statewide, 12 million acres of which would be newly irrigated lands, including 10.3 million acres in the Central Valley.[59] The plan called for the creation of storage reservoirs on the upper Sacramento River and the construction of canals to transport excess water from the Sacramento Valley to the San Joaquin Valley. The plan was not an entirely original idea. Three years earlier, Colonel Robert Bradford Marshall, chief geographer of the U.S. Geological Survey, had proposed a plan to transfer water from the Sacramento Valley to the San Joaquin Valley, part of a vast irrigation scheme to reclaim the Central Valley and to make homes for three million people. Marshall's plan envisaged a dam on the upper Sacramento River near Red Bluff, which would supply two great canals, one on each side of the Central Valley; storage reservoirs would also be built near the canals. Despite promoting it well into the 1920s, Marshall failed to win acceptance for his plan, which was not mentioned in the 1923 report to the legislature.[60]

The Division of Irrigation and Engineering continued to develop its water plan throughout the 1920s. Bulletin no. 9, released in 1925 and authored by State Engineer Paul Bailey, provided for imported Sacramento Valley water to replace downstream flows of the San Joaquin River, which would be diverted for irrigation purposes at Friant, fifteen miles northeast of Fresno at the edge of the foothills of the Sierra Nevada. The plan mentioned a potential reservoir site at Kennett, a small community above Redding at the head of the Sacramento Valley, but did not yet recommend a specific dam for construction.[61] By the time of the release of the Division's Bulletin no. 12 in 1927, also authored by Bailey, the state water plan was emerging as a true multiple-purpose project, with storage dams, reservoirs that would be operated for flood control as well as for water supply, and the development of hydroelectric power generation as an aid to financing.[62]

In response to the concluding recommendation of Bulletin no. 12, the state legislature created the Joint Legislative Water Problems Committee to consider the nonengineering aspects of the plan.[63] The committee addressed major legislative challenges, including the thorny problem that the rights of riparian owners to the full flow of streams abutting their property (upheld in *Lux v. Haggin*) were incompatible with conservation and the full development of water resources. This problem was exacerbated by the California Supreme Court in 1926 with its ruling in *Herminghaus v. Southern California Edison Company*.[64] In that controversial decision, the court held that a downstream riparian owner could command the entire flow of the San Joaquin River to flood pastureland for the reclamation of soil and for irrigation, thereby preventing the upstream development of a power project based on an appropriative right. The court ruled that if a riparian owner's use of water was beneficial—however wasteful it might be—that owner was under no duty to an appropriator on the same stream to use water reasonably. The response to *Herminghaus* was swift. In 1928 the legislature amended the California Constitution to require that all use of water be reasonable as well as beneficial: "It is hereby declared that because of the conditions prevailing in this State the general welfare requires that the water resources of the State be put to beneficial use to the fullest extent of which they are capable, and that the waste or unreasonable use or unreasonable method of use of water be prevented, and that the conservation of such waters is to be exercised with a view to the reasonable and beneficial use thereof in the interest of the people and for the public welfare."[65] This constitutional provision requiring the reasonable and beneficial use of water would prove an important tool in later twentieth-century struggles to save the state's remaining wetlands, both in the Central Valley and beyond.[66] Immediately, however, it helped resolve the issue of conflicting water rights, an important obstacle to the developing state water plan.

In 1929 the Joint Legislative Water Problems Committee endorsed the coordinated state water plan published in the Division of Engineering and Irrigation's Bulletin no. 12. Yet the legislature failed to initiate constitutional amendments to authorize the financing of the project. Instead, it provided for a new Joint Federal-State Commission on Water Resources to investigate a federal role in solving California's water problems.[67] Federal involvement was warranted because, in addition to water storage for irrigation, the emerging state water plan would provide flood control and navigation benefits. The Flood Control Act of 1917, which had cleared the way for federal assistance to the Sacramento Flood Control Project, had added responsibility for flood control to the federal government's historical responsibility for the improvement of navigation; both were now clearly within the federal government's purview. In December 1930 the joint commission, which became known as the Hoover-Young Commission, bearing the names of the president and California's governor, C. C. Young, recommended that the state water plan proceed.[68]

In March 1931 State Engineer Edward Hyatt submitted an updated plan to the legislature, now officially known as the State Water Plan. Published as Bulletin no. 25 by the newly organized Division of Water Resources, the revised State Water Plan was loosely based on State Engineer Bailey's 1927 plan, presented in Bulletin no. 12, but was more comprehensive and detailed, and represented "the culmination of a decade of planning for the comprehensive development of California's water resources."[69] The plan proposed for immediate development both Kennett Reservoir on the Sacramento River and Friant Reservoir on the San Joaquin River, as well as canals to deliver water from Friant Reservoir to the upper San Joaquin Valley. A pump system in the Delta would deliver substitute water to the lower San Joaquin River to replace part of the river's flow, which would be diverted upstream at Friant Reservoir. A newly added Contra Costa Conduit would provide fresh water for the upper San Francisco Bay region in lieu of a saltwater barrier below the Delta.[70] As a prerequisite to the realization of this large and complex plan, the state would need to secure substantial water rights, particularly for the waters of the upper San Joaquin River that would be impounded and exported at Friant, leaving the river below the dam essentially dry. These water rights included the ones attached to the "grass lands," which the state ultimately obtained from the firm of Miller and Lux in 1939, initiating decades of controversy over the water supply to the overflow grasslands of the San Joaquin Basin.[71]

As was the case with earlier versions of the State Water Plan, the 1931 plan included provisions for Southern California as well as for the Central Valley. Hyatt's plan envisaged an aqueduct across the desert from the Colorado River to the Southern California coastal plain. This provision was quickly dropped because of opposition from Southern Californians who had already negotiated for Colorado River water on their own. Fearing delays and complications from federal involvement, Southern Californians requested exclusion from the project. At that point, Hyatt's plan became de facto a Central Valley plan, rather than a true statewide plan.[72]

Severe drought in 1931 lent urgency to the implementation of the State Water Plan. At the height of the drought, the flow of the Sacramento River past the city of Sacramento fell for a short time to zero. Under these conditions, tidal salinity with a chloride concentration at or above 1,000 ppm—the generally accepted limit for irrigation purposes—spread over 90 percent of the Delta, reaching as far inland as Stockton, the greatest extent ever recorded.[73] Finally, in August 1933 the legislature passed the Central Valley Project Act. The act provided for the construction of the facilities outlined in the State Water Plan. The dam at Kennett—later to be renamed Shasta Dam—was to be operated "primarily for the improvement of navigation on the Sacramento River . . ., for increasing flood protection in the Sacramento Valley, for salinity control in the Sacramento–San Joaquin Delta, and for storage and stabilization of the water supply of the Sacramento River for irrigation and domestic use, and secondarily for the generation of electric energy and other beneficial uses."[74] Closely following Edward Hyatt's 1931 plan in Bulletin no. 25, the Central Valley Project Act also authorized a dam, reservoir, and power plant at Friant; a canal leading north from Friant Dam to the Chowchilla River, to be known as the Madera Canal; and a canal extending south from Friant Dam to the Kern River near Bakersfield, to be known as the Friant-Kern Canal. To replace some of the flow of the upper San Joaquin River that these canals would siphon away for the development of agriculture, the San Joaquin Pumping System was to deliver substitute water from the Delta to the lower San Joaquin River at Mendota, near the great bend in the river. For the benefit of San Francisco Bay region water users, the act also included the Contra Costa Conduit (see map 13).[75] The act authorized state construction of the project's hydroelectric plants and power transmission lines, a provision bitterly opposed by the powerful Pacific Gas and Electric Company (PG&E), which steadfastly opposed public power. PG&E launched a referendum campaign against the Central Valley Project Act, but in the referendum vote of December 1933 Californians supported the legislation by a count of 459,712 to 426,109, with most of the opposition coming, as expected, from Southern California, which did not stand to benefit directly from the project.[76]

Having legislated the Central Valley Project into existence, California failed to place on sale the bonds necessary to finance it. Beleaguered by the Depression and hopeful of federal aid, the state lobbied the federal government for funding. Congress responded in 1935, including in the River and Harbor Act of that year the initial authorization for Central Valley Project works, to be constructed by the U.S. Army Corps of Engineers under its responsibility for the maintenance and improvement of navigation.[77] Later that year, however, on the recommendation of Secretary of the Interior Harold Ickes, President Franklin Delano Roosevelt approved the Central Valley Project as a federal reclamation project, in effect assuming the entire fiscal responsibility for the project, and exceeding the hopes of most state officials.[78] The River and Harbor Act of 1937 subsequently reauthorized the Central Valley Project for construction by the U.S. Bureau of Reclama-

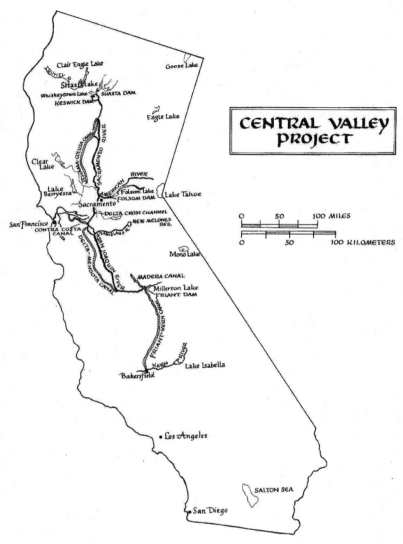

CENTRAL VALLEY
PROJECT

MAP 13. The main features of the Central Valley Project. Note especially the
locations of Shasta Dam, which regulates the flow of the Sacramento River to the
Delta; the Friant-Kern Canal and Madera Canal, which siphon off almost
the complete flow of the San Joaquin River immediately below Friant Dam;
and the Delta-Mendota Canal, which delivers "replacement" water from
the Delta to the lower San Joaquin Valley. Source: Norris Hundley Jr., *The Great
Thirst: Californians and Water, a History,* rev. ed. (Berkeley and Los Angeles:
University of California Press, 2001). Used with permission.

tion (the successor to the Reclamation Service), subject to the Reclamation Act, including the restriction on excess lands.[79] Work on the project began that year. Three years later, the River and Harbor Act of 1940 extended the authorization to include irrigation distribution systems as well.[80]

The Central Valley Project had indeed become a multiple-purpose development, its successive authorizations implicitly acknowledging the interconnectedness of navigation, flood control, irrigation, and reclamation, issues that residents of the Central Valley had attempted to resolve for the better part of a century by local, regional, and finally, statewide planning. Yet in the end, only the federal government possessed the resources and expertise necessary to develop the valley fully.[81]

It seemed as if the project offered something for everyone in the Central Valley, and perhaps it did. But neither the engineers who designed the plan nor the federal officials who oversaw its construction considered the needs of the nonhuman inhabitants of the valley. Conspicuously absent from the project purposes was the protection of fish and wildlife. The Central Valley Project tied together the Sacramento Valley, the Delta, the San Joaquin Basin, and the Tulare Basin both physically and symbolically. The transition to rice culture in the Sacramento Valley had depleted the Sacramento River's inflow to the Delta. When Delta interests fought against the consequent intrusion of salinity, the state launched a series of investigations, the political groundwork for which had long been prepared, which led, ultimately, to the Central Valley Project. That project—so extensive that its initial features were not fully completed until the early 1950s—protected the Delta from salt water, delivered fresh water from the Sacramento Valley across the Delta to the San Joaquin Basin, and exported San Joaquin Basin water to the Tulare Basin.[82] Yet, lacking provisions for fish and wildlife, the project threatened to decimate both the lower San Joaquin River, with its famed salmon runs, and one of the most important wetland areas remaining in the valley, the overflow grasslands of the San Joaquin Basin. Unintended consequences such as these weigh heavily in the story of the Central Valley Project and of California water development as a whole.

Flood control, irrigation, and reclamation exacted a profound cost from the Central Valley's wetlands. By 1939 the valley's 4 million acres of wetlands had been reduced by almost 85 percent to just 619,400 acres.[83] The Sacramento Valley's wetlands had been devastated in the wake of the Sacramento Flood Control Project; the Delta's wetlands had been almost entirely reclaimed by levees; and in the San Joaquin Valley, irrigation canals in the Tulare Basin had eliminated entire lakes as well as the wetlands that surrounded them. In the entire Central Valley, only the Butte Basin in the Sacramento Valley and the overflow grasslands in the San Joaquin Basin remained relatively intact. Throughout the valley, vast wetlands had once provided food and rest for millions of migratory birds arriving from their northern breeding grounds. Yet by the early twentieth century, for the snow geese from the Arctic Archipelago, the ducks from the prairie potholes, and the waterfowl of all kinds from the Yukon-Kuskokwim Delta and from all the rest of the breeding grounds of the Pacific Flyway, wetland habitat in California's Central Valley had become increasingly scarce. Instead of wetlands, agricultural fields now dominated and defined the landscape. But the fortunes of the valley's wetlands were about to change.

PART THREE

The Rise

6

Turning the Tide

Federal and State Responses to the Waterfowl Crisis

By the dawn of the twentieth century, the worsening plight of the country's game birds, including waterfowl, had drawn national attention. California's early attempts to pass more restrictive game laws would be aided by a new federal presence in wildlife protection that would culminate in the Migratory Bird Treaty with Canada in 1916. The discovery of the four migratory flyways during the first decades of the twentieth century, followed by the prolonged drought of the 1930s, would bring together private organizations and state and federal agencies in attempts to protect and restore the most important breeding and wintering grounds for waterfowl. In California, such newly focused attention would lead to the protection of the Central Valley's most endangered wetlands as well as the creation of new federal and state wildlife refuges.

THE MIGRATORY BIRD TREATY

Before the federal government could effectively enter the realm of wildlife protection, a fundamental change in the notion of wildlife ownership would be necessary. During the second half of the nineteenth century, the prevailing legal doctrine in the United States was that the individual states, not the federal government, "owned" the wildlife within their borders. The doctrine of state ownership reached its apogee in the 1896 case of *Geer v. Connecticut,* which upheld the right of the individual states to prohibit the exportation of game taken legally within their borders.[1] States also desired greater authority to restrict the importation of game legally killed in other states, in large part because the presence of imported

game provided a cover for market hunters to continue to deplete local populations.[2] Regulation of the importation of game, however, fell within interstate
commerce, the regulatory province of the federal government. In part to address
this issue of the states' right to restrict the import of game, and thus to inhibit the
activities of market hunters, in 1900 Congress passed the Lacey Act, the first significant federal wildlife law that was national in scope.[3] Named after its author,
Congressman John F. Lacey of Iowa, the act prohibited the transport of any "animals or birds, the importation of which is prohibited" by the states. The Lacey
Act thus brought the weight of the federal government, through its powers over
the regulation of interstate commerce, to the enforcement of state game laws. In
so doing, the act set a precedent for federal involvement in nationwide wildlife
protection.[4]

The Lacey Act prohibited illegal interstate trade in game but still did little to
protect game, including waterfowl, from excessive hunting. Spring shooting, in
particular, was devastating to waterfowl populations, and its deleterious effects
were recognized as early as the 1880s. The killing of one member of a mating pair
in early spring "almost invariably meant one less brood produced before summer."[5] In 1899 drought spread across the breeding grounds in the prairie potholes, exacerbating the demographic effects of uncontrolled spring shooting.
Waterfowl flights plummeted to an all-time low, and drastic steps seemed necessary. In December 1904 Congressman George Shiras III introduced "A Bill to Protect the Migratory Birds of the United States."[6] The legislation asserted that "migratory game birds which do not remain permanently the entire year within the
borders of any State or Territory shall hereafter be deemed to be within the cus-
tody and protection of the Government of the United States." The bill gave the
Department of Agriculture authority for determining and mandating closed
hunting seasons; its decisions would be based on birds' breeding habits and migratory patterns. But despite the Lacey Act's initiation of the federal government
into national wildlife protection, the regulation of hunting had always been a
matter for the individual states, and attitudes in Washington had not yet shifted
sufficiently to accept this leap in the scope of federal regulatory authority.

Nearly a decade later, in 1912, Congressman John W. Weeks and Senator George
P. McLean introduced an expanded version of Shiras's bill that included protection for all species of insectivorous birds and songbirds that migrated across
national and state borders. This more inclusive bill drew wide support, especially
from the U.S. Bureau of Biological Survey, which had been promoting the value
of insectivorous birds as protectors of agriculture.[7] President Taft signed the bill
into law on March 4, 1913, just before leaving office, although he was apparently
unaware of its existence, as it was hidden as a rider on a lengthy agricultural appropriations bill. Taft reportedly regarded the bill as an unconstitutional extension
of federal power.[8] The Weeks-McLean Migratory Bird Act came under heavy

attack, especially by market hunters and advocates of spring shooting. Two federal district courts found the act unconstitutional on the grounds that the states owned the migratory birds found within their borders.[9]

To neutralize the political and judicial opposition to the Migratory Bird Act, Senator Elihu Root, formerly secretary of state under Theodore Roosevelt, introduced a Senate resolution, passed in 1913, authorizing the president to enter into international conventions for the protection of migratory birds. After a delay caused by the outbreak of World War I, President Woodrow Wilson signed the "Convention between the United States and Great Britain [on behalf of Canada] for the Protection of Migratory Birds" in Washington, D.C., on August 16, 1916.[10] The treaty established a closed season on migratory game birds from March 10 to September 1, and on migratory insectivorous birds and other migratory nongame birds year-round; it also prohibited the "taking of nests or eggs of migratory game or insectivorous or nongame birds." Wilson signed the enabling act necessary for the enforcement of the treaty, the Migratory Bird Treaty Act, on July 3, 1918.[11]

Opposition to the treaty remained strong, particularly among market hunters and large duck clubs in the Midwest, especially in Missouri. The matter came to a head when federal game warden Ray P. Holland arrested the attorney general of Missouri, Frank McAllister—a staunch opponent of the Migratory Bird Treaty—for violating the ban on spring shooting. The contest reached the Supreme Court in the landmark case of *Missouri v. Holland*.[12] The decision, delivered by Associate Justice Oliver Wendell Holmes, reaffirmed the constitutionality of the Migratory Bird Treaty and firmly established the federal authority to regulate the hunting of migratory birds. Denying state ownership of such birds, the Court reasoned, "But for the treaty and the [enabling] statute there might soon be no birds for any powers to deal with. We see nothing in the Constitution that compels the government to sit by while a food supply is cut off and the protectors of our forests and our crops are destroyed. It is not sufficient to rely upon the States."[13]

With the Migratory Bird Treaty established as the law of the land, federal officials promulgated regulations that ended the worst abuses against migratory bird populations. The international precedent set by this landmark treaty for the protection of transnational and transcontinental migratory birds would soon extend far beyond the borders of the United States and Canada.[14]

MAPPING THE FLYWAYS

Much as the Migratory Bird Treaty provided protection from indiscriminate killing for waterfowl and other migratory birds, the identification of the four great North American waterfowl flyways—Atlantic, Mississippi, Central, and Pacific—provided the framework necessary for protecting the breeding and wintering habitat on which the waterfowl relied, and finally made it possible to manage

waterfowl populations and wetlands on regional scales. The U.S. Bureau of Biological Survey (USBS) laid the foundation for identifying the flyways during the
early years of the twentieth century. Wells W. Cooke, a USBS biologist described
as the father of bird migration studies in North America, compiled vast amounts
of waterfowl migration and abundance data in his 1906 bulletin, *Distribution
and Migration of North American Ducks, Geese, and Swans.* Cooke wrote of the
principal causes of diminished numbers of waterfowl at that time, citing market
hunting, spring shooting, and, since 1885, the loss of breeding habitat in the prairie pothole region, as millions of acres were converted from wetlands to wheat
fields. Working from field observations, Cooke sketched out with remarkable
accuracy the distribution patterns and travel routes of seventy-one species of
North American waterfowl.[15] Cooke called nationwide attention to California's
particular importance for waterfowl, writing, "One of the principal winter homes
of North American ducks and geese is the State of California, where congregates
during this season the larger part of all the individuals that breed west of the
Rocky Mountains."[16]

The results of bird banding studies soon confirmed and extended Cooke's
work on the existence and location of the flyways. By capturing migrating birds
and placing an identifying band on their bodies, usually on a leg, and then recap-
turing the birds at a later date, it proved possible to identify migration patterns.
Apparently, the first attempt at banding was carried out by naturalist John James
Audubon, who used silver wires to leg-band a brood of phoebes in 1803. But it
was not until the early years of the twentieth century that banding became widespread, with the creation of the American Bird Banding Association in 1909.
With its resources overburdened, the private association turned over its records
to the USBS in 1920, which assumed responsibility for administering the banding program under the leadership of Frederick C. Lincoln. By 1930 the rapid accumulation of banding data had made it possible to map out the breeding and
wintering grounds, along with the complicated series of migration routes that
connected them, of each of the four flyways (see map 14).[17] Banding studies had
made clear the significance of the flyways for the conservation of migratory
birds. In his 1935 report, *The Waterfowl Flyways of North America,* Lincoln wrote,
"Conservationists now know that the birds have a strong attachment for their
ancestral flyways. . . . This fact indicates that if the birds should be exterminated
in any one of the four major flyways now definitely recognized, it would at best
be a long time before that region could be repopulated, even though birds of the
species affected should continue over other flyways to return to their great breeding grounds of the North."[18]

Lincoln carefully distinguished between the terms *migration route* and *flyway*, which in the past had often been used interchangeably. Migration routes
were "the individual lanes of avian travel from breeding grounds to winter quar-

ters." Flyways, in contradistinction, were "those broader areas into which certain migration routes blend or come together in a definite geographical region."[19] The four flyways are not yet well defined in the northern interior breeding grounds, but from approximately 45 degrees of latitude, corresponding to the northernmost tier of the United States, southward to the coast of the Gulf of Mexico, they are well marked. Thus the portion of migratory waterfowl routes that fall within distinct flyways largely coincides with the latitudes of the contiguous United States, and it was there that the first waterfowl refuges were created.

THE REFUGE CONCEPT AND PROTECTION FOR WATERFOWL BREEDING GROUNDS

In 1903 President Theodore Roosevelt established the country's first national wildlife refuge on Florida's Pelican Island to protect the last remaining breeding grounds of the brown pelican along the entire eastern coast of the state. Plume hunters serving the millinery trade had by that time extirpated other species of waterbirds native to Pelican Island, especially egrets and herons, and were then threatening the pelicans as well. Five years later, in 1908, Roosevelt set aside the first refuges specifically for migratory waterfowl, Lower Klamath Lake on the California-Oregon border and Malheur Lake in eastern Oregon. Public and private drainage projects nearly obliterated these refuges during their early years, however, and resuscitation began only decades later.[20] Although additional refuges were created during subsequent years, the real basis for a national system of waterfowl refuges was not established until Congress passed the Migratory Bird Conservation Act, also known as the Norbeck-Andreson Act, in 1929.[21] The Migratory Bird Treaty had established strict limitations on the taking of migratory birds, but it had not authorized acquisition of migratory bird habitat. The Migratory Bird Conservation Act addressed this shortcoming, providing the authority for the systematic acquisition of federal wildlife refuges. With the onset of the Great Depression, however, Congress failed to immediately fund that mandate.

Years of severe and protracted drought then brought the importance of high-quality breeding habitat for migratory waterfowl into sharp focus. The parched years of the 1930s dried up waterfowl nesting grounds, especially those of North America's "duck factory," the prairie pothole region, and caused waterfowl populations across the continent to plummet.[22] In the midst of this unprecedented waterfowl crisis, in January 1934 President Franklin D. Roosevelt created his President's Committee on Wildlife Restoration, appointing three men—Thomas Beck, Jay N. "Ding" Darling, and Aldo Leopold—to devise a wildlife restoration plan that would address habitat shortages for waterfowl while at the same time serving the administration's goal of resolving the national farm crisis brought on by drought and deflationary prices. If submarginal agricultural lands could be

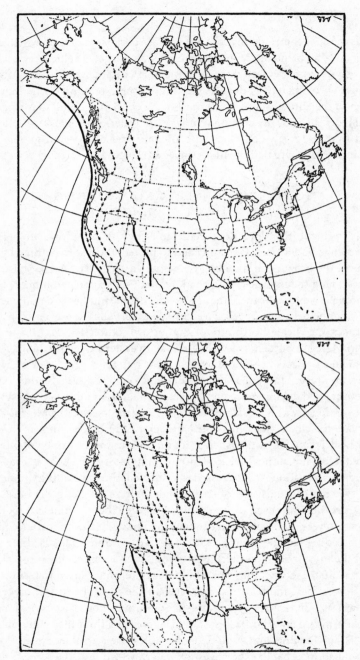

MAP 14. The major migratory routes of the four North American flyways. This page: Pacific Flyway (top), Central Flyway (bottom). Facing page: Mississippi Flyway (top), Atlantic Flyway (bottom).

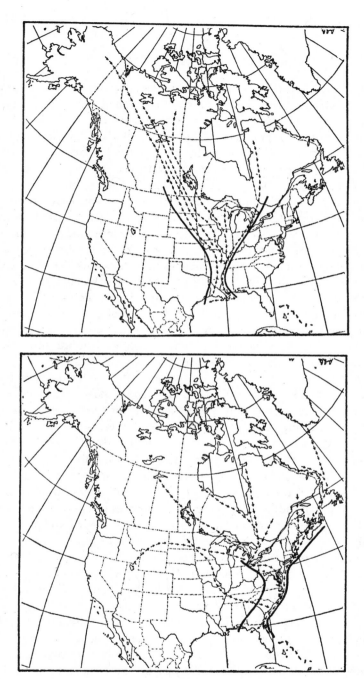

Source: Frederick C. Lincoln, *The Waterfowl Flyways of North America* (Washington, D.C.: U.S. Department of Agriculture, Circular no. 342, 1935).

converted to wildlife refuges, then both wildlife and the nation's farmers would benefit.[23]

The members of the Committee on Wildlife Restoration formed a talented, if eclectic, group. Thomas Beck was editor of *Collier's* magazine, and his conservation qualifications included membership on the Connecticut State Board of Fisheries and Game and the presidency of More Game Birds in America, the forerunner of Ducks Unlimited. Organized by "ardent duck hunters with considerable means" and incorporated in October 1930, More Game Birds was dedicated not simply to the conservation of the remaining game birds on the North American continent, but to applying management techniques directed toward increasing game bird populations.[24] During its decade of existence, More Game Birds published at least twelve books and pamphlets on game birds and game bird breeding, including *More Waterfowl by Assisting Nature* in 1931.[25] This prescient book called for the international management of migratory waterfowl by the United States and Canada; the acquisition of refuges to serve as additional breeding, resting, and wintering grounds along the migratory routes; and the extensive management of these grounds, including the control of water levels to supply food and cover, the control of natural predators where necessary, the restriction of unauthorized grazing, and the cessation of shooting on the breeding grounds.[26] As drought deepened in the early 1930s, More Game Birds lobbied for federal action on behalf of waterfowl. The organization drafted a "Memorandum for Consideration," which Beck presented to Roosevelt. The president responded by establishing the Committee on Wildlife Restoration, appointing Beck as its chairman.[27]

Jay "Ding" Darling and Aldo Leopold brought differing strengths to the committee. Darling, a two-time Pulitzer Prize–winning editorial cartoonist nationally famous for his pro-conservation drawings, was a member of Iowa's Fish and Game Commission and a key organizer, in 1932, of the Iowa Cooperative Wildlife Research Unit, the first such institution for professional wildlife management, research, and administration in the country. He had become an outspoken advocate of game preservation and restoration during the years after World War I, and his artwork had garnered popular support for the Migratory Bird Conservation Act of 1929.[28] Leopold, the only technically trained member of the committee, was a professional forester. Having witnessed firsthand the draining of marshes in the prairie pothole region of the north-central states, he had become convinced that the preservation of habitat was the key to waterfowl's future, and that significant changes in land use philosophy would be required to preserve that habitat.[29] In 1933 Leopold accepted an appointment at the University of Wisconsin to chair the nation's first university program in game management. His text, *Game Management,* published that year, became a classic in the field for its integration of ecological principles and conservation methods.[30]

The Committee on Wildlife Restoration submitted its report to Secretary of Agriculture Henry Wallace in February 1934. The committee proposed the acquisition of 4 million acres, suitable as nesting and breeding grounds, for migratory waterfowl and shorebirds, and more than 12 million acres in total for all kinds of wildlife. Following these recommendations, in March Congress passed the Migratory Bird Hunting Stamp Act. Known informally as the Duck Stamp Act, this measure allocated proceeds from the sale of new federal migratory bird hunting stamps to the acquisition of federal waterfowl refuges under the authority of the Migratory Bird Conservation Act of 1929. Initially priced at one dollar, the stamps were required of each hunter of migratory waterfowl above sixteen years of age.[31] During the 1934–1935 hunting season, more than 635,000 duck stamps were purchased nationwide.[32] Funding was now assured for a new national wildlife refuge program designed largely to benefit migratory waterfowl.

With both an administration and a funding mechanism in place for federal acquisition and protection of wildlife habitat, the one missing ingredient for a comprehensive national policy was federal aid to the *states* for the acquisition, restoration, and maintenance of such habitat. The passage of the Federal Aid in Wildlife Restoration Act, more commonly known as the Pittman-Robertson Act, resolved this deficiency in 1937 and established a formalized cooperative federal and state wildlife program.[33] The program took effect in July 1938, under the administration of Albert M. Day, future director of the U.S. Fish and Wildlife Service. In the first ten years of the program, thirty-eight states either began or completed projects specifically to aid migratory waterfowl. In addition to supporting direct acquisition of refuges, Pittman-Robertson funds have also been directed toward management and research investigations, including surveys, banding, biological studies, and habitat inventory and evaluations.[34]

The passage of the Migratory Bird Conservation Act of 1929, the Migratory Bird Hunting Stamp Act of 1934, and the Pittman-Robertson Act of 1937 demonstrated the federal government's willingness to move beyond the Progressive legislation of the early twentieth century, which had primarily protected waterfowl against unrestrained hunting. This new legislation went further, establishing the ways and means to protect and restore wetland habitat. Such efforts were limited to the United States, however, and most North American waterfowl breed and spend the warmer months of each year in Canada. The plight of Canadian wetlands was yet to be addressed. In 1935 More Game Birds in America carried out the first international wild duck census of the breeding grounds of the prairie potholes and regions to the north. Experimental flights over the marshes of Lake Winnipeg and the Saskatchewan River delta in 1934 had confirmed that it was possible to conduct a waterfowl census from the air, and in remote and sparsely populated northern areas an aerial census was indeed the only practicable method of counting birds. Combining newly developed techniques of aerial survey with traditional ground surveying, in August 1935 More Game Birds tallied 42.7 million ducks, all but 2.2 million of which were in Canada, and an estimated 65 million ducks on the continent as a whole.[35] This first international duck census confirmed the necessity of preserving Canadian breeding grounds if the waterfowl resource were to survive. But there was no extant mechanism by which U.S. public funds could be spent in Canada. To solve this dilemma, Ducks Unlimited, the successor organization to More Game Birds, was created.

While the majority of waterfowl on the North American continent were bred in Canada, the majority of waterfowl hunted each year were in the United States. Therefore, to the members of More Game Birds it seemed appropriate for U.S. sportsmen to bear the brunt of the cost of maintaining the waterfowl supply. To achieve this end, in early 1937 More Game Birds organized two Ducks Unlimited foundations. In the United States, Ducks Unlimited, Inc., was to receive funds contributed by U.S. sportsmen and transfer them to the Canadian foundation, Ducks Unlimited Canada. Through cooperation with provincial and Dominion of Canada officials, Ducks Unlimited's funds would be spent on both the preservation of unspoiled northern breeding grounds and the restoration of degraded breeding grounds farther to the south, especially in the prairie pothole region.[36] Having successfully launched Ducks Unlimited, Inc., and Ducks Unlimited Canada, in 1940 More Game Birds turned over its assets to Ducks Unlimited, Inc., and was absorbed by that organization.

Aided by nature, the Ducks Unlimited foundations achieved considerable success. The effects of habitat restoration, combined with the cessation of drought by the late 1930s, allowed waterfowl populations to rebound. Ducks Unlimited Canada carried out waterfowl censuses from 1938 to 1947, by which time the estimated continental duck population had risen to greater than one hundred million.[37]

THREATS ON THE WINTERING GROUNDS

Efforts by the federal government and the duck hunters and wildlife enthusiasts who founded More Game Birds in America and Ducks Unlimited concentrated primarily on northern breeding grounds and represented a significant advancement in waterfowl and wetland conservation. Yet while the Pacific Flyway's breeding grounds in the Far North have been less disturbed by anthropogenic forces than those of the other flyways, the main problem along the Pacific Flyway was the loss of wintering habitat, particularly in the Central Valley of California.[38] During the 1930s and 1940s it became apparent that in order to protect migratory waterfowl populations, wintering grounds needed to be preserved as well. The wintering grounds provide not only resting habitat for waterfowl, but also the nutrition necessary for waterfowl to return to the breeding grounds in the spring in adequate physical condition to reproduce, and hence maintain species populations. However, on the wintering grounds, which comprise the smallest area occupied by waterfowl at any season, densely concentrated avian populations are most vulnerable to three major threats: overshooting, exposure to disease, and a shortage of food.[39] All of these problems became especially evident in the Central Valley, where few natural wetlands remained.

Despite the prohibitions of the Migratory Bird Treaty, as well as restrictions on hunting methods and the establishment of daily bag limits, the years from the 1930s to the early 1950s witnessed a resurgence of market hunting in the Central Valley. Avian diseases, particularly botulism and cholera, were particularly virulent in the Central Valley during the late 1930s and late 1940s, respectively, and accentuated the need for increased habitat in the Pacific Flyway's most important wintering area. The shortage of food on the wintering grounds, and the intense crop depredations that resulted from it, became a perennial problem in the Central Valley during the middle third of the century, leading, more than any other single factor, to the creation of state and federal refuges to keep birds out of agricultural fields. As market hunting, disease outbreaks, and food shortages afflicted Pacific Flyway waterfowl concurrently on their wintering grounds in the Central Valley, the survival of flyway populations appeared uncertain.

Market Hunting

The eradication of market hunting posed one of the greatest challenges in the multipronged effort to protect wintering waterfowl of the Pacific Flyway. The Migratory Bird Treaty had outlawed the sale of migratory birds throughout the United States, but it proved extremely difficult to enforce its provisions in California's Central Valley, where millions of waterfowl annually gathered on their wintering grounds. Illegal market hunting increased to epidemic proportions in the valley from the 1930s to the early 1950s, largely coinciding with the period of intense crop depredations. There were many reasons, material as well as cultural, why illicit hunting, especially of ducks, was able to proliferate during these years. Falling wages and rising unemployment brought on by the Depression caused some to turn to the underground economy of market hunting. Public support for wildlife protection laws intended to stem such activity was not yet as widespread as it would later become, and many hunters, recalling the days of legal hunting for the market prior to the implementation of the Migratory Bird Treaty, refused to recognize the treaty's authority. There were few game wardens to cover the large wintering areas of the state, and their effectiveness was curtailed by nearly constant surveillance by gangs of market hunters who tracked their every move. Most market hunting occurred under cover of darkness, when it was most difficult to apprehend violators. In the face of serious crop depredations, many farmers allowed, and even encouraged, market hunters to come onto their land. In those instances when lawbreakers were arrested, local courts, not inclined to convict or impose adequate fines on members of the community, often acquitted them.[40]

It was in this context that the U.S. Bureau of Biological Survey established a law enforcement office in Berkeley, California, in 1934. Hugh M. Worcester, who had been serving as reservation protector of the Tule Lake National Wildlife Refuge in the California portion of the Klamath Basin, was recruited to serve as the game management agent in charge of enforcement for this Berkeley office, the jurisdiction of which included all of California and Nevada. At that time, according to Worcester, there were no less than 150 men in the Central Valley actively engaged in the illegal killing and selling of migratory waterfowl on a commercial basis. The majority of these men operated either in the San Joaquin Valley, near the city of Los Banos in the Merced County grasslands, or in the Sacramento Valley. The machinery and methods employed by the market hunters guaranteed the destruction of the largest possible number of ducks. They did not use the ordinary shotguns of legitimate hunters of the day, which by federal law were allowed to hold no more than two shells in the magazine and one in the barrel. Rather, they used a variety of illegal guns and devices, including an extension magazine called a Long Tom that allowed a shotgun to hold nine or thirteen shells, which could all be fired in a few seconds. The hunt itself was known as a drag. Often in teams of three, but sometimes solo, market hunters approached areas where ducks were heavily concentrated during their nocturnal feedings. An initial shot was fired to rouse the birds; then, as they took flight, all the hunters began shooting with their Long Toms, swinging through the flock. Three hunters, using a total of twenty-seven shells, could kill by this method an average of three hundred to four hundred ducks, and cripple and abandon perhaps 20 percent more.[41] Having prearranged the sale of these ducks to restaurants, hotels, and steamship lines in the San Francisco Bay region, as well as additional markets as far away as Los Angeles and Reno, Nevada, the hunters then rapidly transported the dead birds by car, bus, and airplane to these locations. Because the market hunters would have lacked an incentive without the complicity of these willing buyers, the San Francisco Bay region became the third focal point, along with the San Joaquin and Sacramento valleys, of the Biological Survey's investigations.

During the twenty years that Hugh Worcester served as game management agent for the U.S. Biological Survey and its successor, the U.S. Fish and Wildlife Service, he participated in approximately 2,500 cases involving violations of game laws.[42] Two of these cases in particular, the Los Banos Case and the Smith-Zeigler Case, were largely responsible for bringing about the end of illegal market hunting in the San Joaquin Valley and the Sacramento Valley, respectively. The most notorious market hunter in the Los Banos area of the San Joaquin Valley during the 1930s was Howard Blewett, known locally as "Bluejay" Blewett. He hunted primarily in the San Luis Island area of the Merced County grasslands, an area defined by the San Joaquin River on the east and Salt Slough, a channel of the river, on the west. This vast expanse of open overflow country, the future site of a national wildlife refuge, was composed of many depressions containing substantial seasonal ponds that attracted ducks in large numbers. After an undercover operation lasting several months, Worcester and his team of state and federal agents arrested Blewett in December 1935 for the sale of illegally killed wild ducks. Blewett had been arrested for game violations twice before, in 1932 and 1934, but had been acquitted in Los Banos Justice Court for the first violation and fined a modest ten dollars in federal court in Fresno for the second offense. In January 1936 Blewett faced trial for his 1935 arrest, once again in Los Banos Justice Court. Despite the overwhelming evidence that he had illegally sold seventeen wild ducks, representing a minuscule percentage of his annual kill, he was acquitted as before. But the tide of public opinion was changing. Many residents of Los Banos expressed dismay and disappointment over the flagrant miscarriage of justice. A mere three weeks later, Blewett was arrested again, this time for hunting sandhill cranes. For this offense he found himself once again in federal court in Fresno, where, in April 1936, he was sentenced to one and a half years in jail and two years' probation, the heaviest sentence in California history to that date for a game law conviction. With the stern warning it offered to other violators, the Los Banos Case effectively ended illegal market hunting in the region and took on national significance as a turning point in the federal government's efforts to wipe out the market hunting of wild ducks.[43]

The market-hunting situation in the Sacramento Valley proved much more intractable, even as state game wardens and federal agents attempted to disrupt the commercial link between market hunters and their San Francisco Bay Area clients. During the 1940s and early 1950s, market hunters in the vicinity of the city of Gridley, near the Butte Sink, are estimated to have taken more than eighty thousand waterfowl annually. For the Sacramento Valley as a whole, a conservative estimate places the annual figure at more than a quarter of a million birds.[44] The ability of market hunters in the Sacramento Valley to operate with impunity was seriously curtailed, though not entirely eliminated, in the wake of the Smith-Zeigler Case of 1949. Of the nine men arrested and convicted in this extensive operation, the most serious offenders were Donald E. Smith and his partner, Edward L. Zeigler, notorious killers and distributors of wild game. Smith's arrest record for market hunting dated from 1936, and he had served six months in a federal penitentiary in 1948. Zeigler had served two six-month jail sentences, in 1940 and 1945. Following a two-month investigation, both men were arrested in February 1949, and subsequently convicted in federal court in Sacramento. Smith received two and a half years for killing, possessing, transporting, and selling 839 ducks. Zeigler was sentenced to one year for buying, possessing, transporting, and selling 1,016 ducks, the largest number procured to that date by enforcement officers in the western United States. Nevertheless, this number paled in comparison to the fifty thousand ducks that Smith claimed to have killed illegally in his lifetime.[45]

One more large undercover operation, lasting from 1952 to 1954, would still be required to bring about the effective end of market hunting in the Sacramento Valley. During this investigation, federal agents of the Fish and Wildlife Service purchased a total of 4,760 ducks from market hunters in the valley. In March 1954, with cooperation from California Department of Fish and Game officials, the agents arrested seventeen market hunters and five owners and managers of Bay Area establishments. All twenty-two men were convicted. Nine received prison terms, totaling seven years and three months; the remaining men received probation and fines totaling $7,750.[46] After two decades of efforts by the state and federal governments, the era of illegal market hunting in California had effectively come to an end.

Disease

Waterfowl that survived the ravages of market hunting still faced death from avian diseases. Botulism, originally known as alkali poisoning or western duck sickness, has been documented in the western United States since the early 1900s.[47] The first historical record of a substantial die-off caused by botulism occurred in the Bear River marshes, north of Utah's Great Salt Lake, in 1910. Three years later Alexander Wetmore, a young biologist with the U.S. Biological Survey, was assigned to study the cause of widespread duck mortality there. In November 1914 Wetmore visited Tulare Lake in the San Joaquin Valley, where a malady similar to that at the Bear River marshes had been causing massive waterfowl losses for several years. Wetmore's final report, *The Duck Sickness in Utah,* published in 1918, was the federal government's first comprehensive study of disease among waterfowl. Wetmore noted that the losses were almost always associated with declining water levels during the late summer and fall, at which time water temperatures were highest. Although he identified the environment in which disease outbreaks were most likely to occur, Wetmore failed to discover the actual cause of the disease.[48] Western duck sickness was not correctly identified until 1930, by E. R. Kalmbach and others, as a form of botulism, caused by a toxin released by the bacterium *Clostridium botulinum,* type C. The bacterium forms extremely resilient spores that are capable of lying dormant in the soil for years, and then germinating when environmental conditions are appropriate.[49] It proliferates in warm, shallow, stagnant water under anaerobic conditions within dead or decomposing protein-rich organic matter such as vegetation, aquatic insects, and animal carcasses. When waterfowl consume these materials, the toxin from *Clostridium* incapacitates the birds, leading to death: "Birds infected with the disease become weakened in the wing, leg and neck muscles. The inability to fly is ordinarily the first incapacitating symptom, followed by the loss of the ability to walk and the swinging of the head from side to side or back and forth. The nictitating membrane of the eye and in advanced cases the eyelids fail to function and the eyes remain closed and sealed by excretions. The bird finally remains prone and breathing is slow and in gasps."[50]

Avian botulism appears to be endemic to the Central Valley and other wetland regions throughout the world.[51] Because the disease can be spread by the infected bodies of already-dead waterfowl, it proliferates most quickly when large numbers of waterfowl are densely concentrated on limited habitat. The disease struck the Tulare Lake Basin with particular severity following the great flood year of 1937–1938. Record precipitation led to floods that inundated the basin, destroyed its system of levees, and reincarnated Tulare Lake. By the summer of 1938 the lake, which had been dry because of irrigation diversions for at least the past fifteen years, rose to cover 140,000 acres—more than two hundred square miles—and caused crop losses on more than 40,000 of those acres.[52] Reminiscent of former times, the lake once again became a haven for migratory waterfowl. Duck populations peaked that fall at one hundred thousand. As the water slowly receded, either by evaporation or by pumping, temperatures increased in the shallower waters and decomposition of organic matter accelerated, creating an optimal environment for the multiplication of the *Clostridium* bacterium and an outbreak of botulism.[53] An estimated fifteen thousand to twenty thousand ducks perished during the late summer and fall of 1938. Drawn to the resurgent lake, waterfowl nevertheless continued to flock to the Tulare Lake Basin. Numbers peaked annually in late September or early October, reaching 250,000 in the fall of 1939, and 600,000 in the fall of 1940. Exceptionally wet winters in 1940 and 1941 caused further flooding and attracted still greater numbers of waterfowl. Meanwhile, the outbreak raged on, with losses for 1941 estimated at 250,000 ducks out of a peak population of approximately 2 million. Northern pintail and green-winged teal accounted for the greatest share of the mortality, although losses were also high for northern shovelers, mallards, and cinnamon teal.[54]

Environmental conditions at Tulare Lake are particularly well suited for the proliferation of *Clostridium*. The lake's widely fluctuating shorelines historically have advanced and receded according to local flood conditions, creating vast areas of shallow water filled with decaying vegetation. Agricultural practices in the Tulare Lake Basin compounded the problem. During the late summer months following the harvest of the basin's spring planting of cotton, wheat, barley, and other crops, farmers preirrigated their fields for the fall planting. This process involved shallow flooding of the fields to soak the soil and to drive salts below the root zone. The water was allowed to remain standing in the fields for several weeks at a time, which inadvertently re-created the conditions necessary for the spread of botulism. In response to the epidemic in their midst, farmers changed their irrigation practices in 1942, flooding their fields progressively, for only a few days at a time, by breaking restraining levees to allow the water to flow sequentially from one field onto the next. This method prevented water stagnation and limited the decomposition of vegetable matter. As a result, despite peak waterfowl numbers that reached an astonishing 3.5 million in 1942 and 4 million in 1943, the incidence of botulism during those two years was dramatically curtailed.[55] Nevertheless, subsequent flood years have led to additional outbreaks in the Tulare Lake Basin and elsewhere in the Central Valley, repeatedly calling attention to the problems with the concentration of huge numbers of waterfowl on inadequate amounts of habitat.[56]

Unlike avian botulism, which has long affected waterfowl in the Central Valley, avian cholera was not reported in California until January and February 1944, marking the first year that this disease was diagnosed as a cause of mortality in North American waterfowl. Avian cholera has been recognized as a distinct disease for about two hundred years and was first studied in the United States in 1880, but was known to have caused losses only to chickens, turkeys, and domestic geese. In 1944 the bacterial disease appears to have been passed to wild waterfowl in both the Texas Panhandle and California's San Francisco Bay immediately following outbreaks among domestic fowl. Twelve additional outbreaks of avian cholera were reported in California during the 1940s, with losses most heavily concentrated in the Lower Klamath Basin and the Central Valley. The peak season was the winter of 1948–1949, during which an estimated forty thousand waterfowl succumbed.[57] This disease, caused by the bacterium *Pasteurella multocida,* directly attacks internal organs and can cause death in as little as six to twelve hours after exposure. Healthy birds may become infected either through bird-to-bird transmission or from bacteria released into the environment by dead or dying birds. Infected birds that survive initial exposure may carry the disease, complicating efforts to prevent outbreaks. White geese (snow geese and Ross's geese) in particular appear to introduce the disease into the Central Valley on a regular basis; there it affects not only geese but also ducks, American coots, swans, and shorebirds. Mortality in California often begins in mid-November, coinciding with the arrival of white geese, and peaks between December and February. By contrast, mortality from botulism may begin in mid-July, and peaks between August and October.[58] Taking into account both botulism and cholera, migratory waterfowl in the Central Valley are therefore continuously at risk of disease from their arrival in late summer until their departure in late winter. Water levels can be controlled on managed lands to minimize the risk of botulism outbreaks; but overall, the most certain way to protect wintering waterfowl from these diseases has been to reduce their concentration by providing more widely dispersed habitat throughout the valley.

Food Shortages, Crop Depredations, and the First Central Valley Waterfowl Refuges

By the late 1920s California was moving gradually toward accepting state responsibility for providing greater habitat for wildlife. The first state refuge in California designed specifically to protect fish and game was Lake Merritt, in the city of Oakland, created by legislative act in 1870.[59] Yet almost five decades were to pass before the state began an active program of acquiring additional wildlife refuges. In 1917 California set aside sixteen large areas within its national forests as "Big Game Refuges" to protect the state's declining deer herds, but acquisition of habitat for waterfowl lagged behind that for large game animals. In 1927 the legislature replaced a 1907 act that had required licenses for the hunting of game birds and animals with a broader measure that required licenses for game fishes as well and, significantly, provided that for a five-year period beginning in 1928, no less than one-third of all revenue collected under the act was to be expended for "the purchase, lease, or rental" of "game refuges or public shooting grounds, or both," within the state.[60]

At this juncture in California history, a belated recognition of the need to provide winter habitat for waterfowl coincided with an increasingly urgent need to protect crops, especially rice, from waterfowl depredation. The earliest refuges along the Flyway had been established to provide inviolate resting grounds, "sanctuaries where the then diminishing numbers of waterfowl could go to escape gunfire."[61] In the Central Valley, the expansion of agriculture in general, and of rice production in particular, destroyed natural wetland food sources for waterfowl and forced them to turn to whatever food became available. The crop depredations that inevitably followed altered the rationale for refuges from protection *for* waterfowl to protection of farmers' fields *from* waterfowl. Depredation of rice fields by waterfowl had become a problem within a few years of the beginning of commercial rice production in the Central Valley in 1912. With varying degrees of success, rice growers attempted to ward off waterfowl with flares, fireworks, noise bombs, revolving searchlights, carbide guns, and airplanes, but as the acreage planted to rice expanded, the losses continued to mount. An average flock of ducks consumes grain at a rate of one bushel per day for every 125 birds, but the amount of grain damaged or wasted may be more than five times the amount actually eaten.[62] The establishment of refuges specifically as feeding grounds for waterfowl therefore offered the promise of relief for the beleaguered rice growers of the state. Hunting would be prohibited at first on these new refuges, as it had been on the long-established ones, but now the prohibition was intended more to ensure that waterfowl would remain concentrated on the refuges and away from the surrounding fields than to protect their numbers. Given a choice between rice fields where they may be shot, either as part of a hazing process or with lethal intent, and refuge lands with a similarly attractive food supply where they will not be disturbed, waterfowl consistently choose the safer haven.

By the end of 1932, utilizing revenues from hunting license fees, California acquired four state waterfowl refuges: Los Banos in the San Joaquin Valley, Gray Lodge in the Sacramento Valley, Joice Island in Suisun Marsh, and Imperial at the southern end of the Salton Sea, in the extreme southeastern part of the state. All except Joice Island were located in rice-growing areas, and all were sold to the state by local gun clubs, many of whose members were facing economic hardship from the Depression. Los Banos Waterfowl Refuge, purchased in 1929, was the first to be established. Located in Merced County in the heart of the San Joaquin Valley's overflow grasslands, the 3,000-acre refuge was the first parcel in the grasslands to be reserved as public land. In Butte County in the Sacramento Valley, Gray Lodge Waterfowl Refuge, located on the eastern boundary of the Butte Sink, was purchased in 1931 from the Gray Lodge Gun Club. The sixty members of the club (see figure 7)—having suffered the burning down of their gray lodge building and lacking the funds to replace it—sold their 2,540-acre property to the state, thereby allowing for the creation of what would eventually become one of the preeminent waterfowl refuges in the Central Valley.[63] Joice Island Waterfowl Refuge, purchased in 1932, was a natural tidal wetland on the northern shore of Suisun Bay in Solano County. The 1,100-acre refuge provided important habitat for waterfowl and helped hold them in Suisun Marsh, away from the Central Valley, until after the rice harvest.[64] Imperial Waterfowl Refuge, in Imperial County, was also purchased in 1932. Farmers in the Imperial Valley, a rice-growing area from 1927 to 1953, suffered from the same depredation problems as their Central Valley counterparts, and the approximately 1,100 original acres of the refuge were intended as a partial remedy for the problem.[65]

These small and underfunded refuges were scattered like tiny dots in the midst of millions of acres of agricultural fields. Alone, they were inadequate to provide sufficient habitat or food for California's wintering waterfowl. Additional, larger refuges, and the federal funding to purchase them, were urgently needed. Acquisition of these refuges began in 1937, when—under the authority of the Migratory Bird Conservation Act of 1929 and with approximately $155,000 in funds from the Migratory Bird Hunting Stamp Act of 1934—the U.S. Biological Survey purchased a 10,776-acre parcel in Glenn and Colusa counties on the western side of the Sacramento Valley in an open, treeless expanse then known as the Colusa Plains. The USBS had taken advantage of a rare opportunity to purchase a large block of private land, but it was not a natural wetland and therefore was

FIGURE 7. Members of the Gray Lodge Gun Club, circa 1920s. Source: John B. Cowan, *A Jewel in the Pacific Flyway: The Story of Gray Lodge Wildlife Area* (Sacramento: California Waterfowl Association, 2002). Used with permission.

an unlikely site for a waterfowl refuge. Nevertheless, in time it was successfully developed as the Sacramento Migratory Waterfowl Refuge.[66]

The land on the Colusa Plains that became the Sacramento Migratory Waterfowl Refuge, later renamed the Sacramento National Wildlife Refuge, represents a microcosm of the history of the Sacramento Valley and the forces that shaped its development. The refuge land had formed a small part of the territory of the Wintuan-speaking peoples of the western side of the Sacramento Valley.[67] As was the case with Native American peoples throughout the valley, their numbers were decimated by the malaria epidemic of 1833, leaving the region nearly uninhabited. Prior to the influx of population to California during and after the Gold Rush, the region had been largely unexplored by Europeans. The Spanish expended few resources in the exploration of the Sacramento Valley, and only the Argüello-Ordaz expedition of 1821 is known to have reached this stretch of the valley.[68] Early-nineteenth-century fur trappers extensively explored and hunted the Butte Sink across the Sacramento River to the east, but they appear to have spent little time in this section of the Colusa Plains, perhaps because the relatively dry conditions, especially during the summer, did not provide suitable habitat for beaver.

The land remained sparsely settled for decades, and was first used intensively by Norman Dunning Rideout, who purchased it in 1877. Rideout hoped to cash in on the wheat boom that was sweeping the Sacramento Valley in the 1870s and had brought great riches to his neighbor to the north, Dr. Hugh Glenn. In a recapitulation of a common sequence of events, the completion of a rail line along the western side of the Sacramento Valley during the 1870s had provided the impetus for settlement and the expansion of wheat production beyond a relatively narrow strip adjacent to the Sacramento River.[69] Rideout attempted to grow wheat throughout much of the 1880s, but the alkali soil was poorly suited to this crop, and vast numbers of geese destroyed much of the wheat that he did produce, consuming it as green browse when it first sprouted, and then again when it ripened. In the late 1880s Rideout switched to cattle grazing, but the geese devoured his pastures. Resigned, he sold the ranch in 1894, and in 1900 it was sold again to Z. L. Spalding, a member of a wealthy sugar plantation family in the United States' newly acquired territory of Hawaii.[70]

Changes in land use on the Spalding Ranch had profound effects on its utilization by migratory waterfowl. Spalding began to develop artesian wells in 1910, at first growing alfalfa. Beginning about 1915, and paralleling changes in the northern Sacramento Valley as a whole, Spalding began intensive rice farming. He supplemented his water supply with deliveries from the Sacramento Valley Irrigation Company, which was reorganized as the Glenn-Colusa Irrigation District in 1920.[71] The first rice harvest on newly cultivated land on the ranch was always the best, but yields of subsequent crops fell progressively. Despite declining yields, by 1920 Spalding Ranch was the largest agricultural operation in Glenn and Colusa counties, a distinction it was to retain until 1935. The presence of standing water on thousands of acres of rice fields increasingly attracted ducks, which quickly replaced geese as the main depredator in the region.[72]

Hunting patterns changed in turn. The Colusa Plains had become a popular goose-hunting destination, especially for market hunters, upon the opening of the west-side railroad line in the 1870s. Sport hunting became increasingly popular after the turn of the century, particularly after state and federal laws restricted the activities of market hunters. Spalding Ranch offered public access to waterfowling until 1915, after which time hunting was limited to Spalding family members, their guests, and high-level company employees. In 1929, to help offset diminishing revenues from declining rice yields, the Spaldings established a commercial hunting club on the southern half of the ranch, developing ten lakes to attract waterfowl, six on uncultivated lands containing natural depressions, and four on rice fields. Unlike the conditions that prevailed on the ranch in the era before 1915, when public access was unimpeded and free of charge, daily shooting rights were now sold for ten dollars, a prohibitive fee for many would-be hunters. By 1931 the ranch's financial position was becoming precarious, and the entire operation was opened to commercial hunting. A combination of falling prices for rice during the Depression, decreased yields on land that was marginal to begin with, and relatively fixed costs for water from the Glenn-Colusa Irrigation District finally prompted the sale of the ranch to the federal government in January 1937, initiating the era of federal wildlife refuges in the Central Valley.[73]

Development of the Sacramento Migratory Waterfowl Refuge proceeded quickly. Unlike refuges such as Gray Lodge, established by the state, the Sacramento Refuge was able to utilize manpower from the federal Civilian Conservation Corps (CCC), the New Deal program that provided vocational training and work related to conservation for three million men during the Depression.[74] Camp Sacramento was initiated in May 1937. More than 150 CCC workers labored to turn the new refuge into suitable habitat for migratory waterfowl. Initial projects included the remodeling of buildings, removal of cattle fences, construction of boundary fences, repair and construction of dikes and levees, clearing and cleaning of tule-choked channels, excavation of canals, construction of water control structures, planting of trees, and development of lakes and ponds.

The new refuge had the potential to become a biologically diverse wetland ecosystem, but it was clear that a great deal of restoration would be necessary. A biological inventory report completed in June 1937 noted the presence of approximately seventy-five common plants on the refuge, ten of which accounted for 90 percent of the vegetation. Alkali-tolerant plants, such as saltgrass and gum plant, along with foxtail, formed most of the ground cover. Little of this vegetation was useful for waterfowl. The aquatic grass wild millet grew in moist places, and other emergent and moist-soil plants included tule, cattail, smartweed, spike-rush, water plantain, and arrowhead. The floating plant duckweed was present, but the only important submergent plant was sago pondweed. Animal life was depauperate as well. Few nesting ducks were present; these were primarily mallards, northern pintail, and cinnamon teal. Predator species were skewed toward mammals, and winged predators were almost completely absent, except for a few ravens and a pair of bald eagles.[75]

In tension with attempts to establish wetland diversity on the refuge was the need to produce large quantities of a small number of waterfowl crop foods to inhibit depredation on the surrounding rice fields. The local rice crop was most in danger when the fall harvest was delayed by unusually cool weather or early rains. Such a delay, even of only a few weeks, meant that the rice would still be in the fields when the fall flights of ducks arrived from the north. Narrative reports, prepared at first quarterly and later annually by the refuge managers, leave little doubt about the importance of depredation prevention. Peter J. Van Huizen, the refuge's first manager, wrote, "It is highly essential that plenty of food be available on the refuge to hold the ducks here as much as possible. Next year all efforts will be made to raise as much feed as possible. It was hoped that artificial feeding [of bulk grains] could be carried on to avoid crop damage and adverse criticism of the refuge."[76]

In the fall of 1937, in preparation for the refuge's first winter, refuge staff made the first plantings of wheat and barley, a modest 12 and 28 acres, respectively, and collected 1,360 pounds of wild millet seed for planting in the spring. From October to December, a peak number of 36,811 ducks and 72,320 geese descended on the property. The ducks were primarily of six species—northern pintail, mallard, American wigeon, green-winged teal, cinnamon teal, and northern shoveler—with pintail, the most numerous species on the flyway, constituting by far the greatest number. The goose species included snow goose, greater white-fronted goose, Ross's goose, and several subspecies of Canada goose. More than seven hundred tundra swans, then known as whistling swans, were present as well.[77] As impressive as these 1937 figures may have been, they were but a harbinger of the millions of waterfowl that were to winter on the refuge within a decade.

Waterfowl use of the refuge soared in 1938, with peak numbers of 1.2 million ducks and 200,000 geese present in the fall. Van Huizen observed, "These are probably the largest concentrations of ducks seen in this Valley in 20 years." In large part, these numbers reflected the greater availability of waterfowl foods on the refuge, particularly those favored by ducks. Rice and millet had been planted for the first time that year. Nevertheless, the vast numbers of waterfowl easily outstripped the food supply. During three consecutive nights in October, a half-million ducks consumed the refuge's 80 acres of rice and 115 acres of millet in their entirety. Depredation off the refuge was widespread. Van Huizen's comments shed light on the nature of the problem and local reactions to it: "There are some people however who do not complain, but shoot the birds illegally, or invite market hunters to shoot them."[78]

The number of waterfowl food crops available on the refuge continued to increase, with plantings of smartweed, wild oats, and alfalfa added in 1939.[79] In response to the greater availability and variety of food, numbers of waterfowl present on the refuge continued to trend upward, with peak numbers of ducks surpassing two million in 1942.[80] The number of waterfowl that descended on the refuge in 1947, however, dwarfed all previous gains. By the end of July, there were already more than a hundred thousand northern pintail on the refuge. During a normal year, the number at that time might have been five thousand. Van Huizen wrote with amazement, "Nothing like this has ever happened in the history of the refuge. . . . Whatever has happened up North to cause this excessively heavy migration is unknown—whether it is lack of food, drought, or cold weather. Present duck populations would be normal for late October."[81] Peak concentrations were reached on December 24, with 3.36 million ducks and 445,000 geese present on the refuge. Rice and other food crops were inadequate to supply such numbers. Van Huizen predicted great depredation problems on surrounding lands. Writing with a candor that is rarely found in more recent refuge narratives, he lamented the hostility the refuge faced from the local population, as well as "propaganda [that] blamed the refuges for not having any feed, and [that] predicted dire consequences, such as Congressional investigations, abolishment of refuges, and the like. . . . We get the blame when anything goes wrong, but no credit for any relief afforded to the farmers."[82] Van Huizen's forebodings proved premature, however. Heavy supplemental feeding alleviated the situation, and damage from depredation turned out to be not nearly as severe as he had anticipated.

There would be other years of extremely heavy waterfowl use on the refuge, including the banner year of 1954, when more than 3.3 million ducks and geese, combined, wintered on the refuge; but the 1947 total has never been surpassed (see figure 8).[83] Waterfowl concentrations in the Sacramento Valley have since been dispersed by the creation of additional national wildlife refuges and by the eventual development of the state's Gray Lodge refuge, all of which have contributed to reducing the depredation of the valley's rice crop. The Colusa and Sutter national wildlife refuges were established in the Sacramento Valley in 1945, also under authority of the Migratory Bird Conservation Act and with Migratory Bird Hunting Stamp Act funds. These two refuges contain essentially the entirety of extant wetland habitat in the former vast tule marshes of the Colusa and Sutter basins, drained in the early twentieth century as part of the Sacramento Flood Control Project. Their combined area, approximately 3,500 acres initially, was expanded to slightly in excess of 7,000 acres by 1953 with purchases under the newly passed Lea Act.[84]

FIGURE 8. Snow geese at the Sacramento National Wildlife Refuge, with the Sutter Buttes rising in the distance. As a result of the destruction of most of their ancestral natural habitat in the Central Valley, wintering waterfowl have become increasingly dependent on carefully managed public refuges and private duck club lands. Photo by the author.

NEW REFUGES AND NEW HUNTING GROUNDS

The federal Lea Act of 1948 ushered in a new phase in the history of waterfowl refuges in California. It represented the convergence, in federal waterfowl policy, of three interrelated issues, the importance of which was particularly manifest in California.[85] The act's three purposes were "the protection of farmers' crops through the establishment of duck feeding and management areas, the conservation and protection of waterfowl, and the maintenance of a proper balance between hunting and waterfowl conservation."[86] Passed after four years of effort by California congressman Clarence F. Lea, the act authorized the secretary of the interior to purchase or rent up to 20,000 acres of land in California "for the management and control of migratory waterfowl and other wildlife," provided that California first set aside and make available funds for the purchase of equivalent acreage. A joint federal-state program, partnered by the U.S. Fish and Wildlife Service and the California Division of Fish and Game, was quickly established to carry out this provision. Unlike the Pittman-Robertson Act of 1937, which offered federal assistance to the states for the purchase and management of state wildlife areas, the Lea Act provided for the direct federal purchase of national wildlife refuges, and was limited to the state of California.[87]

There is irony in the fact that agricultural development in California has been responsible, in significant measure, for both the destruction and the reestablishment of waterfowl habitat, especially in the Central Valley. Agriculture converted millions of acres of wetlands into irrigated fields, in the process dramatically diminishing natural waterfowl habitat, while at the same time providing an almost unlimited waterfowl food source. Rice acreage, in particular, skyrocketed during and after World War II. In 1946 the total exceeded a quarter of a million acres for the first time. By 1954 rice cultivation reached a peak of 477,000 acres, a figure that would not be exceeded for twenty years.[88] Albert M. Day, director of the Fish and Wildlife Service from 1946 to 1953, evocatively described the situation in the late 1940s:

> I flew over the entire northern Sacramento Valley . . . in the early fall of 1947. The situation from the air was startling. We could see mile after mile of rice fields pointed up by the irrigation ditches and rice checks which wove intricate patterns on the landscape below. But those were privately-owned rice fields. . . . In more than three hours of flying over this whole section, we saw mighty little for the birds. There were two tiny spots of green vegetation on the Colusa and Sutter Federal Refuges, a larger patch as we flew over the Sacramento Refuge, and another small one to the eastward on the state's Grey [sic] Lodge Refuge. Interspersed throughout the general area we spotted a few duck clubs where water had been spread in anticipation of the forthcoming hunting season. These represented the sum total of all the places available for birds in that vast level stretch of productive farm land. Everywhere else ducks were about as welcome as grasshoppers.[89]

The rice industry thus inevitably created the conditions for widespread crop depredation, the solution to which lay in the reestablishment of waterfowl habitat on marginal agricultural lands. This part of California's history represents only one of many of the unexpected consequences that have arisen in the Central Valley as a result of the unrestrained manipulation of nature.[90]

The irony of the waterfowl situation in the Central Valley is compounded by the fact that waterfowl hunting, so prolific during the late nineteenth and early twentieth centuries that it threatened waterfowl populations along the Pacific Flyway, had become so restricted by the mid-twentieth century that the federal government deemed it necessary to provide hunting opportunities on refuges.[91] The Lea Act broke new ground by explicitly exempting lands acquired under its provisions from the prohibition against hunting contained in the Migratory Bird Conservation Act of 1929.[92] The hunting clause of the Lea Act was an answer to the complaints of legitimate hunters, who had been increasingly disenfranchised during the decades preceding the act. Membership in exclusive private hunting clubs was affordable only to the wealthiest hunters. During the 1949–1950 hunting season, all except an estimated 6,000 of approximately 180,000 purchasers of duck stamps in California were "unattached" hunters, those not associated with private hunting clubs.[93] Commercial clubs, such as the one on Spalding Ranch, had blossomed on California waterfowling areas in the late 1920s and 1930s, but their high daily shooting fees were still beyond the financial reach of most hunters with limited means. The creation of inviolate state and federal refuges since 1929 had further restricted hunting opportunities. Hunters could do little to change the situation on private lands, but they increasingly demanded access to the public waterfowl refuges that their hunting license fees, duck stamp purchases, and taxes on arms and ammunition were creating and maintaining. These demands for public access to waterfowling led to a reassessment of the nature and purpose of refuges.

In response to the hunters' protestations, in 1950 the U.S. Fish and Wildlife Service and the California Division of Fish and Game developed a program to provide low-cost hunting opportunities for the general public on California's federal refuges. Having been enlarged with Lea Act funds, the Colusa and Sutter national wildlife refuges were partially opened to hunting in 1950 and 1953, respectively.[94] Public hunting opportunities expanded further in the early 1960s. The Sacramento Valley's fourth national wildlife refuge, Delevan, was established in 1962 on the Colusa Plains a few miles to the south of the Sacramento National Wildlife Refuge, thereby adding almost 5,800 wetland acres to the valley.[95] Delevan was opened to hunting in 1963, the same year that the Sacramento National Wildlife Refuge, after more than twenty-five years as an inviolate sanctuary, opened more than 4,000 acres to sport hunting.[96]

While the Lea Act of 1948 provided a federal response to the multifaceted waterfowl crisis along the Pacific Flyway in California, the Wildlife Conservation Act, passed by the California legislature in 1947, marked the beginning of the state's concerted response to that waterfowl crisis and to the crisis of California wildlife as a whole. The act created the Wildlife Conservation Board to select lands and waters suitable for the preservation, protection, and restoration of wildlife habitat, and to allocate funds for their purchase.[97] The Wildlife Conservation Board's first—and monumental—task was to conduct a survey of all areas of the state, involving all aspects of wildlife and recreation. The board chose Seth Gordon as chief consultant for this far-reaching project. Gordon, who was later appointed director of the California Department of Fish and Game, brought extensive conservation experience to the position from a career that had already spanned more than three decades. After serving since 1913 as a game protector for the state of Pennsylvania, in 1926 Gordon became conservation director of the Izaak Walton League of America, an association founded by anglers in 1922 and dedicated to the preservation of fish and wildlife. Beginning in 1931, Gordon served as president of the American Game Protective Association and then first head of its successor organization, the American Wildlife Institute. In 1936 he returned to Pennsylvania as executive director of the State Game Commission, a position that he held until shortly before beginning his assignment with the Wildlife Conservation Board.[98]

The mandate of the Wildlife Conservation Board represented a significant expansion of state responsibility for waterfowl management. Early in its deliberations, the board recognized the waterfowl crisis as the most urgent of the state's wildlife problems, and in 1948 it ordered a survey of the state's waterfowl areas to determine the requirements for waterfowl management in California and to propose specific projects to meet those requirements. Everett E. Horn of the U.S. Fish and Wildlife Service and Roland E. Curtis of the California Division of Fish and Game carried out the waterfowl survey.[99]

The final results of Horn and Curtis's study were presented in Gordon's *California's Fish and Game Program: Report to the Wildlife Conservation Board* in 1950. This document is perhaps the single best statement of the rationale for the preservation of waterfowl and wetland habitat in California, as well as a blueprint for the conservation gains that would be achieved in the Central Valley during the second half of the twentieth century. The report confirmed that California constitutes the principal wintering ground for the ducks and geese of the Pacific Flyway, and stated simply and eloquently,

> The breeding grounds of the Pacific Flyway waterfowl, in Alaska and Canada, have suffered less from man's interference than those of the other major flyways. Extensive restoration of breeding grounds in Canada, through the efforts of the Canadian Government, Ducks Unlimited, and nature itself, has resulted in a breeding territory far greater than the area available as wintering grounds for these birds. Wintering grounds and breeding grounds are *sadly out of balance,* and the greatest need at the present time is to bring the wintering areas to a point where they are more nearly in line with the breeding potential.[100]

The Sacramento and San Joaquin valleys and the Suisun Bay–Delta region were those portions of the state in greatest need of additional areas for wintering waterfowl. The refuge shortage was particularly acute in the grasslands of the San Joaquin Valley, which contained "the principal remaining waterfowl areas" in that valley. To address the deficiency of protected waterfowl habitat, the report recommended the acquisition of 26,703 acres by the federal government, 18,343 of which would be in the Central Valley, and the acquisition of 40,240 acres by the state, 19,460 of which would be in the Central Valley and 8,600 of which would be in Suisun Marsh. The proposed allocation for the state acquisitions was more than $4 million.[101]

The refuge acquisition plan was ambitious, and was to be only partially realized at first. In 1951 the U.S. Fish and Wildlife Service utilized Lea Act funds to establish the 2,561-acre Merced National Wildlife Refuge in the San Joaquin Valley, approximately fifteen miles to the northeast of the Los Banos Waterfowl Refuge.

The Merced National Wildlife Refuge, the second refuge to be created in the grasslands, protected habitat especially important for geese and sandhill cranes.[102] Approximately 1,000 acres of this new refuge were opened to hunting upon its creation. For California's part, Wildlife Conservation Board funds made it possible for the Division of Fish and Game—restructured as the Department of Fish and Game in 1951—to acquire private land for three new protected areas: the 8,600-acre Grizzly Island Waterfowl Management Area, created in Suisun Marsh in 1950; the 8,500-acre Mendota Waterfowl Management Area, created in the San Joaquin Valley, near the great bend of the San Joaquin River, in 1954; and the 5,600-acre Wister Unit, created in the Imperial Valley as an addition to the Imperial Waterfowl Management Area, also in 1954.[103] The designation as *waterfowl management areas,* rather than the older term *waterfowl refuges,* reflected the noninviolate status of the new state waterfowl areas.

In what would prove to be one of the Wildlife Conservation Board's most important purchases, a plan to enlarge the Gray Lodge Waterfowl Refuge was approved in 1952, with crucial support from the U.S. Fish and Wildlife Service and the California Department of Fish and Game under its new director, Seth Gordon. Acquisitions began that year, and by 1955 a dozen adjoining farms and gun clubs, encompassing 4,160 acres, were added to the refuge, which now totaled approximately 6,700 acres.[104] Hunting was first allowed on portions of the refuge in 1953, and in 1955 its name was correspondingly changed to the Gray Lodge Waterfowl Management Area. Fifteen years later, in 1970, Gray Lodge's name changed again to the Gray Lodge Wildlife Area, this time in recognition of the expansion of state responsibility from protecting waterfowl specifically to protecting all wildlife.[105]

John Cowan, who had taken the reins as refuge manager in November 1947, oversaw the management and maturation of Gray Lodge until 1980. Following expansion, under Cowan's leadership Gray Lodge entered a period of intensive development. The refuge's lands contained three main soil types—loam, adobe, and alkali—and each type was managed intensively for waterfowl and other migratory waterbirds. Loam soils, which hold moisture well and drain adequately, were the sites of most of the refuge's dryland crops, including wheat and barley. Planted in the fall, these crops were sprouting to three or four inches in height when the birds arrived from the north. They provided grazing for geese, American wigeon, and American coots.

Adobe soils, which have high clay content and are usually underlain by a nearly impermeable hardpan layer, served best for marshlands and were well suited for the growth of millet, a favorite duck food. At first, the expanded refuge grew rice as well, in large part because the local farmers believed that rice would better attract waterfowl to the refuge and away from their fields. But millet, which grew as a weed in rice fields, possesses several advantages over rice. It is less expensive, requires less field preparation, matures in about 70 days as compared to up to 160 days (at that time) for rice, and will come up voluntarily in a field after flooding for two to three years before reseeding is necessary.[106] Ducks appear to like millet and rice equally, so after five years the decision was made to cease the production of rice in favor of millet.

Finally, alkali soils, high in mineral salts, composed the smallest portion of the refuge. They were managed for the development of shallow ponds favored by many species of shorebirds, including black-necked stilts, dunlins, dowitchers, yellowlegs, and American avocets. In addition to optimizing the use of its soils for the greatest benefit to waterbirds, Gray Lodge provided milo, a grain sorghum resembling millet, to draw blackbirds and European starlings, significant depredators of ripening rice, away from the rice fields.[107]

STUDIES OF FOOD HABITS

The decisions made at Gray Lodge, the Sacramento National Wildlife Refuge, and other refuges in the Central Valley concerning the most appropriate waterfowl foods to grow, and the ratios in which to grow them, were based in part on trial and error, but mostly they were the result of a long history of waterfowl food habits studies for the birds of the North American flyways that dated back to the beginning of the twentieth century. The U.S. Biological Survey began compiling records of stomach analyses of wild ducks in 1901. Of the many federal biologists who studied waterfowl plant foods and other plants useful to waterfowl, the preeminent researcher was Waldo L. McAtee. Assigned to head the Biological Survey's new Division of Food Habits Research in 1916, McAtee wrote more than a thousand technical publications during his career, and for five years served as editor of *Wildlife Review,* the first sustained periodical to summarize the latest wildlife literature.[108] McAtee's 1939 book, *Wildfowl Food Plants: Their Value, Propagation, and Management,* was a seminal study that marked the first major work on that broad subject in North America.[109] The information on waterfowl food habits and plant propagation published by McAtee and his colleagues was essential to the intensive management of waterfowl on federal and state refuges as well as on private duck clubs.[110] Armed with knowledge of the importance of various aquatic plants to waterfowl, biologists were able to assess the value of marshes for waterfowl and to develop them for optimal use.[111]

Food habits studies intended to aid wetland management proliferated during the depredation-plagued decade of the 1950s. Much of the work in California was carried out by the state Department of Fish and Game with funding from the Pittman-Robertson Act. One of the most exhaustive of the studies involved examining the stomach contents of thousands of waterfowl in California's five major waterfowl areas: the Klamath Basin, the Sacramento Valley, Suisun Marsh, the San Joaquin Valley, and the Imperial Valley.[112] From 1953 to 1959, the project was under the leadership of Department of Fish and Game biologist Howard R. Leach, who performed or supervised the microscopic analysis of 9,562 duck gizzards, of which 8,457 were taken from six species of dabbling ducks (northern pintail, mallard, green-winged teal, gadwall, American wigeon, and northern shoveler) and 1,105 from three species of diving ducks (ruddy duck, redhead, and canvasback). The voluminous data, which documents well over one hundred separate animal and plant food items, point to a tremendous diversity in the diet of waterfowl, and a distinct difference in the dietary preferences of individual species. Animal matter included aquatic invertebrates such as insects, mollusks, and crustaceans. Seeds from aquatic plants, especially bulrush, smartweed, pondweed, millet, sprangletop, spikerush, and arrowhead, accounted for a significant portion of the ducks' diet in the Sacramento Valley and San Joaquin Valley study areas. In the brackish Suisun Marsh, plant species of greatest importance included alkali bulrush, saltbush, pickleweed, several species of dock, saltgrass, brass buttons, and rabbitsfoot grass. In addition to these natural foods, Central Valley ducks consumed a variety of cultivated crops, including rice, oats, barley, alfalfa, milo, wheat, and, in the Suisun Marsh, corn. Ducks had adapted to these foods as the valley was converted to agriculture, but by the 1950s they were able to find them growing on refuges as well, a result of the valleywide effort to limit depredations.[113]

Studies of food habits identified plants consumed by waterfowl, and clearly demonstrated the effectiveness of growing them on refuges and private duck clubs statewide. However, more recent research has conclusively demonstrated that these studies cannot be used to assess fully the overall waterfowl diet, as they significantly underestimate the consumption of invertebrate animal matter. The problem lies in the use of gizzard contents to draw conclusions about diet. The gizzard—the hard, muscular part of a bird's stomach—is where food is ground, often with the aid of grit swallowed by the bird. Since birds do not have teeth, this operation is analogous to chewing in mammals. Soft foods, such as invertebrates, are broken down into unidentifiable form within minutes of consumption, while hard seeds are retained for days. Therefore, studies that used gizzard contents significantly underestimated the importance of animal protein in birds' diets, probably accounting for the failure of most early studies to document the importance of invertebrate foods to wintering waterfowl.[114] More recent studies are based on esophageal contents taken from birds that are actively feeding, and have shown that during late winter, prior to the birds' northward migration to the breeding grounds, aquatic invertebrates may form in excess of 65 percent of the diet of northern pintail in the Sacramento Valley.[115] Similar results have been documented for pintail and other duck species in the San Joaquin Valley as well.[116] These studies, which utilize bioenergetic models, have shown that dietary protein acquired from increased consumption of invertebrates in late winter provides essential amino acids and may contribute to an increase in body weight and the rapid growth of reproductive organs, so it may directly affect reproductive performance. The degree of biological diversity in Central Valley wetlands, and in particular the presence of wetland plants that harbor invertebrates, therefore appears to have repercussions for recruitment of future generations of Pacific Flyway waterfowl. The management of artificially created refuge wetlands, and of privately held wetlands that have seen severe hydrological alterations, becomes ever more complex as attempts are made to re-create the kind of biological diversity that was once present in the Central Valley's primeval wetlands.

THE LIMITS OF PROTECTION

By the mid-1950s, the main outlines for flyway management on a continental scale were largely in place, and separate flyway councils had been established to manage the Pacific, Central, Mississippi, and Atlantic flyways.[117] The numerous perils facing migratory waterfowl had revealed the importance of the proper management and protection of wetlands. From providing appropriate food sources on individual wetlands, such as those within the patchwork of new refuges in the Central Valley, to preventing the destruction of wetlands across entire ecosystems, such as those within the transnational prairie potholes, advances in wetland protection and management during the first half of the twentieth century had been substantial. These new approaches represented significant progress from the prevailing nineteenth-century belief that wetlands were no more than an obstacle to the progress of civilization, the best use of which was drainage and conversion to productive agriculture. Yet—as the battles against market hunting, disease, and crop depredation make clear—during the mid-twentieth century wetlands were valued most for the habitat they provided for migratory waterfowl, rather than for the preservation of biodiversity of all wetland-dependent organisms or for the ecological services that they provide. The scientific study of wetlands as ecosystems was still in its infancy, and few conservationists or ecologists had arrived at a more holistic view of this resource.

The protections offered to wetlands, even within this restricted understanding of their importance, were not absolute. As a further irony in California's wetland history, while the state and federal governments were creating *public* wetland refuges for waterfowl up and down the Central Valley, they were also launching the Central Valley Project, which would dam the San Joaquin River and threaten to extirpate the *privately* held overflow grasslands of the San Joaquin Basin and to displace the millions of waterfowl dependent on them. The battle to save these grasslands, waged during the 1940s and early 1950s, altered the trajectory of California water planning and development and resulted in the protection of the largest remaining wetland area in the Central Valley. The San Joaquin River itself would not be so fortunate.

7

Battles for the Grasslands
and the San Joaquin River

Henry Miller and Charles Lux, the most powerful landowners in the San Joaquin Basin during the late nineteenth century, had carefully cultivated the development and protection of their water rights along the San Joaquin River.[1] The fact that they did so would have tremendous repercussions for the basin's wetlands long after the death of the partners. Beginning about 1925, duck clubs and cattle interests purchased 98,234 acres of the struggling company's grassland properties in the San Joaquin Basin (see chapter 3). The two groups of new owners coexisted symbiotically; the cattlemen leased shooting privileges to the duck clubs, and the duck clubs leased grazing privileges to the cattlemen.[2] However, in almost every purchase deed, the firm of Miller and Lux retained title to the riparian and appropriative water rights for these lands, reserving in the deeds the right to use the water on the lands "until such time as it could be diverted to other lands of higher agricultural productivity or disposed of otherwise."[3] In this way, Miller and Lux protected its water rights from loss by nonuse and left open the possibility of a future disposition of those rights. After the declining firm sold its cattle herds to a subsidiary of Swift and Company, a leading Chicago meatpacking enterprise, in 1930, no longer needed water to flood its irrigated pastures, and its economic calculus changed.[4] Because appropriative water rights depended on "beneficial use" under California's *Civil Code,* Miller and Lux now faced the prospect of the forfeiture of those water rights.[5] Furthermore, because riparian rights were attached to the land by law, Miller and Lux's claim to have reserved those rights upon the sale of its riparian lands was dubious. Thus, for several reasons, the firm needed to sell its water rights before it lost them. It was soon presented with a historic opportunity to do so.

The Central Valley Project planned the construction of a dam and reservoir on the San Joaquin River at Friant, and the consequent diversion of the river's flow from the dam to agricultural lands in Madera County to the north and in Tulare and Kern counties to the south. Before the project could proceed, it was necessary for the government to acquire water rights along the stretch of the San Joaquin River below the dam that was to be dewatered by the diversions. Miller and Lux was the primary holder of those rights. The firm entered into negotiations with the Bureau of Reclamation, the federal agency that would build Friant Dam, to sell its "excess" waters that flooded its "uncontrolled," or undeveloped, overflow lands along the San Joaquin River. On July 27, 1939, Miller and Lux entered into a purchase contract with the Bureau of Reclamation by which it sold its so-called Grassrights, or overflow water rights, to more than a quarter-million acres of land, including the 98,234 acres of "uncontrolled" lands in the grasslands, for $2.45 million.[6] The "uncontrolled" lands were those that were irrigated by the natural seasonal overflow of the San Joaquin River, as distinguished from croplands and "controlled" grasslands, which were maintained by developed sloughs and canals.[7] On the same date, Miller and Lux also entered into a "Contract for Exchange of Waters" with the bureau to provide substitute water for its croplands and "controlled," or developed, grasslands.[8] This contract guaranteed a flow schedule from the new reservoir at Friant, as well as the provision of replacement water originating from the Sacramento River. This replacement water would be delivered via the Delta to the San Joaquin River at the river's great bend at Mendota, by the Central Valley Project's planned Delta-Mendota Canal. Providing for the upstream diversion of the San Joaquin River and the downstream replacement of a portion of that water from the Sacramento River, the purchase and exchange contracts between Miller and Lux and the Bureau of Reclamation "represent the very essence" of the Central Valley Project.[9]

These contracts opened a new chapter in the history of the San Joaquin Basin's overflow grasslands, where seasonal wetlands had continued to support millions of wintering waterfowl during the long dominion of Miller and Lux. As the San Joaquin Basin was drawn into California's modern era of government-orchestrated, large-scale water development, its wetlands faced unprecedented threats. The construction of Friant Dam and the sale and exchange of water rights threatened to desiccate the region's natural overflow lands and thus extirpate this winter paradise for waterfowl. Although Miller and Lux agreed to continue to provide free water to the uncontrolled grasslands until September 1944, the year in which the San Joaquin River would first be impounded in Millerton Lake behind Friant Dam, the duck clubs and cattle companies of the grasslands now faced the impending loss of their water supply. These grassland interests quickly organized and began a fifteen-year struggle to secure a permanent water supply for their lands. What exactly were they trying to protect?

THE GRASSLANDS AND THE SAN JOAQUIN RIVER

THE ECOLOGY OF THE GRASSLANDS

In the lower San Joaquin Valley, the term *grasslands* has several overlapping meanings. In its largest sense, the lowercase *grasslands* refers to well over 200,000 acres of the "flat, monotonous, grassy floor of the lower San Joaquin Valley" that lie on both sides of the San Joaquin River in Fresno, Merced, and Stanislaus counties.[10] The bulk of this 200,000-acre area lies in a floodplain on the western side of the river, and is centered in Merced County. This region lies downstream from the great bend in the San Joaquin River at Mendota, where the river's course changes from west to north, and stretches for about sixty miles from Dos Palos in the south to Gustine in the north. The city of Los Banos lies approximately in the center. Within this part of the grasslands, Miller and Lux sold the federal government its water rights to the 98,234 "uncontrolled" acres. By mid-century, this portion of the larger surrounding grasslands was commonly distinguished by the capitalized term *Grasslands* (see map 15).[11]

At first glance the Grasslands appear flat, but a closer inspection of the region's microtopography reveals both knolls and swales, each containing a distinctive pattern of vegetation. The knolls are sandy, have high concentrations of salts, and support saltgrass, alkali heath, gum plant, iodine bush, and spikerush. The swales, which are subject to inundation, are less heavily vegetated than the knolls, and, when dry, may contain surface deposits of white or black alkali salts. Crabgrass, rushes, joint grass, and filaree are present among the sparse cover. In general, the soils of the Grasslands are saline and high in alkali, especially toward the south, and contain a high percentage of clay, which causes them to drain poorly. For these reasons, the Grasslands have never been well suited for agriculture, and the majority of the region is classified as "non-tillable cropland."[12]

Because of its unsuitability for conversion to agriculture, the Grasslands have historically provided prime waterfowl habitat, sustained by both natural events and human manipulations. Each winter and spring the wetlands in the Grasslands were renewed, first by seasonal rains and then by the San Joaquin River, which, swollen with snowmelt, rose and overflowed its banks, inundating its floodplain. This seasonal water provided habitat for both migratory and resident species of waterfowl and shorebirds. However, because the natural permanent and intermittent ponds and marshes of the Grasslands are often quite shallow, they are subject to desiccation during the long, hot, dry San Joaquin Valley summer. The permanent water areas shrink considerably in size during this time, while the seasonal water areas usually dry completely and support only scrub vegetation or turn into barren alkali mudflats. This natural seasonal pattern was first altered during the nineteenth century by the enterprises of Henry Miller and Charles Lux.

As early as the 1870s, Miller and Lux had introduced the practice of fall flood irrigation, which nurtured winter grasses for their cattle and, at the same time,

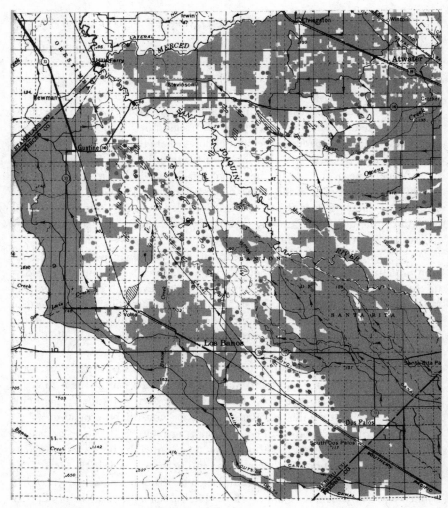

MAP 15. Land use map of western Merced County, 1957–58. The shaded areas represent croplands and unshaded areas represent the Grasslands, which often served dual purposes as cattle ranches and duck hunting clubs. Small dots represent individual duck clubs. Note the concentrations of clubs north and south of Los Banos, as well as to the east of the San Joaquin River. Courtesy of the California Department of Water Resources, Division of Resources Planning.

FIGURE 9. Flooded grassland. This photograph, taken in late August 1958, on flooded duck club lands, illustrates the marshy conditions and excellent waterfowl habitat in the Grasslands that is created by controlled flooding in the late summer and fall, and then sustained by seasonal rains until the spring. Photo courtesy of Howard R. Leach, California Department of Fish and Game, retired.

attracted millions of migratory waterfowl arriving from the north. Most of this fall water, except that which was lost by seepage, transpiration, and evaporation, ultimately flowed into the nearby permanent and seasonal ponds and marshes.[13] The duck clubs that purchased these lands in the 1920s and 1930s continued the practice of fall flood irrigation (see figure 9), maintaining the annual cycle that made the Grasslands a haven for waterfowl.[14] In early August and September, the duck club owners began to "flood their lands with water in preparation for the arrival of the migratory waterfowl. These ponded areas at first give the appearance of discontinuous man-made impoundments; but once the full delivery of water is made and the fall rains fill the swales, sloughs, and overflow lands, the whole area takes on the appearance of a vast, marshy inland sea."[15]

The northern pintail is the first of the migratory birds to arrive in the Grasslands, appearing in late July or early August and often reaching a concentration of fifty thousand by the end of August. Occasionally the pintail are accompanied by a vanguard of green-winged teal, long before the rest of that population arrives in October and November. Mallards increase noticeably in September and October, followed by the remainder of the duck species and the geese. White-fronted

FIGURE 10. Dry grassland. This photograph, taken in 1958, illustrates the typical condition of the Grasslands during the late spring and early summer months. Photo courtesy of Howard R. Leach, California Department of Fish and Game, retired.

geese arrive in October, followed by snow, Ross's, Canada, and cackling geese. Numerous other species of migratory birds accompany the waterfowl, including thousands of sandhill cranes and hundreds of thousands of shorebirds, such as sandpipers, phalaropes, long-billed dowitchers, greater yellowlegs, and common snipe, as well as terns, common moorhens, and American coots. With the arrival of spring, the waterfowl and shorebirds depart from the Grasslands, and by late April all but the resident birds are en route to the Pacific Flyway breeding grounds to the north. As most of the ponded areas evaporate, the Grasslands once again take on their summer visage of dry alkali mudflats and salt-tolerant vegetation (see figure 10).[16]

THE BATTLE FOR GRASSLANDS WATER: AN UNUSUAL ALLIANCE

In early March 1939, a few months prior to the sale of Miller and Lux's water rights to the U.S. Bureau of Reclamation, representatives of the Grasslands owners arranged to meet with Harold Ickes, secretary of the interior, and John Page, U.S. commissioner of reclamation, in Fresno to discuss the impending water crisis. Ickes and Page advised the Grasslands owners to form some type of public

FIGURE 11. Al Jessen, president
of the Grass Lands Association
and its successor, the Grass
Lands Water Association, on a
good hunting day. Courtesy of
the J. Martin Winton Special
Collection on Water Use and
Land Development, San Joaquin
College of Law, Clovis,
California.

body for the purpose of applying for water from the Bureau of Reclamation, suggesting that such provision would need to be included in the Central Valley Project plan if they hoped to acquire water subsequent to the completion of Friant
Dam. Responding to this advice, representatives of the various duck clubs and
cattle-ranching interests in the Grasslands met at the California Hotel in Fresno
on March 15 and voted to create the San Joaquin Grass Lands Mutual Water Users
Association, the name of which was quickly shortened to the Grass Lands
Association.[17]

The officers and board of directors of this new organization were men of influence in the Grasslands and surrounding communities. Most were duck hunters.
Al Jessen, president of the Security First National Bank in Fresno, became president of the association (see figure 11). Henry Wolfsen, a prominent cattleman
from Dos Palos, assumed the office of vice president. George Fink, a banker from

the small town of Crow's Landing and president of the Gustine Gun Club since
its founding in 1926, joined the board of directors. Fink had long been a propo-
nent of waterfowl habitat protection, and had attended the founding meeting of
Ducks Unlimited in Chicago in 1937.[18] Claude Rowe, an attorney for the City of
Fresno, joined the board and served as counsel for the association. Rowe was a
member of the national board of directors for the Izaak Walton League and a director of the Fresno County Sportsmen's Association. During the next decade and
a half, he would file several important federal lawsuits on behalf of the Grasslands
as well as for the preservation of the San Joaquin River.

From 1939 to 1944, the Grass Lands Association delivered water to its members through the canal system of Miller and Lux's old San Joaquin & Kings River
Canal and Irrigation Company, but made little progress toward securing a long-
term water supply. The duck clubs received free water for flooding the land during the fall and winter waterfowl season, but the Grass Lands Association splin-
tered over the high cost of spring and summer water to flood native pasture for
cattle. The San Joaquin & Kings River Canal and Irrigation Company proposed
delivering spring and summer water at the Class I rate—the rate for agricultural
water, the supply of which is guaranteed—of $3.50 per acre-foot.[19] The cattle in-
terests withdrew from the Grass Lands Association over this inequality in the
cost of water, and interest in the organization waned.[20]

In 1944, as the deadline for the cutoff of Grasslands water from Miller and Lux
approached, cattleman Henry Wolfsen launched an initiative on behalf of the
cattle interests that ultimately rejuvenated the Grasslands coalition. In May of
that year, Wolfsen wrote to Charles Carey, regional director of the Bureau of Reclamation, in an attempt to negotiate a temporary water supply. After meeting with
fifty to sixty cattlemen in Los Banos, Carey agreed to the release of 35,000 acre-
feet from Friant Dam's Millerton Lake for use on 90,000 acres of the Grasslands
for the remainder of that year. The water would irrigate pasture for livestock, and
would benefit the duck clubs as well. The livestock interests then formed the
Cattlemen's Water Committee and solicited the support of the local sportsmen,
both to raise funds from the Grasslands duck clubs to assist in the purchase of
the water and to develop a united front for future negotiations. As a direct result
of this outreach, during the summer of 1944 the Cattlemen's Water Committee
merged with two sportsmen's groups, the Gustine Conservation Association and
the remnant Grass Lands Association, to form the Grass Lands Water Association, Inc., a mutual water company, and in the process reestablished the alliance
between the duck clubs and the cattle interests.[21] The executives and board members of the new organization were familiar: Al Jessen, president; Henry Wolfsen,
vice president; George W. Fink, treasurer; Claude Rowe, board member. At the
association's first meeting on August 2, 1944, the board passed a resolution "to
immediately enter into negotiations for the purchase of sufficient water . . . from

the Bureau of Reclamation . . . for years subsequent to 1944."[22] By late 1944 the Grass Lands Water Association encompassed more than 62,000 acres and represented more than five thousand individuals.[23]

The members of the Grass Lands Water Association were initially hopeful that they would be able to negotiate a water contract with the Bureau of Reclamation that would be acceptable to the bureau as part of its overall plan for the Central Valley Project. The hope for negotiation and accommodation resulted from a number of statements written by Charles Carey during the fall of 1944, suggesting that the bureau would be able to provide water to the Grasslands in the future, either by releases from Friant Dam or by delivery from the Sacramento–San Joaquin Delta.[24] Unfortunately for the Grasslands interests, Carey died during the summer of 1945 and was replaced as the bureau's regional director by Richard Boke, who would take a much less sympathetic stance toward providing water for the Grasslands.[25]

Throughout the remainder of the 1940s, the Grass Lands Water Association, with support from the U.S. Fish and Wildlife Service, attempted to negotiate a permanent settlement with the Bureau of Reclamation. Although both agencies were housed within the U.S. Department of the Interior, the Fish and Wildlife Service often found its conservation mission to be at odds with the bureau's reclamation mission. In June 1945 the service's director, Ira Gabrielson, wrote a memo to the bureau's commissioner, Harry Bashore, in which he recommended that the Grasslands receive 100,000 acre-feet of water annually and urged that "the grasslands area must be preserved or the migratory waterfowl of the Pacific Flyway, a national resource, will suffer seriously."[26] Yet neither the association's lobbying effort nor support from the Fish and Wildlife Service was adequate to secure a permanent contract from the bureau. Anticipating a time when the full supply of the Central Valley Project's water would be required on agricultural lands elsewhere, the bureau was willing to negotiate only annual contracts for releases from Friant Dam, leaving the Grasslands interests in a continual state of uncertainty about their economic future and the fate of the region's wildlife.

By 1947, its efforts to negotiate with the bureau still fruitless, the Grass Lands Water Association prepared to use the courts.[27] In October 1947 Claude Rowe filed the suit *Hollister Land and Cattle Company and Yellowjacket Cattle Company v. Julius A. Krug et al.* in U.S. District Court.[28] In addition to Secretary of the Interior Julius A. Krug, Bureau of Reclamation commissioner Michael W. Straus, and the bureau's regional director Richard Boke, Rowe's complaint in the Hollister suit named as defendants the Madera Irrigation District and the San Joaquin Municipal Utility District, each of which had contracted with the bureau for San Joaquin River water from Friant Dam. The plaintiffs—the Hollister Land and Cattle Company and the Yellowjacket Cattle Company—were both located within the boundaries of the Grass Lands Water Association, and both were owners of lands riparian to the San Joaquin River. Rowe argued that the plaintiffs and their predecessors in title had "reasonably and beneficially" used San Joaquin River water for more than sixty years for domestic use, drinking water for cattle, and the irrigation of pasture. Rowe contended that Julius Krug and the other federal officials had illegally, and in excess of the authority of their respective offices, constructed Friant Dam across the San Joaquin River, impounded and stored the waters of the river behind it, and, with the 36-mile-long Madera Canal and 152-mile-long Friant-Kern Canal nearing completion, would soon transport nearly the full volume of the river away from the lands of the plaintiffs. The physical removal of the San Joaquin River waters was particularly grievous because these waters were to be used on lands that neither were riparian to the San Joaquin River nor possessed any appropriative rights to the river's flow. In the case of the San Joaquin Municipal Utility District, San Joaquin River water would be diverted not only to lands not riparian to the river, but to an entirely different watershed—the Tulare Basin to the south. With the filing of the Hollister suit, the Grass Lands Water Association had thrown down the gauntlet to the Bureau of Reclamation.[29]

A SMALL GREEN BOOK RAISES THE STAKES

In March 1947, as construction of the Central Valley Project proceeded, the U.S. Fish and Wildlife Service and the U.S. Bureau of Reclamation agreed to conduct a joint study to determine the importance of the 98,234 acres of the Grasslands to waterfowl and to recommend measures for perpetuating the waterfowl habitat of the lower San Joaquin Valley. Three and a half years would pass before the release of the final report, *Waterfowl Conservation in the Lower San Joaquin Valley, California: Its Relation to the Grasslands and the Central Valley Project,* in October 1950.[30] Known as the Green Book, the report enumerated several highly controversial recommendations unfavorable to the Grasslands owners, and effectively propelled the battle to the U.S. Congress, where hearings on the future of the Grasslands would be held for three consecutive years.[31] The Green Book thus served as linchpin in the Grasslands conflict and as catalyst for the conflict's eventual resolution.

The Green Book reviewed how the operations of the massive Central Valley Project would directly affect the Grasslands. With the San Joaquin River impounded behind Friant Dam and diverted to agricultural lands elsewhere in the upper San Joaquin Valley, replacement water for the lower San Joaquin Valley would be imported from the Sacramento Valley through the Sacramento–San Joaquin Delta. Pumps near the Delta city of Tracy would lift the water approximately two hundred vertical feet into the Delta-Mendota Canal, which would transport it 117 miles to the San Joaquin River at Mendota, on the river's great

bend. Canal companies owned or controlled by Miller and Lux would then distribute this water to croplands in the lower San Joaquin Valley.[32] The "uncontrolled" Grasslands had never acquired cropland water rights, and were not to
receive any of the substitute water from the Delta-Mendota Canal.[33] The interim
period, begun in 1944, during which the Grass Lands Water Association had
contracted annually with the Bureau of Reclamation for water deliveries from
Friant Dam's Millerton Lake, was scheduled to end in July 1951, at which time the
Tracy pumping plant was expected to commence operation. However, in order to
support the joint waterfowl program (established to fulfill the 1948 Lea Act) of
the state of California and the U.S. Fish and Wildlife Service and "to give private
owners opportunity to develop other water sources," the bureau planned to provide to the Grass Lands Water Association, for waterfowl purposes only, 30,000
acre-feet in 1951, 20,000 acre-feet in 1952, and 10,000 acre-feet in 1953.[34] After 1953
there would be no more water for the Grasslands.

The Green Book left little doubt about the ecological importance for waterfowl of privately owned wetlands such as those in the Grasslands. The report acknowledged, "The vast bulk of waterfowl habitat in California is in private ownership, with much of it under the control of duck clubs. Consequently, duck clubs
will always shoulder a share of the responsibility for perpetuating the waterfowl
resource with their Federal and State governments." This joint responsibility was
especially apparent in the lower San Joaquin Valley, where the lone public refuge
in 1950, the Los Banos Waterfowl Refuge, was limited in its ability to provide for
vast numbers of waterfowl by its small size, only 3,000 acres. Aerial counts conducted by the California Department of Fish and Game and the U.S. Fish and
Wildlife Service between October 1947 and October 1948 indicated a maximum
number of 32,835 geese and 308,400 ducks present on the Grasslands at any one
time. As significant as these numbers were, they were almost certainly below
average for the Grasslands; both the continental and the Pacific Flyway waterfowl populations were below normal during the winter of 1947–1948. In addition
to the geese and ducks, the Green Book noted that the Grasslands supported
substantial populations of other resident and migratory species, including long-
billed curlews, black-necked stilts, American avocets, long-billed dowitchers,
killdeer, white pelicans, sandhill cranes, great and snowy egrets, black-crowned
night herons, and great blue herons.[35]

Despite documenting the importance of habitat in the Grasslands for both
breeding and wintering waterfowl, the Green Book recommended the provision
of water only for a proposed expansion of the Los Banos Waterfowl Refuge and
for a proposed federal waterfowl management area to the east of the San Joaquin
River, which in 1951 would become the Merced National Wildlife Refuge. It did
not recommend water deliveries from the Central Valley Project to private lands in
the Grasslands. Instead, in what would prove to be its most inflammatory passage,

the report recommended that the Grassland owners develop, at their own expense, irrigation drainage water and groundwater sources "to perpetuate the Grasslands area as waterfowl habitat." By promoting the feasibility of developing these water sources in the Grasslands, the Green Book apparently ignored its own findings concerning the problems of the excessive salinity and alkalinity of drainage water and groundwater in much of the lower San Joaquin Valley.[36]

In light of the assurances that the Grasslands interests had received that they would be provided Central Valley Project water—from the Bureau of Reclamation's Charles Carey in 1944 and from the Fish and Wildlife Service's Ira Gabrielson in 1945—it is hardly surprising that the Grass Lands Water Association and its members reacted bitterly to the 1950 Green Book's recommendation that they rely on drainage water and groundwater to maintain their seasonal wetlands. Indeed, the decision to withhold Central Valley Project water appeared to the Grasslands interests to be a change in policy and an abrogation of promises and statements of support that various federal officials had made to them during the preceding years. The Green Book's recommendation indicated a retreat from more recent statements as well, including a letter from Secretary of the Interior Julius A. Krug to President Truman in which Krug stated that the Central Valley Project included plans for the preservation and propagation of fish and wildlife, and that "every effort will be made to preserve fish and wildlife resources."[37]

Economic considerations played a role in the decision to withhold Central Valley Project water from the Grasslands. In a report issued in 1948, two years before the release of the Green Book, the Bureau of Reclamation, citing studies conducted by the U.S. Department of Agriculture's Bureau of Agricultural Economics, had argued that water utilized for the irrigation development of agricultural lands in the San Joaquin Valley would return an overall average net benefit of approximately $15 per acre, compared to only $1.25 for the Grasslands. Hence "the Grasslands does not appear to be in position to compete favorably with better agricultural areas which can more efficiently and beneficially utilize the limited available water supplies of the Central Valley Project."[38]

A "class" element may also have influenced the Green Book's recommendations to supply water to public waterfowl refuges but not to private wetlands. The Green Book noted that there was little public hunting in the Grasslands. Most of the land that had once been available for public waterfowl hunting in the lower San Joaquin Valley had been reclaimed. Unattached hunters, those not affiliated with private duck clubs, therefore experienced increasingly limited hunting opportunities. Demands from these dispossessed hunters for more public waterfowl hunting in California had led, in part, to the passage of California's Wildlife Conservation Act in 1947 and the federal Lea Act in 1948. The Green Book suggested that more publicly owned waterfowl areas, on which controlled hunting could be permitted, would offer a solution to this problem.[39]

TO WASHINGTON!

Having failed to sway the bureau, and now that the formerly supportive Fish and Wildlife Service, under its new director, Albert Day, had accepted the conclusions of the Green Book, the duck hunters and cattle ranchers of the Grasslands took their fight to Washington, D.C. They hoped that they would be able to influence Congress to pass legislation that would override the bureau's resistance to protecting private wetlands in California. In April 1951 Congress held the first of three pivotal hearings on the Grasslands water situation. Called by California Congressmen Jack Anderson and (Allan) Oakley Hunter, the hearing was held before the House Subcommittee on Irrigation and Reclamation. Clair Engle of California, chairman of the subcommittee, presided. There were two issues at stake: the immediate provision of summer emergency water for cattle during that drought year, and the permanent provision of fall water for waterfowl. Rice growers, cattle ranchers, and duck clubs, each for their own reasons, supported the Grasslands; opposition originated primarily from agricultural interests outside of the Grasslands that feared a reduction in their water deliveries should the Grasslands win a larger share of the scant resource.

Among those testifying for the Grasslands was Earl Harris, a prosperous haberdasher by profession, and a member of the Santa Cruz Land and Cattle Company, one of the larger Grasslands properties that served as both cattle ranch and duck club. Since 1949 he had been a member of the Grass Lands Water Association's board of directors.[40] Harris expressed his frustration with the "arrogant and dictatorial policy of the Bureau of Reclamation" in its administration of the Central Valley Project, a theme that would be often repeated at the hearings.[41] Harris presented numerous letters in support of continued delivery of water to the Grasslands. R. E. Des Jardins, president of Cal-Oro Rice Growers, Inc., based in the southern Grasslands, had written to Harris of the importance of Grasslands water in preventing severe crop depredations by migrating ducks every September and October.[42] John Baumgartner, president of the California Cattlemen's Association, had written to the new secretary of the interior, Oscar Chapman, stressing the need for livestock water, without which hundreds of head of cattle would need to be moved out of state to, quite literally, greener pastures.[43] Harris offered a particularly damning statement by George W. Fink, now secretary-manager of the Grass Lands Water Association. Fink enumerated the broken promises by federal officials, arguing that the recommendations of the Green Book represented a complete reversal of these earlier positions and that the federal government had abandoned its responsibilities to the Grasslands, leaving its owners to "take care of the Pacific coast flight of wild ducks and geese which under congressional statutes is the duty of the Secretary of the Interior, the Commissioner of Reclamation, and the United States Fish and Wildlife Service."[44]

FIGURE 12. J. Martin Winton, lifelong advocate for the waterfowl and wetlands of the Grasslands. Courtesy of the J. Martin Winton Special Collection on Water Use and Land Development, San Joaquin College of Law, Clovis, California.

Speaking next for the Grasslands was J. Martin Winton, who was destined to become one of the most important—and most vocal—spokesmen for the preservation of the Grasslands (see figure 12). Born in 1909 in the hamlet of Oleander a few miles south of Fresno, Winton grew up hunting ducks and geese with his family in the vanishing wetlands of the Tulare Basin and in the wetlands around Los Banos, in the heart of the Grasslands. A pharmacist by profession, Winton became a lifelong duck hunter devoted to the protection of waterfowl lands. Intimidating to those whose loyalties he questioned, Winton was self-assured and driven, and did not shy away from making personal calls to politicians, directors of federal and state agencies, and heads of private conservation organizations to request, and often demand, support for the Grasslands. In his uncompromising fashion, Winton was known to interrogate potential allies when first meeting them to determine to his satisfaction their degree of commitment to waterfowl and their habitat. Contemporaries describe these unsettling encounters, which in many cases initiated a lifelong bond, with a vividness that reflects the lasting impression left on them by Winton's indomitable personality. Winton was a force to be reckoned with for anyone involved—on either side—in the struggle over Grasslands water.[45]

By the time he journeyed to Washington to speak before the Subcommittee on Irrigation and Reclamation, Winton had already established significant conservation credentials. A member of the Hollister Land and Cattle Company duck club, Winton was chairman of the waterfowl committee for the Sportsman's Council of Central California, chairman of the San Joaquin Valley committee for Ducks Unlimited, and a member of the Izaak Walton League. Later, in 1952, he would join the board of directors of the Grass Lands Water Association and then that of the association's successor, the Grassland Water District, and would serve as president of that new organization for more than twenty years, from 1957 until his retirement in 1978.[46]

Most of Winton's accomplishments on behalf of the Grasslands still lay ahead when, despite his already impressive credentials, he introduced himself to the subcommittee as "just a duck hunter." Winton explained the importance of the Pacific Flyway and the ways in which hunters supported the maintenance of flyway populations, by contributions to Ducks Unlimited and by fees paid for state hunting licenses and federal duck stamps. He pointed out that since 1944 the Grass Lands Water Association had been purchasing the water necessary to protect the waterfowl lands of the Grasslands and in some years had provided the water needed by the adjacent Los Banos Waterfowl Refuge as well. Winton was critical of the Green Book's recommendation to create a new federal refuge in the lower San Joaquin Valley, while at the same time denying water to the private waterfowl lands there. He also called attention to the rice growers who were reclaiming marginal land on the fringes of the Grasslands, and the unusual support that they were now providing for the maintenance of Grasslands water. With more land under cultivation and less land for waterfowl, the rice growers were suffering from increasingly serious crop depredations. Every fall, enormous flocks of ducks, seeking resting and feeding areas, descended on the rice fields and devoured part of the maturing crop before it could be harvested. Therefore, even as they reclaimed the waterfowl lands of the Grasslands, the rice growers lobbied to protect those lands that remained. Winton was fiercely opposed to agricultural development in the Grasslands area, and he argued that water should be made available only "for the growing of natural grass and waterfowl management," not for agricultural crop use.[47]

Winton had raised a key point about the threat agriculture posed to the Grasslands. Not only was the rice economy consuming ever more critical wetlands, but, more important, agricultural enterprises beyond the Grasslands were poised to carry away its historical water supply. These agricultural interests throughout the San Joaquin Valley had their own concerns over the provision of additional water for the Grasslands, which they expressed to the subcommittee in the form of telegrams and letters. Irrigation districts in the San Joaquin Basin, served by the Madera Canal, and in the Tulare Basin, served by the Friant-Kern Canal, argued that especially in the current drought year, water should not be released from Friant Dam for wildlife when it was so desperately needed for croplands. The agriculturalists contended that, as an irrigation and reclamation agency, the bureau's highest priority should be to deliver water to croplands and not to wetlands, highlighting the fact that the crux of the Grasslands issue was how limited supplies of water would be distributed among competing claimants.[48]

Regional Director Richard L. Boke addressed the subcommittee on behalf of the Bureau of Reclamation.[49] Boke attempted to refute the contentions of the Grasslands representatives, arguing that despite Director Carey's assurances, any permanent water supply to the Grasslands would be contingent on increasing the delivery capacity of the Central Valley Project by the construction of additional storage reservoirs. Boke maintained that the bureau had been able to provide interim contracts to the Grasslands since 1944 only because the Central Valley Project had not yet become fully operational. Now that the Madera and Friant-Kern canals, which would carry away most of the flow of the San Joaquin River, were completed, the interim period was over; except for the diminishing deliveries, which would continue until 1953, the Grass Lands Water Association would be forced to rely on groundwater and irrigation drainage water, as per the conclusions of the Green Book.[50] Ten days after the hearing, Boke wrote to Clair Engle, denying the Grasslands' request for summer emergency water.[51]

Facing recalcitrance from the bureau, and with the Hollister suit moving glacially through the courts, the Grasslands interests and their political representatives continued to seek legislation that would secure a permanent water supply and that would compel the bureau to expand its mission to include the protection of fish and wildlife. In March 1952 Congressmen Clair Engle and Jack Anderson introduced bills in the House of Representatives "to authorize works for development and furnishing of water supplies for waterfowl management" in the lower San Joaquin Valley.[52] Significantly, the bills called for the reauthorization of the Central Valley Project. To the project's previous stated purposes of improving navigation, river regulation, flood control, and storage and delivery of water would be added the purpose of "delivering and furnishing water supplies for fish and wildlife conservation and management and for other beneficial uses." Both bills were referred to the Subcommittee on Interior and Insular Affairs; a hearing was scheduled for June 1952.

During the months prior to the hearing, the Grass Lands Water Association lobbied for the passage of these bills, although both the association and its supporters had serious reservations. The bills clearly expanded the beneficial use of water to include the conservation and management of fish and wildlife, but did not explicitly provide for a permanent water supply to the private lands in the Grasslands. They were designed instead to provide a water supply for state waterfowl management areas and national wildlife refuges in the lower San Joaquin Valley. The California Department of Fish and Game, then under Seth Gordon, thus supported the bills, as did the Fish and Wildlife Service, under Albert Day. But Al Jessen, president of the Grass Lands Water Association, wrote to Clair Engle to remind him that the bill failed to protect the Grasslands, and that the association had been spending private funds to purchase water from the Bureau of Reclamation to preserve this important link in the Pacific Flyway.[53] Jessen's position received support from sympathetic state representatives. California assemblyman Wallace D. Henderson pointedly wrote to Engle about the concerns of the Grasslands owners: "While . . . these Bills will allocate water . . . for public lands, there is grave doubt as to the effect this legislation will have on private property. . . . If water had not been purchased by the land owners for the waterfowl, the area would have been lost to the Flyway many years ago. The land owners assumed responsibility of this natural resource at their own expense; and I believe that if this area is to remain part of the Flyway, some relief must be given them in regards to the cost of water and supply."[54]

Martin Winton reemphasized the contributions of the Grasslands owners in his testimony during the hearing. Drawing a parallel to perhaps the most widely known human-caused extinction in American wildlife history, he argued that "if it had not been for the Grass Lands Water Association, the ducks and geese of this all important wintering ground would have vanished with the passenger pigeon."[55] After the hearing, the legislation advanced to the full House Committee on Interior and Insular Affairs, but there it stalled, and Clair Engle could do little more than promise to reintroduce it at the beginning of the 1953 session.

During the fall of 1952, the shortsightedness of denying water to the Grasslands became apparent. Like the state and federal refuges that had been created in the Sacramento Valley to the north, the waterfowl lands of the Grasslands played a crucial role in reducing crop depredations. Allowed to purchase only 20,000 acre-feet of water from the Bureau of Reclamation in 1952, the Grass Lands Water Association was unable to flood its lands sufficiently to create suitable habitat at the start of the waterfowl season.[56] Thus the Grasslands could not draw migrating waterfowl away from the region's rice fields. The massive crop depredations that followed led to an emergency agreement, forged on September 11 at a meeting in Dos Palos, by which the Grasslands would make private land available for one month to the state of California for feeding and harboring waterfowl, by the end of which time most of the rice crop would have been harvested. Only after the declaration of a state of emergency by Governor Earl Warren did the bureau finally agree to deliver up to 6,000 acre-feet of water to flood the Grasslands, allowing the agreement to be fulfilled and thereby alleviating the depredation.[57]

Shortly after coming to the aid of beleaguered rice growers in the lower San Joaquin Valley, the Grasslands owners turned the congressional legislative delay to their advantage by transforming the Grass Lands Water Association from a mutual water company into a public water district. Under the *California Water Code,* such a district would possess clear legal authority to negotiate long-term contracts with the Bureau of Reclamation once Congress passed legislation compelling the bureau to enter into such negotiations. On December 27, 1952, at the annual meeting of its stockholders, the association initiated the formation of a new Grassland Water District.[58] Nearly one year later, on December 22, 1953, the Merced County Board of Supervisors granted its approval and the Grassland Water District, the state's only such district created expressly for the preservation of waterfowl, came into existence.[59]

While the Grassland Water District was being organized, in early 1953 Governor Warren called a conference of representatives of federal and state agencies to draft a revised bill for the public and private wetlands of the lower San Joaquin Valley that would be acceptable to all parties concerned.[60] Clair Engle and Oakley Hunter introduced this new bill, which would become known as the Grasslands bill, in the House of Representatives, and in March the Subcommittee on Irrigation and Reclamation held a hearing on the new legislation, marking the third consecutive year that Congress addressed the Grasslands problem.[61] The bill was intended to provide water supplies not only to state and federal management areas, but also to the privately owned Grasslands. It contained a seminal new provision that its predecessors lacked, one for which the Grasslands interests had been lobbying for years and in anticipation of which they had created the Grassland Water District. The provision authorized the secretary of the interior to contract with public organizations for delivery of Central Valley Project water for waterfowl purposes in the Grasslands area of the San Joaquin Valley.

The House of Representatives passed the Grasslands bill on August 1, the day after President Eisenhower delivered a forceful message to Congress on the responsibility of the federal government to conserve natural resources, including fish and wildlife, on public lands.[62] The Senate followed a year later, on August 11, 1954. All that now stood between the Grasslands and the legal right to negotiate for a guaranteed supply of water was the signature of the president. On August 27, Eisenhower signed into law the Grasslands Development Authorization Act, paving the way for the Grasslands to enter into a long-term water contract with the Bureau of Reclamation and ending fifteen years of uncertainty and struggle that had begun with Miller and Lux's sale of its water rights to the bureau in 1939.[63] In a fitting tribute to the man who had been the most unrelenting force behind the passage of the Grasslands legislation, Martin Winton was presented with the pen Eisenhower used to sign the document.[64]

The Grasslands Development Authorization Act of 1954 reauthorized the Central Valley Project, explicitly stating that in addition to the purposes enumerated in prior authorizing acts, the waters of the project are intended "for fish and wildlife purposes."[65] Water for fish and wildlife was thus added for the first time as a project purpose, albeit with the understanding that "delivery of water from the Central Valley Project for waterfowl purposes is to be subordinate to the priority of deliveries of water for agricultural purposes."[66] Despite this caveat, the language of the 1954 act signified a marked advance from that of the 1937 act that had first authorized the construction of the Central Valley Project by the Bureau of Reclamation, which required only that the project "shall include a due regard for wildlife conservation."[67] The duck hunters and cattle ranchers of the Grasslands and their congressional allies had prevailed in forcing the Bureau of Reclamation to reconsider the purposes and goals of the Central Valley Project and begin to take into account the effects of the project on wildlife. More broadly, their accomplishments call attention to the often overlooked role that protest from relatively small, locally based organizations of conservation-minded citizens has played in influencing national environmental policy.[68]

WATER AT LAST

The most important task facing the newly established Grassland Water District was the negotiation of a permanent contract with the Bureau of Reclamation for Central Valley Project water.[69] Martin Winton led the negotiations for the Grasslands beginning shortly after the passage of the 1954 Grasslands Act, but final execution of the contract would be subject to the prior resolution of the Hollister suit, first filed by Claude Rowe in 1947, which had initiated the legal struggle over Grasslands water rights. Toward that end, in January 1956 the Grassland Water District passed a resolution for the dismissal of the suit, and on September 13 of that year the district and the U.S. Bureau of Reclamation entered into a permanent contract for 50,000 acre-feet of fall water to be delivered annually from the Delta-Mendota Canal.[70] Although this quantity of water was only about half of what was desirable for optimal management, the Grasslands owners would be able to continue the tradition of fall flood irrigation and the annual transformation of the region into wetland habitat for Pacific Flyway waterfowl.[71]

The Grasslands interests were ecstatic at the culmination of their long battle with the Bureau of Reclamation, but this chapter in the history of the Grasslands was not yet closed. Beginning in 1967, newly developed agricultural enterprises, principally rice fields, on lands adjacent to the southern Grasslands began to inundate the Grassland Water District with increased flows of summer drainage water, precipitating an investigation by the U.S. Department of the Interior into the problems facing the Grasslands with regard to the maintenance of waterfowl habitat.[72] By 1969, drain flows amounted to 80,000 to 90,000 acre-feet annually and were expected to continue to increase. These summer flows of agricultural drainage water dramatically increased the district's costs of maintenance and repair of ditches, canals, and related irrigation works, and they diverted funds intended for the development of waterfowl management facilities. Combined with increased taxes associated with rising land prices, these additional costs reduced the district's ability to provide suitable wetland habitat. The Department of the Interior's report concluded, "Without some form of economic aid, the ability of the landowners to maintain their contribution to the waterfowl resources of the Pacific Flyway will be lost."[73] As a result of these changes in the district's fortunes, the 1956 water contract with the Bureau of Reclamation was renegotiated in 1969.[74] The new contract reduced the price of the District's Central Valley Project water from $1.50 to 10 cents per acre-foot, provided that the district's landowners agreed to reserve their land for wildlife habitat and irrigated pasture by the execution of covenants of restrictive use.[75] Martin Winton, now president of the Grassland Water District, spearheaded the effort to enroll the district's landowners in the plan. The majority of landowners voluntarily signed the restrictive covenants, agreeing to "use and maintain" their lands "in a manner compatible with wildlife use and waterfowl habitat."[76]

In addition to the protective covenants, three important federal laws—part of the wave of new environmental legislation that swept Capitol Hill during the 1970s—helped the Grasslands owners to remain solvent and continue to protect their lands for the benefit of waterfowl. In 1970 Congress passed the Water Bank Act "to prevent the serious loss of wetlands, and to preserve, restore, and improve such lands." Landowners participating in the Water Bank Program were offered annual payments, under ten-year contracts, for maintaining marsh habitat into the spring waterfowl breeding season each year and for growing waterfowl food plants. By 1978, 15,700 acres in the Grassland Water District were enrolled in the program.[77] Further assistance came via the Wetlands Loan Extension Act of 1976, which provided funding for the U.S. Fish and Wildlife Service to initiate conservation easement programs for wetlands.[78] In California, the primary focus of these programs was the Grassland wetlands. By 1977 the Fish and Wildlife Service had organized an easement program for the Grasslands, with the goal that "the West [of the San Joaquin River] Grasslands will remain in private ownership and continue to be managed for waterfowl." The service purchased the first easements in the West Grasslands in 1979, the year in which the agency established the Grasslands Wildlife Management Area. Two years later the new wildlife management area included 11,650 acres of wetland habitat under easement on thirty-four duck clubs.[79] Finally, Congress in 1978 passed the Fish and Wildlife Improvement Act, which amended the water contract between the Grasslands and the Bureau of Reclamation once again, to provide that the 50,000 acre-feet of water be delivered annually to the Grasslands free of charge in perpetuity.[80] The provision of water to the Grasslands had thus come full circle. Free water that in the days of Miller and Lux had overflowed onto the Grasslands from the San Joaquin River had been replaced by free water delivered to the Grasslands from the Delta, provided by the Bureau of Reclamation's Central Valley Project.

Attitudes about the Grasslands had changed considerably since the landowners first organized in 1939, when the Central Valley Project had threatened the obliteration of the Grasslands for the "greater good" of agricultural development. During the intervening years, the Central Valley Project had been reauthorized to include the preservation of fish and wildlife as a project purpose, and the Grasslands had been guaranteed a permanent water supply. The federal government, once willing to sacrifice the Grasslands and its resident and migratory waterfowl, now offered landowners annual payments under the Water Bank Program and conservation easements under the Wetlands Loan Extension Act to protect the historic wetlands of the Grasslands and the wildlife they supported. Such dramatic changes would not have taken place without years of dedicated, and often frustrating, effort by the duck hunters of the Grasslands and their allies. Nevertheless, such efforts were not always successful in the face of the overarching development scheme of the Central Valley Project. The San Joaquin River upstream from the Grasslands was destined to become a significant casualty of that project.

THE SORRY FATE OF THE SAN JOAQUIN RIVER

The 1950 Green Book was concerned primarily with waterfowl conservation in the wetlands of the lower San Joaquin Valley. Perhaps the report's emphasis on wetlands accounts for one of its most striking sentences going largely unnoticed at the time: "After meeting remaining existing [water] rights, the San Joaquin River above the Mendota Pool will be dry to all intents and purposes."[81] In this brief statement, the Green Book acknowledged that with almost the entire flow of the San Joaquin River impounded behind Friant Dam and exported to the agricultural lands served by the Madera and Friant-Kern canals (see figure 13), the fifty-nine-mile stretch of river between Friant Dam and the Mendota Pool— where the Delta-Mendota Canal joins the river—would be almost completely dewatered. Gone would be the last vestiges of the river's once-prodigious salmon runs, the southernmost on North America's Pacific Coast.[82] Lost also would be the riparian wetlands along the river that supported nesting waterfowl and a variety of other types of wildlife, including rabbits, badgers, skunks, raccoons, coyotes, and deer. Amid the valleywide enthusiasm for the Central Valley Project and the agricultural bounty it promised, few voices rose to object to the obliteration of a mighty river whose annual average flow was nearly 1.8 million acre-feet, and of the fish and wildlife the river supported.[83]

Aside from the landowners directly affected by the dewatering of the river, most of the limited number of protests came from sportsmen decrying the effects of

FIGURE 13. Friant Dam on the San Joaquin River, with Lake Millerton beyond. The Madera Canal is in the upper left, and the Friant-Kern Canal is in the right foreground, dwarfing the trickle of the river that remains below the dam. Courtesy of the J. Martin Winton Special Collection on Water Use and Land Development, San Joaquin College of Law, Clovis, California.

Friant Dam and the diversionary canals on the salmon and the wildlife of the river. G. W. Philpott, president of the Sportsmen's Council of Central California, addressed several of the threats posed by the project: "We believe every drop of water in the San Joaquin River should be conserved, but to physically take a river out of one area, killing an untold salmon run value *[sic]*, destroying waterfowl nesting and resting habitat and thereby reducing the waterfowl population which belongs to all the people of North and South America, and driv[ing] farmers out of business by removing the water which produced pasture land for cattle, is a program that many of us fail to comprehend."[84] William Voigt Jr., executive director of the Izaak Walton League, emphasized that the water manipulations on the river would prevent the successful spawning of salmon. He predicted quite accurately that "if the damaging manipulations are allowed to continue, it is highly probable that the race of salmon of the San Joaquin River will be wiped out."[85]

Salmon are anadromous fish. They spend their adult lives at sea, but return to the fresh water of their parent stream to spawn. Prior to the construction of dams and diversion canals, the rivers of the Central Valley supported prodigious numbers of four native races of Chinook salmon, each with its own seasonal run (winter, spring, fall, and late-fall), as well as another important anadromous salmonid, the steelhead.[86] An astonishing one million to two million adult salmon could be found annually in the valley's river systems. Before the rivers were constricted by levees and cut off from their floodplains, one of the contributing factors to this historic abundance was the presence of winter floodplain wetlands, which provided high-quality, protected habitat for the rearing of juvenile salmon. Also important for providing spawning as well as rearing habitat for a variety of additional native fish species, these floodplains demonstrate the value of wetlands not only for waterfowl and other aquatic bird species, but for fish as well.[87]

Historically, the San Joaquin River had supported one of the finest salmon spawning areas in the state and, although dams had been constructed across the river since the nineteenth century, none had completely sealed off the river as Friant Dam would. Miller and Lux had constructed a brush dam at Mendota as well as Sack Dam—so named because it was built of brush and sacks of sand— fourteen miles farther downstream. Despite these impediments to their migrations, salmon remained numerous in the San Joaquin River, especially during the spring run, which was aided by high flows. During the 1930s, salmon counts exceeded eighty thousand, and the river continued to support other game fish, including steelhead, white sturgeon, and the introduced striped bass, largemouth and smallmouth bass, catfish, crappie, and sunfish. Although salmon migrating upstream to spawn were capable of navigating the fish ladders at Sack and Mendota dams, which had been rebuilt as permanent structures early in the twentieth century, after 1944 it was impossible for them to pass beyond the massive new 319-foot-high Friant Dam to their ancestral spawning grounds. In 1945 the California Division of Fish and Game recorded fifty-six thousand spring-run salmon ascending the fish ladder at Mendota. But it was to be one of the last large runs. With the San Joaquin River impounded behind Friant Dam, adult salmon migrating upstream became stranded in the low water beyond Sack and Mendota dams. The juvenile offspring, or smolt, of those few salmon that did survive to spawn in the gravels below Friant Dam also faced a fatal obstacle. Lacking the high river flows necessary to carry them downstream and out to sea, the young salmon perished in the irrigation diversions at Mendota and Sack dams.[88] The Fish and Wildlife Service had foreseen such an eventuality, and had recommended in 1944 that "a minimum flow below Friant Dam be set in the immediate future" and that "the Mendota pool be isolated from the main channel of the San Joaquin River for protection of salmon."[89] These recommendations went unheeded by the Bureau of Reclamation, and by the late 1940s the salmon were largely gone.

Years before the Green Book was produced, landowners along the thirty-six-mile stretch of the San Joaquin River between Friant Dam and Gravelly Ford, the last diversion point upstream from Mendota Pool, had suspected that the Bureau of Reclamation's plan to construct the canals at Friant would dewater the river below the dam. By the late 1940s, with Friant Dam completed and work progressing on the canals, it had become clear that these suspicions were not unwarranted. The landowners along the threatened stretch of the river organized the San Joaquin River Riparian Owners Association and secured the legal services of Claude Rowe, who was also serving as attorney to the Grass Lands Water Association and was preparing to file the Hollister suit. Despite having received repeated reassurances from the bureau that their water rights would not be taken or disturbed by either the construction or the operation of Friant Dam or its diversionary canals, the landowners were informed for the first time in July 1947, in a letter signed by Richard Boke, that unless they accepted an offer by the bureau for the "adjustment" of their water rights on terms fixed by the bureau, or filed suit for damages before October 20, 1947, their water rights would be taken without compensation.[90] As a direct result of this action on the part of the Bureau of Reclamation, Rowe filed suit on September 25, 1947, on behalf of Everett G. Rank of Fresno and eleven other owners of land riparian to the San Joaquin River, seeking to prevent the diversion of San Joaquin River water to areas not riparian to the river.[91] The primary defendants were identical to those named in the Hollister suit: Secretary of the Interior Julius A. Krug, Bureau of Reclamation Commissioner Michael W. Straus, Regional Director Richard Boke, and the Madera Irrigation District and South San Joaquin Municipal Utility District. Shortly thereafter, the case was removed from state to federal court, where the litigation of *Rank v. Krug* would continue for the next sixteen years.

The U.S. District Court, with Justice Pierson M. Hall presiding, first heard the case in March 1950.[92] Rank and the other plaintiffs argued that they had the right to the use of the waters of the San Joaquin River, as guaranteed by the California Constitution and by the state's *Water Code,* which specifically preserved all riparian and appropriative rights to the owners of land for reasonable and beneficial use.[93] The plaintiffs asserted several categories of rights to the flow of the river, the most important of which were use for agriculture and domestic purposes, and use for the spawning of salmon and protection of commercial and noncommercial fishing. The Bureau of Reclamation countered by claiming that Friant Dam and the diversionary canals were erected for the improvement of navigation and flood control, and that therefore the plaintiffs did not possess any rights against the impounding and diversion of the flow of the San Joaquin River. However, as the court noted, the text of the acts of Congress relating to the Central Valley Project, which required the secretary of the interior to respect existing water rights established by state law, did not support the bureau's claim.[94] The court therefore confirmed the rights of Rank and the other plaintiffs to the water of the San Joaquin River for agriculture and domestic use, but held that only the state of California was entitled to enforce the right of use for the spawning of salmon and the protection of fisheries.[95] California's role in this matter would prove decisive.

California's attorney general and future governor, Edmund G. ("Pat") Brown, issued a legal opinion in July 1951 to determine the state's position in *Rank v. Krug* regarding the preservation of fish life in the San Joaquin River below Friant Dam.[96] That opinion sealed the fate of the San Joaquin River's salmon runs. Most of Brown's analysis focused on a key provision, section 525 (later renumbered as section 5937) of California's *Fish and Game Code*, which appeared to offer the necessary protection for fish below the dam. The law required that "the owner of any dam shall allow sufficient water at all times to pass through a fishway, or in the absence of a fishway, allow sufficient water to pass over, around or through the dam, to keep in good condition any fish that may be planted or exist below the dam."[97] Brown refuted the applicability of section 525 to Friant Dam. He argued that California's *Water Code* provided that irrigation was one of the highest uses of water, second only to domestic use, and that therefore there was no restriction against taking the entire supply of a stream for irrigation purposes, even to the detriment of fish life. Brown also cited the state's Water Resources Act of 1945, which required that water development projects make adequate provision for the protection of migratory fishes only "when engineering and economic features of the project make it practicable" to do so.[98] Thus the California attorney general's official position was that the United States was not required by state law to provide adequate flows from Friant Dam to preserve fish life in the San Joaquin River.[99] The state of California would not challenge the Bureau of Reclamation's operation of Friant Dam.[100]

The trial of *Rank v. Krug* began in Fresno in January 1952 and lasted for nearly three years, until December 1954. After reviewing approximately thirty thousand pages of transcript, including the testimony of more than seventy witnesses, as well as more than eight hundred exhibits admitted into evidence, Justice Hall issued an opinion, exceeding 150 pages in length, in February 1956. The weighty opinion ranged broadly over California water law and held that Rank and the other plaintiffs had vested rights to the full natural flow of the San Joaquin River, and that the impounding at Friant Dam constituted an unauthorized and unlawful invasion of those rights.[101] Nearly a year and a half later, in June 1957, Justice Hall issued his judgment. The ruling enjoined the defendants from "impounding, or diverting, or storing for diversion, or otherwise impeding or obstructing the full natural flow of the San Joaquin River."[102] This injunction, of course, threatened the bureau's entire operation of the Central Valley Project in the San Joaquin Valley. However, the injunction would not go into effect if the United States or the defendant irrigation districts were to provide a physical solution that would simulate the natural flow of the San Joaquin River and thus satisfy the plaintiffs' water rights. Furthermore, a sufficient flow was to be released from Friant Dam to provide for the needs of all water users as far downstream as Gravelly Ford, thirty-six miles below Friant. Such a minimum flow would still leave the river essentially dry from Gravelly Ford to Mendota, approximately twenty-three miles farther downstream. In light of Attorney General Brown's 1951 opinion that the United States was not responsible for maintaining the salmon runs in its operation of Friant Dam, the court's ruling did not need to address the fact that salmon could not swim across twenty-three miles of dry river channel.

While preparing to appeal Justice Hall's injunction, the Bureau of Reclamation applied to the California State Water Rights Board in 1958 for the rights to the remaining unappropriated water of the San Joaquin River, and the right to store and divert that water at Friant Dam. The California Department of Fish and Game, represented by a private attorney, Wilmer W. Morse, challenged the bureau's application, arguing that the public interest required the reestablishment and maintenance of the San Joaquin River's salmon runs, which had been destroyed by the construction of Friant Dam and the bureau's storage and diversion for irrigation of the river's waters. Nonetheless, in June 1959 the State Water Rights Board issued its ruling, which dismissed the Department of Fish and Game's protest and decided in favor of the bureau's claim to the rights to all unappropriated water in the San Joaquin River and the right to divert nearly all of the water entering Millerton Lake behind Friant Dam into the Madera and Friant-Kern canals.[103]

The State Water Rights Board's ruling regarding salmon reflected a fait accompli. The board noted that because the San Joaquin River's salmon runs above the confluence of the Merced River—the first major tributary to join the river below Friant Dam—were now essentially extinct, "failure to take action *at this time* will not destroy any existing runs nor prevent a possible later reestablishment" of those runs. Such reasoning led the board to conclude that "to require the United States to by-pass water down the channel of the San Joaquin River for the re-establishment and maintenance of the salmon fishery at this time is not in the public interest."[104] The Department of Fish and Game immediately prepared to appeal the decision. As the deadline approached, however, Governor Brown's office telephoned the department's attorney, Morse, and ordered him not to file the appeal.[105]

The fate of the salmon had been sealed, but the long proceedings in *Rank v. Krug* had not yet been resolved. The Bureau of Reclamation still faced Justice Hall's 1957 federal injunction against impounding and diverting the flow of the river on the grounds that the agency had not legally obtained the water rights of Rank and his fellow claimants. Joined by the United States and the state of California, the bureau appealed Justice Hall's ruling to the U.S. Court of Appeals, which heard the case in 1961. The court issued its decision in August, affirming Hall's injunction, though on different technical grounds.[106]

Still thwarted in its attempt to fully legalize the operations of Friant Dam, the Bureau of Reclamation then challenged the Court of Appeals' decision in the U.S. Supreme Court. Claude Rowe, who had argued the case for Rank and the other plaintiffs at every level of review, represented them one final time in 1963, before the high Court. On April 15 the Supreme Court issued its decision, finally bringing this episode of the saga of the San Joaquin River to a close.[107] The Court set aside the judgments of both the U.S. District Court and the Court of Appeals, ruling that United States had in fact legally seized the plaintiffs' water rights. Therefore, the Court vacated the injunction prohibiting the storage and diversion of the San Joaquin River at Friant Dam, reasoning that "to require the full natural flow of the river to go through the dam would force the abandonment of this portion of a project which not only has been fully authorized by the Congress but paid for through its continuing appropriations." The Court also held that the proposed physical solution—the construction of a series of collapsible dams along the San Joaquin River channel, releases from which would simulate the flow of the river—would have no less of a direct, and unacceptable, effect on the bureau's operations. Rank and the other riparian owners were therefore entitled only to financial compensation, based on the difference in market value of their lands before and after the taking of their water rights to the full flow of the river, an avenue of redress that they were free to pursue.[108]

The San Joaquin River and its salmon had been sacrificed to the Central Valley Project and the promotion of irrigated agriculture, echoing the earlier fate of California wetlands in the Sacramento Valley in the face of the Sacramento Flood Control Project, and in the Delta and the Tulare Basin in the face of private reclamation. Once the diversion of nearly the entire flow of the San Joaquin River to agricultural enterprises in Madera, Tulare, and Kern counties was deemed legal by the federal courts, with the consent of the government of the state of California, little could be done to save the river, its fish, or its riparian wetlands.[109] Another half-century would have to pass, and a profound shift in public attitudes about free-flowing rivers would have to take place, before the restoration of the San Joaquin River could become a realistic possibility.

8

Conflicting Agendas

New Refuges and Water Projects for the
San Joaquin Valley

THE TULARE BASIN: DUCKS DO NOT EAT COTTON

The efforts to protect the Grasslands during the 1940s and 1950s called attention to the paucity of wetland habitat remaining in the San Joaquin Valley as a whole. The distribution of those remaining wetlands was far from uniform, however; the San Joaquin Basin to the north had fared considerably better than the Tulare Basin to the south. In addition to the extensive, privately held Grasslands, the San Joaquin Basin in the mid-1950s contained the state-owned Los Banos and Mendota waterfowl management areas, as well as the federal Merced National Wildlife Refuge.[1] The Tulare Basin, in comparison, lacked both refuges and large, contiguous tracts of privately held wetlands. With its lakes and wetlands largely drained and converted to agriculture, the basin's wildlife had been displaced, and populations of breeding and migratory waterfowl had plummeted.

During the early twentieth century, much of the Tulare Basin was converted from wheat to large-scale cotton production, and the bed of Tulare Lake itself had become a cotton plantation that stretched, tabletop-flat, to the horizon. The Tulare Basin was not the first center of cotton agriculture in California, but it has proved the most enduring. After several failed nineteenth-century attempts to introduce cotton into the state, the crop first took hold about 1910 in the Imperial Valley, where U.S. Department of Agriculture scientists experimented successfully with growing long-staple Egyptian varieties. By 1920 cotton covered more than 100,000 acres in the Imperial Valley, before its gradual replacement by vegetable crops and date culture.[2] Cotton would prove far less evanescent in the Tulare Basin, largely thanks to the work of South Carolinian Wofford B. Camp, who was sent to the San Joaquin Valley by the Department of Agriculture in 1917. The influential Camp, who promoted cotton cultivation and breeding experiments in the valley for the next two decades, discovered that Acala cotton, a medium-staple variety that originated in Mexico, was well suited to the basin's high summer temperatures and alkali soils.[3] Farmers began to grow cotton by 1919 in the Tulare Basin near the city of Corcoran, to the east of the remnants of Tulare Lake. Cotton cultivation then spread westward across the basin, following the expansion of irrigation systems. In 1920 a mere 937 acres were planted to cotton in the basin; by 1930 that figure had risen to 90,184 acres.[4]

The cultivation of cotton in the Tulare Basin yielded great fortunes, most notably that of Lieutenant Colonel James Griffin Boswell. Choosing not to return to the cotton plantations in his native Georgia, which had been ravaged by the boll weevil, Boswell, a recently retired army officer, arrived in California in 1921. Relying on the fortune of his wife, Alaine Buck, within a few years Boswell began to amass a cotton empire that would eventually stretch over tens of thousands of acres in and around the leveed Tulare Lake bed. After Buck's premature death, Boswell married Ruth Chandler of the *Los Angeles Times*-owning family, dramatically increasing his political and financial connections. Boswell embraced all aspects of the cotton industry, from growing to ginning to marketing. This vertical integration set the colonel apart from the other large-scale cotton farmers in the region and laid the foundations for a family dynasty that remains powerful to the present day.[5]

Neither the wealth they accumulated nor the levees they constructed, however, could protect Boswell and the other major farmers in the basin from the vicissitudes of nature. Sporadic years of heavy rain and snow in the Sierra Nevada engorged the rivers—the Kings, Kaweah, Tule, and Kern—that drained into the basin and revitalized Tulare Lake, threatening to obliterate agricultural operations on and around the lake bed. From 1922 to 1936, the bed of Tulare Lake lay dry and exposed. During this period of below-average precipitation, the lake itself began to fade from memory and farmers were generally more concerned with drought than flooding. Then the rains returned in the winter of 1936–1937, and they resumed with a ferocious intensity the next year. Floodwaters from the four rivers inundated the basin, covering more than 140,000 acres by the spring and summer of 1938 and destroying 40,000 acres of crops before they could be harvested. The resuscitated lake expanded to a length of twenty-two miles and a width of sixteen miles, threatening to inundate the city of Corcoran.[6]

For decades, farmers in the Tulare Basin had sought the construction of dams on the basin's rivers for irrigation purposes. After the high waters of 1938, however, farmers increasingly thought of these proposed dams as flood control, rather than irrigation, measures. Especially desirable was a dam on the Kings River, to be located at Pine Flat in the foothills of the Sierra Nevada. After a protracted struggle between the U.S. Army Corps of Engineers and the U.S. Bureau of Reclamation over which agency would build Pine Flat Dam, Congress authorized the corps to construct the dam, with its one million acre-foot reservoir, as part of the Flood Control Act of 1944.[7] The act authorized the construction of dams on the Kaweah, Tule, and Kern rivers as well, which, together with Pine Flat Dam, were intended to provide flood protection for the entire Tulare Basin. The corps completed Pine Flat Dam on the Kings River in 1954, a year after finishing Isabella Dam on the Kern River. Terminus Dam on the Kaweah River and Success Dam on the Tule River followed in 1962. Although the dams still could not render the Tulare Basin entirely immune from occasional flooding caused by swollen below-dam tributaries, after their construction the last remnants of the Tulare Lake bed were reclaimed, completing a process that had begun a century earlier with the first large-scale wheat farms in the basin. Tulare Basin's once-rich endowment of hundreds of thousands of acres of wetlands, along with the wildlife they supported, was now almost completely gone.

With the exception of the small acreage controlled by private duck clubs, the landscape of the Tulare Basin had been too radically reordered to serve as habitat for migratory waterfowl. Since the 1920s, when many of the duck clubs were organized, they had provided waterfowl with enough water and food to compensate in part for the loss of wetlands in the Tulare Basin as a whole. During the 1950s, however, rising demand for irrigation water in the basin increased the cost to the clubs of maintaining wetland acreage, and rising land values encouraged club owners to sell their lands for agricultural development.[8] By 1960 the 124 remaining duck clubs controlled less than 27,000 acres, of which only 6,660 acres were actively managed for waterfowl.[9] These clubs were largely concentrated in two locations in the basin's Kern County. The larger of the two groups lay to the south of the Tulare Lake bed; the smaller group was located south of Bakersfield on the eastern side of the Kern Lake bed. Both areas, largely untilled, were subject to increasing pressures for development. It appeared that nothing short of the creation of new wetland refuges could prevent the almost complete disappearance of migratory waterfowl from the southernmost part of California's Great Central Valley.

PIXLEY AND KERN NATIONAL WILDLIFE REFUGES

As wetland acreage in the Tulare Basin dwindled during the 1950s, the U.S. Fish and Wildlife Service actively sought land in the basin suitable for establishing national wildlife refuges. Pacific Flyway wintering waterfowl populations averaged 7.6 million birds from 1955 to 1959, and more seasonal wetlands were urgently needed in the basin to help accommodate the approximately 60 percent of those birds that wintered in the Central Valley.[10] The effort by the Fish and Wildlife

Service to expand available waterfowl habitat culminated in the creation of two new national wildlife refuges, Pixley and Kern.

The circumstances that made it possible to establish the Pixley National Wildlife Refuge date to the 1920s and 1930s, when farmers had abandoned large tracts of land to the east of the former Tulare Lake, largely because of the high alkali content and generally submarginal quality of the soil. The major portion of this land reverted back to the government and was retired from agricultural use under the New Deal's Bankhead-Jones Farm Tenant Act.[11] Administration of the land was assigned to the U.S. Department of Agriculture's Soil Conservation Service until 1958, when President Eisenhower transferred more than two million acres nationwide, including approximately 4,350 acres in Tulare County, to the U.S. Department of the Interior.[12] The next year the Department of the Interior, in turn, transferred the Tulare County land, about five miles southwest of the town of Pixley, to the U.S. Fish and Wildlife Service, officially establishing the Pixley National Wildlife Refuge in November 1959.[13]

The Pixley National Wildlife Refuge is situated within the historic floodplain of Deer Creek, one of the smaller Sierran streams that once nourished Tulare Lake. The extreme western portion of the refuge may have been part of the actual lake, while the majority of the remaining area most likely consisted of riparian habitat, seasonally flooded wetlands, vernal pools, and wet meadows, depending on annual levels of precipitation.[14] By the time of the refuge's creation, decades of reclamation and conversion to cropland had altered the landscape, and water had become scarce. Vegetation characteristic of dry grasslands, such as saltgrass, iodine bush, and saltbush, covered the refuge's saline soils.[15] The only available sources of water for development of the refuge were Deer Creek, a negligible source except in flood years, and groundwater, the level of which was dropping rapidly year after year because of pumping by farmers in the surrounding area.

The Pixley Refuge encountered persistent opposition from nearby irrigation districts, which claimed that groundwater pumping on the refuge would threaten their own supplies. Leon C. Snyder, the first manager of both Pixley and Kern national wildlife refuges, expressed his frustration over the water politics of the region: "Irrigation districts depending on underground water for irrigation have protested vigorously to Congressmen and senators asking that our Service delay development until water conditions improve or until such time as surface water is available. It is hard to determine when these conditions will come to pass."[16] Snyder bitterly objected as well to the apparent hypocrisy of those who wished to postpone the development of the refuge: "While local farmers cry to high heaven if our Service even thinks about developing one or two wells, they apparently think nothing of developing thousands of acres of submarginal lands and drilling dozens of new wells each year themselves."[17]

There is evidence to support Snyder's contentions. In April 1960 the Tulare County Water Commission recommended that the lands of the Pixley Refuge "be retained in government ownership as native pasture, and out of agricultural production [i.e., production for waterfowl crops], until such time as a firm supplemental water supply can be obtained by the Pixley Irrigation District."[18] Formed in 1958, the Pixley Irrigation District in August 1960 stridently urged Clair Engle, now a California senator, to support delaying the development of the Pixley Refuge because of declining groundwater supplies.[19] In May 1960 the board of directors of the Alpaugh Irrigation District—located between the Pixley and Kern refuges, but adjacent to neither—passed a resolution urging the Department of the Interior to "defer action upon the establishment of the [Pixley and Kern] Game Refuges until such time as [they] can be supplied with water obtained from sources other than underground pumping."[20] Such resistance delayed by three decades the effective development of the Pixley National Wildlife Refuge for waterfowl. During those years, however, the refuge was to become an important provider of upland habitat for several endangered grassland species, including the blunt-nosed leopard lizard and the Tipton kangaroo rat.

The Kern National Wildlife Refuge came into existence a little more than a year after its beleaguered counterpart. In 1957 the Fish and Wildlife Service began negotiations for the purchase of sixteen sections of privately owned land, in one square block, south of the Tulare Lake bed. The next year the Migratory Bird Conservation Commission, under the authority of the Migratory Bird Conservation Act, formally approved the acquisition of the land for a new refuge, and in November 1960 the service purchased the 10,544-acre property. The Kern National Wildlife Refuge was formally established in March 1961.[21]

Historically, the lands that became the Kern National Wildlife Refuge had supported seasonal wetlands and riparian habitat. During wet years, when the Kern River filled Buena Vista Lake to overflowing, the river had backed out of its channel and flowed northward across the Tulare Basin and through the lands of the future refuge, covering its lower-lying portions, before emptying into Tulare Lake. Nineteenth-century diversions of the Kern River and the construction of the Goose Lake Canal, which bisects the refuge into eastern and western halves, decreased the frequency of spring floods and eliminated most of its natural wetlands. In place of wetland vegetation, drought-resistant shrubs and grasses covered the new refuge. Much of the soil was alkali and supported saltbush and iodine bush.[22] Except for occasional overflow from Poso Creek, a small stream entering the refuge from the southeast, there was no supply of surface water with which to develop ponds for waterfowl management purposes. The Kern Refuge was forced at first to rely on groundwater, and refuge personnel oversaw the drilling of ten wells; but with an average depth in excess of eight hundred feet, the cost of those wells was prohibitive. The refuge then began to purchase fall and spring irrigation water from local water districts. This imported water was adequate to flood only one-quarter of the refuge in years of normal rainfall, and much less in dry years. Under these constraints, the Kern Refuge developed slowly.

The Kern and Pixley national wildlife refuges had been established not only to restore part of the once-vast migratory waterfowl habitat of the Tulare Basin, but also to alleviate crop depredations elsewhere in the Central Valley. By attracting and holding large numbers of waterfowl through the fall and winter months, the refuges would reduce heavy waterfowl pressure on the wetlands farther north in the San Joaquin Basin and the Sacramento Valley, and would reduce depredation pressure on the rice lands in those regions. The new refuges would also help reduce crop depredations locally and, as an added benefit, would provide new public hunting grounds in the Tulare Basin.[23]

A major challenge for the two refuges would be to provide wintering habitat for early-migrating northern pintail of the Pacific Flyway, an estimated quarter of a million of which arrived in the Tulare Basin during August and September, drawn to vast expanses of flooded agricultural fields. Several hundred thousand acres of cotton lands in the Tulare Lake and Buena Vista Lake areas were flooded, or pre-irrigated, during this time and then drained, usually by late September or early October, for the planting of fall barley.[24] As the water disappeared, migrating pintail required alternative resting and feeding areas, which they sought most frequently in the Grasslands of the San Joaquin Basin and, to a lesser extent, in the Sacramento Valley.[25] Despite limited water supplies, within the first decade of their existence, both the Kern and the Pixley refuges achieved some degree of success in holding these waterfowl in the Tulare Basin. Peak numbers of ducks, primarily pintail, reached 250,550 on Kern and 212,300 on Pixley in the wet year of 1965.[26] Numbers were much lower, however, in dry years, and the refuges could not consistently meet their management objectives without a firm water supply. It would not be until the 1992 passage of the Central Valley Project Improvement Act that Kern, Pixley, and the other Central Valley refuges were finally guaranteed an adequate water supply.[27]

THE SAN JOAQUIN BASIN: SAN LUIS ISLAND

In the San Joaquin Basin, just to the north and east of the Grassland Water District and the city of Los Banos, lies an area known, not altogether accurately, as San Luis Island. Occupying thousands of acres of the historic floodplain of the San Joaquin River, the area is composed of elevated alluvial soil deposited by the river. Situated between the San Joaquin River to the east and Salt Slough to the west, the land historically became an island when the river was at flood stage. San Luis Island, the largest area of unplowed grassland in the Central Valley, is a remnant of the valley grassland community, and contains a matrix of Central

Valley habitats, including alkali grasslands interspersed with alkali sink, vernal pools, valley oak and riparian woodland communities, and freshwater marsh.[28] During the 1960s San Luis Island would become the core of a national wildlife refuge destined to become the largest in the Central Valley.

San Luis Island is located in the heart of the old Rancho Sanjon de Santa Rita, the cornerstone of Henry Miller and Charles Lux's empire in the San Joaquin Basin, and had long been recognized for its importance to waterfowl. Seth Gordon's 1950 report to the Wildlife Conservation Board had authorized the acquisition of a substantial part of it by the state, under the proposed name of the Lower San Joaquin Waterfowl Management Area.[29] As the firm of Miller and Lux continued to divest, in 1942 it had sold its remaining holdings on San Luis Island, and in 1953 California initiated negotiations to purchase the property from the new owners to create the waterfowl management area. Disagreement over the appraised value of the land scuttled the sale, however, and the state missed its opportunity to purchase San Luis Island.[30]

Developments during the early 1960s ensured that San Luis Island would join the ranks of the national wildlife refuge system rather than become a state waterfowl management area. In 1961 Congress passed the Wetlands Loan Act, which authorized federal funds "to promote the conservation of migratory waterfowl and to offset or prevent the serious loss of important wetlands and other waterfowl habitat."[31] The Wetlands Loan Act provided an important first step toward the purchase of San Luis Island as a national wildlife refuge. The next, and decisive, step would be overcoming local opposition to the creation of a federal refuge in the Grasslands area. Many duck clubs, particularly those closest to the proposed refuge, were apprehensive that a new refuge, partially closed to hunting, would draw birds away from their clubs and diminish their shooting. The duck hunters who had fought so hard to protect the privately held Grasslands now found themselves conflicted. As waterfowl enthusiasts, they wanted to see wetland habitat protected, but as investors in the maintenance and operation of duck clubs, they wanted to be able to hunt ducks on their land. Also opposed to a new federal refuge was the Merced County Board of Supervisors, which was concerned not with diminished hunting opportunities, but with the loss of tax revenues for local governments that would ensue when private lands in the county passed into federal ownership.[32]

Ultimately, changes in the distribution of federal funds to local governments, combined with grassroots lobbying, would overcome resistance to a new refuge on San Luis Island. In 1964 Congress passed the Refuge Revenue Sharing Act, which authorized payments, expendable for public schools and roads, to counties in which private lands have been acquired by the United States.[33] Meanwhile, several influential individuals were calling attention to the importance of preserving the unique habitat of San Luis Island. Howard Leach, a prominent biologist with the California Department of Fish and Game who had begun his career conducting studies of waterfowl food habits, initiated an annual public tour of the Grasslands in 1962, which attracted attention from conservationists across the state. The next year Alvaro Sousa, a soil scientist and lifelong resident of Los Banos, began conducting tours of San Luis Island, highlighting the importance of the area's rookery, where willow trees in a five-acre wetland supported approximately fifteen hundred great blue herons, snowy and great egrets, and black-crowned night herons. Leach and Sousa solicited, and gained, the support of the National Audubon Society. During the society's 1963 Western Regional Conference, national conservation leaders participated in an overflight of the area supervised by Martin Winton, now president of the Grassland Water District. Local, regional, and national support for the acquisition of San Luis Island continued to swell; in March 1966, bowing to public pressure but also influenced by the Refuge Revenue Sharing Act, the Merced County Board of Supervisors finally approved the federal purchase of San Luis Island. The new 7,340-acre San Luis National Wildlife Refuge, occupying much of the southern part of San Luis Island, was dedicated in April 1966.[34]

Although historically the refuge lands had been spared the plow, they had been severely degraded as waterfowl habitat by decades of grazing and would require intensive management to recover. The marsh was "practically devoid of any submergent aquatics," cattle having pulled out these important waterfowl food plants by their root systems. Emergent plants, including Baltic rush, smartweed, spikerush, and alkali bulrush, had suffered from grazing as well, producing few seed heads. Within a few years, however, wetland management on the refuge had yielded an abundance of waterfowl foods including sprangletop, wild millet, spikerush, alkali bulrush, swamp timothy, and smartweed.[35] By 1970 the San Luis National Wildlife Refuge hosted a peak number of more than one-half million ducks and approximately ten thousand geese.[36]

The wetlands and uplands of the San Luis National Wildlife Refuge offered food and respite not only to waterfowl, but also to many other types of wildlife, including waterbirds such as herons, egrets, and lesser sandhill cranes; numerous species of reptiles and amphibians; and mammals, including the endangered San Joaquin kit fox and the majestic tule elk. Saved from probable extinction by the efforts of Henry Miller, tule elk had survived in the state in low numbers throughout the first two-thirds of the twentieth century. As early as 1964, before the refuge was approved, Alvaro Sousa had initiated an effort to bring tule elk to San Luis Island.[37] But it was not until February 1974 that the U.S. Fish and Wildlife Service signed a cooperative agreement with the California Department of Fish and Game to reintroduce the tule elk. The agencies constructed an enclosure on the San Luis Refuge, and in December they introduced eighteen elk—eleven bulls and seven cows—to the refuge from the San Diego Wild Animal Park. By

the middle of 1975 the herd numbered twenty-five animals and has since continued to thrive, providing surplus animals for relocation elsewhere in California.[38]

PRELUDE TO DISASTER

In fits and starts, public and private efforts were protecting and restoring portions of the wetlands of the San Joaquin Basin. Still greater promise for the
basin's wetlands appeared on the horizon when, in July 1970, officials of the U.S.
Bureau of Reclamation and the U.S. Fish and Wildlife Service created the new
5,900-acre Kesterson National Wildlife Refuge twelve miles north of Los Banos,
along the northeastern boundary of the Grassland Water District.[39] But at Kesterson, wetland restoration took an unexpected turn, and nearly fifteen years
later, in March 1985, Secretary of the Interior Donald Hodel ordered the immediate closure of the refuge's Kesterson Reservoir, in large part because he feared
that the federal government could be sued for killing wildlife in direct violation
of the Migratory Bird Treaty.

Hodel's alarm was rooted in the June 1983 discovery, by senior Fish and Wildlife Service biologists, of dozens of horribly deformed waterbird embryos and
newly hatched chicks at Kesterson. Scientists from the Fish and Wildlife Service
and the U.S. Geological Survey quickly identified selenium, a trace element, as
the probable cause of the developmental defects. Selenium—an essential nutrient
in small doses—had been leached by irrigation water from poorly drained soils
on the western side of the San Joaquin Valley, primarily in western Fresno
County. The selenium-laden drainwater was transported away from these lands
and ultimately deposited into Kesterson Reservoir, nearly a hundred miles to the
north, at levels toxic to wildlife.

The disaster at Kesterson, which unfolded throughout most of the 1980s and
drew widespread national attention, marked a serious reversal of fortune for the
San Joaquin Valley's wetlands, particularly those in the Grasslands area. The
events leading up to the morbid discovery at Kesterson are complex, and are
rooted in the tightly interwoven development of California's water projects and
irrigated agriculture. As was the case in the Grasslands a generation before, the
culprit was once again the Bureau of Reclamation's Central Valley Project—
specifically its 1960s extension, the San Luis Unit.

WATER FOR THE WESTSIDE

Since the nineteenth century, the arid and remote western side of the southern
San Joaquin Valley has lagged behind the eastern side in almost every measure of
development. Drier and hotter than the eastern half of the valley, the Westside
hosted fewer and smaller towns, supported less-diverse economic development,

and witnessed a much greater concentration of landownership.[40] As a result, the Westside developed a distinct regional identity, the legacy of which is still apparent. By 1957 approximately 3.7 million acres out of a total irrigable area of 8.0 million acres in the San Joaquin Valley had been placed under irrigation; but on the Westside, especially in the Tulare Basin, the lack of all but intermittent streams created a near-total dependence on groundwater for irrigation and placed limits on the prospects for future expansion.[41] The depletion of the region's aquifers had been recognized since the 1920s, and in the 1950s the Westside became the focus of plans for both an expanded Central Valley Project and a new State Water Project.

Agriculture had come late to the Westside of the southern San Joaquin Valley.[42] During the second half of the nineteenth century, Basque sheepherders, not farmers, dominated the regional economy of the Westside. The discovery of oil in 1864, and coal shortly thereafter, near the present-day city of Coalinga added a new dimension to the region's economy. Oil and coal eventually brought the railroad to the Westside, and during the late 1880s Southern Pacific tracks reached Coalinga from the east.[43] A major oil field at Coalinga was tapped in the late 1890s, initiating an oil boom and bringing in thousands of prospectors to the tiny hamlet. Production stabilized by about 1910, and most of those drawn to the region after that date came with hopes of farming its fertile soils. In 1909 G. T. Willis drilled the first deep well on the Westside, at a time when the groundwater table lay only fifty feet below the surface. Using the newly developed turbine pump, which allowed greater lift than older centrifugal pumps and therefore allowed access to deeper, higher-quality groundwater zones, Willis drilled down more than seven hundred feet. Significant irrigation development began in about 1915, and expanding agricultural operations gradually pushed sheepherders off the valley floor and into the Coast Range foothills. Cotton, already established farther south in the Tulare Basin, arrived on the Westside in 1923. Total irrigated acreage in the area, which had encompassed only 33,000 acres in 1922, exploded to 484,000 acres by 1948. In addition to cotton, the dominant crops by this time were hay and grain, each of which required less water than cotton and could be grown in winter; alfalfa and sugar beets were harvested as well.[44]

Groundwater could not serve the Westside's irrigation needs in perpetuity. By 1929 groundwater overdraft of the region's aquifers—measured as the amount by which withdrawals from pumping exceeded natural recharge—was already approaching 100,000 acre-feet annually, and groundwater levels were dropping noticeably.[45] Responding to diminishing supplies of groundwater and increasing pumping costs, in 1942 farmers from western Fresno County and adjacent northwestern Kings County formed the Westside Landowners Association "to urge and help finance studies of the feasibility of developing and constructing water supply systems to serve the west side."[46] During the next year, the Westside Landowners

Association entered into a contract with the Bureau of Reclamation to investigate the possibility of supplying water to the Westside from the Central Valley Project. The bureau determined that developed water supplies from the project's facilities at Shasta Dam on the Sacramento River and Friant Dam on the San Joaquin River would be inadequate to provide water on a permanent basis to the Westside. If the Westside landowners hoped to receive Central Valley Project water, the project's facilities would have to be expanded.[47]

Meanwhile, the groundwater situation on the Westside grew increasingly dire. Between 1946 and 1952, the depth to groundwater increased at an average rate of twenty-five feet per year, groundwater overdraft reached 500,000 acre-feet annually, and well-water levels dropped to an average of 423 feet below the surface. Seeking greater leverage with the Bureau of Reclamation as an official state entity, in 1952 Westside farmers organized the Westlands Water District, the successor of the Westside Landowners Association.[48] From its inception, Westlands would be exceptional for its size, influence, and concentration of large incorporated enterprises.[49] Stretching southward for nearly seventy miles from Mendota in Fresno County to Kettleman City in Kings County, the district originally encompassed 399,000 acres. Later, following its 1965 merger with the Westplains Water Storage District, which lay nestled between Westlands' western boundary and the foothills of the Coast Ranges, the district expanded to approximately 600,000 acres, well over nine hundred square miles, making it the largest agricultural irrigation district in the nation.[50]

The leaders of the new Westlands Water District were powerful men, whose standing within the private and public sectors symbolizes the nexus of wealth and influence that lay behind the district. The first board of directors in 1952 unanimously elected Jack E. O'Neill as president. O'Neill had arrived in the San Joaquin Valley in 1926 after trying his hand at growing and ginning cotton in the Imperial Valley, and had since risen to be a leader in the Westside's cotton and cattle industries. In 1953 the board named Jack W. Rodner, former manager of the Bureau of Reclamation's Fresno District office, Westlands' first manager. Rodner had already been active in the pursuit of a supplemental water supply for the Westside, and he now continued that pursuit on behalf of Westlands. After guiding the Westlands Water District during the formative years of the 1950s, both O'Neill and Rodner were succeeded by a second generation of forceful leaders. Cotton entrepreneur Russell Giffen followed O'Neill as president after the latter's death in 1961, and Ralph M. Brody, special counsel on water matters to Governor Edmund G. ("Pat") Brown, took over as Westlands' manager after Rodner returned to the bureau in 1960.[51] These men—O'Neill, Rodner, Giffen, and Brody—were instrumental in bringing federally subsidized water to the Westside in the late 1960s.

While the growers on the Westside were organizing, both the Bureau of Reclamation and the state of California were developing plans for massive water projects to bring water to the Westside and other water-deficient regions of the state. In 1949 the Bureau of Reclamation released a comprehensive plan for multiple-purpose development of the water resources of the entire Central Valley Basin.[52] The bureau envisioned extending the Central Valley Project farther south in the San Joaquin Valley by delivering winter surplus water from the Sacramento–San Joaquin Delta via the Delta-Mendota Canal, pumping it into a new storage reservoir, and releasing it as needed into a new gravity canal along the Westside. By 1955 the bureau's plan had located a site for a dam and a one million acre-foot storage reservoir, to be named the San Luis Reservoir, on San Luis Creek in the foothills of the inner Coast Range, almost due west from Los Banos and the Grasslands.[53] This "off-stream" site differed from the sites of previously constructed major reservoirs in the state in that most of the water stored behind the dam would not come from the watercourse behind the dam—in this case the inconsequential San Luis Creek—but rather would be imported from elsewhere. The bureau's dam, reservoir, canal, and pumping plants, to be known as the San Luis Unit of the Central Valley Project (or simply the San Luis Project), would serve not only the Westlands Water District, but also two smaller water districts immediately to the north.[54]

Significant portions of the lands along the Westside suffered from poor drainage, and the Bureau of Reclamation presciently noted that the operation of the San Luis Project "may create a general drainage problem along the lower, or eastern, edge of the service area and perhaps in a few isolated spots elsewhere. It appears probable, too, that this drainage water may be of such poor quality that it will have to be removed from the area."[55] The cause of the drainage problem was the largely impermeable Corcoran clay layer, ranging in depth from approximately eight hundred feet on the far western side of the San Joaquin Valley to as little as one hundred feet near the San Joaquin River in the valley's trough.[56] Formed as a lakebed about six hundred thousand years ago, the Corcoran clay layer prevents drainage of irrigation water, with the result that the soil has become fully saturated along much of the Westside, and the water table along its eastern fringe rises to within several feet of the surface.[57] Consequently, the bureau anticipated that a system of underground drains would be necessary for approximately 96,000 acres of the San Luis Unit's service area to drain saline groundwater away from lower-lying croplands.[58] The proposed drains would link to a surface interceptor drain that would convey the water 197 miles northward from the San Luis Unit service area to the Sacramento–San Joaquin Delta for disposal. The Bureau of Reclamation estimated the cost for this drainage system to be $20 million.[59]

As the bureau refined its San Luis Unit plan for the Westside during the 1950s, California was developing a remarkably similar plan of its own. In 1947 the legislature provided the funding for a statewide water investigation and, after ten years of studies, in 1957 the newly reorganized Department of Water Resources produced the California Water Plan, "a comprehensive master plan for the control, protection, conservation, distribution, and utilization of the waters of California."[60] The California Water Plan included the Feather River Project, the first phase of California's State Water Project, which rivaled the Central Valley Project in size and scope (see map 16). The Feather River Project proposed the world's tallest dam (at that time) at Oroville on the Feather River, the largest tributary of the Sacramento, and an aqueduct system that would deliver water to the San Francisco Bay region as well as to the Westside of the San Joaquin Valley and beyond, to Southern California.[61] Water released from the 770-foot-high Oroville Dam would flow down the Feather and Sacramento rivers and then through the Sacramento–San Joaquin Delta, where it would be lifted by pumps into the aqueduct system. Reaching the same conclusion as the bureau, the state determined that the San Luis site was the only suitable location for a reservoir to store the water destined for the Westside.[62] From the planning stages, therefore, the federal and state plans were in potential conflict, as each envisioned the same location for the reservoir that would be the linchpin of its project.

A sense of urgency about the Feather River Project developed after the tragic flood of late December 1955. Following a week of storms that deposited thirty or more inches of torrential rainfall across the region, levees along both the eastern and western banks of the Feather River collapsed on December 23 and just after midnight on December 24, respectively. The second breach flooded the entire community of Yuba City under as much as twenty-five feet of water.[63] The deluge inundated a total of one hundred thousand square miles, mostly in Sutter and Yuba counties astride the Feather River, claimed sixty-four lives, and caused hundreds of millions of dollars in property damage. Because it was evident that the flood and its impacts could have been greatly reduced had there been a dam in place, the California legislature appropriated more than $25 million to begin work immediately on the Feather River Project.[64]

Despite California's extensive water investigations and detailed planning, many growers on the Westside held greater confidence in a federal, rather than a state, project. Recalling how the state in the 1930s had been unable to finance and construct its earlier grand State Water Project—which had become instead the federal Central Valley Project—a group calling itself the San Luis Boosters, led by J. E. O'Neill, Russell Giffen, and other prominent Westside farmers, lobbied for federal authorization of the San Luis Project. Both the House and the Senate held hearings on the matter in 1956, but legislation did not advance at that time, in large part because California was not yet able to provide a united front in sup-

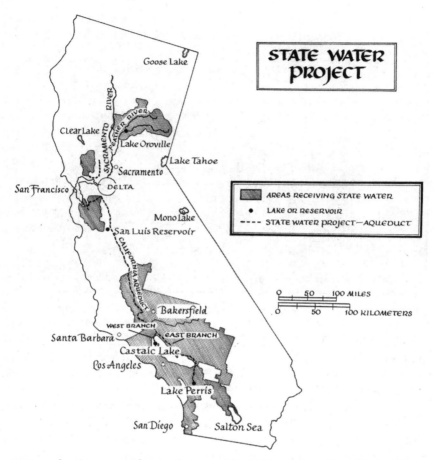

MAP 16. Service areas and major features of the California State Water Project. The California Aqueduct delivers water from the Sacramento Valley to the southern San Joaquin Valley and beyond to densely populated Southern California. Source: Norris Hundley Jr., *The Great Thirst: Californians and Water, a History*, rev. ed. (Berkeley and Los Angeles: University of California Press, 2001). Used with permission.

port of the project. The state faced internal opposition from those who objected to the provision of federal funds for a reclamation project that would serve an area dominated by large landowners whose holdings far exceeded the 160-acre limit of the Reclamation Act. The most adamant opposition came from water agencies with lands located downstream from the San Luis Project's service area, which would be the natural recipients of the project's salt-laden drainage flows.

They insisted that provision for drainage to protect their lands be included in the legislation. Each concern would need to be addressed before the federal project could advance.

In 1957 San Joaquin Valley congressman Bernie Sisk, a staunch ally of the San Luis Boosters, introduced legislation in the House that explicitly stated that the 160-acre limitation of the Reclamation Act would apply to all lands served by the San Luis Project, thereby addressing one major source of opposition to the federal project.[65] The Central California Irrigation District (CCID), a sprawling district formed in 1951 from the last vestiges of Miller and Lux's holdings, led the fight for the provision of drainage. The CCID lay immediately to the north of the water districts to be served by the San Luis Project and in the path of their drainage flow.[66] Represented by a prominent Merced water lawyer, C. Ray Robinson, the farmers of the CCID forced a 1958 amendment to the authorizing legislation for the San Luis Project that provided for a drainage disposal channel to carry away the wastewater to be generated by the project.[67]

Finally, with compromises in place regarding the application of reclamation law and the provision of drainage, in May 1960 Congress passed the San Luis Act, authorizing the U.S. Bureau of Reclamation to construct the San Luis Unit of the Central Valley Project. President Eisenhower signed the act in June.[68] The San Luis Act authorized the export of approximately 1.25 million acre-feet of water annually to the Westside to irrigate roughly 500,000 acres in Merced, Fresno, and Kings counties. After being collected by an underground drainage system, much of that irrigation water would be returned to the Sacramento–San Joaquin Delta as wastewater via the bureau's interceptor drain.

In a little-noticed but portentous decision, in 1962 the Bureau of Reclamation then expanded the service area of the San Luis Unit to include more than 112,000 additional acres, mostly along the low-lying eastern fringe of the Westlands Water District. The bureau had excluded these lands from the original service area in its 1955 feasibility report, noting that the "eastern boundary of the proposed service area . . . represent[s] the eastern edge of the better quality soils." Beyond this line, the soils were categorized as unsuitable for irrigation because of their high salinity and poor drainage characteristics.[69] After a new round of land classification studies urged by Westlands, however, the bureau reclassified these lands as irrigable and determined that they would be included within the San Luis service area (see map 17).[70] Lying in the trough of the San Joaquin Valley, much of this land is situated on or between extensive alluvial fans developed by three watercourses draining the Coast Ranges: Panoche, Little Panoche, and Cantua creeks. The Panoche fan was later found to produce drainage with the highest concentrations of selenium.[71]

During the late 1950s, while the San Luis Act was advancing through Congress, California continued to promote its State Water Project. In July 1959 the

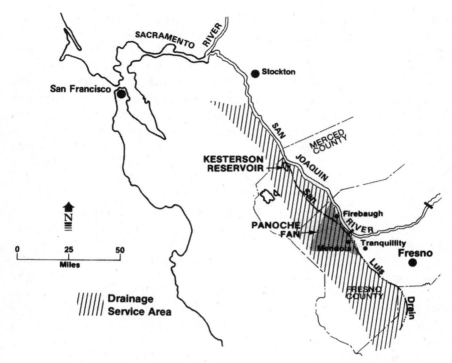

MAP 17. Drainage service area of the San Luis Unit of the Central Valley Project, including the location of the Panoche Fan, the source of much of the selenium that drained into Kesterson Reservoir. Courtesy of the U.S. Bureau of Reclamation.

state legislature brought the project one step closer to realization when it approved—subject to ratification by the voters in the 1960 general election—the Water Resources Bond Development Act, known as the Burns-Porter Act.[72] The act authorized $1.75 billion in bonds to help finance the construction of the first phase of the California Water Plan, which was essentially the Feather River Project. The act also provided for the Department of Water Resources to construct "facilities for removal of drainage water from the San Joaquin Valley." The state, like the Bureau of Reclamation, understood the necessity of providing adequate drainage for the Westside. Irrigation without drainage would be unsustainable; the accumulation of saline water would progressively render otherwise arable Westside land unsuitable for cultivation. In the 1957 California Water Plan, the Department of Water Resources had concluded, "At the present time, the most serious unsolved drainage problem in California is in the west side of the San Joaquin Valley. It is considered probable that full solution will require a master drainage channel extending from Buena Vista Lake in Kern County [at the southern end of the valley] to Suisun Bay [immediately west of the Delta]."[73]

Governor Brown, working with his special counsel on water issues, Ralph Brody, had lobbied fiercely for the passage of the Burns-Porter Act. An activist governor, presiding over California's protracted postwar boom years, Brown was adamant in his belief that the state's future prosperity depended on the continuing development of its water resources. This position was reflected in his 1951 legal opinion, during his tenure as California's attorney general, which had sacrificed the San Joaquin River's salmon runs to the Central Valley Project. Despite Brown's convictions, appeasing regional fears about water rights and convincing the voters to support the bond measure would pose a challenge.[74]

Support was strongest in the San Joaquin Valley, where agricultural landowners had suffered a defeat in 1958 when the U.S. Supreme Court, in *Ivanhoe v. McCracken,* refused to grant an exemption from the 160-acre limitation of the Reclamation Act to lands serviced by the Central Valley Project.[75] The State Water Project would impose no such limitation. Opposition to the bond measure was strongest in the Sacramento Valley and the Delta because Northern Californians remained wary that additional future water facilities might result in the export of more water to the south. Butte County, where Oroville Dam would be constructed and would boost the local economy, provided the only exception in the northern portion of the state to this pattern.

In Southern California, allegiances were more complicated. The Metropolitan Water District, representing most of the coastal population from greater Los Angeles to the border with Mexico, remained hesitant to endorse the State Water Project until days before the election. Although its subscribers would receive most of the water from the state project, the Metropolitan Water District feared that accepting this water would weaken the position of Southern California cities and water agencies before the Supreme Court in ongoing litigation with the state of Arizona over water allocations from the Colorado River.[76] When the election finally took place in November 1960, voters, reflecting these regional divisions, approved the bonds by a margin of only 173,944 votes out of a total of eight million cast.[77]

The passage of the bond measure guaranteed that California would construct the State Water Project at the same time that the federal government would construct the San Luis Unit of the Central Valley Project. Because there was only one suitable site for a dam to serve the Westside, and because it would be redundant and unnecessarily expensive to construct parallel federal and state aqueducts, California had a clear interest in sharing the facilities of the San Luis Unit with the federal government and incorporating those shared facilities into the State Water Project.[78] In December 1961 Secretary of the Interior Stewart L. Udall approved an agreement between the U.S. Bureau of Reclamation and the state of

California for the joint operation of the San Luis Unit. The bureau would construct, and the California Department of Water Resources would operate, the joint-use facilities, including the San Luis Dam and Reservoir, which would be enlarged to slightly more than two million acre-feet.

The Bureau of Reclamation would deliver water from the Delta to the San Luis Reservoir via the Delta-Mendota Canal. The state of California, for its part, would bring water from the Delta to the San Luis Reservoir via a new California Aqueduct, part of the State Water Project.[79] The California Aqueduct would continue south from the San Luis Reservoir, but for approximately the next 102 miles it would be known as the San Luis Canal and would deliver federal water to the service area of the San Luis Unit of the Central Valley Project. As it passed beyond Kettleman City and the southern boundary of the Westlands Water District, the San Luis Canal would continue once again as the California Aqueduct, supplying the service area of the State Water Project in Kings and Kern counties in the western Tulare Basin, and beyond the Tehachapi Mountains in Southern California.

Supporters of this massive federal-state project held high hopes for the bounty it promised. Senator Clair Engle spoke at the San Luis Dam site in August 1962 and echoed the thoughts of many boosters when he proclaimed that the San Luis Project "marks an economic renaissance for the west side of the San Joaquin Valley." Anticipating the breakup of the large landholdings that had dominated the Westside for decades, Engle declared, "I predict that in due course water from San Luis will transform the west side of the southern San Joaquin Valley into a prosperous belt of diversified agriculture, dotted with thriving cities and towns like we see today on the east side of the valley along the Friant-Kern Canal."[80] A half-century later, agriculture has indeed flourished, but the family farms and the thriving cities and towns they would support have yet to appear.

PROVIDING DRAINAGE

The San Luis Act had provided for two possibilities for drainage: either California was to construct a master drain that would serve all portions of the San Joaquin Valley receiving water from the State Water Project and the San Luis Unit of the Central Valley Project, or the federal government was to construct a smaller interceptor drain to serve only the lands irrigated by the San Luis Unit. This requirement of the San Luis Act remained unfulfilled for nearly a decade, as both the state and the federal governments were reluctant to take on the responsibility and cost of constructing the drain.

After opting out of constructing a master drain in June 1961 and therefore leaving the drainage responsibility to the Bureau of Reclamation, the California Department of Water Resources reversed its position in April 1964. The agency now assured the bureau that it would construct a master drain for the entire San Joaquin Valley, including the San Luis Unit service area, and would allow for participation by the bureau in the enterprise. The master drain would extend approximately 280 miles from Bakersfield to a discharge point near the city of Antioch in Contra Costa County in the western Delta. The concrete-lined drain would enlarge steadily from its southern end to its northern terminus, its capacity increasing from approximately sixty cubic feet per second to nine hundred cubic feet per second. This terminal capacity would be well in excess of one-third of the average flow of the San Joaquin River, and would create, in effect, a new river to drain the San Joaquin Valley—a river composed nearly entirely of agricultural wastewater. The Department of Water Resources estimated that by the year 2000 the drain would convey approximately 500,000 acre-feet of this saline drainage water to the Delta annually.[81]

The Department of Water Resources and the Bureau of Reclamation cooperated on plans and designs for the master drain from mid-1964 until late 1966. In 1967, however, Ronald Reagan replaced Edmund "Pat" Brown in the governor's office. The new administration determined that California would not be able to cover its share of the capital costs for the drain. Therefore, in March Governor Reagan's new director of the Department of Water Resources, William Giannelli, informed the Bureau of Reclamation that despite its earlier assurances, the state would not participate in the construction of the master drain after all. The bureau should instead proceed alone with the construction of the smaller interceptor drain that would serve only the Central Valley Project's San Luis Unit.[82] Full responsibility for drainage thus fell once again on the bureau, which was being sued by the Central California Irrigation District for its failure to construct the drain, even as it prepared to begin water deliveries.[83] The bureau's legally tenuous position stemmed from the fact that in January 1963, while plans for a drain were at a standstill, the Department of the Interior had approved a contract with the Westlands Water District for the delivery of up to one million acre-feet of Central Valley Project water annually, the largest water contract ever approved by the federal government.[84] In 1966 the bureau had begun construction of water distribution works throughout the San Luis service area, and was poised to begin major water deliveries in 1968 as soon as the San Luis Canal was completed.[85]

In January 1968 the Bureau of Reclamation finally committed to building the interceptor drain.[86] Acting alone, over the next seven years the bureau constructed the first 85-mile segment of a planned 188-mile San Luis Drain, which would stretch from Kettleman City, at the southern end of the San Luis Unit's service area, northward to the Delta (see map 18). This initial section of the drain began in the south near the small town of Five Points in the Westlands Water District; its terminus was in the northern Grasslands at Kesterson Reservoir within the new Kesterson National Wildlife Refuge. The refuge had been planned

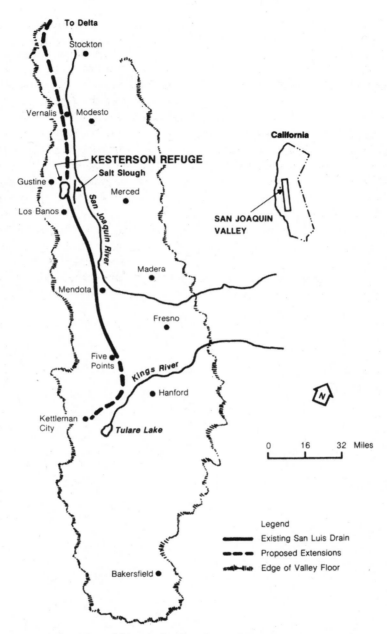

To Delta
Stockton
Vernalis
Modesto
KESTERSON REFUGE
Salt Slough
Gustine
Merced
Los Banos
San Joaquin River
Madera
Mendota
Fresno
Five Points
Kings River
Hanford
Kettleman City
Tulare Lake
Bakersfield

California

SAN JOAQUIN VALLEY

N

0   16   32   Miles

Legend
━━━━━ Existing San Luis Drain
▄ ▄ ▄ Proposed Extensions
⟋⟍ Edge of Valley Floor

MAP 18. Location of the initial eighty-five-mile segment of the U.S. Bureau of Reclamation's San Luis Drain, from Five Points to Kesterson Reservoir, as well as that of the proposed full-length 188-mile drain, from Kettleman City to the Delta. Courtesy of the U.S. Bureau of Reclamation.

to operate in conjunction with the bureau's San Luis Drain project, and, at a cost of $10 million, the bureau had constructed Kesterson Reservoir to receive the agricultural wastewater from the drain. The reservoir consisted of twelve inter-connected evaporation and seepage ponds, averaging three and one-half feet deep, and covering 1,283 acres of the refuge's 5,900 acres.[87]

The potential environmental impacts of Kesterson Reservoir generated few initial concerns. Studies of those impacts focused primarily on potential seepage of the drainwater into underlying aquifers and the waterlogging of adjacent lands. Ecological apprehensions regarding the reuse of drainwater to supply wetlands were not for the most part publicly expressed, and those that were voiced were narrowly limited to potential problems of excessive salinity. Therefore, based on the premise that Kesterson Reservoir could be managed beneficially for resident and migratory waterfowl of the Pacific Flyway, in July 1970 the bureau and the U.S. Fish and Wildlife Service signed a cooperative agreement for the manage-ment of the Kesterson National Wildlife Refuge.[88] The flaw in this plan would prove to be selenium in the drainwater.

9

Tragedy at Kesterson Reservoir

The new Kesterson National Wildlife Refuge had much in common with the recently established San Luis National Wildlife Refuge, located just a few miles to the southeast. The land within the Kesterson refuge was native grassland that had never been used for agricultural purposes. Bisected by Mud Slough, a tributary of the San Joaquin River, the land had been utilized for cattle ranching and waterfowl hunting for many years, with private duck clubs leasing hunting privileges from the landowners. Nearly half of the fall and winter marsh acreage at Kesterson was seasonally flooded grassland. These seasonal wetlands provided an abundance of food for early Pacific Flyway migrants, especially northern pintail. Upland grasses, appearing after the first winter rains, provided an important food source for grazing geese and American wigeon. Grasses and their nutritious seeds were available in copious amounts, but because of the scarcity of summer water prior to development of the refuge, aquatic plants for waterfowl forage "were almost nonexistent."[1] As a partial remedy for this seasonal water shortage, the Grassland Water District, under its water contract with the U.S. Bureau of Reclamation and the U.S. Fish and Wildlife Service, was to furnish the nascent refuge, without charge, several thousand acre-feet of water annually.[2]

While new water supplies were enhancing the refuge's seasonal wetlands, surface agricultural drainage water, delivered via the U.S. Bureau of Reclamation's partially completed San Luis Drain, began flowing into the ponds of Kesterson Reservoir in 1972.[3] This surface drainage, diluted with irrigation-quality water, was of similar quality to the water that had been used for years to flood the surrounding duck club lands. The water provided high-quality wetland habitat, including breeding habitat, on the reservoir ponds. Mallards, gadwalls, cinnamon teal, ruddy ducks, redheads, and other duck species nested in the spring and raised their young there. Together with the San Luis Drain, Kesterson Reservoir attracted tens of thousands of migratory and resident waterfowl and other aquatic birds, and supported numerous species of fish.[4] The new Kesterson National Wildlife Refuge—including its reservoir—appeared to be a success, but the success proved illusory.

Budget constraints and effective political opposition prevented completion of the lower segment of the San Luis Drain from Kesterson to the Delta by the Bureau of Reclamation. Resistance to a drain that would discharge into the Delta had developed as early as 1964, when the state had announced that it would build a master drain. After the bureau assumed responsibility for the drain, local residents and officials, especially Congressman George Miller, elected in 1974, continued to object to the proposed dumping of saline agricultural drainage flows into the Delta, which could negatively affect the region's freshwater supplies as well as the biological integrity of the Delta itself.[5] With little possibility of quickly completing the San Luis Drain, in 1975 the bureau made the fateful decision to change Kesterson's status from a regulating reservoir to a terminal holding reservoir that would store and concentrate drainage water. When the flow of the San Joaquin River was considered sufficiently high to dilute contaminants present in the drainwater in the Kesterson ponds, water from Kesterson would be discharged into the river for transport to the Delta.[6]

There was an inherent disjunction between the recognition by both the state and the federal governments that water development projects in the San Joaquin Valley should not be detrimental to wildlife, and the decision by those same governments to store and concentrate agricultural drainwater on a national wildlife refuge. The Bureau of Reclamation's 1955 feasibility report on the San Luis Project had noted that fish and wildlife were to be protected from adverse effects, and the California Department of Water Resources had repeatedly stressed the same point.[7] The department's 1957 California Water Plan stated, "The necessity for protection and enhancement of fish and wildlife resources and for the development of the recreational potential are important considerations that must be borne in mind in further development of the surface water resources of the [Central Valley] basin."[8]

Despite these acknowledgments of responsibility for fish and wildlife, with the State Water Project anticipated ultimately to import more than 8.5 million acre-feet of irrigation water annually into the San Joaquin Valley, bringing into agricultural production as much as 2.5 million acres of undeveloped land, the state began to think of the agricultural wastewater that would result from the project as an asset rather than a liability.[9] In a 1965 drainage investigation report, the Department of Water Resources adopted the position that it was possible to reuse agricultural drainwater beneficially to preserve the valley's fish and wildlife. The use of agricultural wastewater would contribute to the management of marshlands in the valley, maintaining waterfowl habitat for both resident wildlife and migratory birds of the Pacific Flyway.[10]

In reaching this conclusion, the department relied in part on a 1960 report by California Department of Fish and Game biologist Howard Leach. Mindful of the fact that land development and reclamation to be made possible by the State Water Project would destroy most of the remaining wildlife habitat in the San Joaquin Valley, Leach pointed out the potential value of reusing drainage water in the development of wetland habitat on marginal lands that would not be reclaimed, including duck club lands. He believed that the beneficial reuse of this water would be possible if good-quality dilution water from the California Aqueduct made it acceptable for fish and wildlife. Although he did not specifically mention selenium, Leach was careful to point out that beneficial reuse was based on the presumption that "toxic industrial wastes or excessive amounts of pesticides are not included in the drain water."[11]

While the California Department of Water Resources was developing its policy during the 1960s on the beneficial reuse of drainwater, it paid little heed to other reports, from both within and outside the agency, that began to suggest that the reuse of drainwater might pose significant risks. In December 1960 one of the department's own reports identified drainage from irrigated agriculture as an important cause of water quality degradation in the lower San Joaquin Valley and explicitly stated that waters draining from the area of the Panoche Fan in the northern portion of the Westlands Water District "are highly concentrated from a quality standpoint and are unusable for beneficial purposes."[12] In 1961 soil scientist H. W. Lakin of the U.S. Department of Agriculture, who along with H. G. Bryers had discovered selenium in two Coast Range locations as early as 1939, reported that selenium would be present in soluble, bioavailable forms in alkali soils.[13] Such soils are widespread in the more arid parts of the San Joaquin Valley, particularly on the Westside, where they have been formed by the erosion of the adjacent Coast Ranges.[14] In 1962 the U.S. Fish and Wildlife Service warned the Bureau of Reclamation about the bioaccumulation of toxins in organisms, including fish and waterfowl, exposed to agricultural drainage, and the subsequent health threat to humans who might consume them.[15] The next year the service issued another warning to the bureau that contaminants in drainwater would make such water unfit for enhancing waterfowl habitat. In 1964 the Department of Water Resources discovered selenium in a water sample from the Panoche Drain, which runs into the Grassland Water District, and reported the results to the Bureau of Reclamation.[16]

Meanwhile, as early as 1963 the Fish and Wildlife Service warned that drainwater, if impounded, could also contaminate groundwater. This warning was reissued in 1977, when a study prepared for the California State Water Resources

Control Board—the entity responsible for setting statewide water quality policy and acting as the state's water pollution control agency—found that if Kesterson remained the terminus of the San Luis Drain, "the underlying confined aquifer would ultimately be contaminated."[17] The same year, a study performed for the Fish and Wildlife Service reported that a closed marsh system supplied with sub-surface agricultural drainage, as Kesterson was, would provide good wildlife habitat for no longer than three years and would eventually be destroyed.[18] Neither Bureau of Reclamation nor Fish and Wildlife Service officials acted on these warnings about the potential risks of drainwater to wildlife and human populations as they created the Kesterson National Wildlife Refuge, and as the bureau turned Kesterson Reservoir into a terminal sump for agricultural drainage water flowing from the San Joaquin Valley's Westside.

To address the drainage problem on the Westside, where irrigation water trapped by the Corcoran clay layer threatened to saturate the root zone of crops, between 1976 and 1980 the Bureau of Reclamation constructed the Westlands Drainage Collector System, a network of plastic drains lying six to eight feet below the ground surface. The system was to serve an initial 42,000 acres in the northeastern part of the Westlands Water District, where the drainage problems were most severe. On-farm drains, provided by the landowners, discharged directly into the bureau's collector pipes, which in turn discharged to larger carrier pipes, which conveyed the water to the San Luis Drain and thence to Kesterson Reservoir.[19]

The bureau had little choice but to deliver the subsurface agricultural drain-water from the Westlands Drainage Collector System to Kesterson Reservoir. Bound by the 1960 San Luis Act to provide drainage to Westlands, and lacking both funds and public support for completing the drain to the Delta, in 1978 the bureau began deliveries of subsurface drainage to Kesterson. A crucial difference between surface and subsurface drainage is that, unlike surface drainage, subsurface drainage has percolated down through the soil profile, picking up leachates, including salts and trace elements such as arsenic, boron, chromium, molybdenum, and selenium along the way.[20] Unfortunately for the wildlife at Kesterson, the acreage of the Westlands Water District included in the collector system yielded subsurface drainage heavily contaminated by one such trace element—selenium. These lands are located on the lower fringe of the Panoche Fan, the area from which the Department of Water Resources had warned in 1960 that drainage could serve no beneficial purpose.

The prospects for the completion of the bureau's drain to the Delta appeared to improve in 1979. In June of that year, the San Joaquin Valley Interagency Drainage Program (IDP), which had been formed in 1975 by the U.S. Bureau of Reclamation, the California Department of Water Resources, and the California State Water Resources Control Board, issued its final report, *Agricultural Drain-*

age and Salt Management in the San Joaquin Valley. The IDP had evaluated numerous potential solutions for managing saline drainwater in the valley, including the creation of in-valley evaporation ponds; discharge to the Pacific Ocean via a pipeline over the Coast Ranges, possibly to ecologically rich Monterey Bay; discharge to the San Joaquin River; and discharge via drain directly to the western Delta or Suisun Bay. Ultimately, the IDP recommended the completion of the drain from Kesterson to the Delta, with the discharge location now changed from Antioch to a point several miles west at Chipps Island, near the boundary between the Delta and Suisun Bay.[21] This plan theoretically represented the most economical and environmentally acceptable solution to the San Joaquin Valley's need for drainage and management of salts.[22] Based on the IDP's report, the Bureau of Reclamation requested a waste discharge permit from the State Water Resources Control Board; the board in turn required that the bureau first conduct technical studies of San Luis Drain wastewater. The bureau began its studies in May 1981, the same year in which the agency instructed the Westlands Water District to cease any further connections of on-farm drains to the main San Luis Drain because Kesterson Reservoir was already operating at full capacity, receiving between 6,500 and 8,500 acre-feet of agricultural drainage flows annually. Inflow to the reservoir now consisted almost entirely of subsurface drainage, undiluted by surface flows.[23]

MONSTROSITIES

It was not long before contaminated subsurface drainwater began to affect wildlife at Kesterson. In June 1981, one month after the wastewater studies began, a Bureau of Reclamation field researcher discovered high levels of selenium at Kesterson, but these findings were not released to the public or reported to the State Water Resources Control Board.[24] In April 1982 Gary Zahm, manager of the San Luis National Wildlife Refuge Complex, of which the Kesterson National Wildlife Refuge was a part, reported that in the four years since the introduction of subsurface drainage waters to the holding ponds, cattails were dying, algal blooms were occurring, fewer waterfowl were present, and all but one species of fish— mosquitofish—had been extirpated.[25] Tests conducted in 1982 by U.S. Fish and Wildlife Service scientists on the remaining mosquitofish indicated selenium concentrations higher than ever recorded in a living fish. Fisheries biologist Michael Saiki found that these levels were nearly one hundred times greater than those found in fish at the state Volta Wildlife Area, about six miles southwest of Kesterson.[26] Receiving fresh irrigation water from the Sacramento–San Joaquin Delta via the Delta-Mendota Canal, the Volta Wildlife Area served as an effective reference site for comparing naturally occurring, or background, levels of toxins. The Fish and Wildlife Service provided the toxicity data on the mosquitofish to

FIGURE 14. Felix Smith of the U.S. Fish and Wildlife Service holding a coot hatchling, the first deformed bird found at Kesterson Reservoir, June 7, 1983. The bird lacked eyes, a lower bill, and feet. Photo courtesy of Harry Ohlendorf, U.S. Fish and Wildlife Service, retired.

the Bureau of Reclamation in December, but the bureau failed to recognize the significance of the findings. Instead, the bureau questioned the ability of the Fish and Wildlife Service to detect and test for selenium.[27]

During the spring of 1983, the Fish and Wildlife Service increased the scope of its studies at Kesterson. Although Kesterson and the other public and private Central Valley wetlands served primarily as wintering grounds for migratory waterfowl, there remained a small but significant population of resident breeding birds. From April through July, the service monitored hundreds of nests of these aquatic birds, including the American coot, mallard, northern pintail, cinnamon teal, gadwall, black-necked stilt, American avocet, and eared grebe. On June 7 biologists Harry Ohlendorf and Felix Smith found the first of hundreds of dead and dying horribly deformed embryos and chicks (see figure 14). By the end of the summer breeding season, the Fish and Wildlife Service had discovered that one nest in ten contained one or more deformed chicks, a percentage of developmental abnormalities far greater than normally expected in an uncontaminated population of wild birds. The deformities (see figure 15) included missing or abnormal eyes, beaks, wings, legs, and feet, as well as exencephaly (the brain

FIGURE 15. Deformed black-necked stilt from Kesterson Reservoir. This bird lacked eyes and a lower bill, and its upper bill was corkscrewed. Photo courtesy of the U.S. Fish and Wildlife Service.

protruding through eye sockets) and hydrocephaly (excess fluid within the skull resulting in compression of the brain).[28]

Ohlendorf and Smith, highly respected career scientists with the service, soon found themselves embroiled in a controversy that would profoundly affect their careers. During most of the 1970s, Ohlendorf had been assistant director of the Fish and Wildlife Service's Patuxent Wildlife Research Center in Maryland. Since 1980 he had been director of Patuxent's new Pacific field station, located on the campus of the University of California, Davis, close to the state capital at Sacramento. Ohlendorf and his staff were responsible for several areas of research, including potential uses of agricultural return flows.[29] Felix Smith, Ohlendorf's companion on that fateful day in June, was a fish and wildlife biologist, and a nationally recognized conservationist.[30] In 1983 he was working out of the service's Sacramento office as an environmental assessment specialist.

Harry Ohlendorf found close parallels between the deformities observed at Kesterson and those reported in chickens raised on seleniferous soils in South Dakota during the 1930s.[31] Experiments conducted at the South Dakota Agricultural Experiment Station as early as 1937 demonstrated the occurrence of deformed embryos when chickens were fed rations containing as little as 3.5 parts per million (ppm) of selenium. Reports of acute and chronic selenium toxicity in livestock date back further, to the nineteenth century, when thousands of cattle and horses died across the western states as a result of grazing on forage with high selenium content. Acute poisoning, known as the blind staggers, occurs when animals are brought into a seleniferous area for the first time. After suffering impaired mobility and disorientation, livestock may die from respiratory failure within a day or two. A chronic, less intense form of selenium toxicity is known as alkali disease, reflecting the nineteenth-century belief that it was caused by drinking alkaline waters. Early in the twentieth century, researchers found that alkali disease was caused by selenium, when present in vegetation or feed at levels as low as 5 ppm. Symptoms of the disease include lack of vitality, loss of hair, growth retardation, and hoof deformities. Death results from anemia and the general wasting away of the body.[32] Although the biochemical pathways of its transmission were not thoroughly understood, selenium had thus been known for many years to be toxic to animals. These early studies involved terrestrial ecosystems only. At the time of the first discoveries at Kesterson, little was known about the movement of selenium through aquatic ecosystems. The implications of this earlier generation of terrestrial research had not yet been explored.

Realizing the potential dimensions of the selenium threat, on June 10, 1983, three days after finding the first deformed chick at Kesterson, Felix Smith issued his first of numerous and increasingly strident internal Fish and Wildlife Service memoranda expressing concern over the use of agricultural wastewater for marsh management.[33] On June 13 Dave Lenhart—a Fish and Wildlife Service contaminant specialist in the Portland, Oregon, regional office—provided a "concern alert" to Deputy Regional Director Joseph Blum.[34] This memorandum summarized the findings at Kesterson, stressed the dangers of selenium-laced drainwater to fish and wildlife, and recommended setting aside funding for further studies. In July the Fish and Wildlife Service notified the Bureau of Reclamation of the elevated frequency of embryo and chick developmental abnormalities at Kesterson and forwarded a copy of the concern alert. Unpersuaded by these warnings, the bureau's response was to downplay the significance of the threat, cast doubt that selenium was responsible for the waterfowl problems, and continue to question the service's ability to analyze for selenium.[35]

Scientific evidence contrary to the Bureau of Reclamation's position quickly accumulated. After the bureau had first questioned the Fish and Wildlife Service's findings in December 1982, the service contacted the U.S. Geological Survey (USGS) and requested assistance in validating the data. In August 1983, highly esteemed USGS geologist Ivan Barnes and chemist Theresa Presser conducted an independent analysis for selenium in Kesterson collection ponds, the San Luis Drain, drainage effluents, and shallow groundwater. Preliminary results of the analysis indicated dangerous levels of selenium. The USGS released its data at an agricultural wastewater workshop held at the University of California, Davis, in

February 1984. Presser and Barnes found that selenium concentrations in irrigation water entering the San Luis Drain from the Westlands Water District ranged from 140 to 1,400 micrograms per liter (μg/L), as compared to concentrations in typical fresh water of 0.2–0.4 μg/L.[36] Furthermore, their findings demonstrated levels of selenium significantly higher than the bureau's figures. The USGS reported gross errors in the bureau's laboratory and field techniques, and found that the bureau had used techniques neither approved by the U.S. Environmental Protection Agency nor generally accepted by the scientific community.[37] The USGS also tested sites throughout the Westside, and found that the problem of elevated selenium levels extended from Los Banos south to Kettleman City, with the highest concentrations found in the Panoche Fan area.[38]

By the time the USGS published its findings, both the media and private citizens were challenging the Bureau of Reclamation. Reporter Deborah Blum of the *Fresno Bee* first broke the Kesterson story on September 21, 1983.[39] Quickly the other major newspapers in the state took up the developing saga, and public outrage, fed by disturbing images of grotesquely malformed birds, rose to a crescendo.[40] On March 16, 1984, James and Karen Claus, owners of a combination duck hunting club and cattle ranch adjacent to Kesterson, initiated a petition to the Central Valley Regional Water Quality Control Board to take enforcement action against the Bureau of Reclamation.[41] The Clauses reported finding sick and deformed birds on their property; other wildlife, such as fish and frogs, were suddenly absent. When the regional board, historically dominated by and beholden to local agricultural interests, declined to take action, the Clauses appealed to the more powerful State Water Resources Control Board on May 18, 1984.[42] Meanwhile, media pressure intensified. In August 1984 United Press International journalists Lloyd Carter and Gregory Gordon prepared a five-part series on the Kesterson problem, which the *Fresno Bee* carried in its entirety.[43] In October San Francisco's public television station, KQED, presented a powerful documentary on Kesterson, titled *Down the Drain*.[44] The film challenged the veracity of the Bureau of Reclamation, and in particular that of its new regional director, David Houston, an appointee of President Reagan's interior secretary, James Watt. Facing this barrage of challenges, the bureau found itself in an increasingly defensive position.

There were growing suspicions among U.S. Fish and Wildlife Service and California Department of Fish and Game scientists that the selenium toxicity at Kesterson posed a danger not only to wildlife, but to humans as well. By 1984 the Kesterson ponds were leaking approximately three million gallons per month into Merced County groundwater, threatening local water supplies and devastating properties adjacent to the refuge.[45] The Clauses were not alone in reporting deteriorating conditions on their property. The Freitas family, whose ranch was also adjacent to Kesterson, reported that they lost dozens of cattle from contaminated drinking water, their sheep suffered spontaneous abortions, and their vegetable plants died. After suffering negative health effects, the family was forced to move off their ranch.[46] In response to high levels of contamination, in August 1984 the Fish and Wildlife Service developed an occupational health and safety program for its personnel at Kesterson. The program required breathing masks to prevent respiratory problems, frequent showers and changes of clothes, and monitoring of selenium levels in bodily fluids. In September the service began a waterfowl-hazing program at Kesterson, for the protection of both waterfowl and hunters. Citing the results of tests on birds collected at Kesterson by the Department of Fish and Game in October 1984, the California Department of Health Services issued a warning to hunters about consuming ducks shot in western Merced County. Pregnant women and children under the age of ten were advised to avoid duck meat completely, while others were instructed to eat no more than two meals of duck per week.[47]

THE SCIENCE OF SELENIUM

The chemistry of selenium reveals why it is highly toxic above certain thresholds. First discovered by Jon Jakob Berzelius in 1817, selenium has an atomic structure and chemical properties that are similar to sulfur. Several biochemical reactions do not discriminate between selenium and sulfur, and in the presence of excess selenium organisms bind it, rather than sulfur, into amino acids, the building blocks of proteins. In embryos, incorporated selenium interferes with the ability to utilize oxygen, resulting in deformities. In adults, selenium damages internal organs and the respiratory system.[48] From water and sediments, the latter of which act as a sink or collecting medium, selenium enters the aquatic food chain as it is accumulated by phytoplankton, algae, rooted vegetation, and invertebrates. Eventually the selenium moves to organisms in the higher trophic levels, or categories of consumers, including birds and terrestrial predators, where it accumulates in their organs or tissues. It is the bioavailability of selenium, determined by its metabolic pathways, rather than its concentration per se, that determines the expected level of toxic effects, including teratogenesis, or embryonic malformation.[49]

The effects of selenium on plant and animal communities in aquatic environments were essentially unknown before the Fish and Wildlife Service conducted studies at Kesterson from 1983 through 1985. The main focus was on aquatic bird species, chosen for their differing food habits and abundance during the nesting season, but the service also studied mosquitofish, bullfrogs, gopher snakes, and mice and voles to assess selenium's impact on fish, amphibian, reptile, and mammal populations. At least 39 percent of the 579 waterbird nests monitored to hatching from 1983 through 1985 contained at least one dead or deformed embryo or chick. Whereas the 1983 discoveries were of embryos and newly hatched chicks only, beginning in 1984 the Fish and Wildlife Service found adult birds dead from selenium poisoning as well. These discoveries at Kesterson are particularly revealing when compared to observations from the nearby Volta Wildlife Area. During the three years of the study, the service found only 4 dead embryos, and none with deformities, in 339 eggs (1 percent) at Volta. By contrast, the service identified 604 dead or deformed embryos in 2,689 eggs (22 percent) at Kesterson. Furthermore, there were no signs of survival at Kesterson among the nearly 440 black-necked stilt and American avocet chicks that hatched in 1984 and 1985.[50]

Expanding the selenium research beyond Kesterson, the U.S. Fish and Wildlife Service, the California Department of Fish and Game, and the U.S. Geological Survey conducted additional studies in the Grasslands area west of the San Joaquin River during 1984. The Grassland Water District was then supplementing its 50,000 acre-feet of guaranteed fresh water from the Bureau of Reclamation with approximately 80,000 acre-feet of irrigation return flows, including both surface and subsurface drainage. In June the USGS found selenium concentrations as high as $4,200 \mu g/L$ in drainage water flowing into the Grassland Water District.[51] Elevated levels of selenium were found in aquatic plants, fish, and birds throughout the area. In aquatic birds, particularly American coots, gallinules (common moorhens), black-necked stilts, and American avocets, selenium concentrations "were sufficiently elevated to assume that reproductive problems were likely to have occurred there."[52] As a result of these findings, in 1985 the Grassland Water District ended its practice, in place since 1954, of contracting with local drainage entities for agricultural drainwater for spring and summer flooding of wetland habitat.[53] Instead, with few choices available, the district channeled the drainwater that crossed its boundaries into canals and natural sloughs for discharge directly into the San Joaquin River. Such engineering modifications relocated, but did not solve, the selenium problem. By the end of 1985 researchers had confirmed problematic levels of selenium in water, fish, and wildlife throughout the Grasslands area—in the waterways of the Grassland Water District, Mud Slough, Salt Slough, and the San Joaquin River.[54]

Selenium toxicity was taking a toll at Kesterson and on neighboring lands. Based on his observations, Harry Ohlendorf conservatively estimated that at least one thousand migratory birds, including adults, chicks, and embryos, died at Kesterson alone from 1983 to 1985. The probable cause of death was selenium toxicosis brought on by the bioaccumulation of that element. Recent research findings have persuasively shown that the toxicity threshold for waterborne selenium is less than or equal to $5 \mu g/L$.[55] Selenium concentrations in water entering Kesterson from the San Luis Drain between 1983 and 1985 averaged $300 \mu g/L$, at least sixty times greater than the toxicity threshold and approximately three orders of magnitude greater than the average concentration for uncontaminated surface waters. The danger to wetland birds of these exceedingly high levels of selenium is exacerbated by the nature of aquatic ecosystems, in which selenium bioaccumulates to a greater extent than in terrestrial ecosystems. In a terrestrial environment, bioaccumulation occurs primarily by ingestion of contaminated food or water, but in aquatic systems, bioaccumulation occurs by direct adsorption by surface tissue as well as by ingestion. The ducks and other waterbirds of Kesterson died from feeding on plants, invertebrates, and fish that had bioaccumulated selenium at from 12 to 120 times normal levels.[56]

THE POLITICS OF DRAINWATER

On December 3, 1983, the Department of Conservation and Resource Studies at the University of California at Berkeley sponsored the first of four public symposia on the environmental implications of the crisis at Kesterson.[57] At these symposia, which highlighted presentations by leading scientific and legal experts, concerns quickly turned to the apparent suppression of scientific information under what some participants characterized as federal "gag orders," and the apparent retribution against government scientists who were calling attention to pollution problems at Kesterson. As early as the first symposium, Congressman George Miller warned against censorship of scientific information by government agencies.[58]

During the summer of 1983, prior to the publication of the first newspaper article on the Kesterson crisis, the Sacramento office of the U.S. Fish and Wildlife Service had prepared a report for release to the press that disclosed the Kesterson findings. Known internally as a "white paper," the report was never approved for release by Department of the Interior officials in Washington. Felix Smith contends that Joseph Blum, deputy regional director of the Fish and Wildlife Service, acting under pressure from the Bureau of Reclamation as well as his superiors in the Department of the Interior, ordered him to destroy the report. Smith continued to speak out publicly about the dangers posed to wildlife and human health by the drainage water flowing into Kesterson, and by 1985 he faced the abolition of his position with the Fish and Wildlife Service in Sacramento and an imminent transfer to Portland, Oregon. At this point, Hamilton Candee of the Natural Resources Defense Council, with whom Smith had been in close contact, alerted attorney Louis Clark, executive director of the private, nonprofit Government Accountability Project in Washington, D.C., to the situation. Clark volunteered to represent Smith, and succeeded in enjoining the service from transferring or harassing him.[59]

Felix Smith was not the only Fish and Wildlife Service scientist whose professional integrity was threatened by the politics surrounding the Kesterson affair. William Sweeney, whose position as California area manager for the Fish and

Wildlife Service was later abolished, contended that a 1982 decree prohibiting employees from corresponding with the state of California or issuing public testimony without first routing such material through the Interior Department's regional solicitor for review amounted to a gag order. Sweeney would later testify that "within the Department of the Interior hierarchy, the Fish and Wildlife Service is simply trampled on by the Bureau of Reclamation, generally with the support of both the Solicitor's office and a powerful western political constituency."[60] Jim Foster, an appraiser for the Grasslands conservation easement program from 1977 until 1982, also encountered bureaucratic opposition when he discovered that the drainage water that duck clubs had been accepting frequently violated the Grassland Water District's water quality standards. Foster claimed that he was told by his superiors at the Fish and Wildlife Service not to tell the duck club owners about the harmful effects of the drainwater, and to "develop amnesia" about the water quality problems in the Grasslands.[61]

At the official request of San Joaquin Valley congressman Tony Coelho, in late 1984 the Department of the Interior began a ten-month internal investigation into allegations of a federal government cover-up at Kesterson. These allegations were made by landowner James Claus, who was awaiting the results of his petition to the State Water Resources Control Board for enforcement action against the bureau, and by Carla Bard, chairwoman of the State Water Resources Control Board from 1979 to 1982.[62] In September 1985 the Interior Department's Office of the Inspector General issued its final report, which stated that the investigation did not disclose any official acts to suppress information or hinder the progress of toxicity studies. However, it noted that mistrust and bickering between the Bureau of Reclamation and the Fish and Wildlife Service complicated the task of detecting the contamination problem at Kesterson from 1981 to 1983.[63]

The Department of the Interior's report satisfied few of the principals directly involved with Kesterson. A February 1986 letter from Congressman George Miller to Louis Clark, requesting Clark's help in investigating continuing allegations of a federal cover-up, nearly six months after the release of the exculpatory report, is illuminating:

> We are advised continually by press accounts and by government scientists that agency officials have sometimes gone to extraordinary lengths to prevent public disclosure of the severity of some of these contamination problems. For example, employees have been forbidden to talk with the press, and others have been prevented from attending or delivering professional papers at scientific conferences. Instances also exist where employees have been given new assignments, and one employee of the Fish and Wildlife Service has been advised that his job has been eliminated. Finally, agencies have used heavy-handed techniques to silence employees and frustrate their efforts to document the extent of the contamination problems.[64]

Considerable evidence supports the thrust of Miller's contentions. Harry Ohlendorf had discovered abnormalities in ducks, black-necked stilts, American avocets, and killdeer, and dead and deformed chicks and embryos in nests of stilts, at Kesterson in 1985. Orders from David L. Trauger, director of the Fish and Wildlife Service's Patuxent Wildlife Research Center, which exercised supervisory authority over its Pacific field station in California, prevented Ohlendorf from discussing the implications of his research findings at the Third Selenium Symposium held in Berkeley in March 1986.[65] Symposium organizer Arnold Schultz wrote to Trauger to protest. Trauger replied to Schultz that "1985 observations constitute 'raw data' and were too tenuous to release for open forum."[66] Ohlendorf, always cautious and conservative in his public comments, contends that he tried to present "solid data with a reasonable interpretation. There was not a proven cause and effect relationship necessarily, but there was circumstantial evidence that [the cause] was selenium."[67] Schultz also challenged Trauger's restriction that prevented Ohlendorf from discussing the failure of a hazing program at Kesterson, designed to frighten birds away from the reservoir by firing blanks from shotguns and other firearms. Trauger responded, "there have been no studies conducted by our staff to evaluate the efficiency of this activity." This statement was problematic at best; during the weeks before the symposium, Deputy Regional Director Joseph Blum had testified before the State Water Resources Control Board and sworn in a court affidavit that the hazing program had been monitored and that it was "largely unsuccessful in keeping American coots, water birds, and tricolored blackbirds [at that time a candidate for the federal endangered species list] from using the reservoir during any season."[68]

The questionable repression of scientific evidence extended beyond the waterbirds of Kesterson to mammals as well. Joseph Blum had also testified that samples taken in 1985 by the Fish and Wildlife Service showed selenium concentrations from ten to one thousand times higher than normal in small rodents captured near Kesterson.[69] This discovery implied that selenium was beginning to move up the terrestrial, as well as the aquatic, food chain. Elevated selenium levels in voles, mice, and shrews posed a potential threat to their predators—raccoons, coyotes, gray foxes, and federally endangered San Joaquin kit foxes. Despite the significance of the findings, orders from Patuxent prevented Fish and Wildlife Service research scientist Donald Clark from discussing them at all during the 1986 symposium.[70]

Eminent avian ecologist John Terborgh aptly describes the type of difficulties that confront scientists like Smith, Ohlendorf, and Clark: "When scientists obtain results that are contrary to the goals of a bureaucratic organization, their results may be suppressed, or buried deep in a report so thick and tedious that no one reads it."[71] In the deeply conservative atmosphere of the Reagan administration, in which the protection of the environment was not a priority, the Bureau of

Reclamation, far larger and more powerful than the Fish and Wildlife Service, appeared able to impose its will on its sister agency within the Interior Department, thereby compromising the integrity of the service, at least in matters relating to Kesterson and the San Luis Drain. In this milieu, in which President Reagan threatened to disband the Fish and Wildlife Service's research division for publicly exposing problems with drainwater, officials were not likely to jeopardize their careers by supporting scientists who championed wildlife at the expense of Bureau of Reclamation projects that benefited agribusiness.[72]

An external review of the Patuxent Wildlife Research Center, conducted during 1990 and 1991, severely criticized the Fish and Wildlife Service's leadership at Patuxent for politicizing the selenium issue through its malfeasance. The review panel—representing research scientists and administrators from academia, private conservation organizations, state and federal agencies, and other Fish and Wildlife Service research centers—noted that while the agency's "scientists unanimously agreed that the drainwater issue is one of the most important issues facing American wildlife today," a perception existed among them that upper-level management did not want "to risk career development for resource protection." The investigation found that "competent staff have been caught between their professional interpretations and the conservatism of the agency, which reflects the federal administration's view." For its work on drainwater, the California field staff in particular had "paid a personal price for upholding good science in the face of heavy political, bureaucratic and social pressures."[73] Indeed they had paid a heavy price; by 1990, both Harry Ohlendorf and Felix Smith, facing greatly diminished prospects for career advancement, left the Fish and Wildlife Service, Ohlendorf for private consulting and Smith for an early retirement.[74]

CLOSING IT DOWN AND CLEANING IT UP

Vindication by the Patuxent review for Ohlendorf, Smith, and their colleagues still lay in the future when in October and December 1984, amid the barrage of new research discoveries about selenium, the State Water Resources Control Board held two evidentiary hearings on the Claus petition against the Bureau of Reclamation. During these hearings it became clear that four types of material within Kesterson Reservoir—surface water, groundwater, vegetation, and sediment and shallow soils—were, or may have been, contaminated. Approximately 50 percent to 60 percent of the inflow to Kesterson Reservoir was seeping into underlying groundwater, polluting an aquifer that was used extensively to supply drinking water. In February 1985 the board ordered the Department of the Interior to resolve the problem at Kesterson. The Bureau of Reclamation was to submit a cleanup and abatement plan within five months, and to implement the cleanup plan within three years.[75] In the face of overwhelming and irrefutable scientific evidence, the tide of government resistance to the regulation of drain-water appeared to be turning.

It is no coincidence that action against the Bureau of Reclamation at this time originated from a California state regulatory board rather than from Congress. Irrigation return flows had been exempted from the Clean Water Act, the federal water protection law, since 1977, when they were defined as a "nonpoint source" of pollution.[76] Because the Clean Water Act regulated only "point sources," western irrigated agriculture had been able to operate largely free from federal controls for years.[77] This lack of oversight has had profound consequences; in 1992 the Environmental Protection Agency attributed 81 percent of the pollution affecting wetlands in California to agriculture alone.[78]

A month after the State Water Resources Control Board ruling, the Kesterson story reached a national audience. On March 10, 1985, CBS television's investigative reporting program *60 Minutes* featured the toxicity problems in and around the reservoir. Five days later, Congressman George Miller, the new chairman of the House Subcommittee on Water and Power Resources, called a congressional hearing in Los Banos, California, to discuss agricultural drainage problems and the contamination at Kesterson Reservoir. Early in the hearing, Carol Hallett, the western representative of the secretary of the interior, delivered the shocking announcement that Secretary Hodel, fearing a possible lawsuit under the Migratory Bird Treaty Act, had ordered the immediate closure of Kesterson Reservoir and the San Luis Drain, as well as the termination of irrigation water deliveries to the 42,000 acres of Westlands that drained into Kesterson.[79] The decision had been reached only the night before; Hallett herself had been informed of Hodel's order only that morning. Neither the Westlands farmers nor the Central Valley congressmen had been forewarned of this momentous decision.

The implications of closing the San Luis Drain and ceasing irrigation water deliveries to Westlands were potentially devastating to the growers. At the Second Selenium Symposium, which met in Berkeley only eight days after the hearing in Los Banos, renowned marine biologist Joel Hedgpeth predicted, "Whoever writes the history of all this will doubtless call the Ides of March of 1985 at Los Banos the Black Friday of California agriculture."[80] For a short time, at least on the Westside, it did indeed seem that the world had been turned upside down. But the Westlands Water District immediately threatened to take Donald Hodel to court, and on March 29 the Department of the Interior and the Westlands Water District announced an agreement that rescinded the immediate closure of Kesterson Reservoir and restored the delivery of irrigation water to Westlands' 42,000 acres. Under a less draconian arrangement, Westlands was to reduce the export of wastewater to the San Luis Drain by 20 percent every two months, beginning in September 1985. By June 30, 1986, the process was to be completed and the subsurface drains emptying into the San Luis Drain would be plugged.[81]

Even with this respite, the consequences to Westlands' growers were severe. With their subsurface drains plugged, growers were once again faced with the prospect of rising water tables and the need to dispose of their saline, seleniferous drainage water onsite.[82]

The agreement between the Department of the Interior and the Westlands Water District to halt the flow of effluents into the San Luis Drain and Kesterson Reservoir brought the first chapter of the Kesterson saga to a close. The Bureau of Reclamation now faced the challenge of cleaning up the toxic environment at Kesterson that those effluents had created. There would be no easy solution. In October 1986 the bureau, in cooperation with the Fish and Wildlife Service and the U.S. Army Corps of Engineers, provided to the State Water Resources Control Board its environmental impact statement for the Kesterson program. The bureau examined four options, in order of increasing cost and complexity: a flexible response plan, an immobilization plan, a wetland restoration/on-site disposal plan, and an off-site disposal plan. Under the flexible response plan, the southernmost ponds, where selenium concentrations were highest, were to be flooded with fresh water from the Central Valley Project, while the northernmost ponds were to be dewatered, reverting to seasonal wetlands only. Under the immobilization plan, which was an extension of the flexible response plan, all the ponds of Kesterson Reservoir were to be flooded with fresh water. In both instances, the bureau maintained that this "cap" of fresh water would maintain the anaerobic conditions necessary to keep the selenium immobilized in the bottom sediments and soils. The more comprehensive wetland restoration/on-site disposal plan called for the uppermost six inches of soil, with the existing vegetation, to be excavated and disposed of in a lined and capped on-site landfill. After removal of the most contaminated soils, topsoil would be imported from neighboring lands, and wetland habitat would be reestablished at the Kesterson Reservoir site, which would continue to function as part of the Kesterson National Wildlife Refuge. Finally, the off-site disposal plan entailed the removal of contaminated soils and vegetation to an off-site landfill as well as the extraction and removal of groundwater for off-site treatment.[83]

The bureau proposed a phased approach, beginning with the flexible response plan, and incorporating the immobilization plan and the on-site disposal plan, which would be implemented in succession as and if necessary; the off-site disposal plan would not be attempted. Cost was a major factor in the bureau's decision-making process. The bureau estimated capital costs alone, exclusive of costs for monitoring and operations, at $300,000 for the flexible response plan, $4.2 million for the immobilization plan, and $16.15 million for the on-site disposal plan.[84] To the bureau's dismay, studies conducted at the University of California at Berkeley and by the Fish and Wildlife Service invalidated both the flexible response and the immobilization plan. These findings demonstrated that although levels of selenium in the food chain decreased with freshwater inflow, the rate of decrease slowed at a level that was still too high. Although selenium levels trended downward over time, an insufficient amount was being withdrawn from circulation and immobilized in sediments.[85] On March 19, 1987, the State Water Resources Control Board therefore rejected the phased approach and ordered the bureau to clean up Kesterson Reservoir by August 19, 1988, using the on-site disposal plan.[86]

New evidence soon became available, however, suggesting that not even the on-site disposal plan would be effective in cleaning up Kesterson. Researchers at the University of California's Lawrence Berkeley Laboratory found that selenium in shallow groundwater had concentrated to levels as high as those in the drainage water in the original Kesterson Reservoir ponds. These findings implied that even if the bureau excavated the topsoil in the ponds according to the on-site disposal plan, contaminated shallow groundwater would be released into the renovated wetlands, rendering them as toxic as the original ponds and presenting a continuing threat to wildlife.[87] Therefore, with the on-site disposal plan having been discredited as well, on July 5, 1988, the State Water Resources Control Board ordered the bureau to follow a different plan of action, one not included in the agency's four initial options. The bureau was to fill all low-lying areas where it expected ephemeral pools to form, and to fill all areas to six inches above the expected seasonal rise in groundwater level. The deadline was January 1, 1989.[88]

The bureau's contractors completed the filling of Kesterson Reservoir in November 1988. Approximately 710 low-lying acres of the 1,283-acre reservoir were covered with a total of 1,050,437 cubic yards of earth, at a cost of approximately $6.5 million.[89] Grassland habitat covered an additional 400 acres of higher-elevation areas that had not been filled; open habitat—cattail areas that had been disked to prevent nesting by tricolored blackbirds—accounted for the remaining 170 acres. The dewatering and filling of Kesterson Reservoir reduced or eliminated use by ducks, American coots, and shorebirds. As Kesterson reverted to upland habitat, their place was taken by terrestrial species, including the western meadowlark, horned lark, white-crowned sparrow, mourning dove, barn swallow, ring-necked pheasant, northern harrier, and red-tailed hawk.[90]

Kesterson Reservoir had been buried. But had it been killed? After Kesterson was dewatered, research continued under the Kesterson Reservoir Biological Monitoring Program, developed by the Fish and Wildlife Service and the Central Valley Regional Water Quality Control Board. The main concern was that surface pools formed in low-lying areas during particularly wet years would still contain selenium concentrations high enough to pose a continued threat to wildlife. If pools were to form during late winter or early spring and persist during the nesting season, they might support selenium-laden plants and invertebrates on which birds would then feed. Research conducted at Kesterson during the late 1980s and early 1990s revealed that, although ephemeral pooling of rainwater still occurred, selenium concentrations in plant and animal tissues had stabilized at elevated, but nontoxic, levels.[91] In the Grassland Water District, by contrast, although drainwater used for management of wetlands was replaced by fresh water in 1985, contaminated sediments generally were not buried beneath imported soil. As a result, selenium continued to cycle through the food chain, and selenium concentrations in the tissues of some aquatic birds, though declining, remained above levels associated with reproductive impairment well into the 1990s. By the mid-2000s, more than two decades after the initial contamination of the Grasslands, selenium levels remained above threshold levels for reproductive impairment for black-necked stilts, and above species-specific background levels for numerous other aquatic birds.[92]

BEYOND KESTERSON: SELENIUM IN THE TULARE BASIN

The selenium problem in California's Central Valley was not limited to Kesterson and the Grasslands. To the south, the Tulare Basin, which receives its irrigation water from the State Water Project but lacks a natural outlet, was facing drainage problems of its own. In 1966 the J. G. Boswell Company—the sprawling agribusiness concern that had been founded by the colonel during the 1920s—and other large growers on the Tulare Lake bed formed the 213,000-acre Tulare Lake Drainage District to construct a system of underground drains that would channel excess groundwater from their fields into shallow evaporation ponds.[93] Between 1972 and 1985, growers in the Tulare Basin as a whole constructed more than twenty pond systems, which collectively covered approximately 7,000 acres, or nearly eleven square miles.[94] Though devoid of emergent marsh vegetation and not intended to provide wildlife habitat, these ponds attracted large numbers of waterbirds, including populations of nesting birds.

As early as August 1985, the U.S. Fish and Wildlife Service reported elevated levels of selenium in plants, insects, fish, and birds in the Tulare Basin drainage ponds, some comparable to levels found at Kesterson in 1983. By December 1985 the California Department of Fish and Game and the Fish and Wildlife Service were engaged in a waterfowl-hazing program at Tulare Basin evaporation ponds near the Kern National Wildlife Refuge.[95] In 1987 Harry Ohlendorf sent Joseph Skorupa, an avian biologist with the Fish and Wildlife Service's Patuxent Wildlife Research Center, to the Tulare Basin to investigate whether the basin's evaporation ponds might be creating the same reproductive problems associated with selenium that had been found at Kesterson and in the Grasslands.[96] The selenium content of drainage water entering these ponds spanned four orders of magnitude, ranging from less than 1 µg/L to greater than 1,000 µg/L. At four sites from 1987 to 1989, Skorupa and other biologists found selenium concentrations in eggs and incidences of embryonic deformities as high as, or higher than, those at Kesterson.[97] The deformities were of the same disturbing nature as those found at Kesterson—corkscrewed beaks, missing eyes, and shriveled limbs—and were found in four species of ducks (mallard, gadwall, northern pintail, and redhead) and five species of other waterbirds (American avocet, black-necked stilt, eared grebe, killdeer, and western snowy plover) that nested on the evaporation ponds.[98] In light of these toxicity problems (widely referred to as the "Kesterson syndrome") and of the unwillingness of state regulatory authorities to address them, Skorupa has referred to the Tulare Lake Drainage District as the "skeleton in the closet" of the State Water Project.[99]

The hesitancy of the state to respond to the crisis in the Tulare Basin with the same level of determination that it eventually demonstrated at Kesterson became apparent during the late 1980s. In 1988 the Tulare Lake Drainage District applied to the State Water Resources Control Board for a loan of $1 million to build additional evaporation ponds. In considering such a request, the board was required to review the findings and recommendations of any federal or state studies submitted to it concerning "drainage water management units" and to determine the relevancy of those studies to its decision-making process.[100] The Fish and Wildlife Service presented evidence to the board demonstrating that the abnormally high avian embryonic deformity rates in the Tulare Basin were caused by selenium.[101] The State Water Resources Control Board ruled that these findings were "not relevant." Overall, the board considered relevant only five of the fifty-six scientific articles submitted to it. The board approved the Tulare Lake Drainage District's loan request, subject only to new waste discharge requirements to be issued by the Central Valley Regional Water Quality Control Board.[102] When those requirements were finally issued in 1993, they demanded little more than that the growers steepen the sides of their ponds to make them less attractive to shorebirds, haze waterbirds away from the ponds, and provide one acre of unpolluted mitigation habitat for waterbirds for every ten acres of toxic ponds.[103] These lenient restrictions did little to improve water quality in the ponds. By the late 1990s, however, improved methods of irrigation in the Tulare Basin reduced the quantity of agricultural wastewater that was generated, and about half of the drainage water evaporation facilities had ceased operating. The remaining evaporation ponds nonetheless continue to pose a substantial ecotoxicological threat to aquatic birds.[104]

Although the State Water Resources Control Board had taken substantive action to ensure the cleanup of Kesterson Reservoir, a different calculus prevailed in the Tulare Basin, where the toxic ponds were on private property, and where the death and deformity of waterbirds was farther from the public eye. The state and regional water boards would not challenge the basin's powerful agribusinesses. Such resistance to address drainwater issues in the Tulare Basin was systemic. As Joseph Skorupa amassed increasingly damning evidence, the Tulare Lake Drainage District attempted to have his research grant revoked by the California Department of Water Resources, the agency that manages the State Water Project. Failing in that effort, the district tried to have Skorupa removed as principal investigator of avian deformities. The Department of Water Resources refused to comply, but Skorupa also faced obstacles from his superiors at the Patuxent Wildlife Research Center, which was soon to be critically reviewed for politicizing drainwater issues. David Trauger, now Patuxent's deputy director, challenged Skorupa for reporting information to the press before his data appeared in peer-reviewed publications. Ultimately, Patuxent barred him from making any further trips to the Tulare Basin evaporation ponds.[105]

The resistance encountered by those conducting research on drainage issues, including selenium toxicity, must be understood in light of the tremendous influence of California's multibillion-dollar agricultural industry, which uses approximately 80 percent of the state's developed surface water supply.[106] The influence of the agricultural sector, however, is disproportionate to its actual contribution to California's economy.[107] Despite the fact that much of the state's developed water is utilized to irrigate low-value pasture, alfalfa, rice, and cotton, rather than the much more frequently touted high-value crops, such as almonds, peaches, and grapes, California agribusiness has been successful at creating and maintaining the perception that agriculture drives the state's current economy.[108] This perception, in turn, perpetuates the "agricultural mystique" of the West, the unexamined assumption that agriculture remains the natural and optimal use for western lands even in the face of environmental constraints.

In California's San Joaquin Valley—where the limits of the environment's ability to absorb the effects of destructive agricultural practices were becoming ever more apparent—as the crisis at Kesterson was approaching fever pitch, California's governor, George Deukmejian, and Secretary of the Interior William Clark established the San Joaquin Valley Drainage Program in August 1984 to investigate alternative solutions to the valley's twin problems of salinity and selenium toxicity.[109] The principal participating agencies included the California Department of Fish and Game, the California Department of Water Resources, the U.S. Fish and Wildlife Service, the U.S. Bureau of Reclamation, and the U.S. Geological Survey. In September 1990 the San Joaquin Valley Drainage Program issued its final report, *A Management Plan for Agricultural Subsurface Drainage and Related Problems on the Westside San Joaquin Valley.*[110] This study, which represented years of political consensus building, focused on in-valley solutions, avoiding the question of exporting drainage to the Delta or another point of discharge.

The San Joaquin Valley Drainage Program's report specified eight recommendations for management of agricultural subsurface drainage from 1990 to 2040, most of which were directed toward the reduction, treatment, and disposal of that drainage. The recommendations called for on-farm improvements in the application of irrigation water, known as source control; the reuse of drainage water on salt-tolerant plants; the construction of drainage evaporation ponds that would function as electricity-generating solar ponds; the retirement of land, or the cessation of irrigation, in areas with drainage problems and shallow seleniferous groundwater; the use of groundwater, rather than imported water, where appropriate; and the carefully regulated discharge of drainwater to the San Joaquin River. Some of these recommendations have met with measurable, but limited, success. The Westlands Water District has been active in implementing source control, in the form of drip, rather than furrow, irrigation; experimenting with drainage water reuse on salt-tolerant crops; and implementing groundwater management programs.[111] However, land retirement has been inhibited by the high productive value of San Joaquin Valley soils, including soils with drainage problems and high concentrations of selenium, as well as by thorny legal issues concerning rights to contracted water on land that has been taken out of production.[112]

Observing the difficulty of enacting a truly far-reaching solution to the valley's drainage and toxicity problems, one researcher has referred to the "cognitive dissonance" that must be maintained by irrigation and drainage bureaucracies when they simultaneously uphold inherently incompatible positions that pit the continued profitability of irrigated agriculture against the protection of the environment from the byproducts of that agriculture. Placed in such an untenable position, the agencies prefer that the drainage problem should be solved, but operate on a day-to-day assumption that it will not be.[113] The drainage issue, and the toxicity problem that it creates for waterfowl and other waterbirds of the Pacific Flyway, may ultimately need to be settled by the California state legislature or by the courts.

SELENIUM IN THE WEST: LARGER IMPLICATIONS

The issues raised by Kesterson and repeated in the Tulare Basin had ramifications that extended far beyond the San Joaquin Valley of California. Kesterson raised public concerns about the ecological integrity of other national refuges, while at the same time suggesting a link between federal irrigation projects on seleniferous soils and environmental contamination. Ivan Barnes of the U.S. Geological Survey predicted that the situation at Kesterson would be repeated "in dozens of places over thousands of square miles throughout the West."[114]

In March 1985 Secretary of the Interior Donald Hodel ordered an expanded search for any problems on federal water projects that were similar to those that had caused death and deformity of wildlife at Kesterson. Scientists from the U.S. Geological Survey and the U.S. Fish and Wildlife Service, as well as officials from the U.S. Bureau of Reclamation, met in April to draft a plan to comply with Hodel's order, but the plan stalled upon reaching the office of Robert Broadbent, assistant interior secretary for water and science and a former commissioner of the Bureau of Reclamation, which had built many of the federal projects.[115] Federal investigation of selenium problems was infused with new momentum in September, however, when the *Sacramento Bee,* following a detailed on-location investigation by science journalists Tom Harris and Jim Morris, ran a series of articles concerning possible selenium contamination at twenty-three additional sites in the West.[116] The *Bee's* assertion of detrimental effects of elevated selenium concentrations at thirteen of those locations led Congress to request that the Department of the Interior address these concerns.

In response, the Interior Department developed its National Irrigation Water Quality Program (NIWQP) to investigate irrigation projects and drainage facilities constructed or managed by the federal government that might have been harming national wildlife refuges or other areas important to migratory birds and endangered species.[117] Between the mid-1980s and the mid-1990s, scientists conducted reconnaissance investigations for potentially toxic concentrations of trace constituents, particularly selenium, in the water, sediment, and biota at twenty-six NIWQP study areas in fourteen of the seventeen contiguous western states. Deformities from selenium toxicosis were found at five sites, and three of them—the Tulare Lakebed Area, the Kendrick Reclamation Project Area in Wyoming, and the Ouray National Wildlife Refuge within the Middle Green River Area in Utah—were as seriously poisoned as Kesterson.[118] Based on concentrations of selenium found in fish and bird tissues, toxicity was also predicted, if not directly found, at six additional sites.[119] In terms of the population-level effects of such widespread selenium contamination, probably less than 1 percent of breeding birds in the West as a whole suffer selenium-induced reproductive impairment, but even this relatively small percentage can push Pacific Flyway species populations that are near a stable, or break-even, point into decline. Furthermore, selenium poisoning can have devastating effects on local populations, as witnessed at Kesterson and in the Tulare Basin.[120]

There are legal obstacles as well as scientific challenges to responding to this widespread problem of selenium contamination. The U.S. Fish and Wildlife Service, responsible for the administration of the national wildlife refuge system, lacks authority to set enforceable water quality standards for fish or wildlife habitat. That responsibility lies with the Environmental Protection Agency (EPA), under the provisions of the Clean Water Act. Although the EPA lowered the freshwater chronic criteria for selenium from 35 to 5 parts per billion (ppb) in 1987, irrigation return flows, still classified under the Clean Water Act as nonpoint source pollution, are not subject to this regulation.[121] Even if the EPA's more stringent standard of 5 ppb were enforceable for irrigation drainwater, this water quality criterion fails to take bioaccumulation into account and therefore may not be protective of higher food-chain organisms, including waterfowl.[122] Additionally, as Kesterson made clear, because selenium can enter the food chain from sediments, selenium concentrations in the substrate as well as those in standing water need to be taken into account in any attempt to reduce toxic risk. Despite the clear need for continued study, in 2005 Congress significantly curtailed funding for the NIWQP, leading to the suspension of a majority of its activities.[123]

Selenium toxicity thus remains problematic in wetlands scattered across much of the U.S. West, including California's San Joaquin Valley. However, the dramatic events that occurred at the Kesterson National Wildlife Refuge during the 1980s, which marked both a profound reversal of fortune and a crucial turning point in the environmental history of the Central Valley, were of long-term significance for several reasons. The Bureau of Reclamation's inept handling of the Kesterson affair, and its disregard for the ecological constraints of the Central Valley, eroded its previously unquestioned hegemony. At the same time, Kesterson raised the profile and increased the influence of the expertise of Fish and Wildlife scientists and other natural resource specialists dedicated to the protection of wetlands. Among the promising developments that took place in the wake of Kesterson, the issue of selenium poisoning in aquatic ecosystems gained the attention of the scientific community nationwide. At universities as well as an array of state and federal agencies, research on selenium remediation proliferated. In California Kesterson led, more broadly, to an enhanced awareness of the fragile condition of Central Valley wetlands and ushered in a new era of public and private incentives to protect and restore them. Those initiatives developed within the context of a national and international sea change in attitudes about wetlands that had been gaining momentum for several decades.

10

Wetlands Resurgent

The Central Valley in the Twenty-First Century

CHANGING ATTITUDES ABOUT WETLANDS

When the U.S. Fish and Wildlife Service presented one of the first scientific definitions of wetlands in its 1956 Circular no. 39 publication, *Wetlands of the United States,* the document emphasized wetlands primarily as waterfowl habitat, and assigned values to each state's wetlands according to their importance to waterfowl.[1] But change toward a broader appreciation of wetlands for protecting biodiversity, for providing ecological services, and for appealing to aesthetic sensibilities was on the horizon, in large part aided by significant advances in the discipline of wetland ecology, as well as by the efforts of ecologists to popularize knowledge about wetlands and call attention to the consequences of their destruction.

Among the most prominent of the many scientists who launched modern wetland ecology were the brothers Eugene P. Odum and Howard T. Odum, who conducted pathbreaking experiments in the salt marshes of Sapelo Island, Georgia, and the cypress swamps of Florida, respectively. Beginning during the 1950s, as coastal marshes were rapidly being destroyed by development, their studies of nutrient cycling and energy flow through marshes broadened our understanding of wetlands as functional ecosystems and advanced the subdiscipline of ecosystem ecology. In addition to making tremendous contributions to wetland science, the Odums were pioneers of attempts to quantify the nonmarket values of wetlands in the form of the ecosystem services they provide. The quantification of the values of those services—a partial list of which includes flood mitigation, storm abatement, aquifer recharge, improvement of water quality, nutrient recycling, aquatic productivity, aesthetic and recreational opportunities (including birdwatching, hunting, and fishing), and opportunities for education and scientific research—has since become an important component of the discipline of ecological economics.[2]

During the 1950s and 1960s, a number of accomplished ecologists and other scientists were writing popular books intended to increase public awareness and appreciation of wetlands. In 1957 Paul Errington published *Of Men and Marshes,* which described marsh life in the prairie potholes in intimate detail through the changing of the seasons. Errington, a professor of wildlife management in Iowa's Cooperative Wildlife Unit program, which "Ding" Darling had helped to establish, stressed not only the importance of the marshes in the threatened pothole region, but also the sense of wonder and awe that humans could experience by learning the natural history of the marshes and exploring their secrets. Errington's hauntingly beautiful book, reminiscent of the poetic essays of Aldo Leopold's *A Sand County Almanac,* nudged public attitudes a step closer to a holistic, ecological appreciation of wetlands. In 1966 William A Niering, director of the Connecticut Arboretum and professor of botany at Connecticut College, published *The Life of the Marsh,* the first popular natural history of wetlands in general. The answer to Niering's rhetorical question "Wetlands or Wastelands?" was clear; the long period of American history during which wetlands were viewed as an obstacle to settlement and development was rapidly drawing to a close. In 1969 ecologist John Teal, a colleague of Eugene Odum at Sapelo Island, published, with his wife Mildred, *Life and Death in the Salt Marsh.* This important book, released on the eve of the first Earth Day in 1970, educated readers about the natural history of marshes and the need for their conservation in the face of development pressures and pollution.[3]

As scientists popularized the notion that wetlands have intrinsic value, interest in wetland protection began to be reflected in national policy. In May 1977 President Jimmy Carter issued Executive Order no. 11990, which established the protection of wetlands as the official policy of the federal government. The order required that "each agency shall provide leadership and shall take action to minimize the destruction, loss or degradation of wetlands, and to preserve and enhance the natural and beneficial values of wetlands."[4] President Carter's executive order assumed a greater sense of urgency during the 1980s, when continental waterfowl populations plummeted. Along the Pacific Flyway, population indices of wintering waterfowl in the United States, which had oscillated between 6 million and 9 million since modern midwinter waterfowl surveys began in 1955, declined precipitously to between 4 million and 6 million, approximately 30 percent below long-term averages, during that decade.

In response to the waterfowl crisis—the result of a combination of generalized habitat destruction and a severe, prolonged drought in the prairie pothole region of south-central Canada and the north-central United States—Congress passed the Emergency Wetlands Resources Act in 1986, which expanded and enhanced sources of revenue for acquiring wetlands and required the U.S. Fish and Wildlife Service to report every ten years on the status and trends of the nation's wetlands.[5] An important U.S. policy directive was launched in 1987 when, at the request of the U.S. Environmental Protection Agency, the National Wetlands Policy Forum was convened to investigate the issue of wetland management in the United States. The overriding objective that emerged from the forum was "to achieve no overall net loss of the nation's remaining wetland base and to create and restore wetlands, where feasible, to increase the quantity and quality of the nation's wetland resource base."[6] While this agenda has not yet succeeded in completely halting the loss of wetlands nationally, it has provided an impetus for the construction of artificial wetlands to replace natural wetlands that are destroyed by new development. During the 1990s this process, known as wetland mitigation, became a cornerstone of wetland conservation in the United States.[7]

The most far-reaching response to the waterfowl crisis of the 1980s was the creation of the North American Waterfowl Management Plan (NAWMP), signed on May 14, 1986, by the secretary of the interior for the United States and the minister of environment for Canada. Mexico became a full partner in 1994. The NAWMP provides a broad framework for waterfowl conservation and habitat goals, based on restoring and maintaining the diversity, abundance, and distribution of waterfowl that had existed during the 1970s, before numbers had plummeted.[8] Funding and administrative structure for the implementation of the NAWMP is provided by the North American Wetlands Conservation Act of 1989.[9] During the 1990s alone, nearly 650 projects in Canada, Mexico, and the United States were approved for funding under the act, and approximately 8.6 million acres of wetlands and adjacent uplands were acquired, restored, or enhanced in Canada and the United States.[10]

Direct implementation of the NAWMP is the responsibility of nearly twenty joint ventures, collaborative efforts in which government agencies and private organizations pool their resources to solve waterfowl habitat problems. To carry out the objectives of the NAWMP in the Central Valley, the Central Valley Habitat Joint Venture (CVHJV) was established in 1988. When the CVHJV issued its implementation plan in 1990, it estimated that only 59 percent of remaining Central Valley freshwater wetlands—172,655 of a total of 291,555 acres—was protected. To aid in the restoration of waterfowl populations, the CVHJV sought the protection of existing wetland habitat through perpetual conservation easements and outright purchase, the restoration and protection of former wetlands, the enhancement of all existing wetlands, and the enhancement of waterfowl habitat on agricultural lands.[11]

The CVHJV has been largely successful. By 2003, venture partners had protected 56,778 acres and restored 65,191 acres of wetlands, enhanced between

50,000 and 75,000 acres of wetlands annually, and enhanced a total of 384,121 acres of agricultural lands, primarily through winter flooding of grain (rice and corn) fields to provide for the food energy needs of wintering waterfowl. Its name shortened in 2004, the Central Valley Joint Venture (CVJV) has expanded and refined its objectives. No longer simply aimed at protecting waterfowl, the new CVJV objectives seek to protect all wetland-dependent birds, including shorebirds, other waterbirds, and riparian songbirds.[12]

THE CENTRAL VALLEY PROJECT IMPROVEMENT ACT

Initiatives launched during the 1980s, such as the national "no net loss" policy for wetlands and the joint ventures created to fulfill the North American Waterfowl Management Plan, were all part of the shift in attitudes about wetlands that was taking place in the United States as the twentieth century was drawing to a close. In the Central Valley of California this attitudinal change was given further impetus by the fiasco at Kesterson Reservoir. The crisis at Kesterson played a central role in placing the Central Valley Project, then a half-century old, in the crosshairs of public scrutiny, resulting in substantial reform of that irrigation and reclamation enterprise. Although the Central Valley Project had brought water to three million acres of agricultural land and more than two million urban residents, it had done so at a high cost. The project damaged much of the Central Valley's riparian habitat and kept native Chinook salmon from reaching their ancestral spawning grounds on the Sacramento and San Joaquin river systems. The San Luis Unit extension of the Central Valley Project had exacerbated drainage problems, particularly on the Westside of the San Joaquin Valley, and had led to the tragedy at Kesterson. Furthermore, the Central Valley Project came under increasing criticism for selling low-cost water to farmers at a time when prolonged drought, spiraling urban growth, and new laws to protect the environment all placed an unprecedented demand on the state's limited developed water supply. In this context, Congress passed the Central Valley Project Improvement Act (CVPIA) as Title 34 of the Reclamation Projects Authorization and Adjustment Act of 1992, a large omnibus water bill authorizing a total of $2.4 billion for projects in sixteen western states.[13]

The far-reaching CVPIA ushered in a new era in California's water history. The purposes of the act included the protection and restoration of fish and wildlife habitat in the Central Valley and the protection of the estuary that extended from San Francisco Bay to the Sacramento–San Joaquin Delta. The act aimed "to achieve a reasonable balance among competing demands for use of Central Valley Project water," including the requirements of fish and wildlife, and of agricultural, municipal, industrial, and power contractors.[14] Of paramount importance, the CVPIA reauthorized the Central Valley Project once again, modifying it to provide protections that surpassed those offered to fish and wildlife by the Grass-lands Act of 1954. The culmination of the struggle to save the privately held Grassland wetlands, the Grasslands Act had for the first time included the use of the waters of the Central Valley Project for fish and wildlife as a project pur-pose. The 1992 CVPIA offered a much higher level of protection, adding the "mitigation, protection, and restoration of fish and wildlife" as an *equal* priority among the Central Valley Project's purposes.[15] The act dedicated 800,000 acre-feet of project water annually (600,000 acre-feet in dry years) to fish and wildlife purposes, including increased flows to the San Francisco Bay–Delta and in-creased water supplies to the Central Valley's national wildlife refuges, several state wildlife areas, and the Grassland Resource Conservation District.[16] The act also called on the secretary of the interior to develop a feasible plan to address the restoration of stream flows on the dewatered portion of the San Joaquin River below Friant Dam.[17] This measure set the stage for the reestablishment of salmon runs and opened a new phase in the history of the San Joaquin River.

The passage of the CVPIA illustrates both a transformation in public values concerning wetlands and a realignment of California's traditional alliance be-tween agricultural and urban interests. At a time when new water development projects faced increasing environmental and economic hurdles and the state was suffering through a sixth year of drought, urban leaders looked toward agricul-ture for more reliable supplies of water for metropolitan areas. Environmental groups pushing for passage of the bill thus found unlikely allies in urban lobby-ists, including those of the Metropolitan Water District of Southern California, who successfully sought provisions for water transfers, permitting them access to water that had traditionally been earmarked for agriculture. This alliance of convenience between environmental and urban interests helped secure the pas-sage of the act and represented a seismic shift in California water politics.[18] The long-term efficacy of this alliance, however, remains in question, in part because of the policies of the administration of President George W. Bush. The Bush ad-ministration pushed for early renewal of Central Valley Project contracts for agricultural water, in effect locking up much of the state's future water supply before all of the environmental provisions of the CVPIA had been met.[19] Most notable among the places where the goals of the CVPIA remain unfulfilled is the Sacramento–San Joaquin Delta, where the restoration of wetlands remains in-tractably woven into issues of water quality.

THE DELTA DILEMMA

As the Central Valley Project and, later, the State Water Project increased fresh-water diversions from the Delta to the San Joaquin Valley and Southern California, saltwater intrusion from the Pacific Ocean reemerged as a significant problem.

During periods of low flow and drought, ocean water advances far enough inland to be drawn into the federal and state aqueducts, the Delta-Mendota Canal and the California Aqueduct, respectively, at the pumping plants on the southern edge of the Delta.[20] In addition to posing threats to the quality of irrigation and drinking water for Californians served by the aqueducts, saltwater intrusion poses immediate problems for the fish and waterfowl of the Delta and adjacent Suisun Marsh.

In response to the salinity problem, in 1965 federal and state agencies released a plan that signaled the initiation of the second phase of California's State Water Project. The plan called for a canal that would transport fresh Sacramento River water around, rather than through, the Delta. The unlined canal—43 miles long, 400 feet wide, and 30 feet deep—would swing in an eastward arc beginning fifteen miles south of Sacramento, skirt the eastern periphery of the Delta, and then curve westward to the pumping plants for the Delta-Mendota Canal and the California Aqueduct (see map 19). Gates along the length of the canal would release fresh water into the Delta to protect it from saltwater intrusion. This Peripheral Canal appealed to residents of the San Joaquin Valley and Southern California because it guaranteed that their water supply would remain of high quality. Northern Californians and Delta residents, on the other hand, feared that the canal amounted to a water grab by the southern part of the state, including its large agribusiness concerns. Those opposed to the canal argued that the project contained no provisions for effective water conservation, and they expressed concern that the canal would not adequately protect the ecological resources of the Delta or of Suisun Marsh, which remains a major wintering ground for the Pacific Flyway.[21]

The Peripheral Canal became a flashpoint in north-south tensions over water resources for the next seventeen years, spanning the governorships of Edmund G. "Pat" Brown, Ronald Reagan, and Edmund G. "Jerry" Brown. In 1980 the Peripheral Canal bill finally passed the state Senate and Assembly, by approximately two-to-one margins that largely reflected regional divisions. Governor Jerry Brown signed the Peripheral Canal bill into law, citing the legacy of his father, Pat Brown, who had won passage of the State Water Project two decades earlier.[22] Despite legislative and gubernatorial approval, however, the Peripheral Canal battle was not over. Only a few weeks before the legislature had passed the Peripheral Canal bill, it had voted to put on the ballot a proposed constitutional amendment, Proposition 8, that would protect the Delta and the rivers of California's north coast.[23] This measure was designed to assuage Northern Californians' fears of future water transfers to the south, and would take effect only if the Peripheral Canal legislation were to pass. The electorate approved Proposition 8 in November 1980, after which the California Farm Bureau Federation reversed its previous support for the Peripheral Canal, as did the J. G. Boswell

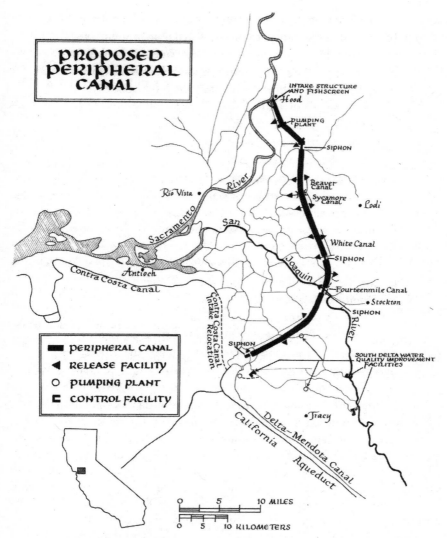

MAP 19. The proposed Peripheral Canal, circa 1980. The purpose of the canal was to route Sacramento River water directly to the pumping plants for the Delta-Mendota Canal and the California Aqueduct, rather than through the channels of the Delta. Source: Norris Hundley Jr., *The Great Thirst: Californians and Water, a History*, rev. ed. (Berkeley and Los Angeles: University of California Press, 2001). Used with permission.

Company and the Salyer Land Company, two of the largest agribusiness concerns in the state. Although these agricultural interests would have directly benefited from the freshwater supply ensured by the canal, they did not want to sacrifice potential access to the state's north coast rivers at some point in the future. If they could defeat the Peripheral Canal, they could nullify Proposition 8.[24] The efforts of agribusiness were rewarded when, in June 1982, voters approved a statewide referendum repealing the Peripheral Canal legislation by a 63 percent majority.[25]

The defeat of the Peripheral Canal did little to solve water quality issues in the Delta, and the decade of political and legal wrangling that followed produced few tangible results.[26] But when Congress passed the Central Valley Project Improvement Act in 1992, it required operation of the federal project to include protective measures for the Delta and Suisun Marsh. The next year, the U.S. Fish and Wildlife Service and the California Fish and Game Commission declared the Delta smelt, a small native fish endemic to the San Francisco Bay–Delta estuary, an endangered species, largely thanks to the efforts of biologist Peter Moyle of the University of California, Davis.[27] Resource problems in the Bay-Delta thus quickly evolved into a joint federal and state responsibility. In December 1994 federal and state agencies, as well as stakeholders representing local water agencies and environmental organizations, signed the Bay-Delta Accord, inaugurating a new phase in California water management under CALFED, an interagency program designed to address four issues crucial to the long-term restoration and management of the Bay-Delta estuary: ecosystem restoration, water supply reliability, water quality, and levee rehabilitation.[28]

Despite high initial hopes, the first decade of CALFED's operational stage, which began in 2000, fell short of the program's goals. Ecosystem restoration efforts in areas upstream from the Delta have achieved notable successes, but within the Delta itself the achievements in wetland restoration have not been sufficient to offset the continuing problems of crumbling levees, an unreliable water supply, and worsening in-stream conditions. Despite spending $3 billion overall between 2000 and 2005, CALFED seemed unable to halt the decline of the Delta ecosystem. Fish populations decreased dramatically, especially that of the endangered Delta smelt. There appears to be no single cause for the collapse of the system; rather, a combination of invasive species, water pollution, and water exports from the Delta is to blame.[29] It is for this last point that CALFED has come under the most intense criticism. CALFED allowed exports from the Delta to the south to increase, and was accused of becoming inappropriately aligned with southern water interests.[30] The future of CALFED became increasingly uncertain as the agency reeled from the often conflicting demands of enhancing the state's developed water supply while at the same time preserving the compromised ecosystem of the Delta through which much of that water supply passes.

As CALFED was struggling, a new moment of possibility and promise for solving the Delta's seemingly intractable problems was taking shape. In September 2006 Governor Arnold Schwarzenegger issued an executive order creating a Delta Vision Blue Ribbon Task Force "to develop a durable vision for sustainable management of the Delta."[31] Shortly thereafter, in February 2007, the nonprofit Public Policy Institute of California (PPIC) issued an extensive report, *Envisioning Futures for the Sacramento–San Joaquin Delta.*[32] This bold study argued for a fundamental reformulation of Delta policy that would alter the way the Delta has been managed since the initiation of the Central Valley Project in the 1930s. The PPIC report suggested that because the Delta historically was heterogeneous and variable in terms of its salinity levels and water flows, it has been a mistake to try to manage it as a static freshwater environment. Such management has led to a decline of native species and an increase in invasive alien species. Instead of managing the Delta as a single homogeneous unit and attempting to achieve simultaneous improvements in habitat, levees, water quality, and water supply reliability, the report recommended that it should be managed as a mosaic for different uses, with the inevitable trade-offs that this would entail. The Delta Vision Blue Ribbon Task Force incorporated much of the philosophy behind the PPIC's study into its final report to the governor in 2008, including the need to elevate the protection of the Delta ecosystem to equal priority with the maintenance of a reliable water supply for the 23 million Californians who rely on the Delta for drinking and irrigation water.[33]

These developments represent a historic break in how Californians have thought about their Sacramento–San Joaquin Delta and provide an instructive example of the gradually increasing recognition of the importance of the state's historical wetlands and the tremendous biodiversity they support. Nevertheless, the Delta remains a complicated place that has been called on to serve a variety of functions, from providing high-quality habitat for endangered fish species to providing water for irrigated agriculture in the San Joaquin Valley and quenching the thirst of Southern California. No solution, however nuanced, to the Delta's problems is likely to satisfy all stakeholders, but these emerging reconceptualizations of the Delta are hopeful signs.[34]

WETLAND PROTECTION ON THE EDGES
OF THE DELTA

One consequence of the complexity of issues concerning the core of the Delta has been that wetland restoration efforts have been more successful along the Delta's margins than in its heart. The Nature Conservancy and its partners have achieved a clear success on the eastern fringes of the Delta with the Cosumnes River Preserve. The last undammed river flowing out of the Sierra Nevada, the Cosumnes

River joins the Mokelumne River on the eastern edge of the Delta before flowing into the San Joaquin River.[35] In 1984 the Nature Conservancy acquired an initial 86 acres of riparian oak forest along the Cosumnes River, one of the healthiest remnant examples of valley oak riparian forest in the state. After acquiring 1,400 additional acres, the Nature Conservancy formally dedicated the Cosumnes River Preserve in 1987. Since that time, the Nature Conservancy has taken on partners, beginning with Ducks Unlimited and the U.S. Bureau of Land Management, and by 2009 the preserve had expanded to approximately 50,000 acres, containing seasonal and permanent wetlands as well as private agricultural and grazing lands that are managed in wildlife-compatible ways to attract wintering waterfowl.[36]

The vision, as well as the size, of the Cosumnes River Preserve has been expanded and now includes floodplain restoration. Accidental and intentional breaching of levees on the preserve has resulted in a proliferation of cottonwood and willow trees and has demonstrated that the restoration of flood regimes is a cost-effective means to accelerate habitat restoration. Recent studies of the Cosumnes River floodplain have found that it is of particular importance for native fish species, including the Chinook salmon and Sacramento splittail. Juvenile salmon experience higher growth rates in the floodplain than in adjacent river habitats, while the splittail is dependent for successful spawning on the flooded vegetation found in the floodplain. These and other native fish species have developed the ability to find their way off the floodplain before receding waters disconnect it from the river, and in this way they benefit from the temporary floodplain habitat but avoid fatal stranding.[37] The Cosumnes River Preserve is thus managed as a natural floodplain, not only for the protection and restoration of riparian habitat and of wintering habitat for migratory waterfowl and other waterbirds of the Pacific Flyway, but also for the protection of endangered species of native fish. The striking success of the preserve has shown that the apparently conflicting land uses of agriculture, grazing, habitat restoration, and floodplain management can be reconcilable.[38]

One of the prerequisites for the success of the Cosumnes River Preserve has been the relative lack of nearby development pressures. The Stone Lakes National Wildlife Refuge, created in 1994 and located only a few miles to the north, offers a telling contrast. Composed of a mosaic of habitats, including wetlands, vernal pools, grasslands, valley oak woodlands, and riparian forests, the refuge is threatened by the rapidly growing suburbs of Sacramento. Soaring land prices and real estate speculation have made land acquisition difficult and have hindered the full expansion of the refuge to its authorized boundary of nearly 18,000 acres. Facing urban encroachment and receiving the runoff from much of the adjacent city of Elk Grove, Stone Lakes has been declared among the six most endangered of the country's national wildlife refuges.[39]

Proximity to urban areas, however, need not be de facto an impediment to wetland protection. Along the northwestern fringes of the Delta, between the cities of Davis and Sacramento, wetland protection has advanced despite such proximity. In 1997 President Bill Clinton formally dedicated the new 3,700-acre Yolo Bypass Wildlife Area, located within the Yolo Bypass in the shadow of Sacramento's skyline.[40] For the past century, the nearly 60,000-acre leveed Yolo Bypass, constructed during the 1910s as part of the Sacramento Flood Control Project, has served to channel Sacramento Valley winter floodwaters through the Yolo Basin, past the city of Sacramento, and toward the Delta. The Yolo Bypass Wildlife Area is managed to be completely compatible with the bypass's flood control function, and restoration has been initiated to return part of the bypass land to wetland habitat for Pacific Flyway ducks, geese, and shorebirds. The wildlife area was expanded in 2001 to approximately 16,000 acres with the purchase—approved by the California Wildlife Conservation Board—of more than 12,000 additional acres, including a 10,000-acre cattle ranch studded with vernal pools. The new parcels increased the ecological diversity of the Yolo Bypass Wildlife Area, which includes permanent and seasonal wetlands, vernal pool grasslands, riparian forests, and managed agricultural lands, all of which possess significant value to wildlife. In addition, the Yolo Bypass seasonal floodplain itself—much like the Cosumnes River floodplain—has been found to support juvenile Chinook salmon and spawning Sacramento splittail, as well as thirteen other native fish species and forty-two fish species in total. Here, as elsewhere in the Central Valley, wetlands—once drained and reclaimed as an obstacle to development—are proving compatible with other land uses, including the maintenance of California's hydraulic infrastructure.[41]

RESTORING WETLANDS AND RIPARIAN FORESTS IN THE SACRAMENTO VALLEY

Beyond the fringes of the Delta, in the Sacramento Valley to the north and in the San Joaquin and Tulare basins to the south, wetlands and riparian forests are rebounding as well. The degree to which this wetland resurgence has taken place varies from region to region, ranging from relatively modest gains in the Tulare Basin to significant restoration of riparian forests along the Sacramento River and the history-making impending restoration of the San Joaquin River itself. Throughout the Central Valley, the drive to protect and restore wetlands is ascendant.

In the Sacramento Valley, the move to establish protected wetland areas that had begun with the creation of the state's Gray Lodge Waterfowl Refuge in 1931 and the Sacramento National Wildlife Refuge in 1937 gained renewed momentum during the 1980s. The U.S. Fish and Wildlife Service created the Butte Sink

National Wildlife Refuge and the Butte Sink Wildlife Management Area in 1980, as well as the Sacramento River National Wildlife Refuge in 1989, bringing thousands of acres of wetlands and riparian habitat, on public and private land, under protection. All are managed as part of the Sacramento National Wildlife Refuge Complex.

Since 1922, when agreements between rice farmers in the upper Butte Basin and landowners in the Butte Sink removed the impetus for the reclamation of the Butte Basin by the Sacramento Flood Control Project, the Butte Sink has been managed primarily as a mix of permanent, semipermanent, and seasonal wetland habitat, as well as riparian forest (see chapter 4).Wetland and riparian habitat are now more extensive than they were in the early 1900s, when agricultural uses were more prevalent, and most of the Butte Sink remains in the ownership of several dozen private duck clubs, "including some of the most exclusive clubs in the United States."[42] The Butte Sink supports the greatest density of waterfowl anywhere in the Central Valley, and it is not uncommon for one million to two million waterfowl to be present during the peak of the fall migration.[43] The Butte Sink National Wildlife Refuge was established in an area of particularly high ecological value, known locally as the Beanfield. The 733 acres of this small refuge support one of the greatest concentrations of waterfowl in the world on a per-acre basis; more than three hundred thousand ducks and one hundred thousand geese have typically been recorded there. Riparian woodland vegetation on the refuge provides habitat diversity and roosting sites for great and snowy egrets, black-crowned night and great blue herons, and various raptors, especially red-tailed hawks.[44] The Butte Sink National Wildlife Refuge is the only public parcel in the approximately 18,000-acre Butte Sink Wildlife Management Area. Under its conservation easement program, by 2009 the Fish and Wildlife Service had purchased perpetual easements on more than 10,000 acres of natural wetlands and restored agricultural lands in the management area, representing more than 75 percent of Butte Sink properties.[45] The creation of the Butte Sink National Wildlife Refuge and Butte Sink Wildlife Management Area thus continues a tradition of wetland protection and management in the region that dates back to the early decades of the twentieth century, and that has set the Butte Basin apart from the Sacramento Valley's other great tule basins.

The creation of the Sacramento River National Wildlife Refuge addressed the problem of more than a century of degradation of riparian habitat along the Sacramento River. The refuge established protection for diverse riparian habitats important to migratory birds, anadromous fish, and a wide variety of native plants and animals, including several threatened and endangered species. As of 2009, the refuge extended along a seventy-seven-mile stretch of the Sacramento River's historic meander zone, and its more than two dozen units encompassed nearly 12,000 acres of riparian and agricultural habitats, including sand and gravel bars, willow scrub, cottonwood forest, mixed riparian forest, valley oak woodlands and savannas, grasslands, freshwater wetlands, pastures, cover crops, and almond and walnut orchards. The agricultural lands are managed by private farmers through cooperative land management agreements until habitat restoration plans can be put into effect. The Sacramento River National Wildlife Refuge is expected to continue to expand to its proposed boundary of 18,000 acres and to extend along the Sacramento River for more than one hundred miles between the cities of Red Bluff and Colusa, spanning Tehama, Butte, Glenn, and Colusa counties. When fully restored, the refuge will create a linked network of flood-plain forests, wetlands, and grasslands that will provide a semblance of the extensive and well-developed riparian corridors that so impressed visitors and settlers during the nineteenth century.[46]

RICE FIELDS AS WETLANDS

The waterfowl depredation problems that plagued the rice industry during its early decades, and that led in large part to the creation of state and federal refuges during the '30s, '40s, and '50s, have been effectively solved by the development of faster-maturing varieties, which can be harvested prior to the fall migration of millions of Pacific Flyway waterfowl into the Central Valley. In yet another turn in the complicated relationship between rice growers and waterfowl, beginning in the 1990s, growers in the Sacramento Valley—who account for more than 90 percent of the rice grown in California—began to flood hundreds of thousands of acres of their fields for use by wintering waterfowl.[47] The driving force behind the rice growers' newfound hospitality toward waterfowl has been a strict limitation placed on the burning of post-harvest fields.

Historically, rice growers have employed open-field burning to dispose of the three to four tons of rice straw per acre that can remain in the fields after harvest. Burning is inexpensive and helps control fungal diseases such as stem rot and aggregate sheath spot.[48] However, the burning of rice contributes substantially to air pollution, and in the early 1990s, on a typical autumn burn day, rice straw burning accounted for 10 percent of the Sacramento Valley's total PM_{10}, or small particulate matter, pollution.[49] On heavy burn days, Sacramento-area physicians reported increased complaints from patients suffering from asthma, bronchitis, and allergies.[50] In 1991 the California legislature responded to complaints about air quality and to petitions to curtail rice burning by passing the Rice Straw Burning Reduction Act.[51]

Facing annual reductions of their burning allowances under the new act, rice farmers sought alternative methods to dispose of their straw. Rice plants can be chopped and disked and left in the field to decompose naturally, but the effectiveness of this dry method of disposal depends heavily on suitable temperature and soil moisture content. During the early 1990s Ducks Unlimited, the California Wildlife Conservation Board, and a consortium of other conservation groups began working with the California Rice Industry Association to develop a waterfowl-friendly approach to straw management. This technique, which has proved effective for decomposition, entails flooding harvested rice fields with two to six inches of water and then using a specially designed straw roller or cage roller to incorporate straw and stubble into the mud. Since the early 1990s, the seasonal flooding of post-harvest rice fields has opened up hundreds of thousands of acres of suitable new habitat for migratory waterfowl and shorebirds.[52] By 2003, rice growers in the Sacramento Valley were annually flooding more than 350,000 acres, approximately 70 percent of all rice acreage in the valley. The extent of flooded rice fields exceeded the combined total acreage of all public refuges and private wetlands in the Central Valley.[53]

The flooding of post-harvest rice fields has proved beneficial for both farmers and waterfowl. Rice farmers receive substantial benefits from the presence of large numbers of waterfowl and shorebirds, which are drawn to their flooded fields. The feeding activity of the birds, especially the larger waterfowl, further mixes the straw and soil, contributing to the decomposition process. At the same time, the waterfowl reduce the presence of "weed" species found in and around rice fields by feeding on seeds of wild millet, sprangletop, and smartweed, and tubers of ricefield bulrush, smallflower umbrella sedge, and arrowhead.[54] Waterfowl benefit from access to the 300 to 350 pounds of waste rice that remain on each acre, 30 percent more than would be present in the aftermath of fall burning. In addition to post-harvest rice, the flooded fields provide approximately 250 pounds per acre of naturally occurring food sources such as small invertebrates (especially midge larvae), tubers, edible shoots, and seeds. Rice fields that are flooded and managed as wetlands, generally from October to March, can therefore provide as much as 600 pounds of food per acre, approximately 80 percent of the 750 pounds per acre, on average, that are found in natural wetlands.[55] This food supply is important for other avian species as well. Within the Sacramento Valley, flooded rice fields have been found to hold as much as 68 percent of the migratory shorebirds present during the early winter months. These shorebird and waterfowl concentrations in turn attract raptors, especially the northern harrier, peregrine falcon, and bald eagle.[56]

Despite these significant ecological contributions, flooded rice fields cannot be considered the complete equivalent of the aboriginal wetlands of the Central Valley. The fields cannot provide suitable conditions for the full suite of species that used those wetlands. However, for many of the 235 animal species known to use California rice lands, they can come close. Although the rice fields produce a smaller volume of natural foods than wetlands, when complemented by the sixty

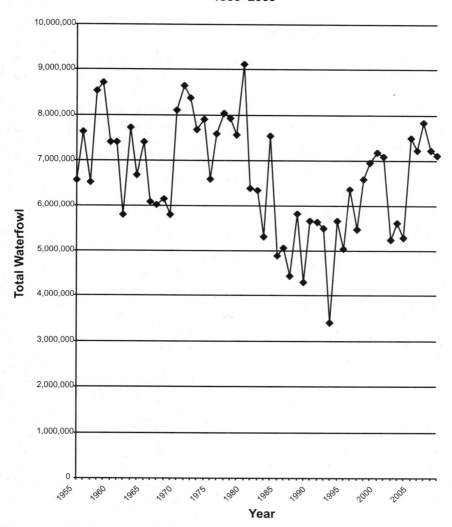

FIGURE 16. Midwinter waterfowl indices (population estimates) for the Pacific Flyway, 1955–2009. Source: Data compiled from Daniel P. Collins and Robert E. Trost, *2009 Pacific Flyway Data Book: Waterfowl Harvests and Status, Hunter Participation and Success in the Pacific Flyway and United States* (Portland, Ore.: U.S. Fish and Wildlife Service, 2009).

thousand tons of waste grain present annually, California rice fields appear able to meet the dietary requirements for a wide range of waterfowl, shorebird, and other waterbird species.[57] For these species, flooded rice fields may be functionally equivalent to contemporary managed wetlands in the valley.[58]

The conservation implications for winter waterbird communities in the Central Valley are profound. By more than doubling the available seasonal wetland habitat, the flooded rice fields of the Central Valley, and particularly those of the Sacramento Valley, have contributed substantially to a reversal in the decline of California's wintering waterfowl population. In conjunction with the increased water supply to wetlands mandated by the Central Valley Project Improvement Act and the restoration initiatives of the Central Valley Joint Venture, the flooding of rice fields has helped boost overall Pacific Flyway populations to levels not seen since the 1970s (see figure 16).[59]

PUBLIC REFUGES AND PRIVATE WETLANDS IN THE TULARE BASIN

In the Tulare Basin, at the opposite end of the Central Valley from the Sacramento Valley, acreage of waterfowl-friendly flooded fields has declined dramatically, but the basin's remnant wetlands have been boosted both by changes wrought by the Central Valley Project Improvement Act and by the creation of a new Tulare Basin Wildlife Management Area. The 1992 CVPIA has substantially increased water allocations for the historically underwatered Pixley and Kern national wildlife refuges, which had been established in an attempt to restore a small portion of the once-vast wetland habitat in the Tulare Basin. The Tulare Basin Wildlife Management Area, established in 2007, is expected to expand wetland habitat by thousands of acres.

The CVPIA incrementally increased the annual water allotment for the Kern National Wildlife Refuge to 25,000 acre-feet, allowing the refuge in 2004 to flood its entire 6,400 acres of wetland habitat for the first time in its history, nearly tripling its previous annual average. The dramatic increase in water availability has changed both the objectives and the appearance of the refuge, which is now managed for a greater quantity and variety of wetland habitats, including summer habitat for colonial nesting birds such as the great blue heron and white-faced ibis; late-summer habitat for early migrant ducks, especially northern pintail; and moist-soil habitat for the production of waterfowl food plants, especially wild millet and swamp timothy. The Pixley National Wildlife Refuge, historically more starved for water than the Kern Refuge, never had sufficient water to provide any significant marsh habitat on a regular basis. The CVPIA began to remedy this problem by providing 6,000 acre-feet annually to Pixley for the development and maintenance of more than 750 acres of seasonal wetlands, including 25 acres of riparian habitat, and more than 500 acres of irrigated pasture and cropland for the benefit of migratory sandhill cranes.[60]

The several thousand acres of managed wetland habitat on the Kern and Pixley national wildlife refuges, while ecologically valuable, are inadequate to provide fully for the needs of waterfowl in the Tulare Basin or to meet the objectives of the Central Valley Joint Venture. Compounding the shortfall of wetland acreage in the basin, water deliveries from the Central Valley Project and State Water Project have resulted in the conversion of thousands of acres of seasonal wetlands to irrigated agriculture. At the same time, agricultural lands, which once provided tens of thousands of acres of flooded temporary waterfowl habitat during fall pre-irrigations, have diminished in their importance to waterfowl. As a result of a shift in crops from grains to cotton and of increases in water prices, fewer acres have been subject to pre-irrigation flooding, and the size of individual flooded areas has declined. By the late 1980s, pre-irrigated acreage had fallen to 5,000 acres.[61] This reduction in temporary fall waterfowl habitat has reduced waterfowl numbers in the basin, and has particularly affected early-migrating northern pintail.[62]

In response to the steep decline in privately owned wetland habitat in the Tulare Basin, most of which is under the control of a few dozen surviving duck clubs, the Fish and Wildlife Service proposed the creation of a new Tulare Basin Wildlife Management Area.[63] Approved in December 2007, the management area—located to the south and east of historic Tulare Lake near the Kern and Pixley national wildlife refuges—will protect up to 22,000 acres of wetland and associated upland habitat, primarily through the purchase of permanent conservation easements, and will maintain the long-term viability of private wetlands in the Tulare Basin.[64] The management area will provide habitat for wetland-dependent species, including the five species of waterfowl—northern pintail, gadwall, green-winged teal, cinnamon teal, and northern shoveler—that rely extensively on Tulare Basin wintering habitat, as well as threatened and endangered species, including the San Joaquin kit fox, Tipton kangaroo rat, and blunt-nosed leopard lizard, that rely on upland habitat.[65]

Neither the establishment of the Tulare Basin Wildlife Management Area nor enhanced water supplies to the Kern and Pixley national wildlife refuges will restore the Tulare Basin to the wetland paradise it once was. Tulare, Buena Vista, and Kern lakes, the marshes of Buena Vista Slough, and the miles of wetland edges that once existed in the basin are gone, converted almost entirely into cotton, tomato, and alfalfa fields, vineyards and almond orchards, and irrigated pasture. The Kings, Kaweah, Kern, and Tule rivers that once filled the basin are contained behind U.S. Army Corps of Engineers dams. But a small remnant of the historic Tulare Basin wetlands still exits, though now measured in thousands, rather than hundreds of thousands, of acres. The contribution of the Tulare Basin's wildlife refuges and protected private wetlands will be to halt the decline of the basin's wetlands and return them from the brink of oblivion.

THE GRASSLANDS: REJUVENATION
AND INTERNATIONAL RECOGNITION

To the north of the Tulare Basin, in the Grasslands of the San Joaquin Basin, waterfowl and the wetlands that support them have witnessed a remarkable recovery. Striking ecological successes have been achieved on both private duck club and public refuge lands. Encompassing the largest contiguous block of wetlands remaining in the entire Central Valley, and containing one-third of the all of the valley's extant wetlands, the Grasslands continues to be of paramount importance not only for migratory waterfowl, populations of which have surged, but also for shorebirds and other waterbirds, as well a variety of threatened and endangered species of animals and plants.

Since the 1980s, when the Grasslands was tainted by selenium in drainwater flowing from lands to the south, tens of thousands of additional acres have been protected, even as land use patterns have changed and the region faces threats from urban expansion. Private landowners within the Grassland Water District have been gradually moving away from the integration of waterfowl and cattle toward exclusive management for waterfowl, bringing to a close an era of mixed land use that dates back to the nineteenth century, when Henry Miller and Charles Lux dominated the Westside of the San Joaquin Basin. Over the course of a century, in several stages, management priorities in the Grasslands have essentially reversed. The flood irrigation practiced by Miller and Lux was intended to benefit their cattle by supporting the growth of moist-soil grasses; the boon to waterfowl was a fortunate by-product of Miller and Lux's land management practices. After 1925, when joint cattle companies and duck clubs purchased the old Miller and Lux tracts, the Grasslands was managed for both cattle and waterfowl. Since the late 1980s, falling beef prices have made grazing less profitable at the same time that the ecological importance of the Grasslands for the wintering waterfowl of the Pacific Flyway has become ever more apparent. As increasing costs of both habitat enhancement and water have driven up the cost of duck club memberships, club owners have sought to improve their club's hunting potential by eliminating cattle and dedicating themselves to a waterfowl management plan.[66] Many clubs have opted for a year-round system of wetland management that includes pond improvements, the development of water control structures, disking, mowing, the cultivation of native waterfowl foods, and irrigation.[67] These practices, in conjunction with the acquisition of additional state and federal refuge lands, have contributed to a waterfowl renaissance in the greater Grasslands area, which has more than doubled the number of wintering waterfowl found there during the 1980s (see figure 17). As a result of these incremental land use changes, the Grasslands have been converted from a cattle empire to a "duck and wetland empire."[68]

One of the keys to the recent ecological gains in the Grasslands has been the ability of the Grassland Water District to reroute selenium-tainted drainwater around, rather than through, the Grasslands. In 1985, at the height of the selenium crisis, the Grassland Water District had ended its practice, in place for three decades, of employing agricultural drainwater that flowed through its wetland channels to supplement its freshwater supply. However, because the Grassland Water District shared its water conveyance systems with the upslope agricultural districts that generated the tainted drainwater, the district still faced the burden of transporting that drainwater through its canals and channels to the San Joaquin River for discharge. This arrangement became increasingly problematic after the Central Valley Project Improvement Act of 1992 increased the freshwater supply to the Grasslands. The district's conveyance system lacked the capacity to handle both drainwater and the enhanced freshwater supply simultaneously.[69]

The Grasslands Bypass Project offered a solution to the problem of dual conveyance of agricultural drainwater and freshwater through the Grasslands. The plan for the project, first proposed in 1985 by San Luis National Wildlife Refuge Complex manager Gary Zahm, called for reopening a portion of the San Luis Drain to convey contaminated drainage along the eastern side of the Grasslands for ultimate discharge into the San Joaquin River.[70] Finally opened in 1996, the Grasslands Bypass reroutes drainwater from approximately 97,000 acres of farmland adjacent to the Grassland Water District through a refurbished section of the concrete-lined San Luis Drain. Upon reaching the North Grasslands, the drain discharges into Mud Slough, a tributary of the San Joaquin River. The Bypass Project by necessity degraded the water quality in the six miles of Mud Slough that now linked the San Luis Drain to the San Joaquin River, and in the San Joaquin River itself at and below the point of discharge. Evidence of selenium accumulation was quickly found in fish and aquatic invertebrates in both Mud Slough and adjoining reaches of the San Joaquin River.[71] Nevertheless, the Bypass Project significantly improved the water quality in more than ninety-three miles of channels used to deliver water to wetlands in the Grassland Water District and adjacent state and federal refuges. As a result of its initial success, the project was extended in 2001 for eight additional years through 2009, and is expected to remain in operation.[72]

With the Grasslands Bypass Project in place, the 75,000-acre Grassland Resource Conservation District has been able to optimize its use of the increased water supplies that the Central Valley Project Improvement Act committed to

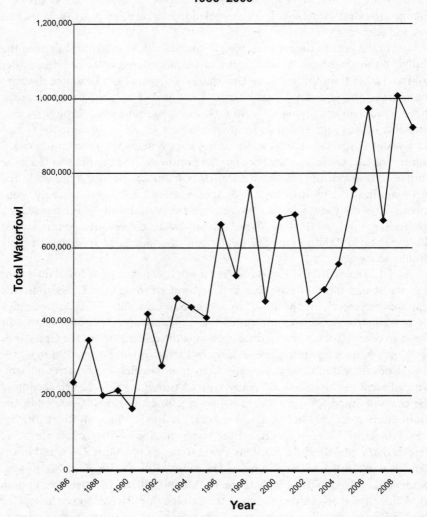

FIGURE 17. Midwinter waterfowl populations for the Grasslands and surrounding areas of the northern San Joaquin Valley, 1986–2009. Source: Data compiled from unpublished California Midwinter Waterfowl Surveys, provided by the U.S. Fish and Wildlife Service, San Luis National Wildlife Refuge Complex, Los Banos, California.

the region. This supplemental water has allowed landowners and refuge managers in the Grasslands not only to manage wetlands for wintering waterfowl, but also to maintain permanent and semipermanent wetlands as spring and summer breeding habitat, important for the provision of invertebrate food resources.[73] The year-round availability of water has allowed for earlier fall flooding of wetlands as well. August and September flooding provides habitat for resident species and for species of early migrating waterfowl, especially the northern pintail. Under the CVPIA, more water also became available for the irrigation of moist-soil waterfowl food plants, as well as for greater flow through the wetlands, which has decreased the potential for the outbreak of the avian diseases botulism and cholera.[74]

The ecological enhancements in the privately held Grasslands mirror the successes achieved on the surrounding San Joaquin Basin refuges. New state wildlife areas have been created and existing ones augmented.[75] National wildlife refuges have expanded significantly. The Merced National Wildlife Refuge, created in 1951, has been enlarged to more than 10,200 acres, including the nearly 2,500-acre Arena Plains Unit, added to the refuge in 1992, which contains the San Joaquin Valley's largest block of undisturbed sand dunes, perched wetlands (which are created by an impervious layer that lies above the water table), and vernal pools.[76] The San Luis National Wildlife Refuge, established in 1966 on the native grassland of San Luis Island between Salt Slough and the San Joaquin River, has tripled in size to more than 26,600 acres.[77] The state and federal acquisitions were in large part a direct mitigation response to the disaster at Kesterson Reservoir, and were abetted by the 1989 San Joaquin Basin Action Plan, implemented by a cooperative agreement among the U.S. Bureau of Reclamation, the U.S. Fish and Wildlife Service, and the California Department of Fish and Game to acquire and enhance wetlands in the San Joaquin Basin.[78] The result has been the protection of most of the remaining contiguous wetland habitat in the Grasslands.

One of the greatest success stories on the public lands in the Grasslands has been the expansion and rebirth of the Kesterson National Wildlife Refuge. Two properties, once devastated by selenium, have been added to the refuge. In 1990 the U.S. Fish and Wildlife Service purchased the 555-acre property formerly owned by James and Karen Claus, who had led the fight against the U.S. Bureau of Reclamation in the Kesterson affair, and in 1991 the service acquired the adjacent 5,600-acre Freitas Ranch, whose owners had retreated from their contaminated land to take up residence in nearby Los Banos.[79] In 1996, at the suggestion of refuge manager Gary Zahm, 4,460 acres of the Kesterson Refuge—almost all of the property except for the 1,283 acres of the former Kesterson Reservoir—and the Claus and Freitas acquisitions were incorporated into the new Kesterson Unit of the San Luis National Wildlife Refuge, consisting of approximately 11,000 acres of seasonal and permanent wetlands, riparian habitat, native grasslands, flood-plain habitat, and an extensive network of vernal pools.[80] The redesignation of Kesterson was in part an attempt to downplay the prominence of the tainted Kesterson name, but also reflected the rejuvenation of this refuge after its check-ered beginnings. With its freshwater supply guaranteed by the Central Valley Project Improvement Act, the reconfigured Kesterson Unit has recovered and thrived. The biological diversity of the area has increased, and, as early as 1997, signs of revival included the return of ground cover, which provides habitat for songbirds, and the sprouting of young cottonwood and oak trees, which will ultimately provide more habitat for wood ducks and hawks.[81]

More than three-quarters of a century of efforts to protect the Grasslands, dating back to the creation of the public Los Banos Waterfowl Refuge in 1929 and the formation of the private Grass Lands Association in 1939, have brought inter-national recognition to this region of the San Joaquin Basin. As an acknowledg-ment of the Grasslands' importance not only to migratory waterfowl but also to the hundreds of thousands of migratory shorebirds that feed on the abundance of invertebrates found along its wetland edges, in 1991 the Western Hemisphere Shorebird Reserve Network officially recognized the Grasslands region as an In-ternational Reserve.[82] In the late 1990s, at the urging of Gary Zahm, the public and private lands of the Grasslands were collectively designated the Grasslands Ecological Area, consisting of more than 160,000 acres of wetlands and wetland-related habitat distributed among national wildlife refuges, state wildlife areas, a state park, and nearly two hundred privately owned parcels, most of which are waterfowl hunting clubs.[83] Further underscoring the importance of the Grass-lands, in February 2005 the newly designated Grasslands Ecological Area was recognized as a Ramsar Wetland of International Importance. This coveted sta-tus was awarded under the Convention on Wetlands of International Importance, the official title of the Ramsar Convention, named after its place of adoption in Iran in 1971. Ratified by the United States in 1986, the Ramsar Convention, with nearly 160 signatory nations, provides the framework for the international protec-tion of wetlands as habitats for migratory fauna that do not observe international boundaries, and for the benefit of human populations dependent on wetlands.[84]

The Ramsar designation recognized the unique ecological contribution of the Grasslands Ecological Area, which supports up to one million Pacific Flyway waterfowl and shorebirds each winter, including nineteen duck species and six goose species. In addition to its wetlands, the area contains a variety of ecological communities, including riparian cottonwood and willow forests, riparian oak woodlands, vernal pools, alkali sinks, and native alkali grasslands. This matrix of habitats supports numerous species of wading birds, raptors, and other wild-life species. Several of these species are classified as federally threatened or en-dangered, including the San Joaquin kit fox, western snowy plover, and giant garter snake. A number of threatened and endangered species of animals and plants are also associated with the Grasslands Ecological Area's vernal pool complexes, including four species of fairy shrimp, the California tiger salamander, and the rare Colusa grass.[85] The number and variety of protected species in the Grasslands Ecological Area reflect the importance of the area not only for waterfowl but also for overall biodiversity.

THE RESURRECTION OF THE SAN JOAQUIN RIVER

While sweeping changes were leading to the enhancement of wetlands in the Grasslands of the San Joaquin Basin, two developments were taking place that would result in the protection and restoration of the San Joaquin River itself. A new national wildlife refuge would protect part of the river's historic floodplain and riparian corridor, and a protracted legal battle would lead to the restoration of the river's flows, bringing the long-dead section of the river below Friant Dam back to life. In the process, an endangered waterfowl species was brought back from the brink of extinction, and California reversed a half-century-old policy of sacrificing its second-longest river, including the salmon runs it had once supported, for the benefit of irrigated agriculture.

In 1987 the Fish and Wildlife Service added the new San Joaquin River National Wildlife Refuge, located within the historical floodplain of the San Joaquin River between its confluences with the Stanislaus and Tuolumne rivers, to its San Luis National Wildlife Refuge Complex. From its original size of approximately 3,100 acres, the refuge had expanded by 2009 to more than 7,000 acres within its proposed boundary of more than 10,000 acres. Like its northern counterpart on the Sacramento River, the San Joaquin River National Wildlife Refuge consists of a variety of habitats, including permanent and seasonal wetlands, riparian woodlands, grasslands, vernal pools, and irrigated pastures and agricultural lands managed under conservation easements. Along the refuge's river channels, sloughs, and oxbows can be found mixed stands of willow, cottonwood, and box elder, composing some of the largest expanses of riparian habitat remaining in the San Joaquin Valley.[86]

Though intended to protect a wide range of plant and animal species, one of the initial primary objectives of the San Joaquin River National Wildlife Refuge was to ensure the wintering habitat requirements of the then-endangered Aleutian Canada goose (now classified as the Aleutian cackling goose).[87] The mosaic of refuge lands is the primary wintering site of 98 percent of the world's population of these geese, essentially all of which winter in California's Central Valley. Once numerous, the Aleutian Canada goose had been decimated by the introduction of arctic and red foxes on its breeding grounds in the Aleutian and nearby island chains. In 1967 the federal government listed the Aleutian Canada goose as an endangered species, and by 1975 fewer than eight hundred of the birds were sighted in California.[88] By protecting and enhancing the wintering grounds for the Aleutian cackling goose, the San Joaquin River National Wildlife Refuge has played a key role in the recovery of this species, which was downlisted from endangered to threatened status in 1991 and delisted entirely in 2001.[89]

Despite the notable successes of the refuge, the restoration of a substantial section of the floodplain of the San Joaquin River still did not address the fact that much of the river contained no water at all. The San Joaquin River had not fared as well as the Grasslands during the San Joaquin Valley water wars of the mid-twentieth century. When the San Joaquin River below Friant Dam was sacrificed during the 1940s for the operation of the Central Valley Project, approximately sixty miles of the river below the dam were left nearly or completely dry, destroying the river's historic salmon runs, cutting it off from its floodplain, and withering its riparian forests. The failure of the U.S. Bureau of Reclamation to release water downstream from Friant Dam has affected the entire lower course of the San Joaquin River, but particularly the 153-mile stretch from the dam to the river's confluence with its first major tributary, the Merced River. Much of this environmental damage to the San Joaquin River, however, appears poised to be reversed. After a struggle lasting two decades, the restoration of flows in the river has begun—an outcome almost unimaginable a half-century ago.

The battle to revive the San Joaquin River began in 1988, when the U.S. Bureau of Reclamation initiated negotiations to renew its forty-year delivery contracts for Central Valley Project water stored behind Friant Dam, the first of which was scheduled to expire the following year. The Natural Resources Defense Council (NRDC), leading a coalition of fifteen environmental groups, filed suit against the bureau for renewing the long-term contracts without first preparing an environmental impact statement, as required by the National Environmental Policy Act, and for violating the Endangered Species Act, the Reclamation Act, and the California Fish and Game Code.[90] While the matter remained in litigation, the 1992 Central Valley Project Improvement Act mandated that the Department of the Interior address the restoration of the San Joaquin River.[91] In 1994 the Friant Water Users Authority, which represents nearly two dozen water agencies that hold contracts for San Joaquin River water stored behind Friant Dam, petitioned unsuccessfully for dismissal of the NRDC's case. Rebuffed by the courts, in 1999 the Friant Water Users Authority entered into negotiations with the NRDC to determine how much water would be needed to restore the river. The difficult negotiations between the water users and the environmental groups broke down in 2003, however, and the issue was returned to the courts.[92]

The stalemate over the river's restoration ended in 2004 when U.S. District Judge Lawrence K. Karlton ruled that the U.S. Bureau of Reclamation had violated both state and federal law by diverting most of the San Joaquin River out of its channel for agricultural purposes over the span of more than half a century.[93] Karlton's ruling required the Bureau of Reclamation to comply with state law by maintaining adequate water in the San Joaquin River below Friant Dam to sustain the river's fishery. The ruling was based in large part on California's *Fish and Game Code* section 5937, which had become the focal point of the litigation, and which required that the amount and timing of water to be released from Friant Dam should be sufficient to maintain in "good condition" any fish that exist below the dam. Significantly, this was the same provision—formerly known as *Fish and Game Code* section 525—that California Attorney General Edmund "Pat" Brown had argued in 1951 was inapplicable to Friant Dam, thus paving the way for state acquiescence to the dewatering of the San Joaquin River as a necessary consequence of the Central Valley Project (see chapter 7).

Prompted back into negotiations by Karlton's ruling, in 2006 the parties reached a historic settlement on most issues concerning the San Joaquin River restoration, thereby ending the eighteen-year legal dispute.[94] The agreement provides for substantial river channel improvements and sufficient releases from Friant Dam to sustain naturally reproducing spring-run and fall-run Chinook salmon and other fish populations on the San Joaquin River from the dam downstream to the confluence with the Merced River.[95] At the same time, the settlement is intended to minimize water supply impacts to San Joaquin River water users, who will give up approximately 15 percent of their current withdrawals from Friant Dam.[96] This river restoration project, the most ambitious in California's history, was approved by Congress and signed by President Barack Obama on March 30, 2009, as the San Joaquin River Restoration Settlement Act.[97] The legislation authorizes the federal government to spend $250 million on this multiyear project, which is expected to cost between $600 million and $1.2 billion; the remainder of the funding will come from the state and the area's water districts.[98]

Amid widespread media coverage, increased releases into the river from Friant Dam began on October 1, 2009. Downstream flows, which had been a mere 117 cubic feet per second (cfs), only enough to satisfy the remaining water rights of those landowners situated along the river between the dam and the last diversion point at Gravelly Ford, were increased to 350 cfs. In March 2010, as interim restoration flows approached 1,000 cfs, the San Joaquin River filled its historical channels below Friant Dam and flowed continuously to San Francisco Bay for the first time in more than six decades—a milestone in the history of the river's restoration. Releases from the dam continued to increase throughout the spring, peaking at approximately 1,600 cfs, the target for the first year of restoration. If all goes according to plan, salmon, taken from the Sacramento River, will be reintroduced in 2012. Full restoration flows of up to 4,500 cfs are expected by 2014, and the full restoration of the San Joaquin River channel is scheduled to be completed by 2016.[99]

The San Joaquin River, a desiccated remnant of its former self for more than half a century, thus appears poised to be the locus of one of the nation's largest and most expensive fishery and river restoration projects. The project will revitalize the most degraded of California's major rivers and usher in the next generation of fish and wildlife protection in the San Joaquin Basin. Occurring more than sixty years after Everett G. Rank and his fellow riparian landowners first filed suit in 1947 against the Bureau of Reclamation for damming and diverting the San Joaquin River, the imminent restoration of the river, its fish and wildlife, its floodplain, and its riparian habitat is both a product and a reflection of a stronger public resolve to protect the Central Valley's wetland resources into the twenty-first century and beyond.

Epilogue

Global Climate Change and the Wetlands of the Great Central Valley

The Great Central Valley portion of the Pacific Flyway at the beginning of the twenty-first century is far different than it was at the time of California statehood. It has been profoundly changed from its natural state, and its wetlands are now intensively managed, from the delivery and drawdown of water to the types and amount of waterfowl food planted. Human intervention has become a permanent and necessary component of the maintenance and perpetuation of the premier wintering grounds of the Pacific Flyway.

Despite the need for artificial regulation, the Central Valley's contribution to the Pacific Flyway is stronger in many ways than it was only a half-century ago. The long, steep decline of California's Central Valley wetlands—the "fall," which began as early as the passage of the Swamp and Overflowed Lands Act of 1850—has been reversed. The number of acres of wetlands in the valley decreased from more than 4 million at the time of statehood to approximately 300,000 acres of freshwater wetlands, and fewer than 400,000 acres of wetlands overall, by 1990.[1] But the rate of loss slowed substantially during the twentieth century, as state and federal wetland refuges were established throughout the valley, and private wetlands, primarily on duck club lands, were protected by conservation easements and enhanced by increased water supplies. In recent decades, tens of thousands of acres of wetlands and associated uplands have been added to state and federal refuges, and the Central Valley Project Improvement Act has dramatically increased their water supplies. Riparian corridors have been protected and enhanced along both the Sacramento and the San Joaquin rivers, and the San Joaquin River below Friant Dam has begun flowing once again. Private nonprofit organizations, including the Nature Conservancy and Ducks Unlimited, have protected important habitat in the Delta and throughout the Central Valley as a whole.[2] The majority of private lands within the Grasslands Ecological Area—now recognized as a Ramsar Wetland of International Importance—and within the Butte Sink in the Sacramento Valley are situated within wildlife management areas and are protected by conservation easements. Similar protection is being established for private lands in the Tulare Basin. The Central Valley Joint Venture, as part of its mission to implement the North American Waterfowl Management Plan, has protected, enhanced, and restored tens of thousands of acres of wetlands, and enhanced hundreds of thousands of acres of agricultural lands to render them compatible with waterfowl use. Flooded rice fields, especially in the Sacramento Valley, have added hundreds of thousands of acres of seasonal wetland habitat. These victories of wetland protection and restoration are substantial, but collectively they represent only a fraction of the Central Valley's wetland heritage. Their significance rests primarily in the fact that they demonstrate that wetland loss can be halted and reversed, and the means by which this reversal can be achieved. The "rise" of the Central Valley's wetlands is a work in progress (see map 20).

All of these accomplishments are tremendously important not only for the future of the wetlands of the Central Valley, but also for the migratory waterfowl, shorebirds, and other waterbirds of the Pacific Flyway, as well as for the protection of a wide range of endangered, threatened, and sensitive species. The extent to which the wetland gains of recent years in the Central Valley can be sustained and furthered will depend on a variety of regional demographic and economic factors, including rapid population increase, urban sprawl, and the disappearance of agricultural lands, and, ultimately, on the degree to which California is affected by global climate change.

California's population continues to grow rapidly, with the greatest growth occurring in the Central Valley. Between 1990 and 2000, the state's population grew by 4.1 million to 33.9 million, an increase of 13.8 percent.[3] Of the eighteen Central Valley counties, thirteen exceeded the statewide average for population growth during that decade, and of those, six experienced growth in excess of 20 percent.[4] As the Central Valley is transformed from a bucolic region dominated by agriculture and cattle grazing to a region of rapid urbanization and economic development, both public and private wetlands will face the dual challenge of encroachment by burgeoning cities and increased competition for finite water supplies. Representative of these changes, in the San Joaquin Valley's Merced County the spheres of influence of three cities—Los Banos, Gustine, and Dos Palos—now overlap a two-mile buffer around the Grasslands Ecological Area.[5]

The loss of agricultural land to urban sprawl poses additional threats to wetlands and wildlife. Between 1990 and 2002, the Central Valley counties lost 283,000 acres of irrigated farmland, approximately 3.7 percent of their total irri-

**Major Protected
Wetland Areas
in the
Central Valley
of California**

Red Bluff

Chico

*Sacramento
Valley*

Sacramento River NWR ★

Sacramento NWR ★
Delevan NWR ★   ★ Gray Lodge WA
Colusa NWR ★   ★ Butte Sink NWR
            ★ Sutter NWR

Yolo Bypass WA ★   ● Sacramento

Stone Lakes NWR ★

            ★ Cosumnes
Suisun   Grizzly   River
            ★ Island WA Preserve
Marsh   Stockton

Delta

San Francisco ●   ★ San Joaquin River NWR

                    *San Joaquin
                    Basin*
            ★ San Luis NWR
Los Banos WA ★   ★ Merced NWR
            Grasslands Ecological Area

            Mendota WA ★ Fresno ●

N   *Tulare
W   E   Basin*
S

*Pacific
Ocean*

                    ★ Pixley NWR

            ★ Kern NWR

LEGEND   Bakersfield
★ Major Wetland Area
Abbreviations:
NWR - National Wildlife Refuge
WA - State Wildlife Area

0 12.5 25   50   75   100
                        Miles
Credit: Kevin Petrik, Ducks Unlimited, Western Regional Office

MAP 20. The locations of the major federal, state, and other protected wetland areas
discussed in the text. All of these areas have come into existence since 1929, demonstrating the revival of the Central Valley's wetlands that began in the twentieth century and
that continues in the twenty-first. To avoid overly cluttering the map, numerous
additional protected areas are not shown. Map created courtesy of Kevin Petrik, Ducks
Unlimited, Western Regional Office, Rancho Cordova, California.

gated acreage.[6] Although it is desirable that some irrigated land in the Central Valley be taken out of production, particularly on the seleniferous Westside, the conversion of agricultural land to urban environments reduces the amount of open space available to wildlife, destroys isolated wetlands such as vernal pools, and reduces the land area available for seasonal flooding. The most prominent effort to preserve agricultural land in California has been the Land Conservation Act of 1965.[7] More commonly known as the Williamson Act, this measure allows owners of agricultural land to enter into contracts with participating county governments to forgo development of their land for at least ten years in return for reduced tax liability. The state provides payments to the counties to compensate for lost revenues. At the end of 2007, more than 16 million acres of California's 45 million acres of farm and ranch land were enrolled in Williamson Act programs, nearly 10 million of which were in the Central Valley.[8] By helping landowners to maintain their properties in agricultural production, the Williamson Act also preserves the amount of land eligible for conservation easements within wildlife management areas. The lands slated for inclusion within the Tulare Basin Wildlife Management Area, for example, overlap with Williamson Act lands in Kern County.[9] In the form of tax relief and payments for conservation easements, landowners therefore have a double incentive to preserve agricultural land and to manage that land in wildlife-compatible ways.

It may well be possible to protect the Central Valley's revitalized wetlands and the wildlife they harbor from population pressures and land conversion. In the long run, however, it may prove much more difficult to protect the valley's wetlands from the effects of global climate change, which appear poised to dwarf all other environmental challenges.[10] Freshwater marshes in the Central Valley will be at risk as increased temperatures and seasonal changes in rainfall reduce the amount of water available from runoff. Vernal pools, among California's rarest and most sensitive wetland habitats, are especially vulnerable and may suffer a loss of shallow pools, a decrease in the size of deeper pools, the loss of species that are growing at the present ecological limits of their ranges, and the endangerment of rare endemic species. Anticipated rapid climate change—measured in decades rather than thousands of years—will affect the composition of riparian corridors as well. Current riparian tree species may no longer experience the conditions necessary for germination, establishment, and growth.[11]

For agriculture, changing weather patterns will translate to reduced irrigation water supplies at the same time that higher temperatures increase demand. Under these conditions, the continued production of low-value, water-intensive crops such as cotton, alfalfa, and rice would be at risk.[12] A reduction in the number of acres devoted to rice production would prove detrimental to migratory waterfowl that have come to depend on the availability of flooded post-harvest fields for food and habitat. Private owners of wetlands, including duck club owners, would face increasing costs and changes in seasonal availability of water and might be unable to continue to maintain wetland habitat on their properties.

Climate change predictions for California indicate that impacts will be greatest in the Sacramento–San Joaquin Delta. As sea levels rise from the melting of polar ice and the thermal expansion of the oceans, the salinity gradient in the San Francisco Bay–Delta estuary will be shifted inland. The brackish waters of Suisun Marsh will become more saline, and currently fresh waters in the Delta will become brackish. Such changes will alter habitat conditions and affect species composition throughout the region.[13] The danger to the Delta of rising sea levels is compounded by the continuing subsidence of Delta islands, a process begun during the second half of the nineteenth century when Delta tracts were first drained and converted to agriculture.

Nowhere is the subsidence of the Delta islands more apparent than from the roads that have been constructed atop the levees that ring them. Water in some Delta channels laps almost to the roadside, while toward the interior of the islands, green fields and orchards lie far below. This scenario is akin to that presented by the low-lying city of New Orleans, Louisiana, devastated by Hurricane Katrina in 2005, where one must look up from ground level and over the levees to watch the riverboats pass by on the Mississippi River above. Like that of New Orleans, the present hydrology of the Delta is both surreal and dangerous. Because the Delta serves as the conduit through which the Central Valley Project and State Water Project transport fresh irrigation and drinking water from the Sacramento Valley to more than 20 million people in the San Joaquin Valley and Southern California, the integrity of its eleven hundred miles of levees is of paramount importance for the preservation of water quality in the state.

Delta levees have collapsed repeatedly, and from 1900 to 2007 there were 166 levee breaches on the Delta's sinking islands and tracts.[14] While most breaches occurred during winter floods, the breaching of a levee on the below-sea-level Upper Jones Tract in the south-central Delta on June 3, 2004, at a time of low flow, pointed to the vulnerability of the Delta's aging, eroding infrastructure. Within three days, both Upper Jones Tract and the adjacent Lower Jones Tract were flooded to an average depth of twelve to sixteen feet. Approximately 11,000 acres of cropland were inundated, along with dozens of homes and barns. After the three-hundred-foot levee breach was repaired in July, the process of pumping out the water required five months and cost $90 million.[15]

Conservative global climate models estimate an increase in sea level of eight to twelve inches for California by the end of the twenty-first century, which will place continuous additional pressure on the Delta's fragile levee system and exacerbate high tide events. A one-foot rise in sea level would transform the current storm surge peak on the lower San Joaquin River in the Delta from an event that occurs once every one hundred years on average to an event that occurs once every ten years.[16] Under this scenario, levees will be breached and islands will be inundated with increasing frequency. The problems of levee erosion, island subsidence, and rising sea levels caused by global warming are so severe that University of California scientists Jeffrey Mount and Robert Twiss have predicted a two-in-three chance of massive levee failure, from a devastating flood, earthquake, or combination of the two, in the Delta by 2050. The simultaneous failure of multiple levees in the Delta would draw brackish water inland from San Francisco Bay, while submerging the below-sea-level islands behind the breached levees. This brackish water would be drawn toward the state and federal pumps for the California Aqueduct and the Delta-Mendota Canal in the southern Delta. Supplies of irrigation and drinking water would become contaminated, and delivery to the south would be halted for an indeterminate, but probably lengthy, period of time.[17]

A warming climate will also profoundly affect the freshwater sources for the Delta—the Sacramento and San Joaquin rivers and their tributaries, which will run higher in winter and lower in summer. The flows of the rivers of the Central Valley are bound in large part to the melting of the Sierra Nevada snowpack. Increased winter temperatures will cause more precipitation to fall as rain rather than snow, resulting in an increase in winter runoff, a reduction in the overall volume of the snowpack, and the earlier melting of the snowpack that remains. To avoid overflowing, reservoirs will be forced to release more water in the winter, which in turn will mean that less water will be available for release during the spring and summer, when demand, especially for irrigation water, is highest.[18] Water supplies in the spring and summer will be further stretched by the need to compensate for reduced river flows by releasing yet more water from Central Valley reservoirs to drive back salinity encroachment in the Delta.[19]

Global climate change thus presents a litany of serious challenges for the wetlands and riverine systems of the Central Valley. At first glance, these potential future scenarios threaten to turn the tale of progress in the protection and restoration of the valley's wetlands into a declension story after all. A historian writing a generation or a century from now may perhaps feel compelled to discuss the "fall and rise and fall" of the Central Valley's wetlands. However, while little can be done to compensate for the physical changes that are becoming manifest under an altered climate regime, management decisions to protect and preserve wetlands remain under our control. Momentum to restore wetlands in the valley has been building for several generations across both the public and the private sectors, and the policies driving that momentum are unlikely to be reversed quickly or arbitrarily. Furthermore, although there is consensus on the predictions of many of the effects of global climate change on the Central Valley, those predictions are based on the continuance of current policies and practices. As a society, we can still choose to make the sweeping changes necessary to reduce the intensity of future climate change impacts. As governments at all levels and the private sector increasingly realize that climate change affects everything from the ability to provide utility services to the ability to generate a profit, they may attempt to minimize the degree and therefore the consequences of climate change. The government of the state of California has begun to move forcefully in that direction.[20]

Coming to terms with climate change and its effects on wetlands—and, of course, on virtually everything else—will be the next step in the evolution of our attitudes about the natural world. As this book has argued, changes in how we perceive wetlands have allowed us to appreciate their intrinsic values. We have come to realize that waterfowl and other fauna and flora that depend on wetlands have an inherent right to exist within intact ecosystems. Furthermore, after first abandoning the Native American perspective of wetlands as sources of bounty and conceptualizing wetlands as "wastelands" that impede the progress of civilization, we now view wetlands not only as habitat for wildlife but also as fonts of human recreation and aesthetic pleasure—benefits that arguably help us to remain civilized.

The history of the wetlands of California's Great Central Valley offers many lessons that are applicable far beyond the confines of the valley. Indiscriminate conversion of wetlands to agricultural use has resulted in numerous and at times unexpected ecological consequences, from the loss of habitat for a wide variety of species of both plants and animals, to crop depredations, to the spread of the avian diseases botulism and cholera, to the outright poisoning of wildlife from exposure to contaminated irrigation drainwater. In response to these challenges to the agricultural mystique of western lands, efforts to control nature in the service of agriculture have been superseded by methods through which agriculture works with, rather than against, nature. Contemporary agriculture in much of the Central Valley now operates in wildlife-compatible ways, such as the post-harvest flooding of fields for the benefit of waterfowl.

Changing priorities regarding the allocation of scarce water resources have resulted in the enactment of policies that offer economic incentives to protect, rather than destroy, wetlands on private lands, especially in the form of conservation easements. In the public sector, the national wildlife refuges and state wildlife areas that have been created across the length and breadth of the Central Valley offer testimony to a commitment to wetland protection on the part of the federal government, the state government, and the public. The most recent plans for the management of the Sacramento–San Joaquin Delta demonstrate that even as Californians have continued to struggle to meet their water needs, environmental protection has gained greater legitimacy. Rivers such as the San Joaquin have been reconceptualized from a source of irrigation water, divorced from the wildlife that inhabit them, to valuable living systems, complete with their riparian wetlands and floodplains, that support runs of wild salmon, steelhead, and other native fish, as well as the entire web of life on which these species depend.

Along with that reconceptualization have come changes in the operation of irrigation and reclamation projects, most notably the Central Valley Project, which has legally recognized the protection of fish and wildlife as intrinsic to its purpose. As both cause and consequence of these changing perceptions, the expertise of scientists—ecologists and wildlife biologists of every stripe—has gained influence in decisions regarding the construction and operation of the dams, reservoirs, canals, and pumping plants that compose the Central Valley's engineered hydraulic system. Whether spurred by ecological research and the dissemination of knowledge about wetlands, or by protests against the prospective loss of entire wetland regions to hydraulic engineering projects, or by the horrific poisoning of wildlife as a direct consequence of irrigated agriculture, there has been a tangible change in our understanding of the nature and purpose of wetlands.

Behind these changes in both outlook and policy lies the discovery, early in the twentieth century, of the great migratory flyways. These chains of lakes, rivers, and wetlands of every variety revealed the interconnectedness of all avian life, from the breeding grounds of the Far North to—in the case of Pacific Flyway—the wintering grounds of the Central Valley. The rejuvenation of California's Great Central Valley wetlands, though unique in its details and in the particular insights it offers, is part of a broader national and international trend toward reversing wetland decline.[21] The lessons learned in the Central Valley's wetlands about the unexpected and undesirable consequences of heedlessly manipulating nature on local and regional scales will need to be applied on a global scale as well. If we can achieve a sustainable climatic future, the gains of the past century to protect wetlands, waterfowl, and other wetland-dependent species in the Central Valley, and along the entirety of the Pacific Flyway, will not be lost.[22] The migratory ducks, geese, swans, shorebirds, and other waterbirds of the Pacific Flyway arriving from their northern breeding grounds will still find wetlands in which to land, and food upon which to survive, when they descend on the Central Valley every fall, as they have done for millions of years.

Animals and Plants of the Central Valley Discussed in the Text

Scientific names of birds follow David Allen Sibley, *The Sibley Guide to Birds* (New York: Alfred A. Knopf, 2000), except for more recent reclassifications, noted as (*).

Scientific names of plants follow James C. Hickman, ed., *The Jepson Manual: Higher Plants of California* (Berkeley and Los Angeles: University of California Press, 1993), except for more recent reclassifications, noted as (*). Classification is either by genus or by species.

BIRDS

Common Name	Scientific Name
Aleutian cackling goose	*Branta hutchinsii leucopareia**
American avocet	*Recurvirostra americana*
American bittern	*Botaurus lentiginosis*
American coot	*Fulica americana*
American wigeon	*Anas americana*
bald eagle	*Haliaeetus leucophalus*
barn swallow	*Hirundo rustica*
black-crowned night heron	*Nycticorax nycticorax*
black-necked stilt	*Himantopus mexicanus*
Brewer's blackbird	*Euphagus cyanocephalus*
brown-headed cowbird	*Molothrus ater*
bufflehead	*Bucephala albeola*
cackling goose	*Branta hutchinsii**
Canada goose	*Branta canadensis*
canvasback	*Aythya valisineria*
cinnamon teal	*Anas cyanoptera*

common goldeneye	*Bucephala clangula*
common merganser	*Mergus merganser*
common moorhen	*Gallinula chloropus*
common snipe	*Gallinago gallinago*
double-crested cormorant	*Phalacrocorax auritus*
dunlin	*Calidris alpina*
eared grebe	*Podiceps nigricollis*
European starling	*Sturnus vulgaris*
gadwall	*Anas strepera*
great blue heron	*Ardea herodias*
great egret	*Ardea alba*
greater white-fronted goose	*Anser albifrons*
greater yellowlegs	*Tringa melanoleuca*
green heron	*Butorides virescens*
green-winged teal	*Anas crecca*
horned lark	*Eremophila alpestris*
killdeer	*Charadrius vociferus*
least sandpiper	*Calidris minutilla*
lesser scaup	*Aythya affinis*
long-billed curlew	*Numenius americanus*
long-billed dowitcher	*Limnodromus scolopaceus*
mallard	*Anas platyrhynchos*
mourning dove	*Zenaida macroura*
northern harrier	*Circus cyaneus*
northern pintail	*Anas acuta*
northern shoveler	*Anas clypeata*
peregrine falcon	*Falco peregrinus*
redhead	*Aythya americana*
red-tailed hawk	*Buteo jamaicensis*
red-winged blackbird	*Agelaius phoeniceus*
ring-necked duck	*Aythya collaris*
ring-necked pheasant	*Phasianus colchicus*
Ross's goose	*Chen rossii*
ruddy duck	*Oxyura jamaicensis*
sandhill crane	*Grus canadensis*
snow goose	*Chen caerulescens*
snowy egret	*Egretta thula*
tricolored blackbird	*Euphagus cyanocephalus*
tundra swan	*Cygnus columbianus*
western grebe	*Aechmophorus occidentalis*
western meadowlark	*Sturnella neglecta*
western sandpiper	*Calidris mauri*
western snowy plover	*Charadrius alexandrinus nivosus*
white-crowned sparrow	*Zonotrichia leucophrys*

white pelican   *Pelecanus erythrorhynchos*
white-faced ibis   *Plegadis chihi*
wood duck   *Aix sponsa*
yellow-headed blackbird   *Xanthocephalus xanthocephalus*

FISH

Common Name   *Scientific Name*
Chinook salmon   *Oncorhynchus tshawytscha*
Delta smelt   *Hypomesus transpacificus*
mosquitofish   *Gambusia affinis*
Sacramento perch   *Archoplites interruptus*
Sacramento splittail   *Pogonichthys macrolepidotus*
steelhead   *Oncorhynchus mykiss*
white sturgeon   *Acipenser transmontanus*

MAMMALS

Common Name   *Scientific Name*
riparian brush rabbit   *Sylvilagus bachmani riparius*
tule elk   *Cervus elaphus nannodes*
San Joaquin kit fox   *Vulpes macrotis mutica*
Tipton kangaroo rat   *Dipodomis nitratoides nitratoides*

REPTILES AND AMPHIBIANS

Common Name   *Scientific Name*
blunt-nosed leopard lizard *Gambelia silus*
California tiger salamander *Ambystoma californiense*
giant garter snake   *Thamnophis gigas*

PLANTS

Common Name   *Scientific Name*
alder   *Alnus rhombifolia*
alkali bulrush   *Schoenoplectus maritimus**
alkali heath   *Frankenia salina*
arrowhead   *Sagittaria latifolia*
Baltic rush   *Juncus balticus*
blackberry   *Rubus* spp.
bluegrass   *Poa* spp.
box elder   *Acer negundo*
brass buttons   *Cotula coronopifolia*
bur-reed   *Sparganium eurycarpum*

California burclover	*Medicago polymorpha*
cattail	*Typha* spp.
Colusa grass	*Neostapfia colusana*
common tule	*Schoenoplectus acutus**
common water-nymph	*Najas guadalupensis*
crabgrass	*Digitaria* spp.
ditch-grass	*Ruppia maritima*
dock	*Rumex* spp.
downingia	*Downingia* spp.
duckweed	*Lemma* spp.
fescue	*Festuca* spp.
filaree	*Erodium* spp.
foxtail	*Hordeum jubatum*
Fremont cottonwood	*Populus fremontii*
golden dock	*Rumex maritimus*
goldfields	*Lasthenia* spp.
gum plant	*Grindelia* spp.
hornwort	*Ceratophyllum demersum*
interior live oak	*Quercus wislizenii*
iodine bush	*Allenrolfia occidentalis*
joint grass	*Paspalum distichum*
knotweed	*Polygonum* spp.
meadowfoam	*Limnanthes* spp.
needlegrass	*Nassella* spp.
Oregon ash	*Fraxinus latifolia*
pickleweed	*Salicornia* spp.
poison oak	*Rhus diversiloba*
pondweed	*Potamogeton* spp.
popcornflower	Plagiobothrys spp.
rabbitsfoot grass	*Polypogon monspeliensis*
ricefield bulrush	*Schoenoplectus mucronatus**
ripgut brome	*Bromus diandrus*
rush	*Juncus* spp.
ryegrass	*Elymus* and *Lolium* spp.
sago pondweed	*Potamogeton pectinatus*
saltbush	*Atriplex* spp.
saltgrass	*Distichlis spicata*
smallflower umbrella sedge	*Cyperus difformis*
smartweed	*Polygonum* spp.
soft chess	*Bromus hordeaceus*
spikerush	*Eleocharis* spp.
sprangletop	*Leptochloa* spp.
swamp timothy	*Crypsis schoenoides*
three-awn grass	*Aristida* spp.

valley oak	*Quercus lobata*
water plantain	*Alisma plantago-aquatica*
waterlily	*Nymphaea* spp.
western sycamore	*Platanus racemosa*
wild grape	*Vitis californica*
wild millet (or barnyard grass)	*Echinochloa crus-galli*
wild oat	*Avena barbata* and *A. fatua*
wild rose	*Rosa californica*
willow	*Salix* spp.

NOTES

ABBREVIATIONS

CEP   Clair Engle Papers, Meriam Library Special Collections, California State University, Chico

FLC   Frank Latta Collection, Huntington Library, San Marino, California

GWD   Grassland Water District Archives, Los Banos, California

JMW   J. Martin Winton Special Collection on Water Use and Land Development, San Joaquin College of Law, Clovis, California

KCWHC   Kern County Water History Collection, Walter W. Stiern Library Special Collections, California State University, Bakersfield

KNWRC   Kern National Wildlife Refuge Complex Archives, Delano, California

MLR   Miller and Lux Collection, Bancroft Library, University of California, Berkeley

MSRB   Minutes of the State Reclamation Board, California State Reclamation Board Records, California State Archives, Sacramento

NLP   National Land for People Collection, Henry Madden Library Special Collections, California State University, Fresno

SAC   Spanish Archives Collection, United States Surveyor General for California Records, California State Archives, Sacramento

SLNWRC   San Luis National Wildlife Refuge Complex Archives, Los Banos, California

SNWRC   Sacramento National Wildlife Refuge Complex Archives, Willows, California

SPR   Southern Pacific Records, California State Railroad Museum Library, Sacramento

INTRODUCTION

1. Linda Nash, *Inescapable Ecologies: A History of Environment, Disease, and Knowledge* (Berkeley and Los Angeles: University of California Press, 2006), 2.

2. T. E. Dahl, *Wetland Losses in the United States, 1780s to 1980s* (Washington, D.C.: U.S. Department of the Interior, Fish and Wildlife Service, 1990), 1. Dahl's estimates indicate that there were an additional 170 million acres in Alaska and 59,000 acres in Hawaii. In 1986 Congress passed the Emergency Wetlands Resources Act (100 *Stat.* 3582; Public Law 99–645) to promote the conservation of the nation's wetlands. The act requires the U.S. Fish and Wildlife Service to update wetland status and trends information every ten years.

3. T. E. Dahl, *Status and Trends of Wetlands in the Conterminous United States 1986–1997* (Washington, D.C.: U.S. Department of the Interior, Fish and Wildlife Service, 2000), 9.

4. W. J. Mitsch and J. G. Gosselink, *Wetlands*, 3rd ed. (New York: John Wiley & Sons, 2000), esp. 571–609; J. Scott Feierabend and John M. Zelazny, *Status Report on Our Nation's Wetlands* (Washington, D.C.: National Wildlife Federation, 1987), 6–15.

5. Dahl, *Wetland Losses*, 6. Florida has lost the most acreage of any state (9.3 million acres), yet this figure represents a loss of only 46 percent of its original wetlands.

6. W. E. Frayer, D. D. Peters, and H. R. Pywell, *Wetlands of the California Central Valley: Status and Trends—1939 to Mid-1980s* (Portland, Ore.: U.S. Department of the Interior, Fish and Wildlife Service, 1989), 17–18. The figure of 379,000 acres excludes deepwater habitats (rivers and lakes), which accounted for an additional 166,000 acres.

7. In the contiguous states, the average annual rate of loss was 458,000 acres from the mid-1950s to the mid-1970s, 290,000 acres from the mid-1970s to the mid-1980s, and 58,000 acres from 1986 to 1997. Dahl, *Status and Trends . . . 1986–1997*, 9. In 2006 the U.S. Fish and Wildlife Service reported an average rate of *gain* of approximately 32,000 acres per year from 1998 to 2004, but these figures are based on the controversial inclusion of a number of types of artificial freshwater ponds, including residential ponds created for aesthetics, that are not ecologically equivalent replacements for natural vegetated wetlands. Exclusive of such artificially created ponds, overall wetland acreage continued to be lost during the period 1998 to 2004, but it is difficult to calculate the annual rate of loss because the 2006 report does not differentiate between the acreages of the types of freshwater ponds that have traditionally been included in the *Status and Trends* reports and the types that were included in the 2006 report for the first time. T. E. Dahl, *Status and Trends of Wetlands in the Conterminous United States 1998 to 2004* (Washington, D.C.: U.S. Department of the Interior, Fish and Wildlife Service, 2006), 15–17, 43–44, 74–76; Jeffrey K. Stine, *America's Forested Wetlands: From Wasteland to Valued Resource* (Durham, N.C.: Forest History Society, 2008), 77–78.

8. Frayer, Peters, and Pywell, *Wetlands of the California Central Valley*, 4. It is difficult to define precisely the boundaries of the Central Valley; its biological communities grade irregularly into adjacent communities, and its elevational contours at the margins are not linear.

9. The age of the modern Sierra Nevada remains controversial, as geologists are divided into "Young Sierra" and "Old Sierra" schools. Estimates for the period of major

uplift range from tens of millions of years ago to only a few million years ago. For a contribution to this debate, see Andreas Mulch, Stephan A. Graham, and C. Page Chamberlain, "Hydrogen Isotopes in Eocene River Gravels and Paleoelevation of the Sierra Nevada," *Science* 313, no. 5783 (2006). For an environmental history of the Sierra Nevada, see David Beesley, *Crow's Range: An Environmental History of the Sierra Nevada* (Reno and Las Vegas: University of Nevada Press, 2004).

10. Allan A. Schoenherr, *A Natural History of California* (Berkeley and Los Angeles: University of California Press, 1992), 75–76, 264–269, 520.

11. Smaller parts of four additional counties are also located in the Central Valley. Solano and Contra Costa counties lie within both the Central Valley and the San Francisco Bay area; the eastern portion of Napa County falls within the Sacramento Valley; and the northeastern portion of Alameda County falls within the San Joaquin Valley.

12. The Sacramento River is 447 miles long from its mouth in Suisun Bay to the confluence of its Middle and South forks; the San Joaquin River is 330 miles long from its mouth to its headwater lake.

13. Schoenherr, *Natural History of California,* 520. The Pleistocene and Holocene epochs together compose the Quaternary period of geologic time, which extends from 1.6 million years ago to the present.

14. A member of the sedge (Cyperaceae) family, the tule grows to heights in excess of ten feet and can form virtually impenetrable stands in shallow water at wetland edges. The tule, *Schoenoplectus acutus* (var. *occidentalis*), was formerly classified as *Scirpus acutus.*

15. Jeffrey F. Mount, *California Rivers and Streams: The Conflict between Fluvial Process and Land Use* (Berkeley and Los Angeles: University of California Press, 1995), 313. An acre-foot is 325,851.4 gallons, or 43,560 cubic feet—enough water to cover one acre of land to a depth of one foot.

16. U.S. Fish and Wildlife Service, *Concept Plan for Waterfowl Wintering Habitat Preservation: Central Valley, California* (Portland, Ore.: U.S. Department of the Interior, Fish and Wildlife Service, 1978), 11 (60 percent figure); U.S. Department of the Interior, *The Impact of Federal Programs on Wetlands,* vol. 2: *A Report to Congress by the Secretary of the Interior* (Washington, D.C.: U.S. Department of the Interior, 1994), 13 (19 percent figure), 191.

17. 9 *Stat.* 519.

18. Arthur S. Hawkins, "The U.S. Response," in *Flyways: Pioneering Waterfowl Management in North America,* ed. A. S. Hawkins et al. (Washington, D.C.: U.S. Department of the Interior, Fish and Wildlife Service, 1984), 2.

19. The history and purpose of Ducks Unlimited are discussed in chapter 6.

20. The Fish and Wildlife Service defined wetlands as "lowlands covered with shallow and sometimes temporary or intermittent waters. They are referred to by such names as marshes, swamps, bogs, wet meadows, potholes, sloughs, and river-overflow lands. Shallow lakes and ponds, usually with emergent vegetation as a conspicuous feature, are included in the definition, but the permanent waters of streams, reservoirs, and deep lakes are not included. Neither are water areas that are so temporary as to have little or no effect on the development of moist-soil vegetation." Samuel P. Shaw and C. Gordon Fredine,

Wetlands of the United States: Their Extent and Their Value to Waterfowl and Other Wild-life (Washington, D.C.: U.S. Fish and Wildlife Service, Circular no. 39, 1956), 3; Mitsch and Gosselink, *Wetlands*, 25–26.

21. The technical definition reads, "Wetlands are lands transitional between terrestrial and aquatic systems where the water table is usually at or near the surface, or the land is covered by shallow water. For the purposes of this classification, wetlands must have one or more of the following three attributes: (1) at least periodically, the land supports predominantly hydrophytes; (2) the substrate is predominantly undrained hydric soil; and (3) the substrate is nonsoil and is saturated with water or covered by shallow water at some time during the growing season of each year." Lewis M. Cowardin, Virginia Carter, Francis C. Golet, and Edward T. LaRoe, *Classification of Wetlands and Deepwater Habitats of the United States* (Washington, D.C.: U.S. Department of the Interior, Fish and Wildlife Service, 1979), 3.

22. Estuarine wetlands included those of the Sacramento–San Joaquin Delta and, to the immediate west, Suisun Bay and Suisun Marsh. Frayer, Peters, and Pywell, *Wetlands of the California Central Valley . . . 1939 to Mid-1980s*, 10–13, 18. The Fish and Wildlife Service divides deepwater habitats and wetlands into five systems, or categories: marine, lacustrine, riverine, estuarine, and palustrine. All except the marine system, which extends from the coastline to the outer edge of the continental shelf, are present in the Central Valley. The remaining deepwater habitats fall within the lacustrine system, which includes permanently flooded lakes and reservoirs, as well as intermittent lakes such as playa lakes, and the riverine system, which is restricted to those habitats within a river or stream channel. Cowardin et al., *Classification of Wetlands*, 4–10.

23. The Sacramento Valley is also subdivided into a number of basins with important topographical and ecological distinctions, as discussed in chapter 4. Unlike the two basins of the San Joaquin Valley, however, the basins of the Sacramento Valley have not been historically considered distinctly separate regions.

24. See William L. Preston, *Vanishing Landscapes: Land and Life in the Tulare Lake Basin* (Berkeley and Los Angeles: University of California Press, 1981).

25. Mount, *California Rivers and Streams*, 209.

26. The decision was issued by Judge Lorenzo Sawyer in *Woodruff, Edwards v. North Bloomfield Gravel Mining Co. et al.*, 18 F. 753 (9th Cir. 1884).

27. 1911 (Extra Session) *Statutes of California* ch. 25; 39 *Stat.* 948.

28. See Robert Kelley, "Taming the Sacramento: Hamiltonianism in Action," *Pacific Historical Review* 34, no. 1 (1965); Robert Kelley, *Battling the Inland Sea: American Political Culture, Public Policy, and the Sacramento Valley, 1850–1986* (Berkeley and Los Angeles: University of California Press, 1989).

29. John Thompson, "The Settlement Geography of the Sacramento–San Joaquin Delta, California," PhD diss., Stanford University, 1957, 238.

30. 50 *Stat.* 844.

31. 68 *Stat.* 879. See Philip Garone, "Rethinking Reclamation: How an Alliance of Duck Hunters and Cattle Ranchers Brought Wetland Conservation to California's Central Valley Project," in *Natural Protest: Essays on the History of American Environmentalism*, ed. Michael Egan and Jeff Crane (New York and London: Routledge, 2009).

32. See Philip Garone, "The Tragedy at Kesterson Reservoir: A Case Study in Environmental History and a Lesson in Ecological Complexity," *Environs: Environmental Law and Policy Journal* 22, no. 2 (1999).

33. For historical studies of wetlands, see Ann Vileisis, *Discovering the Unknown Landscape: A History of America's Wetlands* (Washington, D.C.: Island Press, 1997); Nancy Langston, *Where Land and Water Meet: A Western Landscape Transformed* (Seattle: University of Washington Press, 2003); and Robert M. Wilson, *Seeking Refuge: An Environmental History of the Pacific Flyway* (Seattle: University of Washington Press, 2010). The scientific literature on wetland ecology is vast. A number of major journals, including *Wetlands* and *Wetland Ecology and Management*, publish scientific and management papers on wetlands.

34. For a discussion of the importance of scale in the management of waterfowl on federal refuges, see Robert M. Wilson, "Directing the Flow: Migratory Waterfowl, Scale, and Mobility in Western North America," *Environmental History* 7, no. 2 (2002).

35. See Frieda Knobloch, *The Culture of Wilderness: Agriculture as Colonization in the American West* (Chapel Hill: University of North Carolina Press, 1996).

36. For seminal U.S.-based and global critiques, respectively, of the social and ecological consequences of large-scale attempts to control nature, see Donald Worster, *Rivers of Empire: Water, Aridity, and the Growth of the American West* (New York: Pantheon Books, 1985); James C. Scott, *Seeing Like a State: How Certain Schemes to Improve the Human Condition Have Failed* (New Haven, Conn.: Yale University Press, 1998).

37. The Nature Conservancy is a private, nonprofit conservation organization founded in 1951 that operates in all fifty states and dozens of countries.

38. U.S. Fish and Wildlife Service, *Status Report for the National Wetlands Inventory Program: 2009* (Arlington, Va.: U.S. Fish and Wildlife Service, Division of Habitat and Resource Conservation, Branch of Resource and Mapping Support, 2009), 1. For the *Status and Trends* reports, see Dahl, *Status and Trends . . . 1998 to 2004*; Dahl, *Status and Trends . . . 1986–1997*; T. E. Dahl and C. E. Johnson, *Status and Trends of Wetlands in the Conterminus United States, Mid-1970s to Mid-1980s* (Washington, D.C.: U.S. Department of the Interior, Fish and Wildlife Service, 1991); Dahl, *Wetland Losses*; W. E. Frayer, T. J. Monahan, D. C. Bowden, and F. A. Graybill, *Status and Trends of Wetlands and Deepwater Habitats in the Conterminous United States, 1950's to 1970's* (Fort Collins: Colorado State University, 1983).

39. See Ramsar Convention Bureau, *Directory of Wetlands of International Importance* (Gland, Switzerland: Ramsar Convention Bureau, 1990).

1. THE NATURE OF THE GREAT CENTRAL VALLEY AND THE PACIFIC FLYWAY

1. Schoenherr, *Natural History of California*, 516. See also Elna Bakker, *An Island Called California: An Ecological Introduction to Its Natural Communities*, 2nd ed. (Berkeley and Los Angeles: University of California Press, 1984), 143.

2. The perennial bunchgrass paradigm had been established by influential plant ecologist Frederic E. Clements during the 1920s. Since the late twentieth century, researchers have contended that there is no conclusive evidence that perennial bunchgrasses ever

dominated the grasslands of the Central Valley. The issue is more than an academic debate, because it brings into question the most appropriate means to "restore" California grasslands. For a more detailed treatment of this argument, see Jason G. Hamilton, "Changing Perceptions of Pre-European Grasslands in California," *Madroño* 44, no. 4 (1997). For various perspectives, see Mark A. Blumler, "Some Myths about California Grasses and Grazers," *Fremontia* 20, no. 3 (1992); L. Wester, "Composition of Native Grassland in the San Joaquin Valley, California," *Madroño* 28, no. 4 (1981); James W. Bartolome and Barbara Gemmill, "The Ecological Status of *Stipa pulchra* (Poaceae) in California," *Madroño* 28, no. 3 (1981); F. Thomas Griggs, Jack M. Zaninovich, and Grant D. Werschkull, "Historic Native Vegetation Map of the Tulare Basin, California," in *Endangered and Sensitive Species of the San Joaquin Valley, California: Their Biology, Management, and Conservation,* ed. D. F. Williams, S. Byrne, and T. A. Rado (Sacramento: California Energy Commission, 1992); Glen Holstein, "Pre-Agricultural Grassland in Central California," *Madroño* 48, no. 4 (2001).

3. John Muir, *The Mountains of California* (New York: Century Company, 1894; repr. New York: Penguin Books, 1985), 234–235.

4. Schoenherr, *Natural History of California,* 516.

5. William L. Preston, "Serpent in the Garden: Environmental Change in Colonial California," in *Contested Eden: California before the Gold Rush,* ed. Ramón A. Gutiérrez and Richard J. Orsi (Berkeley and Los Angeles: University of California Press, 1998), 272.

6. Michael Barbour et al., *California's Changing Landscapes: Diversity and Conservation of California Vegetation* (Sacramento: California Native Plant Society, 1993), 76–80; Preston, "Serpent in the Garden," 268–269, 273; Schoenherr, *Natural History of California,* 539; James W. Bartolome et al., "Valley Grassland," in *Terrestrial Vegetation of California,* ed. Michael Barbour, Todd Keeler-Wolf, and Allan A. Schoenherr (Berkeley and Los Angeles: University of California Press, 2007), 372.

7. John C. Ewers, *Adventures of Zenas Leonard, Fur Trader* (Norman: University of Oklahoma Press, 1959), 88.

8. Edwin Bryant, *What I Saw in California: Being the Journal of a Tour in the Years 1846, 1847* (Palo Alto, Calif.: Lewis Osborne, 1967), 300.

9. U.S. Census Office, *Agriculture of the United States in 1860* (Washington, D.C.: Government Printing Office, 1864), 10.

10. Native perennial bunchgrasses require periodic disturbances, particularly burning, to grow vigorously and reproduce competitively. Native Americans practiced controlled burning extensively, and the decimation of the Native American populations in the Central Valley by European diseases to which they lacked immunity led to a significant reduction of controlled burning, which may have further diminished the competitive abilities of the perennial bunchgrasses. Preston, "Serpent in the Garden," 269.

11. Barbour et al., *California's Changing Landscapes,* 80.

12. R. Earl Storie and Bruce C. Owen, *Soil Survey of the Pixley Area, California* (Washington, D.C.: U.S. Department of Agriculture, Bureau of Plant Industry, 1942), 5; Bartolome et al., "Valley Grassland," 369–370.

13. William H. Brewer, *Up and Down California in 1860–1864,* 3rd ed. (Berkeley and Los Angeles: University of California Press, 1966), 512–513.

14. Vernal pools are classified as palustrine seasonal emergent wetlands.

15. M. C. Rains et al., "The Role of Perched Aquifers in Hydrological Conductivity and Biogeochemical Processes in Vernal Pool Landscapes," *Hydrological Processes* 20, no. 5 (2006).

16. Ayzik I. Solomeshch, Michael G. Barbour, and Robert F. Holland, "Vernal Pools," in *Terrestrial Vegetation of California*, ed. Michael G. Barbour, Todd Keeler-Wolf, and Allan A. Schoenherr (Berkeley and Los Angeles: University of California Press, 2007), 394–398; Michael G. Barbour and Carol W. Witham, "Islands within Islands: Viewing Vernal Pools Differently," *Fremontia* 32, no. 2 (2004): 5. See also M. Barbour et al., "Vernal Pool Vegetation in California: Variation within Pools," *Madroño* 50, no. 3 (2003); David F. Bradford, "Biogeography and Endemism in the Central Valley of California," in *Endangered and Sensitive Species of the San Joaquin Valley, California: Their Biology, Management, and Conservation*, ed. D. F. Williams, S. Byrne, and T. A. Rado (Sacramento: California Energy Commission, 1992); Jon E. Keeley and Paul H. Zedler, "Characterization and Global Distribution of Vernal Pools," in *Ecology, Conservation, and Management of Vernal Pool Ecosystems, Proceedings from a 1996 Conference*, ed. Carol W. Witham (Sacramento: California Native Plant Society, 1998).

17. Solomeshch, Barbour, and Holland, "Vernal Pools," 417. Notable vernal pool complexes are found at the Vina Plains Preserve in Tehama County, Jepson Prairie Preserve in Solano County, in eastern Merced County, and in Kings and Tulare counties east of the former Tulare Lake. The last is former marshland that has partially dried as water tables have fallen, creating new vernal pool habitat. Robert F. Holland, "Great Valley Vernal Pool Distribution, Photorevised 1996," in *Ecology, Conservation, and Management of Vernal Pool Ecosystems, Proceedings from a 1996 Conference*, ed. Carol W. Witham (Sacramento: California Native Plant Society, 1998), 73.

18. Sylvia Wright, "Splendor in the Grass," *UC Davis Magazine* (Spring 2002): 19.

19. The cackling goose *(Branta hutchinsii)*, once considered a subspecies of the Canada goose *(Branta canadensis)*, was reclassified in 2004 as a distinct species.

20. Joseph G. Silveira, "Avian Uses of Vernal Pools and Implications for Conservation Practice," in *Ecology, Conservation, and Management of Vernal Pool Ecosystems, Proceedings from a 1996 Conference*, ed. Carol W. Witham (Sacramento: California Native Plant Society, 1998), 92; Cliff Feldheim, "A Glimpse into California's Past," *California Waterfowl* 25, no. 6 (1999): 41.

21. Frayer, Peters, and Pywell, *Wetlands of the California Central Valley . . . 1939 to Mid-1980s*, 4; Mitsch and Gosselink, *Wetlands*, 79. Riparian forests are classified as palustrine forested wetlands. They are far more prevalent in moister regions of the country, such as the southeastern United States, where they are known as bottomland hardwood forests.

22. Mehrey G. Vaghti and Steven E. Greco, "Riparian Vegetation of the Great Valley," in *Terrestrial Vegetation of California*, ed. Michael G. Barbour, Todd Keeler-Wolf, and Allan A. Schoenherr (Berkeley and Los Angeles: University of California Press, 2007), 430.

23. Edwin F. Katibah, "A Brief History of Riparian Forests in the Central Valley of California," in *California Riparian Systems: Ecology, Conservation, and Productive Management*, ed. Richard E. Warner and Kathleen M. Hendrix (Berkeley and Los Angeles: University of California Press, 1984), 23–25; Kenneth Thompson, "Riparian Forests of the

Sacramento Valley, California," in *Riparian Forests in California: Their Ecology and Conservation, Proceedings from a 1977 Symposium,* ed. Anne Sands (Davis, Calif.: Regents of the University of California, 1980), 36–37; Kenneth Thompson, "Riparian Forests of the Sacramento Valley, California," *Annals of the Association of American Geographers* 51, no. 3 (1961); Schoenherr, *Natural History of California,* 534. See also Bruce M. Pavlik et al., *Oaks of California* (Los Olivos, Calif.: Cachuma Press, 1991).

24. Captain Sir Edward Belcher, R.N., *Narrative of a Voyage round the World Performed in Her Majesty's Ship Sulphur during the Years 1836–1842* (London: Henry Colburn, 1843), 1:123.

25. Katibah, "Brief History of Riparian Forests," 27.

26. Vaghti and Greco, "Riparian Vegetation of the Great Valley," 426–428. One of the finest remaining stands of riparian oak woodland is found along the lower Stanislaus River in Caswell Memorial State Park, which opened to the public in 1958.

27. David Gaines, "The Valley Riparian Forests of California: Their Importance to Bird Populations," in *Riparian Forests in California: Their Ecology and Conservation, Proceedings from a 1977 Symposium,* ed. Anne Sands (Davis, Calif.: Regents of the University of California, 1980), 63; Chris S. Elphick, John B. Dunning Jr., and David Allen Sibley, eds., *The Sibley Guide to Bird Life & Behavior* (New York: Alfred A. Knopf, 2001), 192.

28. Mitsch and Gosselink, *Wetlands,* 739. Frayer, Peters, and Pywell, *Wetlands of the California Central Valley . . . 1939 to Mid-1980s,* 18.

29. Milton W. Weller, *Wetland Birds: Habitat Resources and Conservation Implications* (Cambridge: Cambridge University Press, 1999), 121–123; William A. Niering, *Wetlands,* The Audubon Society Nature Guides (New York: Alfred A. Knopf, 1985), 46–52; James C. Hickman, ed., *The Jepson Manual: Higher Plants of California* (Berkeley and Los Angeles: University of California Press, 1993); Herbert L. Mason, *A Flora of the Marshes of California* (Berkeley and Los Angeles: University of California Press, 1957).

30. A sixth, smaller basin, the Sacramento Basin, lies below Sacramento on the east side of the river. Unlike the other five basins, this basin drains not toward the Sacramento River but southward toward the lower Mokelumne River and the Sacramento–San Joaquin Delta.

31. Joseph A. McGowan, *History of the Sacramento Valley* (New York: Lewis Historical Publishing, 1961), 1:5.

32. U.S. Fish and Wildlife Service, *Concept Plan for Waterfowl Wintering Habitat Preservation,* 30.

33. The gradient of the Sacramento River, which is seven feet to the mile between Redding and Red Bluff in the northern Sacramento Valley, decreases to less than one-half foot to the mile as it approaches the Delta below Sacramento. The gradient of the lower San Joaquin River is so slight that as it approaches the Delta, the river distributes its flow between its main stem and two former main channels, known as Middle River and Old River. McGowan, *History of the Sacramento Valley,* 1:6.

34. Thompson, "Settlement Geography," 2, 22; John Thompson and Edward A. Dutra, *The Tule Breakers: The Story of the California Dredge* (Stockton, Calif.: Stockton Corral of Westerners International, University of the Pacific, 1983), 13; U.S. Fish and Wildlife Service, *Concept Plan for Waterfowl Wintering Habitat Preservation,* 36, 47.

35. Brenda J. Grewell, John C. Calloway, and Wayne R. Ferren Jr., "Estuarine Wetlands," in *Terrestrial Vegetation of California*, ed. Michael G. Barbour, Todd Keeler-Wolf, and Allan A. Schoenherr (Berkeley and Los Angeles: University of California Press, 2007), 139.

36. See Frayer, Peters, and Pywell, *Wetlands of the California Central Valley . . . 1939 to Mid-1980s*; U.S. Fish and Wildlife Service, *Concept Plan for Waterfowl Wintering Habitat Preservation*.

37. California Department of Water Resources, *Sacramento–San Joaquin Delta Atlas* (Sacramento: California Department of Water Resources, 1993), 77. In addition to many of the wetland plants found further inland, Suisun Marsh offers a suite of salt-tolerant wetland species, including pickleweed, saltbush, golden dock, and brass buttons. Howard Leach, California Department of Fish and Game, retired, personal correspondence; Hickman, ed., *Jepson Manual*; Mason, *Flora of the Marshes of California*.

38. U.S. Fish and Wildlife Service, *Concept Plan for Waterfowl Wintering Habitat Preservation*, 51–56.

39. U.S. Fish and Wildlife Service, *Concept Plan for Waterfowl Wintering Habitat Preservation*, 57.

40. Bruce D. J. Batt, "Introduction: The Waterfowl," in *Ecology and Management of Breeding Waterfowl*, ed. Bruce D. J. Batt et al. (Minneapolis and London: University of Minnesota Press, 1992), xiii.

41. Elphick, Dunning, and Sibley, eds., *Sibley Guide to Bird Life & Behavior*, 191.

42. Paul A. Johnsgard, *Waterfowl of North America* (Bloomington: Indiana University Press, 1975), 61–62.

43. U.S. Fish and Wildlife Service, *Concept Plan for Waterfowl Wintering Habitat Preservation*, 9.

44. Phylogenetic interpretations of the family Anatidae have evolved, but as of the early 2000s, Anatidae was classified into subfamilies and tribes as follows: The subfamily Anserinae consists of geese and swans, which are classified into the tribes Anserini and Cygnini, respectively. The subfamily Anatinae includes four tribes of true ducks. Dabbling ducks constitute the tribe Anatini; diving ducks comprise the tribes Aythyini (pochards, or bay ducks), Oxyurini (stiff-tailed ducks), and Mergini (sea ducks and mergansers). This classification follows Elphick, Dunning, and Sibley, eds., *Sibley Guide to Bird Life & Behavior*, 190–193.

45. Weller, *Wetland Birds*, 90.

46. Johnsgard, *Waterfowl of North America*, 181.

47. U.S. Fish and Wildlife Service, *Concept Plan for Waterfowl Wintering Habitat Preservation*, 9.

48. John E. Chattin, "Pacific Flyway," in *Waterfowl Tomorrow*, ed. Joseph P. Linduska (Washington, D.C.: U.S. Department of the Interior, Fish and Wildlife Service, Bureau of Sport Fisheries and Wildlife, 1964), 243.

49. Johnsgard, *Waterfowl of North America*, 301, 361.

50. U.S. Fish and Wildlife Service, *Concept Plan for Waterfowl Wintering Habitat Preservation*, 9; Johnsgard, *Waterfowl of North America*, 361, 519.

51. The flyways are both biological and administrative concepts. Unlike the biological flyways, which span the continent, the administrative flyways are defined only for the United States.

52. A number of environmental historians have written about the importance of scale. Dan Flores has called for transcending traditional history by following in the tradition of those disciplines—ecology, geography, ecological anthropology, and bioregionalism— that define the boundaries of the places they study in ways that make ecological and topographical sense. These disciplines explicitly recognize that ecological boundaries rarely coincide with political entities, such as the state or nation. Dan Flores, "Place: An Argument for Bioregional History," *Environmental History Review* 18 (1994): 5–6. Richard White has pointed out that because histories of environmental change rarely are confined to national borders, environmental historians must consider transnational scales as well. Richard White, "The Nationalization of Nature," *Journal of American History* 86, no. 3 (1999): 980. Robert M. Wilson has applied this methodology in his treatment of the U.S. Fish and Wildlife Service's management of national wildlife refuges along the Pacific Flyway. Wilson, "Directing the Flow," 249. For the use of appropriate terminology for discussing various scales, see Joseph E. Taylor III, "Boundary Terminology," *Environmental History* 13, no. 3 (2008). For a primer on bioregionalism, see Robert L. Thayer Jr., *Life-Place: Bioregional Thought and Practice* (Berkeley and Los Angeles: University of California Press, 2003).

53. As one prominent ecologist has written, scale is "the fundamental conceptual problem in ecology, if not in all of science"; Simon A. Levin, "The Problem of Pattern and Scale in Ecology," *Ecology* 73, no. 6 (1992): 1944. Because ecology is a predictive science based on the observation of patterns, the ability to make accurate predictions—and hence management decisions—rests on the selection of the proper scales of analysis. Timothy F. H. Allen and Thomas W. Hoekstra, *Toward a Unified Ecology* (New York: Columbia University Press, 1992), 11.

54. Tundra swans *(Cygnus columbianus)* were formerly known as American whistling swans.

55. For an accessible discussion of the formal meanings of *niche* in ecology, see Peter J. Morin, *Community Ecology* (Oxford: Blackwell Science, 1999), 53–66.

56. See R. H. MacArthur and E. O. Wilson, *The Theory of Island Biogeography* (Princeton, N.J.: Princeton University Press, 1967).

57. Mike Brown and James J. Dinsmore, "Implications of Marsh Size and Isolation for Marsh Bird Management," *Journal of Wildlife Management* 50, no. 3 (1986).

58. J. H. Patterson, "The Role of Environmental Heterogeneity in the Regulation of Duck Populations," *Journal of Wildlife Management* 40, no. 1 (1976): 28.

59. U.S. Fish and Wildlife Service, *Concept Plan for Waterfowl Wintering Habitat Preservation,* 10, 23.

60. These policies are discussed beginning in chapter 6.

61. Weller, *Wetland Birds,* 183–186.

62. Daniel P. Collins and Robert E. Trost, *2009 Pacific Flyway Data Book: Waterfowl Harvests and Status, Hunter Participation and Success in the Pacific Flyway and United States* (Portland, Ore.: U.S. Fish and Wildlife Service, 2009), 83.

63. U.S. Fish and Wildlife Service, *Concept Plan for Waterfowl Wintering Habitat Preservation*, 11. These numbers represent an average of 69 percent of the entire Pacific Flyway goose population, 63 percent of the dabbling duck population, and 12 percent of the diving duck population.

64. U.S. Fish and Wildlife Service, *Concept Plan for Waterfowl Wintering Habitat Preservation*, 9–10.

65. During the summer postbreeding period, prior to fall migration, adult North American ducks undergo a simultaneous primary wing- and tail-feather molt that leaves them flightless for a period of several days to several weeks, during which time they are extremely vulnerable to predators. Elphick, Dunning, and Sibley, eds., *Sibley Guide to Bird Life & Behavior*, 194–196.

66. Wilson, "Directing the Flow," 260.

67. Patrick Dugan, ed., *Wetlands in Danger: A World Conservation Atlas* (New York: Oxford University Press, 1993), 62.

68. Dahl, *Wetland Losses in the United States*, 6. Because there are 640 acres per square mile, the conversion factor from acres, as presented by Dahl, to square miles is 1/640.

69. Robert H. Smith, Frank Dufresne, and Henry A. Hansen, "Northern Watersheds and Deltas," in *Waterfowl Tomorrow*, ed. Joseph P. Linduska (Washington, D.C.: U.S. Department of the Interior, Fish and Wildlife Service, Bureau of Sport Fisheries and Wildlife, 1964), 61; Dugan, ed., *Wetlands in Danger*, 62.

70. Russell D. Butcher, *America's National Wildlife Refuges: A Complete Guide* (Lanham, Md.: Roberts Rinehart, 2003), 62–64.

71. Frederick C. Lincoln, *The Waterfowl Flyways of North America* (Washington, D.C.: U.S. Department of Agriculture, Circular no. 342, 1935), 8.

72. John B. Cowan, *A Jewel in the Pacific Flyway: The Story of Gray Lodge Wildlife Area* (Sacramento: California Waterfowl Association, 2002), 21. Elsewhere in Alaska, the Susitna River Delta and Copper River Delta, west and southeast of Anchorage, respectively, serve as important staging areas for waterfowl and shorebirds about to cross the Gulf of Alaska on their way to the Pacific Coast.

73. Butcher, *America's National Wildlife Refuges*, 64–65; Smith, Dufresne, and Hansen, "Northern Watersheds and Deltas," 62–63.

74. Smith, Dufresne, and Hansen, "Northern Watersheds and Deltas," 63; Hugh Boyd, "Waterfowl Population Levels in North America and Their Use in Identifying Canadian Wetlands of Importance for Breeding Waterfowl," in *Flyways and Reserve Networks for Water Birds*, ed. H. Boyd and J.-Y. Pirot (Slimbridge, Gloucester, Eng.: International Waterfowl and Wetlands Research Bureau, 1989), 77; S.C. Zoltai et al., "Wetlands of Subarctic Canada," in *Wetlands of Canada*, Ecological Land Classification Series no. 24 (Montreal: Environment Canada and Polyscience Publications, 1988), 92.

75. The Saskatchewan River Delta lies to the southeast, but is associated with the Central and Mississippi flyways. It has been significantly degraded by hydroelectric and agricultural development. Despite the remoteness of the Peace-Athabasca Delta, it too has been negatively affected by development. Since 1967, when it began to fill, the W.A.C. Bennett Dam, upstream on the Peace River in British Columbia, has caused a deterioration of the delta's waterfowl habitat. Boyd, "Waterfowl Population Levels in North America," 77.

76. Mitsch and Gosselink, *Wetlands,* 103; S. C. Zoltai et al., "Wetlands of Boreal Canada," in *Wetlands of Canada,* Ecological Land Classification Series no. 24 (Montreal: Environment Canada and Polyscience Publications, 1988), 148.

77. Smith, Dufresne, and Hansen, "Northern Watersheds and Deltas," 60; Cowan, *Jewel in the Pacific Flyway,* 17.

78. Lincoln, *Waterfowl Flyways of North America,* 9.

79. Edward G. Wellein and Harry Gordon Lumsden, "Northern Forests and Tundra," in *Waterfowl Tomorrow,* ed. Joseph P. Linduska (Washington, D.C.: U.S. Department of the Interior, Fish and Wildlife Service, Bureau of Sport Fisheries and Wildlife, 1964), 67–69. For an overview of contemporary threats to North American boreal forests, see Nancy Langston, "Paradise Lost: Climate Change, Boreal Forests, and Environmental History," *Environmental History* 14, no. 4 (2009).

80. Wellein and Lumsden, "Northern Forests and Tundra," 72–73.

81. Smith, Dufresne, and Hansen, "Northern Watersheds and Deltas," 65; C. Tarnocai and S. C. Zoltai, "Wetlands of Arctic Canada," in *Wetlands of Canada,* Ecological Land Classification Series no. 24 (Montreal: Environment Canada and Polyscience Publications, 1988), 50; Chattin, "Pacific Flyway," 245. A smaller group of twenty thousand snow goose nesting pairs breeds on Wrangell Island in eastern Siberia; most winter in the Skagit/Fraser Delta near the border between Washington and British Columbia, but one-quarter to one-half of the population continues on into the Central Valley. The blue goose, the symbol of the National Wildlife Refuge System, was once considered a separate species from the snow goose, but is actually a color phase of that species. The blue phase is extremely rare in the Pacific Flyway, accounting for perhaps one of every thousand birds, but is much more common in the more easterly flyways. Greg Mensik, deputy refuge manager, Sacramento National Wildlife Refuge, public lecture, 4th Annual Snow Goose Festival, Chico, California, January 24, 2003.

82. Mensik, 2003; IBA [Important Bird Areas] Canada Web site, http://ibacanada.com.

83. William A. Niering, *The Life of the Marsh: The North American Wetlands* (New York: McGraw-Hill, 1966), 176.

84. Dugan, ed., *Wetlands in Danger,* 66.

85. Allen G. Smith, Jerome H. Stoudt, and J. Bernard Gollup, "Prairie Potholes and Marshes," in *Waterfowl Tomorrow,* ed. Joseph P. Linduska (Washington, D.C.: U.S. Department of the Interior, Fish and Wildlife Service, Bureau of Sport Fisheries and Wildlife, 1964), 39; Mitsch and Gosselink, *Wetlands,* 96–97.

86. Chattin, "Pacific Flyway," 238–244.

87. Wells W. Cooke, *Distribution and Migration of North American Ducks, Geese, and Swans* (Washington, D.C.: U.S. Department of Agriculture, Bureau of Biological Survey, Bulletin no. 26, 1906), 11.

88. Dugan, ed., *Wetlands in Danger,* 66.

89. C. D. A. Rubec et al., "Wetland Utilization in Canada," in *Wetlands of Canada,* Ecological Land Classification Series no. 24 (Montreal: Environment Canada and Polyscience Publications, 1988), 389, 406.

90. G. D. Adams, "Wetlands of the Prairies of Canada," in *Wetlands of Canada,* Ecological Land Classification Series no. 24 (Montreal: Environment Canada and Polyscience

Publications, 1988), 192–193. To protect the prairie pothole region and to achieve the conservation goals of the North American Waterfowl Management Plan of 1986 (discussed in chapter 10), the U.S.-based Prairie Pothole Joint Venture and the Canadian-based Prairie Habitat Joint Venture were established in the late 1980s.

91. G. Hortin Jensen and John E. Chattin, "Western Production Areas," in *Waterfowl Tomorrow,* ed. Joseph P. Linduska (Washington, D.C.: U.S. Department of the Interior, Fish and Wildlife Service, Bureau of Sport Fisheries and Wildlife, 1964), 84–86; Holly Doremus and A. Dan Tarlock, *Water War in the Klamath Basin: Macho Law, Combat Biology, and Dirty Politics* (Washington, D.C.: Island Press, 2008), 27. For histories of the Klamath Basin, in addition to Doremus and Tarlock see William Kittredge, *Balancing Water: Restoring the Klamath Basin* (Berkeley and Los Angeles: University of California Press, 2000). For a history of Malheur National Wildlife Refuge, see Langston, *Where Land and Water Meet.*

92. Lincoln, *Waterfowl Flyways of North America,* 9.

93. Weller, *Wetland Birds,* 51–52.

94. Chattin, "Pacific Flyway," 238–242.

95. Grassland Water District, "Estimates of Waterfowl That Breed in Grasslands Ecological Area Tops 66,000," *Grassland Today* 15, no. 4 (2005): 1.

96. For the evolution of environmental thought toward biocentrism, see Roderick Frazier Nash, *The Rights of Nature: A History of Environmental Ethics* (Madison: University of Wisconsin Press, 1989); Lisa Mighetto, *Wild Animals and American Environmental Ethics* (Tucson: University of Arizona Press, 1991); Donald Worster, *Nature's Economy: A History of Ecological Ideas,* 2nd ed. (Cambridge: Cambridge University Press, 1994).

97. Johnsgard, *Waterfowl of North America,* 30.

2. FROM NATIVE AMERICAN LANDS OF PLENTY TO "WASTE" LANDS

1. Warren A. Beck and Ynez D. Haase, *Historical Atlas of California* (Norman: University of Oklahoma Press, 1974), 15–18.

2. The settlement at Fort Ross was hindered by several factors, including a cool climate unsuitable for large-scale agricultural production, Spanish resistance to the Russian presence in California, and, in the end, a drastic decline in the populations of sea otters, the skins of which formed the basis for trade. For Russian hunting from the base at Fort Ross, see Adele Ogden, "Russian Sea-Otter and Seal Hunting on the California Coast 1803–1841," *California Historical Society Quarterly* 12 (1933). For the overall Russian fur trade in North America, see James R. Gibson, *Imperial Russia in Frontier America: Changing Geography of Supply of Russian America, 1784–1867* (New York: Oxford University Press, 1976).

3. Sherburne F. Cook, "The Epidemic of 1830–1833 in California and Oregon," *University of California Publications in American Archaeology and Ethnology* 43, no. 3 (1955): 321–322.

4. This key point about the essence of irrigation and reclamation is articulated in David Igler, *Industrial Cowboys: Miller & Lux and the Transformation of the Far West, 1850–1920* (Berkeley and Los Angeles: University of California Press, 2001), 93. Extensive

bodies of scholarship exist for these interrelated topics. The following monographs are among those that treat, in whole or large part, the broad issues of irrigation and reclamation in the Central Valley. For a statewide view, see Norris Hundley Jr., *The Great Thirst: Californians and Water, a History*, rev. ed. (Berkeley and Los Angeles: University of California Press, 2001); Lawrence J. Jelinek, *Harvest Empire: A History of California Agriculture*, 2nd ed. (San Francisco: Boyd & Fraser, 1982); Donald J. Pisani, *From the Family Farm to Agribusiness: The Irrigation Crusade in California and the West, 1850–1931* (Berkeley and Los Angeles: University of California Press, 1984); Worster, *Rivers of Empire*. For the Sacramento Valley, see Robert L. Kelley, *Gold vs. Grain: The Hydraulic Mining Controversy in California's Sacramento Valley* (Glendale, Calif.: Arthur H. Clark, 1959); Kelley, *Battling the Inland Sea*. For the Delta, see W. Turrentine Jackson and Alan M. Paterson, *The Sacramento–San Joaquin Delta: The Evolution and Implementation of Water Policy, an Historical Perspective* (Davis: California Water Resources Center, University of California, Davis, Contribution no. 163, 1977); Thompson, "Settlement Geography of the Sacramento–San Joaquin Delta"; Thompson and Dutra, *Tule Breakers*. For the San Joaquin Basin, see Igler, *Industrial Cowboys;* Wallace Smith, *Garden of the Sun: A History of the San Joaquin Valley, 1772–1939*, ed. William B. Secrest Jr., 2nd ed. (Fresno, Calif.: Linden Publishing, 2004). For the Tulare Basin, see Preston, *Vanishing Landscapes*.

5. Robert F. Heizer and Albert B. Elsasser, *The Natural World of the California Indians* (Berkeley and Los Angeles: University of California Press, 1980), 27.

6. Of those Native American groups living in whole or in large part in the Central Valley, the Nomlaki and Patwin, on the western side of the Sacramento Valley, were Wintuan-speaking peoples. The Konkow and Nisenan, on the eastern side of the Sacramento Valley, were Maiduan-speaking peoples. The Plains Miwok, who occupied the Delta region and territory to the north and east, were a Miwokan-speaking people. The Northern Valley and Southern Valley Yokuts, who occupied the San Joaquin Basin and the Tulare Basin, respectively, of the San Joaquin Valley, were Yokutsan-speaking peoples. Heizer and Elsasser, *Natural World of the California Indians*, 14–16. For a classic account of California's Native American peoples, see A. L. Kroeber, *Handbook of the Indians of California* (Washington, D.C.: Smithsonian Institution, Bureau of American Ethnology, Bulletin no. 78, 1925).

7. Henry T. Lewis, "Patterns of Indian Burning in California: Ecology and Ethnohistory," in *Before the Wilderness: Environmental Management by Native Californians*, ed. Thomas C. Blackburn and Kat Anderson (Menlo Park, Calif.: Ballena Press, 1993), 80–86.

8. M. Kat Anderson, Michael G. Barbour, and Valerie Whitworth, "A World of Balance and Plenty: Land, Plants, Animals, and Humans in a Pre-European California," in *Contested Eden: California before the Gold Rush*, ed. Ramón A. Gutiérrez and Richard J. Orsi (Berkeley and Los Angeles: University of California Press, 1998), 14–16, 35.

9. See Kat Anderson, *Tending the Wild: Native American Knowledge and the Management of California's Natural Resources* (Berkeley and Los Angeles: University of California Press, 2005), especially 334–357.

10. Kroeber, *Handbook of the Indians of California*, 410. Francis A. Riddell, "Maidu and Konkow," 375, 384; Norman L. Wilson and Arlean H. Towne, "Nisenan," 391; Patti J.

Johnson, "Patwin," 355; Richard Levy, "Eastern Miwok," 403–404; William J. Wallace, "Northern Valley Yokuts," 464; and William J. Wallace, "Southern Valley Yokuts," 450, all in *Handbook of North American Indians*, vol. 8: *California*, ed. Robert F. Heizer (Washington, D.C.: Smithsonian Institution, 1978); Silveira, "Avian Uses of Vernal Pools," 92.

11. Thomas Jefferson Mayfield, *Indian Summer: Traditional Life among the Choinumne Indians of California's San Joaquin Valley* (Berkeley, Calif.: Heyday Books and the California Historical Society, 1993), 10. Latta's original self-published 1928 version of Mayfield's account is titled *San Joaquin Primeval: Uncle Jeff's Story, a Tale of a San Joaquin Valley Pioneer and His Life with the Yokuts Indians*. Such ethnographies, recorded decades after the events they describe, must always be read with caution, but much of Mayfield's tale seems authentic, and his descriptions of hunting and fishing with the Yokuts have been corroborated by other sources.

12. Mayfield, *Indian Summer*, 75.

13. Mayfield, *Indian Summer*, 98. See also the description of Yokut tule rafts by John Barker, a white pioneer of the early 1850s, in Frank F. Latta, *Handbook of Yokuts Indians*, 2nd ed. (Santa Cruz, Calif.: Bear State Books, 1977), 504–506.

14. Albert L. Hurtado, *Indian Survival on the California Frontier* (New Haven, Conn.: Yale University Press, 1988), 164–165.

15. Preston, *Vanishing Landscapes*, 83.

16. Hurtado, *Indian Survival on the California Frontier*, 24–26. For a history of Spanish California in the context of Spain's frontier colonies in North America as a whole, see David J. Weber, *The Spanish Frontier in North America* (New Haven, Conn.: Yale University Press, 1992), especially 236–265.

17. Beck and Haase, *Historical Atlas of California*, 21.

18. Letter from José Argüello to Governor Arrillaga, San Francisco, October 31, 1813, in Sherburne F. Cook, "Colonial Expeditions to the Interior of California: Central Valley, 1800–1820," *University of California Publications: Anthropological Records* 16, no. 6 (1960): 266.

19. Beck and Haase, *Historical Atlas of California*, 21. See the diaries of Juan Ortega and José Dolores Pico for the year 1815, in Cook, "Colonial Expeditions to the Interior of California," 267–271.

20. Hurtado, *Indian Survival on the California Frontier*, 33–35.

21. See Jack Holterman, "The Revolt of Estanislao," *The Indian Historian* 3, no. 1 (1970).

22. Cook, "Epidemic of 1830–1833"; Nash, *Inescapable Ecologies*, 22. Cook effectively ruled out other possible maladies, including smallpox, cholera, measles, typhus, and plague. There exists at least one suggestion in the literature that influenza, more than malaria, may have been responsible for the symptoms and the high mortality rate reported during the epidemic. See Herbert C. Taylor Jr. and Lester L. Hoaglin Jr., "The 'Intermittent Fever' Epidemic of the 1830's on the Lower Columbia River," *Ethnohistory* 9, no. 2 (1962).

23. John Work, *Fur Brigade to the Bonaventura*, ed. Alice Bay Maloney (San Francisco: California Historical Society, 1945), 19, 69, 70, 72.

24. Warner's account is reproduced in Cook, "Epidemic of 1830–1833," 318; Walter Goldschmidt, "Nomlaki," in *Handbook of North American Indians*, vol. 8: *California*, ed. Robert F. Heizer (Washington, D.C.: Smithsonian Institution, 1978), 342.

25. Cook, "Epidemic of 1830–1833," 320–322; Sherburne F. Cook, "Historical Demography," in *Handbook of North American Indians,* vol. 8: *California,* ed. Robert F. Heizer (Washington, D.C.: Smithsonian Institution, 1978), 92.

26. For those who survived the malaria epidemic, the worst was yet to come. During the decade of 1845–1855—during which California witnessed the Bear Flag Revolt, independence from Mexico, the Gold Rush, and statehood—Native Americans in California as a whole suffered their sharpest demographic decline of any single ten-year period. Perhaps one hundred thousand individuals, two-thirds of their remaining number, perished. The litany of causes for this breathtaking decline includes disease, starvation, homicide, and new social and domestic situations that contributed to a declining birthrate among Native American women. Women's reproductive ability was curtailed by separation from their families and segregation of the sexes in the workforce, as well as sterility resulting from venereal diseases brought on by rape, prostitution, and forced concubinage. By the last two decades of the nineteenth century, only twenty thousand Native Americans survived in the state, a decline of well over 90 percent since 1769. Cook, "Historical Demography," 91. See Robert F. Heizer, ed., *The Destruction of the California Indians* (Santa Barbara, Calif., and Salt Lake City: Peregrine Smith, 1974); Hurtado, *Indian Survival on the California Frontier.*

27. The law provided for land grants of up to eleven square leagues, divided into one league of irrigable soil, four leagues arable with adequate rainfall, and six leagues suitable for grazing. Smith, *Garden of the Sun,* 164–165. A single square league equals 4,438.44 acres.

28. W. W. Robinson, *Land in California: The Story of Mission Lands, Ranchos, Squatters, Mining Claims, Railroad Grants, Land Scrip, Homesteads* (Berkeley and Los Angeles: University of California Press, 1948), 63.

29. The term *manifest destiny* is attributed to journalist John L. O'Sullivan.

30. 9 *Stat.* 922.

31. 9 *Stat.* 631.

32. Beck and Haase, *Historical Atlas of California,* 24; Robinson, *Land in California,* 67, 100, 106. The loss of land resulting from litigation stemming from the Land Act of 1851 contributed to the economic, political, and social decline of the Californios, a group that included California inhabitants of Spanish or Mexican descent as well as Americans from the United States who had settled in California prior to statehood and adopted Hispanic culture.

33. Kenneth Thompson, "Insalubrious California: Perception and Reality," *Annals of the Association of American Geographers* 59, no. 1 (1969): 51. Diseases present in nineteenth-century California as a whole included—in addition to malaria—cholera, smallpox, scarlet fever, measles, diphtheria, influenza, typhoid fever, consumptive diseases including tuberculosis, and dysentery and other intestinal diseases. Nash, *Inescapable Ecologies,* 37.

34. Kenneth Thompson, "Irrigation as a Menace to Health in California," *The Geographical Review* 59, no. 2 (1969): 195–196.

35. The belief that marshes or, more particularly, marsh vapor caused febrile diseases dates back at least to Greek and Roman times and changed little before modern times. During the eighteenth century, Italians first referred to the cause of fever as *mal'aria,*

"bad air." Gordon Harrison, *Mosquitoes, Malaria and Man: A History of the Hostilities since 1880* (New York: E. P. Dutton, 1978), 5; Thompson, "Irrigation as a Menace to Health," 196.

36. John Thomas Metcalfe, *Report of a Committee of the Associate Medical Members of the United States Sanitary Commission on the Subject of the Nature and Treatment of Miasmatic Fevers* (Washington, D.C.: United States Sanitary Commission, 1863), 5.

37. J. L. Tyson, *Diary of a Physician in California* (New York: D. Appleton, 1850), 54–55.

38. Central Pacific Railroad, *Statement of the Workings of the Railroad Hospital, at Sacramento, Cal. for the Year 1883* (Sacramento: H. S. Crocker, 1884), 5–9.

39. "Southern Pacific Company—Railroad Lands for Sale. California as Sanitarium," *San Francisco Wave*, 1892, MS 10, Series 7, Public Relations, Scrapbook 1888–1892, SPR; emphasis added.

40. There are four main species of *Plasmodium* that cause malaria. *Plasmodium vivax*, the species primarily responsible for malaria in the Central Valley, is the commonest form and, except for populations lacking inherited immunity, is rarely fatal. The other malaria-inducing species of *Plasmodium* are *P. ovale*, *P. malariae*, and *P. falciparum*, the most lethal of the four.

41. Thompson, "Irrigation as a Menace to Health," 196. While the *Anopheles* mosquito is indigenous to California, *Plasmodium vivax* is not, and was apparently introduced by Europeans.

42. Harrison, *Mosquitoes, Malaria and Man*, 59.

43. Thompson, "Insalubrious California," 63.

44. Thomas M. Logan, *Report of the Permanent Secretary to the State Board of Health. Second Biennial Report, State Board of Health of California for the Years 1871, 1872, and 1873* (Sacramento: State Printer, 1873), 54.

45. George P. Marsh, *Irrigation: Its Evils, the Remedies, and the Compensations*, Senate Miscellaneous Document no. 55, 43d Congress, 1st session, 1874, 7, 18–19, 22; emphasis in original. One of the great intellectuals of the nineteenth century, Marsh was the first significant writer to call attention to human-caused degradation of the environment and its consequences. See George P. Marsh, *Man and Nature; or, Physical Geography as Modified by Human Action* (New York: Charles Scribner, 1864). For Marsh's biography, see David Lowenthal, *George Perkins Marsh: Prophet of Conservation* (Seattle: University of Washington Press, 2003).

46. Nash, *Inescapable Ecologies*, 14; Linda Nash, "Finishing Nature: Harmonizing Bodies and Environments in Late-Nineteenth-Century California," *Environmental History* 8, no. 1 (2003): 27. See also Conevery Bolton Valencius, *The Health of the Country: How American Settlers Understood Themselves and Their Land* (New York: Basic Books, 2002).

47. This figure would more than triple, to slightly more than a million acres, by 1889. Thompson, "Irrigation as a Menace to Health," 208.

48. Jas. D. Schuyler, "Report on the Works and Practice of Irrigation in Kern County," Appendix B to the *Report of the State Engineer to the Legislature of California, Session of 1880* (Sacramento: State Printer, 1880), 109. See also William Hammond Hall's statement to this effect in U.S. Senate, *Report of the Special Committee of the U.S. Senate on the Irrigation and Reclamation of Arid Lands*, part 2: *The Great Basin Region and California*, Senate Report no. 928, 51st Congress, 1st session, 1890, 217. Malarial conditions throughout

the Central Valley improved markedly in subsequent years, especially after the cause of the disease was scientifically understood. Mosquito control campaigns were initiated during the early years of the twentieth century, and in 1915 the California State Legislature passed the Mosquito Abatement Act, which allowed for the creation of local public mosquito abatement districts. *California Health and Safety Code*, sec. 2000–2093.

49. 9 *Stat.* 352.

50. Paul W. Gates, *History of Public Land Law Development* (Washington, D.C.: U.S. Government Printing Office, 1968; repr. 1979), 323.

51. Those states were Ohio, Indiana, Illinois, Missouri, Alabama, Mississippi, Michigan, Arkansas, Wisconsin, Iowa, Florida, and California. In 1860 the act was extended to include the recently admitted states of Minnesota and Oregon.

52. 9 *Stat.* 519.

53. Gates, *History of Public Land Law Development*, 324.

54. California State Surveyor-General, "Annual Report of the Surveyor-General of California for the Year 1862," Appendix to *Journals of Senate and Assembly of the Fourteenth Session of the Legislature of the State of California*, 1862, 10, 13. The counties, with acreages, were Sacramento, 9,797.62 acres; Sutter, 22,241.74 acres; Colusa, 15,069.72 acres; Yolo, 35,830.00 acres; and San Joaquin, 1,600.00 acres.

55. The federal government sold the land under the Preemption Act of 1841 (5 *Stat.* 453). Richard H. Peterson, "The Failure to Reclaim: California State Swamp Land Policy and the Sacramento Valley, 1850–1866," *Southern California Quarterly* 56, no. 1 (1974): 47–48.

56. 14 *Stat.* 218.

57. Paul W. Gates, "Public Land Disposal in California," *Agricultural History* 49, no. 1 (1975): 161. The Swamp and Overflowed Lands Act was one of many federal land policies designed to settle the land as quickly as possible by transferring the public domain into private hands, and to provide for internal improvements. Federal grants of the public domain to the state of California included 5,534,293 acres for public schools; 6,400 acres for public buildings; 46,080 acres for seminaries; 500,000 acres for canals and river improvements; and—under the Agricultural College Act, commonly known as the Morrill Act, of July 2, 1862—150,000 acres for agricultural and mechanical colleges. Together with the 2,193,965 acres of swampland and a small number of miscellaneous acres, the total federal grant to the state of California equaled 8,852,140 acres, or approximately 8.7 percent of the state's total area. Interestingly, this figure pales in comparison to the 11,588,626 acres, or approximately 11.6 percent of the state's total area, that the federal government granted directly to railroads. Gates, *History of Public Land Law Development*, 385, 804–806.

58. 1855 *Statutes of California* ch. 151.

59. 1858 *Statutes of California* ch. 235.

60. 1859 *Statutes of California* ch. 314.

61. 1861 *Statutes of California* ch. 352.

62. Kelley, *Battling the Inland Sea*, 40–41. For mid-nineteenth-century Republican political philosophy and the party's relation to its Whig predecessors, see Eric Foner, *Free Soil, Free Labor, Free Men: The Ideology of the Republican Party before the Civil War* (New York: Oxford University Press, 1995).

63. Kelley, *Battling the Inland Sea*, 48.

64. California Board of Swamp Land Commissioners, "First Annual Report of Swamp Land Commissioners," Appendix to *Journals of Senate and Assembly of the Thirteenth Session of the Legislature of the State of California*, 1862, 10, 27.

65. Petition by the owners of one-third of the land in a reclamation district was required in order for a county board of supervisors to levy an assessment. California Department of Public Works, *Financial and General Data Pertaining to Irrigation, Reclamation and Other Public Districts in California* (Sacramento: California Department of Public Works, Division of Water Resources, Bulletin no. 37, 1930), 109–110.

66. See, for example, Thompson & West, *History of Sacramento County, California* (Oakland, Calif.: Thompson & West, 1880; repr. 1960).

67. Brewer, *Up and Down California*, 242.

68. Brewer, *Up and Down California*, 244.

69. Peterson, "Failure to Reclaim," 54; Kelley, *Battling the Inland Sea*, 52.

70. The issue of hydraulic mining, and its eventual resolution, will be further discussed in chapter 4.

71. California Board of Swamp Land Commissioners, "Annual Report of the Swamp Land Commissioners for the Year 1862," Appendix to *Journals of Senate and Assembly of the Fourteenth Session of the Legislature of the State of California*, 1863, 3–4; Peterson, "Failure to Reclaim," 51–52.

72. California Board of Swamp Land Commissioners, "Annual Report . . . for the Year 1862," 5.

73. California Board of Swamp Land Commissioners, "Report of the Board of Swamp Land Commissioners, for the Years 1864 and 1865," Appendix to *Journals of Senate and Assembly of the Sixteenth Session of the Legislature of the State of California*, 1865–1866, 2:3.

74. Peterson, "Failure to Reclaim," 53.

75. 1865–1866 *Statutes of California* ch. 570.

76. Peterson, "Failure to Reclaim," 54–55; California Department of Public Works, *Financial and General Data Pertaining to Irrigation*, 110–111; Kelley, *Battling the Inland Sea*, 56.

77. 1867–1868 *Statutes of California* ch. 415.

78. Will S. Green, *The History of Colusa County, California* (San Francisco: Elliott & Moore, 1880; repr. 1950), 75–76.

79. Kelley, *Battling the Inland Sea, 1850–1986*, 58.

80. Kelley, *Battling the Inland Sea*, 58–60; Cynthia F. Davis, *Where Water Is King: The Story of Glenn-Colusa Irrigation District* (Willows, Calif.: Glenn-Colusa Irrigation District, 1984), 5.

81. 1867–1868 *Statutes of California* ch. 415.

82. California Department of Public Works, *Financial and General Data Pertaining to Irrigation*, 111.

83. For a discussion of abuses in the California State Land Office in general, and concerning the sale of swamp and overflow lands in particular, see Gerald D. Nash, "The California State Land Office," *Huntington Library Quarterly* 27, no. 4 (1964).

84. *Political Code of California* (1872), sec. 3440 et seq. See sec. 3443 for the acreage restriction.

85. California State Surveyor-General, "Statistical Report of the Surveyor-General of California, for the Years 1869, 1870, and 1871," Appendix to *Journals of Senate and Assembly of the Nineteenth Session of the Legislature of the State of California,* 1871–1872, 6–7.

86. Gates, *History of Public Land Law Development,* 327. In fairness to these baronial landowners, Gates did argue that they expended large amounts of money over many years to bring these lands into production "and should not be thought of as sheer speculators." Nevertheless, by refusing to partition and sell the land, they also prevented the development of small-scale farms. Gates, "Public Land Disposal in California," 176.

3. THE SAN JOAQUIN VALLEY

1. The Tulare Basin encompasses Kings County, the valley floor portions of Tulare and Kern counties, and all except the northwestern part of the valley floor portion of Fresno County.

2. Schoenherr, *Natural History of California,* 526; U.S. Fish and Wildlife Service, *Concept Plan for Waterfowl Wintering Habitat Preservation,* 69.

3. Gerald Haslam, "The Lake That Will Not Die," *California History* 72, no. 3 (1993): 257–258.

4. Griggs, Zaninovich, and Werschkull, "Historic Native Vegetation Map of the Tulare Basin," 113; Gerald R. Ogden, *Agricultural Land Use and Wildlife in the San Joaquin Valley, 1769–1930: An Overview* (Sacramento: U.S. Bureau of Reclamation, San Joaquin Valley Drainage Program, 1988), 19.

5. Preston, *Vanishing Landscapes,* 18–19; Wallace, "Southern Valley Yokuts," 448.

6. Ogden, *Agricultural Land Use and Wildlife,* 22; Richard E. Warner and Kathleen M. Hendrix, *Final Draft: Riparian Resources of the Central Valley and California Desert* (Sacramento: California Department of Fish and Game, 1985), 5.14. The maximum depth of the lake in 1862 is often cited as forty-one feet, based on State Engineer William Hammond Hall's figure of 220 feet above sea level as the highest surface level. However, using the datum of the United States Geological Survey, that figure has since been revised to 216 feet, resulting in a maximum depth of thirty-seven feet above the 179-foot elevation of the lake bed. Robert R. Brown, *History of Kings County* (Hanford, Calif.: A. H. Cawston, 1940), 112.

7. Preston, *Vanishing Landscapes,* 14–18.

8. See George R. Brooks, ed., *The Southwest Expedition of Jedediah S. Smith: His Personal Account of the Journey to California 1826–1827* (Glendale, Calif.: Arthur H. Clark, 1977).

9. George H. Derby, *Report of the Secretary of War, Communicating, in Compliance with a Resolution of the Senate, a Report of the Tulare Valley, Made by Lieutenant Derby,* Senate Executive Document no. 110, 32d Congress, 1st session, 1852, 6–7. For more on Derby, see Peter Browning, ed., *Bright Gem of the Western Seas: California 1846–1852* (Lafayette, Calif.: Great West Books, 1991).

10. Derby, *Report of the Secretary of War,* 9.

11. Derby, *Report of the Secretary of War,* 13.

12. M. E. Heitmeyer, D. P. Connelly, and R. L. Pederson, "The Central, Imperial, and Coachella Valleys of California," in *Habitat Management for Migrating and Wintering Waterfowl in North America,* ed. L. M. Smith, R. L. Pederson, and R. M. Kaminski (Lubbock: Texas Tech University Press, 1989), 479.

13. Mary Austin, *The Land of Little Rain* (Cambridge, Mass.: Houghton Mifflin, 1903; repr. New York: Dover Publications, 1996), 66.

14. Ogden, *Agricultural Land Use and Wildlife,* 23, 58; David Igler, "When Is a River Not a River? Reclaiming Nature's Disorder in *Lux v. Haggin,*" *Environmental History* 1, no. 2 (1996): 61.

15. C. E. Grunsky, "Water Appropriation from Kings River," in *Report of Irrigation Investigations in California* (Washington, D.C.: U.S. Department of Agriculture, Office of Experiment Stations. Bulletin no. 100, 1901), 265–266.

16. Preston, *Vanishing Landscapes,* 95–96.

17. Adobe soils are heavy-textured clay soils that harden when dry. These soils are widely distributed in the troughs of the Sacramento and San Joaquin valleys.

18. Sources vary slightly as to the date of the final overflow. For 1876 and 1878 dates, respectively, see Grunsky, "Water Appropriations from the Kings River," 265; Ogden, *Agricultural Land Use and Wildlife,* 23, citing local historian Frank Latta.

19. Brown, *History of Kings County,* 115; Preston, *Vanishing Landscapes,* 118.

20. Jelinek, *Harvest Empire,* 40.

21. There is little question about the tremendous importance of the railroad for developing California's economy during the late nineteenth century. Renowned social critic Henry George, even while decrying the concentration of wealth and power, differentiation of classes, and destruction of small towns and businesses that the railroad threatened to bring to California, could not deny that it would also increase land values and access to resources, as well as opportunities for labor and immigration. Henry George, "What the Railroad Will Bring Us," *The Overland Monthly* 1, no. 4 (1868).

22. California's connection to the global wheat market was in large part the accomplishment of Isaac Friedlander, who had immigrated to California in 1849 and had risen to become one of the wealthiest land speculators in the state. Friedlander assembled a shipping empire that stretched from San Francisco to England and Australia, and that made it profitable for California farmers to rely on wheat monoculture. Jelinek, *Harvest Empire,* 42.

23. During the next two years, the Southern Pacific crossed the Tehachapi Mountains, and on September 5, 1876, it linked Los Angeles with the state's northern railroad lines.

24. On May 11, 1880, Mussel Slough was the site of a bloody confrontation between settlers and the Southern Pacific Railroad that left seven people dead and has been immortalized in California history by Frank Norris's 1901 novel *The Octopus.* Recent scholarship has added a great deal of complexity to Norris's David versus Goliath interpretation as well as that of earlier California historians. See William Conlogue, "Farmers' Rhetoric of Defense: California Settlers versus the Southern Pacific Railroad," *California History* 78, no. 1 (1999). For an introduction to revisionism in California railroad history, see Richard J. Orsi, "The Octopus Reconsidered: The Southern Pacific and Agricultural Modernization in California," *California Historical Quarterly* 54, no. 3 (1975). For a more

expansive treatment of the role of the Southern Pacific in developing the West, see Richard J. Orsi, *Sunset Limited: The Southern Pacific Railroad and the Development of the American West, 1850–1930* (Berkeley and Los Angeles: University of California Press, 2005).

25. Brown, *History of Kings County*, 218.

26. Preston, *Vanishing Landscapes*, 135–145.

27. Grunsky, "Water Appropriations from the Kings River," 265.

28. Much of this work was carried out by the Tulare Lake Basin Water Storage District, organized in 1926. California Department of Public Works, *Financial and General Data Pertaining to Irrigation*, 119, 242. A township consists of thirty-six sections, each of which is one square mile. The township designated for impoundment of the lake was T22S R20E, Mt. Diablo Meridian.

29. Preston, *Vanishing Landscapes*, 143.

30. The clay layer is known as the Corcoran Clay. Corcoran is a Tulare Basin city that once bordered Tulare Lake.

31. U.S. Census Office, *Agriculture—Artesian Wells for Irrigation* (Washington, D.C.: U.S. Department of the Interior, Census Office, Bulletin no. 193, 1892), 11–12.

32. Preston, *Vanishing Landscapes*, 141–144. The depletion, and subsequent collapse, of aquifers in the San Joaquin Valley has led to widespread land subsidence. In parts of the southern valley, land subsidence caused by aquifer collapse approaches fifty feet. Stephen Johnson, Gerald Haslam, and Robert Dawson, *The Great Central Valley: California's Heartland* (Berkeley and Los Angeles: University of California Press, 1993), 184.

33. Igler, *Industrial Cowboys*, 101. At the height of their empire, Haggin and his associates owned 1.4 million acres of grasslands in California, Arizona, and New Mexico. Pisani, *From the Family Farm to Agribusiness*, 202. In 1967 Tenneco Corporation—an oil, petrochemical, and natural gas conglomerate—acquired the Kern County Land Company for $432 million. Norman Berg, *A History of Kern County Land Company* (Bakersfield, Calif.: Kern County Historical Society, 1971), 48–49.

34. James Ben Ali Haggin, *The Desert Lands of Kern County, California* (San Francisco: C.H. Street, 1877), v.

35. 19 *Stat.* 377. Section 2 of the Desert Land Act provided that "all lands exclusive of timber lands and mineral lands which will not, without irrigation, produce some agricultural crop, shall be deemed desert lands within the meaning of this act." The act applied to California, Oregon, and Nevada, as well as to the territories of Washington, Idaho, Montana, Utah, Wyoming, New Mexico, and Dakota.

36. Haggin, *Desert Lands of Kern County*, 305. Because precipitation in most of California falls primarily during the fall and winter, annual precipitation totals are calculated from July 1 to June 30 of the following year.

37. Igler, *Industrial Cowboys*, 102; Pisani, *From the Family Farm to Agribusiness*, 194–195.

38. Paul W. Gates, "Land Policies in Kern County," in *Land and Law in California: Essays on Land Policies*, ed. Richard S. Kirkendall (Ames: University of Iowa, 1991), 281.

39. Haggin, *Desert Lands of Kern County*, v.

40. "Kern County Canals," *Bakersfield Californian*, April 9, 1892; Pisani, *From the Family Farm to Agribusiness*, 195–200.

41. Igler, *Industrial Cowboys*, 16, 97.

42. Berg, *History of Kern County Land Company*, 9.

43. "Kern County Canals"; Wallace W. Elliott & Co., *History of Kern County, California* (San Francisco: Wallace W. Elliott, 1883), 157.

44. This landmark case in California water law has generated considerable scholarship. See Pisani, *From the Family Farm to Agribusiness*, 191–249; Igler, *Industrial Cowboys*, 92–121; Igler, "When Is a River Not a River?" For a history of litigation involving Miller and Lux, see M. Catherine Miller, *Flooding the Courtrooms: Law and Water in the Far West* (Lincoln: University of Nebraska Press, 1993).

45. "Kern County Canals"; Igler, *Industrial Cowboys*, 98; Igler, "When Is a River Not a River?" 63.

46. 1850 *Statutes of California* ch. 95.

47. Hundley, *Great Thirst*, 85.

48. 1851 *Statutes of California* ch. 5; 14 *Stat.* 251. The California Supreme Court also recognized both riparian and appropriative rights in the cases of *Irwin v. Phillips*, 5 Cal. 140 (1855), and *Crandall v. Woods*, 8 Cal. 136 (1857), respectively.

49. *Civil Code of California* (1872), sec. 1410 et seq.; sec. 1411 (quote).

50. For a discussion of the ways in which the arguments in this case hinged on definitions of watercourses—and by extension, nature—as fixed and eternal, or as fluid and mutable, see Igler, "When Is a River Not a River?"

51. 4 *Pacific Reporter* 919.

52. 69 Cal. 255; 10 *Pacific Reporter* 674.

53. Pisani, *From the Family Farm to Agribusiness*, 211–229. The first California irrigation district act was passed in 1872, but the irrigation district did not become a viable entity until the passage of the Wright Act in 1887, just one year after the final decision in *Lux v. Haggin*. (1887 *Statutes of California* ch. 34.) See chapter 4.

54. Hundley, *Great Thirst*, 97. The more arid states of the intermountain West, where water was scarcer and where riparian rights would more seriously impede development, chose appropriation as their sole water law. Nevada, Idaho, Montana, Wyoming, Utah, Colorado, Arizona, and New Mexico all went this route, as did Alaska.

55. For details of the compromise, ratified in 1888, see Pisani, *From the Family Farm to Agribusiness*, 243.

56. The Tulare Basin supported a tremendous range of native species. William Preston lists twenty-four species of mammals, sixteen species of fish, and thirty-eight species of birds for the Tulare Lake Basin alone. Preston, *Vanishing Landscapes*, 248–250. The inclusion of reptile and amphibian species would significantly expand this list.

57. Handwritten notes by F. F. Latta, in his copy of Edward F. Treadwell, *The Cattle King: A Dramatized Biography* (New York: Macmillan, 1931), 213. This volume is located in the Miller and Lux Papers, FLC.

58. C. Hart Merriam, "A California Elk Drive," *Scientific Monthly* 13 (1921). See Gerhard Bakker, *History of the California Tule Elk* (Los Angeles: Los Angeles City College Press, 1965).

59. Elliott, *History of Kern County*, 176; Brown, *History of Kings County*, 121.

60. "Piscatorial Plundering," *Tulare Daily Register,* January 29, 1889, 3, typescript copy, box 16(4), folder 21, Skyfarming Collection, FLC; Schoenherr, *Natural History of California,* 603.

61. Frank Latta, "William J. Browning: Personal Recollections after More Than 60 Years," 1938, box 7(1), folder 1, Miller & Lux Papers, FLC.

62. Preston, *Vanishing Landscapes,* 161.

63. Brown, *History of Kings County,* 117.

64. *Kern Standard,* August 18, 1899, 2, typescript copy, box 16(3), folder 1, Skyfarming Collection, FLC. The "brown ibis" was presumably the darkly colored white-faced ibis, *Plegadis chihi.*

65. Ogden, "Agricultural Land Use and Wildlife," 66–67.

66. These diseases, and their effect on waterfowl populations, are discussed in chapter 6.

67. The San Joaquin Basin encompasses San Joaquin County south and east of the Delta, Merced and Stanislaus counties, the valley floor portion of Madera County, and the northwestern part of Fresno County.

68. Katibah, "Brief History of Riparian Forests," 26–27.

69. Heitmeyer, Connelly, and Pederson, "Central, Imperial, and Coachella Valleys," 479.

70. Ogden, *Agricultural Land Use and Wildlife,* 22.

71. The profound influence of Miller and Lux is apparent from the numerous interviews of long-time San Joaquin Valley Westside residents, conducted over two decades—from the 1920s to the 1940s—by Ralph Milliken, a local San Joaquin Valley historian. See Ralph Milliken Oral History Notebooks, JMW. For a local history that portrays life in the Westside during the early years, see Wayne Pimentel, *Dogtown and Ditches: Life on the Westside* (Los Banos, Calif.: Loose Change Publications, 1987).

72. "Rancho Sanjon de Santa Rita," MSS 70/154c, MLR.

73. Vol. 7, 55 (microfilm), SAC.

74. Igler, *Industrial Cowboys,* 55.

75. "Map of Merced County, West Side," map 12, Miller and Lux Papers, FLC; "Rancho Sanjon de Santa Rita," MSS 70/154c, MLR. Collier mapped out twenty-four townships, including eight that were, in whole or in part, included in Rancho Sanjon de Santa Rita.

76. Igler, *Industrial Cowboys,* 56, 66–67, 207 n.33.

77. Elliott & Moore, *History of Merced County, California* (San Francisco: Elliott & Moore, 1881), 96.

78. Treadwell, *Cattle King,* 323.

79. Igler, *Industrial Cowboys,* 71–85; Pisani, *From the Family Farm to Agribusiness,* 105–119. See also Jeff R. Bremer, "To Water the Valley: The San Joaquin and Kings River Canal and Irrigation Company, 1866–1875," MA thesis, California State University, Bakersfield, 1995; R. M. Brereton, *Reminiscences of Irrigation-Enterprise in California* (Portland, Ore.: Irwin-Hodson, 1903).

80. B. S. Alexander, George Davidson, and G. H. Mendell, *Report of the Board of Commissioners on the Irrigation of the San Joaquin, Tulare, and Sacramento Valleys of the State of California,* House of Representatives Executive Document no. 290, 43d Congress, 1st session, 1874, 28.

81. "The West Side," *Merced Star,* April 30, 1885, typescript copy, Ralph Milliken Oral History Notebooks, JMW.

82. Latta, "William J. Browning."

83. Ralph Milliken, interview with L. A. Sischo, Los Banos, California, May 7, 1938, Ralph Milliken Oral History Notebooks, JMW.

84. Treadwell, *Cattle King,* 319.

85. Latta, "William J. Browning."

86. Igler, *Industrial Cowboys,* 113, 176.

87. Miller, *Flooding the Courtrooms,* 120.

88. In an attempt to salvage the firm's finances, in 1922 Miller and Lux entered into an agreement with a local irrigation district and water storage district to create the San Joaquin River Water Storage District. The new district was to purchase Miller and Lux's water rights and construct a dam on the San Joaquin River where it emerges from the foothills of the Sierra Nevada at Friant, just above Millerton, the original seat of Fresno County. The dam would supply water to Miller and Lux and expand irrigation in the surrounding region. But the San Joaquin River Water Storage District died on the drawing board in 1928, scuttled by lingering disputes over water rights, flow schedules from the dam, and the acquisition by the district of the San Joaquin and Kings River Canal and Irrigation Company. Miller, *Flooding the Courtrooms,* 134–171. The chief engineer of the San Joaquin and Kings River Canal and Irrigation Company, Robert Maitland Brereton, had proposed a dam in the vicinity of Friant as early as 1871. Brereton, *Reminiscences of Irrigation-Enterprise,* 69; Bremer, "To Water the Valley," 30.

89. Miller and Lux pamphlet, "California Irrigated Lands in the Western San Joaquin Valley," no date but circa mid-1920s, box 12(2), Skyfarming Collection, FLC. Even Rancho Sanjon de Santa Rita went to the chopping block. A 1931 Miller and Lux pamphlet offered 40,983 acres, or about five-sixths of the original grant, for sale. "Rancho Sanjon de Santa Rita," MSS 70/154c, MLR.

4. RECLAMATION AND CONSERVATION IN THE SACRAMENTO VALLEY

1. The eleven counties that, in whole or in part, form the floor of the Sacramento Valley are Shasta, Tehama, Butte, Glenn, Colusa, Sutter, Yuba, Placer, Yolo, Sacramento, and Solano. Of these, Yolo, Sacramento, and Solano counties also form part of the Delta.

2. Michael J. Gillis and Michael F. Magliari, *John Bidwell and California: The Life and Writings of a Pioneer 1841–1900* (Spokane, Wash.: Arthur H. Clark, 2003), 130–151; Ian Tyrrell, *True Gardens of the Gods: Californian-Australian Environmental Reform, 1860–1930* (Berkeley and Los Angeles: University of California Press, 1999), especially 42. The reformers' ideal of diversified horticulture in the Sacramento Valley gradually gave way by the early years of the twentieth century to the industrialized production of single specialty crops. See Steven Stoll, *The Fruits of Natural Advantage: Making the Industrial Countryside in California* (Berkeley and Los Angeles: University of California Press, 1998); David Vaught, *Growers, Specialty Crops, and Labor, 1875–1920* (Baltimore, Md.: Johns Hopkins University Press, 1999).

3. Gillis and Magliari, *John Bidwell and California*, 116.

4. California State Agricultural Society, *Transactions of the California State Agricultural Society, during the Years 1866 and 1867* (Sacramento: State Printer, 1868), 422.

5. Heitmeyer, Connelly, and Pederson, "Central, Imperial, and Coachella Valleys," 477.

6. For the most comprehensive treatment of the attempts to prevent flooding in the Sacramento Valley and of the development of the Sacramento Flood Control Project, see Kelley, *Battling the Inland Sea*. For a compendium of the federal and state legislative actions that led to the Sacramento Flood Control Project, see E. A. Bailey, "Historical Summary of Federal Action and Its Resulting Effect upon the Sacramento Flood Control Project," Appendix C to *Sacramento Flood Control Project, Revised Plans* (Sacramento: State Printer, 1927); E. A. Bailey, "Historical Summary of State Legislative Action with Results Accomplished in Reclamation of Swamp and Overflowed Lands of Sacramento Valley, California," Appendix D to *Sacramento Flood Control Project, Revised Plans* (Sacramento: State Printer, 1927).

7. The Corps of Engineers had been responsible for maintaining and improving navigability of the nation's waterways ever since the U.S. Supreme Court had ruled in 1824 that, pursuant to the commerce clause of the Constitution, the federal government possessed authority over the country's navigable rivers. *Gibbons v. Ogden*, 22 U.S. 1 (1824).

8. Kelley, *Battling the Inland Sea*, 128–129.

9. It was not until after 1905 that the state, in cooperation with the U.S. Geological Survey, acquired truly comprehensive data on river flows.

10. Will S. Green, J. W. Bost, and Amos Matthews, "Report of the Commissioners on the Reclamation of Swamp Lands in the Sacramento Valley," Appendix to *Journals of Senate and Assembly of the Eighteenth Session of the Legislature of the State of California*, 1870.

11. Kelley, *Battling the Inland Sea*, 129–135.

12. Kelley, *Battling the Inland Sea*, 104.

13. *Woodruff, Edwards v. North Bloomfield Gravel Mining Co. et al.*, 18 F. 753 (9th Cir. 1884).

14. The definitive work on this epic struggle remains Kelley, *Gold vs. Grain*.

15. 1877–1878 *Statutes of California* ch. 429.

16. See William Hammond Hall, "The Irrigation Question in California," Appendix to the *Report of the State Engineer to the Governor of California* (Sacramento: State Printer, 1880).

17. William Hammond Hall, *Report of the State Engineer to the Legislature of California, Session of 1880* (Sacramento: State Printer, 1880), part 1, 10; emphasis in original. See also Kenneth Thompson, "Historic Flooding in the Sacramento Valley," *Pacific Historical Review* 29, no. 4 (1960): 350–352.

18. For the mathematical relations among discharge, velocity of flow, and the area (depth and width) of a river channel, see Mount, *California Rivers and Streams*, 18–19.

19. Hall, *Report of the State Engineer*, part 1, 10.

20. Hall, *Report of the State Engineer*, part 2, 14, 15.

21. 1880 *Statutes of California* ch. 117.

22. *The People v. Parks*, 58 Cal. 624 (1881).

23. Kelley, *Battling the Inland Sea*, 216.

24. 27 *Stat.* 507; Kelley, *Battling the Inland Sea*, 228–230.

25. 1893 *Statutes of California* ch. 232.

26. California Commissioner of Public Works, *Report to the Governor of California* (Sacramento: State Printer, 1895), 59.

27. Kelley, *Battling the Inland Sea*, 238–240.

28. T. G. Dabney et al., "Report of the Commission of Engineers to the Commissioner of Public Works," in the *Annual Report* of the California Commissioner of Public Works, 1905, 20.

29. Kelley, *Battling the Inland Sea*, 277.

30. California Debris Commission, *Reports on the Control of Floods in the River Systems of the Sacramento Valley and the Adjacent San Joaquin Valley, Cal.,* House of Representatives Document no. 81, 62d Congress, 1st session, 1911, 4.

31. 1911 (Extra Session) *Statutes of California* ch. 25.

32. 1913 *Statutes of California* 252; Kelley, *Battling the Inland Sea*, 288–289; California Department of Public Works, *Financial and General Data Pertaining to Irrigation,* 231; Kelley, "Taming the Sacramento," 41.

33. 39 *Stat.* 948. Kelley, *Battling the Inland Sea*, 269, 282–292. Although the corps accepted an expansion of its responsibilities from navigation to flood control, it continued to resist the concept of multiple use for water projects, which also encompassed irrigation and power production.

34. California Debris Commission, *Reports on the Control of Floods*, 14–15; Kelley, *Battling the Inland Sea*, 283. Additional features of the Sacramento Flood Control Project include Tisdale Weir, below Colusa, which allows additional Sacramento River water to flow into the Sutter Bypass; and the Sacramento Weir, which can release Sacramento River water into the Yolo Bypass, relieving pressure on the Sacramento River just above the point at which the American River empties into it.

35. To date, the Sacramento Flood Control Project has been successful in keeping the Sacramento River from turning the valley once again into an inland sea. But as recently as 1986 the system was sorely tested when a week of torrential February rainstorms sundered a major levee on the Yuba River, inundating the town of Linda, and threatened levees throughout the valley. At the flood's peak, 650,000 cubic feet per second of water passed through the Sacramento River at the capitol, 50,000 cfs more than the project had ever been designed to manage. The system held—barely. Ominously, however, were it not for the dams that have been constructed in the Sacramento Valley since the completion of the project (Shasta Dam on the Sacramento River in the 1940s, Folsom Dam on the American River in the 1950s, and Oroville Dam on the Feather River in the 1960s), which received more water during the storms than they released, the flow down the Sacramento River would have been greater still, exceeding a truly frightening one million cubic feet per second. Kelley, *Battling the Inland Sea*, 311–314.

36. McGowan, *History of the Sacramento Valley*, 2:174–176; Thompson and Dutra, *Tule Breakers*, 299–300, 304; Kelley, *Battling the Inland Sea*, 292; Thompson, "Settlement Geography of the Sacramento–San Joaquin Delta," 177.

37. Thompson and Dutra, *Tule Breakers*, 33, 101, 302, 314.

38. McGowan, *History of the Sacramento Valley*, 2:178. There were 32,000 additional acres of tule marsh in the smaller Sacramento Basin, south of the city of Sacramento and east of the Sacramento River.

39. Thompson and Dutra, *Tule Breakers*, 13. The level of the Sacramento River at the basin's southern outlets regulated the quantity of water retained in these basins. Only as the level of the Sacramento River fell below the water level in the basins at these points could the basins drain back into the river.

40. Thompson and Dutra, *Tule Breakers*, 288.

41. Thompson and Dutra, *Tule Breakers*, 288–294; McGowan, *History of the Sacramento Valley*, 1:286; Kelley, *Battling the Inland Sea*, 144–145; George Basye, "Short History of Reclamation District No. 108," in *Reclamation District No. 108 125th Anniversary, 1870–1995* (Grimes, Calif.: Reclamation District No. 108, 1995), 6–8; California Department of Water Resources, *Colusa Basin Investigation* (Sacramento: California Department of Water Resources, Bulletin no. 109, 1964), 24.

42. Thompson and Dutra, *Tule Breakers*, 303–304; McGowan, *History of the Sacramento Valley*, 2:177.

43. McGowan, *History of the Sacramento Valley*, 2:175; U.S. Fish and Wildlife Service, *Concept Plan for Waterfowl Wintering Habitat Preservation*, 33.

44. *Moulton v. Parks*, 64 Cal. 166 (1883). Kelley, *Battling the Inland Sea*, 146, 155–174.

45. Thompson and Dutra, *Tule Breakers*, 294–303.

46. Thompson and Dutra, *Tule Breakers*, 286–288; McGowan, *History of the Sacramento Valley*, 2:174–175. Much of the land in the American Basin is currently undergoing absorption into the greater Sacramento metropolis. The lowest-lying part, and the area most in danger of flooding in the case of levee failure, is known as the Natomas Basin, and is rapidly being converted to residential housing developments and large retail outlets.

47. California Department of Fish and Game, *Water Requirements for the Waterfowl of Butte Basin, California* (Sacramento: California Department of Fish and Game, 1967), 9; Kelley, *Battling the Inland Sea*, 115.

48. Butte Sink, with its chemical neutrality (neither acidic nor alkaline) and fresh water, differs from the alkaline marshes of the Grasslands of the San Joaquin Basin and from the brackish marshes of Suisun Bay.

49. California Department of Fish and Game, *Water Requirements for the Waterfowl of Butte Basin*, 13, 32, 41.

50. MSRB, November 16, 1913, 1:46.

51. MSRB, October 21, 1915, 2:755.

52. MSRB, June 27, 1918, 3:1602–1603.

53. Pisani, *From the Family Farm to Agribusiness*, 383.

54. Jones & Stokes, *Butte Sink Cooperative Management Plan: Final* (Sacramento: prepared in association with MBK Engineers and Lennihan Law for the California Waterfowl Association, Willows, Calif., 2001), 1–3.

55. MSRB, November 21, 1923, 6:3466–3467; emphasis added.

56. MSRB, November 25, 1924, 7:3844.

57. MSRB, November 25, 1924, 7:3845.

58. 1913 *Statutes of California* ch. 170.

59. MSRB, November 24, 1925, 8:4384. The lower part of the Butte Basin, including all of the Butte Sink, is located in northern Sutter County.

60. MSRB, November 24, 1925, 8:4386. In addition to the West Butte Country Club, the member organizations were the Sacramento Outing Club, North Butte Country Club, Buttes Land Company, South Butte Gun Club, and Maverick Club.

61. MSRB, November 24, 1925, 8:4385.

62. Jones & Stokes, *Butte Sink Cooperative Management Plan*, 1 - 3 - 1 - 4.

63. John B. Cowan, "Waterfowl History in the Sacramento Valley," *Outdoor California* 46, no. 1 (1985): 3.

64. Nicholas Wilson Hanson, *As I Remember* (Chico, Calif.: Broyles & Camper, 1944), 121.

65. Joseph G. Silveira, "Hunting Wild Geese in an Era before Sacramento National Wildlife Refuge," *California Waterfowl* 28, no. 5 (2001): 33; Tracy I. Storer, "Fish and Wildlife of the Sacramento Valley—Past and Present," *Outdoor California* 26, no. 8 (1965): 15; McGowan, *History of the Sacramento Valley*, 1:364–365. Glenn's estate, which he began to acquire in 1867 with the purchase of 7,000 acres of the Jacinto Mexican land grant, fronted the Sacramento River for twenty miles in northern Colusa (now Glenn) County and, by 1880, produced an astonishing one million bushels of wheat annually. Green, *History of Colusa County*, 52; Gillis and Magliari, *John Bidwell and California*, 134.

66. Cowan, "Waterfowl History in the Sacramento Valley," 5; McGowan, *History of the Sacramento Valley*, 1:364; Silveira, "Hunting Wild Geese," 34.

67. 1913 *Statutes of California* ch. 579; Seth Gordon, *California's Fish and Game Program: Report to the Wildlife Conservation Board* (Sacramento: Senate of the State of California, 1950), 26–27; Howard R. Leach, "An Historical Account of Waterfowling, San Joaquin Valley, California: 1870–1970" (unpublished), 34–35; Joseph Grinnell, Harold Child Bryant, and Tracy Irwin Storer, *The Game Birds of California* (Berkeley: University of California Press, 1918), 11–12; W. P. Taylor, "Synopsis of the Recent Campaign for the Conservation of Wild Life in California," *The Condor* 15, no. 3 (1913).

68. McGowan, *History of the Sacramento Valley*, 1:369; Grinnell, Bryant, and Storer, *Game Birds of California*, 11–12, 55–60. A new federal presence in wildlife protection, expanding since 1900 and culminating in the 1916 Migratory Bird Treaty with Canada, would finally end the legal wholesale slaughter of waterfowl. See chapter 6.

69. Historian Samuel Hays demonstrated that the key issue in the turn-of-the-century conservation movement was resource use rather than resource ownership. See Samuel P. Hays, *Conservation and the Gospel of Efficiency: The Progressive Conservation Movement, 1890–1920* (Cambridge, Mass.: Harvard University Press, 1959; repr. Pittsburgh, Pa.: University of Pittsburgh Press, 1999), especially 262.

70. For studies that investigate the dispossession of subsistence hunters in the face of externally imposed hunting restrictions, see Louis S. Warren, *The Hunter's Game: Poachers and Conservationists in Twentieth-Century America* (New Haven, Conn.: Yale University Press, 1997); Karl Jacoby, *Crimes against Nature: Squatters, Poachers, Thieves, and the Hidden History of American Conservation* (Berkeley and Los Angeles: University of California Press, 2001). For the dispossession of Native Americans in particular, see Mark

David Spence, *Dispossessing the Wilderness: Indian Removal and the Making of the National Parks* (New York: Oxford University Press, 1999).

71. George Bird Grinnell and Charles B. Reynolds, "A Plank," *Forest and Stream* 62, no. 5 (1894): 89. Among his many conservation credentials, Grinnell founded the Audubon Society in 1886 and was a cofounder, along with Theodore Roosevelt, of the Boone and Crockett Club in 1887. For the prominent role of sportsmen in the genesis of the conservation movement in the United States, see John F. Reiger, *American Sportsmen and the Origins of Conservation,* 3rd ed. (Corvallis: Oregon State University Press, 2001); James B. Trefethen, *An American Crusade for Wildlife* (New York: Winchester Press, 1975).

72. James A. Tober, *Who Owns the Wildlife? The Political Economy of Conservation in Nineteenth-Century America* (Westport, Conn.: Greenwood Press, 1981), 55, 130. See also John B. Cowan, "Outlaw Hunters Waged War on Ducks," *Outdoor California* 53, no. 1 (1992); John B. Cowan, "Federal War on Market Hunters," *Outdoor California* 53, no. 2 (1992); Albert M. Day, *North American Waterfowl,* 2nd ed. (Harrisburg, Pa.: Stackpole, 1959).

73. Grinnell, Bryant, and Storer, *Game Birds of California,* 6.

74. Grinnell, Bryant, and Storer, *Game Birds of California,* 9–10.

75. Grinnell, Bryant, and Storer, *Game Birds of California,* 11, 13, 18. Just four years later, with these new game restrictions in place, the number of ducks sold in San Francisco and statewide fell to 75,000 and 125,000, respectively.

76. Grinnell, Bryant, and Storer, *Game Birds of California,* 23–28.

77. Southern Pacific and other railroads actively promoted hunting of all kinds in California. By routing lines through or near the best hunting grounds, railroads could serve the needs of sportsmen while increasing the volume of their traffic. Southern Pacific in particular published a number of books and pamphlets to entice sportsmen to explore California in search of fish and game, including Southern Pacific, *California Game: Marked Down* (San Francisco: Southern Pacific, 1896); and Southern Pacific, *California for the Sportsman: Being a Collection of Hints as to the Haunts of the Wild Things of Hoof, Claw, Scale and Feather of California's Land and Water—the Way to Reach Them, and Some Suggestions as to Approved Methods of Capture* (San Francisco: Southern Pacific, 1911). The latter volume extols the virtues of goose and duck hunting in the Central Valley at length, devoting nearly ten pages of closely spaced text to this topic alone.

78. M. Hall McAllister, "The Early History of Duck Clubs in California," *California Fish and Game* 16, no. 4 (1930): 283–284; Anthony Arnold, *Suisun Marsh History: Hunting and Saving a Wetland* (Marina, Calif.: Monterey Pacific, 1996), 17–29.

79. M. Hall McAllister, "Wild Goose Shooting in California Twenty-Five Years Ago," *California Fish and Game* 15, no. 3 (1929): 217.

80. McGowan, *History of the Sacramento Valley,* 1:367; Leach, "Historical Account of Waterfowling," 46.

81. Grinnell, Bryant, and Storer, *Game Birds of California,* 25, 28.

82. California State Agricultural Society, *Transactions of the California State Agricultural Society during the Year 1858* (Sacramento: State Printer, 1859), 70; J. H. Willson, "Rice in California," in *Rice in California,* ed. Jack H. Willson (Richvale, Calif.: Butte County Rice Growers Association, 1979), 24.

83. Sucheng Chan, *This Bittersweet Soil: The Chinese in California Agriculture, 1860–1910* (Berkeley and Los Angeles: University of California Press, 1986), 82.

84. Willson, "Rice in California," 24–25.

85. Willson, "Rice in California," 35–37. Cool temperatures in the Delta are a consequence of the so-called Delta breeze, a flow of cool air from the Pacific Ocean that passes through the Golden Gate and significantly lowers temperatures in the San Francisco Bay region as well as the Delta and adjacent portions of the Central Valley, especially in the late afternoon and evening.

86. Willson, "Rice in California," 37–38; Masakazu Iwata, *Planted in Good Soil: A History of the Issei in United States Agriculture*, 2 vols. (New York: Peter Lang, 1992), 1:306–307; Chan, *This Bittersweet Soil*, 269–270.

87. Morton D. Morse and Gary M. Lindberg, "The Rice Experiment Station," in *Rice in California*, ed. Jack H. Willson (Richvale, Calif.: Butte County Rice Growers Association, 1979), 41–42, 45.

88. With the exception of the period from 1927 to 1953 when rice was grown on a limited scale in the Imperial Valley at the extreme southern end of the state, the Central Valley has produced the entire California commercial rice crop. Within the Central Valley, rice did not become as important in the San Joaquin Valley as in the Sacramento Valley because the former generally has better soils, which can support higher-value crops. Nevertheless, the San Joaquin Valley counties of Fresno, San Joaquin, and Merced produce sizable quantities of rice, and smaller acreages are harvested in Kern, Kings, Madera, Stanislaus, and Tulare counties. Willson, "Rice in California," 39.

89. Milton D. Miller and D. Marlin Brandon, "Evolution of California Rice Culture," in *Rice in California*, ed. Jack H. Willson (Richvale, Calif.: Butte County Rice Growers Association, 1979), 79–80. More technically, many of these basin soils are saline and sodic. Sodic soils are alkaline soils with a pH greater than 8.3 and with a high concentration of sodium. Sodic soils may be nonsaline or saline, and historically were classified as black alkali and white alkali, respectively. Black alkali soils have extremely poor structure, a consequence of their chemistry, and are generally unsuitable for agriculture. White alkali soils can be farmed, providing the crop is salt-tolerant, and preferably if the excess salts can be leached from the soil profile. For a more detailed discussion of problems associated with saline and sodic soils, see Michael J. Singer and Donald N. Munns, *Soils: An Introduction* (Upper Saddle River, N.J.: Prentice Hall, 1999), 297–302.

90. Miller and Brandon, "Evolution of California Rice Culture," 127.

91. McGowan, *History of the Sacramento Valley*, 2:248–249.

5. THE SACRAMENTO–SAN JOAQUIN DELTA AND THE CENTRAL VALLEY PROJECT'S ORIGINS

1. California Department of Water Resources, *Sacramento–San Joaquin Delta Atlas*, 91. The Delta comprises parts of six counties: eastern Solano and southern Yolo and Sacramento counties at the southern extreme of the Sacramento Valley, and eastern Contra Costa, northeastern Alameda, and western San Joaquin counties at the northern extreme of the San Joaquin Valley. The major portion of the Delta lies within San Joaquin County.

2. Heitmeyer, Connelly, and Pederson, "Central, Imperial, and Coachella Valleys," 480; Thompson and Dutra, *Tule Breakers*, 18; California Department of Water Resources, *Sacramento–San Joaquin Delta Atlas*, 26.

3. Thompson, "Settlement Geography of the Sacramento–San Joaquin Delta," 39, 52; Thompson and Dutra, *Tule Breakers*, 327; John Thompson, *Discovering and Rediscovering the Fragility of Levees and Land in the Sacramento–San Joaquin Delta, 1870–1879 and Today* (Sacramento: California Department of Water Resources, Central District, 1982), 4–6.

4. George H. Tinkham, *History of San Joaquin County California* (Los Angeles: Historic Record Company, 1923), 35–36.

5. Tinkham, *History of San Joaquin County*, 35.

6. Thompson, "Settlement Geography of the Sacramento–San Joaquin Delta," 153–155. See also Mount, *California Rivers and Streams*, 202–226.

7. Thompson and Dutra, *Tule Breakers*, 19.

8. The details of Delta reclamation were meticulously documented by historical geographer John Thompson in "Settlement Geography of the Sacramento–San Joaquin Delta," 218–238, 468–509.

9. In addition to the vast freshwater wetlands of the Delta itself, an estimated additional 197,000 acres of brackish marshland historically lay at about the level of mean high tide in Suisun, San Pablo, and San Francisco bays. Thompson and Dutra, *Tule Breakers*, 13, 327; Heitmeyer, Connelly, and Pederson, "Central, Imperial, and Coachella Valleys," 480; California Department of Water Resources, *Sacramento–San Joaquin Delta Atlas*, 91.

10. These extreme measures followed in the wake of the Foreign Miners' Tax Law of 1852, which targeted the Chinese by imposing a monthly fee on "aliens ineligible for citizenship." When the law failed to displace the Chinese, angry whites took matters into their own hands. Hostility toward the Chinese culminated in the federal Chinese Exclusion Act of 1882, which barred the admission of Chinese laborers. The Chinese Exclusion Act was not repealed until 1943, at which time China was a World War II ally of the United States. Chinese immigrants then became eligible for naturalized citizenship.

11. George Chu, "Chinatowns in the Delta: The Chinese in the Sacramento–San Joaquin Delta, 1870–1960," *California Historical Society Quarterly* 49, no. 1 (1970): 24 (quote), 25. For the role of the Chinese in the development of California's agriculture, see Chan, *This Bittersweet Soil,* and for the Delta specifically, see 158–191.

12. Thompson, "Settlement Geography of the Sacramento–San Joaquin Delta," 290–293.

13. W. A. Slocum & Co., *History of Contra Costa County, California* (San Francisco: W. A. Slocum, 1882), 54; emphasis in original.

14. J. P. Whitney, *Fresh Water Tide Lands of California* (Cambridge, Mass.: Riverside Press, 1873), 17.

15. Reclamation required not only the construction of levees, but also drainage of inundated tracts. The first drainage pump was installed at Ryde, on Grand Island in 1876, and by 1879 steam-powered pumps began to be added to the drainage systems of Delta tracts. Thompson, "Settlement Geography of the Sacramento–San Joaquin Delta," 265, 277; Thompson and Dutra, *Tule Breakers*, 130, 172.

16. Thompson and Dutra, *Tule Breakers*, 18.

17. Thompson, "Discovering and Rediscovering the Fragility of Levees and Land," 27, 30; California Department of Water Resources, *Sacramento–San Joaquin Delta Atlas*, 28.

18. Walker R. Young, *Report on Salt Water Barrier below Confluence of Sacramento and San Joaquin Rivers, California* (Sacramento: California Department of Public Works, Division of Water Resources, Bulletin no. 22, 1929), 46; Thompson, "Settlement Geography of the Sacramento–San Joaquin Delta," 57.

19. John Hart and David Sanger, *San Francisco Bay: Portrait of an Estuary* (Berkeley and Los Angeles: University of California Press, 2003), 81; Heitmeyer, Connelly, and Pederson, "Central, Imperial, and Coachella Valleys," 480–481; Arnold, *Suisun Marsh History*, 77–83.

20. The Sacramento River carries its peak monthly flows from January to May; the San Joaquin River peaks from March to June. Salt water generally reaches its maximum penetration by September 1, toward the end of the Central Valley's long dry season. Thompson, "Settlement Geography of the Sacramento–San Joaquin Delta," 22, 30. The San Joaquin Valley watershed provided 21 percent of Delta inflow; the remaining 5 percent came from local watercourses that flowed directly into the Delta. Thompson, "Settlement Geography of the Sacramento–San Joaquin Delta," 25.

21. Jackson and Paterson, *Sacramento–San Joaquin Delta*, 2; Pisani, *From the Family Farm to Agribusiness*, 383.

22. Jackson and Paterson, *Sacramento–San Joaquin Delta*, 5–6; Pisani, *From the Family Farm to Agribusiness*, 384–385.

23. *Town of Antioch v. Williams Irrigation District*, 188 Cal. 451, 465 (1922). Under California law, incorporated municipalities may refer to themselves as a "city" or a "town" (*California Government Code*, sec. 34500–34504). For consistency in the text, however, I have used the word *city* to refer only to incorporated municipalities, and *town* to refer only to settlements that either became incorporated after the time period under discussion or remain unincorporated.

24. Jackson and Paterson, *Sacramento–San Joaquin Delta*, 7.

25. Jackson and Paterson, *Sacramento–San Joaquin Delta*, 7–8.

26. Igler, *Industrial Cowboys*, 72–79; W. Turrentine Jackson, Rand F. Herbert, and Stephen R. Wee, eds., *Engineers and Irrigation: Report of the Board of Commissioners on the Irrigation of the San Joaquin, Tulare, and Sacramento Valleys of the State of California, 1873* (Fort Belvoir, Va.: U.S. Army Corps of Engineers, 1990), 9–14; Pisani, *From the Family Farm to Agribusiness*, 105–112.

27. Alexander, Davidson, and Mendell, *Report of the Board of Commissioners on the Irrigation of the San Joaquin, Tulare, and Sacramento Valleys*, 4.

28. Alexander, Davidson, and Mendell, *Report of the Board of Commissioners on the Irrigation of the San Joaquin, Tulare, and Sacramento Valleys*, 78.

29. Lawrence B. Lee, "Environmental Implications of Government Reclamation in California," in *Agriculture in the Development of the Far West*, ed. James H. Shideler (Washington, D.C.: Agricultural History Society, 1975), 224.

30. For the early failures of irrigation district plans, see Pisani, *From the Family Farm to Agribusiness*, 129–153.

31. Hall, "Irrigation Question in California," 18 (quote); William Hammond Hall, "Irrigation in California," *National Geographic Magazine* 1, no. 4 (1889): 13.

32. 1887 *Statutes of California* ch. 34.

33. Pisani, *From the Family Farm to Agribusiness,* 252–256.

34. For the shortcomings of the Wright Act, see Pisani, *From the Family Farm to Agribusiness,* 256–273. Of the seven irrigation districts formed in the Sacramento Valley, only one—the Browns Valley District near Marysville—succeeded. In the San Joaquin Valley, the Turlock and Modesto irrigation districts, the first two districts formed under the act in 1887, were successful and are still in existence. Frank Adams, *Irrigation Districts of California 1887–1915* (Sacramento: California Department of Engineering, Bulletin no. 2, 1916), 9.

35. 1897 *Statutes of California* ch. 189.

36. Hundley, *Great Thirst,* 101–102.

37. Pisani, *From the Family Farm to Agribusiness,* 278.

38. John Wesley Powell, *Report on the Lands of the Arid Region of the United States* (Washington, D.C.: Government Printing Office, 1879).

39. Donald Worster, *A River Running West: The Life of John Wesley Powell* (Oxford and New York: Oxford University Press, 2001), 475–477, 504–506.

40. William E. Smythe, *The Conquest of Arid America,* ed. Lawrence B. Lee (Seattle: University of Washington Press, 1969), 266–267. For Smythe's views on the benefits that irrigation would bring to California, see 121–160.

41. Lawrence B. Lee, "Introduction to Smythe," in Smythe, *Conquest of Arid America,* xxi–xxxv; Martin E. Carlson, "William E. Smythe: Irrigation Crusader," *Journal of the West* 12, no. 1 (1968).

42. Smythe, *Conquest of Arid America,* 273–274.

43. 32 *Stat.* 388.

44. Pisani, *From the Family Farm to Agribusiness,* 290–301; Hundley, *Great Thirst,* 117; Lee, "Environmental Implications of Government Reclamation," 225. Support for the Newlands Act was far from universal. Opposition to the act came not only from eastern politicians, who feared agricultural competition from the West, but also from those who believed that reclamation should be organized and promoted by individual states. Prominent among the latter critics was Elwood Mead, in charge of the Office of Irrigation Investigations (established in 1898 within the U.S. Department of Agriculture's Office of Experiment Stations), who argued that federal reclamation should be restricted to federal public lands. See U.S. Department of Agriculture, *Report of Irrigation Investigations in California;* Donald J. Pisani, *To Reclaim a Divided West: Water, Law, and Public Policy, 1848–1902* (Albuquerque: University of New Mexico Press, 1992), 298–319.

45. The Reclamation Act applied to the thirteen states of California, Colorado, Idaho, Kansas, Montana, Nebraska, Nevada, North Dakota, Oregon, South Dakota, Utah, Washington, and Wyoming, and the territories of Oklahoma (admitted to statehood in 1907) and Arizona and New Mexico (both admitted to statehood in 1912). Texas, which had no federal lands, was included in the Reclamation Act in 1906.

46. 32 *Stat.* 389, sec. 5.

47. 12 *Stat.* 410.

48. Although the bureau soon relaxed the 160-acre requirement to allow that a husband and wife could each claim water for 160 acres of irrigable land, thereby increasing the size of a family farm on reclamation projects to 320 acres, the issue of excess lands was to remain contentious throughout most of the twentieth century.

49. William E. Warne, *The Bureau of Reclamation* (New York: Praeger, 1973), 70–76. Two acts, the Reclamation Extension Act of 1914 (38 *Stat.* 686) and the Omnibus Adjustment Act of 1926 (44 *Stat.* 649), attempted to resolve the excess land problem by requiring the sale of excess lands at nonspeculative prices, upon penalty of project water being withheld from such lands. The acts met with only limited success.

50. Acreage figures for the Orland Project are from Pisani, *From the Family Farm to Agribusiness,* 329–330. The acreage figure for the Sacramento Valley is from California Department of Public Works, *Report to the Legislature of 1931: State Water Plan* (Sacramento: California Department of Public Works, Division of Water Resources, Bulletin no. 25, 1930). Two additional reservoirs, Stony Gorge Reservoir and Black Butte Lake, were later impounded on Stony Creek below East Park Dam. Both are in Glenn County.

51. Pisani, *From the Family Farm to Agribusiness,* 331–334.

52. 1911 *Statutes of California* ch. 408.

53. 1913 *Statutes of California* ch. 586. The Water Commission became the Water Rights Division of the Department of Public Works in 1921.

54. See California State Water Problems Conference, *Report of the State Water Problems Conference* (Sacramento: State Printer, 1916). The conference was convened pursuant to a legislative act of the previous year: 1915 *Statutes of California* ch. 359.

55. 1921 *Statutes of California* ch. 889.

56. The expansion of state authority over water management that had begun under Hiram Johnson's administration continued with the creation of water storage districts in 1921 and water conservation districts in 1923. 1921 *Statutes of California* ch. 914; 1923 *Statutes of California* ch. 426.

57. Hundley, *Great Thirst,* 247–252.

58. California Department of Public Works, *Water Resources of California: A Report to the Legislature of 1923* (Sacramento: California Department of Public Works, Division of Engineering and Irrigation, Bulletin no. 4, 1923).

59. U.S. House of Representatives, *Central Valley Project Documents,* part 1: *Authorizing Documents,* House Document no. 416, 84th Congress, 2d session, 1956, 5; California Department of Public Works, *Report to the Legislature of 1931: State Water Plan,* 56.

60. Robert Bradford Marshall, *Irrigation of Twelve Million Acres in the Valley of California* (Sacramento: California State Irrigation Association, 1920). For more on the history and fate of Marshall's plan, see Pisani, *From the Family Farm to Agribusiness,* 394–408; Hundley, *Great Thirst,* 243–244.

61. California Department of Public Works, *Supplemental Report on Water Resources of California: A Report to the Legislature of 1925* (Sacramento: California Department of Public Works, Division of Engineering and Irrigation, Bulletin no. 9, 1925); U.S. House of Representatives, *Central Valley Project Documents,* part 1: *Authorizing Documents,* 5.

62. California Department of Public Works, *Summary Report on the Water Resources of California and a Coordinated Plan for Their Development: A Report to the Legislature of 1927* (Sacramento: California Department of Public Works, Division of Engineering and Irrigation, Bulletin no. 12, 1927).

63. 1927 *Statutes of California* ch. 30.

64. 200 Cal. 81.

65. 1927 *Statutes of California* ch. 67. This provision was adopted as part of article XIV, sec. 3 of the Constitution of California on November 6, 1928.

66. In a groundbreaking 1983 decision (*National Audubon Society v. Superior Court*, 33 Cal. 3d 419), the California Supreme Court first ruled that the California Constitution's requirement of reasonable use applied to public-trust resources, including the waters of Mono Lake, the second largest lake in California after Lake Tahoe and an important avian feeding ground along the Pacific Flyway. At the time of the decision, for four decades the Los Angeles Department of Water and Power had been siphoning the tributary streams of Pleistocene age Mono Lake, on the eastern side of the Sierra Nevada, to serve the needs of its urban population, thereby causing grave deterioration of the lake's ecosystem. See John Hart, *Storm over Mono: The Mono Lake Battle and the California Water Future* (Berkeley and Los Angeles: University of California Press, 1996); California State Water Resources Control Board, Mono Lake Basin Water Right Decision no. 1631 (1994).

67. 1929 *Statutes of California* ch. 561.

68. In its 1927 report, the Division of Engineering and Irrigation had not yet dropped the saltwater barrier concept, which had resurfaced in the wake of the Antioch lawsuit, but had concluded that at least initially, it would not be necessary. Both the Joint Legislative Water Problems Committee and the Hoover-Young Commission went a step further and rejected the saltwater barrier as impractical and excessively expensive. Instead, the Delta would be protected from salinity intrusion by freshwater releases from a dam and reservoir on the upper Sacramento River. Jackson and Paterson, *Sacramento–San Joaquin Delta*, 21–24. See California Department of Public Works, *Economic Aspects of a Salt Water Barrier below Confluence of Sacramento and San Joaquin Rivers* (Sacramento: California Department of Public Works, Division of Water Resources, Bulletin no. 28, 1931).

69. California Department of Public Works, *Report to the Legislature of 1931: State Water Plan;* Jackson and Paterson, "*Sacramento–San Joaquin Delta,* 29 (quote). In 1929 the Division of Engineering and Irrigation was incorporated into a new Division of Water Resources.

70. The Contra Costa Conduit was necessary because the operation of Kennett Dam, without the saltwater barrier, would guarantee fresh water only as far as Antioch, at the western edge of the Delta, and not to points farther west in Contra Costa County. California Department of Public Works, *Report to the Legislature of 1931: State Water Plan,* 35–47, 56.

71. California Department of Public Works, *San Joaquin River Basin* (Sacramento: California Department of Public Works, Division of Water Resources, Bulletin no. 29, 1931), 66.

72. Hundley, *Great Thirst,* 246–247.

73. Jackson and Paterson, *Sacramento–San Joaquin Delta*, 6, 30; California Department of Water Resources, *Sacramento–San Joaquin Delta Atlas*, 22.

74. 1933 *Statutes of California* ch. 1042.

75. The Central Valley Project Act allowed for the construction of additional units in the future. During the early years of the project, Congress authorized three additional divisions: the American River Division in 1949, which consisted of the Folsom and Nimbus dams on the American River, along with their reservoirs and power plants; the Sacramento Canals Division in 1950, which provided a canal system to serve the area between Red Bluff and Colusa; and the Trinity River Division in 1955, which includes Whiskeytown Reservoir and power plants that deliver Trinity River water into the Sacramento Valley from the northwest. U.S. House of Representatives, *Central Valley Project Documents*, part 1: *Authorizing Documents*, 13.

76. U.S. House of Representatives, *Central Valley Project Documents*, part 1: *Authorizing Documents*, 409; Pisani, *From the Family Farm to Agribusiness*, 434–436.

77. 49 *Stat.* 1028.

78. U.S. House of Representatives, *Central Valley Project Documents*, part 1: *Authorizing Documents*, 562–567; Pisani, *From the Family Farm to Agribusiness*, 437.

79. 50 *Stat.* 844. In 1923, the Reclamation Service was renamed the Bureau of Reclamation. The director's title was abolished, and replaced by that of commissioner.

80. 54 *Stat.* 1198.

81. In addition to the sources previously cited, a useful study of the genesis and early years of the Central Valley Project is Mary Montgomery and Marion Clawson, *History of Legislation and Policy Formation of the Central Valley Project* (Berkeley, Calif.: U.S. Department of Agriculture, Bureau of Agricultural Economics, 1946). See also Robert de Roos, *The Thirsty Land: The Story of the Central Valley Project* (Stanford, Calif.: Stanford University Press, 1948); Paul S. Taylor, "Central Valley Project: Water and Land," *The Western Political Quarterly* 2 (1949); William L. Kahrl, ed., *The California Water Atlas* (Sacramento: Governor's Office of Planning and Research, 1979), 47–50.

82. Shasta and Friant dams were completed in 1944; the Delta-Mendota Canal made its first delivery of water to the San Joaquin Valley in 1951. During the late 1940s, the Bureau of Reclamation's position on salinity control gradually shifted away from protection for the Delta as a whole to only providing that fresh water be available at the diversion points for the Delta Mendota and Contra Costa canals, based on the operational requirements of the export pumps. Jackson and Paterson, *Sacramento–San Joaquin Delta*, 50. This development accounts, in part, for unresolved water quality issues in the Delta that have continued into the twenty-first century. See chapter 10 for further discussion of this point.

83. Frayer, Peters, and Pywell, *Wetlands of the California Central Valley*, 17.

6. TURNING THE TIDE

1. *Geer v. Connecticut*, 161 U.S. 519 (1896).

2. Tober, *Who Owns the Wildlife?* 150.

3. 31 *Stat.* 187. The full name of the act was the Lacey Game and Wild Birds Preservation and Disposition Act.

4. Michael J. Bean and Melanie J. Rowland, *The Evolution of National Wildlife Law*, 3rd ed. (Westport, Conn.: Praeger, 1997), 15–16; Kurkpatrick Dorsey, *The Dawn of Conservation Diplomacy: U.S.-Canadian Wildlife Protective Treaties in the Progressive Era* (Seattle: University of Washington Press, 1998), 180–181. Amended and expanded in 1981 (Public Law 97–79, 95 *Stat.* 1073), the Lacey Act remains an important tool in the regulation of the illegal take of fish and wildlife.

5. Trefethen, *American Crusade for Wildlife*, 147.

6. H.R. 15601.

7. The origins of the Bureau of Biological Survey date back to 1885, when Congress created the Division of Economic Ornithology and Mammalogy within the Department of Agriculture. Reorganized as the Division of Biological Survey in 1896, the agency was elevated to the status of the Bureau of Biological Survey in 1905.

8. Dorsey, *Dawn of Conservation Diplomacy*, 183–191; Trefethen, *American Crusade for Wildlife*, 149–152.

9. *United States v. Shauver*, 214 F. 154 (E.D. Ark. 1914) and *United States v. McCullagh*, 221 F. 288 (D. Kan. 1915); Tober, *Who Owns the Wildlife?* 161.

10. 39 *Stat.* 1702, T.S. no. 628.

11. 40 *Stat.* 755; Dorsey, *Dawn of Conservation Diplomacy*, 192–231. See also Bean and Rowland, *Evolution of National Wildlife Law*, 15–18; Day, *North American Waterfowl*, 42–49; Trefethen, *American Crusade for Wildlife*, 153–155.

12. Dorsey, *Dawn of Conservation Diplomacy*, 231–236.

13. *State of Missouri v. Holland, United States Game Warden*, 252 U.S. 416, 435 (1920).

14. The United States has since entered into three additional protective covenants, with Mexico, Japan, and the former Soviet Union. Respectively, these treaties are the Convention for the Protection of Migratory Birds and Game Mammals, February 7, 1936, United States–Mexico, 50 *Stat.* 1311, T.S. no. 912; Convention for the Protection of Migratory Birds and Birds in Danger of Extinction, and Their Environment, March 4, 1972, United States–Japan, 25 U.S.T. 3329; and Convention Concerning the Conservation of Migratory Birds and Their Environment, November 19, 1976, United States–U.S.S.R., 29 U.S.T. 4647.

15. The number of North American waterfowl species would later be altered by modern taxonomic methods.

16. Cooke, *Distribution and Migration of North American Ducks, Geese, and Swans*, 15.

17. Day, *North American Waterfowl*, 58; Hawkins, "U.S. Response," 2. The USBS had undertaken its study of bird migration four years earlier, in 1916, when biologist Alexander Wetmore banded several hundred ducks, herons, and other marsh and shore birds in the Bear River Marshes of Utah's Great Salt Lake. Lincoln, *Waterfowl Flyways of North America*, 2.

18. Lincoln, *Waterfowl Flyways of North America*, 1.

19. Lincoln, *Waterfowl Flyways of North America*, 2.

20. See Robert M. Wilson, "Seeking Refuge: Making Space for Migratory Waterfowl and Wetlands along the Pacific Flyway," PhD diss., University of British Columbia, 2003, especially 67–96; Langston, *Where Land and Water Meet*, especially 63–90.

21. Clear Lake and Tule Lake national wildlife refuges in northeastern California, for example, were created in 1911 and 1928, respectively; both served the waterfowl of the Klamath Basin. The Norbeck-Andreson Act (45 *Stat.* 1222) was named after its sponsors, South Dakota senator Peter Norbeck and Minnesota congressman August Andreson.

22. W. B. Bell and Edward A. Preble, *Status of Waterfowl in 1934* (Washington, D.C.: Department of Agriculture, Miscellaneous Publication no. 210, 1934). The continental waterfowl population is estimated to have fallen to a nadir of approximately 27 million by the winter of 1934–1935. W. G. Leitch, *Ducks and Men: Forty Years of Co-Operation in Conservation* (Winnipeg, Manitoba: Ducks Unlimited [Canada], 1978), 9. This widely cited figure is based on the first organized inventory of waterfowl wintering grounds in the United States, conducted in January 1935. The survey was later expanded to include wintering areas in Alaska, Canada, Mexico, and the West Indies. As described in the text below, the first continental survey of waterfowl breeding grounds was not completed until the summer of 1935. Surveys of breeding grounds return much higher population numbers than surveys of wintering grounds because the former are conducted prior to seasonal losses caused by migration, hunting, predation, and winter weather.

23. Jared Orsi, "From Horicon to Hamburgers and Back Again: Ecology, Ideology, and Wildlife Management, 1917–1935," *Environmental History Review* 18, no. 4 (1994): 30–31.

24. Day, *North American Waterfowl*, 300; Jon R. Tennyson, *A Singleness of Purpose: The Story of Ducks Unlimited* (Chicago: Ducks Unlimited, 1977), 13–14.

25. More Game Birds in America, *More Waterfowl by Assisting Nature* (New York: More Game Birds in America, 1931).

26. Tennyson, *Singleness of Purpose*, 20–23; Leitch, *Ducks and Men*, 14; Day, *North American Waterfowl*, 300–301.

27. Leitch, *Ducks and Men*, 14; Tennyson, *Singleness of Purpose*, 36.

28. Philip A. Du Mont and Henry M. Reeves, "The Darling-Salyer Team," in *Flyways: Pioneering Waterfowl Management in North America*, ed. A. S. Hawkins et al. (Washington, D.C.: U.S. Department of the Interior, Fish and Wildlife Service, 1984), 107–108.

29. Arthur S. Hawkins, "Portraits: Aldo Leopold," in *Flyways: Pioneering Waterfowl Management in North America*, ed. A. S. Hawkins et al. (Washington, D.C.: U.S. Department of the Interior, Fish and Wildlife Service, 1984), 103.

30. Aldo Leopold, *Game Management* (New York: Charles Scribner's Sons, 1933). Outside the circle of wildlife management professionals, Leopold is perhaps best known for *A Sand County Almanac*, published posthumously in 1949. This collection of timeless essays prescribes an ethical foundation for human relationships with the land and its nonhuman inhabitants, and remains a seminal work in support of environmentalism. Aldo Leopold, *A Sand County Almanac* (New York: Oxford University Press, 1949).

31. 48 *Stat.* 451; Bean and Rowland, *The Evolution of National Wildlife Law*, 284. The Migratory Bird Conservation Act established the Migratory Bird Conservation Fund. The fund was supplemented in 1961 by the Wetlands Loan Act (75 *Stat.* 813), which authorized an advance appropriation, without interest, to be used to accelerate the acquisition of wetlands. To encourage nonhunters to contribute to the Migratory Bird Conservation

Fund, a 1976 amendment to the Wetlands Loan Act changed the name of the stamp to the "migratory bird hunting *and conservation* stamp" (emphasis added).

32. This figure comes from the U.S. Fish and Wildlife Service, Federal Duck Stamp Program, www.fws.gov/duckstamps/federal/sales/sales.htm.

33. The Pittman-Robertson Act was named after its sponsors, Nevada senator Key Pittman and Virginia congressman A. Willis Robertson.

34. Henry M. Reeves, "FWS Operating Branches," in *Flyways: Pioneering Waterfowl Management in North America,* ed. A.S. Hawkins et al. (Washington, D.C.: U.S. Department of the Interior, Fish and Wildlife Service, 1984), 357.

35. Leitch, *Ducks and Men,* 16; Tennyson, *Singleness of Purpose,* 41–51.

36. Leitch, *Ducks and Men,* 19, 21; Tennyson, *Singleness of Purpose,* 65. In 1970 Mexico joined the Ducks Unlimited partnership, with the formation of Ducks Unlimited de México; Tennyson, *Singleness of Purpose,* 111.

37. Leitch, *Ducks and Men,* 67–71. After 1947, owing to discrepancies between Ducks Unlimited's figures and the lower figures of the U.S. Fish and Wildlife Service, the two organizations, along with the Dominion Wildlife Service (succeeded by the Canadian Wildlife Service in 1950), decided that instead of publishing annual population figures, they would express changes in populations from year to year as trends or indices. Victor E.F. Solman, "The Canadian Response," in *Flyways: Pioneering Waterfowl Management in North America,* ed. A.S. Hawkins et al. (Washington, D.C.: U.S. Department of the Interior, Fish and Wildlife Service, 1984), 12.

38. Day, *North American Waterfowl,* 167.

39. Ira N. Gabrielson, *Wildlife Refuges* (New York: Macmillan, 1943), 137.

40. Hugh M. Worcester, *Hunting the Lawless* (Berkeley, Calif.: American Wildlife Associates, 1955), especially 50–51.

41. Worcester, *Hunting the Lawless,* 47–49, 55–58.

42. In 1939 the Bureau of Biological Survey in the Department of Agriculture was transferred to the Department of the Interior. The next year, the Bureau of Biological Survey was consolidated with the Bureau of Fisheries and reorganized as the Fish and Wildlife Service.

43. Worcester, *Hunting the Lawless,* 69–116.

44. Cowan, "Outlaw Hunters Waged War on Ducks," 2. By comparison, waterfowl taken legally on the Sacramento National Wildlife Refuge after it was opened to public hunting in 1963 averaged only one-tenth of this figure annually. Frank Arthur Hall Jr., "An Environmental History of the Sacramento National Wildlife Refuge," MA thesis, California State University, Chico, 1975, 106.

45. Worcester, *Hunting the Lawless,* 214–250. See also "Memo to Regional Director L.L. Laythe, Region No. 1, from Game Management Agents Hugh M. Worcester and C.G. Fairchild," March 9, 1949, in Day, *North American Waterfowl,* 120–123.

46. Cowan, "Federal War on Market Hunters," 19–21.

47. Ducks Unlimited, *Diseases of Waterfowl Wintering in the Central Valley of California,* in Valley Habitats: A Technical Guidance Series for Private Land Managers in California's Central Valley, no. 12 (Sacramento: Ducks Unlimited, 1995), 3.

48. Alexander Wetmore, *The Duck Sickness in Utah* (Washington, D.C.: U.S. Department of Agriculture, Bulletin no. 672, 1918); Henry M. Reeves, "Portraits: Alexander Wetmore," in *Flyways: Pioneering Waterfowl Management in North America*, ed. A.S. Hawkins et al. (Washington, D.C.: U.S. Department of the Interior, Fish and Wildlife Service, 1984), 75–77.

49. "Type C Botulism among Wild Birds—A Historical Sketch," presented by E.R. Kalmbach, director (retired), Denver Wildlife Research Library, Bureau of Sport Fisheries and Wildlife, Department of the Interior, in U.S. House of Representatives, Subcommittee on Fisheries and Wildlife Conservation of the Committee on Merchant Marine and Fisheries, *Hearing on the Recent Outbreak of Botulism in the Tulare Lake Basin of California's San Joaquin Valley*, 91st Congress, 1st session, July 31, 1969, 4, 6–11. Prior to 1930 only two types of botulism, A and B, were known. Both affect humans but not wildfowl.

50. Donald D. McLean, "Duck Disease at Tulare Lake," *California Fish and Game* 32, no. 2 (1946): 72.

51. Statement of Dr. Joseph P. Linduska, associate director, Bureau of Sport Fisheries and Wildlife, Department of the Interior, in U.S. House of Representatives, Subcommittee on Fisheries and Wildlife Conservation, *Hearing on the Recent Outbreak of Botulism*, 4.

52. The vertical files of the main branch of the Kings County Public Library in Hanford, California, contain numerous clippings of local newspaper articles from 1937 and 1938 documenting the spread and retreat of Tulare Lake at that time, from which these figures were taken. Unfortunately, the clippings were prepared in such a way as to omit the names of the newspapers in which the articles appeared.

53. Studies of this outbreak by the California Division of Fish and Game, conducted between 1938 and 1945, indicated that incidence of disease was heaviest in areas where the water was less than one foot deep and nearly motionless, and where surface water temperatures ranged above 72 degrees Fahrenheit. McLean, "Duck Disease at Tulare Lake." Summer daytime temperatures in the Tulare Basin regularly exceed 100 degrees Fahrenheit.

54. McLean, "Duck Disease at Tulare Lake," 72–75.

55. McLean, "Duck Disease at Tulare Lake," 75; Leach, "Historical Account of Waterfowling," 64.

56. The year 1969 was a particularly notable flood year, when spring flooding submerged well over a hundred square miles of the Tulare Lake bed. By late July, with early fall migrants (mostly northern pintail) poised to arrive within a matter of weeks, botulism in the Tulare Lake Basin had reached severe enough proportions to warrant a congressional hearing concerning the imminent problem. "Run-Off Spreads over Much More Farm Land: 130 Square Miles Now under Water," *Corcoran Journal*, March 6, 1969, n.p; "Lake Nearing 190 Foot Elevation," *Corcoran Journal*, April 24, 1969, n.p. See U.S. House of Representatives, Subcommittee on Fisheries and Wildlife Conservation, *Hearing on the Recent Outbreak of Botulism*.

57. Milton Friend, "Waterfowl Get Sick, Too," in *Flyways: Pioneering Waterfowl Management in North America*, ed. A.S. Hawkins et al. (Washington, D.C.: U.S. Department of the Interior, Fish and Wildlife Service, 1984), 478–480.

58. Greg Mensik and Jennifer Isola, "Avian Cholera Takes Toll on Wintering Waterfowl," *California Waterfowl* 26, no. 2 (1999): 26; Ducks Unlimited, *Diseases of Waterfowl*, 3, 5.

59. 1870 *Statutes of California* ch. 224.

60. 1907 *Statutes of California* ch. 206; 1927 *Statutes of California* ch. 798.

61. Gordon, *California's Fish and Game Program*, 152.

62. Merrill C. Hammond, "Ducks, Grain, and American Farmers," in *Waterfowl Tomorrow*, ed. Joseph P. Linduska (Washington, D.C.: U.S. Department of the Interior, Fish and Wildlife Service, Bureau of Sport Fisheries and Wildlife, 1964), 423.

63. Cowan, *Jewel in the Pacific Flyway*, 48–50.

64. The Joice Island property now forms the Joice Island Unit of Suisun Marsh's Grizzly Island Wildlife Area.

65. Today rice is no longer grown in the Imperial Valley, but the expanded and renamed Imperial Wildlife Area, located on the edge of the Salton Sea, continues to provide wintering habitat for waterfowl and shorebirds, and to reduce depredation of other crops. This habitat has become increasingly important as the wetlands of the Central Valley— and especially of the Tulare Basin, several hundred miles to the north and the closest former freshwater waterfowl area—have been severely curtailed. Patrick Moore, "Imperial Wildlife Area and the Wister Unit," *Outdoor California* 62, no. 4 (2001): 34. For a history of the Salton Sea and its environs, including its myriad contemporary ecological problems, see William deBuys and Joan Myers, *Salt Dreams: Land & Water in Low-Down California* (Albuquerque: University of New Mexico Press, 1999).

66. Hall, "Environmental History of the Sacramento National Wildlife Refuge," 84, 112–114. The refuge was later expanded slightly to 10,819 acres, its size as of 2009.

67. Heizer and Elsasser, *Natural World of the California Indians*, 14.

68. Beck and Haase, *Historical Atlas of California*, 18.

69. This Central Pacific Railroad line was known as the Northern California Railroad. McGowan, *History of the Sacramento Valley*, 1:231–234.

70. Hall, "Environmental History of the Sacramento National Wildlife Refuge," 22–23, 34–36, 41–42.

71. For the history of the influential Glenn-Colusa Irrigation District, see Davis, *Where Water Is King*.

72. Hall, "Environmental History of the Sacramento National Wildlife Refuge," 50, 58, 67.

73. Hall, "Environmental History of the Sacramento National Wildlife Refuge," 70, 75–76, 79.

74. For an analysis of the role of the CCC in shaping the environmental movement in the United States, see Neil M. Maher, *Nature's New Deal: The Civilian Conservation Corps and the Roots of the American Environmental Movement* (New York: Oxford University Press, 2008).

75. Narrative Report, June 1937, Sacramento National Wildlife Refuge, SNWRC.

76. Narrative Report, July–September 1937, Sacramento National Wildlife Refuge, SNWRC, 4. Van Huizen was manager of the Sacramento Refuge from 1937 until early 1948.

77. Narrative Report, October–December 1937, Sacramento National Wildlife Refuge, SNWRC. Peak numbers of waterfowl present at any particular time are not equivalent to

the total number of waterfowl that are present over the course of a season. Total numbers would invariably be higher. By modern taxonomy, some of the subspecies listed as Canada geese in the narrative report would now be classified as cackling geese.

78. Narrative Report, August–October 1938, Sacramento National Wildlife Refuge, SNWRC, 1, 2.

79. Narrative Report, February–April 1939, Sacramento National Wildlife Refuge, SNWRC, 7.

80. Narrative Report, September–December 1942, Sacramento National Wildlife Refuge, SNWRC.

81. Narrative Report, May–August 1947, Sacramento National Wildlife Refuge, SNWRC, 3.

82. Narrative Report, September–December 1947, Sacramento National Wildlife Refuge, SNWRC, 22–23.

83. Narrative Report, 1954, Sacramento National Wildlife Refuge, SNWRC, 3.

84. Gordon, *California's Fish and Game Program,* 150. As of 2009, the Colusa National Wildlife Refuge encompassed 4,567 acres and the Sutter National Wildlife Refuge encompassed 2,591 acres.

85. 62 *Stat.* 238.

86. U.S. Senate, *Wildlife Management and Control Areas, California,* Senate Report no. 1217, 80th Congress, 2d session, 1948, 1547.

87. Gordon, *California's Fish and Game Program,* 153–154; Day, *North American Waterfowl,* 171.

88. Miller and Brandon, "Evolution of California Rice Culture," 131.

89. Day, *North American Waterfowl,* 170–171.

90. For a trenchant argument, based elsewhere in the irrigated West, about the inability of humans to control nature precisely, and of the unexpected ecological consequences of such attempts, see Mark Fiege, *Irrigated Eden: The Making of an Agricultural Landscape in the American West* (Seattle: University of Washington Press, 1999).

91. Hunting had been allowed on state, as opposed to federal, refuges in California for several years prior to the passage of the Lea Act, but none of these refuges was in the Central Valley. In 1953 Los Banos Waterfowl Refuge became the first state refuge in the Central Valley (exclusive of Suisun Marsh) to be opened to hunting. Frank M. Kozlik, "Waterfowl Hunting Areas Operated by the California Department of Fish and Game," *California Fish and Game* 41, no. 1 (1955): 35–36.

92. The exemption was valid provided that such hunting was consistent with the provisions of the Migratory Bird Treaty Act of 1918. In 1949 Congress provided for the hunting of waterfowl on refuges acquired under the Migratory Bird Conservation Act of 1929 as well. Bean and Rowland, *Evolution of National Wildlife Law,* 296.

93. Gordon, *California's Fish and Game Program,* 147.

94. Cowan, *Jewel in the Pacific Flyway,* 130; Kozlik, "Waterfowl Hunting Areas," 36.

95. Sacramento, Colusa, Sutter, and Delevan national wildlife refuges, as well as subsequent federal acquisitions in the Sacramento Valley, are managed as part of the Sacramento National Wildlife Refuge Complex.

96. The hunting program, initiated by the U.S. Fish and Wildlife Service and the California Department of Fish and Game, required a fee of $2.50 per day for each adult hunter, an amount far below the daily shoot fees of commercial clubs. By 1964, 8,525 hunters on the Sacramento National Wildlife Refuge took 21,338 waterfowl over the course of the season's thirty-five hunt days. Hall, "Environmental History of the Sacramento National Wildlife Refuge," 105–106. In exchange for this harvest, hunters, via their fees, provided a significant portion of the refuge's revenue for operations.

97. 1947 *Statutes of California* ch. 1325. The Wildlife Conservation Board was originally created within the California Department of Natural Resources, and later placed with the California Department of Fish and Game.

98. Gordon, *California's Fish and Game Program*, unnumbered page.

99. Gordon, *California's Fish and Game Program*, 140.

100. Gordon, *California's Fish and Game Program*, 148; emphasis in original.

101. Gordon, *California's Fish and Game Program*, 144 (quote), 154, 159, 161–162. In California as a whole, only 189,851 of the state's more than 100 million acres were designated waterfowl areas in 1950. Federal refuges accounted for 166,647 acres of this total, more than half of which lay on open water incapable of appreciable development for waterfowl. Only 14,433 acres of the federal areas lay in the Central Valley, on the Sacramento, Colusa, and Sutter national wildlife refuges. State waterfowl areas accounted for 23,204 acres, only 5,542 of which were in the Central Valley, distributed between the Gray Lodge and Los Banos waterfowl refuges. The state owned an additional 1,887 acres in Suisun Marsh, including the Joice Island Waterfowl Refuge. Gordon, *California's Fish and Game Program*, 161.

102. Narrative Report, 1997, Merced National Wildlife Refuge, SLNWRC; Kozlik, "Waterfowl Hunting Areas," 36.

103. From 1927 to 1951 the Division of Fish and Game was a part of the Department of Natural Resources. In 1951 it was elevated to the independent status of the Department of Fish and Game.

104. Gray Lodge continued to expand in later years, and as of 2009 encompassed approximately 9,100 acres.

105. Leach, "Historical Account of Waterfowling," 73; Cowan, *Jewel in the Pacific Flyway*, 56–57. Protected areas that were created either as state waterfowl refuges or, later, as state waterfowl management areas became state wildlife areas as well, and many of them, like Gray Lodge, continued to be enlarged. The Grizzly Island Waterfowl Management Area was later incorporated, as the Grizzly Island Unit, into the Grizzly Island Wildlife Area. As of 2009, the Grizzly Island Wildlife Area encompassed approximately 15,300 acres; the Mendota Waterfowl Management Area, renamed the Mendota Wildlife Area, had been expanded to more than 11,800 acres; and the Imperial Waterfowl Management Area, renamed the Imperial Wildlife Area, had been expanded to more than 7,900 acres. See Robert J. Huddleston, "Mendota Wildlife Area," *Outdoor California* 62, no. 4 (2001): 14; Moore, "Imperial Wildlife Area," 34.

106. Beginning in 1969, the Rice Experiment Station near Biggs launched a research program to improve rice varieties in California that resulted in the development of new semidwarf varieties with shorter maturity periods. These new varieties averaged 130,

rather than 160, days to maturity. Early maturity was a particularly important development for reducing crop depredations, as this feature greatly increased the probability that the crop would be fully harvested before the fall flights of ducks arrived in the Central Valley. The peak harvesttime is now September 15 to October 15, although the harvest sometimes stretches into early November, depending on weather conditions. Cowan, *Jewel in the Pacific Flyway*, 72–73; Miller and Brandon, "Evolution of California Rice Culture," 97–98.

107. Cowan, *Jewel in the Pacific Flyway*, 69–73. The main species of blackbirds that feed on rice in the Central Valley are the red-winged blackbird, tricolored blackbird, Brewer's blackbird, and yellow-headed blackbird. The closely related brown-headed cowbird is implicated as well. Miller and Brandon, "Evolution of California Rice Culture," 127–128.

108. The U.S. Biological Survey and its successor, the U.S. Fish and Wildlife Service, published *Wildlife Review* for sixty years, from 1935 to 1995.

109. Waldo L. McAtee, *Wildfowl Food Plants: Their Value, Propagation, and Management* (Ames, Iowa: Collegiate Press, 1939). McAtee's work was complemented by two publications of the same year. See Clarence Cottam, *Food Habits of North American Diving Ducks* (Washington, D.C.: U.S. Department of Agriculture, Technical Bulletin no. 643, 1939); and A. C. Martin and F. M. Uhler, *Food of Game Ducks in the United States and Canada* (Washington, D.C.: U.S. Department of Agriculture, Technical Bulletin no. 634, 1939).

110. Drawing on the results of investigations by the Biological Survey, in 1933 More Game Birds in America published a booklet intended for the management of private waterfowl lands. See More Game Birds in America, *Waterfowl Food Plants* (New York: More Game Birds in America, 1933).

111. Henry M. Reeves, "Portraits: Waldo L. McAtee," in *Flyways: Pioneering Waterfowl Management in North America*, ed. A.S. Hawkins et al. (Washington, D.C.: U.S. Department of the Interior, Fish and Wildlife Service, 1984), 85–86.

112. This study was conducted as Pittman-Robertson Project W25-R and ran concurrently with Pittman-Robertson Project W20-R, sponsored by the California Department of Fish and Game, the U.S. Fish and Wildlife Service, and the Department of Botany of the University of California, Berkeley. The latter project was a floristic survey of the marshes and other feeding and resting areas used by Pacific Flyway waterfowl in California, and led to the publication of Herbert Mason's seminal work *A Flora of the Marshes of California*.

113. Unpublished data, "Waterfowl Summaries, Food Habits Analysis," Howard R. Leach, California Department of Fish and Game. Plant common names (in the text) and scientific names (in the appendix) used in the food habits studies have been updated by the author as necessary, following Hickman, ed., *Jepson Manual*.

114. G. A. Swanson and J. C. Bartonek, "Bias Associated with Food Analysis in Gizzards of Blue-Winged Teal," *Journal of Wildlife Management* 34, no. 4 (1970).

115. Michael R. Miller, "Fall and Winter Foods of Northern Pintails in the Sacramento Valley, California," *Journal of Wildlife Management* 51, no. 2 (1987).

116. D. P. Connelly and D. L. Chesemore, "Food Habits of Pintails, *Anas acuta*, Wintering on Seasonally Flooded Wetlands in the Northern San Joaquin Valley, California,"

California Fish and Game 66, no. 4 (1980); Ned H. Euliss Jr. and Stanley W. Harris, "Feeding Ecology of Northern Pintails and Green-Winged Teal Wintering in California," *Journal of Wildlife Management* 51, no. 4 (1987); Ned H. Euliss Jr., Robert L. Jarvis, and David S. Gilmer, "Feeding Ecology of Waterfowl Wintering on Evaporation Ponds in California," *The Condor* 93, no. 3 (1991).

117. A significant component of flyway management has been the establishment of hunting regulations. The first attempts to coordinate regulations for legal waterfowl hunting on a national basis date from the 1930s, when a system of three latitudinal hunting zones, stretching east to west across the United States, was developed as a means to establish uniform and consistent seasons. Under this system of zonal management, which had been supported by More Game Birds in America, a single bag limit and season length applied nationwide, though opening and closing dates varied depending on zone. One of the most important weaknesses of this management plan was that it allowed for an equal take along each flyway, even though populations varied considerably among them. Frederick C. Lincoln had argued for the importance of the four north-south flyways in 1935, but it was not until 1948 that the U.S. Fish and Wildlife Service adopted a change from latitudinal zone to flyway management. Because each state in a flyway harvested the same population of birds and therefore shared a common interest, flyway management provided the incentive for unprecedented levels of coordination, making it possible to establish a separate bag limit and season length for each flyway, dependent on waterfowl population size and hunting mortality. Hawkins, "U.S. Response," 5; Walter F. Crissey, "Calculators and Ouija Boards," in *Flyways: Pioneering Waterfowl Management in North America,* ed. A.S. Hawkins et al. (Washington, D.C.: U.S. Department of the Interior, Fish and Wildlife Service, 1984), 261; James C. Bartonek, "Pacific Flyway," in *Flyways: Pioneering Waterfowl Management in North America,* ed. A.S. Hawkins et al. (Washington, D.C.: U.S. Department of the Interior, Fish and Wildlife Service, 1984), 395-398. The Pacific Flyway Council's original members were the seven states within the administrative boundaries of the flyway, as delineated by the U.S. Fish and Wildlife Service in 1948: Arizona, California, Idaho, Nevada, Oregon, Utah, and Washington. Alaska was admitted to the council following statehood in 1959. After the administrative boundaries of the flyway were extended eastward to the Continental Divide, Montana was admitted in 1980, Wyoming in 1982, and Colorado in 1987. New Mexico has a representative to the council but is not an active member.

7. BATTLES FOR THE GRASSLANDS AND THE SAN JOAQUIN RIVER

1. As late as 1930, Miller and Lux had filed suit against the Madera Irrigation District, which had been organized to build a dam at Friant and divert the San Joaquin River waters to irrigate about 170,000 acres of land. The ruling, entered in 1933, sustained Miller and Lux's riparian rights to the annual overflow of the river onto its grasslands, and adjudged the proposed appropriation by the Madera Irrigation District invalid. *Miller and Lux v. Madera Irrigation District* (Superior Court, Fresno County, no. 24729, 1933);

G. L. Rogers, "Synopsis of the Riparian, Appropriative, and Prescriptive Rights of Miller & Lux and Its Affiliated Canal Companies (1979), 12, box 9, folder 3, JMW.

2. The cattle industry in the lower San Joaquin Valley was largely bifurcated by the San Joaquin River, with most dairying conducted west of the river and most beef cattle raised to the east of the river. Howard R. Leach, *The Wildlife and Fishery Resources in Relation to Drainage Disposal Problems in the San Joaquin Valley* (Sacramento: California Department of Fish and Game, 1960), 40.

3. U.S. Department of the Interior, *Waterfowl Conservation in the Lower San Joaquin Valley: Its Relation to the Grasslands and the Central Valley Project* (Washington, D.C.: U.S. Department of the Interior, 1950), 18.

4. Igler, *Industrial Cowboys*, 180.

5. Miller, *Flooding the Courtrooms*, 165.

6. The purchase contract for $2.45 million represented the difference between the market value of the uncontrolled lands before and after they were deprived of their rights to seasonal overflow water from the San Joaquin River. Contract for Purchase of Miller & Lux Water Rights, in U.S. House of Representatives, *Central Valley Project Documents*, part 2: *Operating Documents*, House Document no. 246, 85th Congress, 1st session, 1957, 568–589.

7. Miller, *Flooding the Courtrooms*, 173.

8. Contract for Exchange of Waters, in U.S. House of Representatives, *Central Valley Project Documents*, part 2: *Operating Documents*, 555–567.

9. U.S. House of Representatives, *Central Valley Project Documents*, part 2: *Operating Documents*, 555. Also important for the initiation of the Central Valley Project was the Madera Contract, negotiated between the bureau and the Madera Irrigation District, which owned the Friant Dam site, portions of the reservoir area, and additional San Joaquin water rights. The bureau purchased these properties and water rights for $300,000. U.S. House of Representatives, *Central Valley Project Documents*, part 2: *Operating Documents*, 589.

10. U.S. Department of the Interior, *Waterfowl Conservation in the Lower San Joaquin Valley*, 25.

11. The term *Grasslands* has since been expanded to include lands east of the San Joaquin River as well. The Grasslands Wildlife Management Area and the Grasslands Ecological Area, to be discussed later in this chapter and in chapter 10, respectively, reflect this more expansive definition.

12. U.S. Department of the Interior, *Waterfowl Conservation in the Lower San Joaquin Valley*, 26–30.

13. U.S. Department of the Interior, *Waterfowl Conservation in the Lower San Joaquin Valley*, 23.

14. The managers of state and federal refuges in the Central Valley maintain the same annual cycle.

15. Leach, *Wildlife and Fishery Resources*, 56.

16. Leach, *Wildlife and Fishery Resources*, 56.

17. Al Jessen, president, Grass Lands Association, "History," 1939, box 9, folder 3, JMW.

18. Leach, "Historical Account of Waterfowling," 60, 79.

19. Class I water is water guaranteed by contract, and it sells at a higher price than Class II water, which is available only to the extent that supply exceeds demand for Class I water.

20. J. Martin Winton, undated letter, box 9, folder 3, JMW.

21. U.S. Bureau of Reclamation, *Land and Water Utilization in the Westside Grasslands Area of San Joaquin Valley, California* (Sacramento: U.S. Department of the Interior, Bureau of Reclamation, 1948), 8.

22. Minute Book, Grass Lands Water Association, August 2, 1944, GWD.

23. Al Jessen, untitled document, 1944, box 9, folder 3, JMW.

24. Charles E. Carey to Anthony C. Mattos, general manager, Western Cooperative Dairymen's Union, September 22, 1944; Charles E. Carey to Assemblyman S.L. Heisinger, October 10, 1944, box 16, folder 8, JMW.

25. U.S. House of Representatives, Subcommittee on Irrigation and Reclamation of the Committee on Interior and Insular Affairs, *Hearing on Central Valley Project Water Problem Relating to the Grasslands Area in the San Joaquin Valley, Calif.*, 82d Congress, 1st session, April 17 and May 3, 1951, 14.

26. I. N. Gabrielson to Harry W. Bashore, June 5, 1945, reproduced in complaint of *Hollister Land and Cattle Company and Yellowjacket Cattle Company v. Julius A. Krug et al.*, S.D. Cal., no. 680-ND, unpublished, October 20, 1947, 23–25.

27. Minute Book, Grass Lands Water Association, September 11, 1947, GWD.

28. Reflecting the dual nature of land use in the Grasslands, many of the duck clubs were designated as "land and cattle" or "cattle" companies.

29. *Hollister Land and Cattle Company and Yellowjacket Cattle Company v. Julius A. Krug et al.*, S.D. Cal., no. 680-ND, unpublished, October 20, 1947. See chapter 3 for a discussion of riparian and appropriative water rights.

30. U.S. Department of the Interior, *Waterfowl Conservation in the Lower San Joaquin Valley*.

31. The term *Green Book* was adopted simply from the report's green covers.

32. U.S. Department of the Interior, *Waterfowl Conservation in the Lower San Joaquin Valley*, 13.

33. California Department of Public Works, *Report to the Legislature of 1931: State Water Plan*, 45.

34. U.S. Department of the Interior, *Waterfowl Conservation in the Lower San Joaquin Valley*, 16.

35. U.S. Department of the Interior, *Waterfowl Conservation in the Lower San Joaquin Valley*, 36, 42–44, 52–53, 59 (quote).

36. U.S. Department of the Interior, *Waterfowl Conservation in the Lower San Joaquin Valley*, 78, 118 (quote). The Green Book estimated that the Grasslands owners would need to develop 150 wells at a cost of $6,000 per well, for a total development cost of $900,000. After the wells were constructed, the additional cost of pumping the groundwater would be approximately $2.25 per acre-foot. This cost was far higher than the $1.50 per acre-foot that the Grass Lands Water Association had been paying since 1948 in its annual contracts with the bureau for Class II water. Minute Book, Grass Lands Water Association,

November 18, 1947, GWD; U.S. Department of the Interior, *Waterfowl Conservation in the Lower San Joaquin Valley*, 111–112.

37. Krug to Truman, July 29, 1948, in U.S. Bureau of Reclamation, *Central Valley Basin: A Comprehensive Report on the Development of the Water and Related Resources of the Central Valley Basin*, U.S. Department of the Interior, Bureau of Reclamation, Senate Document no. 113, 81st Congress, 1st session, 1949, 6.

38. U.S. Bureau of Reclamation, *Land and Water Utilization in the Westside Grasslands Area*, 12.

39. U.S. Department of the Interior, *Waterfowl Conservation in the Lower San Joaquin Valley*, 62–63.

40. Minute Book, Grass Lands Water Association, November 8, 1949, GWD.

41. U.S. House of Representatives, Subcommittee on Irrigation and Reclamation, *Hearing on Central Valley Project Water Problem*, 7. The Bureau of Reclamation was criticized in California for other aspects of its implementation of the Central Valley Project as well, particularly for its sporadic attempts to enforce the Reclamation Act of 1902, which prohibited the distribution of subsidized reclamation project water to landholdings in excess of 160 acres. The most withering attack on the bureau was by California senator Sheridan Downey, *They Would Rule the Valley* (San Francisco: privately published, 1947). For a contrasting, celebratory, view of the bureau, see Warne, *Bureau of Reclamation*. The closest to a nonpolemical history of the early years of the Central Valley Project is de Roos, *Thirsty Land*.

42. R. E. Des Jardins to Earl Harris, April 11, 1951, in U.S. House of Representatives, Subcommittee on Irrigation and Reclamation, *Hearing on Central Valley Project Water Problem*, 7–8.

43. John Baumgartner to Oscar Chapman, April 10, 1951, in U.S. House of Representatives, Subcommittee on Irrigation and Reclamation, *Hearing on Central Valley Project Water Problem*, 8.

44. George W. Fink, February 20, 1951, in U.S. House of Representatives, Subcommittee on Irrigation and Reclamation, *Hearing on Central Valley Project Water Problem*, 10–12.

45. Howard Leach, California Department of Fish and Game, retired, personal correspondence; Gary Zahm, U.S. Fish and Wildlife Service, retired, personal correspondence; Leach, "Historical Account of Waterfowling," 150.

46. Minute Book, Grass Lands Water Association, July 8, 1952, GWD; Lloyd Carter, "J. Martin Winton: A Short Biography," JMW. Winton was to be the recipient of numerous awards in recognition of his lifelong conservation efforts, including, shortly after his death in 1991, the dedication of the J. Martin Winton Memorial Marsh within the San Luis National Wildlife Refuge, created in the Grasslands in 1966. Winton donated his voluminous collection of professional correspondence to the San Joaquin College of Law in Clovis, California, just outside of Fresno, in 1988. The resulting J. Martin Winton Special Collection on Water Use and Land Development is an important holding that documents California water developments, especially as they relate to waterfowl in the San Joaquin Valley, over four decades.

47. U.S. House of Representatives, Subcommittee on Irrigation and Reclamation, *Hearing on Central Valley Project Water Problem*, 22–27.

48. See, for example, H. V. Eastman, secretary, Chowchilla Water District, to Clair Engle, April 1951, in U.S. House of Representatives, Subcommittee on Irrigation and Reclamation, *Hearing on Central Valley Project Water Problem*, 32.

49. Boke was director of Region 2, which encompassed California from north of the Tehachapi Mountains (the southern boundary of the Central Valley) to the Klamath River Basin in southern Oregon. This area is now included in the Bureau's Mid-Pacific Region.

50. Statement of R. L. Boke, in U.S. House of Representatives, Subcommittee on Irrigation and Reclamation, *Hearing on Central Valley Project Water Problem*, 48–62.

51. Richard L. Boke to Clair Engle, April 27, 1951, in U.S. House of Representatives, Subcommittee on Irrigation and Reclamation, *Hearing on Central Valley Project Water Problem*, 83–84.

52. H.R. 7177 and H.R. 7178.

53. Al Jessen to Clair Engle, May 21, 1952, box 139, folder 2, CEP.

54. Wallace D. Henderson to Clair Engle, May 26, 1952, box 139, folder 2, CEP.

55. Statement of J. Martin Winton to the House Committee on Interior and Insular Affairs, June 6, 1952, box 1, folder 25, JMW. In addition to the considerable scientific literature on the subject of the extinction of the passenger pigeon, see Jennifer Price, *Flight Maps: Adventures with Nature in Modern America* (New York: Basic Books, 1999), 1–55.

56. U.S. House of Representatives, Subcommittee on Irrigation and Reclamation, *Hearing on Central Valley Project Water Problem*, 51.

57. A. J. Jessen, "Emergency Water Fowl Management Program for the Lower San Joaquin Valley," September 11, 1952, box 175, folder 5, CEP.

58. Minute Book, Grass Lands Water Association, December 27, 1952, GWD. The various provisions governing California water districts appear in the *California Water Code*, sec. 34000–38501.

59. Resolution and Order Forming Grassland Water District, Merced County Board of Supervisors, December 22, 1953. Closing the previous chapter of Grasslands history, in November 1955 the Grass Lands Water Association was dissolved and its assets and property transferred and sold to the Grassland Water District. "Agreement of Transfer and Sale," Minute Book, Grass Lands Water Association, November 8, 1955, box 5, folder 1, JMW.

60. Seth Gordon, *A New Milestone in Cooperative Effort—the Grasslands Water Bill* (Sacramento: California Department of Fish and Game, 1954). Box 9, folder 3, JMW; Earl Warren to Oakley Hunter, March 20, 1953, box 139, folder 2, CEP. Warren was serving his last year as governor. President Eisenhower would soon appoint him to the U.S. Supreme Court.

61. H.R. 4213.

62. "Conservation of Natural Resources—Message from the President of the United States," House Document no. 221, in *Congressional Record*, July 31, 1953, 10929.

63. Public Law 674, 68 *Stat.* 879.

64. Lloyd Carter, "J. Martin Winton: A Short Biography," JMW.

65. 68 *Stat.* 879, sec. 1.

66. U.S. Senate, *Authorizing Works for Development and Furnishing of Water Supplies for Waterfowl Management, Central Valley Project, California*, Senate Report no. 1786, 83d Congress, 2d session, 1954, 1.

67. 50 *Stat.* 844.

68. For a collection of essays on this point, see Michael Egan and Jeff Crane, eds., *Natural Protest: Essays on the History of American Environmentalism* (New York: Routledge, 2009).

69. Minutes of the Grassland Water District, January 12, 1954, GWD.

70. Minutes of the Grassland Water District, January 10, 1956, GWD. *Hollister Land and Cattle Company et al. v. Julius A. Krug et al.* was finally dismissed on April 10, 1957. "Grassland Water District: Organization and Description of the District," box 9, folder 3, JMW; "Contract between the United States of America and the Grassland Water District" (no. 14–06–200–6106), September 13, 1956, in U.S. House of Representatives, *Central Valley Project Documents*, part 2: *Operating Documents*, 39–42.

71. The water was to be delivered during the period September 15 through November 30. During critical (drought) years, the delivery would be restricted to not more than 25,000 acre-feet, to be delivered during the period October 1 through November 30.

72. United States General Accounting Office report to the secretary of the interior, December 1, 1972, GWD; U.S. Department of the Interior, *The Grasslands of California: A Plan for Conservation and Development of Waterfowl Habitat* (Washington, D.C.: U.S. Department of the Interior, 1969).

73. U.S. Department of the Interior, *Grasslands of California*, 1 (quote), 3.

74. Cooperative Agreement and Management Plan, Contract no. 14–06–200–4658A, December 27, 1969, GWD.

75. The contract also included the requirement that the district furnish without charge 3,500 acre-feet of winter water, and 4,000 acre-feet of summer water when available, to the new Kesterson National Wildlife Refuge immediately to the north of the Grasslands. Kesterson's checkered history is discussed in detail in chapter 9.

76. Sample Covenant of Restrictive Use, GWD.

77. Public Law 91–559, 84 *Stat.* 1468. The Water Bank Program was administered by the Soil Conservation Service, precursor to the Natural Resources Conservation Service, established in 1994. Agreements under the Water Bank Act are developed in cooperation with local soil and water conservation districts. The Grassland Soil Conservation District had been formed in March 1959, was renamed the Grassland Resource Conservation District (GRCD) in 1972, and includes the lands of the Grassland Water District as well as neighboring private and public lands. Grassland Water District, *Ecological and Water Management Characterization of the Grassland Water District* (Los Banos, Calif.: Grassland Water District, 1986), 10–11.

78. Public Law 94–215, 90 *Stat.* 189, originally passed in 1961 as the Wetlands Loan Act, Public Law 87–383, 75 *Stat.* 813.

79. Narrative Report, 1981, Grasslands Wildlife Management Area, SLNWRC, 1 (quote and figures). In 1987 the easement program was extended to the East Grasslands, across the San Joaquin River. The easement program differed from the earlier restrictive

use covenants in that landowners were paid for the conservation easements, whereas entry into the restrictive use covenants was a precondition for receiving discounted Central Valley Project water.

80. Fish and Wildlife Improvement Act, Public Law 95–616, 92 *Stat.* 3110, sec. 10, "Waterfowl Habitat Conservation in the San Joaquin Valley." The mandate of the act was carried out under the Cooperative Agreement and Habitat Management Plan, Contract no. 14–06–200–4658A Amendatory, December 6, 1980, GWD.

81. U.S. Department of the Interior, *Waterfowl Conservation in the Lower San Joaquin Valley,* 16.

82. Chinook salmon had been important to the subsistence economies and cultures of Native Americans living along both the Sacramento and the San Joaquin rivers. In the decades following the Gold Rush, these subsistence economies were replaced by a commercial fishing industry that, from the mid-1870s to approximately 1910, annually harvested four million to ten million pounds of salmon from the Sacramento–San Joaquin Delta region alone. For a history of California's salmon fisheries, see Ronald M. Yoshiyama, "A History of Salmon and People in the Central Valley Region of California," *Reviews in Fisheries Science* 7, nos. 3–4 (1999). For California fisheries in general, see Arthur F. McEvoy, *The Fisherman's Problem: Ecology and Law in the California Fisheries, 1850–1980* (Cambridge: Cambridge University Press, 1986). For accounts of recreational fishing on the San Joaquin River prior to the construction of Friant Dam, see G. Rose, *San Joaquin: A River Betrayed,* 2nd ed. (Clovis, Calif.: Word Dancer Press, 2000), 113–124.

83. From 1897 to 1944, the annual average flow of the San Joaquin River was 1,797,260 acre-feet, a rate of 2,463 cubic feet per second, measured at Friant. *Rank et al. v. Krug et al.,* 142 F. Supp. 1, 37 (S.D. Cal. 1956).

84. G.W. Philpott to Allan Oakley Hunter, March 22, 1951, box 27, unnumbered folder, JMW.

85. William Voigt Jr. to Willis A. Robertson, chairman, Senate Subcommittee to Investigate Wildlife Conservation, March 5, 1951, box 27, unnumbered folder, JMW.

86. Damming and diversion of rivers has nearly extirpated the winter, spring, and late-fall salmon runs. The fall run, which uses mainly the lower stretches of rivers within the Central Valley and foothills, historically was less dramatically affected than the other runs by the loss and degradation of habitat at higher elevations, but is currently under siege from a variety of environmental threats. See Ronald M. Yoshiyama, Frank W. Fisher, and Peter B. Moyle, "Historical Abundance and Decline of Chinook Salmon in the Central Valley Region of California," *North American Journal of Fisheries Management* 18 (1998); Ronald M. Yoshiyama et al., "Chinook Salmon in the California Central Valley: An Assessment," *Fisheries Management* 25, no. 2 (2000).

87. Peter Moyle, University of California, Davis, personal correspondence; Peter B. Moyle, Patrick K. Crain, and Keith Whitener, "Patterns in the Use of a Restored California Floodplain by Native and Alien Fishes," *San Francisco Estuary and Watershed Science* 5, no. 3 (2007). For a discussion of the importance of floodplain restoration for protecting salmon and other native fish species, see chapter 10.

88. Leland O. Graham, "The Central Valley Project: Resource Development of a Natural Basin," *California Law Review* 38 (1950): 597; Rose, *San Joaquin,* 119–121; Leach, "Historical Account of Waterfowling," 145–146.

89. Report of the Fish and Wildlife Service, Preliminary Report on Fishery Resources, December 27, 1944, in U.S. Bureau of Reclamation, *Central Valley Basin,* 260.

90. *Rank et al. v. Krug et al.,* 90 F. Supp. 773, 783 (S.D. Cal. 1950).

91. Rank and the other eleven plaintiffs had sued on behalf of themselves and approximately 125 additional owners of farms totaling approximately 47,500 acres of land riparian to the San Joaquin River below Friant Dam and above Mendota Dam, as well as for approximately one thousand others owning approximately 600,000 acres of land that overlay underground waters that were historically sustained and replenished by percolating waters along that stretch of the river. *Rank et al. v. Krug et al.,* 90 F. Supp. 773, 781 (S.D. Cal. 1950).

92. *Rank et al. v. Krug et al.,* 90 F. Supp. 773 (S.D. Cal. 1950).

93. Article XIV, sec. 3 of the Constitution of California, adopted on November 6, 1928; *California Water Code,* sec. 101.

94. *Rank et al. v. Krug et al.,* 90 F. Supp. 773, 783, 789–800 (S.D. Cal. 1950). An important legal precedent also belied the bureau's claim. In *Gerlach Livestock Co. v. United States,* 76 F. Supp. 87 (Court of Claims 1948), the Gerlach Livestock Company had sued over the loss of the rights of its uncontrolled grasslands to the overflow water of the San Joaquin River. The U.S. Court of Claims ruled that Friant Dam was constructed for irrigation purposes, not for the improvement of navigation and flood control. Therefore, the Bureau of Reclamation was not immune from liability for taking Gerlach's water rights. The United States appealed the decision to the U.S. Supreme Court, which upheld the ruling. *United States v. Gerlach Live Stock* [sic] *Co.,* 339 U.S. 725, 730 (1950).

95. *Rank et al. v. Krug et al.,* 90 F. Supp. 773, 801 (S.D. Cal. 1950).

96. Edmund G. Brown, Opinion no. 50–89. Friant Dam, in *Opinions of the Attorney General of California* 18 (1951), 31–40.

97. 1933 *Statutes of California* ch. 73. This provision was transferred from the *Penal Code* to the *Fish and Game Code* in 1933; the change to the current numbering of the *Fish and Game Code* was adopted in 1957.

98. 1945 *Statutes of California* ch. 1514.

99. *Rank et al. v. Krug et al.,* 90 F. Supp. 773, 801 (S.D. Cal. 1950); Leach, "Historical Account of Waterfowling," 142–144. Brown's opinion signaled a reversal from the position of his predecessor, Fred Howser, who in a 1949 opinion had argued that the use of water for fish and wildlife was a beneficial use, and who had filed an amicus curiae brief on behalf of the California Division of Fish and Game in support of the plaintiffs' position with respect to fish. Fred N. Howser, Attorney General, Opinion no. 49/68, May 10, 1949, reproduced in part in U.S. House of Representatives, *Central Valley Project Documents,* part 2: *Operating Documents,* 429.

100. Brown's opinion would be reversed twenty-three years later by Attorney General Evelle J. Younger, who argued that new state laws reflected "an increasing awareness of the necessity and importance of preserving California's fishery resources in connection

with water usage and water projects." Evelle J. Younger, Opinion no. SO 73–44. State Water Resources Control Board—Water Appropriator Regulation, in *Opinions of the Attorney General of California* 57 (1974), 577–583.

101. *Rank et al. v. Krug et al.*, 142 F. Supp. 1, 116 (S.D. Cal. 1956). Among the testimony reviewed by Hall was a prescient paper by G. E. P. Smith, an engineer at the University of Arizona, who argued that Friant Dam, with a reservoir capacity of only 520,000 acre-feet, was "far too small to conserve the erratic flow of the [San Joaquin] River" and therefore should never have been built. Smith contended that a dam at Temperance Flat, a site with a storage capacity in excess of 1.8 million acre-feet and located only six miles upstream from Friant Dam, would have been able to provide timely downstream flows to recharge groundwater supplies and satisfy the needs of landowners. G. E. P. Smith, *The Failure of the Keystone of the Arch of the Central Valley Project,* University of Arizona special paper (January 15, 1952), 1, box 22, JMW.

102. See *State of California, United States of America, et al. v. Rank et al.*, 293 F. 2d 340, 346 (9th Cir. 1961).

103. California State Water Rights Board, Decision no. D 935 (1959).

104. California State Water Rights Board, Decision no. D 935, 40–41; emphasis in original.

105. Rose, *San Joaquin,* 106; Leach, "Historical Account of Waterfowling," 146, 149.

106. *State of California, United States of America, et al. v. Rank et al.*, 293 F.2d 340 (9th Cir. 1961).

107. The suit was now named *Dugan et al. v. Rank et al.*, 372 U.S. 609 (1963). Chief Justice Earl Warren, a landowner in Kern County, recused himself from the consideration and decision of this case.

108. Under the Tucker Act (28 U.S.C. sec. 1346) the landowners were entitled to bring a suit for damages against the United States.

109. Diversions to the Madera and Friant-Kern canals, combined with minimal releases to serve water contractors along the thirty-six-mile stretch from Friant to Gravelly Ford, amounted to approximately 98 percent of the river's annual flow. California State Water Rights Board, Decision no. D 935," 84.

8. CONFLICTING AGENDAS

1. Although the Mendota Waterfowl Management Area (later renamed the Mendota Wildlife Area) lies physically on the northern boundary of the Tulare Basin, administratively it has been categorized with the wetlands of the Grasslands area of the San Joaquin Basin. U.S. Fish and Wildlife Service, *Concept Plan for Waterfowl Wintering Habitat Preservation,* 57.

2. Mark Arax and Rick Wartzman, *The King of California: J. G. Boswell and the Making of a Secret American Empire* (New York: Public Affairs, 2003), 36.

3. "History of Cotton in California, and History of California's One Variety Seed Program" (Bakersfield, Calif.: California Planting Cotton Seed Distributors, n.d.), pamphlet, KCWHC. In 1925 the California legislature passed the One Variety Cotton Act (1925 *Statutes of California* ch. 299), which, in an effort to increase overall yields and to

coordinate processing among growers, restricted production to Acala cotton alone. In 1991 the law was finally relaxed to allow the growing of Pima cotton as well.

4. Preston, *Vanishing Landscapes,* 183.

5. After the colonel's nephew, J. G. Boswell II, took over the enterprise following his uncle's death in 1952, the younger Boswell continued to expand operations, so that by the end of the 1990s the Boswells owned approximately 200,000 acres in California and 60,000 acres in Australia and had the largest amount of planted acreage of any farmers in the United States. Arax and Wartzman, *King of California,* 130, 433. J. G. Boswell II died in April 2009.

6. Figures from various Tulare Basin newspapers, 1938, vertical files, Kings County Library, Hanford. In many cases, names of newspapers or exact dates have not been preserved.

7. 58 *Stat.* 887. The wrangling between the two federal agencies was complicated by shifting alliances among those farmers who supported construction by the corps and those who supported the bureau. See Arax and Wartzman, *King of California,* 184–211. For the bureau's perspective, see Warne, *Bureau of Reclamation,* 184–188. In large part, the conflict revolved around whether the 160-acre limitation for receipt of subsidized water under the Reclamation Act would be enforced. Ultimately, reclamation law has never been enforced on the Kings River, but the issue of enforcement generated decades of controversy. National Land for People, an influential organization founded and led by George Ballis, sued the federal government in 1976 and fought until 1982 for the enforcement of reclamation law. For the contrasting perspective of those Kings River water users opposed to the acreage limitation, see Robert E. Leake Jr. and Stanley M. Barnes, *The Pine Flat Project on Kings River, California: Reclamation Law Should Not Apply!* (Fresno, Calif.: Kings River Water Users Committee, 1980), box 1, NLP. For Pine Flat Dam in the context of larger struggles over enforcement of the Reclamation Act, see Arax and Wartzman, *King of California,* 316–360; Hundley, *Great Thirst,* 262–272.

8. Narrative Report, January–April 1961, Kern National Wildlife Refuge, KNWRC, 12. This report, by refuge manger Leon C. Snyder, states that during the 1950s "duck clubs disappeared at an alarming rate," but for most of the 1950s it may be more accurate that wetland acreage managed by the clubs, rather than the number of clubs themselves, was in decline. Frank Hall of the California Department of Fish and Game, retired, who has researched the history of duck clubs on California wetlands, estimates that the number of Tulare Basin duck clubs peaked at approximately 150 during the 1950s, and then began to decline only toward the end of that decade. Personal correspondence.

9. Leach, *Wildlife and Fishery Resources,* 30.

10. Waterfowl populations are from Collins and Trost, *2009 Pacific Flyway Data Book,* 83.

11. 50 *Stat.* 522, July 22, 1937.

12. Executive Order no. 10787, dated November 6, 1958.

13. Secretary of the Interior Order no. 2843; U.S. Fish and Wildlife Service, *Kern and Pixley National Wildlife Refuges: Final Comprehensive Conservation Plan* (Sacramento: U.S. Department of the Interior, Fish and Wildlife Service, 2005), 6.

14. U.S. Fish and Wildlife Service, *Kern and Pixley National Wildlife Refuges,* 29.

15. Narrative Report, January–April, 1960, Pixley National Wildlife Refuge, KNWRC, 1.

16. Narrative Report, May–August, 1960, Pixley National Wildlife Refuge, KNWRC, 5.

17. Narrative Report, May–August, 1960, Pixley National Wildlife Refuge, KNWRC, 3.

18. The statement of April 1960 is referenced in Kenneth A. Kuney, attorney at law, to Board of Supervisors, County of Tulare, September 22, 1961, box 114, folder 2, CEP.

19. W. A. Alexander, engineer-manager, Pixley Irrigation District, to Clair Engle, August 29, 1960, box 161, folder 1, CEP.

20. Resolution before the board of directors of the Alpaugh Irrigation District, County of Tulare, State of California, May, 4, 1960, box 161, folder 1, CEP.

21. The service purchased the 10,544 acres from the Allison Honer Company. U.S. Fish and Wildlife Service, *Kern and Pixley National Wildlife Refuges*, 6.

22. Narrative Report, January–April 1961, Kern National Wildlife Refuge, KNWRC, 2.

23. Narrative Report, January–April 1960, Pixley National Wildlife Refuge, KNWRC, 13; Narrative Report, January–April 1961, Kern National Wildlife Refuge, KNWRC, 13; U.S. Fish and Wildlife Service, *Kern and Pixley National Wildlife Refuges*, 6.

24. Narrative Report, 1981, Kern National Wildlife Refuge, KNWRC, 18.

25. Banding of approximately one thousand ducks in the Tulare Basin during July and August of 1958 had conclusively proved that most pintail relocated to the lower San Joaquin Valley (San Joaquin Basin) during the fall and winter. Narrative Report, January–April 1960, Pixley National Wildlife Refuge, KNWRC, 13. The problem of displaced pintail would become more acute during the 1980s, when changes in irrigation methods in the Tulare Basin led to a drastic reduction in the duration of pre-irrigation inundation, which had previously lasted from two to three weeks on each parcel.

26. Narrative Report, 1965, Kern National Wildlife Refuge and Pixley National Wildlife Refuge, KNWRC.

27. U.S. Fish and Wildlife Service, *Kern and Pixley National Wildlife Refuges*, 26–27. The Central Valley Project Improvement Act is discussed in chapter 10.

28. J. L. Medeiros, "San Luis Island: The Last of the Great Valley," *Fremontia* 7, no. 1 (1979).

29. Gordon, *California's Fish and Game Program*, 245.

30. Miller and Lux sold the property to the Moffat and Noble Cattle Company. Leach, "Historical Account of Waterfowling," 180–181.

31. 75 *Stat.* 813, Public Law 87–383. The funds for wetland purchases were to be allocated as loans against future sales of federal duck stamps.

32. Leach, "Historical Account of Waterfowling," 182–183.

33. 78 *Stat.* 701, Public Law 88–523. Counties would receive an annual payment of 25 percent of the net revenue derived from public lands, or 0.75 percent of the cost of those public lands, whichever was greater.

34. Leach, "Historical Account of Waterfowling," 183–192.

35. Narrative Reports, 1968, San Luis National Wildlife Refuge, SLNWRC, 7; ibid., 1981, 7–8.

36. Narrative Report, 1970, San Luis National Wildlife Refuge, SLNWRC.

37. Leach, "Historical Account of Waterfowling," 189.

38. Narrative Reports, 1974, San Luis National Wildlife Refuge, SLNWRC, 5; ibid., 1975, 9. In 1970 only 500 free-roaming elk existed in the state. By 1994, California's overall tule elk population had grown to 2,700 in twenty-three herds. Carl G. Thelander, ed., *Life on the Edge: A Guide to California's Endangered Natural Resources: Wildlife* (Santa Cruz, Calif.: BioSystems Books, 1994), 103.

39. Cooperative Agreement no. 14–06–200–467–4A; U.S. General Accounting Office, *Wildlife Management: National Refuge Contamination Is Difficult to Confirm and Clean Up*, Report to the chairman, Subcommittee on Oversight and Investigations, Committee on Energy and Commerce, House of Representatives (Washington, D.C.: General Accounting Office, 1987), 20.

40. The eastern side of the valley, particularly in Fresno County, was remarkable for its densely settled agricultural colonies. See Virginia E. Thickens, "Pioneer Agricultural Colonies of Fresno County," *California Historical Quarterly* 25, nos. 1 and 2 (1946).

41. California Department of Water Resources, *The California Water Plan* (Sacramento: California Department of Water Resources, Bulletin no. 3, 1957), 119.

42. The Westside of the southern San Joaquin Valley is south of, and distinct from, the Westside of the San Joaquin Basin identified with the properties of Miller and Lux, discussed in chapter 3.

43. This route was a westward extension of Southern Pacific's line through the Mussel Slough district, from Goshen to Huron, completed in 1877.

44. Ed Simmons, *Westlands Water District: The First 25 Years, 1952–1977* (Fresno, Calif.: Westlands Water District, 1983), 4–24; U.S. Bureau of Reclamation, *Report to the Regional Director—San Luis Unit, Central Valley Project, California: A Report on the Feasibility of Water Supply Development* (Sacramento: U.S. Department of the Interior, Bureau of Reclamation, 1955), 4–5.

45. Annual average recharge in the region is approximately 210,000 acre-feet. U.S. Bureau of Reclamation, *Report to the Regional Director—San Luis Unit*, 5.

46. Simmons, *Westlands Water District*, 24.

47. U.S. Bureau of Reclamation, *Substantiating Report—San Luis Unit, Central Valley Project, California: A Report on the Feasibility of Water Supply Development* (Sacramento: U.S. Department of the Interior, Bureau of Reclamation, 1955), 12–13.

48. U.S. Bureau of Reclamation, *Report to the Regional Director—San Luis Unit*, 5; Simmons, *Westlands Water District*, 29. The Fresno County Board of Supervisors approved the organization of the Westlands Water District on September 8, 1952.

49. In 1959, on the eve of federal authorization of the San Luis Unit expansion of the Central Valley Project, the eight largest holdings in the Westlands Water District encompassed nearly 160,000 of the district's 367,000 irrigable acres. A single corporation, the Southern Pacific Railroad Company, owned more than 58,000 acres of land, not including acreage owned as right-of-way. Jack W. Rodner, manager, Westlands Water District, to California senators Kuchel and Engle, May 8, 1959, box 158, folder 3, CEP.

50. U.S. Bureau of Reclamation, *Special Task Force Report on San Luis Unit, Central Valley Project, California* (Washington, D.C.: U.S. Department of the Interior, U.S. Bureau of Reclamation, 1978), 3; Arax and Wartzman, *King of California*, 382–383.

51. Russell Clemings, *Mirage: The False Promise of Desert Agriculture* (San Francisco: Sierra Club Books, 1996), 85–86; Simmons, *Westlands Water District*, 32.

52. U.S. Bureau of Reclamation, *Central Valley Basin.*

53. U.S. Bureau of Reclamation, *San Luis Unit, Central Valley Project, California: A Report on the Feasibility of Water Supply Development* (Sacramento: U.S. Department of the Interior, Bureau of Reclamation, 1955).

54. The additional districts were the 51,290-acre San Luis Water District and the 40,070-acre Panoche Water District. U.S. Bureau of Reclamation, *Substantiating Report— San Luis Unit,* 8–9.

55. U.S. Bureau of Reclamation, *Substantiating Report—San Luis Unit,* 22.

56. Gerrit Schoups et al., "Sustainability of Irrigated Agriculture in the San Joaquin Valley, California," *Proceedings of the National Academy of Sciences of the United States of America* 102, no. 43 (2005).

57. San Joaquin Valley Drainage Program, *A Management Plan for Agricultural Subsurface Drainage and Related Problems on the Westside San Joaquin Valley: Final Report of the San Joaquin Valley Drainage Program* (U.S. Department of the Interior and California Resources Agency, 1990), 25, 30.

58. The drains were referred to as tile drains, reflecting the fact that they were originally constructed of hollow, cylindrical clay tiles, dug in by hand. During the 1960s, more efficient plastic drainage tile was developed. Available in long coils that are easily connected together, plastic tiles are ridged and contain individual slots between the ridges, allowing for greater infiltration. Although these plastic coils, now buried by plows using laser levels, are hardly "tiles," the term remains in use. For the early development of tile drainage in the United States, see Marion M. Weaver, *History of Tile Drainage in America Prior to 1900* (Waterloo, N.Y.: 1964). For the status of tile drainage in the San Joaquin Valley during the 1960s, see Arthur F. Pillsbury and William R. Johnston, *Tile Drainage in the San Joaquin Valley of California* (Los Angeles: University of California, Department of Irrigation and Soil Science, 1965).

59. U.S. Bureau of Reclamation, *Substantiating Report—San Luis Unit,* 22, 73–76.

60. 1947 *Statutes of California* ch. 1541; California Department of Water Resources, *California Water Plan,* xxv. The water investigation was begun under the direction of the State Water Resources Board, created in 1945 (1945 *Statutes of California* ch. 1514). In 1956 the legislature, meeting in a special session, created the Department of Water Resources, which brought together fifty-two formerly independent agencies responsible for the state's water planning and development. Kahrl, ed., *California Water Atlas,* 51.

61. California Water Resources Board, *Report on Feasibility of Feather River Project and Sacramento–San Joaquin Delta Diversion Projects Proposed as Features of the California Water Plan* (Sacramento: California Water Resources Board, 1951).

62. California Department of Public Works, *Program for Financing and Constructing the Feather River Project as the Initial Unit of the California Water Plan* (Sacramento: California Department of Public Works, Division of Engineering and Irrigation, 1955).

63. Bob Holdaway, "Yuba City Flood: December 24, 1955," vertical files, Sutter County Library, Yuba City; "How Yuba City Flood Was Born," *Sacramento Union,* January 1, 1956, n.p.

64. Hundley, *Great Thirst,* 280; Kahrl, ed., *California Water Atlas,* 51.

65. California senators Knowland and Kuchel simultaneously introduced a similar measure in the Senate.

66. The CCID extends from Stanislaus County in the north, across the length of Merced County (west of the Grassland Water District), to Fresno County in the south.

67. B. F. Sisk, *A Congressional Record: The Memoir of Bernie Sisk* (Fresno, Calif.: Panorama West, 1980), 75–76.

68. 74 *Stat.* 156, Public Law 86–488.

69. U.S. Bureau of Reclamation, *Substantiating Report—San Luis Unit,* 23 (quote), 30.

70. U.S. Bureau of Reclamation, "Soil Classification Studies—San Luis Unit," Appendix D to *Special Task Force Report on San Luis Unit, Central Valley Project, California* (Washington, D.C.: U.S. Department of the Interior, Bureau of Reclamation, 1978), 283. Deliveries of San Luis Project water by the Bureau of Reclamation to 156,000 acres of the Westlands Water District that had not been included in the original service area for the San Luis Unit would generate a contentious struggle over the legality of those deliveries. The 156,000 acres included the 112,000 acres on the eastern side of the district that the bureau reclassified as irrigable in 1962, as well as lands along the extreme western side of the district that had formed part of the annexed Westplains Water Storage District. In 1978, under the Carter administration, Interior Department Solicitor Leo Krulitz issued an opinion that the legitimate service area was restricted to the 1955 delineation. Leo Krulitz, Opinion no. M-36901. Westlands Water District—Legal Questions, in *Decisions of the Department of the Interior* 85 (Washington, D.C.: U.S. Government Printing Office, 1978), 297–326. The issue was not resolved until 1986, when the Reagan administration's solicitor, Ralph Tarr, issued an opinion contending that the entire Westlands Water District was considered part of the authorized service area of the San Luis Unit. Tarr's opinion quieted charges that the bureau had illegally constructed part of its water delivery system on lands unauthorized to receive project water. Bryan J. Wilson, "Westlands Water District and Its Federal Water: A Case Study of Water District Politics," *Stanford Environmental Law Journal* 7 (1987–1988): 202, 213–214.

71. Theresa S. Presser, "Geologic Origin and Pathways of Selenium from the California Coast Ranges to the West-Central San Joaquin Valley," in *Selenium in the Environment,* ed. W. T. Frankenberger Jr. and Sally Benson (New York: Marcel Dekker, 1994), 139–141. An alluvial fan is a fan-shaped deposit formed where a fast-flowing stream slows and spreads, typically at the exit of a canyon or ravine, onto a more level plain.

72. 1959 *Statutes of California* ch. 1762. The Burns-Porter Act was retroactively named after Senator Hugh Burns and Assemblyman Carley Porter, the two legislative leaders on water policy.

73. California Department of Water Resources, *California Water Plan,* 21.

74. The water rights of Northern Californians were guaranteed by the incorporation of the Watershed Protection Act, first passed as part of the Central Valley Project Act (1933 *Statutes of California* ch. 1042), into the Burns-Porter Act. For Southern Californians, the Burns-Porter Act guaranteed that future legislatures could not rescind or alter water contracts entered into with the state. For Delta water users, the separate passage of the Delta Protection Act (1959 *Statutes of California* ch. 1766) guaranteed the quantity

and quality of Delta water supplies. Despite these measures, regional fears and suspicions remained.

75. *Ivanhoe Irrigation District v. McCracken*, 357 U.S. 275 (1958).

76. Southern California would eventually contract with the State Water Project for 2.5 million acre-feet of water annually, out of a project total of 4.2 million acre-feet. Hundley, *Great Thirst*, 293. For the interstate litigation, see *Arizona v. California*, 373 U.S. 546 (1963).

77. Hundley, *Great Thirst*, 278–291; Kahrl, ed., *California Water Atlas*, 51–52.

78. The state had advanced this position during the years the San Luis legislation was evolving, and thus provision for California to enter into negotiations with the United States concerning the joint operation of the San Luis Unit had been written into the San Luis Act.

79. California would have the right to approximately 1.1 million acre-feet of water in the San Luis Reservoir and would pay 55 percent of all the joint-use facilities' construction costs. The federal government would have the right to approximately 1.0 million acre-feet and would pay the remaining 45 percent of the costs. "Interior Approves Federal-State Agreement for $433 Million San Luis Unit in California," U.S. Department of the Interior news release, Office of the Secretary, December 31, 1961, box 158, folder 1, CEP.

80. Clair Engle, "The San Luis Project—Moving Forward Again," speech delivered on August 18, 1962, box 158, folder 2, CEP.

81. The expected cost of construction of the master drain was approximately $92 million, dwarfing that of the bureau's interceptor drain. California Department of Water Resources, *San Joaquin Valley Drainage Investigation: San Joaquin Master Drain* (Sacramento: California Department of Water Resources, Bulletin no. 127, 1965), 34.

82. Jackson and Paterson, *Sacramento–San Joaquin Delta*, 143.

83. The lawsuit was dismissed more than five years later, in May 1973, upon the near-completion of the drain. The CCID had previously sued the agency on the same grounds in 1962. C. Ray Robinson to B. F. Sisk, January 24, 1964, box 1, folder 9, JMW; U.S. Bureau of Reclamation, *Special Task Force Report on San Luis Unit*, 287.

84. United States Department of the Interior news release, Office of the Secretary, "Nation's Largest Water Contract Signed in White House Ceremony," January 28, 1963; Contract between the United States and Westlands Water District providing for water service, Contract no. 14–06–200–495-A, June 5, 1963, box 158, folder 3, CEP. The contract required landowners to enter "recordable contracts" to sell "excess lands," those holdings in excess of the 160-acre limitation of the Reclamation Act, within ten years of receiving project water. Despite the guarantees in the San Luis Act and in the water-service contract that reclamation law would apply, the persistent concentration of land ownership in Westlands would prove contentious for decades. For a discussion of the failure of reclamation law in the Westlands Water District on the eve of the Reclamation Reform Act of 1982 (99 *Stat.* 1261, 1263, Public Law 97–293), which raised the acreage limitation to 960 acres, see Mary Louise Frampton, "The Enforcement of Federal Reclamation Law in the Westlands Water District: A Broken Promise," *UC Davis Law Review* 13, no. 1 (1979–1980).

85. Simmons, *Westlands Water District*, 69–73.

86. Jackson and Paterson, *Sacramento–San Joaquin Delta*, 143.

87. Narrative Report, 1969, Kesterson National Wildlife Refuge, SLNWRC. The bureau had acquired the 5,900-acre site in 1968. A second stage of the reservoir, never completed, was to consist of thirty-nine ponds on 4,000 additional acres. U.S. Department of the Interior, *Kesterson Reservoir Closure and Cleanup Plan* (U.S. Department of the Interior, 1985), 2–3.

88. U.S. Department of the Interior and California Department of Fish and Game, *General Plan for Use of Project Land and Waters for Wildlife Conservation and Management, Kesterson Reservoir, California* (U.S. Department of the Interior and California Department of Fish and Game, 1969); U.S. Bureau of Reclamation, *Special Task Force Report on San Luis Unit*, 288; S. M. Benson, M. Delamore, and S. Hoffman, *Kesterson Crisis: Sorting out the Facts* (Berkeley, Calif.: Lawrence Berkeley Laboratory Report, LBL-30587, 1990), 1.

9. TRAGEDY AT KESTERSON RESERVOIR

1. Narrative Report, 1970, Kesterson National Wildlife Refuge, SLNWRC, 1–2.

2. This agreement, which required the provision of 3,500 acre-feet of winter water and, when available, at least 4,000 acre-feet of summer water, was part of the district's 1969 contract, which had reduced its water costs in exchange for executing covenants of restrictive use.

3. Arnold Schultz, "Background and Recent History," in *Selenium and Agricultural Drainage: Implications for San Francisco Bay and the California Environment, Proceedings of the Second Selenium Symposium, March 23, 1985, Berkeley, California* (Berkeley, Calif.: Bay Institute of San Francisco, 1986), 6.

4. Clemings, *Mirage*, 57; Benson, Delamore, and Hoffman, "Kesterson Crisis," 2.

5. Jackson and Paterson, *Sacramento–San Joaquin Delta*, 140–141. As a representative of Contra Costa County—whose waters between San Francisco Bay and the Delta were the proposed recipient of the wastewater of the San Luis Drain—Miller carried legislation to halt completion of the drain and to provide the first federal water quality protections for the Delta. Alice Q. Howard, ed., *Selenium and Agricultural Drainage: Implications for San Francisco Bay and the California Environment, Proceedings of the Fourth Selenium Symposium, March 21, 1987, Berkeley, California* (Sausalito, Calif.: Bay Institute of San Francisco, 1989), 12–13.

6. Harry M. Ohlendorf, "Bioaccumulation and Effects of Selenium in Wildlife," in *Selenium in Agriculture and the Environment*, ed. L. W. Jacobs, SSSA Special Publication no. 23 (Madison, Wisc.: Soil Science Society of America, 1989), 153.

7. U.S. Bureau of Reclamation, *Report to the Regional Director—San Luis Unit*, 21.

8. California Department of Water Resources, *California Water Plan*, 119.

9. California Department of Water Resources, *California Water Plan*, 143; Janne Ilmari Hukkinen, "Unplugging Drainage: Toward Sociotechnical Redesign of San Joaquin Valley's Agricultural Drainage Management," PhD diss., University of California at Berkeley, 1990, 4–5.

10. California Department of Water Resources, *San Joaquin Valley Drainage Investigation*, 40.

11. Leach, *Wildlife and Fishery Resources in Relation to Drainage Disposal Problems*, x, 117 (quote); Leach, "Historical Account of Waterfowling," 160.

12. California Department of Water Resources, *Lower San Joaquin Valley Water Quality Investigation* (Sacramento: California Department of Water Resources, Bulletin no. 89, 1960), 95.

13. H. W. Lakin, "Geochemistry of Selenium in Relation to Agriculture," in *Selenium in Agriculture* (Washington, D.C.: U.S. Department of Agriculture, Agricultural Research Service, Agriculture Handbook no. 200, 1961), 12; U.S. Department of Agriculture, *Selenium Occurrence in Certain Soils in the United States, with a Discussion of Related Topics: Sixth Report* (Washington, D.C.: U.S. Department of Agriculture, Technical Bulletin no. 783, 1941).

14. The sources of this selenium are the Moreno and Kreyenhagen Shale formations of the Coast Ranges. These formations reach a maximum selenium concentration of 45 parts per million (ppm), with median values of 6.5 and 8.7 ppm, respectively. In comparison, the average selenium concentration in the Earth's crust as a whole is only between 0.03 and 0.08 ppm. Geologists believe that the selenium in the Coast Ranges originated from extensive volcanic eruptions during the Cretaceous period, from 146 million to 65 million years ago. The selenium was deposited in sediments of the inland sea that once covered the Central Valley and that eventually formed the Moreno and Kreyenhagen shales. These shale formations have since been uplifted as the Coast Ranges and exposed to weathering and erosion. Overall selenium transport from the Coast Ranges to the San Joaquin Valley has taken place by both mass wasting (landslides, slumps, or mudflows) and surface runoff. Presser, "Geologic Origin and Pathways of Selenium," 145; Charles G. Wilber, *Selenium: A Potential Environmental Poison and a Necessary Food Constituent* (Springfield, Ill.: Charles C. Thomas, 1983), 4; Ivan Barnes, "Sources of Selenium," in *Selenium and Agricultural Drainage: Implications for San Francisco Bay and the California Environment, Proceedings of the Second Selenium Symposium, March 23, 1985, Berkeley, California* (Berkeley, Calif.: Bay Institute of San Francisco, 1986), 42–46.

15. Bioaccumulation is the accumulation of an element or compound in the tissues of an organism to concentrations that are significantly higher than those found in the environment in which the organism lives. Bioaccumulation may occur via bioconcentration (the bioaccumulation of a chemical directly from the nonliving environment) and biomagnification (the bioaccumulation of a chemical at ever greater concentrations from one trophic level to another up the food chain). Biomagnification can result in tissue concentrations orders of magnitude greater than concentrations in the surrounding environment. S. B. Moore et al., *Fish and Wildlife Resources and Agricultural Drainage in the San Joaquin Valley, California* (Sacramento: San Joaquin Valley Drainage Program, 1990), vol. 1, 3-6.

16. U.S. House of Representatives, Subcommittee on Water and Power Resources of the Committee on Interior and Insular Affairs, *Hearing on Agricultural Drainage Problems and Contamination at Kesterson Reservoir*, 99th Congress, 1st session, March 15, 1985, 233–234. A subsequent change in the department's sampling procedure, however, resulted in no further detections of selenium until 1981.

17. U.S. House of Representatives, Subcommittee on Water and Power Resources, *Hearing on Agricultural Drainage Problems*, 233, 235 (quote). The State Water Resources Control Board was formed in 1967 from the merger of the State Water Quality Control Board and the State Water Rights Board. The duties of the State Water Resources Control Board are enumerated in the Porter-Cologne Water Quality Control Act, 1969 *Statutes of California* ch. 482, division 7.

18. Schultz, "Background and Recent History," 6.

19. Simmons, *Westlands Water District*, 73.

20. San Joaquin Valley Drainage Program, *Management Plan for Agricultural Subsurface Drainage*, 21.

21. San Joaquin Valley Interagency Drainage Program, *Agricultural Drainage and Salt Management in the San Joaquin Valley: Final Report Including Recommended Plan and First-Stage Environmental Impact Report* (Fresno, Calif.: U.S. Bureau of Reclamation, California Department of Water Resources, and California State Water Resources Control Board, 1979), 7-4. An alternative to Monterey Bay as an oceanic discharge point was Estero Bay, located farther south near the town of Cayucos.

22. The San Joaquin Valley suffers from a negative salt balance that increasingly threatens the long-term viability of agriculture on approximately 400,000 acres of the region. San Joaquin Valley Interagency Drainage Program, *Agricultural Drainage and Salt Management*, 1-1. Representative data from 1990 indicate that 1.9 million tons of salt per year enter the valley's groundwater as a result of leaching by irrigation water. Of that amount, 1.4 million tons are not exported. Manucher Alemi, presentation at the Salinity/Drainage Program Annual Meeting, sponsored by the University of California Salinity/Drainage Task Force, Sacramento, Calif. (March 26–27, 1997).

23. J. Letey et al., *An Agricultural Dilemma: Drainage Water and Toxics Disposal in the San Joaquin Valley* (Davis, Calif.: University of California, Division of Natural Resources, Agricultural Experiment Station, Special Publication no. 3319, 1986); U.S. Department of the Interior, *Kesterson Reservoir Closure and Cleanup Plan*, 4.

24. U.S. House of Representatives, Subcommittee on Water and Power Resources, *Hearing on Agricultural Drainage Problems*, 236–237.

25. Letey, *Agricultural Dilemma*. For the next decade and a half, Zahm meticulously documented the events that took place at Kesterson in the refuge's annual narrative reports.

26. Selenium levels were 26.0–31.0 mg/kg wet weight at Kesterson versus 0.39 mg/kg wet weight at Volta. Michael K. Saiki, "Concentrations of Selenium in Aquatic Food-Chain Organisms and Fish Exposed to Agricultural Tile Drainage Water," in *Selenium and Agricultural Drainage: Implications for San Francisco Bay and the California Environment, Proceedings of the Second Selenium Symposium, March 23, 1985, Berkeley, California* (Berkeley, Calif.: Bay Institute of San Francisco, 1986), 27. Volta was originally a Central Valley Project facility known as the San Luis Wasteway Holding Reservoir. In 1952 it was opened as a public hunting area, and its name was later changed to the Volta Wildlife Area.

27. Mark B. Campbell, *Ownership and Recreational Use of Wetlands in the Grassland Water District and Refuges of the Central San Joaquin Valley* (Sacramento: U.S. Bureau

of Reclamation, San Joaquin Valley Drainage Program, 1988), 43; Letey, *Agricultural Dilemma*.

28. Harry M. Ohlendorf et al., "Embryonic Mortality and Abnormalities of Aquatic Birds: Apparent Impacts of Selenium from Irrigation Drainwater," *The Science of the Total Environment* 52 (1986): 50; Ohlendorf, "Bioaccumulation and Effects of Selenium," 159.

29. Harry Ohlendorf, interview with the author, Davis, California, April 9, 1997.

30. In 1978 Smith had been awarded the prestigious American Motors Conservation Award for his efforts to protect wildlife.

31. See, for example, E. J. Thacker, "Effect of Selenium on Animals," in *Selenium in Agriculture* (Washington, D.C.: Agricultural Research Service, Agriculture Handbook no. 200, 1961), 50, displaying a photo of a selenized chick embryo almost identical in appearance to those found at Kesterson.

32. Arthur W. Kilness and Jerry L. Simmons, "Toxic Effects of Selenium on Wildlife Species and Other Organisms," in *Selenium and Agricultural Drainage: Implications for San Francisco Bay and the California Environment, Proceedings of the Second Selenium Symposium, March 23, 1985, Berkeley, California* (Berkeley, Calif.: Bay Institute of San Francisco, 1986), 56; Wilber, *Selenium*, 62; J. E. Oldfield, "Selenium: An Essential Poison," *Science of Food and Agriculture* 4, no. 2 (1986): 23.

33. Felix Smith, *Information Alert—Agricultural Waste Water (AWW) Investigation— Need for Water/Soil/Vegetation/Invertebrate Monitoring* (Sacramento: U.S. Department of the Interior, Fish and Wildlife Service, 1983); U.S. House of Representatives, Subcommittee on Water and Power Resources, *Hearing on Agricultural Drainage Problems*, 239–240.

34. Dave Lenhart, *Concern Alert: Contaminant Problems at Kesterson NWR, California—Selenium* (Portland, Ore.: U.S. Department of the Interior, Fish and Wildlife Service, 1983).

35. Harry Ohlendorf, interview with the author, Davis, California, April 9, 1997; Clemings, *Mirage*, 64; Letey, *Agricultural Dilemma*. In at least one instance, a bureau spokesperson went too far with his denials. Jerry King, the bureau's chief western public relations officer, was fired for dismissing the seriousness of the Kesterson situation on network television. Tom Harris, *Death in the Marsh* (Washington, D.C.: Island Press, 1991), 26.

36. Theresa S. Presser and Ivan Barnes, *Selenium Content in Waters Tributary to and in the Vicinity of Kesterson NWR* (Menlo Park, Calif.: U.S. Geological Survey, 1984), 16; Theresa S. Presser and Ivan Barnes, *Dissolved Constituents, Includes Waters in the Vicinity of Kesterson NWR and the West Grasslands, Fresno and Merced Counties, CA* (Menlo Park, Calif.: U.S. Geological Survey, 1985), 46; K. J. Maier and A. W. Knight, "Ecotoxicology of Selenium in Freshwater Systems," *Reviews of Environmental Contamination and Toxicology* 134 (1994). Until circa 1985, background fresh water concentrations of selenium are often cited as "less than 2 µg/L," reflecting the threshold for detectability at that time.

37. One USGS value for selenium—collected using approved techniques—was 7,000 percent of the bureau's comparable figure. Schultz, "Background and Recent History," 8.

38. Saiki, "Concentrations of Selenium in Aquatic Food-Chain Organisms," 37–38.

39. Deborah Blum, "Mineral Is Linked to Bird Deformities," *Fresno Bee*, September 21, 1983.

40. Other major California newspapers that highlighted the Kesterson story included the *Sacramento Bee, San Jose Mercury News, San Francisco Chronicle*, and *Los Angeles Times*. Despite the wide media coverage that Kesterson generated, it has received little attention from historians, although a few have given it brief mention. See Hundley, *Great Thirst*, 429–431; Worster, *Rivers of Empire*, 323–324. Journalists have paid more attention to Kesterson. See Harris, *Death in the Marsh;* Clemings, *Mirage*. Much of the scientific literature on the subject appears in highly technical journals, but for an accessible article, see Kenneth Tanji, Andre Lauchli, and Jewel Meyer, "Selenium in the San Joaquin Valley," *Environment* 28, no. 6 (1986).

41. U.S. House of Representatives, Subcommittee on Water and Power Resources, *Hearing on Agricultural Drainage Problems*, 241. The Clauses also petitioned the Central Valley Regional Water Quality Control Board to take enforcement action against the Grassland Water District, which transported and discharged contaminated agricultural drainage water, although the district did not actually generate the selenium contamination. The board, with offices in Sacramento and Fresno, is one of nine regional water quality control boards for the state of California.

42. U.S. House of Representatives, Subcommittee on Water and Power Resources, *Hearing on Agricultural Drainage Problems*, 241.

43. Gregory Gordon and Lloyd G. Carter, "Poison in the Valley," *Fresno Bee*, August 13–17, 1984.

44. *Down the Drain* was produced in 1984 by Joseph Kwong and Gray Brechin for the KQED Current Affairs Department.

45. Deborah Blum, "Kesterson Refuge: No Safe Harbor," *Defenders* (November–December 1984): 35.

46. Documented in *Down the Drain*. The San Luis Drain was known to leak at its concrete panel joints, and the highly saline and seleniferous water that escaped was probably the source of the reported problems. Gary Zahm, U.S. Fish and Wildlife Service, retired, personal correspondence.

47. U.S. House of Representatives, Subcommittee on Water and Power Resources, *Hearing on Agricultural Drainage Problems*, 242–243.

48. Presser and Barnes, *Dissolved Constituents*, 10; Blum, "Kesterson Refuge," 30, 34. Selenium exists in nature in four states of biological significance, as selenide, elemental selenium, selenite, and selenate. The oxidation states of the four forms are: selenide (Se^{2-}), elemental selenium (Se^0), selenite (Se^{4+}), and selenate (Se^{6+}). John L. Fio and Roger Fujii, *Comparison of Methods to Determine Selenium Species in Saturation Extracts of Soils from the Western San Joaquin Valley, California* (Sacramento: U.S. Geological Survey, 1988), 2. Selenate is the predominant inorganic form in semiarid areas that possess alkaline soils, such as the San Joaquin Valley. Ohlendorf, "Bioaccumulation and Effects of Selenium," 135. Selenium, insoluble at low to moderate pH, becomes soluble at high pH. The high evaporation rates and generally saline soils of the southern San Joaquin Valley produce high pH soil water conditions associated with high concentrations of soluble selenium. Mount, *California Rivers and Streams*, 263.

49. The percentage of soluble selenium found in soils that enters the food chain is difficult to quantify and depends on a variety of biotic and abiotic factors, including plant species present, rainfall, temperature, soil pH, plant growth rates, root depth, and distribution of selenium in the soil profile. Harry M. Ohlendorf and Gary M. Santolo, "Kesterson Reservoir—Past, Present and Future: An Ecological Risk Assessment," in *Selenium in the Environment,* ed. W. T. Frankenberger Jr. and Sally Benson (New York: Marcel Dekker, 1994), 73.

50. Ohlendorf, "Bioaccumulation and Effects of Selenium," 159, 163-166. For additional data on selenium toxicity at Kesterson, see S. B. Moore et al., *Fish and Wildlife Resources and Agricultural Drainage in the San Joaquin Valley, California* (Sacramento: San Joaquin Valley Drainage Program, 1990), vol. 2, 4 - 23 - 4 - 57.

51. Saiki, "Concentrations of Selenium in Aquatic Food-Chain Organisms," 31. These measurements were taken in the Main Canal, originally part of Miller and Lux's irrigation system.

52. Harry M. Ohlendorf, "Aquatic Birds and Selenium in the San Joaquin Valley," in *Selenium and Agricultural Drainage: Implications for San Francisco Bay and the California Environment, Proceedings of the Second Selenium Symposium, March 23, 1985, Berkeley, California* (Berkeley, Calif.: Bay Institute of San Francisco, 1986), 22. For additional data on selenium toxicity in the Grasslands, see Moore et al., *Fish and Wildlife Resources and Agricultural Drainage,* vol. 2, 4 - 127 - 4 - 138.

53. Grassland Water District, *Ecological and Water Management Characterization,* 2, 10.

54. Narrative Report, 1985, San Luis National Wildlife Refuge, SLNWRC, 1. The rerouting of selenium-contaminated drainwater by the Grasslands Water District into Salt Slough negatively affected the San Luis National Wildlife Refuge, which depended on Salt Slough as a water source. In April 1985 refuge manager Gary Zahm ceased the application of Salt Slough waters on the refuge. In May the regional director of the Fish and Wildlife Service and the director of the California Department of Fish and Game officially announced that federal and state agencies would not utilize toxic drainwaters. Gary Zahm, "Impacts Associated with Grassland Drainage Program," Memorandum to regional director, Portland, Oregon, March 22, 1985; Gary Zahm, "Salt Slough Degradation and Associated Impacts," Memorandum to regional director, Portland, Oregon, September 25, 1985. Personal files of Gary Zahm, made available to the author. Despite the clear language of the 1954 Grasslands Act (68 *Stat.* 879), which had reauthorized the Central Valley Project, to include use of its waters for fish and wildlife purposes, the Bureau of Reclamation had continued to provide primarily drainwater—not fresh Central Valley Project water—to the national wildlife refuges and state wildlife areas in the Grasslands. At the time of the selenium crisis, the bureau still had not fully accepted the fish and wildlife protection purpose of the Central Valley Project, and the Department of the Interior had supported the bureau's restrictive reading of the act. Regional Solicitor Charles R. Penda to field supervisor, Division of Ecological Services, Fish and Wildlife Service, Sacramento, "Fish and Wildlife Purposes of the Central Valley Project," April 14, 1977. Personal files of Felix Smith, made available to the author.

55. Joseph P. Skorupa, "Selenium Poisoning of Fish and Wildlife in Nature: Lessons from Twelve Real-World Examples," in *Environmental Chemistry of Selenium,* ed. William T. Frankenberger Jr. and Richard A. Engberg (New York: Marcel Dekker, 1998), 341.

56. Ohlendorf, "Bioaccumulation and Effects of Selenium," 156, 165.

57. These symposia, titled Selenium and Agricultural Drainage: Implications for San Francisco Bay and the California Environment, are generally referred to as Selenium I, II, III, and IV. Selenium II was held on March 23, 1985; Selenium III on March 15, 1986; and Selenium IV on March 21, 1987. Selenium II, III, and IV were cosponsored by the San Francisco Bay Institute, and Selenium II was also cosponsored by the U.S. Fish and Wildlife Service. The proceedings of all except the first symposium have been published.

58. Schultz, "Background and Recent History," 7–8.

59. Felix Smith, interview with the author, Carmichael, California, April 14, 1997; Clemings, *Mirage,* 64–65; Tom Harris, "Kesterson Whistle-Blower Being Eased Out," *Sacramento Bee,* February 4, 1986, A1; Harris, *Death in the Marsh,* 28.

60. Bill Sweeney, "The Central Valley Project and the Public Trust Doctrine: Some Questions Which Should Be Asked—and Answered," presented at a public meeting on the use of agricultural drainage water on private and public wetlands for waterfowl, Los Banos, California, Fairgrounds, October 6, 1984, box 3, JMW; U.S. House of Representatives, Subcommittee on Water and Power Resources, *Hearing on Agricultural Drainage Problems,* 92, 237–239.

61. Lloyd G. Carter, "Grassland Probe Is Ordered," *Fresno Bee,* November 7, 1985, A1.

62. U.S. House of Representatives, Subcommittee on Water and Power Resources, *Hearing on Agricultural Drainage Problems,* 200–203. In August 1984 James Claus and his wife, Karen, filed a $33 million lawsuit against the United States for the destruction of their 650-acre property by means of contamination with agricultural drainage water. *Claus, James, and Claus, Karen E. v. United States et al.,* Civ. no. S84–1309 LKK (E.D. Cal. 1984). The suit was settled in September 1987 when the U.S. Department of the Interior purchased approximately ninety acres of the Claus property.

63. John Johnson, "Kesterson Cover-up Ruled Out," *Fresno Bee,* September 12, 1985, A12.

64. George Miller to Louis Clark, executive director, Government Accountability Project, Inc., February 26, 1986, reprinted in *Selenium and Agricultural Drainage: Implications for San Francisco Bay and the California Environment, Proceedings of the Third Selenium Symposium, March 15, 1986, Berkeley, California,* ed. Alice Q. Howard (Sausalito, Calif.: Bay Institute of San Francisco, 1989), ix–x.

65. Trauger served as director of the Patuxent Wildlife Research Center from 1983 to 1987 and as deputy director from 1987 to 1996.

66. Arnold Schultz to David L. Trauger, March 17, 1986; David L. Trauger to Arnold Schultz, March 31, 1986. Personal files of Harry Ohlendorf, made available to the author.

67. Harry Ohlendorf, interview with the author, Davis, California, April 9, 1997.

68. Affidavit of Joseph Blum, deputy regional director, U.S. Fish and Wildlife, 2, for *City of Mendota v. Hodel,* Civ. no. F-86–109-REC (E.D. Cal. 1986).

69. Affidavit of Joseph Blum, 3, for *City of Mendota v. Hodel.*

70. Tom Harris, "U.S. Conceals Deformity Study on Kesterson, Scholar Says," *Sacramento Bee,* March 22, 1986, A11. Clark was finally able to present his findings at the 1987 symposium. See Donald Clark, "Selenium and Small Mammal Populations at Kesterson Reservoir," in *Selenium and Agricultural Drainage: Implications for the San Francisco Bay and the California Environment, Proceedings of the Fourth Selenium Symposium, March 21, 1987, Berkeley, California,* ed. Alice Q. Howard (Berkeley, Calif.: Bay Institute of San Francisco, 1989), 82–90.

71. John Terborgh, *Where Have All the Birds Gone? Essays on the Biology and Conservation of Birds That Migrate to the American Tropics* (Princeton, N.J.: Princeton University Press, 1989), 26–27.

72. Reagan's pro-agribusiness policies were continued under the administration of George H. W. Bush, which ended federal funding for drainwater studies in 1991. State agencies were willing to fund the U.S. Fish and Wildlife Service's continuing selenium research. However, Douglas Buffington, director of research for the service's Region 8—which includes the Patuxent Wildlife Research Center and its field stations—forbade scientists to seek nonfederal funding for that research. Joseph Skorupa, U.S. Fish and Wildlife Service, interview with the author, Davis, California, April 24, 1997; Robert H. Boyle, "The Killing Fields," *Sports Illustrated,* March 22, 1993.

73. Patuxent Wildlife Research Center, *Patuxent Research Review Panel Report* (Laurel, Md.: U.S. Fish and Wildlife Service, Patuxent Wildlife Research Center, 1991), 72, 76.

74. Harry Ohlendorf, interview with the author, Davis, California, April 9, 1997; Felix Smith, interview with the author, Carmichael, California, April 14, 1997. Though retired, Smith has remained active in the politics of drainwater and has advanced the legal argument that the provision of irrigation water to seleniferous soils, with its ecologically harmful consequences, constitutes an unreasonable use of water and a violation of the public trust doctrine. See Felix Smith, "The Kesterson Effect: Reasonable Use of Water and the Public Trust," *San Joaquin Agricultural Law Review* 6, no. 1 (1996).

75. U.S. Department of the Interior, *Kesterson Reservoir Closure and Cleanup Plan,* 10; California State Water Resources Control Board, Cleanup and Abatement Order no. WQ 85-1 (1985). Finding that the wastewater entering Kesterson Reservoir constituted a hazardous waste, the board based much of its order on the state's recently passed Toxic Pits Cleanup Act, which prohibits discharge of liquid hazardous wastes into any surface impoundment, such as a reservoir, that lies within one-half mile upgradient from a potential source of drinking water, unless that impoundment is equipped with a double liner and a leachate collection system (1984 *Statutes of California* ch. 1543, article 9.5.). Because the unlined Kesterson Reservoir contained hazardous waste and was located within the half-mile limit from a drinking water source, the bureau was subject to the act.

76. The official designation of the Clean Water Act (CWA) is the Federal Water Pollution Control Act of 1972, 33 *U.S. Code* sec. 1251 et seq.

77. In November 1986 President Reagan pocket-vetoed the Clean Water Act, which was due for reauthorization. In February 1987 both the House and Senate voted by wide margins to override Reagan's veto. Howard, ed., *Selenium and Agricultural Drainage,* 10–11.

78. In 1987 Congress amended the Clean Water Act to emphasize regulation based on water quality, thereby requiring states to address nonpoint source pollution, but did not

actually require states to implement nonpoint source regulatory programs. Terry F. Young and Chelsea H. Congdon, *Plowing New Ground: Using Economic Incentives to Control Water Pollution from Agriculture* (Oakland, Calif.: Environmental Defense Fund, 1994), 4–5.

79. U.S. House of Representatives, Subcommittee on Water and Power Resources, *Hearing on Agricultural Drainage Problems*, 11. During the 1970s the Migratory Bird Treaty Act had been applied to a number of cases involving criminal prosecutions of private individuals and businesses, especially in situations in which harm to migratory birds was caused by pollution. Harrison C. Dunning, "Legal Aspects of the Kesterson Problem," in *Selenium and Agricultural Drainage: Implications for San Francisco Bay and the California Environment, Proceedings of the Second Selenium Symposium, March 23, 1985, Berkeley, California* (Berkeley, Calif.: Bay Institute of San Francisco, 1986), 120. For a list and discussion of such cases, see George Cameron Coggins and Sebastian T. Patti, "The Resurrection and Expansion of the Migratory Bird Treaty Act," *University of Colorado Law Review* 50 (1979): 184–188. However, no suit had ever held the government liable, and there was considerable debate within the Department of the Interior over whether the treaty permitted prosecution of the government.

80. Joel Hedgpeth, "Sense of the Meeting," in *Selenium and Agricultural Drainage: Implications for San Francisco Bay and the California Environment, Proceedings of the Second Selenium Symposium, March 23, 1985, Berkeley, California* (Berkeley, Calif.: Bay Institute of San Francisco, 1986), 168.

81. U.S. Department of the Interior, "Agreement between U.S. Department of the Interior and Westlands Water District Concerning Closure of Kesterson Reservoir, April 3, 1985, Appendix C to *U.S. Department of the Interior Kesterson Reservoir Closure and Cleanup Plan* (U.S. Department of the Interior, 1985). Westlands completed plugging the subsurface drains on the 42,000 affected acres on May 16, 1986.

82. The Westlands Water District and other water districts in the San Joaquin Valley have since gradually been able to increase their water use efficiency and consequently reduce the quantity of wastewater generated, but such measures alone cannot solve the drainage and toxicity problems. Studies of standard evaporation pond systems and ephemeral pools of groundwater in the Westlands Water District have continued to document selenium-induced embryonic deformities in waterbirds at rates significantly higher than those at Kesterson. Joseph Skorupa, "Drainage Solutions: Homage to the Ponds of Folly," presented at the University of California Salinity/Drainage Annual Conference, Sacramento, March 26, 2003. Despite a court ruling in 2000 that the Bureau of Reclamation remains obligated to provide drainage for the San Luis Unit of the Central Valley Project, a satisfactory solution has remained elusive. *Firebaugh Canal Co. v. U.S.*, 203 F. 3d 568 (9th Cir. 2000). For the development of the bureau's preferred alternatives for addressing the ongoing problem of drainage-impaired lands, including land retirement, see U.S. Bureau of Reclamation, *San Luis Drainage Feature Re-Evaluation, Plan Formulation Report* (Sacramento: U.S. Department of the Interior, Bureau of Reclamation, 2002); U.S. Bureau of Reclamation, *Final Environmental Impact Statement, San Luis Drainage Feature Re-Evaluation* (Sacramento: U.S. Department of the Interior, Bureau of Reclamation, 2006); U.S. Bureau of Reclamation, *San Luis Drainage Feature Re-Evaluation: Feasibility Report* (Sacramento: U.S. Department of the Interior, Bureau of Reclamation, 2008).

83. U.S. Bureau of Reclamation, *Final Environmental Impact Statement, Kesterson Program, Merced and Fresno Counties, CA* (Sacramento: U.S. Department of the Interior, Bureau of Reclamation, 1986).

84. U.S. Bureau of Reclamation, *Final Environmental Impact Statement, Kesterson Program,* vi.

85. Harry Ohlendorf, interview with the author, Davis, California, April 9, 1997; Alexander J. Horne, "Kinetics of Selenium Uptake and Loss and Seasonal Cycling of Selenium by the Aquatic Microbial Community in the Kesterson Wetlands," in *Selenium in the Environment,* ed. W. T. Frankenberger Jr. and Sally Benson (New York: Marcel Dekker, 1994).

86. California State Water Resources Control Board, Order no. WQ 87-3 (1987).

87. Harry Ohlendorf, interview with the author, Davis, California, April 9, 1997; Narrative Report, 1988, San Luis National Wildlife Refuge, SLNWRC, 6; Benson, Delamore, and Hoffman, "Kesterson Crisis," 5.

88. California State Water Resources Control Board, Order no. WQ 88-7 (1988).

89. Narrative Report, 1988, San Luis National Wildlife Refuge, SLNWRC, 8–9; U.S. Department of the Interior, *Effectiveness of Filling Ephemeral Pools at Kesterson Reservoir,* U.S. Department of the Interior submission to California State Water Resources Control Board in response to Order no. WQ 88-7 (U.S. Department of the Interior, 1989), 2–3.

90. Narrative Report, 1989, San Luis National Wildlife Refuge, SLNWRC, 23; U.S. Department of the Interior, *Kesterson Program Upland Habitat Assessment,* U.S. Department of the Interior submission to California State Water Resources Control Board in response to Order no. WQ 88-7 (U.S. Department of the Interior, 1989), 1, 11.

91. Ohlendorf and Santolo, "Kesterson Reservoir—Past, Present and Future," 104.

92. Fred L. Paveglio, Kevin M. Kilbride, and Christine M. Bunck, "Selenium in Aquatic Birds from Central California," *Journal of Wildlife Management* 61, no. 3 (1997); Fred L. Paveglio and Kevin M. Kilbride, "Selenium in Aquatic Birds from Central California," *Journal of Wildlife Management* 71, no. 8 (2007).

93. Arax and Wartzman, *King of California,* 397.

94. Skorupa, "Selenium Poisoning of Fish and Wildlife in Nature," 327–331; Joseph P. Skorupa and Harry M. Ohlendorf, *Drainwater Contaminants in Eggs Related to Deformities in Tulare Basin Waterbirds* (U.S. Fish and Wildlife Service, Research Information Bulletin no. 89-04, 1989).

95. Arnold Schultz, "Highlights since Selenium II," in *Selenium and Agricultural Drainage: Implications for San Francisco Bay and the California Environment, Proceedings of the Third Selenium Symposium, March 15, 1986, Berkeley, California,* ed. Alice Q. Howard (Berkeley, Calif.: Bay Institute of San Francisco, 1989), 5, 7.

96. Clemings, *Mirage,* 101.

97. Skorupa, "Selenium Poisoning of Fish and Wildlife in Nature," 327–333; Joseph P. Skorupa and Harry M. Ohlendorf, *Deformed Waterbird Embryos Found near Agricultural Drainage Ponds in the Tulare Basin* (U.S. Fish and Wildlife Service, Research Information Bulletin no. 88-49, 1988); Skorupa and Ohlendorf, *Drainwater Contaminants in Eggs.* Rates of embryo teratogenesis in one or more species of waterbirds at each of the sites ranged from 10 percent to 50 percent.

98. Clemings, *Mirage*, 106–107. For additional data on selenium toxicity in the Tulare Basin evaporation ponds, see Moore et al., *Fish and Wildlife Resources and Agricultural Drainage*, vol. 2, 4-243-4-410.

99. Joseph Skorupa, interview with the author, Davis, California, April 24, 1997.

100. Minutes of the State Water Resources Control Board, Sacramento, December 15, 1988, 1–2. Personal files of Joseph Skorupa, made available to the author.

101. Skorupa and Ohlendorf, *Deformed Waterbird Embryos*.

102. State Water Resources Control Board Resolution no. 88–130, December 15, 1988. Attachments 1 and 2 discuss the determination of "relevant" and "not relevant" research findings.

103. Central Valley Regional Water Quality Control Board, *Waste Discharge Requirements for Tulare Lake Drainage District*, Order no. 93–136 (Fresno, Calif.: Central Valley Regional Water Quality Control Board, 1993).

104. Skorupa, "Selenium Poisoning of Fish and Wildlife in Nature," 331.

105. Joseph Skorupa, interview with the author, Davis, California, April 24, 1997; Arax and Wartzman, *King of California*, 399–400; Clemings, *Mirage*, 98–99.

106. Mount, *California Rivers and Streams*, 247.

107. Less than 4 percent of the state's workers are employed on farms and in farm-related industries, and in 1991, at the time that these events in the Tulare Basin were unfolding, gross farm income of $17.9 billion accounted for only 2.6 percent of California's gross state product of approximately $697 billion. Factoring in "ripple" or multiplier effects, farming and related activities still generated no more than $63.1 billion, or about 9 percent of California's gross state product. Harold O. Carter and George Goldman, "The Measure of California's Agriculture: Its Impact on the State Economy" (University of California, Division of Agriculture and Natural Resources, Leaflet no. 21517, 1992), 2–5, 44.

108. Hukkinen, "Unplugging Drainage," 24. According to the most recent complete figures available from the California Department of Water Resources, in 2001, of an estimated total 9,203,850 acres of irrigated cropland in California, 3,255,000 acres were dedicated to pasture, alfalfa, rice, and cotton (www.water.ca.gov/landwateruse/analglwu.cfm). These low-value crops required more than 48 percent of total irrigation water applied to all crops (approximately 15 million acre-feet of a total of 31 million acre-feet). These figures have been derived by the author from estimates of the number of irrigated acres per crop category and the number of acre-feet per acre of irrigation water required for each crop category.

109. The San Joaquin Valley Drainage Program, founded in 1984, is not to be confused with the previously discussed San Joaquin Valley Interagency Drainage Program (IDP), founded in 1975.

110. San Joaquin Valley Drainage Program, *Management Plan for Agricultural Subsurface Drainage*.

111. Anthony Toto, Central Valley Water Resources Control Board, Fresno, California, personal correspondence; Westlands Water District, *Water Conservation* (Fresno, Calif.: Westlands Water District, 1999).

112. Westlands Water District, *Drainage and Land Retirement* (Fresno, Calif.: Westlands Water District, 1999).

113. Hukkinen, "Unplugging Drainage," 7–8.

114. Tom Harris, "The Kesterson Syndrome," *Amicus Journal* 11, no. 4 (1989): 6.

115. Tom Harris, "U.S. Prevented Selenium Probe," *Sacramento Bee,* reprinted from a *Sacramento Bee* series published September 8–10, 1985.

116. Tom Harris and Jim Morris, "Selenium: Toxic Trace Element Threatens the West; the *Bee* Uncovers Conspiracy of Silence," *Sacramento Bee,* reprinted from a *Sacramento Bee* series published September 8–10, 1985.

117. Richard A. Engberg et al., "Federal and State Perspectives on Regulation and Remediation of Irrigation-Induced Selenium Problems," in *Environmental Chemistry of Selenium,* ed. William T. Frankenberger Jr. and Richard A. Engberg (New York: Marcel Dekker, 1998), 4.

118. The other two sites were the Stillwater National Wildlife Refuge in Nevada and the Sun River Project Area in Montana. A. Dennis Lemly, Susan E. Finger, and Marcia K. Nelson, "Sources and Impacts of Irrigation Drainwater Contaminants in Arid Wetlands," *Environmental Toxicology and Chemistry* 12, no. 12 (1993): 2273; Skorupa, "Selenium Poisoning of Fish and Wildlife in Nature," 327–336.

119. These six sites were the Malheur National Wildlife Refuge in Oregon, the Salton Sea Area in California, the Gunnison River Basin in Colorado, the Riverton Reclamation Project Area in Wyoming, the Belle Fourche Reclamation Unit in South Dakota, and the Middle Arkansas River Basin in Colorado and Kansas. Lemly, Finger, and Nelson, "Sources and Impacts of Irrigation Drainwater Contaminants," 2273. In the Salton Sea Area, selenium concentrations are elevated in water, sediment, and biota in the sea itself and in the rivers and agricultural drains that empty into it. Larger pisciverous birds at the top of the food chain are at greatest risk of reproductive impairment. James G. Setmire and Roy A. Schroeder, "Selenium and Salinity Concerns in the Salton Sea Area of California," in *Environmental Chemistry of Selenium,* ed. William T. Frankenberger Jr. and Richard A. Engberg (New York: Marcel Dekker, 1998), 220.

120. Joseph Skorupa, U.S. Fish and Wildlife Service, public lecture, University of California, Davis, February 5, 1999, and personal correspondence.

121. U.S. Environmental Protection Agency, *Ambient Water Quality Criteria for Selenium* (Washington, D.C.: U.S. Environmental Protection Agency, Office of Water Regulation and Standards, 1987). The measurement ppb is equivalent to μg/L.

122. Engberg et al., "Federal and State Perspectives," 9.

123. www.usbr.gov/niwqp. For a detailed synthesis of the NIWQP's research findings, see Ralph L. Seiler et al., *Irrigation-Induced Contamination of Water, Sediment, and Biota in the Western United States—Synthesis of Data from the National Irrigation Water Quality Program* (U.S. Geological Survey Professional Paper no. 1655, 2003).

10. WETLANDS RESURGENT

1. Shaw and Fredine, *Wetlands of the United States.*

2. Vileisis, *Discovering the Unknown Landscape,* 217–219; Samuel P. Hays, *Beauty, Health, and Permanence: Environmental Politics in the United States, 1955–1985* (Cambridge: Cambridge University Press, 1987), 148–151. For valuation of wetlands based on

the ecological services they provide, see Eugene P. Odum, "The Value of Wetlands: A Hierarchical Approach," in *Wetland Functions and Values: The State of Our Understanding, Proceedings of the 1978 National Symposium on Wetlands,* ed. Phillip E. Greeson, John R. Clark, and Judith E. Clark (Minneapolis, Minn.: American Water Resources Association, 1979); Edward B. Barbier, Mike Acreman, and Duncan Knowler, *Economic Valuation of Wetlands: A Guide for Policy Makers and Planners* (Gland, Switzerland: Ramsar Convention Bureau, 1997); William J. Mitsch and James G. Gosselink, "The Value of Wetlands: Importance of Scale and Landscape Setting," *Ecological Economics* 35, no. 1 (2000). For an overview of ecological economics, see Edward B. Barbier, Joanne C. Burgess, and Carl Folke, *Paradise Lost? The Ecological Economics of Biodiversity* (London: Earthscan Publications, 1994). For a discussion of the role of ecologists, particularly Eugene Odum, in popularizing the notion that ecology could provide the expertise for environmental problem-solving, see Joel B. Hagen, "Teaching Ecology during the Environmental Age, 1965–1980," *Environmental History* 13, no. 4 (2008).

3. Paul L. Errington, *Of Men and Marshes* (New York: Macmillan, 1957); Niering, *Life of the Marsh;* John M. Teal and Mildred Teal, *Life and Death of the Salt Marsh* (Boston: Little, Brown, 1969). In California, scientists had demonstrated concern for the environment since the nineteenth century, but—reflective of the priorities of that earlier era—they were not directly concerned with wetland preservation. For the role of science in late-nineteenth- and early-twentieth-century California, see Michael L. Smith, *Pacific Visions: California Scientists and the Environment* (New Haven, Conn.: Yale University Press, 1987).

4. Executive Order no. 11990, "Protection of Wetlands," May 24, 1977.

5. Public Law 99–645, 100 *Stat.* 3582.

6. One of the most controversial vehicles for wetland protection and regulation in the United States, affecting the fulfillment of the goal of "no net loss," is section 404 of the Clean Water Act (33 *U.S Code* sec. 1344). Section 404 requires that anyone dredging or filling in "waters of the United States" request a permit from the U.S. Army Corps of Engineers. The extent of the corps's section 404 legal authority over wetlands has been bitterly contested in the courts. See, for example, *Solid Waste Agency of Northern Cook County v. U.S. Army Corps of Engineers,* 531 U.S. 159 (2001); *Rapanos v. United States,* 547 U.S. 715 (2006). In this uncertain regulatory environment, since 2005 Congress has been considering legislation, the Clean Water Restoration Act, which would clarify the corps's jurisdiction by including most wetlands as "waters of the United States."

7. Wetland mitigation has been controversial, in part because of disagreement over whether wetland loss can be compensated successfully or it is essentially impossible for constructed wetlands effectively to reproduce the functionality of the natural wetlands that they replace. Despite that caveat, one of the more promising avenues for wetland mitigation involves the operation of wetland mitigation banks. In this approach, wetlands are restored, created, or enhanced in advance of development activities that will cause wetland loss, and developers can then purchase credits of wetland area from public and private mitigation banks. Mitsch and Gosselink, *Wetlands,* 655, 685. For an economic analysis of mitigation banks, see Linda Fernandez and Larry Karp, "Restoring Wetlands through Wetlands Mitigation Banks," *Environmental and Resource Economics* 12, no. 3 (1998).

8. Canadian Wildlife Service and U.S. Fish and Wildlife Service, *North American Waterfowl Management Plan* (Washington, D.C.: Environment Canada and U.S. Department of the Interior, 1986); Central Valley Habitat Joint Venture, *Central Valley Habitat Joint Venture Implementation Plan: A Component of the North American Waterfowl Management Plan* (Central Valley Habitat Joint Venture, 1990), 12.

9. Public Law 101–233, 103 *Stat.* 1968.

10. Mitsch and Gosselink, *Wetlands,* 648.

11. Central Valley Habitat Joint Venture, *Central Valley Habitat Joint Venture Implementation Plan,* 5. The 172,655-acre figure was later found to be an overestimation. More precise estimates by the U.S. Fish and Wildlife Service indicated that as late as 1996, there were only 165,384 acres of managed wetlands in the Central Valley, even with the inclusion of the CVHJV's accomplishments to that date. Central Valley Joint Venture, *Central Valley Joint Venture Implementation Plan: Conserving Bird Habitat* (Central Valley Joint Venture, 2006), 28.

12. Central Valley Joint Venture, *Central Valley Joint Venture Implementation Plan: Conserving Bird Habitat,* 2, 10–15.

13. Public Law 102–575, 106 *Stat.* 4706. Sue McClurg, "Changes in the Central Valley Project," *Western Water* (January–February 1993): 4.

14. CVPIA sec. 3402(f).

15. CVPIA sec. 3406(a)(1).

16. CVPIA sec. 3406(d). The act refers to state "wildlife management areas," but clearly is intended to refer to state wildlife areas. The act applies to the Gray Lodge, Los Banos, Volta, North Grasslands, and Mendota wildlife areas. The CVPIA increased the water supply to refuges, wildlife areas, and the Grassland Resource Conservation District from level 2 supplies, the minimum amount of water necessary to maintain existing wetland habitat, to level 4 supplies, the amount of water needed to permit full habitat development. Level 4 water supplies were to be achieved gradually, by incremental increases of 10 percent annually for ten years, culminating in 2002. Although significant progress has been made toward meeting this goal, progress has been spotty because of chronic funding shortages, rising water costs, and the lack of infrastructure necessary to convey level 4 supplies on some of the refuges and wildlife areas. Central Valley Joint Venture, *Central Valley Joint Venture Implementation Plan: Conserving Bird Habitat,* 11–12.

17. CVPIA sec. 3406(c)(1).

18. CVPIA sec. 3405(a). No water transfers outside the Central Valley Project service area were completed during the 1990s, but in 2003 and 2005 the Metropolitan Water District of Southern California purchased water from a variety of Sacramento Valley irrigation districts, initiating a fledgling private market for Central Valley Project water. Dale Kasler, "Farmers OK Deal to Send Water South," *Sacramento Bee,* January 13, 2005, D1; McClurg, "Changes in the Central Valley Project," 7.

19. Glen Martin, "Big Shift in Flow of Water Policy," *San Francisco Chronicle,* October 23, 2005, A15.

20. The C. W. "Bill" Jones Pumping Plant (formerly the Tracy Pumping Plant) serves the Delta-Mendota Canal, and the Harvey O. Banks Pumping Plant serves the California

Aqueduct. These pumps are powerful enough to reverse the direction of flow in some Delta channels. The pumps also "entrain," or pull, fish into them, where they are killed.

21. Hundley, *Great Thirst*, 319–329. In the early 2000s there were nearly 160 duck clubs in Suisun Marsh, which, together with the California Department of Fish and Game, manage a total of 52,000 acres of private and public wetlands in the marsh. Tidal wetlands (6,300 acres), bays and sloughs (30,000 acres), and upland grasslands (27,700 acres) provide additional wildlife habitat. California Department of Water Resources, *Sacramento–San Joaquin Delta Atlas*, 77; Hart and Sanger, *San Francisco Bay*, 81. Legislative protection for Suisun Marsh is provided by the Suisun Marsh Preservation Act (1977 *Statutes of California* ch. 1155).

22. Hundley, *Great Thirst*, 321–326.

23. Proposition 8 required a two-thirds, rather than a simple majority, vote by the legislature to construct storage facilities on the north coast rivers. In 1981 Governor Jerry Brown obtained protection for these rivers when he successfully appealed to Cecil Andrus, President Jimmy Carter's secretary of the interior, to include them under the provisions of the 1968 federal Wild and Scenic Rivers Act (Public Law 90–542, 82 *Stat.* 906, 16 *U.S. Code* sec. 1271–1287). Andrus's decision was later upheld by both the Ninth Circuit Court of Appeals and the U.S. Supreme Court. *County of Del Norte v. United States*, 732 F. 2d 1462 (9th Cir. 1984); cert. denied 469 U.S. 1189 (1985).

24. Boswell alone spent more than $1.2 million in 1982 to defeat the canal. Eric Schine, "A Cotton-Pickin' Mess in California," *Business Week* (April 29, 1991): 95.

25. Hundley, *Great Thirst*, 325–331.

26. For further discussion of Delta water politics during the period between the defeat of the Peripheral Canal and the passage of the CVPIA, see Alan M. Paterson, "Water Quality, Water Rights, and History in the Sacramento–San Joaquin Delta: A Public Historian's Perspective," *Western Legal History* 9, no. 1 (1996): 84–93; Sue McClurg, "The Delta Dilemma Continues," *Western Water* (March–April 1993).

27. An expert on the native fishes of the Bay-Delta estuary, Moyle prepared the petition that resulted in the endangered species listing of the Delta smelt *(Hypomesus transpacificus)*.

28. Sue McClurg, "Delta Debate," *Western Water* (March–April 1998): 4. The formal name of the Bay-Delta Accord is "Principles for Agreement on Bay-Delta Standards between the State of California and the Federal Government." It was published in January 1995 in the *Federal Register*, at 60 *Fed. Reg.* 4664. For details of CALFED's goals, see CALFED Bay-Delta Program, *California's Water Future: A Framework for Action* (Sacramento: CALFED Bay-Delta Program, 2000); CALFED Bay-Delta Program, *Programmatic Record of Decision* (Sacramento: CALFED Bay-Delta Program, 2000); Hundley, *Great Thirst*, 408–412.

29. Matt Weiser, "Delta Danger," *Sacramento Bee*, July 3, 2005, B1. For further details on CALFED programs, particularly the Ecosystem Restoration Program, see the CALFED Bay-Delta Program Web site, http://calwater.ca.gov/calfed/objectives/Ecosystem_Restoration.html.

30. Part of CALFED's problem can be attributed to the program's lack of leadership responsibility, which led, in part, to the creation of the California Bay-Delta Authority in 2003 to oversee the implementation of CALFED programs.

31. Executive Order no. S-17-06, September 28, 2006.

32. Jay Lund et al., *Envisioning Futures for the Sacramento–San Joaquin Delta* (San Francisco: Public Policy Institute of California, 2007). See also Glen Martin, "Bold Ideas for Delta," *San Francisco Chronicle*, February 8, 2007, A1.

33. Delta Vision Blue Ribbon Task Force, *Our Vision for the Delta* (Sacramento: State of California Resources Agency, 2007); Delta Vision Blue Ribbon Task Force, *Delta Vision Strategic Plan* (Sacramento: State of California Resources Agency, 2008). See also Kelly Zito, "Urgent Warning on Saving Delta," *San Francisco Chronicle*, October 18, 2008, A1. For details of proposed management plans for the ecological restoration of the Delta, see http://baydeltaconservationplan.com.

34. In November 2009 the California legislature approved a new water package comprising five separate bills (S.B. X7 1, S.B. X7 2, S.B. X7 6, S.B. X7 7, S.B. X 7 8) designed to address not only the future of the Delta but also water supply and water quality issues across the state. The legislation created a new Delta Stewardship Council charged with creating a Delta plan to balance environmental and other water needs, along with a Delta Conservancy, charged with overseeing the restoration of habitat. The Conservancy's budget and numerous other aspects of this water plan are dependent on voter approval of an $11 billion bond measure, which, as a consequence of California's severe budget crisis, was postponed in August 2010 from that year's November ballot to the November 2012 ballot. Robin Hindrey, "Water Bond Tough Sell in Current Economy," *Modesto Bee*, August 11, 2010, B3.

35. There are two small dams and a diversion tunnel on tributaries of the Cosumnes River, but none on the river's main stem. The U.S. Bureau of Reclamation planned as many as thirteen dams on the river during the 1950s and 1960s, but public opposition to the bureau's downstream mitigation plans (as opposed to opposition to the dams themselves) blocked the project. Sally K. Fairfax et al., *Buying Nature: The Limits of Land Acquisition as a Conservation Strategy, 1780–2004* (Cambridge, Mass.: MIT Press, 2005), 245.

36. Anna Steding, "Restoring Riparian Forests and Natural Flood Regimes: The Cosumnes River Preserve," in *Sustainable Use of Water: California Success Stories*, ed. Lisa Owens-Viani, Arlene K. Wong, and Peter H. Gleick (Oakland, Calif.: Pacific Institute for Studies in Development, Environment, and Society, 1999), 233.

37. Moyle, Crain, and Whitener, "Patterns in the Use of a Restored California Floodplain"; Carson A. Jeffres, Jeff J. Opperman, and Peter B. Moyle, "Ephemeral Floodplain Habitats Provide Best Growth Conditions for Juvenile Chinook Salmon in a California River," *Environmental Biology of Fishes* 83, no. 4 (2008).

38. Steding, "Restoring Riparian Forests," 237.

39. Anna Steding, "Reviving Central Valley Wetlands: Upper Beach Lake Wildlife Enhancement and the Beach Lake Mitigation Bank," in *Sustainable Uses of Water: California Success Stories*, ed. Lisa Owens-Viani, Arlene K. Wong, and Peter H. Gleick (Oakland, Calif.: Pacific Institute for Studies in Development, Environment, and Society, 1999), 224–225; National Wildlife Refuge Association, *State of the System: An Annual Report on the Threats to the National Wildlife Refuge System* (Washington, D.C.: National Wildlife Refuge Association, 2005), 3, 9. As of 2009, the U.S. Fish and Wildlife Service owned or managed approximately 6,200 acres within the Stone Lakes National Wildlife

Refuge boundary; Sacramento County and several state agencies owned approximately 5,000 additional acres.

40. The Yolo Bypass Wildlife Area was constructed by the U.S. Army Corps of Engineers and Ducks Unlimited, and is managed by the California Department of Fish and Game. In 1999 the original 3,700-acre parcel of the Yolo Bypass Wildlife Area was renamed the Vic Fazio Yolo Wildlife Area, after California congressman Victor H. Fazio, who lobbied for its creation.

41. Peter J. Hayes, "Yolo Bypass Wildlife Area: Birth of a Wintering Waterfowl Wildland," *Outdoor California* 60, no. 1 (1999); Dave Feliz, "Yolo Fly By," *Outdoor California* 65, no. 5 (2004); Ted Sommer et al., "California's Yolo Bypass: Evidence That Flood Control Can Be Compatible with Fisheries, Wetlands, Wildlife, and Agriculture," *Fisheries* 26, no. 8 (2001).

42. Narrative Report, 1995, Butte Sink Wildlife Management Area, SNWRC, i. Waterfowl surveys have shown that historically, some duck clubs in the Butte Sink consistently held more birds than individual state or federal waterfowl refuges. John M. Anderson and Frank M. Kozlik, "Private Duck Clubs," in *Waterfowl Tomorrow*, ed. Joseph P. Linduska (Washington, D.C.: U.S. Department of the Interior, Fish and Wildlife Service, Bureau of Sport Fisheries and Wildlife, 1964), 521.

43. Jones & Stokes, *Butte Sink Cooperative Management Plan*, 2-4.

44. Narrative Report, 1995, Butte Sink National Wildlife Refuge, SNWRC, 3.

45. The Fish and Wildlife Service's conservation easement program is one of many land management programs in the Butte Sink that are intended to protect and restore wetland habitat. For more detail on these programs, see Jones & Stokes, *Butte Sink Cooperative Management Plan*, 3-3-3-8.

46. Narrative Report, 1995, Sacramento River National Wildlife Refuge, SNWRC; U.S. Fish and Wildlife Service, *Sacramento River National Wildlife Refuge: Final Comprehensive Conservation Plan* (Sacramento: U.S. Department of the Interior, Fish and Wildlife Service, 2005), 9, 14, 16. Comprehensive conservation plans (CCPs) were mandated by the National Wildlife Refuge System Improvement Act (111 *Stat.* 1252, Public Law 105-57), which requires that all federal refuges be managed in accordance with an approved CCP by 2012.

47. The primary rice-growing counties are Glenn, Butte, Colusa, and Sutter. Lisa Owens-Viani, "Winter-Flooded Fields Benefit Farmers and Wildlife," in *Sustainable Use of Water: California Success Stories*, ed. Lisa Owens-Viani, Arlene K. Wong, and Peter H. Gleick (Oakland, Calif.: Pacific Institute for Studies in Development, Environment, and Society, 1999), 200. Rice production in California increased steadily throughout most of the twentieth century, reaching a peak of 608,000 acres in 1981. Sylvie M. Brouder and James E. Hill, "Winter Flooding of Ricelands Provides Waterfowl Habitat," *California Agriculture* 49, no. 6 (1995): 58.

48. Stem rot is caused by the fungus *Sclerotium oryzae;* aggregate sheath spot is caused by the fungus *Rhizoctonia oryzae sativae.* These rice pathogens have overwintering structures that develop in and on rice straw residue but can be destroyed by burning. Brouder and Hill, "Winter Flooding of Ricelands," 63.

49. PM_{10} pollution refers to particles between 2.5 and 10 microns in diameter.

50. Owens-Viani, "Winter-Flooded Fields," 203–204.

51. A.B. 1378, *California Health and Safety Code* sec. 41865. A 1997 amendment (S.B. 318) to the Rice Straw Burning Reduction Act removed the original requirement for a complete ban by 2000, and allowed for the burning of up to 25 percent of a farmer's acreage, and up to 125,000 acres in the Sacramento Valley Air Basin as a whole, if the fields targeted for burning are threatened by a pathogen that "will likely cause a significant, quantifiable reduction in yield."

52. Brouder and Hill, "Winter Flooding of Ricelands," 60, 62.

53. Central Valley Joint Venture, *Central Valley Joint Venture Implementation Plan: Conserving Bird Habitat,* 33.

54. Chris S. Elphick and Lewis W. Oring, "Conservation Implications of Flooding Rice Fields on Winter Waterbird Communities," *Agriculture, Ecosystems and Environment* 94 (2003): 18; Ducks Unlimited, *Rice Straw Decomposition and Development of Seasonal Waterbird Habitat on Rice Fields,* Valley Habitats: A Technical Guidance Series for Private Land Managers in California's Central Valley, no. 1 (Sacramento: Ducks Unlimited, 1995), 5.

55. Michael R. Miller and Glenn D. Wylie, "Residual Rice Seed Is Critical Food for Waterfowl," *California Agriculture* 49, no. 6 (1995); Brouder and Hill, "Winter Flooding of Ricelands," 59.

56. Jones & Stokes, *Wildlife Known to Use California Ricelands* (Sacramento: Jones & Stokes, prepared for the California Rice Commission, 2005), 3.

57. Jones & Stokes, *Wildlife Known to Use California Ricelands,* 2–3. This figure of 235 species includes 183 species of birds, 28 species of mammals, and 24 species of amphibians and reptiles.

58. Chris S. Elphick, "Functional Equivalency between Rice Fields and Seminatural Wetland Habitats," *Conservation Biology* 14, no. 1 (2000); Chris S. Elphick and Lewis W. Oring, "Winter Management of California Rice Fields for Waterbirds," *Journal of Applied Ecology* 35 (1998); Elphick and Oring, "Conservation Implications of Flooding Rice Fields."

59. The Midwinter Waterfowl Survey, the oldest of the waterfowl surveys, carried out in one form or another since 1935, serves as the basis for estimating flyway populations. Since the mid-1950s, however, management decisions for the flyways have relied heavily on two aerial surveys, conducted jointly by the U.S. Fish and Wildlife Service and the Canadian Wildlife Service, which have been of particular importance for estimating duck population size and production. These are the Waterfowl Breeding Population and Habitat Survey, conducted since the 1950s in May and June, and the Waterfowl Production and Habitat Survey, conducted since the 1960s in July and August. Crissey, "Calculators and Ouija Boards," 261–262; James C. Bartonek, "Status of Waterfowl, Cranes, and Other Water Birds in North America," in *Flyways and Reserve Networks for Water Birds,* ed. H. Boyd and J.-Y. Pirot (Slimbridge, Gloucester, Eng.: International Waterfowl and Wetlands Research Bureau, 1989), 64.

60. U.S. Fish and Wildlife Service, *Proposed Tulare Basin Wildlife Management Area: Environmental Assessment, Land Protection Plan, and Conceptual Management Plan* (Delano, Calif.: U.S. Department of the Interior, Fish and Wildlife Service, 2004), 9, 26, 29–30. As of 2009, the Kern National Wildlife Refuge encompassed 11,249 acres. Pixley

National Wildlife Refuge has been enlarged several times since its establishment. As of 2009, the approved refuge boundary contained more than 10,300 acres, of which the Fish and Wildlife Service owned 6,939 acres in fee title.

61. Jones & Stokes Associates, *Private Wetlands in the Kern-Tulare Basin, California: Their Status, Values, Protection, and Enhancement* (Sacramento: Jones & Stokes Associates, prepared for the California Department of Fish and Game and California Waterfowl Association, 1988), 4 - 2 - 4 - 4.

62. Douglas A. Barnum and Ned H. Euliss Jr., "Impacts of Changing Irrigation Practices on Waterfowl Habitat Use in the Southern San Joaquin Valley, California," *California Fish and Game* 77, no. 1 (1991); Joseph P. Fleskes, Robert L. Jarvis, and David S. Gilmer, "Distribution and Movements of Female Northern Pintails Radiotagged in San Joaquin Valley, California," *Journal of Wildlife Management* 66, no. 1 (2002). For recommendations of methods to improve the value to waterfowl and other waterbirds of post-harvest flooded fields in the Tulare Basin, see Richard C. Moss et al., "Emergent Insect Production in Post-Harvest Flooded Agricultural Fields Used by Waterbirds," *Wetlands* 29, no. 3 (2009).

63. The number of duck clubs in the Tulare Basin has fallen precipitously over the past half-century. Estimates vary, but probable figures are approximately 150 clubs in the 1950s and only 25 clubs by the 1990s. Frank Hall, California Department of Fish and Game, retired, personal correspondence; Leach, *Wildlife and Fishery Resources,* 30; Jones & Stokes Associates, *Private Wetlands in the Kern-Tulare Basin,* 4 - 5; U.S. Fish and Wildlife Service, *Proposed Tulare Basin Wildlife Management Area,* 1, 18.

64. The Fish and Wildlife Service will seek to purchase permanent conservation easements on approximately 20,000 acres, with the acquisition of up to 2,000 additional acres in fee title or optional conservation easements. U.S. Fish and Wildlife Service, *Tulare Basin Wildlife Management Area, Planning Update #5, December 2007* (Delano, Calif.: U.S. Department of the Interior, Fish and Wildlife Service, 2007).

65. U.S. Fish and Wildlife Service, *Proposed Tulare Basin Wildlife Management Area,* 3, 14.

66. Membership in the private duck clubs of the Grasslands costs about thirty thousand dollars, in addition to annual assessments. Don Marciochi, general manger of the Grassland Water District and Grassland Resource Conservation District, personal correspondence. Though high, these fees pale in comparison to those of some of the exclusive clubs in the Butte Sink.

67. Campbell, *Ownership and Recreational Use of Wetlands,* 11, 26.

68. I am borrowing the phrase used by historian Nancy Langston in her description of historical changes in land use in the Malheur Basin in eastern Oregon, also once owned in substantial part by Miller and Lux. Langston, *Where Land and Water Meet,* 89.

69. U.S. House of Representatives, Committee on Natural Resources, Subcommittee on Oversight and Investigation, *Hearing on the Proposed Use of the San Luis Drain,* October 26, 1993, typescript of presentation of Don Marciochi, general manager of the Grassland Water District and Grassland Resource Conservation District, GWD.

70. Gary Zahm, "Salt Slough Degradation and Associated Impacts," memorandum to regional director, Portland, Oregon, September 25, 1985. Personal files of Gary Zahm,

made available to the author; Narrative Report, 1992, Kesterson National Wildlife Refuge, SLNWRC, 5.

71. William N. Beckon et al., *Biological Effects of the Reopening of the San Luis Drain (Grasslands Bypass Project) to Carry Subsurface Irrigation Drainwater* (Sacramento: U.S. Fish and Wildlife Service, Division of Environmental Contaminants, 1997). The water quality monitoring program for the Grasslands Bypass was a requirement of California's Nonpoint Source Pollution Control Program, which commits the state to develop methods and practices to manage and reduce toxic elements in drainage water and to develop total maximum daily load (TMDL) standards for selenium, salt, and boron for the San Joaquin River. See California State Water Resources Control Board and California Coastal Commission, *Plan for California's Nonpoint Source Pollution Control Program* (Sacramento and San Francisco: State Water Resources Control Board and California Coastal Commission, 2000).

72. Pete Ottesen, "San Luis Drain to Reopen," *California Waterfowl* 23, no. 2 (1996): 33; Grassland Water District, "Agreement to Send Drainwater around Grasslands Is up for Renewal," *Grassland Today* 10, no. 6 (2000): 3–4.

73. Ferenc A. de Szalay et al., "Temporal Overlap of Nesting Duck and Aquatic Invertebrate Abundances in the Grasslands Ecological Area, California, USA," *Wetlands* 23, no. 4 (2003).

74. Stoddard & Associates, *Water Management Plan for Grassland Water District* (Los Banos, Calif.: Stoddard & Associates, 1998), 16–19.

75. State wildlife areas in the Grasslands included, as of 2009, the 6,217-acre Los Banos Wildlife Area, the 2,891-acre Volta Wildlife Area, and the 7,069-acre North Grasslands Wildlife Area.

76. U.S. Fish and Wildlife Service, *Wildland Fire Management Plan: San Luis National Wildlife Refuge Complex* (U.S. Department of the Interior, Fish and Wildlife Service, 2001), 13.

77. In addition to incorporating the former Kesterson National Wildlife Refuge and lands adjacent to it, described in the text below, the San Luis National Wildlife Refuge expanded to include the 4,000-acre East Bear Creek Unit and the 3,892-acre West Bear Creek Unit, both acquired in 1993. These units are located adjacent to the refuge's original northern boundary, on the eastern and western sides of the San Joaquin River, respectively.

78. Narrative Report, 1990, Kesterson National Wildlife Refuge, SLNWRC, 4. The cooperative agreement was signed in 1990. U.S. Department of the Interior, *Impact of Federal Programs on Wetlands*, vol. 2, 200–201.

79. The Claus and Freitas parcels are called the Blue Goose Unit and Freitas Unit, respectively.

80. In 1992, under a cooperative agreement between the Bureau of Reclamation and the Fish and Wildlife Service, 4,460 acres of the original Kesterson National Wildlife Refuge were transferred in fee title to the service. Narrative Report, 1993, Kesterson National Wildlife Refuge, SLNWRC, 1.

81. Gary Voet, "Kesterson Comes Back to Life," *Sacramento Bee*, January 8, 1997, E6.

82. Narrative Reports, 1991, Grasslands Wildlife Management Area, SLNWRC, 43; ibid., 1994, 41–42. According to censuses conducted by the Point Reyes Bird Observatory's Pacific Flyway Project, the Grasslands holds about two hundred thousand shorebirds during the peak of the spring migration, nearly 50 percent of all the shorebirds present in the Central Valley at that time. The species present in greatest numbers are western sandpipers, long-billed dowitchers, dunlins, and least sandpipers. For these figures, as well as shorebird populations during the fall and winter, see the Western Hemisphere Shorebird Reserve Network Web site, http://whsrn.org.

83. Specifically, the Grasslands Ecological Area consists of the San Luis and Merced national wildlife refuges, the Los Banos, Volta, and North Grasslands wildlife areas, the approximately 3,000-acre Great Valley Grasslands State Park (for a total of more than 50,000 acres of public lands), and more than 100,000 acres of private lands in or adjacent to the Grassland Water District or the Grassland Resource Conservation District. "Information Sheet on Ramsar Wetlands (RIS)," January 14, 2005, compiled by Kim Forrest, refuge manager, San Luis National Wildlife Refuge Complex.

84. "Contracting Parties to the Ramsar Convention on Wetlands" and "Ramsar List of Wetlands of International Importance," www.ramsar.org/index_key_docs.htm; Mitsch and Gosselink, *Wetlands*, 649. As of 2009, only twenty-four wetlands in the United States had received Ramsar recognition.

85. "Information Sheet on Ramsar Wetlands (RIS)," January 14, 2005, compiled by Kim Forrest, refuge manager, San Luis National Wildlife Refuge Complex.

86. Narrative Report, 1997, San Joaquin River National Wildlife Refuge, SLNWRC.

87. The cackling goose, which includes the Aleutian cackling goose *(Branta hutchinsii leucopareia)* and three other subspecies, was reclassified in 2004 as a species distinct from the Canada goose.

88. The nonnative foxes were introduced as early as 1750, but primarily between 1915 and 1939, to augment the fur trade. Thelander, ed., *Life on the Edge*, 138–139.

89. The San Joaquin River National Wildlife Refuge, along with Caswell Memorial State Park, is also particularly significant for the protection of one of California's most endangered mammals, the riparian brush rabbit *(Sylvilagus bachmani riparius)*.

90. *Natural Resources Defense Council v. Houston*, 146 F. 3d 1118 (9th Cir. 1998); cert. denied 526 U.S. 1111 (1999). For the National Environmental Policy Act of 1969, see 42 *U.S. Code* sec. 4321 et seq.; for the Endangered Species Act of 1973, see 16 *U.S. Code* sec. 1531 et seq. In 1992 the Natural Resources Defense Council and other plaintiffs amended their original 1988 complaint to add the claim that the Bureau of Reclamation had violated section 8 of the Reclamation Act by not complying with section 5937 of the *California Fish and Game Code*.

91. CVPIA sec. 3406(c)(1).

92. Nathan Matthews, "Rewatering the San Joaquin River: A Summary of the Friant Dam Litigation," *Ecology Law Quarterly* 34, no. 3 (2007): 1122–1129; Jim Nickles, "S.J. River Restoration a 'Wild Ride,' " *Stockton Record*, May 29, 2000, A1.

93. *Natural Resources Defense Council v. Patterson (Patterson II)*, 333 F. Supp. 2d 906 (E.D. Cal. 2004); Denny Walsh, "Diversions Ruined River, Judge Rules," *Sacramento Bee*,

August 28, 2004, A1. The suit underwent a series of name changes, corresponding to the name of the U.S. Bureau of Reclamation's mid-Pacific regional director.

94. Stipulation of Settlement, September 13, 2006, in *Natural Resources Defense Council v. Rodgers*, CV-S-88–1658 LKK/GGH (E.D. Cal.). Judge Karlton approved the settlement on October 23, 2006.

95. For an introduction to some of the issues involved in river restoration, particularly the importance of filling in gravel mining pits along riverbeds that support introduced fish species that prey on juvenile salmon, see G. Mathias Kondolf et al., "Projecting Cumulative Benefits of Multiple River Restoration Projects: An Example from the Sacramento–San Joaquin River System in California," *Environmental Management* 42, no. 6 (2008).

96. Farmers are expected to lose, on average, 170,000 acre-feet of water annually, approximately 15 percent of their current withdrawals from Friant Dam's reservoir, Millerton Lake; but they will be permitted to recapture some of the water released down the river's main channel and will also be provided with discounted water during wet years to compensate for further curtailment of water supplies during dry years.

97. The San Joaquin River Restoration Settlement Act was among more than 160 measures included in a landmark wilderness bill that set aside more than 2 million acres in nine states, the Omnibus Public Land Management Act, Public Law 111–11.

98. Michael Doyle and John Ellis, "Farmers, Congress, Californians Will Foot the Bill," *Fresno Bee*, September 27, 2009, 6, in "A Special Report: A River Reborn." California has committed $200 million for restoration of the San Joaquin River, including $100 million of a nearly $5.4 billion natural resources bond package passed as Proposition 84 in November 2006.

99. Mark Grossi, "Historic Awakening: Opportunities, Challenges Mark River's Revival," *Fresno Bee*, September 27, 2009, 2, in "A Special Report: A River Reborn"; Carolyn Jones, "San Joaquin River: Water Now Flowing Freely Again," *San Francisco Chronicle*, March 31, 2010, A1. Prior to restoration, annual releases from Friant Dam into the San Joaquin River averaged 117,000 acre-feet. Under the settlement agreement, these annual releases will be increased, depending on the type of water year (e.g., wet, normal, dry), to as much as 555,568 acre-feet. Stipulation of Settlement, September 13, 2006, in *Natural Resources Defense Council v. Rodgers*, CV-S-88–1658 LKK/GGH (E.D. Cal.), exhibit B, appendices A–F.

EPILOGUE

1. Central Valley Habitat Joint Venture, *Central Valley Habitat Joint Venture Implementation Plan: A Component*, 5; Frayer, Peters, and Pywell, *Wetlands of the California Central Valley . . . 1939 to Mid-1980s*, 4, 18.

2. Since the 1980s, the California Waterfowl Association—founded in 1945 as the Duck Hunters Association of California—has complemented the work of the Nature Conservancy and Ducks Unlimited by expanding its mission to include habitat restoration projects, many of which are located in the Central Valley, as well as bird banding activities. See www.calwaterfowl.org/.

3. By 2009 California's estimated population had increased to nearly 37 million. Table 1, Annual Estimates of the Resident Population for the United States, Regions, States, and Puerto Rico: April 1, 2000, to July 1, 2009, Population Division, U.S. Census Bureau, www .census.gov/popest/states/NST-ann-est.html.

4. "Counting California," *Sacramento Bee,* April 9, 2001, A3.

5. Karen G. Weissman and David Strong, "Merced County Study Looks at Economic Cost of Urban Sprawl," *California Waterfowl* 27, no. 2 (2000): 21.

6. Mike Lee, "Bumper Crop of Preservationists," *Sacramento Bee,* December 15, 2004, A1.

7. 1965 *Statutes of California* ch. 1443, *California Government Code,* sec. 51200–51297.4.

8. Williamson Act Fact Sheet and Enrollment Statistics, California Department of Conservation, Division of Land Resource Protection, www.conservation.ca.gov/dlrp/lca/ stats_reports/Pages/index.aspx.

9. U.S. Fish and Wildlife Service, *Proposed Tulare Basin Wildlife Management Area,* 16.

10. For the history of the science and politics of global warming, see Spencer R. Weart, *The Discovery of Global Warming* (Cambridge, Mass.: Harvard University Press, 2003). For more technical information, see the reports of the Intergovernmental Panel on Climate Change (IPCC), www.ipcc.ch/ipccreports/index.htm.

11. Daniel B. Botkin et al., "Global Climate Change and California's Natural Ecosystems," in *Global Climate Change and California: Potential Impacts and Responses,* ed. Joseph B. Knox and Ann Foley Scheuring (Berkeley and Los Angeles: University of California Press, 1991), 130–137; Christopher B. Field et al., *Confronting Climate Change in California: Ecological Impacts on the Golden State* (Cambridge, Mass., and Washington, D.C.: Union of Concerned Scientists and Ecological Society of America, 1999), 17–19.

12. Field et al., *Confronting Climate Change in California,* 44–45.

13. Botkin et al., "Global Climate Change," 123, 132; Mount, *California Rivers and Streams,* 345.

14. URS Corporation, *Status and Trends of Delta-Suisun Services* (Sacramento: prepared for the California Department of Water Resources, 2007), 12–13. Whereas newly reclaimed areas once could be drained by gravity after levee breaks, now that the islands have subsided to below sea level the water must be pumped out at considerable expense. One sizable island, Frank's Tract, in the west-central Delta, was inundated in 1938 and has never been reclaimed. Thompson, *Discovering and Rediscovering the Fragility of Levees,* 30.

15. Stuart Leavenworth, "Saltwater Could Spell Disaster for Delta," *Sacramento Bee,* June 14, 2004, A1; California Department of Water Resources, *Jones Tract Flood Water Quality Investigations* (California Department of Water Resources, Division of Environmental Services, 2009), 1-1–1-6.

16. Field et al., *Confronting Climate Change in California,* 33, 49.

17. Jeffrey Mount and Robert Twiss, "Subsidence, Sea Level Rise, and Seismicity in the Sacramento–San Joaquin Delta," *San Francisco Estuary and Watershed Science* 3, no. 1 (2005). Levees are in danger not only in the Delta, but also throughout much of the Central Valley. As recently as 1997, in the Sacramento Valley, a flood on the Feather River near the city of Marysville caused a levee breach that killed six people and forced the

evacuation of 120,000 people from their homes—the largest evacuation in California history. Teri Bachman, "Headed for a Bad Break," *UC Davis Magazine* (Winter 2006). In large part because of concerns about levee failure and compromised freshwater supplies, a 2008 Public Policy Institute of California report recommended a modified peripheral canal around the Delta as the best means to provide both a secure, cost-effective water supply and improved fish viability. The report was later published as Jay R. Lund et al., *Comparing Futures for the Sacramento–San Joaquin Delta* (Berkeley and Los Angeles: University of California Press, 2010).

18. Norman L. Miller, Kathy E. Bashford, and Eric Strem, "Potential Impacts of Climate Change on California Hydrology," *Journal of the American Water Resources Association* 39, no. 4 (2003); Michael G. Anderson and Lisa G. Sorenson, "Global Climate Change and Waterfowl: Adaptation in the Face of Uncertainty," *Transactions of the North American Wildlife and Natural Resources Conference* 66 (2001): 309–310; Field et al., *Confronting Climate Change in California,* 17; Dennis P. Lettenmaier and Thian Yew Gan, "Hydrologic Sensitivities of the Sacramento–San Joaquin River Basin, California, to Global Warming," *Water Resources Research* 26, no. 1 (1990).

19. Botkin et al., "Global Climate Change," 133. One solution to the water shortage problem appears likely to involve building new dams and enlarging existing ones. In 2000 CALFED recommended studies of projects to increase surface water storage in the Central Valley. These projects include Sites Reservoir, a proposed off-stream reservoir on the western side of the Sacramento Valley, which would store up to 1.8 million acre-feet of Sacramento River water, and a proposed 1.3 million acre-foot reservoir on the San Joaquin River at Temperance Flat, located above Friant Dam's Millerton Lake. CALFED Bay-Delta Program, *Programmatic Record of Decision,* 44–45; U.S. Bureau of Reclamation and California Department of Water Resources, *Upper San Joaquin River Basin Storage Investigation: Plan Formulation Report* (U.S. Department of the Interior, Bureau of Reclamation, and California Department of Water Resources, 2008). The construction of major dams in the Central Valley has been halted since 1978, when New Melones Dam, part of the Central Valley Project, was completed on the Stanislaus River despite a decade of protest from environmentalists, most notably the group Friends of the River. See Tim Palmer, *Stanislaus: The Struggle for a River* (Berkeley and Los Angeles: University of California Press, 1982).

20. On June 1, 2005, Governor Arnold Schwarzenegger issued Executive Order no. S-3-05, establishing greenhouse gas emissions targets for California and requiring biennial reports on the effects of climate change. In response, in July 2006 the California Department of Water Resources issued its first report on the potential effects of climate change on the state's water resources. California Department of Water Resources, *Progress on Incorporating Climate Change into Management of California's Water Resources* (Sacramento: California Department of Water Resources, 2006). In December 2009 Governor Schwarzenegger announced the creation of a panel of twenty-three California leaders to recommend specific actions to combat the detrimental effects of climate change in the state. Wyatt Buchanan, "Climate Change: Planning for Warming," *San Francisco Chronicle,* December 3, 2009.

21. In the United States, the most notable—and largest—wetland restoration project is taking place in the Florida Everglades. For details of the Comprehensive Everglades Restoration Plan, see www.evergladesplan.org/about/landing_about.aspx.

22. Just as efforts to reduce the impacts of global climate change will benefit the wetlands of the Central Valley, so too will they assist the rest of the Pacific Flyway, where climate change threatens to increase the frequency and intensity of drought in the prairie potholes, intensify the destructiveness of fires and insect outbreaks in the boreal forests, and accelerate the thawing of the tundra permafrost that currently supports seasonal wetlands and provides high-quality breeding habitat.

BIBLIOGRAPHY

ARCHIVES AND MANUSCRIPT COLLECTIONS

Bancroft Library, University of California, Berkeley
    Miller and Lux Collection, Rancho Sanjon de Santa Rita (MLR)
California State Archives, Sacramento
    California State Reclamation Board Records
        Minutes of the State Reclamation Board (MSRB)
    United States Surveyor General for California Records
        Spanish and Mexican Land Grant Maps, 1855–1875
        Spanish Archives Collection (SAC)
California State Railroad Museum Library, Sacramento
    Southern Pacific Records (SPR)
Grassland Water District Archives, Los Banos, California (GWD)
    Minutes of the Grass Lands Water Association
    Minutes of the Grassland Water District
Henry Madden Library Special Collections, California State University, Fresno
    National Land for People Collection (NLP)
Huntington Library, San Marino, California
    Frank Latta Collection (FLC)
        Miller and Lux Papers
        Skyfarming Collection
Kern National Wildlife Refuge Complex Archives, Delano, California (KNWRC)
    Narrative Reports
        Kern National Wildlife Refuge
        Pixley National Wildlife Refuge

Meriam Library Special Collections, California State University, Chico
    Clair Engle Papers (CEP)
Sacramento National Wildlife Refuge Complex Archives, Willows, California (SNWRC)
    Narrative Reports
        Butte Sink National Wildlife Refuge
        Butte Sink Wildlife Management Area
        Sacramento National Wildlife Refuge
        Sacramento River National Wildlife Refuge
San Joaquin College of Law, Clovis, California
    J. Martin Winton Special Collection on Water Use and Land Development
    (JMW)
        J. Martin Winton Papers
        Ralph Milliken Oral History Notebooks
San Luis National Wildlife Refuge Complex Archives, Los Banos, California (SLNWRC)
    Narrative Reports
        Grasslands Wildlife Management Area
        Kesterson National Wildlife Refuge
        Merced National Wildlife Refuge
        San Joaquin River National Wildlife Refuge
        San Luis National Wildlife Refuge
Walter W. Stiern Library Special Collections, California State University, Bakersfield
    Kern County Water History Collection (KCWHC)

COURT CASES
California

Crandall v. Woods, 8 Cal. 136 (1857)
Herminghaus v. Southern California Edison Company, 200 Cal. 81 (1926)
Irwin v. Phillips, 5 Cal. 140 (1855)
Lux v. Haggin, 4 Pac. 919 (1884); 69 Cal. 255 (1886)
Miller and Lux v. Madera Irrigation District (Superior Court, Fresno County, no. 24729, 1933)
Moulton v. Parks, 64 Cal. 166 (1883)
National Audubon Society v. Superior Court, 33 Cal. 3d 419 (1983)
The People v. Parks, 58 Cal. 624 (1881)
Town of Antioch v. Williams Irrigation District, 188 Cal. 451 (1922)

United States

Arizona v. California, 373 U.S. 546 (1963)
City of Mendota v. Hodel, Civ. no. F-86–109-REC (E.D. Cal. 1986)
Claus, James, and Claus, Karen E., v. United States et al., Civ. no. S84–1309 LKK (E.D. Cal. 1984)
County of Del Norte v. United States, 732 F. 2d 1462 (9th Cir. 1984); cert. denied 469 U.S. 1189 (1985)

Dugan et al. v. Rank et al., 372 U.S. 609 (1963)

Firebaugh Canal Co. v. U.S., 203 F. 3d 568 (9th Cir. 2000)

Geer v. Connecticut, 161 U.S. 519 (1896)

Gerlach Livestock Company v. the United States, 76 F. Supp. 87 (Court of Claims 1948)

Gibbons v. Ogden, 22 U.S. 1 (1824)

Hollister Land and Cattle Company and Yellowjacket Cattle Company v. Julius A. Krug et al. (S.D. Cal., no. 680-ND, 1947)

Ivanhoe Irrigation District v. McCracken, 357 U.S. 275 (1958)

Natural Resources Defense Council v. Houston, 146 F. 3d 1118 (9th Cir. 1998); cert. denied 526 U.S. 1111 (1999)

Natural Resources Defense Council v. Patterson (Patterson II), 333 F. Supp. 2d 906 (E.D. Cal. 2004)

Natural Resources Defense Council v. Rodgers, CV-S-88–1658 LKK/GGH (E.D. Cal.)

Rank et al. v. Krug et al., 90 F. Supp. 773 (S.D. Cal. 1950); 142 F. Supp. 1 (S.D. Cal. 1956)

Rapanos v. United States, 547 U.S. 715 (2006)

Solid Waste Agency of Northern Cook County v. U.S. Army Corps of Engineers, 531 U.S. 159 (2001)

State of California, United States of America, et al. v. Rank et al., 293 F. 2d 340 (9th Cir. 1961)

State of Missouri v. Holland, United States Game Warden, 252 U.S. 416 (1920)

United States v. Gerlach Live Stock Co., 339 U.S. 725 (1950)

United States v. McCullagh, 221 F. 288 (D. Kan. 1915)

United States v. Shauver, 214 F. 154 (E.D. Ark. 1914)

Woodruff, Edwards v. North Bloomfield Gravel Mining Co. et al., 18 F. 753 (9th Cir. 1884)

NEWSPAPERS

Bakersfield Californian
Corcoran Journal
Fresno Bee
Kern Standard
Merced Star
Modesto Bee
Sacramento Bee
Sacramento Union
San Francisco Chronicle
Stockton Record
Tulare Daily Register

THESES, DISSERTATIONS, AND UNPUBLISHED MANUSCRIPTS

Bremer, Jeff R. "To Water the Valley: The San Joaquin and Kings River Canal and Irrigation Company, 1866–1875." MA thesis, California State University, Bakersfield, 1995.

Hall, Frank Arthur, Jr. "An Environmental History of the Sacramento National Wildlife Refuge." MA thesis, California State University, Chico, 1975.

Hukkinen, Janne Ilmari. "Unplugging Drainage: Toward Sociotechnical Redesign of San Joaquin Valley's Agricultural Drainage Management." PhD diss., University of California at Berkeley, 1990.

Leach, Howard R. "An Historical Account of Waterfowling, San Joaquin Valley, California: 1870–1970."

Thompson, John. "The Settlement Geography of the Sacramento–San Joaquin Delta, California." PhD diss., Stanford University, 1957.

Wilson, Robert M. "Seeking Refuge: Making Space for Migratory Waterfowl and Wetlands along the Pacific Flyway." PhD diss., University of British Columbia, 2003.

PUBLISHED PRIMARY SOURCES

Belcher, Captain Sir Edward, R.N. *Narrative of a Voyage round the World Performed in Her Majesty's Ship Sulphur during the Years 1836–1842,* vol. 1. London: Henry Colburn, 1843.

Brereton, R.M. *Reminiscences of Irrigation-Enterprise in California.* Portland, Ore.: Irwin-Hodson, 1903.

Brewer, William H. *Up and Down California in 1860–1864,* 3rd ed. Berkeley and Los Angeles: University of California Press, 1966.

Brooks, George R., ed. *The Southwest Expedition of Jedediah S. Smith: His Personal Account of the Journey to California 1826–1827.* Glendale, Calif.: Arthur H. Clark, 1977.

Browning, Peter, ed. *Bright Gem of the Western Seas: California 1846–1852.* Lafayette, Calif.: Great West Books, 1991.

Bryant, Edwin. *What I Saw in California: Being the Journal of a Tour in the Years 1846, 1847.* Palo Alto, Calif.: Lewis Osborne, 1967.

Central Pacific Railroad. *Statement of the Workings of the Railroad Hospital, at Sacramento, Cal. for the Year 1883.* (Sacramento: H.S. Crocker, 1884).

Ewers, John C. *Adventures of Zenas Leonard, Fur Trader.* Norman: University of Oklahoma Press, 1959.

George, Henry. "What the Railroad Will Bring Us." *The Overland Monthly* 1, no. 4 (1868): 297–306.

Haggin, James Ben Ali. *The Desert Lands of Kern County, California.* San Francisco: C.H. Street, 1877.

Hanson, Nicholas Wilson. *As I Remember.* Chico, Calif.: Broyles & Camper, 1944.

Marsh, George P. *Man and Nature; or, Physical Geography as Modified by Human Action.* New York: Charles Scribner, 1864.

Marshall, Robert Bradford. *Irrigation of Twelve Million Acres in the Valley of California.* Sacramento: California State Irrigation Association, 1920.

Sisk, B.F. *A Congressional Record: The Memoir of Bernie Sisk.* Fresno, Calif.: Panorama West, 1980.

Smythe, William E. *The Conquest of Arid America,* edited by Lawrence B. Lee. Seattle: University of Washington Press, 1969.

Southern Pacific. *California for the Sportsman: Being a Collection of Hints as to the Haunts of the Wild Things of Hoof, Claw, Scale and Feather of California's Land and*

Water—the Way to Reach Them, and Some Suggestions as to Approved Methods of Capture. San Francisco: Southern Pacific, 1911.

———. *California Game: Marked Down.* San Francisco: Southern Pacific, 1896.

Tyson, J. L. *Diary of a Physician in California.* New York: D. Appleton, 1850.

Whitney, J. P. *Fresh Water Tide Lands of California.* Cambridge, Mass.: Riverside Press, 1873.

Work, John. *Fur Brigade to the Bonaventura,* edited by Alice Bay Maloney. San Francisco: California Historical Society, 1945.

GOVERNMENT DOCUMENTS
California

Adams, Frank. *Irrigation Districts of California 1887–1915.* Sacramento: California Department of Engineering, Bulletin no. 2, 1916.

Bailey, E. A. "Historical Summary of Federal Action and Its Resulting Effect upon the Sacramento Flood Control Project." Appendix C to *Sacramento Flood Control Project, Revised Plans.* Sacramento: State Printer, 1927.

———. "Historical Summary of State Legislative Action with Results Accomplished in Reclamation of Swamp and Overflowed Lands of Sacramento Valley, California." Appendix D to *Sacramento Flood Control Project, Revised Plans.* Sacramento: State Printer, 1927.

Bradford, David F. "Biogeography and Endemism in the Central Valley of California." In *Endangered and Sensitive Species of the San Joaquin Valley, California: Their Biology, Management, and Conservation,* edited by D. F. Williams, S. Byrne, and T. A. Rado, 65–79. Sacramento: California Energy Commission, 1992.

Brown, Edmund G. Opinion no. 50–89. Friant Dam. In *Opinions of the Attorney General of California,* vol. 18 (1951), 31–40.

California Board of Swamp Land Commissioners. "Annual Report of the Swamp Land Commissioners for the Year 1862." Appendix to *Journals of Senate and Assembly of the Fourteenth Session of the Legislature of the State of California,* 1863.

———. "First Annual Report of Swamp Land Commissioners." Appendix to *Journals of Senate and Assembly of the Thirteenth Session of the Legislature of the State of California,* 1862.

———. "Report of the Board of Swamp Land Commissioners, for the Years 1864 and 1865." Appendix to *Journals of Senate and Assembly of the Sixteenth Session of the Legislature of the State of California,* vol. 2, 1865–1866.

California Commissioner of Public Works. *Report to the Governor of California.* Sacramento: State Printer, 1895.

California Debris Commission. *Reports on the Control of Floods in the River Systems of the Sacramento Valley and the Adjacent San Joaquin Valley, Cal.* House of Representatives Document no. 81, 62d Congress, 1st session, 1911.

California Department of Fish and Game. *Water Requirements for the Waterfowl of Butte Basin, California.* Sacramento: California Department of Fish and Game, 1967.

California Department of Public Works. *Economic Aspects of a Salt Water Barrier Below Confluence of Sacramento and San Joaquin Rivers.* Sacramento: California Department of Public Works, Division of Water Resources, Bulletin no. 28, 1931.

——. *Financial and General Data Pertaining to Irrigation, Reclamation and Other Public Districts in California*. Sacramento: California Department of Public Works, Division of Water Resources, Bulletin no. 37, 1930.

——. *Program for Financing and Constructing the Feather River Project as the Initial Unit of the California Water Plan*. Sacramento: California Department of Public Works, Division of Engineering and Irrigation, 1955.

——. *Report to the Legislature of 1931. State Water Plan*. Sacramento: California Department of Public Works, Division of Water Resources, Bulletin no. 25, 1930.

——. *San Joaquin River Basin*. Sacramento: California Department of Public Works, Division of Water Resources, Bulletin no. 29, 1931.

——. *Summary Report on the Water Resources of California and a Coordinated Plan for Their Development: A Report to the Legislature of 1927*. Sacramento: California Department of Public Works, Division of Engineering and Irrigation, Bulletin no. 12, 1927.

——. *Supplemental Report on Water Resources of California: A Report to the Legislature of 1925*. Sacramento: California Department of Public Works, Division of Engineering and Irrigation, Bulletin no. 9, 1925.

——. *Water Resources of California: A Report to the Legislature of 1923*. Sacramento: California Department of Public Works, Division of Engineering and Irrigation, Bulletin no. 4, 1923.

California Department of Water Resources. *The California Water Plan*. Sacramento: California Department of Water Resources, Bulletin no. 3, 1957.

——. *Colusa Basin Investigation*. Sacramento: California Department of Water Resources, Bulletin no. 109, 1964.

——. *Jones Tract Flood Water Quality Investigations*. California Department of Water Resources, Division of Environmental Services, 2009.

——. *Lower San Joaquin Valley Water Quality Investigation*. Sacramento: California Department of Water Resources, Bulletin no. 89, 1960.

——. *Progress on Incorporating Climate Change into Management of California's Water Resources*. Sacramento: California Department of Water Resources, 2006.

——. *Sacramento–San Joaquin Delta Atlas*. Sacramento: California Department of Water Resources, 1993.

——. *San Joaquin Valley Drainage Investigation: San Joaquin Master Drain*. Sacramento: California Department of Water Resources, Bulletin no. 127, 1965.

California State Agricultural Society. *Transactions of the California State Agricultural Society during the Year 1858*. Sacramento: State Printer, 1859.

——. *Transactions of the California State Agricultural Society, during the Years 1866 and 1867*. Sacramento: State Printer, 1868.

California State Surveyor-General. "Annual Report of the Surveyor-General of California for the Year 1862." Appendix to *Journals of Senate and Assembly of the Fourteenth Session of the Legislature of the State of California*, 1862.

——. "Statistical Report of the Surveyor-General of California, for the Years 1869, 1870, and 1871." Appendix to *Journals of Senate and Assembly of the Nineteenth Session of the Legislature of the State of California*, 1871–1872.

California State Water Problems Conference. *Report of the State Water Problems Conference*. Sacramento: State Printer, 1916.

California State Water Resources Control Board. Cleanup and Abatement Order no. WQ 85–1. 1985.

———. Mono Lake Basin Water Right Decision 1631. 1994.

———. Order no. WQ 87–3. 1987.

———. Order no. WQ 88–7. 1988.

California State Water Resources Control Board and California Coastal Commission. *Plan for California's Nonpoint Source Pollution Control Program*. Sacramento and San Francisco: State Water Resources Control Board and California Coastal Commission, 2000.

California State Water Rights Board. Decision no. D 935. 1959.

California Water Resources Board. *Report on Feasibility of Feather River Project and Sacramento–San Joaquin Delta Diversion Projects Proposed as Features of the California Water Plan*. Sacramento: California Water Resources Board, 1951.

Central Valley Regional Water Quality Control Board. *Waste Discharge Requirements for Tulare Lake Drainage District*. Order no. 93–136. Fresno, Calif.: Central Valley Regional Water Quality Control Board, 1993.

Dabney, T. G., H. M. Chittenden, H. B. Richardson, and M. A. Nurse. "Report of the Commission of Engineers to the Commissioner of Public Works." In the *Annual Report* of the Commissioner of Public Works, 1905, 1–40.

Delta Vision Blue Ribbon Task Force. *Delta Vision Strategic Plan*. Sacramento: State of California Resources Agency, 2008.

———. *Our Vision for the Delta*. Sacramento: State of California Resources Agency, 2007.

Gordon, Seth. *California's Fish and Game Program: Report to the Wildlife Conservation Board*. Sacramento: Senate of the State of California, 1950.

———. *A New Milestone in Cooperative Effort—the Grasslands Water Bill*. Sacramento: California Department of Fish and Game, 1954.

Green, Will S., J. W. Bost, and Amos Matthews. "Report of the Commissioners on the Reclamation of Swamp Lands in the Sacramento Valley." Appendix to *Journals of Senate and Assembly of the Eighteenth Session of the Legislature of the State of California*, 1870.

Griggs, F. Thomas, Jack M. Zaninovich, and Grant D. Werschkull. "Historic Native Vegetation Map of the Tulare Basin, California." In *Endangered and Sensitive Species of the San Joaquin Valley, California: Their Biology, Management, and Conservation*, edited by D. F. Williams, S. Byrne, and T. A. Rado, 111–118. Sacramento: California Energy Commission, 1992.

Hall, William Hammond. "The Irrigation Question in California. Appendix to *Report of the State Engineer to the Governor of California*, 1–20. Sacramento: State Printer, 1880.

———. *Report of the State Engineer to the Legislature of California, Session of 1880*. Sacramento: State Printer, 1880.

Kahrl, William L., ed. *The California Water Atlas*. Sacramento: Governor's Office of Planning and Research, 1979.

Leach, Howard R. *The Wildlife and Fishery Resources in Relation to Drainage Disposal Problems in the San Joaquin Valley*. Sacramento: California Department of Fish and Game, 1960.

Logan, Thomas M. *Report of the Permanent Secretary to the State Board of Health. Second Biennial Report, State Board of Health of California for the Years 1871, 1872, and 1873*. Sacramento: State Printer, 1873.

Schuyler, Jas. D. "Report on the Works and Practice of Irrigation in Kern County." Appendix B to *Report of the State Engineer to the Legislature of California, Session of 1880*. Sacramento: State Printer, 1880.

Thompson, John. *Discovering and Rediscovering the Fragility of Levees and Land in the Sacramento–San Joaquin Delta, 1870–1879 and Today*. Sacramento: California Department of Water Resources, Central District, 1982.

Warner, Richard E., and Kathleen M. Hendrix. *Final Draft: Riparian Resources of the Central Valley and California Desert*. Sacramento: California Department of Fish and Game, 1985.

Young, Walker R. *Report on Salt Water Barrier below Confluence of Sacramento and San Joaquin Rivers, California*. Sacramento: California Department of Public Works, Division of Water Resources, Bulletin no. 22, 1929.

Younger, Evelle J. "State Water Resources Control Board—Water Appropriator Regulation." Opinion no. SO 73-44. In *Opinions of the Attorney General of California*, vol. 57 (1974), 577–583.

Joint California–United States

CALFED Bay-Delta Program. *California's Water Future: A Framework for Action*. Sacramento: CALFED Bay-Delta Program, 2000.

———. *Programmatic Record of Decision*. Sacramento: CALFED Bay-Delta Program, 2000.

Moore, S. B., J. Winckel, S. J. Detwiler, S. A. Klasing, P. A. Gaul, A. R. Kanim, B. E. Kesser, A. B. DeBevec, A. Beardsley, and L. K. Puckett. *Fish and Wildlife Resources and Agricultural Drainage in the San Joaquin Valley, California*, vols. 1 and 2. Sacramento: San Joaquin Valley Drainage Program, 1990.

San Joaquin Valley Drainage Program. *A Management Plan for Agricultural Subsurface Drainage and Related Problems on the Westside San Joaquin Valley: Final Report*. U.S. Department of the Interior and California Resources Agency, 1990.

San Joaquin Valley Interagency Drainage Program. *Agricultural Drainage and Salt Management in the San Joaquin Valley: Final Report Including Recommended Plan and First-Stage Environmental Impact Report*. Fresno, Calif.: U.S. Bureau of Reclamation, California Department of Water Resources, and California State Water Resources Control Board, 1979.

U.S. Bureau of Reclamation and California Department of Water Resources. *Upper San Joaquin River Basin Storage Investigation: Plan Formulation Report*. U.S. Department of the Interior, Bureau of Reclamation, and California Department of Water Resources, 2008.

U.S. Department of the Interior and California Department of Fish and Game. *General Plan for Use of Project Land and Waters for Wildlife Conservation and Management, Kesterson Reservoir, California.* U.S. Department of the Interior and California Department of Fish and Game, 1969.

United States

Alexander, B. S., George Davidson, and G. H. Mendell. *Report of the Board of Commissioners on the Irrigation of the San Joaquin, Tulare, and Sacramento Valleys of the State of California.* House of Representatives Executive Document no. 290, 43d Congress, 1st session, 1874.

Anderson, John M., and Frank M. Kozlik. "Private Duck Clubs." In *Waterfowl Tomorrow,* edited by Joseph P. Linduska, 519–526. Washington, D.C.: U.S. Department of the Interior, Fish and Wildlife Service, Bureau of Sport Fisheries and Wildlife, 1964.

Bartonek, James C. "Pacific Flyway." In *Flyways: Pioneering Waterfowl Management in North America,* edited by A. S. Hawkins, R. C. Hanson, H. K. Nelson, and H. M. Reeves, 395–403. Washington, D.C.: U.S. Department of the Interior, Fish and Wildlife Service, 1984.

Beckon, William N., John D. Henderson, Thomas C. Maurer, and Steven E. Schwarzbach. *Biological Effects of the Reopening of the San Luis Drain (Grasslands Bypass Project) to Carry Subsurface Irrigation Drainwater.* Sacramento: U.S. Fish and Wildlife Service, Division of Environmental Contaminants, 1997.

Bell, W. B., and Edward A. Preble. *Status of Waterfowl in 1934.* Washington, D.C.: Department of Agriculture, Miscellaneous Publication no. 210, 1934.

Campbell, Mark B. *Ownership and Recreational Use of Wetlands in the Grassland Water District and Refuges of the Central San Joaquin Valley.* Sacramento: U.S. Bureau of Reclamation, San Joaquin Valley Drainage Program, 1988.

Chattin, John E. "Pacific Flyway." In *Waterfowl Tomorrow,* edited by Joseph P. Linduska, 233–252. Washington, D.C.: U.S. Department of the Interior, Fish and Wildlife Service, Bureau of Sport Fisheries and Wildlife, 1964.

Collins, Daniel P., and Robert E. Trost. *2009 Pacific Flyway Data Book—Waterfowl Harvests and Status, Hunter Participation and Success in the Pacific Flyway and United States.* Portland, Ore.: U.S. Fish and Wildlife Service, 2009.

Cook, Sherburne F. "Historical Demography." In *Handbook of North American Indians,* vol. 8: *California,* edited by Robert F. Heizer, 91–98. Washington, D.C.: Smithsonian Institution, 1978.

Cooke, Wells W. *Distribution and Migration of North American Ducks, Geese, and Swans.* Washington, D.C.: U.S. Department of Agriculture, Bureau of Biological Survey, Bulletin no. 26, 1906.

Cottam, Clarence. *Food Habits of North American Diving Ducks.* Washington, D.C.: U.S. Department of Agriculture, Technical Bulletin no. 643, 1939.

Cowardin, Lewis M., Virginia Carter, Francis C. Golet, and Edward T. LaRoe. *Classification of Wetlands and Deepwater Habitats of the United States.* Washington, D.C.: U.S. Department of the Interior, Fish and Wildlife Service, 1979.

Crissey, Walter F. "Calculators and Ouija Boards." In *Flyways: Pioneering Waterfowl Management in North America,* edited by A. S. Hawkins, R. C. Hanson, H. K. Nelson, and H. M. Reeves, 259–271. Washington, D.C.: U.S. Department of the Interior, Fish and Wildlife Service, 1984.

Dahl, T. E. *Status and Trends of Wetlands in the Conterminous United States 1986–1997.* Washington, D.C.: U.S. Department of the Interior, Fish and Wildlife Service, 2000.

———. *Status and Trends of Wetlands in the Conterminous United States 1998 to 2004.* Washington, D.C.: U.S. Department of the Interior; Fish and Wildlife Service, 2006.

———. *Wetland Losses in the United States, 1780s to 1980s.* Washington, D.C.: U.S. Department of the Interior, Fish and Wildlife Service, 1990.

Dahl, T. E., and C. E. Johnson. *Status and Trends of Wetlands in the Conterminus United States, Mid-1970s to Mid-1980s.* Washington, D.C.: U.S. Department of the Interior, Fish and Wildlife Service, 1991.

Derby, George H. *Report of the Secretary of War, Communicating, in Compliance with a Resolution of the Senate, a Report of the Tulare Valley, Made by Lieutenant Derby.* Senate Executive Document no. 110, 32d Congress, 1st session, 1852.

Du Mont, Philip A., and Henry M. Reeves. "The Darling-Salyer Team." In *Flyways: Pioneering Waterfowl Management in North America,* edited by A. S. Hawkins, R. C. Hanson, H. K. Nelson, and H. M. Reeves, 107–112. Washington, D.C.: U.S. Department of the Interior, Fish and Wildlife Service, 1984.

Fio, John L., and Roger Fujii. *Comparison of Methods to Determine Selenium Species in Saturation Extracts of Soils from the Western San Joaquin Valley, California.* Sacramento: U.S. Geological Survey, 1988.

Frayer, W. E., D. D. Peters, and H. R. Pywell. *Wetlands of the California Central Valley: Status and Trends—1939 to Mid-1980s.* Portland, Ore.: U.S. Department of the Interior, Fish and Wildlife Service, 1989.

Frayer, W. E., T. J. Monahan, D. C. Bowden, and F. A. Graybill. *Status and Trends of Wetlands and Deepwater Habitats in the Conterminous United States, 1950's to 1970's.* Fort Collins: Colorado State University, 1983.

Friend, Milton. "Waterfowl Get Sick, Too." In *Flyways: Pioneering Waterfowl Management in North America,* edited by A. S. Hawkins, R. C. Hanson, H. K. Nelson, and H. M. Reeves, 478–485. Washington, D.C.: U.S. Department of the Interior, Fish and Wildlife Service, 1984.

Gates, Paul W. *History of Public Land Law Development.* Washington, D.C.: U.S. Government Printing Office, 1968; repr. 1979.

Goldschmidt, Walter. "Nomlaki." In *Handbook of North American Indians,* vol. 8: *California,* edited by Robert F. Heizer, 341–349. Washington, D.C.: Smithsonian Institution, 1978.

Grunsky, C. E. "Water Appropriation from Kings River." In U.S. Department of Agriculture, *Report of Irrigation Investigations in California,* 259–325. Washington, D.C.: U.S. Department of Agriculture, Office of Experiment Stations, Bulletin no. 100, 1901.

Hammond, Merrill C. "Ducks, Grain, and American Farmers." In *Waterfowl Tomorrow,* edited by Joseph P. Linduska, 417–424. Washington, D.C.: U.S. Department of the Interior, Fish and Wildlife Service, Bureau of Sport Fisheries and Wildlife, 1964.

Hawkins, Arthur S. "Portraits: Aldo Leopold." In *Flyways: Pioneering Waterfowl Management in North America*, edited by A. S. Hawkins, R. C. Hanson, H. K. Nelson, and H. M. Reeves, 103–106. Washington, D.C.: U.S. Department of the Interior, Fish and Wildlife Service, 1984.

———. "The U.S. Response." In *Flyways: Pioneering Waterfowl Management in North America*, edited by A. S. Hawkins, R. C. Hanson, H. K. Nelson, and H. M. Reeves, 2–8. Washington, D.C.: U.S. Department of the Interior, Fish and Wildlife Service, 1984.

Heizer, Robert F., ed. *Handbook of North American Indians*, vol. 8: *California*. Washington, D.C.: Smithsonian Institution, 1978.

Jackson, W. Turrentine, Rand F. Herbert, and Stephen R. Wee, eds. *Engineers and Irrigation: Report of the Board of Commissioners on the Irrigation of the San Joaquin, Tulare, and Sacramento Valleys of the State of California, 1873*. Fort Belvoir, Va.: U.S. Army Corps of Engineers, 1990.

Jensen, G. Hortin, and John E. Chattin. "Western Production Areas." In *Waterfowl Tomorrow*, edited by Joseph P. Linduska, 79–88. Washington, D.C.: U.S. Department of the Interior, Fish and Wildlife Service, Bureau of Sport Fisheries and Wildlife, 1964.

Johnson, Patti J. "Patwin." In *Handbook of North American Indians*, vol. 8: *California*, edited by Robert F. Heizer, 350–360. Washington, D.C.: Smithsonian Institution, 1978.

Kroeber, A. L. *Handbook of the Indians of California*. Washington, D.C.: Smithsonian Institution, Bureau of American Ethnology, Bulletin no. 78, 1925.

Krulitz, Leo. "Westlands Water District—Legal Questions." Opinion no. M-36901. In *Decisions of the Department of the Interior*, vol. 85, 297–326. Washington, D.C.: U.S. Government Printing Office, 1978.

Lakin, H. W. "Geochemistry of Selenium in Relation to Agriculture." In *Selenium in Agriculture*, 3–12. Washington, D.C.: U.S. Department of Agriculture, Agricultural Research Service, Agriculture Handbook no. 200, 1961.

Lenhart, Dave. *Concern Alert: Contaminant Problems at Kesterson NWR, California—Selenium*. Portland, Ore.: U.S. Department of the Interior, Fish and Wildlife Service, 1983.

Levy, Richard. "Eastern Miwok." In *Handbook of North American Indians*, vol. 8: *California*, edited by Robert F. Heizer, 398–413. Washington, D.C.: Smithsonian Institution, 1978.

Lincoln, Frederick C. *The Waterfowl Flyways of North America*. Washington, D.C.: U.S. Department of Agriculture, Circular no. 342, 1935.

Marsh, George P. *Irrigation: Its Evils, the Remedies, and the Compensations*. Senate Miscellaneous Document no. 55, 43d Congress, 1st session, 1874, 1–22.

Martin, A. C., and F. M. Uhler. *Food of Game Ducks in the United States and Canada*. Washington, D.C.: U.S. Department of Agriculture, Technical Bulletin no. 634, 1939.

Metcalfe, John Thomas. *Report of a Committee of the Associate Medical Members of the United States Sanitary Commission on the Subject of the Nature and Treatment of Miasmatic Fevers*. Washington, D.C.: United States Sanitary Commission, 1863.

Montgomery, Mary, and Marion Clawson. *History of Legislation and Policy Formation of the Central Valley Project*. Berkeley, Calif.: U.S. Department of Agriculture, Bureau of Agricultural Economics, 1946.

Ogden, Gerald R. *Agricultural Land Use and Wildlife in the San Joaquin Valley, 1769–1930: An Overview.* Sacramento: U.S. Bureau of Reclamation, San Joaquin Valley Drainage Program, 1988.

Patuxent Wildlife Research Center. *Patuxent Research Review Panel Report.* Laurel, Md.: U.S. Fish and Wildlife Service, Patuxent Wildlife Research Center, 1991.

Powell, John Wesley. *Report on the Lands of the Arid Region of the United States.* Washington, D.C.: Government Printing Office, 1879.

Presser, Theresa S., and Ivan Barnes. *Dissolved Constituents, Includes Waters in the Vicinity of Kesterson NWR and the West Grasslands, Fresno and Merced Counties, CA.* Menlo Park, Calif.: U.S. Geological Survey, 1985.

———. *Selenium Content in Waters Tributary to and in the Vicinity of Kesterson NWR.* Menlo Park, Calif.: U.S. Geological Survey, 1984.

Reeves, Henry M. "FWS Operating Branches." In *Flyways: Pioneering Waterfowl Management in North America,* edited by A. S. Hawkins, R. C. Hanson, H. K. Nelson, and H. M. Reeves, 346–358. Washington, D.C.: U.S. Department of the Interior, Fish and Wildlife Service, 1984.

———. "Portraits: Alexander Wetmore." In *Flyways: Pioneering Waterfowl Management in North America,* edited by A. S. Hawkins, R. C. Hanson, H. K. Nelson, and H. M. Reeves, 75–81. Washington, D.C.: U.S. Department of the Interior, Fish and Wildlife Service, 1984.

———. "Portraits: Waldo L. McAtee." In *Flyways: Pioneering Waterfowl Management in North America,* edited by A. S. Hawkins, R. C. Hanson, H. K. Nelson, and H. M. Reeves, 85–86. Washington, D.C.: U.S. Department of the Interior, Fish and Wildlife Service, 1984.

Riddell, Francis A. "Maidu and Konkow." In *Handbook of North American Indians,* vol. 8: *California,* edited by Robert F. Heizer, 370–386. Washington, D.C.: Smithsonian Institution, 1978.

Seiler, Ralph L., Joseph P. Skorupa, David L. Naftz, and B. Thomas Nolan. *Irrigation-Induced Contamination of Water, Sediment, and Biota in the Western United States—Synthesis of Data from the National Irrigation Water Quality Program.* U.S. Geological Survey, Professional Paper no. 1655, 2003.

Shaw, Samuel P., and C. Gordon Fredine. *Wetlands of the United States: Their Extent and Their Value to Waterfowl and Other Wildlife.* Washington, D.C.: U.S. Fish and Wildlife Service, Circular no. 39, 1956.

Skorupa, Joseph P., and Harry M. Ohlendorf. *Deformed Waterbird Embryos Found near Agricultural Drainage Ponds in the Tulare Basin.* U.S. Fish and Wildlife Service, Research Information Bulletin no. 88–49, 1988.

———. *Drainwater Contaminants in Eggs Related to Deformities in Tulare Basin Waterbirds.* U.S. Fish and Wildlife Service, Research Information Bulletin no. 89–04, 1989.

Smith, Allen G., Jerome H. Stoudt, and J. Bernard Gollup. "Prairie Potholes and Marshes." In *Waterfowl Tomorrow,* edited by Joseph P. Linduska, 39–50. Washington, D.C.: U.S. Department of the Interior, Fish and Wildlife Service, Bureau of Sport Fisheries and Wildlife, 1964.

Smith, Felix. *Information Alert—Agricultural Waste Water (AWW) Investigation—Need for Water/Soil/Vegetation/Invertebrate Monitoring.* Sacramento: U.S. Department of the Interior, Fish and Wildlife Service, 1983.

Smith, Robert H., Frank Dufresne, and Henry A. Hansen. "Northern Watersheds and Deltas." In *Waterfowl Tomorrow,* edited by Joseph P. Linduska, 51–66. Washington, D.C.: U.S. Department of the Interior, Fish and Wildlife Service, Bureau of Sport Fisheries and Wildlife, 1964.

Solman, Victor E. F. "The Canadian Response." In *Flyways: Pioneering Waterfowl Management in North America,* edited by A. S. Hawkins, R. C. Hanson, H. K. Nelson, and H. M. Reeves, 9–14. Washington, D.C.: U.S. Department of the Interior, Fish and Wildlife Service, 1984.

Storie, R. Earl, and Bruce C. Owen. *Soil Survey of the Pixley Area, California.* Washington, D.C.: U.S. Department of Agriculture, Bureau of Plant Industry, 1942.

Thacker, E. J. "Effect of Selenium on Animals." In *Selenium in Agriculture,* 46–53. Washington, D.C.: Agricultural Research Service, Agriculture Handbook no. 200, 1961.

U.S. Bureau of Reclamation. *Central Valley Basin: A Comprehensive Report on the Development of the Water and Related Resources of the Central Valley Basin.* U.S. Department of the Interior, Bureau of Reclamation, Senate Document no. 113, 81st Congress, 1st session, 1949.

———. *Final Environmental Impact Statement, Kesterson Program, Merced and Fresno Counties, CA.* Sacramento: U.S. Department of the Interior, Bureau of Reclamation, 1986.

———. *Final Environmental Impact Statement, San Luis Drainage Feature Re-Evaluation.* Sacramento: U.S. Department of the Interior, Bureau of Reclamation, 2006.

———. *Kesterson Reservoir and Waterfowl.* U.S. Bureau of Reclamation, San Luis Unit, Central Valley Project, California, Information Bulletin no. 2, 1984.

———. *Land and Water Utilization in the Westside Grasslands Area of San Joaquin Valley, California.* Sacramento: U.S. Department of the Interior, Bureau of Reclamation, 1948.

———. *Report to the Regional Director, San Luis Unit, Central Valley Project, California: A Report on the Feasibility of Water Supply Development.* Sacramento: U.S. Department of the Interior, Bureau of Reclamation, 1955.

———. *San Luis Drainage Feature Re-Evaluation: Feasibility Report.* Sacramento: U.S. Department of the Interior, Bureau of Reclamation 2008.

———. *San Luis Drainage Feature Re-Evaluation, Plan Formulation Report.* Sacramento: U.S. Department of the Interior, Bureau of Reclamation, 2002.

———. *San Luis Unit, Central Valley Project, California: A Report on the Feasibility of Water Supply Development.* Sacramento: U.S. Department of the Interior, Bureau of Reclamation, 1955.

———. "Soil Classification Studies—San Luis Unit." Appendix D to *Special Task Force Report on San Luis Unit, Central Valley Project, California.* Washington, D.C.: U.S. Department of the Interior, Bureau of Reclamation, 1978.

———. *Special Task Force Report on San Luis Unit, Central Valley Project, California.* Washington, D.C.: U.S. Department of the Interior, U.S. Bureau of Reclamation, 1978.

———. *Substantiating Report—San Luis Unit, Central Valley Project, California: A Report on the Feasibility of Water Supply Development.* Sacramento: U.S. Department of the Interior, Bureau of Reclamation, 1955.

U.S. Census Office. *Agriculture—Artesian Wells for Irrigation.* Washington, D.C.: U.S. Department of the Interior, Census Office, Bulletin no. 193, 1892.

———. *Agriculture of the United States in 1860.* Washington, D.C.: Government Printing Office, 1864.

U.S. Department of Agriculture. *Report of Irrigation Investigations in California.* Washington, D.C.: U.S. Department of Agriculture, Office of Experiment Stations, Bulletin no. 100, 1901.

———. *Selenium Occurrence in Certain Soils in the United States, with a Discussion of Related Topics: Sixth Report.* Washington, D.C.: U.S. Department of Agriculture, Technical Bulletin no. 783, 1941.

U.S. Department of the Interior. "Agreement between U.S. Department of the Interior and Westlands Water District Concerning Closure of Kesterson Reservoir, April 3, 1985." Appendix C to *U.S. Department of the Interior Kesterson Reservoir Closure and Cleanup Plan.* U.S. Department of the Interior, 1985.

———. *Effectiveness of Filling Ephemeral Pools at Kesterson Reservoir.* U.S. Department of the Interior submission to California State Water Resources Control Board in response to Order no. WQ 88–7. U.S. Department of the Interior, 1989.

———. *The Grasslands of California: A Plan for Conservation and Development of Waterfowl Habitat.* Washington, D.C.: U.S. Department of the Interior, 1969.

———. *The Impact of Federal Programs on Wetlands,* vol. 2: *A Report to Congress by the Secretary of the Interior.* Washington, D.C.: U.S. Department of the Interior, 1994.

———. *Kesterson Program Upland Habitat Assessment.* U.S. Department of the Interior submission to California State Water Resources Control Board in response to Order no. WQ 88–7. U.S. Department of the Interior, 1989.

———. *Kesterson Reservoir Closure and Cleanup Plan.* U.S. Department of the Interior, 1985.

———. *Waterfowl Conservation in the Lower San Joaquin Valley: Its Relation to the Grasslands and the Central Valley Project.* Washington, D.C.: U.S. Department of the Interior, 1950.

U.S. Environmental Protection Agency. *Ambient Water Quality Criteria for Selenium.* Washington, D.C.: U.S. Environmental Protection Agency, Office of Water Regulation and Standards, 1987.

U.S. Fish and Wildlife Service. *Concept Plan for Waterfowl Wintering Habitat Preservation: Central Valley, California.* Portland, Ore.: U.S. Department of the Interior, Fish and Wildlife Service, 1978.

———. *Kern and Pixley National Wildlife Refuges: Final Comprehensive Conservation Plan.* Sacramento: U.S. Department of the Interior, Fish and Wildlife Service, 2005.

———. *Proposed Tulare Basin Wildlife Management Area: Environmental Assessment, Land Protection Plan, and Conceptual Management Plan.* Delano, Calif.: U.S. Department of the Interior, Fish and Wildlife Service, 2004.

———. *Sacramento River National Wildlife Refuge: Final Comprehensive Conservation Plan*. Sacramento: U.S. Department of the Interior, Fish and Wildlife Service, 2005.

———. *Status Report for the National Wetlands Inventory Program: 2009*. Arlington, Va.: U.S. Fish and Wildlife Service, Division of Habitat and Resource Conservation, Branch of Resource and Mapping Support, 2009.

———. *Tulare Basin Wildlife Management Area, Planning Update #5, December 2007*. Delano, Calif.: U.S. Department of the Interior, Fish and Wildlife Service, 2007.

———. *Wildland Fire Management Plan: San Luis National Wildlife Refuge Complex*. U.S. Department of the Interior, Fish and Wildlife Service, 2001.

U.S. General Accounting Office. *Wildlife Management: National Refuge Contamination Is Difficult to Confirm and Clean Up*. Report to the Chairman, Subcommittee on Oversight and Investigations, Committee on Energy and Commerce, House of Representatives. Washington, D.C.: U.S. General Accounting Office, 1987.

U.S. House of Representatives. *Central Valley Project Documents, part 1: Authorizing Documents*. House Document no. 416, 84th Congress, 2d session, 1956.

———. *Central Valley Project Documents, part 2: Operating Documents*. House Document no. 246, 85th Congress, 1st session, 1957.

U.S. House of Representatives, Subcommittee on Fisheries and Wildlife Conservation of the Committee on Merchant Marine and Fisheries. *Hearing on the Recent Outbreak of Botulism in the Tulare Lake Basin of California's San Joaquin Valley*, 91st Congress, 1st session, July 31, 1969.

U.S. House of Representatives, Subcommittee on Irrigation and Reclamation of the Committee on Interior and Insular Affairs. *Hearing on Central Valley Project Water Problem Relating to the Grasslands Area in the San Joaquin Valley, Calif.*, 82d Congress, 1st session, April 17 and May 3, 1951.

U.S. House of Representatives, Subcommittee on Water and Power Resources of the Committee on Interior and Insular Affairs. *Hearing on Agricultural Drainage Problems and Contamination at Kesterson Reservoir*, 99th Congress, 1st session, March 15, 1985.

U.S. Senate. *Authorizing Works for Development and Furnishing of Water Supplies for Waterfowl Management, Central Valley Project, California*. Senate Report no. 1786, 83d Congress, 2d session, 1954.

———. *Report of the Special Committee of the U.S. Senate on the Irrigation and Reclamation of Arid Lands, part 2: The Great Basin Region and California*. Senate Report no. 928, 51st Congress, 1st session, 1890.

———. *Wildlife Management and Control Areas, California*. Senate Report no. 1217, 80th Congress, 2d session, 1948.

Wallace, William J. "Northern Valley Yokuts." In *Handbook of North American Indians*, vol. 8: *California*, edited by Robert F. Heizer, 462–470. Washington, D.C.: Smithsonian Institution, 1978.

———. "Southern Valley Yokuts." In *Handbook of North American Indians*, vol. 8: *California*, edited by Robert F. Heizer, 448–461. Washington, D.C.: Smithsonian Institution, 1978.

Wellein, Edward G., and Harry Gordon Lumsden. "Northern Forests and Tundra." In *Waterfowl Tomorrow*, edited by Joseph P. Linduska, 67–76. Washington, D.C.: U.S.

Department of the Interior, Fish and Wildlife Service, Bureau of Sport Fisheries and Wildlife, 1964.

Wetmore, Alexander. *The Duck Sickness in Utah*. Washington, D.C.: U.S. Department of Agriculture, Bulletin no. 672, 1918.

Wilson, Norman L., and Arlean H. Towne. "Nisenan." In *Handbook of North American Indians*, vol. 8: *California*, edited by Robert F. Heizer, 387–397. Washington, D.C.: Smithsonian Institution, 1978.

Joint United States–Canada

Canadian Wildlife Service and U.S. Fish and Wildlife Service. *North American Waterfowl Management Plan*. Washington, D.C.: Environment Canada and U.S. Department of the Interior, 1986.

SECONDARY SOURCES

Adams, G. D. "Wetlands of the Prairies of Canada." In *Wetlands of Canada*, 155–198. Ecological Land Classification Series no. 24. Montreal: Environment Canada and Polyscience Publications, 1988.

Allen, Timothy F. H., and Thomas W. Hoekstra. *Toward a Unified Ecology*. New York: Columbia University Press, 1992.

Anderson, Kat. *Tending the Wild: Native American Knowledge and the Management of California's Natural Resources*. Berkeley and Los Angeles: University of California Press, 2005.

Anderson, M. Kat, Michael G. Barbour, and Valerie Whitworth. "A World of Balance and Plenty: Land, Plants, Animals, and Humans in a Pre-European California." In *Contested Eden: California before the Gold Rush,* edited by Ramón A. Gutiérrez and Richard J. Orsi, 12–47. Berkeley and Los Angeles: University of California Press, 1998.

Anderson, Michael G., and Lisa G. Sorenson. "Global Climate Change and Waterfowl: Adaptation in the Face of Uncertainty." *Transactions of the North American Wildlife and Natural Resources Conference* 66 (2001): 300–319.

Arax, Mark, and Rick Wartzman. *The King of California: J. G. Boswell and the Making of a Secret American Empire*. New York: Public Affairs, 2003.

Arnold, Anthony. *Suisun Marsh History: Hunting and Saving a Wetland*. Marina, Calif.: Monterey Pacific Publishing, 1996.

Austin, Mary. *The Land of Little Rain*. Cambridge, Mass.: Houghton Mifflin, 1903; repr. New York: Dover Publications, 1996.

Bachman, Teri. "Headed for a Bad Break." *UC Davis Magazine* (Winter 2006): 16–20.

Bakker, Elna. *An Island Called California: An Ecological Introduction to Its Natural Communities*. 2nd ed. Berkeley and Los Angeles: University of California Press, 1984.

Bakker, Gerhard. *History of the California Tule Elk*. Los Angeles: Los Angeles City College Press, 1965.

Barbier, Edward B., Mike Acreman, and Duncan Knowler. *Economic Valuation of Wetlands: A Guide for Policy Makers and Planners*. Gland, Switzerland: Ramsar Convention Bureau, 1997.

Barbier, Edward B., Joanne C. Burgess, and Carl Folke. *Paradise Lost? The Ecological Economics of Biodiversity*. London: Earthscan Publications, 1994.

Barbour, M., et al. "Vernal Pool Vegetation in California: Variation within Pools." *Madroño* 50, no. 3 (2003): 129–146.

Barbour, Michael, Bruce Pavlik, Frank Drysdale, and Susan Lindstrom. *California's Changing Landscapes: Diversity and Conservation of California Vegetation*. Sacramento: California Native Plant Society, 1993.

Barbour, Michael G., and Carol W. Witham. "Islands within Islands: Viewing Vernal Pools Differently." *Fremontia* 32, no. 2 (2004): 3–9.

Barnes, Ivan. "Sources of Selenium." In *Selenium and Agricultural Drainage: Implications for San Francisco Bay and the California Environment: Proceedings of the Second Selenium Symposium, March 23, 1985, Berkeley, California*, 41–51. Berkeley, Calif.: Bay Institute of San Francisco, 1986.

Barnum, Douglas A., and Ned H. Euliss Jr. "Impacts of Changing Irrigation Practices on Waterfowl Habitat Use in the Southern San Joaquin Valley, California." *California Fish and Game* 77, no. 1 (1991): 10–21.

Bartolome, James W., W. James Barry, Tom Griggs, and Peter Hopkinson. "Valley Grassland." In *Terrestrial Vegetation of California*, edited by Michael Barbour, Todd Keeler-Wolf, and Allan A. Schoenherr, 367–393. Berkeley and Los Angeles: University of California Press, 2007.

Bartolome, James W., and Barbara Gemmill. "The Ecological Status of *Stipa pulchra* (Poaceae) in California." *Madroño* 28, no. 3 (1981): 172–185.

Bartonek, James C. "Status of Waterfowl, Cranes, and Other Water Birds in North America." In *Flyways and Reserve Networks for Water Birds*, edited by H. Boyd and J.-Y. Pirot, 64–75. Slimbridge, Gloucester, Eng.: International Waterfowl and Wetlands Research Bureau, 1989.

Basye, George. "Short History of Reclamation District No. 108." In *Reclamation District No. 108 125th Anniversary, 1870–1995*, 6–11. Grimes, Calif.: Reclamation District No. 108, 1995.

Batt, Bruce D. J. "Introduction: The Waterfowl." In *Ecology and Management of Breeding Waterfowl*, edited by Bruce D. J. Batt, Alan D. Afton, Michael G. Anderson, C. Davison Ankney, Douglas H. Johnson, John A. Kadlec, and Gary L. Krapu, xiii–xxi. Minneapolis and London: University of Minnesota Press, 1992.

Bean, Michael J., and Melanie J. Rowland. *The Evolution of National Wildlife Law*. 3rd ed. Westport, Conn.: Praeger, 1997.

Beck, Warren A., and Ynez D. Haase. *Historical Atlas of California*. Norman: University of Oklahoma Press, 1974.

Beesley, David. *Crow's Range: An Environmental History of the Sierra Nevada*. Reno and Las Vegas: University of Nevada Press, 2004.

Benson, S. M., M. Delamore, and S. Hoffman. *Kesterson Crisis: Sorting out the Facts*. Berkeley, Calif.: Lawrence Berkeley Laboratory Report, LBL-30587, 1990.

Berg, Norman. *A History of Kern County Land Company*. Bakersfield, Calif.: Kern County Historical Society, 1971.

Blum, Deborah. "Kesterson Refuge: No Safe Harbor." *Defenders* (November–December 1984): 30–36.

Blumler, Mark A. "Some Myths about California Grasses and Grazers." *Fremontia* 20, no. 3 (1992): 22–27.

Botkin, Daniel B., Robert A. Nisbet, Susan Bicknell, Charles Woodhouse, Barbara Bentley, and Wayne Ferren. "Global Climate Change and California's Natural Ecosystems." In *Global Climate Change and California: Potential Impacts and Responses,* edited by Joseph B. Knox and Ann Foley Scheuring, 123–149. Berkeley and Los Angeles: University of California Press, 1991.

Boyd, Hugh. "Waterfowl Population Levels in North America and Their Use in Identifying Canadian Wetlands of Importance for Breeding Waterfowl." In *Flyways and Reserve Networks for Water Birds,* edited by H. Boyd and J.-Y. Pirot, 76–84. Slimbridge, Gloucester, Eng.: International Waterfowl and Wetlands Research Bureau, 1989.

Boyle, Robert H. "The Killing Fields." *Sports Illustrated* (March 22, 1993): 62.

Brouder, Sylvie M., and James E. Hill. "Winter Flooding of Ricelands Provides Waterfowl Habitat." *California Agriculture* 49, no. 6 (1995): 58–64.

Brown, Mike, and James J. Dinsmore. "Implications of Marsh Size and Isolation for Marsh Bird Management." *Journal of Wildlife Management* 50, no. 3 (1986): 392–397.

Brown, Robert R. *History of Kings County.* Hanford, Calif.: A. H. Cawston, 1940.

Butcher, Russell D. *America's National Wildlife Refuges: A Complete Guide.* Lanham, Md.: Roberts Rinehart, 2003.

Carlson, Martin E. "William E. Smythe: Irrigation Crusader." *Journal of the West* 12, no. 1 (1968): 41–47.

Carter, Harold O., and George Goldman. "The Measure of California's Agriculture: Its Impact on the State Economy." University of California, Division of Agriculture and Natural Resources, Leaflet no. 21517, 1992.

Central Valley Habitat Joint Venture. *Central Valley Habitat Joint Venture Implementation Plan: A Component of the North American Waterfowl Management Plan.* Central Valley Habitat Joint Venture, 1990.

Central Valley Joint Venture. *Central Valley Joint Venture Implementation Plan: Conserving Bird Habitat.* Central Valley Joint Venture, 2006.

Chan, Sucheng. *This Bittersweet Soil: The Chinese in California Agriculture, 1860–1910.* Berkeley and Los Angeles: University of California Press, 1986.

Chu, George. "Chinatowns in the Delta: The Chinese in the Sacramento–San Joaquin Delta, 1870–1960." *California Historical Society Quarterly* 49, no. 1 (1970): 21–37.

Clark, Donald. "Selenium and Small Mammal Populations at Kesterson Reservoir." In *Selenium and Agricultural Drainage: Implications for the San Francisco Bay and the California Environment, Proceedings of the Fourth Selenium Symposium, March 21, 1987, Berkeley, California,* edited by Alice Q. Howard, 82–90. Berkeley, Calif.: Bay Institute of San Francisco, 1989.

Clemings, Russell. *Mirage: The False Promise of Desert Agriculture.* San Francisco: Sierra Club Books, 1996.

Coggins, George Cameron, and Sebastian T. Patti. "The Resurrection and Expansion of the Migratory Bird Treaty Act." *University of Colorado Law Review* 50 (1979): 165–206.

Conlogue, William. "Farmers' Rhetoric of Defense: California Settlers versus the Southern Pacific Railroad." *California History* 78, no. 1 (1999): 41–55.

Connelly, D. P., and D. L. Chesemore. "Food Habits of Pintails, *Anas acuta*, Wintering on Seasonally Flooded Wetlands in the Northern San Joaquin Valley, California." *California Fish and Game* 66, no. 4 (1980): 233–237.

Cook, Sherburne F. "Colonial Expeditions to the Interior of California: Central Valley, 1800–1820." *University of California Publications: Anthropological Records* 16, no. 6 (1960): 239–292.

———. "The Epidemic of 1830–1833 in California and Oregon." *University of California Publications in American Archaeology and Ethnology* 43, no. 3 (1955): 303–325.

Cowan, John B. "Federal War on Market Hunters." *Outdoor California* 53, no. 2 (1992): 17–21.

———. *A Jewel in the Pacific Flyway: The Story of Gray Lodge Wildlife Area*. Sacramento: California Waterfowl Association, 2002.

———. "Outlaw Hunters Waged War on Ducks." *Outdoor California* 53, no. 1 (1992): 1–8.

———. "Waterfowl History in the Sacramento Valley." *Outdoor California* 46, no. 1 (1985): 1–7.

Davis, Cynthia F. *Where Water Is King: The Story of Glenn-Colusa Irrigation District*. Willows, Calif.: Glenn-Colusa Irrigation District, 1984.

Day, Albert M. *North American Waterfowl*. 2nd ed. Harrisburg, Pa.: Stackpole, 1959.

deBuys, William, and Joan Myers. *Salt Dreams: Land & Water in Low-Down California*. Albuquerque: University of New Mexico Press, 1999.

Doremus, Holly, and A. Dan Tarlock. *Water War in the Klamath Basin: Macho Law, Combat Biology, and Dirty Politics*. Washington, D.C.: Island Press, 2008.

Dorsey, Kurkpatrick. *The Dawn of Conservation Diplomacy: U.S.-Canadian Wildlife Protective Treaties in the Progressive Era*. Seattle: University of Washington Press, 1998.

Downey, Sheridan. *They Would Rule the Valley*. San Francisco: privately published, 1947.

Ducks Unlimited. *Diseases of Waterfowl Wintering in the Central Valley of California*. Valley Habitats: A Technical Guidance Series for Private Land Managers in California's Central Valley, no. 12. Sacramento: Ducks Unlimited, 1995.

———. *Rice Straw Decomposition and Development of Seasonal Waterbird Habitat on Rice Fields*. Valley Habitats: A Technical Guidance Series for Private Land Managers in California's Central Valley, no. 1. Sacramento: Ducks Unlimited, 1995.

Dugan, Patrick, ed. *Wetlands in Danger: A World Conservation Atlas*. New York: Oxford University Press, 1993.

Dunning, Harrison C. "Legal Aspects of the Kesterson Problem." In *Selenium and Agricultural Drainage: Implications for San Francisco Bay and the California Environment, Proceedings of the Second Selenium Symposium, March 23, 1985, Berkeley, California*, 118–129. Berkeley, Calif.: Bay Institute of San Francisco, 1986.

Egan, Michael, and Jeff Crane, eds. *Natural Protest: Essays on the History of American Environmentalism*. New York: Routledge, 2009.

Elliott & Moore. *History of Merced County, California*. San Francisco: Elliott & Moore, 1881.

Elliott, Wallace W., & Co. *History of Kern County, California*. San Francisco: Wallace W. Elliott, 1883.

———. *History of Tulare County, California*. San Francisco: Wallace W. Elliott, 1883.

Elphick, Chris S. "Functional Equivalency between Rice Fields and Seminatural Wetland Habitats." *Conservation Biology* 14, no. 1 (2000): 181–191.

Elphick, Chris S., John B. Dunning Jr., and David Allen Sibley, eds. *The Sibley Guide to Bird Life & Behavior.* New York: Alfred A. Knopf, 2001.

Elphick, Chris S., and Lewis W. Oring. "Conservation Implications of Flooding Rice Fields on Winter Waterbird Communities." *Agriculture, Ecosystems and Environment* 94 (2003): 17–29.

———. "Winter Management of California Rice Fields for Waterbirds." *Journal of Applied Ecology* 35 (1998): 95–108.

Engberg, Richard A., Dennis W. Westcot, Michael Delamore, and Delmar D. Holz. "Federal and State Perspectives on Regulation and Remediation of Irrigation-Induced Selenium Problems." In *Environmental Chemistry of Selenium,* edited by William T. Frankenberger Jr. and Richard A. Engberg, 1–25. New York: Marcel Dekker, 1998.

Errington, Paul L. *Of Men and Marshes.* New York: Macmillan, 1957.

Euliss, Ned H., Jr., and Stanley W. Harris. "Feeding Ecology of Northern Pintails and Green-Winged Teal Wintering in California." *Journal of Wildlife Management* 51, no. 4 (1987): 724–732.

Euliss, Ned H., Jr., Robert L. Jarvis, and David S. Gilmer. "Feeding Ecology of Waterfowl Wintering on Evaporation Ponds in California." *The Condor* 93, no. 3 (1991): 582–590.

Fairfax, Sally K., Lauren Gwin, Mary Ann King, Leigh Raymond, and Laura A. Watt. *Buying Nature: The Limits of Land Acquisition as a Conservation Strategy, 1780–2004.* Cambridge, Mass.: MIT Press, 2005.

Feierabend, J. Scott, and John M. Zelazny. *Status Report on Our Nation's Wetlands.* Washington, D.C.: National Wildlife Federation, 1987.

Feldheim, Cliff. "A Glimpse into California's Past." *California Waterfowl* 25, no. 6 (1999): 40–41.

Feliz, Dave. "Yolo Fly By." *Outdoor California* 65, no. 5 (2004): 12–16.

Fernandez, Linda, and Larry Karp. "Restoring Wetlands through Wetlands Mitigation Banks." *Environmental and Resource Economics* 12, no. 3 (1998): 323–344.

Fiege, Mark. *Irrigated Eden: The Making of an Agricultural Landscape in the American West.* Seattle: University of Washington Press, 1999.

Field, Christopher B., Gretchen C. Daily, Frank W. Davis, Steven Gaines, Pamela A. Matson, John Melack, and Norman L. Miller. *Confronting Climate Change in California: Ecological Impacts on the Golden State.* Cambridge, Mass., and Washington, D.C.: Union of Concerned Scientists and Ecological Society of America, 1999.

Fleskes, Joseph P., Robert L. Jarvis, and David S. Gilmer. "Distribution and Movements of Female Northern Pintails Radiotagged in San Joaquin Valley, California." *Journal of Wildlife Management* 66, no. 1 (2002): 138–152.

Flores, Dan. "Place: An Argument for Bioregional History." *Environmental History Review* 18 (1994): 1–18.

Foner, Eric. *Free Soil, Free Labor, Free Men: The Ideology of the Republican Party before the Civil War.* New York: Oxford University Press, 1995.

Frampton, Mary Louise. "The Enforcement of Federal Reclamation Law in the Westlands Water District: A Broken Promise." *UC Davis Law Review* 13, no. 1 (1979–80): 89–122.

Gabrielson, Ira N. *Wildlife Refuges.* New York: Macmillan, 1943.

Gaines, David. "The Valley Riparian Forests of California: Their Importance to Bird Populations." In *Riparian Forests in California: Their Ecology and Conservation. Proceedings from a 1977 Symposium,* edited by Anne Sands, 57–73. Davis, Calif.: Regents of the University of California, 1980.

Garone, Philip. "Rethinking Reclamation: How an Alliance of Duck Hunters and Cattle Ranchers Brought Wetland Conservation to California's Central Valley Project." In *Natural Protest: Essays on the History of American Environmentalism,* edited by Michael Egan and Jeff Crane, 137–162. New York and London: Routledge, 2009.

———. "The Tragedy at Kesterson Reservoir: A Case Study in Environmental History and a Lesson in Ecological Complexity." *Environs: Environmental Law and Policy Journal* 22, no. 2 (1999): 107–144.

Gates, Paul W. "Land Policies in Kern County." In *Land and Law in California: Essays on Land Policies,* edited by Richard S. Kirkendall, 272–299. Ames: University of Iowa, 1991.

———. "Public Land Disposal in California." *Agricultural History* 49, no. 1 (1975): 158–178.

Gibson, James R. *Imperial Russia in Frontier America: Changing Geography of Supply of Russian America, 1784–1867.* New York: Oxford University Press, 1976.

Gillis, Michael J., and Michael F. Magliari. *John Bidwell and California: The Life and Writings of a Pioneer 1841–1900.* Spokane, Wash.: Arthur H. Clark, 2003.

Graham, Leland O. "The Central Valley Project: Resource Development of a Natural Basin." *California Law Review* 38 (1950): 588–637.

Grassland Water District. "Agreement to Send Drainwater around Grasslands Is up for Renewal." *Grassland Today* 10, no. 6 (2000): 3–4.

———. *Ecological and Water Management Characterization of the Grassland Water District.* Los Banos, Calif.: Grassland Water District, 1986.

———. "Estimates of Waterfowl That Breed in Grasslands Ecological Area Tops 66,000." *Grassland Today* 15, no. 4 (2005): 1.

Green, Will S. *The History of Colusa County, California.* San Francisco: Elliott & Moore, 1880; repr. 1950.

Grewell, Brenda J., John C. Calloway, and Wayne R. Ferren Jr. "Estuarine Wetlands." In *Terrestrial Vegetation of California,* edited by Michael G. Barbour, Todd Keeler-Wolf, and Allan A. Schoenherr, 124–154. Berkeley and Los Angeles: University of California Press, 2007.

Grinnell, George Bird, and Charles B. Reynolds. "A Plank." *Forest and Stream* 62, no. 5 (1894): 89.

Grinnell, Joseph, Harold Child Bryant, and Tracy Irwin Storer. *The Game Birds of California.* Berkeley: University of California Press, 1918.

Hagen, Joel B. "Teaching Ecology during the Environmental Age, 1965–1980." *Environmental History* 13, no. 4 (2008): 704–723.

Hall, William Hammond. "Irrigation in California." *National Geographic Magazine* 1, no. 4 (1889): 1–14.

Hamilton, Jason G. "Changing Perceptions of Pre-European Grasslands in California." *Madroño* 44, no. 4 (1997): 311–333.

Harris, Tom. *Death in the Marsh*. Washington, D.C.: Island Press, 1991.

———. "The Kesterson Syndrome." *Amicus Journal* 11, no. 4 (1989): 4–9.

Harrison, Gordon. *Mosquitoes, Malaria and Man: A History of the Hostilities since 1880*. New York: E. P. Dutton, 1978.

Hart, John. *Storm over Mono: The Mono Lake Battle and the California Water Future*. Berkeley and Los Angeles: University of California Press, 1996.

Hart, John, and David Sanger. *San Francisco Bay: Portrait of an Estuary*. Berkeley and Los Angeles: University of California Press, 2003.

Haslam, Gerald. "The Lake That Will Not Die." *California History* 72, no. 3 (1993): 256–271.

Hayes, Peter J. "Yolo Bypass Wildlife Area: Birth of a Wintering Waterfowl Wildland." *Outdoor California* 60, no. 1 (1999): 16–17.

Hays, Samuel P. *Beauty, Health, and Permanence: Environmental Politics in the United States, 1955–1985*. Cambridge: Cambridge University Press, 1987.

———. *Conservation and the Gospel of Efficiency: The Progressive Conservation Movement, 1890–1920*. Cambridge, Mass.: Harvard University Press, 1959; repr. Pittsburgh, Pa.: University of Pittsburgh Press, 1999.

Hedgpeth, Joel. "Sense of the Meeting." In *Selenium and Agricultural Drainage: Implications for San Francisco Bay and the California Environment, Proceedings of the Second Selenium Symposium, March 23, 1985, Berkeley, California*, 165–175. Berkeley, Calif.: Bay Institute of San Francisco, 1986.

Heitmeyer, M. E., D. P. Connelly, and R. L. Pederson. "The Central, Imperial, and Coachella Valleys of California." In *Habitat Management for Migrating and Wintering Waterfowl in North America*, edited by L. M. Smith, R. L. Pederson and R. M. Kaminski, 475–505. Lubbock: Texas Tech University Press, 1989.

Heizer, Robert F., ed. *The Destruction of the California Indians*. Santa Barbara and Salt Lake City: Peregrine Smith, 1974.

Heizer, Robert F., and Albert B. Elsasser. *The Natural World of the California Indians*. Berkeley and Los Angeles: University of California Press, 1980.

Hickman, James C., ed. *The Jepson Manual: Higher Plants of California*. Berkeley and Los Angeles: University of California Press, 1993.

Holland, Robert F. "Great Valley Vernal Pool Distribution, Photorevised 1996." In *Ecology, Conservation, and Management of Vernal Pool Ecosystems, Proceedings from a 1996 Conference*, edited by Carol W. Witham, pp. 71–75. Sacramento: California Native Plant Society, 1998.

Holstein, Glen. "Pre-Agricultural Grassland in Central California." *Madroño* 48, no. 4 (2001): 253–264.

Holterman, Jack. "The Revolt of Estanislao." *The Indian Historian* 3, no. 1 (1970): 43–54.

Horne, Alexander J. "Kinetics of Selenium Uptake and Loss and Seasonal Cycling of Selenium by the Aquatic Microbial Community in the Kesterson Wetlands." In *Selenium in the Environment*, edited by W. T. Frankenberger Jr. and Sally Benson, 223–236. New York: Marcel Dekker, 1994.

Howard, Alice Q., ed. *Selenium and Agricultural Drainage: Implications for San Francisco Bay and the California Environment, Proceedings of the Fourth Selenium Symposium, March 21, 1987, Berkeley, California*. Sausalito, Calif.: Bay Institute of San Francisco, 1989.

———, ed. *Selenium and Agricultural Drainage: Implications for San Francisco Bay and the California Environment, Proceedings of the Third Selenium Symposium, March 15, 1986, Berkeley, California.* Sausalito, Calif.: Bay Institute of San Francisco, 1989.

Huddleston, Robert J. "Mendota Wildlife Area." *Outdoor California* 62, no. 4 (2001): 12–14.

Hundley, Norris, Jr. *The Great Thirst: Californians and Water, a History.* Rev. ed. Berkeley and Los Angeles: University of California Press, 2001.

Hurtado, Albert L. *Indian Survival on the California Frontier.* New Haven, Conn.: Yale University Press, 1988.

Igler, David. *Industrial Cowboys: Miller & Lux and the Transformation of the Far West, 1850–1920.* Berkeley and Los Angeles: University of California Press, 2001.

———. "When Is a River Not a River? Reclaiming Nature's Disorder in *Lux v. Haggin.*" *Environmental History* 1, no. 2 (1996): 52–69.

Iwata, Masakazu. *Planted in Good Soil: A History of the Issei in United States Agriculture.* 2 vols. New York: Peter Lang, 1992.

Jackson, W. Turrentine, and Alan M. Paterson. *The Sacramento–San Joaquin Delta: The Evolution and Implementation of Water Policy, an Historical Perspective.* Davis: California Water Resources Center, University of California, Davis, Contribution no. 163, 1977.

Jacoby, Karl. *Crimes against Nature: Squatters, Poachers, Thieves, and the Hidden History of American Conservation.* Berkeley and Los Angeles: University of California Press, 2001.

Jeffres, Carson A., Jeff J. Opperman, and Peter B. Moyle. "Ephemeral Floodplain Habitats Provide Best Growth Conditions for Juvenile Chinook Salmon in a California River." *Environmental Biology of Fishes* 83, no. 4 (2008): 449–458.

Jelinek, Lawrence J. *Harvest Empire: A History of California Agriculture.* 2nd ed. San Francisco: Boyd & Fraser, 1982.

Johnsgard, Paul A. *Waterfowl of North America.* Bloomington: Indiana University Press, 1975.

Johnson, Stephen, Gerald Haslam, and Robert Dawson. *The Great Central Valley: California's Heartland.* Berkeley and Los Angeles: University of California Press, 1993.

Jones & Stokes. *Butte Sink Cooperative Management Plan: Final.* Sacramento: Jones & Stokes, prepared in association with MBK Engineers and Lennihan Law for the California Waterfowl Association, Willows, California, 2001.

———. *Wildlife Known to Use California Ricelands.* Sacramento: Jones & Stokes, prepared for the California Rice Commission, 2005.

Jones & Stokes Associates, Inc. *Private Wetlands in the Kern-Tulare Basin, California: Their Status, Values, Protection, and Enhancement.* Sacramento: Jones & Stokes Associates, prepared for the California Department of Fish and Game and California Waterfowl Association, 1988.

Katibah, Edwin F. "A Brief History of Riparian Forests in the Central Valley of California." In *California Riparian Systems: Ecology, Conservation, and Productive Management,* edited by Richard E. Warner and Kathleen M. Hendrix, 23–29. Berkeley and Los Angeles: University of California Press, 1984.

Keeley, Jon E., and Paul H. Zedler. "Characterization and Global Distribution of Vernal Pools." In *Ecology, Conservation, and Management of Vernal Pool Ecosystems, Proceedings from a 1996 Conference,* edited by Carol W. Witham, 1–14. Sacramento: California Native Plant Society, 1998.

Kelley, Robert. *Battling the Inland Sea: American Political Culture, Public Policy, and the Sacramento Valley, 1850–1986.* Berkeley and Los Angeles: University of California Press, 1989.

———. "Taming the Sacramento: Hamiltonianism in Action." *Pacific Historical Review* 34, no. 1 (1965): 21–49.

Kelley, Robert L. *Gold vs. Grain: The Hydraulic Mining Controversy in California's Sacramento Valley.* Glendale, Calif.: Arthur H. Clark, 1959.

Kilness, Arthur W., and Jerry L. Simmons. "Toxic Effects of Selenium on Wildlife Species and Other Organisms." In *Selenium and Agricultural Drainage: Implications for San Francisco Bay and the California Environment, Proceedings of the Second Selenium Symposium, March 23, 1985, Berkeley, California,* 52–59. Berkeley, Calif.: Bay Institute of San Francisco, 1986.

Kittredge, William. *Balancing Water: Restoring the Klamath Basin.* Berkeley and Los Angeles: University of California Press, 2000.

Knobloch, Frieda. *The Culture of Wilderness: Agriculture as Colonization in the American West.* Chapel Hill: University of North Carolina Press, 1996.

Kondolf, G. Mathias, Paul L. Angermeier, Kenneth Cummins, Thomas Dunne, Michael Healey, Wim Kimmerer, Peter B. Moyle, Dennis Murphy, Duncan Patten, Steve Railsback, Denise J. Reed, Robert Spies, and Robert Twiss. "Projecting Cumulative Benefits of Multiple River Restoration Projects: An Example from the Sacramento–San Joaquin River System in California." *Environmental Management* 42, no. 6 (2008): 933–945.

Kozlik, Frank M. "Waterfowl Hunting Areas Operated by the California Department of Fish and Game." *California Fish and Game* 41, no. 1 (1955): 33–53.

Langston, Nancy. "Paradise Lost: Climate Change, Boreal Forests, and Environmental History." *Environmental History* 14, no. 4 (2009): 641–650.

———. *Where Land and Water Meet: A Western Landscape Transformed.* Seattle: University of Washington Press, 2003.

Latta, Frank F. *Handbook of Yokuts Indians.* 2nd ed. Santa Cruz, Calif.: Bear State Books, 1977.

Leake, Robert E., Jr., and Stanley M. Barnes. *The Pine Flat Project on Kings River, California: Reclamation Law Should Not Apply!* Fresno, Calif.: Kings River Water Users Committee, 1980.

Lee, Lawrence B. "Environmental Implications of Government Reclamation in California." In *Agriculture in the Development of the Far West,* edited by James H. Shideler, 223–229. Washington, D.C.: Agricultural History Society, 1975.

Leitch, W. G. *Ducks and Men: Forty Years of Co-Operation in Conservation.* Winnipeg, Manitoba: Ducks Unlimited (Canada), 1978.

Lemly, A. Dennis, Susan E. Finger, and Marcia K. Nelson. "Sources and Impacts of Irrigation Drainwater Contaminants in Arid Wetlands." *Environmental Toxicology and Chemistry* 12, no. 12 (1993): 2265–2279.

Leopold, Aldo. *Game Management*. New York: Charles Scribner's Sons, 1933.

———. *A Sand County Almanac*. New York: Oxford University Press, 1949.

Letey, J., et al. *An Agricultural Dilemma: Drainage Water and Toxics Disposal in the San Joaquin Valley*. Davis: University of California, Division of Natural Resources, Agricultural Experiment Station, Special Publication no. 3319, 1986.

Lettenmaier, Dennis P., and Thian Yew Gan. "Hydrologic Sensitivities of the Sacramento–San Joaquin River Basin, California, to Global Warming." *Water Resources Research* 26, no. 1 (1990): 69–86.

Levin, Simon A. "The Problem of Pattern and Scale in Ecology." *Ecology* 73, no. 6 (1992): 1943–1967.

Lewis, Henry T. "Patterns of Indian Burning in California: Ecology and Ethnohistory." In *Before the Wilderness: Environmental Management by Native Californians*, edited by Thomas C. Blackburn and Kat Anderson, 55–116. Menlo Park, Calif.: Ballena Press, 1993.

Lowenthal, David. *George Perkins Marsh: Prophet of Conservation*. Seattle: University of Washington Press, 2003.

Lund, Jay R., Ellen Hanak, William E. Fleenor, William A. Bennett, Richard E. Howitt, Jeffrey E. Mount, and Peter B. Moyle. *Comparing Futures for the Sacramento–San Joaquin Delta*. Berkeley and Los Angeles: University of California Press, 2010.

Lund, Jay, Ellen Hanak, William Fleenor, Richard Howitt, Jeffrey Mount, and Peter Moyle. *Envisioning Futures for the Sacramento–San Joaquin Delta*. San Francisco: Public Policy Institute of California, 2007.

MacArthur, R. H., and E. O. Wilson. *The Theory of Island Biogeography*. Princeton, N.J.: Princeton University Press, 1967.

Maher, Neil M. *Nature's New Deal: The Civilian Conservation Corps and the Roots of the American Environmental Movement*. New York: Oxford University Press, 2008.

Maier, K. J., and A. W. Knight. "Ecotoxicology of Selenium in Freshwater Systems." *Reviews of Environmental Contamination and Toxicology* 134 (1994): 31–48.

Mason, Herbert L. *A Flora of the Marshes of California*. Berkeley and Los Angeles: University of California Press, 1957.

Matthews, Nathan. "Rewatering the San Joaquin River: A Summary of the Friant Dam Litigation." *Ecology Law Quarterly* 34, no. 3 (2007): 1109–1135.

Mayfield, Thomas Jefferson. *Indian Summer: Traditional Life among the Choinumne Indians of California's San Joaquin Valley*. Berkeley, Calif.: Heyday Books and the California Historical Society, 1993.

McAllister, M. Hall. "The Early History of Duck Clubs in California." *California Fish and Game* 16, no. 4 (1930): 281–285.

———. "Wild Goose Shooting in California Twenty-Five Years Ago." *California Fish and Game* 15, no. 3 (1929): 215–218.

McAtee, Waldo L. *Wildfowl Food Plants: Their Value, Propagation, and Management*. Ames, Iowa: Collegiate Press, 1939.

McClurg, Sue. "Changes in the Central Valley Project." *Western Water* (January–February 1993): 4–11.

———. "Delta Debate." *Western Water* (March–April 1998): 4–17.

———. "The Delta Dilemma Continues." *Western Water* (March–April 1993): 3–11.

McEvoy, Arthur F. *The Fisherman's Problem: Ecology and Law in the California Fisheries, 1850–1980.* Cambridge: Cambridge University Press, 1986.

McGowan, Joseph A. *History of the Sacramento Valley.* 3 vols. New York: Lewis Historical Publishing, 1961.

McLean, Donald D. "Duck Disease at Tulare Lake." *California Fish and Game* 32, no. 2 (1946): 71–80.

Medeiros, J. L. "San Luis Island: The Last of the Great Valley." *Fremontia* 7, no. 1 (1979): 3–9.

Mensik, Greg, and Jennifer Isola. "Avian Cholera Takes Toll on Wintering Waterfowl." *California Waterfowl* 26, no. 2 (1999): 26.

Merriam, C. Hart. "A California Elk Drive." *Scientific Monthly* 13 (1921): 465–475.

Mighetto, Lisa. *Wild Animals and American Environmental Ethics.* Tucson: University of Arizona Press, 1991.

Miller, M. Catherine. *Flooding the Courtrooms: Law and Water in the Far West.* Lincoln: University of Nebraska Press, 1993.

Miller, Michael R. "Fall and Winter Foods of Northern Pintails in the Sacramento Valley, California." *Journal of Wildlife Management* 51, no. 2 (1987): 405–414.

Miller, Michael R., and Glenn D. Wylie. "Residual Rice Seed Is Critical Food for Waterfowl." *California Agriculture* 49, no. 6 (1995): 61.

Miller, Milton D., and D. Marlin Brandon. "Evolution of California Rice Culture." In *Rice in California,* edited by Jack H. Willson, 79–134. Richvale, Calif.: Butte County Rice Growers Association, 1979.

Miller, Norman L., Kathy E. Bashford, and Eric Strem. "Potential Impacts of Climate Change on California Hydrology." *Journal of the American Water Resources Association* 39, no. 4 (2003): 771–784.

Mitsch, William J., and James G. Gosselink. "The Value of Wetlands: Importance of Scale and Landscape Setting." *Ecological Economics* 35, no. 1 (2000): 25–33.

———. *Wetlands.* 3rd ed. New York: John Wiley & Sons, 2000.

Moore, Patrick. "Imperial Wildlife Area and the Wister Unit." *Outdoor California* 62, no. 4 (2001): 33–37.

More Game Birds in America. *More Waterfowl by Assisting Nature.* New York: More Game Birds in America, 1931.

———. *Waterfowl Food Plants.* New York: More Game Birds in America, 1933.

Morin, Peter J. *Community Ecology.* Oxford: Blackwell Science, 1999.

Morse, Morton D., and Gary M. Lindberg. "The Rice Experiment Station." In *Rice in California,* edited by Jack H. Willson, 41–65. Richvale, Calif.: Butte County Rice Growers Association, 1979.

Moss, Richard C., Steven C. Blumenshine, Julie Yee, and Joseph P. Fleskes. "Emergent Insect Production in Post-Harvest Flooded Agricultural Fields Used by Waterbirds." *Wetlands* 29, no. 3 (2009): 875–883.

Mount, Jeffrey F. *California Rivers and Streams: The Conflict between Fluvial Process and Land Use.* Berkeley and Los Angeles: University of California Press, 1995.

Mount, Jeffrey, and Robert Twiss. "Subsidence, Sea Level Rise, and Seismicity in the Sacramento–San Joaquin Delta." *San Francisco Estuary and Watershed Science* 3, no. 1 (2005): article 5. http://repositories.cdlib.org/jmie/sfews/vol3/iss1/art5.

Moyle, Peter B., Patrick K. Crain, and Keith Whitener. "Patterns in the Use of a Restored California Floodplain by Native and Alien Fishes." *San Francisco Estuary and Watershed Science* 5, no. 3 (2007): article 1. http://repositories.cdlib.org/jmie/sfews/vol5/iss3/art1.

Muir, John. *The Mountains of California.* New York: Century Company, 1894; repr. New York: Penguin Books, 1985.

Mulch, Andreas, Stephan A. Graham, and C. Page Chamberlain. "Hydrogen Isotopes in Eocene River Gravels and Paleoelevation of the Sierra Nevada." *Science* 313, no. 5783 (2006): 87–89.

Nash, Gerald D. "The California State Land Office." *Huntington Library Quarterly* 27, no. 4 (1964): 347–356.

Nash, Linda. "Finishing Nature: Harmonizing Bodies and Environments in Late-Nineteenth-Century California." *Environmental History* 8, no. 1 (2003): 25–52.

———. *Inescapable Ecologies: A History of Environment, Disease, and Knowledge.* Berkeley and Los Angeles: University of California Press, 2006.

Nash, Roderick Frazier. *The Rights of Nature: A History of Environmental Ethics.* Madison: University of Wisconsin Press, 1989.

National Wildlife Refuge Association. *State of the System: An Annual Report on the Threats to the National Wildlife Refuge System.* Washington, D.C.: National Wildlife Refuge Association, 2005.

Niering, William A. *The Life of the Marsh: The North American Wetlands.* New York: McGraw-Hill, 1966.

———. *Wetlands.* The Audubon Society Nature Guides. New York: Alfred A. Knopf, 1985.

Odum, Eugene P. "The Value of Wetlands: A Hierarchical Approach." In *Wetland Functions and Values: The State of Our Understanding, Proceedings of the 1978 National Symposium on Wetlands,* edited by Phillip E. Greeson, John R. Clark, and Judith E. Clark, 16–25. Minneapolis, Minn.: American Water Resources Association, 1979.

Ogden, Adele. "Russian Sea-Otter and Seal Hunting on the California Coast 1803–1841." *California Historical Society Quarterly* 12 (1933): 217–239.

Ohlendorf, Harry M. "Aquatic Birds and Selenium in the San Joaquin Valley." In *Selenium and Agricultural Drainage: Implications for San Francisco Bay and the California Environment, Proceedings of the Second Selenium Symposium, March 23, 1985, Berkeley, California,* 14–24. Berkeley, Calif.: Bay Institute of San Francisco, 1986.

———. "Bioaccumulation and Effects of Selenium in Wildlife." In *Selenium in Agriculture and the Environment,* edited by L. W. Jacobs, 133–177. SSSA Special Publication no. 23. Madison, Wisc.: Soil Science Society of America, 1989.

Ohlendorf, Harry M., David J. Hoffman, Michael K. Saiki, and Thomas W. Aldrich. "Embryonic Mortality and Abnormalities of Aquatic Birds: Apparent Impacts of Selenium from Irrigation Drainwater." *The Science of the Total Environment* 52 (1986): 49–63.

Ohlendorf, Harry M., and Gary M. Santolo. "Kesterson Reservoir—Past, Present and Future: An Ecological Risk Assessment." In *Selenium in the Environment,* edited by W. T. Frankenberger Jr. and Sally Benson, 69–117. New York: Marcel Dekker, 1994.

Oldfield, J. E. "Selenium: An Essential Poison." *Science of Food and Agriculture* 4, no. 2 (1986): 22–26.

Orsi, Jared. "From Horicon to Hamburgers and Back Again: Ecology, Ideology, and Wild-life Management, 1917–1935." *Environmental History Review* 18, no. 4 (1994): 19–40.

Orsi, Richard J. "The Octopus Reconsidered: The Southern Pacific and Agricultural Modernization in California." *California Historical Quarterly* 54, no. 3 (1975): 196–220.

———. *Sunset Limited: The Southern Pacific Railroad and the Development of the American West, 1850–1930*. Berkeley and Los Angeles: University of California Press, 2005.

Ottesen, Pete. "San Luis Drain to Reopen." *California Waterfowl* 23, no. 2 (1996): 33.

Owens-Viani, Lisa. "Winter-Flooded Fields Benefit Farmers and Wildlife." In *Sustainable Use of Water: California Success Stories,* edited by Lisa Owens-Viani, Arlene K. Wong, and Peter H. Gleick, 199–213. Oakland, Calif.: Pacific Institute for Studies in Development, Environment, and Society, 1999.

Palmer, Tim. *Stanislaus: The Struggle for a River.* Berkeley and Los Angeles: University of California Press, 1982.

Paterson, Alan M. "Water Quality, Water Rights, and History in the Sacramento–San Joaquin Delta: A Public Historian's Perspective." *Western Legal History* 9, no. 1 (1996): 75–96.

Patterson, J. H. "The Role of Environmental Heterogeneity in the Regulation of Duck Populations." *Journal of Wildlife Management* 40, no. 1 (1976): 22–32.

Paveglio, Fred L., and Kevin M. Kilbride. "Selenium in Aquatic Birds from Central California." *Journal of Wildlife Management* 71, no. 8 (2007): 2550–2555.

Paveglio, Fred L., Kevin M. Kilbride, and Christine M. Bunck. "Selenium in Aquatic Birds from Central California." *Journal of Wildlife Management* 61, no. 3 (1997): 832–839.

Pavlik, Bruce M., Pamela C. Muick, Sharon G. Johnson, and Marjorie Popper. *Oaks of California.* Los Olivos, Calif.: Cachuma Press, 1991.

Peterson, Richard H. "The Failure to Reclaim: California State Swamp Land Policy and the Sacramento Valley, 1850–1866." *Southern California Quarterly* 56, no. 1 (1974): 45–60.

Pillsbury, Arthur F., and William R. Johnston. *Tile Drainage in the San Joaquin Valley of California.* Los Angeles: University of California, Department of Irrigation and Soil Science, 1965.

Pimentel, Wayne. *Dogtown and Ditches: Life on the Westside.* Los Banos, Calif.: Loose Change Publications, 1987.

Pisani, Donald J. *From the Family Farm to Agribusiness: The Irrigation Crusade in California and the West, 1850–1931.* Berkeley and Los Angeles: University of California Press, 1984.

———. *To Reclaim a Divided West: Water, Law, and Public Policy, 1848–1902.* Albuquerque: University of New Mexico Press, 1992.

Presser, Theresa S. "Geologic Origin and Pathways of Selenium from the California Coast Ranges to the West-Central San Joaquin Valley." In *Selenium in the Environment,* edited by W. T. Frankenberger Jr. and Sally Benson, 139–153. New York: Marcel Dekker, 1994.

Preston, William L. "Serpent in the Garden: Environmental Change in Colonial Califor- nia." In *Contested Eden: California before the Gold Rush,* edited by Ramón A. Gutiér- rez and Richard J. Orsi, 260–298. Berkeley and Los Angeles: University of California Press, 1998.

———. *Vanishing Landscapes: Land and Life in the Tulare Lake Basin.* Berkeley and Los Angeles: University of California Press, 1981.

Price, Jennifer. *Flight Maps: Adventures with Nature in Modern America.* New York: Basic Books, 1999.

Rains, M. C., G. E. Fogg, T. Harter, R. A. Dahlgren, and R. J. Williamson. "The Role of Perched Aquifers in Hydrological Conductivity and Biogeochemical Processes in Vernal Pool Landscapes." *Hydrological Processes* 20, no. 5 (2006): 1157–1175.

Ramsar Convention Bureau. *Directory of Wetlands of International Importance.* Gland, Switzerland: Ramsar Convention Bureau, 1990.

Reiger, John F. *American Sportsmen and the Origins of Conservation.* 3rd ed. Corvallis: Oregon State University Press, 2001.

Robinson, W. W. *Land in California: The Story of Mission Lands, Ranchos, Squatters, Mining Claims, Railroad Grants, Land Scrip, Homesteads.* Berkeley and Los Angeles: University of California Press, 1948.

Roos, Robert de. *The Thirsty Land: The Story of the Central Valley Project.* Stanford, Calif.: Stanford University Press, 1948.

Rose, G. *San Joaquin: A River Betrayed.* 2nd ed. Clovis, Calif.: Word Dancer Press, 2000.

Rubec, C. D. A., P. Lynch-Stewart, G. M. Wickware, and I. Kessel-Taylor. "Wetland Utilization in Canada." In *Wetlands of Canada,* 379–412. Ecological Land Classifi- cation Series no. 24. Montreal: Environment Canada and Polyscience Publications, 1988.

Saiki, Michael K. "Concentrations of Selenium in Aquatic Food-Chain Organisms and Fish Exposed to Agricultural Tile Drainage Water." In *Selenium and Agricultural Drainage: Implications for San Francisco Bay and the California Environment: Pro- ceedings of the Second Selenium Symposium, March 23, 1985, Berkeley, California,* 25– 33. Berkeley, Calif.: Bay Institute of San Francisco, 1986.

Schine, Eric. "A Cotton-Pickin' Mess in California." *Business Week* (April 29, 1991): 95.

Schoenherr, Allan A. *A Natural History of California.* Berkeley and Los Angeles: Univer- sity of California Press, 1992.

Schoups, Gerrit, Jan W. Hopmans, Chuck A. Young, Jasper A. Vrugt, Wesley W. Wallen- der, Ken K. Tanji, and Sorab Punday. "Sustainability of Irrigated Agriculture in the San Joaquin Valley, California." *Proceedings of the National Academy of Sciences of the United States of America* 102, no. 43 (2005): 15352–15356.

Schultz, Arnold. "Background and Recent History." In *Selenium and Agricultural Drain- age: Implications for San Francisco Bay and the California Environment, Proceedings of the Second Selenium Symposium, March 23, 1985, Berkeley, California,* 3–9. Berkeley, Calif.: Bay Institute of San Francisco, 1986.

———. "Highlights since Selenium II." In *Selenium and Agricultural Drainage: Implica- tions for San Francisco Bay and the California Environment, Proceedings of the Third*

Selenium Symposium, March 15, 1986, Berkeley, California, edited by Alice Q. Howard, 3–9. Berkeley, Calif.: Bay Institute of San Francisco, 1989.

Scott, James C. *Seeing Like a State: How Certain Schemes to Improve the Human Condition Have Failed.* New Haven, Conn.: Yale University Press, 1998.

Setmire, James G., and Roy A. Schroeder. "Selenium and Salinity Concerns in the Salton Sea Area of California." In *Environmental Chemistry of Selenium,* edited by William T. Frankenberger Jr. and Richard A. Engberg, 205–221. New York: Marcel Dekker, 1998.

Sibley, David Allen. *The Sibley Guide to Birds.* New York: Alfred A. Knopf, 2000.

Silveira, Joseph G. "Avian Uses of Vernal Pools and Implications for Conservation Practice." In *Ecology, Conservation, and Management of Vernal Pool Ecosystems: Proceedings from a 1996 Conference,* edited by Carol W. Witham, 92–106. Sacramento: California Native Plant Society, 1998.

———. "Hunting Wild Geese in an Era before Sacramento National Wildlife Refuge." *California Waterfowl* 28, no. 5 (2001): 32–35.

Simmons, Ed. *Westlands Water District: The First 25 Years, 1952–1977.* Fresno, Calif.: Westlands Water District, 1983.

Singer, Michael J., and Donald N. Munns. *Soils: An Introduction.* Upper Saddle River, N.J.: Prentice Hall, 1999.

Skorupa, Joseph P. "Selenium Poisoning of Fish and Wildlife in Nature: Lessons from Twelve Real-World Examples." In *Environmental Chemistry of Selenium,* edited by William T. Frankenberger Jr. and Richard A. Engberg, 315–354. New York: Marcel Dekker, 1998.

Slocum, W. A., & Co. *History of Contra Costa County, California.* San Francisco: W. A. Slocum, 1882.

Smith, Felix. "The Kesterson Effect: Reasonable Use of Water and the Public Trust." *San Joaquin Agricultural Law Review* 6, no. 1 (1996): 45–67.

Smith, Michael L. *Pacific Visions: California Scientists and the Environment.* New Haven, Conn.: Yale University Press, 1987.

Smith, Wallace. *Garden of the Sun: A History of the San Joaquin Valley, 1772–1939,* edited by William B. Secrest Jr. 2nd ed. Fresno, Calif.: Linden Publishing, 2004.

Solomeshch, Ayzik I., Michael G. Barbour, and Robert F. Holland. "Vernal Pools." In *Terrestrial Vegetation of California,* edited by Michael G. Barbour, Todd Keeler-Wolf, and Allan A. Schoenherr, 394–424. Berkeley and Los Angeles: University of California Press, 2007.

Sommer, Ted, Bill Harrell, Matt Nobriga, Randall Brown, Peter Moyle, Wim Kimmerer, and Larry Schemel. "California's Yolo Bypass: Evidence That Flood Control Can Be Compatible with Fisheries, Wetlands, Wildlife, and Agriculture." *Fisheries* 26, no. 8 (2001): 6–16.

Spence, Mark David. *Dispossessing the Wilderness: Indian Removal and the Making of the National Parks.* New York: Oxford University Press, 1999.

Steding, Anna. "Restoring Riparian Forests and Natural Flood Regimes: The Cosumnes River Preserve." In *Sustainable Use of Water: California Success Stories,* edited by Lisa Owens-Viani, Arlene K. Wong, and Peter H. Gleick, 229–239. Oakland, Calif.: Pacific Institute for Studies in Development, Environment, and Society, 1999.

———. "Reviving Central Valley Wetlands: Upper Beach Lake Wildlife Enhancement and the Beach Lake Mitigation Bank." In *Sustainable Uses of Water: California Success Stories,* edited by Lisa Owens-Viani, Arlene K. Wong, and Peter H. Gleick, 215–228. Oakland, Calif.: Pacific Institute for Studies in Development, Environment, and Society, 1999.

Stine, Jeffrey K. *America's Forested Wetlands: From Wasteland to Valued Resource.* Durham, N.C.: Forest History Society, 2008.

Stoddard & Associates. *Water Management Plan for Grassland Water District.* Los Banos, Calif.: Stoddard & Associates, 1998.

Stoll, Steven. *The Fruits of Natural Advantage: Making the Industrial Countryside in California.* Berkeley and Los Angeles: University of California Press, 1998.

Storer, Tracy I. "Fish and Wildlife of the Sacramento Valley—Past and Present." *Outdoor California* 26, no. 8 (1965): 15–16.

Swanson, G. A., and J. C. Bartonek. "Bias Associated with Food Analysis in Gizzards of Blue-Winged Teal." *Journal of Wildlife Management* 34, no. 4 (1970): 739–746.

Szalay, Ferenc A. de, L. Chantelle Carroll, John A. Beam, and Vincent H. Resh. "Temporal Overlap of Nesting Duck and Aquatic Invertebrate Abundances in the Grasslands Ecological Area, California, USA." *Wetlands* 23, no. 4 (2003): 739–749.

Tanji, Kenneth, Andre Lauchli, and Jewel Meyer. "Selenium in the San Joaquin Valley." *Environment* 28, no. 6 (1986): 6–39.

Tarnocai, C., and S. C. Zoltai. "Wetlands of Arctic Canada." In *Wetlands of Canada,* 27–53. Ecological Land Classification Series no. 24. Montreal: Environment Canada and Polyscience Publications, 1988.

Taylor, Herbert C., Jr., and Lester L. Hoaglin Jr. "The 'Intermittent Fever' Epidemic of the 1830's on the Lower Columbia River." *Ethnohistory* 9, no. 2 (1962): 160–178.

Taylor, Joseph E., III. "Boundary Terminology." *Environmental History* 13, no. 3 (2008): 454–481.

Taylor, Paul S. "Central Valley Project: Water and Land." *The Western Political Quarterly* 2 (1949): 228–253.

Taylor, W. P. "Synopsis of the Recent Campaign for the Conservation of Wild Life in California." *The Condor* 15, no. 3 (1913): 125–128.

Teal, John M., and Mildred Teal. *Life and Death of the Salt Marsh.* Boston: Little, Brown, 1969.

Tennyson, Jon R. *A Singleness of Purpose: The Story of Ducks Unlimited.* Chicago: Ducks Unlimited, 1977.

Terborgh, John. *Where Have All the Birds Gone? Essays on the Biology and Conservation of Birds That Migrate to the American Tropics.* Princeton, N.J.: Princeton University Press, 1989.

Thayer, Robert L., Jr. *LifePlace: Bioregional Thought and Practice.* Berkeley and Los Angeles: University of California Press, 2003.

Thelander, Carl G., ed. *Life on the Edge: A Guide to California's Endangered Natural Resources: Wildlife.* Santa Cruz, Calif.: BioSystems Books, 1994.

Thickens, Virginia E. "Pioneer Agricultural Colonies of Fresno County." *California Historical Quarterly* 25, nos. 1 and 2 (1946): 17–38, 169–177.

Thompson & West. *History of Sacramento County, California.* Oakland, Calif.: Thompson & West, 1880; repr. 1960.

Thompson, John, and Edward A. Dutra. *The Tule Breakers: The Story of the California Dredge.* Stockton, Calif.: Stockton Corral of Westerners International, University of the Pacific, 1983.

Thompson, Kenneth. "Historic Flooding in the Sacramento Valley." *Pacific Historical Review* 29, no. 4 (1960): 349–360.

———. "Insalubrious California: Perception and Reality." *Annals of the Association of American Geographers* 59, no. 1 (1969): 50–64.

———. "Irrigation as a Menace to Health in California." *The Geographical Review* 59, no. 2 (1969): 195–214.

———. "Riparian Forests of the Sacramento Valley, California." *Annals of the Association of American Geographers* 51, no. 3 (1961): 294–315.

———. "Riparian Forests of the Sacramento Valley, California." In *Riparian Forests in California: Their Ecology and Conservation, Proceedings from a 1977 Symposium,* edited by Anne Sands, 35–38. Davis, Calif.: Regents of the University of California, 1980.

Tinkham, George H. *History of San Joaquin County, California.* Los Angeles: Historic Record Company, 1923.

Tober, James A. *Who Owns the Wildlife? The Political Economy of Conservation in Nineteenth-Century America.* Westport, Conn.: Greenwood Press, 1981.

Treadwell, Edward F. *The Cattle King: A Dramatized Biography.* New York: Macmillan, 1931.

Trefethen, James B. *An American Crusade for Wildlife.* New York: Winchester Press, 1975.

Tyrrell, Ian. *True Gardens of the Gods: Californian-Australian Environmental Reform, 1860–1930.* Berkeley and Los Angeles: University of California Press, 1999.

URS Corporation. *Status and Trends of Delta-Suisun Services.* Sacramento: prepared for the California Department of Water Resources, 2007.

Vaghti, Mehrey G., and Steven E. Greco. "Riparian Vegetation of the Great Valley." In *Terrestrial Vegetation of California,* edited by Michael G. Barbour, Todd Keeler-Wolf, and Allan A. Schoenherr, 425–455. Berkeley and Los Angeles: University of California Press, 2007.

Valencius, Conevery Bolton. *The Health of the Country: How American Settlers Understood Themselves and Their Land.* New York: Basic Books, 2002.

Vaught, David. *Growers, Specialty Crops, and Labor, 1875–1920.* Baltimore, Md.: Johns Hopkins University Press, 1999.

Vileisis, Ann. *Discovering the Unknown Landscape: A History of America's Wetlands.* Washington, D.C.: Island Press, 1997.

Warne, William E. *The Bureau of Reclamation.* New York: Praeger, 1973.

Warren, Louis S. *The Hunter's Game: Poachers and Conservationists in Twentieth-Century America.* New Haven, Conn.: Yale University Press, 1997.

Weart, Spencer R. *The Discovery of Global Warming.* Cambridge, Mass.: Harvard University Press, 2003.

Weaver, Marion M. *History of Tile Drainage in America Prior to 1900.* Waterloo, N.Y., 1964.

Weber, David J. *The Spanish Frontier in North America.* New Haven, Conn.: Yale University Press, 1992.

Weissman, Karen G., and David Strong. "Merced County Study Looks at Economic Cost of Urban Sprawl." *California Waterfowl* 27, no. 2 (2000): 20–22.

Weller, Milton W. *Wetland Birds: Habitat Resources and Conservation Implications.* Cambridge: Cambridge University Press, 1999.

Wester, L. "Composition of Native Grassland in the San Joaquin Valley, California." *Madroño* 28, no. 4 (1981): 231–241.

Westlands Water District. *Drainage and Land Retirement.* Fresno, Calif.: Westlands Water District, 1999.

———. *Water Conservation.* Fresno, Calif.: Westlands Water District, 1999.

White, Richard. "The Nationalization of Nature." *Journal of American History* 86, no. 3 (1999): 976–986.

Wilber, Charles G. *Selenium: A Potential Environmental Poison and a Necessary Food Constituent.* Springfield, Ill.: Charles C. Thomas, 1983.

Willson, J. H. "Rice in California." In *Rice in California,* edited by Jack H. Willson, 20–40. Richvale, Calif.: Butte County Rice Growers Association, 1979.

Wilson, Bryan J. "Westlands Water District and Its Federal Water: A Case Study of Water District Politics." *Stanford Environmental Law Journal* 7 (1987–1988): 187–224.

Wilson, Robert M. "Directing the Flow: Migratory Waterfowl, Scale, and Mobility in Western North America." *Environmental History* 7, no. 2 (2002): 247–266.

———. *Seeking Refuge: An Environmental History of the Pacific Flyway.* Seattle: University of Washington Press, 2010.

Worcester, Hugh M. *Hunting the Lawless.* Berkeley, Calif.: American Wildlife Associates, 1955.

Worster, Donald. *Nature's Economy: A History of Ecological Ideas.* 2nd ed. Cambridge: Cambridge University Press, 1994.

———. *A River Running West: The Life of John Wesley Powell.* Oxford and New York: Oxford University Press, 2001.

———. *Rivers of Empire: Water, Aridity, and the Growth of the American West.* New York: Pantheon Books, 1985.

Wright, Sylvia. "Splendor in the Grass." *UC Davis Magazine* (Spring 2002): 18–21.

Yoshiyama, Ronald M. "A History of Salmon and People in the Central Valley Region of California." *Reviews in Fisheries Science* 7, nos. 3 and 4 (1999): 197–239.

Yoshiyama, Ronald M., Frank W. Fisher, and Peter B. Moyle. "Historical Abundance and Decline of Chinook Salmon in the Central Valley Region of California." *North American Journal of Fisheries Management* 18 (1998): 487–521.

Yoshiyama, Ronald M., Eric R. Gerstung, Frank W. Fisher, and Peter B. Moyle. "Chinook Salmon in the California Central Valley: An Assessment." *Fisheries Management* 25, no. 2 (2000): 6–20.

Young, Terry F., and Chelsea H. Congdon. *Plowing New Ground: Using Economic Incentives to Control Water Pollution from Agriculture.* Oakland, Calif.: Environmental Defense Fund, 1994.

Zoltai, S.C., C. Tarnocai, G.F. Mills, and H. Veldhuis. "Wetlands of Subarctic Canada." In *Wetlands of Canada,* 55–96. Ecological Land Classification Series no. 24. Montreal: Environment Canada and Polyscience Publications, 1988.

Zoltai, S.C., S. Taylor, J.K. Jeglum, G.F. Mills, and J.D. Johnson. "Wetlands of Boreal Canada." In *Wetlands of Canada,* 97–154. Ecological Land Classification Series no. 24. Montreal: Environment Canada and Polyscience Publications, 1988.

INDEX

Italicized page numbers indicate figures and maps.

acre-foot/acre-feet, defined, 120, 279n15
"Act to provide for the Reclamation and
Segregation of Swamp . . . ," 60
agricultural crops: irrigation of low-value, 233,
347n108; pre-irrigation for, 147–48; refuges
to counter waterfowl depredations of, 109,
154–55, 177, 179, 195–97; specialization in
single, 301n2; tule replaced by, 96–98;
waterfowl depredations of, 11, 83, 102–3,
108–9, 143–44, 149–50, 152–53, 177, 179, 181;
waterfowl protection and hunting balanced
with, 156–61. *See also* agriculture; irrigation
agricultural crops, specific: alfalfa, 152, 155, 201;
barley, 154, 160, 197; cotton, 71, 192–94, 197,
201, 330–31n3; fruit trees, 25; hay, 201; sugar
beets, 201; wheat, 70–71, 102–3, 121, 152,
154–55, 160. *See also* rice growing
Agricultural Drainage and Salt Management
(IDP), 216–17
agriculture: actual jobs and income from,
347n107; diversification and shift from
extensive to intensive, 71; global climate
change and, 266–67; human alteration of
environment for (overview), 9–13, 41;
insectivorous birds as protectors of, 134–35;
mythic vision of, 2, 14; in peat lands of
Delta, 115–16; Peripheral Canal and, 242,
244; politics and power of, 179–80, 232–33;
riparian vegetation used in, 25; smallholdings encouraged in, 120, 121, 311n48; state
crops in global markets, 71, 84, 107, 297n22;
urban encroachment on lands, 264, 266;
waterfowl protection linked to, 157–58;
Westside of San Joaquin River, 83, 201–2.
See also agricultural crops; American
settlers; cattle ranches; sheep ranches
Alaska, waterfowl breeding and staging areas
in, 36, 37–38, 39–40, 287n72
Aleutian cackling goose, refuge lands to
protect, 259–60
Alexander, B. S., 118–19
Alexander Commission report, 118–19, 120
alkali sinks, endangered species in, 258–59
Allen, Timothy F. H., 286n53
alluvial fans, 206, 207, 215, 216, 335n71
Alpaugh Irrigation District, 196
American Basin: acres of marsh in, 26, 96;
bypass of, 95; housing and retail developments in, 304n46; map of, 87; reclamation
of, 98; swampland district of, 62
American Bird Banding Association, 136
American Game Protective Association, 158
American River: dams on, 313n75; overflows
of, 98; riparian woodland along, 23
American settlers: fears of alien landscape, 57;
first organized in Calif. (1841), 55; Mexican
grants for cattle ranches as buffer against,
54; number in nineteenth century, 48;

397

types vs., 317n49; more water flow to prevent, 257; role of diminished habitat in, 14, 32, 79, 143, 269; seasonal mortality from, 148; spread of, 147–48; studies of, 146, 317n53. *See also* cholera (avian)

breeding and staging areas: duck nesting in, 32; forest and tundra, 39–40; overview of, 36, 41–42; prairie potholes, 40–41; refuge concept and protection of, 137, 140–42; waterfowl counts on wintering vs., 315n22; watersheds and deltas, 37–39; wintering grounds out of balance with, 159

Brereton, Robert Maitland, 118

Brewer, William H., 21–22, 61

Bridgeford Act (Calif., 1897), 119

Broadbent, Robert, 235

Brody, Ralph M., 202, 208

Brown, Edmund G. ("Jerry"), 242, 351n23

Brown, Edmund G. ("Pat"): on *Fish and Game Code*, 261; proposed Peripheral Canal and, 242; Reagan's defeat of, 210; water delivery issues and, 189, 190, 202, 208, 329nn99–100

Browning, William J., 78, 83

Brundage, Benjamin, 75

Bryant, Edwin, 21

Bryant, Harold Child, 104–6

Bryers, H. G., 215

Buck, Alaine, 193

Buena Vista Lake: diminished size of, 67, 69; river source of, 66; tule elk refuge along, 76–77; waterfowl hunting on, 78–79

Buena Vista Slough: demise of marshes, 76, 253; description of, 67; diversions of, 73–74; drainage into, 66, 69; landowners along, 80; legal case concerning, 74–76

Buffington, Douglas, 344n72

bull hunting, tactics of, 103, 105

Burns, Hugh, 335n72

Burns-Porter Act (Water Resources Bond Development Act, Calif., 1960), 207–8, 335–36n74, 335n72

Bush, George H. W., 344n72

Bush, George W., 241

Butte Basin: acres of marsh in, 26, 27, 96; agreements concerning water for, 100–101, 305n60; bypass proposed for, 99–100, 101; gun club in, 106; hydrology of, 90; lack of development and reclamation, 98; management of emergent vegetation of, 101–2; map of, *87*; rice-growing experiments in (Butte County), 107–8; riparian yellow-billed

cuckoo in, 33; weirs and bypasses of, 93, *94*; wetland and riparian habitat resurgence in, 248

Butte Creek, riparian woodland along, 23

Butterfield, Justin, 58–59

Butte Sink: agreements concerning water for, 100–101, 305n60; chemical neutrality of, 304n48; conservation easement program in, 248, 353n45; cost of duck club memberships in, 355n66; duck clubs and waterfowl counts in, 248, 353n42; waterfowl hunting as primary use of, 101–2; water sources of, 99

Butte Sink National Wildlife Refuge, 247–48

Butte Sink Wildlife Management Area, 247–48

Buttes Land Company, 305n60

CALFED: agreement for, 244, 351n28; challenges for, 244–45, 360n19; program implementation of, 351n30

California: agriculture as percentage of gross state product, 347n107; federal land grants of public domain to, 294n57; "garden landscape" vision for, 86, 88; maps of, *xvi, 6*; mythology of, 2, 14; statehood for, 65; swamplands deeded to, 59–60; tribal territories in, *49*; U.S. control of, 48

California Agricultural Experiment Station, 107

California Aqueduct (including San Luis Canal section): freshwater for, via proposed Peripheral Canal, 242, *243*, 244; map of, *205*; plan for, 209; pumping plant of, 350–51n20; saltwater intrusion problem in, 242

California Board of Fish and Game Commissioners, 103, 104–5

California Cattlemen's Association, 177

California codes: *Civil Code*, 75, 165; *Fish and Game*, 189, 260–61; *Political*, 64

California Constitution, 124, 312n66

California Debris Commission (federal body), 91, 92, 100

California Department of Agriculture, Division of Biological Survey, 76–77

California Department of Fish and Game (earlier, Division): avian disease studies of, 317n53; food studies of, 161–62, 321n112; market hunting crackdown of, 146; reorganization of, 320n103; salinity and selenium studies of, 221–22, 223, 233–34; San Joaquin River dewatering and, 190; selenium in Tulare drainage ponds and,

Preston, William L., 20, 299n56
Proposition 8 (Calif., 1980), 242, 244, 351n23
public attitudes: anthropocentric to biocentric
    shift, 43; beginnings of wetlands awareness,
    10; changes in, 14, 42–43, 240–41; Grass-
    lands, 185; local, state, or federal control of
    projects, 120–26, 128–29, 204–5, 310n44;
    manifest destiny, 55; market hunting,
    143–44, 145; plight of waterfowl, 133;
    protection, preservation, and restoration,
    237–40, 247, 269–70; reconceptualization of
    Delta, 245; San Luis Island refuge, 199; in
    western history context, 2, 14, 42–43;
    wetlands and waterfowl support, 15;
    wetlands as obstacles, 48, 55–64. See also
    agriculture; waterfowl protection; wetland
    protection; wildlife protection
Public Policy Institute of California (PPIC),
    245, 360n17
Purcell, Sam, 109

railroads and railroad development: Chinese
    laborers on, 113; hunting promoted by, 153,
    306n77; importance of, 297n21; swampy
    areas as obstacles to, 56; Westside lines
    of, 201, 333n43; wheat boom linked to,
    70–71, 152
Ramsar Wetland of International Importance
    (designation), 258, 264
ranches, waterfowl coexisting with, 12. See also
    cattle ranches; sheep ranches
Rancho del Arroyo Chico (Butte County), 88
Rancho Orestimba (San Joaquin Basin), 80
Rancho Sanjon de Santa Rita (San Joaquin
    Basin): grasslands and water rights issues
    of, 80, 82–84; map of, 81; sales pamphlet for,
    301n89; San Luis Island in, 198, 332n30;
    townships included in, 300n75. See also
    Lux, Charles; Miller, Henry
Rank, Everett G., 188–91, 262
Rank v. Krug (1950s), 188–90, 262, 329n91,
    329n94, 329nn99–100, 330n101
Reagan, Ronald, 210, 221, 226–27, 242,
    344n72
reclamation: converting wetlands to agricul-
    tural use in, 1, 8, 11, 14, 32, 48, 65, 69, 110,
    163, 253, 269; decentralized oversight of,
    61–64; meanings of, 48; political support
    for, 121–22. See also irrigation; irrigation
    and reclamation projects; U.S. Bureau of
    Reclamation

Reclamation Act (1902): 160-acre limitation of,
    205–6, 208, 311n48, 331n7, 336n84; Central
    Valley Project and, 128; lawsuits concern-
    ing, 260–61; opposition to, 310n44; Pine
    Flat Dam and, 331n7; provisions of, 121–22,
    311n48; states included in, 310n45
reclamation districts: concept of, 60; legislation
    empowering, 63–64; specific: American
    Basin (Nos. 1000 and 1001), 98; Colusa
    Basin (No. 108), 96–97; Sutter Basin (No.
    1500), 98; Yolo Basin (No. 999), 97. See also
    irrigation districts
Reclamation Extension Act (U.S., 1914), 311n49
Reclamation Projects Authorization and
    Adjustment Act (U.S., 1992), 240. See also
    Central Valley Project Improvement Act
Reclamation Service (USGS), 122. See also U.S.
    Bureau of Reclamation
Reed, Charles, 96–97
Refuge Revenue Sharing Act (U.S., 1964), 198
reptiles and amphibians: Central Valley
    Project's impact on, 128–29; dependence on
    wetlands, 33; endangered species of, 196,
    258–59; riparian woodland habitat of, 25;
    San Luis Island, 199; selenium's effects on,
    222–23; Tulare Lake, 77
reptiles and amphibians, specific species:
    common and scientific names, listed, 273;
    blunt-nosed leopard lizard, 196, 253;
    California tiger salamander, 259; giant
    garter snake, 33; terrapins, 77
Republican Party: Bidwell's role in, 88;
    centralized planning preferred by, 63; on
    economic development, 123; reclamation
    and, 60, 121
reservoirs. See dams and reservoirs
Reynolds, Charles B., 104
Rice Experiment Station (USDA), 108
rice growing: airplane seeding for, 109; Butte
    Basin situation and, 98–102; Colusa Plains
    area, 152–53; declining income from, 153;
    economic prosperity from, 108–9;
    experiments in, 107–8; faster-maturing
    varieties for, 249, 320–21n106; flooded fields
    as wetlands for waterfowl, 249–50, 252;
    fungal disease issues in, 249, 353n48;
    increased water diversions for, 116–17, 123;
    limit on burning harvested fields, 249,
    354n51; millet compared with, 160–61; peak
    in, 157, 353n47; primary counties of, 353n47;
    refuges to counter waterfowl depredations

Smith, G. E. P., 330n101

Smith, Jedediah, 54, 67, 102

Smith-Zeigler Case (market hunting), 144, 145–46

Smythe, William, 120–21

Snyder, Leon C., 195–96, 331n8

Soberanes, Francisco, 80

soil types and characteristics: adobe, 70, 107–8, 160, 297n17; alkali, 21–22, 22, 152, 153, 161, 167, 196, 215; Corcoran Clay, 203, 298n30; hydric, 9; loam, 160; peat, 111, 113, 115–16; riparian woodland, 25; saline and sodic, 108, 167, 195, 206, 307n89, 341n48

Solano County, swampland district in, 62

Sousa, Alvaro, 199

South Butte Gun Club, 305n60

South Dakota, selenium contamination and studies in, 219–20, 340n31, 348n119

Southern California: Colorado River water for, 125, 208; proposed Peripheral Canal and, 242, 244; State Water Project and, 208, 336n76. See also Imperial Valley

Southern Pacific Railroad: hunting promoted by, 105, 306n77; lobbyist for, 73; Los Angeles and link to, 297n23; settlers' confrontation with, 297–98n24; settlers encouraged by, 10; Westside landholdings of, 333n49; Westside lines of, 201, 333n43; wheat boom and, 71

South San Joaquin Municipal Utility District, 188

Spalding, Z. L. (ranch of), 152–53, 158

Spanish period (1769–1821): alien grasses near missions in, 20; establishment of, 51–52; expanding number of settlements in, 47; Native Americans in, 48, 51, 52–53

sport hunting: "class" element in considerations of, 176; conservation movement and, 104–5, 306n71; crop protection and waterfowl protection balanced with, 156–61; fees for, 320n96; market hunting distinguished from, 104–5; popularity increased, 153. See also duck and hunting clubs; gun clubs; waterfowl hunting; and specific clubs

Sportsman's Council of Central California, 179, 186

Stanford, Leland, 60

Stanislaus County: artesian wells of, 72; canals and ditches of, 83. See also Grasslands

Stanislaus River: dam on, 360n19; riparian woodland along, 23, 24, 79, 284n26

Stewart, William Morris, 118

Stillwater National Wildlife Refuge (Nevada), 42, 348n118

Stone Lakes National Wildlife Refuge, 246, 352–53n39

Storer, Tracy Irwin, 104–6

Straus, Michael W., 173–74, 188

submergent (wetland) vegetation, 26, 30, 31, 38, 154, 199

Success Dam (Tule River), 194

Suisun Bay: Delta connected to, 110–11; outflow of Sacramento Flood Control Project into Delta and thence to, 91, 92, 93; refuge shortage in, 159; as San Luis Drain discharge point, 217; tidal marsh areas (map), 112

Suisun Marsh: failure of agriculture and subsequent reflooding of, 116; location and significance of, 27–28, 28; major protected wetland areas of, 265; management of public and private lands in, 351n21; private ownership and market hunting in, 105–6; protective measures for, 244; refuge established in, 160; salt-tolerant plants of, 285n37; saltwater intrusion problem in, 242; waterfowl diet in, 162; waterfowl refuge of, 150, 318n64

Summer Lake (Oregon), 42

Summit Lake: demise of, 69; in wet years, 66

Sun River Project Area (Montana), selenium contamination in, 348n118

Susitna River Delta (Alaska), 287n72

Sutter, John, 47, 88

Sutter Basin: acres of marsh in, 26, 96; hydrology of, 90; map of, 87; reclamation of, 97–98; weirs and bypasses of, 93, 94, 95

Sutter Buttes, geology of, 7

Sutter County, rice crop of, 108

Sutter County Water Users Organization, 101

Sutter National Wildlife Refuge, 155, 157, 158, 319n84

Swamp and Overflowed Lands Act (U.S., 1850): flood control efforts in context of, 58–64; settlement encouraged via, 294n57; states included in, 58, 294n51; wetlands drainage promoted in, 8

Swamp Land Act (U.S., 1849), 8, 58

Swamp Land Commission (Calif.), 60–64, 86, 113

Swamp Land District No. 18, 97

swamplands: coordinated reclamation of, 60–61; decentralization of oversight, 61–64; list and classification of, 58–59; state and

valley grassland: controlled burning of, 282n10; description of, 20–23, 22; percentage remaining, 20; ranchers' use of, 82; as wetlands component, 19. *See also* Grasslands; San Luis National Wildlife Refuge

Van Huizen, Peter J., 154–55

vernal pools: classification of, 283n14; complexes of, listed, 283n17; endangered species in, 258–59; habitat and plants of, 22–23

Vina Plains Preserve, 283n17

Voigt, William, Jr., 186

Volta Wildlife Area, 217, 223, 339n26, 350n16, 356n75, 357n83

Walker, Joseph, 54

Wallace, Henry, 141

wardens. *See* fish and game wardens

Warner, J. J., 53–54

Warren, Earl, 181, 182, 326n60, 330n107

water: accumulation of toxins in, 215–16; assumptions about beneficial reuse of, 214–15; beneficial and reasonable use provision for, 124, 312n66; Classes I and II, price and delivery, 172, 324n19; dedicated for fish and wildlife, 241; groundwater overdraft (Westside), 201–2; reshaped landscape due to pursuit of, 7–8; society's priorities for, 3; wildlife protection juxtaposed to development projects for, 214–15; for wildlife vs. cropland debate, 179–80, 195. *See also* agriculture; rivers; wells; wetlands; *specific locales and projects*

Water Bank Act and Program (U.S., 1970), 184, 185, 327n77

water conservation districts, 311n56

watercourse, defined, 75–76, 299n50

waterfowl: aerial surveys and other counts of, 34, 36, 104–6, 141–42, 238, 315n22, 316n37; ancient origins of, 29; bioaccumulation of toxins in, 215, 223, 224, 236; Butte Sink area, 99–100; cattle ranches inadvertently protecting, 80, 82–84; Central Valley Project's impact on, 128–29; classification of (Anatidae), 30–31, 285n44; community of, 31–32; crop depredations of, 11, 83, 102–3, 108–9, 143–44, 149–50, 152–53, 177, 179, 181; crop production on refuges for, 154–55; endangered species of, 259–60 (*see also* Aleutian cackling goose); freshwater marsh habitat (overview), 25–29; Grasslands'

importance for, 254–55; Kesterson refuge, 213–14; nadir of, 238, 315n22; number of species, 314n15; rice field habitat of, 106–7; riparian woodland habitat of, 25; Sacramento Valley, 102–6; San Luis Island, 199; selenium's effects on, 217–24, 231–33; Tulare and Buena Vista lakes, 78–79; variety of scales in studies of, 13; vernal pool habitat of, 23; Westside of San Joaquin Basin, 83–84. *See also* breeding and staging areas; ducks; food habits and dietary requirements; geese and swans; waterfowl protection; wetlands; wintering grounds

waterfowl hunting: Butte Basin managed for, 98–102; farmers' attitudes toward, 102–3; licenses for, 141–42, 149–50, 157–58; by Native Americans, 50–51, 102, 291n11; railroad company's promotion of, 306n77; regulatory authority over, 134; role in decreased numbers of wild game, 104–6; Sacramento Valley, 102; shift from prohibited to limited hunting on refuges, 157–58; spring shooting banned, 134–35; state restrictions on, 103–5; tactics in Delta, 111; on Tulare Lake, 78–79. *See also* duck and hunting clubs; Ducks Unlimited, Inc.; market hunting; sport hunting

waterfowl management areas, designation of, 160

waterfowl protection: acres designated for, 320n101; breeding ground issues in, 137, 140–42; crop protection and hunting balanced with, 156–61; disease issues in, 143, 146–49; federal legislation for, 133–35, 239–40; food issues in, 149–50, 152–55; identification and mapping of flyways, 135–37, 138–39; as key wildlife problem, 158–59; limits of, 163–64; market hunting issue in, 134, 135, 143–46; refuges and hunting issues in, 156–61; U.S.-Canada treaty concerning, 8, 135, 143, 200, 228, 305n68, 319n92, 345n79. *See also* wildlife and wetland refuges

Water Resources Act (Calif., 1945), 189

Water Resources Bond Development Act (Burns-Porter Act, Calif., 1960), 207–8, 335–36n74, 335n72

Water Resources of California (Bulletin No. 4, 1923), 123

water rights. *See* appropriative rights; riparian rights

wildlife and wetland refuges (*continued*)
    protection; wintering grounds; *and specific refuges*
Wildlife Conservation Act (Calif., 1947), 158–59
Wildlife Conservation Board: departmental home of, 320n97; Gray Lodge Waterfowl Refuge enlarged under, 160–61; San Luis Island and, 198; wildlife and recreation survey of, 158–59
wildlife management issues. *See* game and wildlife management
wildlife protection: absent originally in Central Valley Project, 128–29; attitudinal changes and, 237–40; in CVPIA, 240–41; in Grasslands, 254–55, 257–59; major areas of, *265*; rejuvenation of San Joaquin River, 259–62; rice fields and, 249–50, 252; in Tulare Basin public and private lands, 252–54; water development projects juxtaposed to, 214–15; wetlands and riparian forests in Sacramento Valley, 247–49; wetlands on Delta edges, 245–47. *See also* duck and hunting clubs; waterfowl protection; wetland protection; wildlife and wetland refuges
Wildlife Review, 161, 321n108
Williamson, R. S., 67
Willis, G. T., 201
Wilson, Robert, 286n52
Wilson, Woodrow, 135
wintering grounds: disease threat to, 143, 146–49; food issues and, 149–50, 152–55, 161–63; key role of, 142–43, 159; limits of protecting, 163–64; market hunting threat to, 143–46; overview of nesting, staging, and, 32–34, *35*, 36–42; population estimates for, *251*, 252, *256*; as refuges and hunting grounds, 156–61; in Tulare Basin, 194–97; waterfowl counts on breeding vs., 315n22
Winton, J. Martin: characteristics of, 178, *178*; Grasslands tours by, 199; honored for

Grasslands advocacy, 182; legacy of, 325n46; testimony at congressional hearings on Grasslands, 179, 181; water contract negotiations of, 183, 184
Wister Unit (Imperial Valley Waterfowl Management Area, later Wildlife Area), 160
Wolfsen, Henry, 171, 172
Wood Buffalo National Park (Alberta), 38
woodlands, boreal forests, 39
Woodruff, Edwards v. North Bloomfield Gravel Mining Co. et al. (1884), 90
Worcester, Hugh M., 144–45
Work, John, 53
Wright, C. C., 119
Wright Act (Calif., 1887), 119–20, 121, 299n53

Yasuoka, Tokuya, 108
Yellowjacket Cattle Company, 173–74
Yokuts: controlled burning by, 50; rebellion led by, 52–53; resistance to colonial expeditions, 52, 70; of Tulare Basin (Tachi), 66; waterfowl hunting by, 50–51, 291n11
Yolo Basin: acres of marsh in, 26, 96; map of, *87*; reclamation of, 86, 97; swampland district of, 62; weirs and bypasses of, 93, *94*, 95, 247
Yolo Bypass Wildlife Area, 247, 353n40
Young, C. C., 125
Young, Ewing, 53
Younger, Evelle J., 329–30n100
Yuba River: flood of, 303n35; mining debris in, 89; riparian woodland along, 23
Yukon Delta National Wildlife Refuge (Alaska), 37–38
Yukon Flats National Wildlife Refuge (Alaska), 37–38
Yukon-Kuskokwim Delta (Alaska), 37–38

Zahm, Gary, 217, 255, 257–58, 339n25, 342n54
Zeigler, Edward L., 145–46

TEXT
10/12.5 Minion Pro

DISPLAY
Minion Pro

COMPOSITOR
Westchester Book Group

INDEXER
Margie Towery

PRINTER AND BINDER
Sheridan Books, Inc.